Advances in Vehicular Ad-Hoc Networks:
Developments and Challenges

Mohamed Watfa
University of Wollongong, UAE

Information Science
REFERENCE

INFORMATION SCIENCE REFERENCE

Hershey · New York

Director of Editorial Content:	Kristin Klinger
Director of Book Publications:	Julia Mosemann
Acquisitions Editor:	Lindsay Johnston
Development Editor:	Elizabeth Ardner
Publishing Assistant:	Deanna Zombro
Typesetter:	Michael Brehm
Production Editor:	Jamie Snavely
Cover Design:	Lisa Tosheff
Printed at:	Yurchak Printing Inc.

Published in the United States of America by
Information Science Reference (an imprint of IGI Global)
701 E. Chocolate Avenue
Hershey PA 17033
Tel: 717-533-8845
Fax: 717-533-8661
E-mail: cust@igi-global.com
Web site: http://www.igi-global.com/reference

Library of Congress Cataloging-in-Publication Data

Advances in vehicular ad-hoc networks : developments and challenges / Mohamed Watfa, editor.
       p. cm.
  Includes bibliographical references and index.
  Summary: "This book tackles the prevalent research challenges that hinder a fully deployable vehicular network, presenting a unified treatment of the various aspects of VANETs and is essential for not only university professors, but also for researchers working in the automobile industry"--Provided by publisher.
  ISBN 978-1-61520-913-2 (hardcover) -- ISBN 978-1-61520-914-9 (ebook) 1. Vehicular ad hoc networks (Computer networks) I. Watfa, Mohamed, 1981-
  TE228.37.A38 2010
  388.3'12--dc22
                                    2010010163

British Cataloguing in Publication Data
A Cataloguing in Publication record for this book is available from the British Library.

All work contributed to this book is new, previously-unpublished material. The views expressed in this book are those of the authors, but not necessarily of the publisher.

Table of Contents

Section 1
Introduction to Vehicular Adhoc Networks (VANETs)

Danda Rawat, Old Dominion University, USA
Gongjun Yan, Old Dominion University, USA

Debika Bhattacharyya, Salt Lake Electronics Complex, India
Avijit Bhattacharyya, Salt Lake Electronics Complex, India

Section 2
Applications of VANETs

Yacine Khaled, INRIA Rocquencourt, France
Manabu Tsukada, INRIA Rocquencourt, France
José Santa, University of Murcia, Spain
Thierry Ernst, INRIA Rocquencourt, France

Samy El-Tawab, Old Dominion University, USA
Gongjun Yan, Old Dominion University, USA

Section 3
Communication Protocols in VANETs

Detailed Table of Contents

Section 1
Introduction to Vehicular Adhoc Networks (VANETs)

The first section of the book, Introduction of Vehicular Adhoc Networks, presents introductory materials that are preparatory for what we describe in the rest of the book. It details the basic infrastructure and architecture of a vehicular Adhoc network and what are the possible challenges associated with such architecture.

Chapter 1
Danda Rawat, Old Dominion University, USA
Gongjun Yan, Old Dominion University, USA

The infrastructure of a vehicular Adhoc network plays a major role in order to realize the full potential of vehicular communications. This chapter provides an in-depth survey of the infrastructures and technologies that were recently proposed as part of the future intelligent transportation system (ITS).

Chapter 2
Debika Bhattacharyya, Salt Lake Electronics Complex, India
Avijit Bhattacharyya, Salt Lake Electronics Complex, India

This chapter deals with the basic architecture of VANET where both wired and wireless technologies can be used for intra-vehicular communication. It ultimately explains inter-vehicular communications and the components of a smart vehicle.

Section 2
Applications of VANETs

The second section of the book, Applications of Vehicular Adhoc Networks, presents different categories of vehicular network applications which will motivate researchers to pursue further research in the field by designing new protocols, technologies and implementations.

Chapter 3

Yacine Khaled, INRIA Rocquencourt, France
Manabu Tsukada, INRIA Rocquencourt, France
José Santa, University of Murcia, Spain
Thierry Ernst, INRIA Rocquencourt, France

This chapter provides an in depth analysis of application requirements taking into consideration the available technologies for physical/MAC and network layers.

Chapter 4

Samy El-Tawab, Old Dominion University, USA
Gongjun Yan, Old Dominion University, USA

This chapter gives a background on different applications categories in VANETs that include safety, commercial, monitoring, service and entertainment applications.

Chapter 5

Marco Fiore, INSA Lyon, INRIA, France
Claudio Casetti, Politecnico di Torino, Italy
Carla-Fabiana Chiasserini, Politecnico di Torino, Italy

This chapter focuses on a possible application for data sharing between vehicular users highlighting the main challenges while introducing some mechanisms that can be applied to solve two major issues in content sharing: content query propagation and content caching.

Section 3
Communication Protocols in VANETs

The third section of the book, Communication Protocols in VANETs, presents various data communication protocols used in vehicular networks that include medium access control protocols, different variations of routing protocols and wireless access techniques in vehicular environments.

Chapter 6

Md. Imrul Hassan, Swinburne University of Technology, Australia
Hai L. Vu, Swinburne University of Technology, Australia
Taka Sakurai, University of Melbourne, Australia

In this chapter, an overview of proposed MAC protocols for VANETs is presented and current standardization activities are described. The authors also review prominent existing analytical models and study their advantages, disadvantages and their suitability for performance evaluation of MAC protocols for VANETs.

Chapter 7

Raúl Aquino-Santos, University of Colima, México
Víctor Rangel-Licea, National Autonomous University of México, México
Aldo L. Méndez-Pérez, Universidad Autónoma de Tamaulipas, México
Miguel A. Garcia-Ruiz, University of Colima, México
Arthur Edwards-Block, University of Colima, México
Eduardo Flores-Flores, University of Colima, México

IEEE 802.11 Standard has led to increased research in the areas of wireless ad hoc networks and location-based routing algorithms. This chapter analyzes two prominent technologies, IEEE 802.11g (WiFi) and IEEE 802.16e (WiMAX), for single-hop inter-vehicular communication (SIVC).

Chapter 8

Kevin C. Lee, UCLA, USA
Uichin Lee, UCLA, USA
Mario Gerla, UCLA, USA

Despite many surveys already published on routing protocols in MANETs, a survey of newly developed routing protocols specific to VANETs has long been overdue. This chapter provides a survey of routing protocols in vehicular ad hoc networks highlighting the advantages and disadvantages of these routing protocols while exploring the motivation behind their design.

This chapter introduces geographic routing in vehicular ad hoc networks (VANETs).

Currently, there are five major types of VANETs routing protocols based on the metrics used for routing: 1) flooding based routing, 2) mobility based routing, 3) infrastructure based routing, 4) geographic position based routing, 5) probability model based routing. This chapter gives a survey of each type of routing method presenting probability model based routing as a detailed example.

Vehicular mobility is characterized by acceleration, deceleration, possibility of different lanes and intelligent driving patterns. This chapter provides taxonomy of mobility models and an analysis of their implications.

Many of the applications in VANETs, especially the safety related ones, set up requirements for information dissemination which are different from conventional networks and are thus difficult to fulfill with existing strategies. This chapter reviews recently proposed data dissemination schemes in VANETs and presents novel solutions and analytical evaluation tools.

Section 4
General Research Challenges in VANETs

The fourth and last section of the book, General Research Challenges in VANETs, concludes this book by presenting some research challenges in vehicular networks such as clustering techniques, delay tolerant protocols, and adaptive solutions in Multihop VANETs.

In this chapter, clustering algorithms, solutions appropriate to increase connectivity, and carious algorithms that can detect intruders in VANETs are presented.

Real-time traffic and route updates, traffic monitoring, remote diagnostics, general purpose Internet access and in-car entertainment are examples that require data collection and dissemination analogous to the wired Internet. However, related short-range communications technology would appear to be insufficient for these scenarios. In this chapter, the conditions under which it is feasible to use short range communications are described.

The nature of VANETs demands a flexible multi-hop communication protocol supporting different communications needs and adapting to the network environment and to context elements specified by the application itself. This chapter introduces the reader to these kinds of solutions, show their benefits and also mention the challenges involved.

Preface

A vehicular ad hoc network (VANET) is a non-infrastructure based network that does not rely on a central administration for communication between vehicles. In a vehicular ad hoc network, the overlapping transmission range of each vehicle ensures a unified and common channel for communication between the vehicles. The flexibility of VANETs opens the door to a myriad of applications that contribute to the safety and comfort of the vehicle's passengers. Unfortunately, this versatility does not come for free: there are a large number of computer communication challenges that await researchers and engineers who are serious about the implementation and deployment of vehicular ad hoc networks. Throughout the world, there are many national/international projects in government, industry, and academia devoted to vehicular networks. VANETs represent a rapidly emerging, particularly challenging class of mobile ad hoc network (MANET). They are distributed, self-organizing communication networks built up by moving vehicles, and are thus characterized by very high node mobility and limited degrees of freedom in mobility patterns. Such particular features often make standard networking protocols inefficient or unusable, hence the growing effort in the development of communication protocols which are specific to vehicular networks. Early VANET researchers, who had extensive research experience in MANETs, were very optimistic. They thought that MANETs could be slightly modified and tailored to suit VANET architectures. Unfortunately, things did not turn out to their expectations. The high mobility of communicating vehicles necessitated that protocols be vastly revised or re-written from scratch.

A book about vehicular ad hoc networks is both timely and looked-for. In the last few years there has been an industrial aspiration to roll out VANETs. However, VANETs introduce a lot of challenges that only earnest academic and industrial research can overcome. A comprehensive and unified treatment of the intermingled aspects of VANETs in a book is required. The goal of this book is to explore the developments and current/future challenges in the area of vehicular networks. This book presents techniques and protocols that satisfy the peculiar needs of VANETs. It will tackle the wireless medium access control (WMAC) techniques that are common to all wireless communication systems and provide special treatment of the peculiar aspects of WMAC in VANETs. Proactive, reactive and location-aware routing techniques are also presented. The cross-layer dependencies in VANETs are discussed and ways in which their exploitation will eventually lead to the optimization of communication are shown. This book serves as a powerful reference and background in the area of VANETs by tackling the prevalent research challenges that hinder a fully deployable vehicular network. It will be a pioneer reference in this field and will resonance sharply with researchers who have been craving a unified reference in the field of inter-vehicular communication.

The book is divided into four sections where each section groups several related VANETs research topics starting from a brief introduction to VANETs, to a list of possible applications of VANETS, to VANETs communication protocols, and finally concluding this book with general research problems of VANETs.

SECTION 1: INTRODUCTION TO VEHICULAR AD HOC NETWORKS (VANETs)

The first section of the book, *Introduction to Vehicular Ad Hoc Networks*, presents introductory materials that are preparatory for what we describe in the rest of the book. It details the basic infrastructure and architecture of a vehicular ad hoc network and what are the possible challenges associated with such architecture.

The infrastructure of a vehicular ad hoc network plays a major role in order to realize the full potential of vehicular communications. The first chapter provides an in-depth survey of the infrastructures and technologies that were recently proposed as part of the future intelligent transportation system (ITS).

The second chapter deals with the basic architecture of VANET where both wired and wireless technologies can be used for intra-vehicular communication. It ultimately explains inter-vehicular communications and the components of a smart vehicle.

SECTION 2: APPLICATIONS OF VANETs

The second section of the book, Applications of VANETs, presents different categories of vehicular network applications which will motivate researchers to pursue further research in the field by designing new protocols, technologies and implementations.

The third chapter provides an in depth analysis of application requirements taking into consideration the available technologies for physical/MAC and network layers.

The fourth chapter gives a background on different applications categories in VANETs that include safety, commercial, monitoring, service and entertainment applications.

The fifth chapter focuses on a possible application for data sharing between vehicular users highlighting the main challenges while introducing some mechanisms that can be applied to solve two major issues in content sharing: content query propagation and content caching.

SECTION 3: COMMUNICATION PROTOCOLS IN VANETs

The third section of the book, Communication Protocols in VANETs, presents various data communication protocols used in vehicular networks that include medium access control protocols, different variations of routing protocols and wireless access techniques in vehicular environments.

Chapter 6, an overview of proposed MAC protocols for VANETs is presented and current standardization activities are described. The authors also review prominent existing analytical models and study their advantages, disadvantages and their suitability for performance evaluation of MAC protocols for VANETs.

IEEE 802.11 Standard has led to increased research in the areas of wireless ad hoc networks and location-based routing algorithms. Chapter 7 analyzes two prominent technologies, IEEE 802.11g (WiFi) and IEEE 802.16e (WiMAX), for single-hop inter-vehicular communication (SIVC).

Despite many surveys already published on routing protocols in MANETs, a survey of newly developed routing protocols specific to VANETs has long been overdue. Chapter 8 provides a survey of routing protocols in vehicular ad hoc networks highlighting the advantages and disadvantages of these routing protocols while exploring the motivation behind their design.

Chapter 9 introduces geographic routing in vehicular ad hoc networks (VANETs).

Currently, there are five major types of VANETs routing protocols based on the metrics used for routing: 1) flooding based routing, 2) mobility based routing, 3) infrastructure based routing, 4) geographic position based routing, 5) probability model based routing. Chapter 10 gives a survey of each type of routing method presenting probability model based routing as a detailed example.

Vehicular mobility is characterized by acceleration, deceleration, possibility of different lanes and intelligent driving patterns. Chapter 11 provides taxonomy of mobility models and an analysis of their implications.

Many of the applications in VANETs, especially the safety related ones, set up requirements for information dissemination which are different from conventional networks and are thus difficult to fulfill with existing strategies. Chapter 12 reviews recently proposed data dissemination schemes in VANETs and presents novel solutions and analytical evaluation tools.

SECTION 4: GENERAL RESEARCH CHALLENGES IN VANETs

The fourth and last section of the book, General Research Challenges in VANETs, concludes this book by presenting some research challenges in vehicular networks such as clustering techniques, delay tolerant protocols, and adaptive solutions in Multihop VANETs.

Chapter 13, clustering algorithms, solutions appropriate to increase connectivity, and carious algorithms that can detect intruders in VANETs are presented.

Real-time traffic and route updates, traffic monitoring, remote diagnostics, general purpose Internet access and in-car entertainment are examples that require data collection and dissemination analogous to the wired Internet. However, related short-range communications technology would appear to be insufficient for these scenarios. Chapter 14, the conditions under which it is feasible to use short range communications are described.

The nature of VANETs demands a flexible multi-hop communication protocol supporting different communications needs and adapting to the network environment and to context elements specified by the application itself. Chapter 15 introduces the reader to these kinds of solutions, show their benefits and also mention the challenges involved.

Acknowledgment

The work presented in this book has been made possible though the hard work of the contributors who kept the deadlines and were always enthusiastic. I would also like to thank my editorial assistant, Elizabeth Ardner for her continuous and prompt help through every stage in the publication of this book. A special thanks also goes to the contributor's universities, institutions and organizations who allow them the valuable time to pursue their research interests.

I dedicate this book to my family and many friends. I would like to start by thanking God for his blessings and for sending me two angels from heaven, my beautiful wife, Diana, and my baby boy, Walid. I also present a special feeling of gratitude to my loving parents, Khalil and Habiba whose words of encouragement and push for tenacity ring in my ears. My sister Lana and her gift artist husband Mohamed, my sisters in law Maya and Douja and my idol brothers Walid and Ali who have never left my side and are very special.

Mohamed Watfa
University of Wollongong, UAE

Section 1
Introduction to Vehicular Ad Hoc Networks (VANETs)

Chapter 1
Infrastructures in Vehicular Communications:
Status, Challenges and Perspectives

Danda B. Rawat
Old Dominion University, USA

Gongjun Yan
Old Dominion University, USA

ABSTRACT

Vehicular communication is regarded as a backbone for the development of intelligent transportation system (ITS). Recently vehicular communication has attracted researchers from both academia and industry all over the world, notably, in the United States of America, Japan and European Union. The rapid advances in wireless technologies provide opportunities to utilize them in vehicular communication in advanced road safety applications. The most important feature of vehicular communication is to improve the road traffic safety, efficiency, comfort and quality of everyday road travel. Networking in particular and communication in general are important rudiments in the development of ITS. Generally, in vehicular communication, the information exchange occurs among vehicles not only in an ad-hoc based vehicle-to-vehicle networking but also in a vehicle-to-infrastructure with possible intermediate infrastructure-to-infrastructure networking. Therefore, the infrastructure plays major role in order to realize the full potential of vehicular communications. This chapter provides an in-depth survey of the infrastructures and technologies that are recently proposed as part of future ITS developments as well as tested for vehicular communications in mobile environment. Specifically, we provide an in-depth analysis of wireless technology-applications such as ad-hoc networking and wireless local area network (WLAN), dedicated short-range communication (DSRC), cellular technology and NOTICE Architecture, and compare their characteristics in terms of their abilities to support vehicular communications for development of ITS.

DOI: 10.4018/978-1-61520-913-2.ch001

I. INTRODUCTION

Vehicular communication is an emergent technology that has recently deserve attention of both industry and academic institutions all over the world, notably, in United States of America, Japan and Europe for the development of ITS. The main idea behind ITS is not new since JSK (Association of Electronic Technology for Automobile Traffic and Driving of Japan) was instantiated to work on vehicular communications in the early 1980s. However, the formal development process in the United States of America began in 1990s when the United States Congress mandated the creation of a program called Intelligent Vehicle Highway System (IVHS) based on Intermodal Surface Transportation Efficiency act of 1991 (ISTEA), whose main goal was to improve road safety, efficiency, comfort and quality of everyday life reducing possible pollution and preserving fuel while traveling on the road. The main responsibility of IVHS was assigned to the U.S. Department of Transportation (U.S. DOT), which required the advice of the Intelligent Transportation Society of America (ITSA).

Recently well-known research results on platooning have been demonstrated by California PATH project of USA (Alvarez & Horowitz, 1997) and Chauffeur of EU. Vehicular communication is regarded as a major component for ITS to enhance passenger comfort, traffic efficiency, safety of passengers and so on, by propagating and disseminating the information in a timely and accurate manner towards the region of interest with an aim of automating existing transportation system which will rely on vehicle-to-vehicle (V2V) and vehicle-to-infrastructure (V2I) with possible intermediate infrastructure-to-infrastructure (I2I) communications. Conventional solutions to these issues use mainly automatic control systems using on board unit (OBU) in individual vehicles without any interaction to other vehicles, however, recently proposed vehicular communication could help to make the coordination among participating vehicles more efficiently and effectively with the help of inter-vehicle communication using V2V and/or V2I communications.

Generally speaking, there are four basic types of information or messages that are exchanged among vehicles in vehicular communications:

- *Emergency and warning messages:* These types of messages can be of critical emergency, construction sites, or congestion related messages.
- *Routing and basic safety messages:* This category consists of information used by routing protocols and driving conditions. Information related to sender vehicle's speed, position, direction, identity and so on are some examples.
- *Infotainment (information and entertainment) messages:* These types of messages are basically related to recourses and services available on the roadside, and/or the services offered by other participating vehicles on the road. Information for nearby gas stations, restaurants, and so on are the example of this category.
- *Inter-personal messages:* This category may contain messages related to a profile of a driver and other passengers on the vehicle.

In V2V communication, individual vehicles work as a source, a destination and/or a router to propagate and disseminate the information towards the destination region, and the communication relies on information received from other participating vehicles on the road. Frequent breakage in network connection in V2V communication might happen because of dynamic change in vehicular network topology as a result of high mobility of vehicles in different traffic conditions, such as during traffic jams, accidents, traffic lights, rush hours, late night, school areas, etc. One way of making long time V2V connections for communication is by increasing the transmission range by assigning high transmission power for sparse ad hoc networks such as in rural areas or in urban areas where the application penetration ratio is low, i.e., low number of participating vehicles have communication and computing equipments. However, the high transmission power might result in high interference and high network overhead in vehicular networks in highly dense traffic (*e.g.*, areas with a high penetration ratio, urban areas, or traffic jams). In order to address these problems, Rawat, et al. (2009) has been proposed dynamic adaptation of transmission power based on local vehicle density. In general, it seems that the role of infrastructure is not important for vehicular communication. However, there is vulnerability of security and privacy of drivers traveling on the vehicle from malevolent drivers since vehicles working as routers for the information forwarding need the position, direction and identity of other vehicles who are participating in communications to forward and disseminate the information. If someone else tracks the drivers, nobody will be interested to use vehicular communication. Therefore, security and privacy are critical factors and challenges to take in to account for successful implementation of vehicular communication in future ITS. The different techniques in (Lin, et al., 2008; Parno & Perrig, 2005; Raya & Hubaux, 2005) have been proposed to deal with the security and privacy of the participating vehicles especially of the drivers and passengers on the vehicle. A potential approach in countering malicious attacks in V2V communications would be to use some infrastructures to keep track of participating vehicles as well as to fill communication gap in V2V communication.

On the other hand, in V2I communication, individual vehicles communicate with others through infrastructures installed along the roadside, and each vehicle work as a source and/or a destination. In this case, taking care of infrastructure by some authorized body such as government, the problem associated with the privacy and security

can be solved. Although in theory vehicular ad hoc network (VANET) can exist without a fixed infrastructure or roadside unit (RSU), however, in practice fixed infrastructure will be required to communicate messages to the wider range and to fill in the gaps of communication that may exist during periods of low vehicular traffic density such as in rural areas. Moreover, because of the limitation in transmission range, transmission power and data rate, VANETs cannot be extended to very large area. Therefore the fixed infrastructures will always be needed in the system to address all these issues. However, there are lots of open concerns regarding the cost, trust and ownership of such infrastructures.

The main goal of this chapter is to provide an state-of-the-art of the infrastructures and technologies that are recently proposed (Abuelela, Olariu, & Weigle, 2008; Karpiriski, Senart, & Cahill, 2006; Rosi, Hyder, & Kim, 2008) as part of future ITS developments as well as tested for vehicular communications in the mobile environment (Santa, Moragon, & Gomez-Skarmeta, 2008; Shankar, et al., 2005).

We also provide an in-depth analysis of wireless technology-applications such as cellular technology, ad-hoc networking and DSRC, and compare their characteristics in terms of their abilities to support V2V and V2I communications for ITS. In particular, recently proposed Notification of Traffic Incidents (NOTICE) system (Abuelela, et al., 2008) for vehicular communications will be presented in detail along with some physical layer issues (Rawat, Treeumnuk, Popescu, Abuelela, & Olariu, 2008) required to be addressed in order to make effective implementation of this system in future ITS. Moreover, the NOTICE system is an alternative approach to address both security and privacy issues of participating vehicles in communications by using short-range transmission at low power using V2I communications where sensor belt on each lane of a road works as an infrastructure.

II. BACKGROUND

In ITS, the infrastructures play an important role to realize full potential of vehicular communication in real environment since the information exchange among vehicles rely on vehicular networking where vehicles interact not only with each other based on ad-hoc networking but also with the infrastructure installed along the roadside using V2I communications to enhance road safety, mobility and traffic handling capacity, travel conditions, and adverse environmental effects aiming an automatic transportation systems. The communication performs the forwarding and dissemination of information needed for numerous purposes in timely and accurate manner; communication technologies are central component to ITS infrastructure. A significant number of projects have addressed vehicular communication during the recent years such as VSCC (VSCC, 2005), FleetNet (Franz, Wagner, Maihofer, & Hartenstein, 2004), NoW (Festag, et al., 2008), CVIS (CVIS, 2009), and SafeSpot (SafeSpot, 2009). In the following Section, we first review the technologies applicable for vehicular communication systems.

A) Radio Frequency Spectrum in Vehicular Communications

Basically, both infrared and radio waves *that include VHF (very high frequency), micro, and millimeter waves* have been studied and employed experimentally as a RF (radio frequency) spectra used in different inter-vehicular communication system in the past. The networking for communications with infrared and millimeter waves is usually directional and should be within the range of line-of-site (LOS), whereas those with VHF and microwaves are of telecast and/or broadcast type. Moreover, the VHF waves have been used in communication because of their long communication ranges.

In USA, the ITSA realized that the wireless communication is a milestone of the implemen-

tation of vehicular communication to develop an ITS. Initially assigned band 902 MHz and 928 MHz, used for automated toll collection, was over crowded to implement vehicular communication. Therefore, in 1997, the ITSA appealed the Federal communications Commissions (FCC) for 75 MHz of bandwidth in 5.9GHz with the aim of supporting DSRC applicable for the development of ITS. In October of 1999, FCC granted the request for DSRC with 75 MHz of bandwidth in the range of 5.85 - 5.925GHz. By the time US allocated the continuous spectrum of 75 MHz in DSRC band, unfortunately that band was already occupied and not available for vehicular communication in Europe. Therefore, the different European communities (Car2Car, 2007) have proposed a equivalent of the US approach with allocation of 2 x 10 MHz for primary use of safety critical applications at 5.9 GHz in the range 5.875 - 5.925 GHz. Moreover, because of the availability of an unlicensed frequency band at 2010–2020 MHz in Europe, CarTALK/FleetNet chose UTRA TDD. In Japan, DEMO 2000 has been used 5.8 GHz for DSRC, and 60 GHz wave has been tested to evaluate its performance under the hidden terminal scenario. For recently proposed NOTICE architecture, ZigBee has been proposed (Rawat, et al., 2008) for the communication technology applicable in the physical layer for vehicular communication because of its low connection set up or association time which is less than 30ms, sufficient data rate and availability in commercial market. It is worth to note that in spite of various drawbacks associated with the implementation of infrared, it has been implemented by most projects including JSK, CarTALK and PATH for co-operative driving for testing purpose.

B) Applications of Vehicular Communication and Their Requirements

In vehicular communication systems, generally the applications can be divided into three categories as (Wewetzer, Caliskan, Meier, & Luebke, 2007) safety, traffic efficiency and infotainment with four different types of messages - emergency and warning messages, routing and basic safety messages, infotainment messages, and Inter-personal messages.

Each category of messages has different requirements in vehicular networking. The safety application requires low latency and delay in order to deliver the emergency messages and warnings in time to the destination region for all vehicles in the surrounding of a hazard in a single hop or multi-hop communication. In addition, safety messages need low bandwidth because they are small in size. Traffic efficiency applications, such as parking space broadcasting, gas station information, are more delay tolerant than safety applications but require higher bandwidth. However, it may require distribution of information in large area so that information seeker can easily obtain the information. Applications for infotainment such as audio video sharing among participating vehicles need the highest bandwidth among all applications in the system.

Generally the evaluation of technologies is carried out focusing on maximum achievable data rate and communication range for infotainment applications. Whereas the evaluation is carried out by focusing on low latency and delay for timely reception of time critical emergency messages even in worst cases in order to reduce further accidents and congestions on the road.

It is worth to note that the broadcast communication is desirable in vehicular communication because many vehicles are potentially interested in the same information in order to change their route and/or react according to the received messages. For vehicular networking, different technologies have been proposed in the literature to realize the inter-vehicle communications for the development of future ITS. The communication technologies that could be considered for ITS applications are as following:

- Ad hoc networking techniques such as IEEE 802.11 wireless LAN standards.
- Cellular radio systems, such as UMTS and/ or 3G CDMA cellular technologies.
- Notification of Traffic Incidents (NOTICE) architecture.

C) Wireless LAN Infrastructure

The availability of IEEE 802.11 WLAN technology, vehicular communication is considered as vehicular ad-hoc networks using this technology (Wewetzer, et al., 2007). It is noted that WLAN technology can work in infrastructure-less ad hoc mode and infrastructure-based mode. In an infrastructure-less ad hoc mode, communication between two nodes occurs directly in peer-to-peer basis. On the other hand, in an infrastructure-based approach, communication between two nodes happens through centralized access point (AP). In order to use infrastructure-based approach for vehicular communication, one has to install APs along the road, which is almost infeasible. In this chapter, therefore, we consider ad hoc based networking as a potential candidate for vehicular communication.

The WLAN technology was originally designed to work at 2.4 GHz based on the industrial, scientific and medical (ISM) frequency band with data rate up to 2 Mbps. Among several IEEE 802.11 standards, IEEE 802.11b is widely used since it operates at 2.4 GHz with high data rates up to 11 Mbps. However, an OFDM based 802.11a operates in the 5 GHz band with a maximum net data rate of 54 Mbps. When two vehicles/nodes are within a communication range of each other, WLAN offers the possibility of an ad-hoc V2V communication where the centralized infrastructure like AP is not required, and communication can be occurred directly among participating vehicles as depicted in Figure 1. All participating vehicles should be equipped with communication and computing equipments such as WLAN enabled laptops, GPS, etc.

Figure 1. Ad hoc based networking among vehicles using WLAN technology

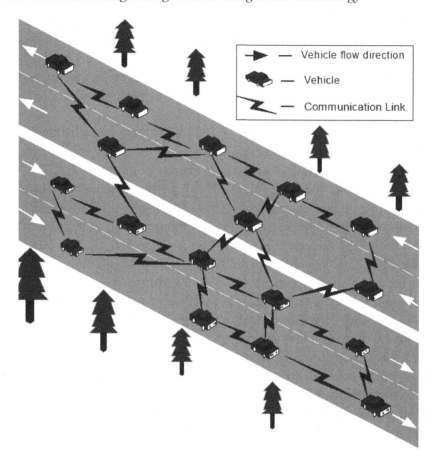

In 2004, an IEEE task group p (TGp) started to develop IEEE 802.11p by amending the IEEE 802.11 standard to include vehicular environment and make applicable for DSRC. Specifically, the IEEE 802.11p is the standard by IEEE for vehicular communication operating at speeds up to 200 km/h (124.27 miles/h) and handling communication range as high as 1000m (0.62 miles), and is designed to work at 5.9 GHz (5.850-5.925 GHz in USA) and allows data rates up to 27 Mbps that would be applied to support V2I communication, or, alternatively, V2V communication. The performance of 802.11p has been evaluated using simulations (Jiang & Delgrossi, 2008; Murray, Cojocari, & Fu, 2008; Wang, Ahmed, Krishnamachari, & Psounis, 2008). Another group formed to set up the standard with four documents IEEE 1609.1, IEEE 1609.2, IEEE 1609.3 and IEEE 1609.4. Collectively IEEE 802.11p and IEEE 1609.x are called wireless access in vehicular environment (WAVE).

It is worth to mention that, in WLAN, there is no guarantee of channel access slots for wireless nodes because of Carrier Sense Multiple Access / Collision Avoidance (CSMA/CA) channel access mechanism.

In order for ad hoc based WLAN technology to be employed effectively in VANETs, the following technical challenges have to be addressed (Valldorf & Gessner, 2005):

- Dynamic and distributed resource allocation for highly dynamic topology of VANET

- Time synchronization among vehicles susceptible to the speeds.
- Assignment and selection of appropriate physical layer specifications for communication system since the ISM bands are unlicensed and may be over crowed soon with a wide variety of applications. Moreover, the IEEE 802.11p addresses the physical layer issues only with single hop communication in a vehicular environment.
- Determining the level of fixed infrastructure required to fill in the gaps in communication that may exist during periods of low vehicle density in VANETs.
- Design appropriate routing protocols to address the particular requirements of VANETs and resistance to worst-case multi-path effects.

It is noted that the most of these problems are because of lack of centralized infrastructure unit installed along the roadside. However, as mentioned in previous, the installation of APs along the roadside is almost infeasible. The next Section deals with cellular infrastructure, which can be a potential candidate for vehicular communication.

D) Cellular Infrastructure

As mentioned in previous Section, the most extended and useful technologies for VANET are the wireless LAN technologies (especially IEEE 802.11a, IEEE 802.11b, IEEE 802.11g and the new standard IEEE 802.11p). In addition, the most of the current researches in vehicular communication are assumed to be based on ad hoc based VANETs. However, the communication among vehicles may not be possible all the time and locations because of the limitation of transmission power and range in low traffic density such as in rural highways. The vehicles move fast with high speed in rural areas resulting moderate to sparse vehicle density. Even in urban area there are chances of low penetration ratio or low

traffic in nighttime that results in sparse vehicle density, and the communication among vehicles using V2V may not be sufficient. This gap can be filled either by installing the infrastructure along the roadside and cross-sections or by using existing cellular infrastructures. In stead of installing new roadside infrastructures, Santa, et al. (2008) has been investigated the performance of vehicular communication using the existing cellular system infrastructures.

Moreover, the computer communication is considered as the major part of telematic services for intelligent transportation system, however, cellular network can be considered as a central part of vehicular communication by addressing some technical and operational issues making some change on them to be suitable for ITS (Santa, et al., 2008). Among many existing cellular network technologies, the mostly used technologies are CDMA (Code Division Multiple Access) in USA and CDMA based UMTS (Universal Mobile Telecommunications System) in Europe. Since the communication is based on centralized base-station and a backbone networks, the cellular network has completely different communication characteristics than those of Wireless LAN. The experimental work of Santa, et al. (2008) has shown that cellular networks based on UMTS can be suitable for both V2V and V2I communications for the development of ITS.

In order to consider cellular network for vehicular communication as a backbone of ITS, it is very important to take an account of the performance measuring parameters. Since the communication and information exchange between participating vehicles happen through a vehicle to base station and a base station to the vehicle with possible intermediate base station-to-station communication, one can expect higher delay/latency compared to wireless ad-hoc communication. Therefore the important and challenging performance parameter is latency in cellular based vehicular communication. The example of use of cellular technology in vehicular communications is depicted in Figure 2.

Figure 2. Cellular infrastructure for vehicular communication

It is well known that the cellular network is suitable for mobile services with regular latencies, and the latency is usually of several hundreds of milliseconds. This latency does not play any major role in voice communication for mobile phone-service users. However, the latency observed in cellular network to send an emergency relates messages from one vehicle to an adjacent vehicle is high. For 50 to 100 meters, current UMTS technology is able to give propagation times suitable to VANET, and an initial studies of future plans on UMTS confirms the latency time of about 60 milliseconds (Santa, et al., 2008). In UMTS system, initially the upper bound of downlink data rate was 384 Kbps and uplink rate was 64 Kbps. However, the data rate has been increased to 7.2 Mbps for downlink and 5.8 Mbps for uplink in the High-Speed Downlink Packet Access (HSDPA) extension. These modified specifications make UMTS technology suitable to vehicular communication for time critical emergency messages as well as for other regular messages.

Shankar, et al. (2005) has been performed an experiment on CDMA-1xEVDO based cellular network which offers an average rate of 300 – 400 kbps and bursts of up to 2 Mbps. The speed of vehicle does not affect the round trip time (RTT). But the latency observed in such cellular system is not in tolerable limit for emergency messages.

In contrast to WLAN based ad-hoc communication, in CDMA based cellular technology, it is worth to note that the vehicles have guaranteed communication channels since the CDMA lets communicate multiple vehicles simultaneously by assigning orthogonal spreading sequences. However, this technology has high delay/latency as communication among vehicles take place using combination of V2I, I2I and I2V communications.

It is almost impossible to implement existing cellular - third generation (3G) - technologies without making any modification in technical specifications suitable for vehicular communications. This is because existing cellular technologies are basically designed for voice communication, which are inherently centralized as they rely on single base station for one cell and multiple base stations along with backbone network to cover large area for communication. The following problems have to be addressed in order to implement and extend 3G technologies for vehicular communications:

- High delay and latency
- Distributed radio resource management
- Time synchronization
- Power control algorithms to determine the transmission range. However, power control is not a major problem in vehicular communication systems whereas this is major concern in cellular systems.

As we noted previously, there are several limitations in existing technologies, such as in WLAN and cellular technologies, to use in vehicular communications. Since the WLAN is especially made for low mobility and to replace wires and make scalable to some extension inside the office or buildings, such technology may not be suitable for highly dynamic and mobile vehicular networking. Similarly, the current 3G cellular technologies are made for voice communication with tolerable latency. However, the latency in cellular technologies when used in vehicular communication is not tolerable especially for the time sensitive emergency messages. Therefore, it is almost impossible to use them as main communication means in ITS because of high latency, relatively high cost and limited bandwidth in case of cellular technology, and limited mobility support in WLAN technologies. However, by making suitable amendment in those existing technologies, one can implement them in ITS. In addition to that, in VANETs, there are high threats in terms of security and privacy of the participating vehicles. In order to overcome all of these challenges, Abuelela, et al. (2008) has been recently proposed the NOTICE architecture. The following Section deals with details of NOTICE architecture, which is a possible candidate for vehicular communication.

III. THE NOTICE ARCHITECTURE

In vehicular communication, as we noted in previous Section, ad hoc based vehicular communication has many problems because of lack of centralized infrastructure. In order to address those problems and realize the full potential of vehicular networking in all scenarios for ITS, some experiments has been performed exploiting the existing cellular 3G technologies. However, without modifying existing cellular technology specifications, it is impossible to use in vehicular communication because of its high latency, which is undesirable for emergency and time sensitive information. In addition, in both technologies, there is vulnerability of security and privacy for participating vehicles and/or passengers. Recently proposed NOTICE architecture addresses all these issues (Abuelela, et al., 2008). The NOTICE system assumes that vehicles are equipped with a tamper-proof Event Data Recorder (EDR) designed to store basic information about the vehicle's movement such as information related to lane changes, speed variation, specific driver input about road conditions, and so on. The information stored in EDR will be exchanged with sensors embedded in a belt in the roadway.

In the NOTICE architecture, the sensor belts are plotted under the road in each lane at regular intervals, *e.g.,* every km or so, as shown in Figure 3 (a). All lanes are not interconnected with each other and two sides of a road are interconnected by wire through the median in order also to disseminate the information in opposite direction of the road.

The vehicle taking part in communication consists of EDR with two radio transceivers; one #1 in the front sedan and the other #2 at backside of the vehicle as shown in Figure 4. The front radio transceiver is placed at about 1 meter from front wheel of the vehicle. A sensor belt in each lane plotted underneath the highways will have one transceiver, which will transmit with low power so as to ensure security and privacy of participants. It works as a detector of possible candidate for communication with the help of two-way handshaking mechanism with #1 radio in a vehicle. The available time, for one-meter distance with the speed at about highest legal

Figure 3. (a) Two-lane roadway with vehicles and sensor belts in NOTICE architecture (b) Two-way two-lane roadway with incident in one lane (Abuelela, et al., 2008)

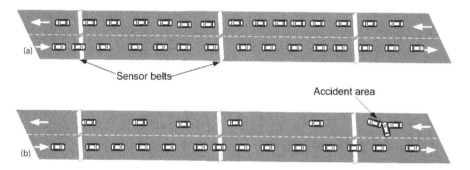

Figure 4. Sketch of two instances of a vehicle while communicating with a particular sensor belt in NOTICE System (Rawat, et al., 2008). The vehicle has #1 as a front radio for handshaking and # 2 as the second/rear radio for actual message exchange with the belt

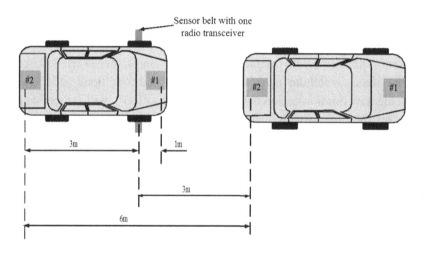

speed 65miles/h in USA, is approximately 36 milliseconds (≈1meter/65miles/h). The second transceiver is placed at the backside of the car at about 3 meter from the front wheel so that the total distance will be about 6 meter. This distance provides the time for actual information exchange between a vehicle and a belt. With the highest legal speed (65miles/h) the time available for information exchange is about 216 milliseconds (≈6meter/65miles/h). First of all, when a sensor belt on the road senses the front wheel of a vehicle, it tries to handshake with the front transceiver radio of the vehicle (if it is equipped with transceiver

radio) with low transmission power. If the handshake between the vehicle and the belt becomes successful, the belt uploads the information (if available) to the vehicle and vehicle delivers the information (if available) to the belt. In order to confirm an event related to a traffic incident a given belt aggregates information reported by multiple vehicles to report the incident and alert traffic participants, as vehicles cannot usually alert each other directly about incidents. Information flow in the NOTICE system is based upon the following communication scenarios:

A) Vehicle-to-Belt Communications

The most important part of NOTICE system is the communication between a vehicle and a sensor belt or vice versa. This vehicle-to-belt communication scenario is described schematically in Figure 4 and 5. In vehicle-to-belt communication, the process start after a sensor belt senses the front wheels of a vehicle when a vehicle arrived at the belt, and the transceiver of sensor belt tries to communication with a #1 transceiver of a vehicle. That is, as soon as the belt senses a vehicle passing over, a radio transceiver on the belt will attempt to establish communication with #1 transceiver in the vehicle by sending a short message with low transmit power for the purpose of handshaking. As mentioned previously, the speed of vehicles determines the available time for handshaking. With highest legal speed in US, the available time to respond by radio #1 with an acknowledgement message to the short message from the belt for handshaking has limited time about 36 milliseconds. The transceiver of a belt may or may not get the acknowledgement from a vehicle because of different reasons such as high speed of vehicle. If the belts does not get acknowledgement from the vehicle, it will assume that vehicle either does not have communication equipment or could not become successful handshaking because of high speed. In such scenario, the transceiver of the sensor belt will not attempt for actual information exchange for a particular vehicle. However, the belt will try the same approach for next incoming vehicle to transfer the data from one belt to the other belt. It is worth noting that there is no need of any encryption for handshaking data since it has short available time to make handshaking and no one will be able to make successful communication except the intended vehicle.

After having successful handshaking between a transceiver of a belt and #1 transceiver of a vehicle, a wireless radio link would be established with #2 radio transceiver of the vehicle, and information will be exchanged using symmetric key encryption technique (Abuelela, et al., 2008) in order to make secure communication. It is also important to note that the NOTICE architecture has been proposed to address the security and privacy of participants. Therefore, the transmission range of #1 radio and transceiver at sensor belt are chosen very low just to cover up to 1 meter for handshaking so that other unintended vehicles on the other lanes or on the same lane could not hear it. However, the transmission range for actual information exchange will be made higher up to 3 meter by increasing the transmit power than that used in handshaking, so that a longer time interval will be available for actual data exchange. The low transmission range and/or power protect the flow of information to unintended vehicle-receivers, and thus protect the system from malicious drivers.

The highway with embedded transceivers in sensor belts is the main infrastructure of the NOTICE system. The available time for both handshaking and information exchange is central concern because it depends on speed of the vehicle. Moreover, the connection set up time of the technology used in the transceivers of a sensor belt with two transceivers on a vehicle is another challenge to make successful communication. The existing technologies such as Blue tooth, WLAN and infrared are not suitable technologies for transceivers in the NOTICE architecture because the association or connection set up time for these technologies are greater than one second. We need the communication technology with association time having less than 36 milliseconds for first radio on the board. One possible technology for physical layer for the NOTICE architecture is ZigBee (Rawat, et al., 2008), which has an association time of about 30 milliseconds and sufficient data rate. As the installed sensor belts with transceivers are major component in NOTICE system, the installation cost of those components along the highways would be significantly high. It has not been discussed about the installation and operating cost for such sensor belts in NOTICE. The installa-

Figure 5. Sketch of timing diagram for handshaking and data exchange for vehicle-to-belt communication in NOTICE (Rawat, et al., 2008)

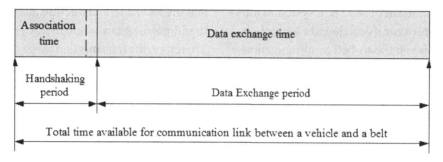

tion cost might be one of the major disadvantages in the implementation of the NOTICE system.

B) Sensor Belt-to-Belt Communications

This is a major means of information dissemination in NOTICE system. As mentioned previously, adjacent belts on the different lanes of a road are not connected with each other in order to deal with lane specific information, and the belts on opposite sides of highways will be connected by direct-wired link under the median of the road in order to disseminate the information in opposite direction of vehicle flow. Two adjacent sensor belts on the same lane do not directly communicate with each other but may exchange information using passing vehicles, and the communication between two sensor belts can be considered as belt-to-vehicle and vehicle-to-belt communications. This scenario assumes that one belt uploads the information for the next belt to a passing vehicle using belt-to-vehicle communication as described in Section III-A and that vehicle should deliver this information to the next incoming belt. As the vehicle gets information from one belt for the next coming belt, vehicles work as information carriers. It is worth to note that, in this scenario with an assumption of successful communications between vehicles and belts, the information travels from one belt to the other with a speed of vehicle.

In this scenario, with an assumption of tamper proof EDR on the vehicle, driver cannot change the information according to his own desire. However, installation of such black box in a vehicle as in an airplane would increase the cost of vehicle itself. This might be another major concern in the implemen-tation of the NOTICE system.

C) Vehicle-to-Vehicle Communications

This is the least desirable option of communication in NOTICE system since the security and privacy of participants in vehicular communications are major issues to be addressed by utilizing minimum V2V communications. However, in order to have information forwarding and disseminations even in worst cases where V2V communication is desirable for timely dissemination of information towards the intended region, NOTICE system support this type of communications. For instances, the information intended for next coming belt is uploaded to a vehicle using belt-to-vehicle communication, and a message-carrying vehicle is unable to reach to that destination belt to deliver the information due to congestion or other factors such as traffic lights at inter-sections, the vehicle will forward its content to the other vehicles, which are in front of it and are heading towards the destination belt. In this case the information flow will occur using multi-hop communication to the destination belt. The vehicle works as a source, router and/or destination in multi-hop communication whereas the vehicle works as a source and a destination in a single-hop communication.

In this scenario, the NOTICE system is as vulnerable as V2V communication, and it can be thought as a disadvantage in the implementation of this system. In order to implement V2V communication in NOTICE system, one has to address and adopt security and privacy solutions proposed in the literature.

D) Incident Detection Time

Incident or event detection time is unseen but the most important part in vehicular communication since the information does not come automatically to a vehicle or a sensor belt. In case of NOTICE system, the incident detection time can be defined as the time required by a sensor belt to determine that a traffic incident has occurred. This time depends on several parameters such as how much conservative the belt inference mechanism is, the spatial density of the vehicles (vehicles/km), how many instances of a received message can confirm the incident. Abuelela, et al. (2008) has been investigated the incident detection time under different scenarios. Generally speaking, all nominal vehicles arriving to a sensor belt successfully establish handshaking and do exchange the information. However, this assumption may be failed at the moment if the vehicle changes the lane when one belt of a lane has specific information to the next belt of the same lane. Moreover, incident detection time may be longer in some cases when some of the vehicles may be failed to establish a successful connection with the belt.

For reliability and trust of information which is received from the vehicles, the sensor belt collects the information from all passing and communicating vehicles, and aggregates the information after getting it from sufficient number of vehicles to upload that message to the next incoming vehicle in order to forward that information to the next

destination belt. If the sensor belt does not get the information from sufficient number of vehicles, the transceiver of a belt assumes that there is no incident happened, and will assume that the message received was from bad drivers who gave wrong information to the belt. In sparse vehicle density scenarios as well as when only a fraction of the vehicles are able to exchange information with the belts, the incident detection time required by the system will be affected. Using simulation results, Rawat, et al. (2008) has shown that the mean incident detection time is about 1 minute for the case when 70% of the vehicles communicate successfully with the belt. It is worth to note that the incident detection time for 100% successful vehicle-to-belt communication is only 7% higher than the time for 80% successful communication. In addition, according to the simulation results of Rawat, et al. (2008), it is concluded that the incident detection mean time is about 2 minutes for 30% successful vehicle-to-belt communication.

It is important to point out that the association or connection set up time plays central role in incident detection time. The NOTICE Architecture assumes that there is perfect technology to make association between the transceiver of a sensor belt and transceivers of a vehicle. We again mention that, for the legal highest speed of about 65 mph in US highways, the available time for association for front radio is about 36 milliseconds for handshaking, and for rear radio it is about 216 milliseconds for information exchange. These time values are calculated using standard relationship, that is, the distance is product of velocity and time. In NOTICE system the distances of both transceivers are fixed since the both transceivers are mounted on the vehicle rigidly so that the available distance for first radio is about 1 meter and for second radio is about 6 meter from a sensor belt as shown Figure 3. From the relationship among distance, time and velocity, it is clear that as the velocity/speed of a vehicle increases, the available time decreases for given distance. As a result the vehicle could not make handshake and successful communication with vehicles traveling with a speed higher than the highest US legal speed that is greater than 65 miles/h. In such cases, currently proposed NOTICE system might not be able to have successful communication between a belt and a vehicle. In order to address these issues, one can mount the radio at around 1 meter back from front wheel of a vehicle so that the total effective distance will be nearly 2 meters for the first radio and consequently the available time for handshaking will be high.

As mentioned previously, the less available time for handshaking and communication which is because of high speed of vehicle, and high association time of technologies used in transceivers play major role in incident detection time and are very serious concern in the implementation of NOTICE system. Recently, Rawat, et al. (2008) has been proposed ZigBee technology as a suitable physical layer air interface in the implementation of NOTICE environment without changing the position of two transceivers since the ZigBee has association or connection set up time approximately 30 milliseconds, (i.e., less than the time available for handshaking in NOTICE).

In order to increase the probability of successful communication between a transceiver of a belt and transceivers of a vehicle in NOTICE system implementation, the following modifications might be needed:

- Feasible physical layer air interface technology.
- Position and number of radio transceivers in a vehicle.
- Position of a transceiver in a sensor belt on each lane of highways.

E) *Security and Privacy Issues*

The main idea of information forwarding and dissemination in NOTICE system is based on belt-to-belt communication with the help of passing vehicles, and vehicles are assumed to be equipped with tamper-proof devices so that no one can damage or alter the information. Therefore, NOTICE system is least susceptible technology in terms of security and privacy issues. Moreover, a single belt aggregates the information received from multiple vehicles in a lane to confirm the validity of the information. After installing NOTICE system, there will not be any problem associated with ownership and trust of owners since the interactive sensor belts works as an information holder, and the information are actual messages rather than messages related to vehicles' identity. Therefore, we conclude that the NOTICE system offers best solution to the problems related to security and privacy in vehicular communications.

F) Solutions and Recommendations

The NOTICE system addresses the security and privacy issues with successful information forwarding and dissemination towards the destination region. However, it has not given the essential physical layer specifications, which are important in the implementation of the system.

Modification of system configuration such as position of radios on the vehicle as well as on the sensor belt can be done in order to increase the available time to make successful handshaking and data exchange using the available technologies. Without changing any system configurations of NOTICE system proposed by Abuelela, et al. (2008), one has to design a technology such as ultra-wide band which has less association or connection set up time compared to ZigBee, i.e., less than 30ms, and at least as high data rates as of ZigBee technology. Multimedia communication is not possible in the proposed NOTICE system. However, with the modification of the technical specifications, it might be possible in the future. Even though, the NOTICE system is perfect for information forwarding and dissemination in the case of safety and other applications in vehicular networks.

Table 1. Comparison of three different systems applicable in vehicular communications

Technologies Parameters	WLAN system	Cellular System	NOTICE System
1. Security and privacy	This is vulnerable since the vehicles working as a router need the identity of others.	Less vulnerable compared to WLAN since one can assign ID and keep the records of individual vehicles and can track malevolent one.	Least vulnerable because messages are not related to vehicles' identity except in V2V communication.
2. Latency, delay etc.	It has low delay since communication takes place between vehicles directly.	It has highest delay or latency than others since vehicle communicates with others through base station.	It has least delay or latency for all types of messages.
3. Reliability	Less reliable for emergency messages because of CSMA/CA mechanism.	Least reliable for emergency messages because of high latency.	Best for all types of messages once the incident is detected.
4. Support for multimedia content	Yes.	Yes.	No. But possible by amending specifications
5. Cost: installation, etc.	Less. Since we need to install WLAN enabled devices as an OBU.	No installation cost for infrastructure since one can use existing one, but there will be cost for an OBU.	Cost may be high to embed sensor belts at regular intervals in the road and to install EDR on the vehicle.
6. Modifications on specifications	Need to change according to DSRC.	Need to amend the specifications to reduce latency.	No need of major change in technical specifications.
7. Time synchronization	Need to be addressed.	Need to be addressed.	Not needed.
8. Distributed Resource allocation	Need to be performed.	Need to be performed.	No need of distributed resource allocation.

The feasibility analysis of the NOTICE system might be major concern in order to realize and implement it in real vehicular networking for the development of ITS.

IV. COMPARISON AMONG WLAN, CELLULAR AND NOTICE SYSTEMS

In this Section, we compare WLAN technology, cellular technology and NOTICE architecture from the prospective of implementation issues in vehicular communication for future ITS. We have taken in to account of metrics, which are important in vehicular communication, to compare these technologies as shown in Table 1.

V. CONCLUSION

In this chapter, we presented the survey of infrastructures and technologies that are applicable in vehicular communications for the development of future ITS. VANET is generally regarded as purely ad hoc based networking, however, it does not fulfill the requirement in low vehicle density region such as in rural area and in night time in urban areas. In such scenarios, the information exchange among vehicles might not always be possible using an ad-hoc based vehicle-to-vehicle networking but may also need a vehicle-to-infrastructure with possible intermediate infrastructure-to-infrastructure communications. As the vehicular communication is central component of ITS, in order to fill the gap created by sparse ad hoc networking, infrastructure plays a central role to realize the full potential of vehicular networking. In addition, by keeping the records of participants in centralized infrastructure, we can solve possible threats related to security and privacy issues by back tracing for malicious participants. We note that the existing cellular technology is not suitable for vehicular communication because of its high latency since the high latency makes almost impossible to forward and disseminate the time critical emergency information towards the destination region on time in accurate manner. However, with some modification in technical specifications, it is possible to use the existing cellular system as an infrastructure for vehicular communication. We have listed problems to be addressed and amendment recommendations in WLAN and cellular systems to implement in vehicular networking.

In this chapter, we mainly focused in the NO-TICE architecture where both sensor belts and highways work as an infrastructure for vehicular communication. As mentioned in this chapter, the NOTICE system is the remedy of the problems associated with WLAN based ad hoc networking and existing cellular technologies while used in vehicular communication. Moreover, it addresses the problems associated with privacy and security issues of participants in vehicular communication. We also presented the challenges, solutions and recommendations for NOTICE system in order to realize it in real vehicular environment.

All in all, we provided a survey of wireless technology-applications such as wireless LAN based ad-hoc networking, cellular technologies and NOTICE Architecture, and compared their characteristics in terms of their abilities to support vehicular communications for development of ITS.

REFERENCES

Abuelela, M., Olariu, S., & Weigle, M. C. (2008). *NOTICE: An Architecture for the Notification of Traffic Incidents*. Paper presented at the VTC Spring 2008. *IEEE Vehicular Technology Conference*, 2008.

Alvarez, L., & Horowitz, R. (1997). *Safe Platooning In Automated Highway Systems*.

Car2Car (2007). *Car2Car Project*. Retrieved from http://www.car-to-car.org/

CVIS. (2009). *CVIS Project*. Retrieved from http://www.cvisproject.org/

Festag, A., Noecker, G., Strassberger, M., Lübke, A., Bochow, B., Torrent-Moreno, M., et al. (2008). *'NoW – Network on Wheels': Project Objectives, Technology and Achievements*. Paper presented at the 5rd International Workshop on Intelligent Transportation (WIT).

Franz, W., Wagner, C., Maihofer, C., & Hartenstein, H. (2004). *Fleetnet: Platform for inter-vehicle communications*. Paper presented at the 1st Intl. Workshop on Intelligent Transportation.

Hartenstein, H., & Laberteaux, K. P. (2008, June). A tutorial survey on vehicular ad hoc networks. *IEEE Communications Magazine, 46*(6), 164–171. doi:10.1109/MCOM.2008.4539481

Jakubiak, J., & Koucheryavy, Y. (2008, January 10-12). State of the Art and Research Challenges for VANETs. Presented at the *5th IEEE Consumer Communications and Networking Conference, 2008. CCNC 2008* (pp.912-916).

Jerbi, M., & Senouci, S. M. (2008, April). Characterizing Multi-Hop Communication in Vehicular Networks. *IEEE Wireless Communications and Networking Conference, 2008. WCNC 2008* (pp.3309 – 3313).

Jerbi, M., Senouci, S. M., Doudane, Y. G., & Beylot, A. (2008, October 24). Geo-localized virtual infrastructure for urban vehicular networks. Presented at the *8th International Conference on ITS Telecommunications, 2008. ITST '08* (pp.305-310).

Jiang, D., & Delgrossi, L. (2008). *IEEE 802.11p: Towards an International Standard for Wireless Access in Vehicular Environments*. Paper presented at the IEEE Vehicular Technology Conference, 2008. VTC Spring 2008.

Kapadia, S., Krishnamachari, B., & Ghandeharizadeh, S. (2004, October). PAVAN: A Policy Framework for Availability in Vehicular Ad-Hoc Networks. Presented at the *First ACM Workshop on Vehicular Ad Hoc Networks (VANET 2004), Held in conjunction with ACM MobiCom,* Philadelphia, PA.

Karpiriski, M., Senart, A., & Cahill, V. (2006). *Sensor Networks for Smart Roads*. Paper presented at the PerCom Workshops 2006 - Fourth Annual IEEE International Conference on Pervasive Computing and Communications Workshops, 2006.

Kchiche, A., Kamoun, F., Makram, S. A., & Gunes, M. (2008, September 29-October 4). A Traffic-Aware Infrastructure-Based Architecture for Inter-vehicles File Sharing. Presented at *The Second International Conference on Mobile Ubiquitous Computing, Systems, Services and Technologies, 2008. UBICOMM '08* (pp.44-49).

Lin, X., Lu, R., Zhang, C., Zhu, H., Ho, P.-H., & Shen, X. (2008). 2008). Security in Vehicular ad hoc. *Networks, 46*(4), 88–95.

Marfia, G., Pau, G., Giordano, E., De Sena, E., & Geria, M. (2007, May 11). On Mobility Scenarios and Urban Infrastructure. In *Proceedings of A Case Study 2007 Mobile Networking for Vehicular Environments* (pp. 31–36). VANET.

Murray, T., Cojocari, M., & Fu, H. (2008). *Measuring the Performance of IEEE 802.11p Using ns-2 Simulator for Vehicular Networks*. Paper presented at the IEEE International Conference on Electro/Information Technology, 2008. EIT 2008.

Nekoui, M., Eslami, A., & Pishro-Nik, H. (2008, April). The capacity of Vehicular Ad Hoc Networks with infrastructure. Presented at the *6th International Symposium on Modeling and Optimization in Mobile, Ad Hoc, and Wireless Networks and Workshops, 2008. WiOPT 2008* (pp. 267-272).

Olariu, S., & Weigle, M. C. (Eds.). (2009). *Vehicular Networks: From Theory to Practice*. Boca Raton, FL: CRC Press.

Park, S., & Zou, C. C. (2008, April 28-30). Reliable Traffic Information Propagation in Vehicular Ad-Hoc Networks, *IEEE Sarnoff Symposium 2008* (pp. 16).

Parno, B., & Perrig, A. (2005). *Challenges in securing vehicular networks*. Paper presented at the Fourth Workshop on Hot Topics in Networks (HotNets-IV).

Petit, B., Ammar, M., & Fujimoto, R. (2006, April). Protocols for Roadside-to-Roadside Data Relaying over Vehicular Networks, *In Proc. of IEEE WCNC*.

Rawat, D. B., Treeumnuk, D., Popescu, D., Abuelela, M., & Olariu, S. (2008). *Challenges and Perspectives in the Implementation of NOTICE Architecture for Vehicular Communications*. Paper presented at the MASS 2008. 5th IEEE International Conference on Mobile Ad Hoc and Sensor Systems, 2008.

Rawat, D. B., Yan, G., Popescu, D., Weigle, M., & Olariu, S. (2009). *Dynamic Adaptation of Joint Transmission Power and Contention Window in VANET*. Paper presented at the IEEE Vehicular Technology Conference 2009 - Fall'09.

Raya, M., & Hubaux, J. P. (2005). *The Security of Vehicular ad hoc Networks*.

Rosi, U. T. Chowdhury, S. H., & Tai-hoon, K, A. (2008). Novel Approach for Infrastructure Deployment for VANET. *Future Generation Communication and Networking*, vol. *1*, 234-238. Presented at the 2nd International Conference on Future Generation Communication and Networking, 2008.

Rosi, U. T., Hyder, C. S., & Kim, T. (2008). *A Novel Approach for Infrastructure Deployment for VANET*. Paper presented at the FGCN '08. Second International Conference on Future Generation Communication and Networking, 2008.

SafeSpot. (2009). *SafeSpot Project*. Retrieved from http://www.safespot-eu.org

Santa, J., Moragon, A., & Gomez-Skarmeta, A. F. (2008). *Experimental Evaluation of a Novel Vehicular Communication Paradigm Based on Cellular Networks*. Paper presented at the IEEE Intelligent Vehicles Symposium 2008.

Shankar, P., Alam, M. T., Musharoff, S., Ravi, N., Prados, C. V., Gradinescu, V., et al. (2005). *Outdoor Experience with the Traffic View Application*.

Valldorf, U., & Gessner, W. (Eds.). (2005). *Advanced Microsystems for Automotive Applications 2005*. Springer Berlin Heidelberg. doi:10.1007/b139105

Verma, M., & Huang, D. (2009, January 10-13). SeGCom: Secure Group Communication in VANETs. Presented at the *6th IEEE Consumer Communications and Networking Conference, 2009*. (pp. 1-5).

VSCC. (2005). *Vehicle Safety Communications Project Task 3 Final Report: Identify Intelligent Vehicle Safety Applications Enabled by DSRC* (No. *DOT HS, 809, 859*.

Wang, Y., Ahmed, A., Krishnamachari, B., & Psounis, K. (2008). *IEEE 802.11p Performance Evaluation and Protocol Enhancement*. Paper presented at the IEEE International Conference on Vehicular Electronics and Safety.

Wegener, A., Hellbruck, H., Wewetzer, C., & Lubke, A. (2008, November 30-December 4). VANET Simulation Environment with Feedback Loop and its Application to Traffic Light Assistance. In Proceedings of the IEEE GLOBECOM Workshops, 2008 (pp. 1-7).

Wewetzer, C., Caliskan, M., Meier, K., & Luebke, A. (2007). *Experimental Evaluation of UMTS and Wireless LAN for Inter-Vehicle Communication*. Paper presented at the ITST '07. 7th International Conference on ITS Telecommunications, 2007. ADDITIONAL READINGS Ghandeharizadeh, S., & Krishnamachari, B. (2004). C2P2: A Peer-to-Peer Network for On-Demand Automobile Information Services. *In First International Workshop on Grid and Peer-to-Peer Computing Impacts on Large Scale Heterogeneous Distributed Database Systems (Globe'04)*.

Xu, Q., Mak, T., & Sengupta, R. (2004). *Vehicle-to-Vehicle Safety Messaging in DSRC*. ACM VANET, Oct 2004.

Yousefi, S., Mousavi, M. S., & Fathy, M. (2006). Vehicular Ad Hoc Networks (VANETs): Challenges and Perspectives, In *Proceeding of ITS Telecommunications s, 2006 6th International Conference on June 2006* (pp. 761-766).

Yuen, W. H., Yates, R. D., & Sung, C. W. (2003). Performance evaluation of highway mobile infostation network. Presented at the IEEE GLOBECOM 2003 at San Francisco, December, 2003.

Zhao, J., & Cao, G. (2006). VADD: Vehicle-Assisted Data Delivery in Vehicular Ad Hoc Networks. *InfoCom, 2006*, 16.

Chapter 2
Architecture of Vehicular Ad Hoc Network

Debika Bhattacharyya
Salt Lake Electronics Complex, India

Avijit Bhattacharyya
Salt Lake Electronics Complex, India

ABSTRACT

Over the last few years Vehicular Ad hoc Networks (VANETs) have gained much attention within the automobile industry and the research applications. Vehicular Ad hoc networks (VANETs) are a subgroup of mobile adhoc networks (MANETs) with the distinguishing property that the nodes are vehicles like cars, trucks, buses and motorcycles. Nodes are expected to communicate by means of North American direct short-range communication (DSRC) standard [1] that employs the IEEE 802.11p standard for wireless communication and describes a MAC and PHY specifications for wireless connectivity. This chapter deals with the basic architecture of VANET and wired and wireless technology for intra-vehicular communication. Two prominent networking technologies such as Local Interconnect Network (LIN) and the Controller Area Network (CAN) for wired intra-vehicular communication have also been discussed. The objective of this chapter is to explain inter-vehicular communication and the components of a smart vehicle.

INTRODUCTION

A Vehicular Ad hoc Network (VANET) is a special type of short-range wireless communication mobile ad hoc network (MANET) in which all nodes are vehicles that move generally at high speed. The VANET is a decentralized, self organizing and infrastructure less network unlike Wi-Fi, Wimax, GSM technology.

Modern vehicles are often designed as local area networks, with the ability to connect multiple embedded computers which can communicate among themselves as well as with other vehicles via multiple wireless connections. The VANET is thus being used in many commercial applications like providing efficient routing information to the other vehicles, informing the drivers about the

DOI: 10.4018/978-1-61520-913-2.ch002

Figure 1. Vehicular ad hoc network

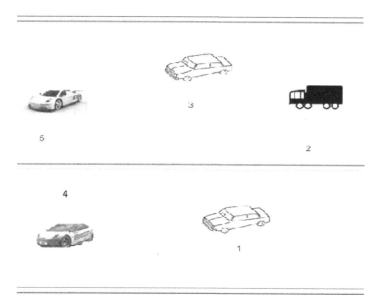

traffic conditions, accidents, road conditions etc. For this purpose the VANET uses sensor devices to monitor the network conditions such as vibration, pressure, motion, pollution, temperature and sound. Each sensor is capable of collecting relevant information and transmits the data to others. These sensor devices are very small, low cost and can be deployed in a large numbers in the network. Federal Communications Commission (USA) has recently allocated 75MHz in 5.9GHz band for short range communication for vehicle-to-vehicle and vehicle-to-infrastructure communications.

In VANET, radio communication among vehicles is complex [4] for three main reasons:

1. The environment in which the vehicles move has many radio reflective surfaces.
2. Vehicles travel at a wide range of speeds, resulting in disruption of radio communication.
3. Radio frequency (RF) interference is common from both in-car sources and other nearby transmitters.

Generally, Vehicular communication in VANET can be of two types:

1. Inter-vehicle communication
2. Intra-vehicle communication.

The *intra-vehicle communications* is used to describe communications within a vehicle, whereas the term *inter-vehicle communications* [3] [6] represents communications between vehicles or vehicles and sensors placed in or on various locations, such as roadways, signs, parking areas, and even the home garage. Inter-vehicle communications can be considered to be more technically challenging because in this case the vehicle communications need to be supported both when vehicles are stationary and when they are moving.

Figure 1 illustrates an example of a Vehicular Ad Hoc Network. In the figure we see three cars

Figure 2. Vehicular Mesh structure

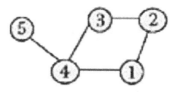

Figure 3. Vehicle mobility can result in broken links, which dynamically rearranges the paths between nodes

2, 3 and 5 in one lane and another two cars 1, 4 in another lane of a highway. The cars 1, 2, 3, 4 and 5 are in close proximity with one another and accordingly they can form a Vehicular Ad Hoc Network or VANET. In this example the car 2 and 3 in the first lane and cars 1 and 4 in the second lane are within direct communication to each other. Again cars 2 and 1, cars 3 and 4 and cars 5 and 4 are also within communications range of one another.

In the Figure 2, the vehicles have been treated as nodes and corresponding to *Figure 1*, mesh structure is shown in the *Figure 2* which can be used to relay information from one member of VANET to another member. Each vehicle will use wireless local area network (WLAN) technology as a mechanism to form a Vehicle Ad Hoc Network. Because the IEEE 802.11 LANs use 48-bit Media Access Control (MAC) addresses to identify nodes, those addresses would be used

to form the ad hoc network. As vehicles move on the highway, the connections between vehicles will dynamically change. Vehicle mobility can thus result in broken links, which dynamically rearranges the path between nodes. For example say car 2 moves out of network then the corresponding structure is shown in *Figure 3*. In that case the VANET will dynamically reconfigure itself and the corresponding mesh structure is shown in *Figure 4*.

Figure 4. Modified vehicular mesh structure

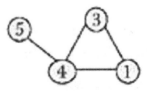

DIFFERENCES BETWEEN VANET AND MANET

As discussed, the term vehicular Ad hoc network (VANET) is used for a subgroup of mobile Ad hoc networks (MANETs). Both VANET and MANET are characterized by the movement and self-organization of the nodes. But they are also different in some ways. MANET can contain many nodes that have un-controlled moving patterns. But since VANET is formed mainly by vehicles so node movement is restricted by factors like road course, traffic and traffic regulations. Because of the restricted node movement it is quite likely that the VANET will be supported by some fixed infrastructure that provide some services and access to stationary networks. The fixed infrastructure will be deployed at critical locations like slip roads, service stations, dangerous intersections or places well-known for hazardous weather conditions. Nodes are expected to communicate by means of North American DSRC standard that employs the IEEE 802.11p standard for wireless communication. Vehicles that are not subjected to the strict energy, space and computing capabilities restrictions normally adopted MANETs. The very high speed of the nodes (up to 250 km/h) and the large dimensions of the VANET are more challenging problems in recent research areas [2].

INTRA-VEHICLE COMMUNICATIONS

In this section we would discuss Intra-vehicle communications which may be done using wired technology or wireless technology as explained below.

Wired Technology

Nowadays, general vehicles include electronic luxuries. For example, top-of-the range vehicles adopt sophisticated electronics, such as intelligent cruise controls that automatically maintain a safe distance from the vehicle ahead. Estimates suggest that the electronics content of an average car now accounts for no less than 22% of its manufacturing cost, creating markets for the embedded controllers. The automotive industry uses two main networking technologies: Local Interconnect Network (LIN) and Controller Area Network (CAN). In this section we will study the technology associated with the Local Interconnect Network (LIN), its use in automobiles and other vehicles, the role of the LIN consortium, and its use as a bridge into a Controller Area Network (CAN). CAN was introduced by Bosch for intra-vehicle networks in 1986. LIN supports the interoperability of network nodes from the viewpoint of hardware and software. CAN is more robust and costly network than LIN. In this context it is worth mentioning that the LIN protocol is specified by the LIN Consortium. The founding members of the LIN Consortium were Volvo Car Corporation, Daimler Chrysler, European car manufacturers as BMW, Volkswagen Audi Group.

LIN Application

LIN is a single wire serial communication protocol based on common UART (universal asynchronous receiver-transmitter) interface. It uses a single master, multiple slave networking architecture. Body controlled electronics improve the comfort and safety of vehicle occupants. To produce smarter vehicles, advancement of body control electronics is an essential element for the car manufacturers so that the car becomes pleasing to drive, reliable and safer. Body control electronics also improve the safety factor of a vehicle by simplifying the operation of the vehicle and releasing the driver of distractions from secondary activities

Typical applications for the LIN bus include assembly units such as doors, steering wheel, seats, and motors and sensors in climate control, lighting, rain sensors, smart wipers, intelligent alternators, switch panels and RF receivers. They can be easily connected to the car network and become accessible to all types of diagnostics and services. Nowadays the commonly used analog coding of signals is being replaced by digital signals, leading to an optimized wiring control.

LIN and CAN Connectivity

In a centralized body control system, actuators and sensors are hardwired to one electronic control unit (ECU) with CAN connectivity. One ECU exchanges signals via a CAN link with other main ECUs. In systems where the local performance can be low, an alternative distributed system based on smart actuators and sensors can be used. This architecture is cost effective if the additional expenditure for the local intelligence and networking can be compensated by cost savings due to fewer total electronic components. The key enablers for this architecture are the sub-bus LIN standard, low-cost mechatronic assembly and semiconductor integration.

LIN being the key technology for low-end applications, two factors are critical: (a) the communication cost per node must be significantly low compared with CAN and (b) the performance, bandwidth and versatility of CAN are not required. The main cost savings of LIN versus CAN are derived from: (1) the single-wire transmission of LIN, (2) the low cost of implementation as hardware or software in silicon, and (3) the avoidance of crystals or ceramic resonators in slave nodes. These advantages are compromised with a lower bandwidth and the restrictive single-master bus access scheme.

LIN Specification

The LIN specification covers the transmission protocol, the transmission medium, and the tools for interface development and application software. LIN represents an open standard that provides a low-cost alternative to the use of the Controller Area Network (CAN). LIN uses a single conductor wire to form a 12-V bus. It is a relatively low-cost serial communication system developed to provide communication between electronic systems and sensors in vehicles. LIN can be applied in forward/backward, horizontal position motor, light control (light sensor) for interior light, navigation control, wiper control, window lift, door lock etc. In LIN communication is based upon the serial communications interface (SCI) universal asynchronous receiver-transmitter (UART) data format.

The LIN specification has three parts, LIN protocol Specification describing physical and data link layers, LIN Configuration Language and LIN Application Programming Interface (API). LIN Configuration file configures the network whereas LIN API gives the interface between the network and the application program. The maximum data rate supported in LIN is 20 kbps and the maximum distance supported in LIN is 40 m.

A LIN consists of 1 master and 16 slave nodes. Since the message transmitted by the master reaches all nodes so LIN forms a broadcast network. Here no collision detection mechanism exist and the master node initiates all communication. Consequently a powerful microcontroller is considered as the master node whereas for slave nodes less powerful nodes can be chosen as slave node. In the modern automobile several LINs are connected to a Controller Area Network (CAN). The operation principles of CAN are discussed later. This interconnection to a central location is done via the master node. This must be done in order to provide warning information on a console display, performing testing and controlling other activities.

The master initiates and stops the transmission of data with the help of a scheduling table. The slave task is rather simple. The slave task responds to a master task when any data is sent by the master for that slave otherwise the slave ignores it.

Nodes can be added to the LIN network without requiring hardware or software changes in other slave nodes. The size of a LIN network is typically under 16 nodes (though not restricted to this), resulting from the small number of identifiers and the relatively low transmission speed. The clock synchronization, the simplicity of UART communication, and the single-wire medium are the major factors for the cost efficiency of LIN.

COMMUNICATION CONCEPT

A LIN network is comprised of one master node and one or more slave nodes. All nodes include a slave communication task that is split into a transmit and a receive task, while the master node includes an additional master transmit task. The communication in an active LIN network is always initiated by the master task.

Unlike CAN, LIN's master/slave architecture avoids data-traffic collisions and the need for arbitration logic by having the master supervise message transmissions, thus ensuring that only one message transmits at any time. To initiate a data transfer following an interframe space or bus-idle condition, the master transmits a header comprising a synchronization-break period, a single-byte-synchronization field, and an identifier byte. The identifier byte carries six bits of information and two parity bits, allowing 64 message identifiers. In normal operation, there is no addressing as such; rather like CAN, the identifier byte uniquely defines the purpose of the frame. Exactly one slave task is activated upon reception and filtering of the identifier, and starts the transmission of the message response. The response contains two, four or eight data bytes and one checksum byte. The header and the response form one message frame.

The identifier of a message denotes the content of a message but not the destination. This communication concept enables the exchange of data in various ways: from the master node (using its slave task) to one or more slave nodes, and from one slave node to the master node and/or other slave nodes. It is possible to send signals directly from slave to slave without the need for routing through the master node, or broadcasting messages from the master to all nodes in a network. The sequence of message frames is controlled by the master. The number, sequence and frequency of messages in the scheduling frame of the master determine, along with the baud rate, the system response time and time behaviour. Because it's imperative to preserve battery power when the vehicle is inoperative, slaves automatically enter sleep mode if the bus is idle for more than four seconds. Careful system design is necessary since, if the master missed a slave message, this message will reach the master earliest at the next schedule sequence due to the master-slave concept. The requirement for the master node can be covered by high-performance 8-bit microcontrollers with CAN interface and USART/Enhanced USART. Memory requirement and package size demand depend on the software functions, CAN software stack and hardware I/O requirements.

Slave node functions in this example are typically within the scope of lower performance but cost-effective 8-bit microcontrollers. Generally, I/O demand is covered in 14-pin to 28-pin packages while program memory ranges from 2 KB to 16 KB, depending on the complexity of control functions.

LIN Slave Implementation

Depending on the complexity of the LIN slave application and budget allocated for the slave microcontroller, LIN can be implemented in software, by using a Standard USART, with an Enhanced LIN USART or with dedicated LIN hardware.

A LIN frame can transport from one to eight data bytes, with each data byte transmitted in a byte field. When more than one data byte is transmitted the least significant byte (LSB) is transmitted first while the most significant byte (MSB) is transmitted last.

OVERVIEW OF CONTROLLER AREA NETWORK (CAN)

The Controller Area Network (CAN) is a serial, asynchronous, multimaster communication protocol for connecting control modules in the vehicle designed by Bosch in 1986. Actually Mercedes Benz had planned for a car model with a communications system that would be capable of interconnecting three electronic control units (ECUs). Then Bosch understanding this requirement determined that as the UART was designed for point-to-point communications, so it was not suitable for this type of vehicle. Recognizing the need for a multi-master communications system, Intel Corporation fabricated the first CAN silicon chip, and then subsequently it was designed by from Phillips and other vendors. Different transceivers are used with different physical layers of CAN so the cost of CAN becomes higher and this result in the use of LIN as a mechanism to provide a lower-cost communications capability.

The CAN communications protocol describes the method by which information is passed between devices. It conforms to the Open Systems Interconnection model which is defined in terms of layers. Each layer in a device apparently communicates with the same layer in another device. Actual communication is between adjacent layers in each device and the devices are only connected by the physical medium via the physical layer of the model. The CAN architecture defines the lowest two layers of the model: the data link and physical layers. The application levels are linked to the physical medium by the layers of various emerging protocols, dedicated to particular industry areas plus any numbers of propriety schemes defined by individual CAN users. The physical and data link layers will normally be transparent to the system designer and are included in any component that implements the CAN protocols. There are some microcontrollers with integral CAN interfaces, for example, the Philips 8051-compatible 8xC592 processor and the Siemens SABC167CR. The 80C200 is a standalone CAN controller which directly interfaces to many microcontrollers. The connection to the physical medium can be implemented with discrete components or with the 82C250 integrated circuit. Standalone CAN controllers are also available from Siemens, NEC and Intel.

There are two methods by which a CAN controller is programmed. The first initial CAN controller was the Intel 82526 CAN controller that provided a dual-port random access memory (DPRAM) interface for programming. Phillips discovered 82C200 CAN controller, which used a first-in, first-out (FIFO) queue programming model. Intel CAN controller was referred to as full CAN whereas Phillips method is referred to as basic CAN. Nowadays most CAN controllers support both full CAN an and basic CAN. Also there are other two CAN versions *standard CAN* and *extended CAN* that support 11-bit identifiers and 29 bit identifiers in a frame respectively.

The subdivision of CAN into standard and enhanced versions resulted in two ISO standards. ISO 11519 has an upper limit of 125 kbps, while ISO 11898 provides for data rates up to 1 Mbps. To specify different maximum data rates, the two ISO specifications differ primarily in their definition of the physical layer.

There are two versions of CAN, one supporting data rates up to 125 kbps while the other versions of CAN support data rates up to 1 Mbps which is much higher than the maximum data rate supported by LIN. CAN operates at the physical and data-link layers of the Open Systems Interconnection (OSI) Reference Model. Under CAN a broadcast transmission method is employed for placing frames on the bus. In LIN, the number of slave nodes is limited to 16 which are controlled by a master node, whereas CAN theoretically has the ability to link up to 2032 devices on a single network. But due to hardware transceiver constraints CAN can connect up to 110 nodes on a single network.

Figure 5. Connection between CAN controller and CAN bus

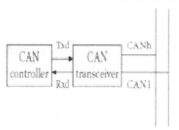

CAN Controllers and CAN Bus

There are three types of CAN controllers which are referred to as Part A, Part B, and Part B passive. All of the three controllers support the standard version of CAN, which uses 11-bit identifiers. But for extended CAN with the 29-bit identifier, only Part B controller should be used because Part A controller will generate errors.

The two-wire CAN bus represents the most popular implementation of CAN. The two-wire CAN bus uses non-return-to-zero (NRZ) signaling with bit stuffing. Bit stuffing prohibits the transmission of a string of six consecutive zero (000000) or six consecutive one (111111) bits by inserting an opposite bit in the data stream to prevent the transmission of six bits set to a 0 or 1. A CAN transceiver has two connections to the bus. The first connection (CANh) is used to transmit a differential signal, while the second connection (CANl) is used to monitor the CAN bus, which also provides for the receipt of the receiver signal by the CAN controller

Figure 5. illustrates the connection of a CAN controller to a two-wire CAN bus.

The figure 6 shows the corresponding timing diagram of the signal for communication between CAN controller and CAN bus. The CAN controller is usually integrated on a digital signal processor (DSP) chip, which in turn is built into an electronic control unit (ECU). Thus, the CAN controller provides the mechanism whereby one

Figure 6. Timing diagram of the signal for communication between CAN controller and CAN bus

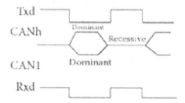

ECU can communicate with another to check its status or exchange information.

In CAN a modified carrier sense multiple access with collision detection (CSMA/CD) method is used for transmission of data in which each device listens to the bus to determine if the message flowing on the bus is the same as it is trying to transmit. If it is different, the device will immediately release the bus. This process ensures that one master will always win and results in no messages lost due to a collision.

To place data on the bus arbitration free transmission is used where a CAN message transmitted with the lower-priority messages will sense the existence of higher priority message and back off and wait for access to the bus. In this method a dominant bit (logical 0) will always win the arbitration whereas a recessive (logical 1) bit loses.

During the arbitration process each transmitting node will monitor the state of the CAN bus

Table 1. Comparing features of CAN and LIN

Feature	LIN	CAN
Network topology	Bus	Bus
Number of wires	2	1
Maximum data rate	20 kbps	1Mbps
Communications method	UART based	Controller based
Network access	Master-initiated transmission	Nondestructive
Node support	1 master, up to 15 slaves	64-128; typically limited by physical layer or higher layer protocol

and compare the received bit with the transmitted bit. If a dominant bit is received when a recessive bit is transmitted the node will stop transmitting.

In the actual arbitration process in the message frame the identifier field is transmitted by each node with a dominant bit as binary 0 and beginning with the high-order bit. As soon as the node ID becomes a larger number it indicates that it has a lower priority. Then the node will transmit a binary 1 (recessive) and if it observes a binary 0 (dominant), then the node will back off and wait. So we can see that the node with the highest priority continues its transmission and all other nodes will be backed off and they will automatically retransmit in the next bus cycle or in a subsequent bus cycle, if there are other higher-priority messages waiting to gain access to the bus.

Network Comparison

Table 1 provides a comparison of the major features of LIN and CAN. In the table five key technologic features of each networking technology has been compared.

Form the above Table 1; it is apparent that though both LIN and CAN support a bus topology, yet they have significant differences in other features. Those differences include the number of wires used, maximum data rate achieved, method of network access supported, and number of nodes that can be in a network. By further examining the comparative entries in the Table 1 it is apparent that CAN is a more robust networking

technology that can support four to eight times the maximum number of nodes than in a LIN environment at a maximum operating rate. However, to achieve this higher level of performance, CANs have a controller based design, whereas LINs are universal asynchronous receiver-transmitter (UART) based. This result in the cost of a LIN, to include the chips required to connect nodes to the bus, being significantly less than the cost of the electronics required to attach nodes to the bus in a CAN environment.

In the above section we have discussed wired communications that is primarily used to support intra-vehicle communications. In the next section we will explain the wireless technology used for intra-vehicle communications.

WIRELESS INTRA-VEHICULAR COMMUNICATIONS

With the rapid use of wireless technology, the modern vehicles are increasingly using wireless technology for communication purposes. Among different applications using wireless technology some of the popular applications are hands-free cell phone operation, remote door unlocking, updated navigation, and traffic reporting etc. Although some wireless communications technologies extend beyond a vehicle, such as satellite communications, we will consider them to represent a wireless intra-vehicle communications method. So now we will turn our attention to Bluetooth and satellite services such as satellite radio and satellite-based vehicle services.

Bluetooth Introduction

Bluetooth is a low-power, short-range wireless technology originally developed for replacing cables when connecting devices like mobile phones, headsets and computers. It has since evolved into a wireless standard for connecting electronic devices to form Personal Area Networks (PANs) as well as ad hoc networks. Not only will cables be unnecessary for connecting devices, but connections will also be done seamlessly without the need for installations and software drivers. With this technology, devices will be able to discover any other Bluetooth-enabled device, determine its capabilities and applications, and establish connections for data exchange. The key features of Bluetooth technology are robustness, low power, and low cost. A fundamental Bluetooth wireless technology strength is the ability to simultaneously handle both data and voice transmissions. The Bluetooth technology operates in the open 2.4 GHz ISM band. With adaptive frequency hopping (AFH), the signal "hops" and thus limits interference from other signals. Further, Bluetooth technology has built-in security such as 128bit encryption and PIN code authentication.

How Bluetooth Works

Bluetooth operates on the unlicensed Industrial Scientific Medical (ISM) band at 2.4 GHz, which ensures worldwide communication compatibility. Since the ISM band is open to anyone, systems operating on this band must deal with several unpredictable sources of interference, such as microwave ovens, baby monitors and 802.11 wireless networks. Hence, to minimize the risk of such interference, Bluetooth uses a Frequency Hopping Spread Spectrum (FHSS) technology for its air interface. During a connection, radio transceivers hop from one channel to another. This

means that after one packet is sent on a channel, the two devices retune their frequencies (hop) to send the next packet on a different channel. When the transmission encounters a disturbance due to interference, the packet will simply be retransmitted on a different channel. Hence, if one frequency channel is blocked, there will be a limited disturbance to the Bluetooth communication. This allows several Bluetooth networks to run concurrently without interrupting one other. The link rate offered by Bluetooth is 1 Mbps, but with overhead, this effectively becomes 721 kbps. The typical range for Bluetooth is 10m, but it can reach up to 100m depending on the power class of the device.

Bluetooth devices can interact with one or more other Bluetooth devices in several different ways. The simplest scheme is when only two devices are involved. This is referred to as "point-to-point". One of the devices acts as the master and the other as a slave. When there is just one Master and one Slave the system is called a Point to Point connection. When many Slaves are connected to one Master, the system is called a Point to Multipoint. Both these types sharing the same channel form a Piconet. The Slaves in the Piconet only have links to the Master and no direct links between Slaves. There can be up to seven active slaves in a Piconet. Each of the active slaves has an assigned 3-bit Active Member address. Apart from the active slaves there can be additional slaves which remain synchronized to the master, but do not have an Active Member address. These slaves are not active and are referred to as parked. In case of both active and parked units, all channel access is regulated by the master. A parked device has an 8-bit Parked Member Address, so the maximum number of parked members is 256. A parked device remains synchronized to the master clock and can very quickly become active and begin communicating in the piconet.

Every Bluetooth device has a unique Bluetooth device address and a 28-bit Bluetooth clock. The baseband part of the Bluetooth System uses a

Figure 7. Piconet and Scatternet of Bluetooth

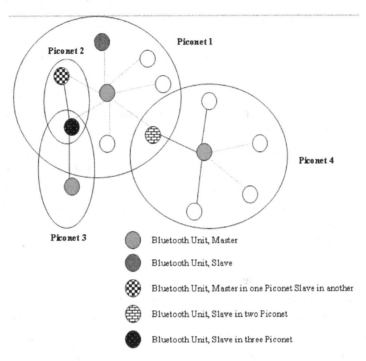

special algorithm, which calculates the frequency hop sequence from the masters clock and device address which can be found from the FHS packet. A set of two or more interconnected Piconets form Scatternet. In a Scatternet a device can be a Master in one Piconet and a Slave in another. Figure 7 explains the piconet and scatternet of Bluetooth.

The Bluetooth specification defines 3 power classes for radio transmitters with an output power shown in Table 2.

In examining the entries in Table 2 we can see that the most powerful Bluetooth class is Class 1, as it provides a maximum power level that can extend the range of transmission to approximately 100 m. For most in-vehicle operations, Class 2 Bluetooth should be more than sufficient, as it enables a transmission range of up to approximately 10 m.

There are four types of addresses that can be assigned to a Bluetooth device. One address is a three-bit number referred to as the MAC address. This address is valid only when a slave is active

Table 2. Output power of different classes of radio transmitter

Power Class	Maximum Output Power (mW)
Class 1	100
Class 2	2.5
Class 3	1

on a channel. The other Bluetooth addresses include a device address, parked member address, and access request address.

The Bluetooth device address is a unique 48-bit address. The parked member address is an eight-bit address used to identify up to 255 parked slaves. This address is only valid as long as the slave is parked. The access request address is used by a parked slave to determine the slave-to-master half slot in the access window it can use to transmit access request messages. Similar to the parked member address, the access request address is only valid when the slave is parked.

There are two major operational modes for a Bluetooth device standby and connection. The standby state represents the default low-power state in a Bluetooth device. In this state there is no interaction between devices. To obtain connectivity between devices, one device (master) will transmit an inquiry packet that the destination (slave) will respond to with an inquiry response. Once this is accomplished, the source will page the destination. In response, the destination will transmit a slave response. The master will then transmit a frequency hop sequence to the slave, allowing the two devices to exchange information as they hop through a pseudo-random sequence of frequencies.

As devices exchange information, a series of functions are performed that are transparent to the device operations. Those functions include three types of forward error correction schemes to reduce transmission errors, flow control to prevent the loss of data as queues fill, and synchronization of devices to the master's clock.

Bluetooth Applications in Vehicles

There are several existing and potential Bluetooth applications that can be used within a vehicle. The most frequently used application involves the extension of the use of a cell phone to a hands-free environment.

Hands-Free Cell Phone Use

The most common use of Bluetooth within a vehicle is for the driver or passenger to use a hands-free headset that is used to wirelessly control many cell phone operations. For example, by pressing a button on the headset, the driver or passenger can answer an incoming call without the necessity to touch the cell phone. Likewise, pressing the button a second time will disconnect the call. A microphone that extends below the ear allows the driver or passenger to communicate with the caller.

A second type of hands-free vehicle communication involving the use of a cell phone is the integration of the vehicle's radio system with the phone. A Bluetooth-compliant cell phone may be integrated into the vehicle's electronic circuit through the use of a Bluetooth adapter typically mounted in the interior of the vehicle's central console. This integration allows the driver or operator to use buttons on the radio to call another telephone, with the radio speakers used to provide audio reception of the distant party. When an incoming call is received, any sound generated by the radio or CD player is temporarily muted, allowing the speakers to be used for the audio generated by the caller. This capability may be enhanced further to a higher level, for example some vehicle manufacturers that support high-end cell phones enable the driver or passenger to use his or her voice to initiate and disconnect calls, as well as to utilize additional such functions as adding and editing the phone book entries in the cell phone.

Evolving Applications

Bluetooth represents a low-cost, limited-distance transmission technology and it is well suited to enable mobile devices to be integrated into a vehicle's prewired entertainment system in the vehicle's console. This means that with appropriate software the following functionality (for example) may be possible:

1. To move mobile navigation systems from one vehicle to another and use the console display to provide a map of the route to a specific destination,
2. To allow the key pad and phone list of a cell phone to operate a mobile navigation system,
3. To enable debit cards to be used to pay tolls via their insertion into a reader integrated into a miniature transponder located within a vehicle.

Thus, the use of Bluetooth technology within a vehicle can be used in connecting different mobile devices within a vehicle.

SATELLITE SERVICES

This section on wireless applications with a vehicle will be incomplete if we do not discuss about the satellite services. Next we will briefly mention several existing and evolving satellite-based applications that are being marketed for use within a vehicle.

Satellite Radio

A satellite radio is a digital radio signal that is broadcast by a communications satellite, which covers a much wider geographical range than terrestrial radio signals. Most popular satellite-based service is satellite radio, which provides subscribers with a large number of stations to listen to. Many mobile satellite radio receivers that are built into modern vehicles can be easily moved from a vehicle into a home or office. This is generally offered as a subscription-based service and makes sense to purchase because only a small portion of the day is spent in most vehicles.

INTER-VEHICLE COMMUNICATION

Inter-vehicle communications means the flow of communications between vehicles as well as from a vehicle to sensors or transponders located on a highway, road, or street that is used by a vehicle. For inter-vehicular communication the use of Mobile Ad Hoc Networking for vehicle safety which enable groups of vehicles traveling on a road or highway to dynamically form a network through which different types of information can be relayed from vehicle to vehicle. Also a combination of ad hoc networking and intelligent roads can be used

to extend the range of safety and other information provided by roadway devices.

Now we will explain the intelligent road. In doing so, we will examine how intelligence can be provided to vehicles that use highways, roads, and streets.

TRANSMISSION METHODS

There are two types of communication in inter-vehicle communication one from infrastructure to vehicle and the other from vehicle to vehicle. When a Vehicle Mobile Ad hoc Network is formed, it also becomes possible for the initial infrastructure-to-vehicle transmission to be relayed through the formed VANET.

Infrastructure to Vehicle

In Figure 8, note that of the five vehicles shown on the highway, only one is within range of a roadside transmitter. In addition, although that vehicle is within range of the transmitter, it may or may not have the capability to receive data broadcast. At first only a small number of vehicles will be equipped with networking capability. Then, as more vehicles become equipped with a VANET capability, the range of roadway transmission will be extended via mobile mesh networks.

Vehicle to Vehicle

In the vehicle-to-vehicle transmission method the vehicle nearest to the roadside transmitter receives the broadcast of information and relays that data to other vehicles in the Vehicle Ad Hoc Mobile Network.

In the example shown in Figure 9, three vehicles are close enough together to form a mesh network. Thus, the transmission from the roadway can be extended, allowing vehicles with a VANET capability to have much more information to be displayed.

Figure 8. Infrastructure-to-vehicle communication

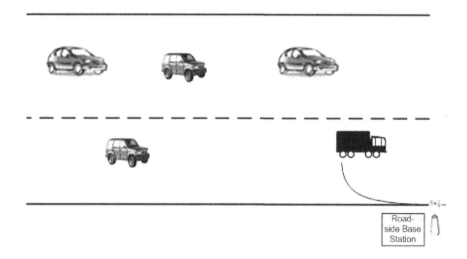

Figure 9. Extending roadway communication transmission distance via a vehicle-to-vehicle network

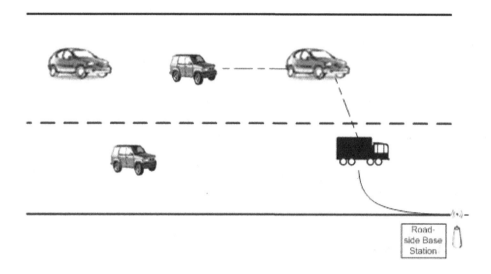

COMPONENTS OF A SMART VEHICLE

The term intelligent transportation system (ITS) [14] [15] refers to a system having computing equipment and algorithms to enhance comfort of occupant/driver, transporting safety messages to other vehicles, thus enhancing road safety. Such enhancements may provide increased safety, lowered cost (temporal, environmental), increased comfort, or have a greater efficiency. For road vehicles, two categories of system can be identified: intelligent infrastructure and intelligent vehicles, the classification depending on where the bulk of processing takes place (as in all cases communication will take place between the infrastructure and the vehicles).

The general components of the future smart vehicles are

a. Event data recorder
b. Cellular transmitter/receiver
c. Side radar GPS
d. Forward-looking radar
e. Wireless networking transmitter/receiver
f. Microprocessor

Now we will discuss each of the communications components of the emerging smart vehicle.

Event Data Recorder (EDR)

An event data recorder is a device that records certain information from a vehicle immediately before and/or during a crash — not all crashes but most of the serious ones. Police, crash investigators, and others can download the data from the EDR's memory to help them better understand what happened to the vehicle and how the safety systems performed, and in some cases, help establish culpability.

Cellular Transmitter/Receiver

A vehicle has a navigation system including a controller, a display, a wireless transmitter/receiver and a global positioning unit to determine the location of the navigation system. The controller is configured to transmit, to an off-vehicle system the location of the navigation system, a unique identifier of the navigation system and a list of other navigation systems. In addition, the controller is configured to receive, via the transmitter/receiver, the location of any other navigation systems which listed that navigation system and to display the locations of the other navigation systems on the display.

The Global Positioning System (GPS)

The Global Positioning System (GPS) is a worldwide radio-navigation system formed from

a constellation of 24 satellites and their ground stations. A GPS system includes the following:

1. A frame having a window
2. A GPS navigator supported by the frame, wherein a display of the GPS navigator is facing opposite to the window of the frame,
3. A radar detector received in the frame to align with the window thereof,
4. An attaching element attaching the GPS system to an interior side surface of a vehicle such that the display of the GPS navigator is backwardly facing towards the driver while the radar detector is forwardly sending out detecting signal through the window of the frame.

The GPS system integrates the two important driving assistant equipments together, occupies minimal mounting space, and utilize only one car power outlet.

Side Radar and Forward Radar

Forward radar is used to detect any forward obstacles at distances up to 400 to 500 ft, depending upon the contour of the terrain. This radar may operate in the unlicensed wideband (UWB) frequency range in the 60-GHz spectrum and is generally integrated into a vehicle's braking system. Thus, the sudden appearance of an obstacle in front of a vehicle or the rapid braking of a leading vehicle would result in the forward radar immediately detecting a closing of the distance between vehicles, which would result in either an automatic adjustment to the vehicle's cruise control, if enabled, or initiation of the vehicle's braking.

The purpose of side radar is to detect the presence of vehicles in a vehicle's blind spots. Because the primary purpose of side radar is to look for obstacles in the blind spots of a vehicle, it will operate on low power and have a transmission range of less than 10 ft.

Wireless Networking Transmitter/Receiver

The wireless network transmitter/receiver enables the vehicle to receive roadway broadcasts as well as relay such broadcasts if the vehicle is within range of other VANET-compatible vehicles. There are significant benefits that can occur by integrating the VANET system with a GPS, that is why the probability of the two be interconnected in the emerging smart vehicle is very likely.

Microprocessor

The microprocessor receives input from the various communications devices. This input is used to display warnings and other information on a display, via an audio alarm, and perhaps eventually via a voice synthesis system.

Another function of the microprocessor will be to operate any routing protocol selected for the formation of a Vehicle Ad hoc Mobile Network. Thus, vehicle manufacturers could elect to use one high-performance processor or subdivide work by using two or more microprocessors.

CONCLUSION

Vehicular Ad hoc Networks (VANETs), like MANETs (mobile Ad hoc networks) embody the objective of providing useful communications among arbitrarily-formed collections of vehicles. There are multiple technologies evolving around this concept of VANET. In this chapter we have explained the Local Interconnect Network (LIN) and Controller Area Network (CAN) technologies that provide a robust, low-cost mechanism for controlling electronic-based devices distributed throughout a vehicle. The evolving VANET gives lot of opportunities for inter-vehicular as well as intra-vehicular communication for significant enhancement of both road safety and driver and passenger requests for information. Although

the true smart vehicle is yet to evolve, and at the present time we do not know the exact components of the smart vehicle of the future, still after reading this chapter the reader will get an idea of what we can expect from a smart vehicle and intelligent roadway.

REFERENCES

Artimy, M. M., Robertson, W., & Phillips, W. J. (2004, May). Connectivity in inter-vehicle ad hoc networks. In *Proceedings of the Engineering Canadian Conference on Electrical and Computer* (pg. 293-298).

Bianchi, G., Campbell, A. T., & Liao, R. R. F. (1998, May). On utility-fair adaptive services in wireless networks. In *Proceedings of the. 6th International Workshop on Quality of Service (IEEE/IFIP IWQOS'98)*. Napa Valley, CA.

Blum, J., Eskandarian, A., & Hoffman, L. (2003). Performance Characteristics of Inter- Vehicle Ad Hoc Networks". *The IEEE 6th International Conference on Intelligent Transportation Systems*, Shanghai, China, page 114-119, 2003.

Briesemeister, L., & Hommel, G. (2000, August). Role-based multicast in highly mobile but sparsely connected ad hoc networks. *MobiHOC First Annual Workshop on Mobile and Ad Hoc Networking and Computing* (pp. 45-50).

Car2Car (n.d.). *Car2Car Communication Consortium*. Retrieved from http://www.carto-car.org/

DSRC. (n.d.). *The DSRC Project*. Retrieved from http://www.leearmstrong.com/-DSRC/DSRCHomeset.htm

FleetNet. (n.d.). *The FleetNet Project*. Retrieved from http://www.fleetnet.de

IEEE. (n.d.). *IEEE 802.11p Task Group*. Retreived from http://grouper.ieee.org/-groups/scc32/dsrc/index.html

Internet, I. T. S. (n.d.). *Internet ITS*. Retrieved from http://www.internetits.org

Korkmaz, G., Ekici, E., Özgüner, F., & Özgüner, U. (2004). Urban multihop broadcast protocol for inter-vehicle communication systems. In *Proceedings of the first ACM workshop on Vehicular ad hoc networks* (pp. 76–85). Philadelphia: ACM Press.

Namboodiri, V., Agarwal, M., & Gao, L. (2004, October). A study on the feasibility of mobile gateways for vehicular ad-hoc networks. In *Proceedings of the first ACM workshop on Vehicular ad hoc networks* (pp. 66-75). Philadelphia.

Network-on-Wheels. (n.d.). *The Network-on-Wheels Project*. Retrieved from http://www.networkon-wheels.de

PATH. (n.d.). *The PATH Project*. Retrieved from http://www.path.berkeley.edu

PReVENT. (n.d.). *The PReVENT Project*. Retrieved from http://www.prevent-ip.org

Saha, A. K., & Johnson, D. B. (2004, October). Modeling mobility for vehicular ad-hoc networks. In *Proceedings of the first ACM workshop on Vehicular ad hoc networks*. Philadelphia.

Wang, S. Y. (2004, September). Predicting the lifetime of repairable unicast routing paths in vehicleformed mobile ad hoc networks on highways. *PIMRC 2004. 15th IEEE International Symposium on Personal, Indoor and Mobile RadioCommunications,* Volume: 4, (pg2815-2819).

Wischhof, L., Ebner, A., Rohling, H., Lott, M., & Halfmann, R. (2003, April). SOTIS –a self-organizing traffic information system. In *Proceedings of the 57th IEEE Semiannual Vehicular Technology Conference* (pp. 2442-2446). Jeju, South Korea.

Wu, H., Fujimoto, R., Guensler, R., & Hunter, M. (2004). MDDV: a mobility-centric data dissemination algorithm for vehicular networks. In *Proceedings of the 1st ACM International Workshop on Vehicular Ad Hoc Networks (VANET'04)*, Philadelphia: ACM Press.

Zhu, J., & Roy, S. (2003, December). MAC for dedicated short range communicatins in intelligent transport system. *IEEE Communications Magazine*, 41.

KEY TERMS AND DEFINITIONS

Event Data Recorder (EDR): An event data recorder is a device that records certain information from a vehicle immediately before and/or during a crash — not all crashes but most of the serious ones.

Intelligent Transportation Systems (ITS): The term intelligent transportation system (ITS) refers to a system having computing equipment and algorithms to enhance comfort of occupant/driver, transporting safety messages to other vehicles thus enhancing road safety.

Inter-Vehicle Communication: Inter-vehicle communications represents communications between vehicles or vehicles and sensors placed in or on various locations or vehicles and roadside base station

Intra-Vehicle Communications: Intra-vehicle communications refer to the communications that occur within a vehicle which is achieved by connecting its processors using LIN and CAN technology.

Local Interconnect Network (LIN): LIN is a single wire serial communication protocol based on common UART interface used in VANET.

The Controller Area Network (CAN): The Controller Area Network (CAN) is a serial, asynchronous, multimaster communication protocol for connecting control modules in the vehicle designed by Bosch in 1986.

Vehicular Ad-Hoc Network: A Vehicular Ad-Hoc Network, or VANET, is a kind of Mobile ad-hoc network (MANET) which enable communications among nearby vehicles and between vehicles and nearby fixed radio equipment, usually called as roadside unit.

Section 2
Applications of VANETs

Chapter 3
The Role of Communication Technologies in Vehicular Applications

Yacine Khaled
INRIA Rocquencourt, France

Manabu Tsukada
INRIA Rocquencourt, France

José Santa
University of Murcia, Spain

Thierry Ernst
INRIA Rocquencourt, France

ABSTRACT

Vehicular networks attract a lot of attention in the research world. Novel vehicular applications need a suitable communication channel in order to extend in-vehicle capabilities and, be aware of surrounding events. However, these networks present some peculiarities, such as high mobility or specific topologies. These features affect the performance of applications; hence, more effort should be directed to identify the final necessities of the network. Few works deal with application requirements that should be considered when vehicular services are designed. In this chapter this gap is filled, proposing an analysis of application requirements mapped with suitable communication technologies for physical/MAC and network layers. This study contains key factors that must be taken into account not only at the design stage of the vehicular network, but also when applications are evaluated.

INTRODUCTION

Nowadays, communications become essential in the information society. Everyone can get information anywhere, even in mobility environments, using different kinds of devices and communication technologies. In this frame the vehicle is another place where users stay for long periods. Thus, in addition to safety applications, considered as the most important services, other networked applications could bring an additional value for the

DOI: 10.4018/978-1-61520-913-2.ch003

comfort of drivers and passengers, as well as for driving efficiency, in terms of mobility, traffic fluency and environment preservation. However, such kinds of networks are characterized by a strong mobility, a high dynamicity of vehicles and specific topology patterns. Moreover, these networks experience significant rates of packet losses and very short communication periods. These properties affect the performance and feasibility of vehicular applications. The proper operation of vehicular applications remains a great challenge nowadays, and specific requirements should be considered. In our opinion, such kind of applications should be initially studied from the communication technology point of view. An analysis of the requirements, in terms of technologies at different abstraction levels, should help to design efficient applications. In this chapter an analysis of available communication and network technologies is given, and a study about how they can fulfill main networking requirements of ITS applications is stated.

This chapter scrutinizes of the vehicular application requirements in terms of communication technologies. First, broad background and our point of view are presented. In order to explain the main focus of our chapter, we started by describing vehicular applications and services, selecting, thus, the most representative ones as cases of study and defining their networking requirements. So, before analyzing the application requirements against the capabilities offered by current communication possibilities, we introduce the most common communication technologies in the vehicular field as solutions issues, as well as and some of the most standardized level-three. Finally, some concluding remarks end the chapter.

BACKGROUND

Numerous research works deal with vehicular services, essentially those related to traffic safety, but also traffic efficiency and infotainment are of special importance. However, the achievement of the functional goals of these applications is strongly linked to technological requirements, which vary from one application to another. For instance, safety applications should operate with good location accuracy, and real-time and scalable communications; distributed games or talk applications, however, do not require great scalability or real-time features.

To ensure the appropriate operation of these applications regarding networking, new technological requirements, far away from those identified in fixed networks, appear in vehicular communications. This kind of solutions usually needs to cover many networking necessities for their efficient operation. In this chapter, the most important ones are studied, being identified as: location awareness, geocast capabilities, penetration rate dependency, time awareness, permanent access and mobility.

To meet these demands, a number of communication technologies at access level are currently available. The most important ones are briefly introduced, such as Bluetooth, DSRC (IEEE 802.11p), cellular networks and satellite. Moreover, these technologies are analyzed according to the covered communication paradigms, vehicle to vehicle (V2V), vehicle to infrastructure (V2I) or infrastructure to vehicle (I2V), and the destination nodes involved in the communication (1-to-1 or 1-to-n). In the same way, some of the main network (level-three) technologies studied in standardization bodies of vehicular communications are discussed, in order to determine which of the networking requirements can be covered with them. NEMO [Devarapalli, Wakikawa, Petrescu, & Thubert et al.2005] as well as some common MANET and VANET proposals are briefly described, but also more specialized concepts, like Multihoming [Ernst, Montavont, Wakikawa, Ng, & Kuladinithi et al.2007], Flow distribution [Soliman, Montavont, Fikouras, & Kuladinithi et al.2007, Larsson, Eriksson, Mitsuya, Tasaka, & Kuntz et al.2008], Route Optimization

[Ng, Thubert, Watari, & Zhao, et al.2007] and MANEMO, are analyzed. Finally, an overlay architecture using cellular networks shows the feasibility of this technology to enable vehicular communications.

DESIGN OF EFFICIENT VEHICULAR APPLICATIONS

Vehicular Applications and Services

Vehicular services and applications can be classified into three main families: safety, traffic management and monitoring, and comfort. Road safety certainly is the main motivation of many researchers and represents the major issue in Intelligent Transportation Systems (ITS). About 40.000 people die on roads every year in the European Union alone, with around 1.7 million people incurring several injuries. These accidents are often caused by a faulty driver behavior, bad weather conditions or mechanical problems. One of the most important solutions to this problem relies on using vehicular communications to anticipate road accidents, extend road visibility and disseminate safety information. In addition to road safety applications, traffic information and monitoring systems are another important application field of vehicular networks. They aim at improving traffic flow and road usage, providing timely information about the traffic state along many kilometers. Finally, the goal of comfort applications is to offer novel on board services to improve the travel experience, improving common multimedia capabilities of current commercial vehicles.

In order to analyze this wide world of vehicular applications, some of the most representative ones have been chosen as cases of study. Thus, three reference applications which best represent these three families are described, such as Cooperative Collision Warning, Platooning or Parking Place Management. Next, a discussion about how net-working requirements of vehicular application and services can be fulfilled by means of several communication technologies is included in the chapter.

Since there is no any specific technology which can satisfy all these networking requirements, our opinion is that future On Board and Road Side Units (OBU and RSU) should combine, in the same platform, some of them to enable the deployment of different ITS applications. Having the requirements and technologies in mind, vehicular network solutions can be designed by means of new communication architectures or integrating current ones. In this frame, our contribution should help in the design of both vehicular applications/ services and technologies for testing scenarios, evaluations, or commercial developments.

Safety Applications

- Cooperative collision warning. It is considered as the most important safety application. It allows enhancing the driver capabilities by monitoring the distance between vehicles and, depending on the case, warns the driver or automatically brakes the vehicle when the distance decreases under a threshold. These systems also take into account the post-collision situation, when vehicles on the road must be warned.

- Incident management. The aim of this system is to successfully manage current accidents on the road. First, by detecting road problems (e.g. obtaining location and nature of the accident) via positioning devices or other sensors. The next point is to manage vehicle flows during and after the accident, through vehicular communications.

- Emergency video streaming. It deals with video transmission in emergency contexts. Some vehicles are equipped with video cameras and have enough storage capabilities to buffer multimedia content. This service can be provided over V2V schemes

[Guo, M-H., & Zegura et al.2005] or 3G [Qureshi, Carlisle, & Guttag et al.2006].

Traffic Management and Monitoring Systems

- Platooning. Such systems allow vehicles to travel together closely and safely. This leads to a reduction in the space used by vehicles on a highway. As a consequence, more vehicles can use the highway without provoking congestion. This kind of solutions increase comfort levels of passengers, and can allow a higher level of safety due to constant monitoring of the road state by the vehicles in the platoon. Although the operation of these systems requires, essentially, a direct communication between vehicles, some enhancements could be obtained by using other technologies, which can improve location accuracy or overcome the lack of V2V communication.

- Vehicle tracking. This service enables car manufacturers, logistic companies and other trusted parties, to remotely monitor vehicle status. Data is collected by an Application Unit (AU), and sent by the On Board Unit (OBU) to the data center through network technologies.

- Notification services. It consists of providing travel information to subscribers through an Internet access. As application examples, we can quote weather and traffic forecasting.

Comfort Applications

- Parking place management. This service enables drivers to discover an available parking place and book it. Additionally, a vehicle could automatically park, without the need of driver assistance.

- Distributed games and/or talks. This kind of entertainment applications comprises

the management of activities among a limited number of vehicles, in a distributed fashion and via a pure V2V link. For instance, we can quote card games, sharing draws or instantaneous talks.

- Peer to peer applications. Using these services it is possible to exchange data between vehicles, without contacting any application server. This exchange operates, essentially, by means of V2I communications and complementary through V2V. In this context, we have some possible applications such as instantaneous messaging, file transfer and voice over IP.

The achievement of the functional goals of the previous applications is strongly linked to technological requirements, which vary from one application to another. For instance, safety applications should operate with good location accuracy, and real-time and scalable communications; distributed games or talk applications, however, do not need great scalability or real-time features. The following section summarizes the most important application requirements, and use the services described above as a reference point.

NETWORKING REQUIREMENTS OF VEHICULAR APPLICATIONS

In this section main technological requirements of vehicular applications and services, regarding networking, are carefully examined. This kind of solutions needs to cover many needs for their efficient operation in most of the cases. However, in our study we will treat only the most important ones.

Location Awareness

Next generation vehicles are expected to exchange information not only beyond their immediate surroundings and line-of-sight with other vehicles, but also with the road infrastructure and Internet databases. This will allow vehicles to anticipate trajectories, coordinate merging manoeuvres, notify a braking action to vehicles behind, warn oncoming traffic of an icy patch, report road traffic conditions, locate parking lots, or simply entertain passengers. In this context, the knowledge of their actual position and trajectory is necessary, and it is only meaningful to vehicles in a particular geographic area. The exchange of information among vehicles in a particular geographic area requires reliable and scalable communication capabilities, which we call geographical routing and addressing. This function mainly relies on the information given by GPS receivers. However, GPS imposes some constraints such as lack of coverage in some environments or its weak robustness for some critical applications. For these reasons, other positioning techniques such as cellular or WiFi localization, dead reckoning (by using last known position and velocity) [King, Füßler, Transier, & Effelsberg et al.2006], and image/video localization, have been proposed in the vehicular field [Boukerche, Oliveira, Nakamura, Jang, & Loureiro et al.2008]. Critical safety services such as cooperative collision warning and incident management need a high accurate localization, as well as some comfort applications such as parking booking. Note that an accurate positioning system can help us to define the zone of relevance more precisely. Other services, however, require a low accurate localization, like peer to peer applications and vehicle tracking.

Geocast Capability

Geocast provides the capability to deliver a message to nodes within a geographical region [Maihöfer 2004]. The shape and size of this area depend on the application aims. The complexity of defining this region can be as high as the set of vehicles behind or in front of the subject one. Other times this constraint is relaxed, and defining this region as the vehicles inside a geographic area, or near a designated spot (such as a smog area), is enough. In order to design a general communication architecture, where services which require both unicast and geocast capabilities can be deployed, an hybrid networking architecture can be proposed [Khaled, Ducourthial, & Shawky, 2007]. This way, services such as platooning, which need unicast communications, do not experience bad performances. Geocast is considered efficient if messages are forwarded in both sparse and dense geographical areas, while efficiently leveraging the available bandwidth. This criterion, scalability, was introduced in [Clifford Neuman 1994], and was defined as the ability to handle the addition of nodes or objects without suffering a noticeable loss in performance or increase in administrative complexity.

Penetration Rate Dependency

Penetration rate is defined as the percentage of vehicles equipped with the necessary OBU on the road. This parameter may have important consequences in the operation of some applications [Breitenberger, Grber, Neuherz, Kates et al.2004], especially in critical and safety ones. Although a low penetration rate is obviously a problem in safety applications, such as collision avoidance, an excess of equipped vehicles also arises transmission problems. In cellular networks, situations of high penetration are also a problem. The system performance is not affected when the number of equipped vehicles is low, but in high load circumstances the network connection starts to give a poor performance, when the time slot scheduler need to serve too much users [Landman & Kritzinger2005]. Note that penetration rate has a direct bearing on the wireless bandwidth used. The higher the penetration rates the higher the wireless bandwidth that should be used to allow vehicles communication.

Time Awareness

Vehicular applications often require a reliable communication channel that supports time-critical message transmissions [Meier, Hughes, Cunningham, & Cahill et al.2005]. One of the most important criterions for measuring the quality of the network, regardless of the application type, is the communication delay. Although most applications have time constraints, those related with road safety are critical. Due to this, providing a real-time behavior in vehicular networks is a key challenge. In order to enable the driver to react quickly, information must reach the destination with a minimum. However, this requirement is not easy to ensure in mobile networks, and even more difficult to address if vehicular network characteristics are considered, particularly the high mobility. Thus, real-time communications can only be assured by the presence of an efficient and robust communication system.

Permanent Access

Permanent access to the network is one of the main drawbacks of vehicular communications. In VANET designs, a physical infrastructure is not necessary, due to the inherent decentralized design. Regarding infrastructure-based networks, operators do not offer the same service over the entire terrestrial surface. For instance, in urban environments, the coverage is excellent, and the amount of base stations where the mobile terminal could be connected is really high. At rural locations, however, the deployment is poor. A vehicle equipped with a VANET system, however, is always able to emit messages because the vehicle itself is part of the infrastructure. Moreover, in cellular network connections, it is also important to differentiate between two important concepts regarding the access to the network: coverage and capacity. The coverage can be understood as the possibility of the mobile terminal to use the network, because at a particular location opera-

tors have deployed the necessary infrastructure. However, the user can be rejected to establish a call or a data connection, even under good coverage circumstances, if the capacity of the network has been exceeded. Depending on several technological issues, such as modulation, frequency allocation, time slot scheduling, etc., this effect has a different impact. This way, the number of users who are concurrently using the network restricts the potential cellular network usage. At the application level, some services such as file transfer need a permanent communication channel. In this kind of applications, the election of a suited vehicular network is essential.

Mobility

Wireless network technologies allow devices to move freely. However, this mobility affects the potential permanent access to the network (see the previous point) and causes other problems. In [Wewetzer, Caliskan, Meier, & Luebke et al.2007], experimental evaluations give real results of these effects. In 802.11 transmissions, the distance between sender and receiver is an important factor; the more the distance, the smaller the delivery rate, as also show [ElBatt, Goel, Holland, Krishnan, & Parikhl.2006, Khaled, Ducourthial, & Shawky.2005]. In infrastructure-based technologies, handoffs between base stations are also relevant, due to the potential decrease of performance in the process. Poor latency and throughput results are obtained if the mobile terminal is moving at locations far away from the UMTS Node B without performing a handoff [Alexiou, Bouras, & Igglesis et al.2004]. Nevertheless, the distance between two devices during the communication is not the only noticeable effect of mobility. Interference with other radio equipments in the case of VANET should also be taken into account, due to the wide usage of the 2.4 GHz frequency band [Wewetzer, Caliskan, Meier, & Luebke et al.2007]. The presence of the equipment at locations of bad orography could also cause

Table 1. Application requirements (none-not needed, ★ needed, and ★★ strongly needed)

Applications/App. Req.	Location awareness	Geocast capability	Penetration rate dependence	Time Awareness	Permanent access	Mobility
Safety						
Cooperative Collision Warning	★★	★★	★★	★★	★	★★
Incident management	★★	★★	★★	★★	★	★★
Emergency video streaming	★★	★★	★★	★★	★	★★
Traffic management and Monitoring						
Platooning	★★	★★	★★	★★	★	★★
Vehicles tracking	★		★	★	★★	★
Notification Services	★		★	★	★	★
Comfort						
Parking place management	★★	★★	★	★	★	★★
Distributed games and/ or talk	★	★★	★★	★	★	★★
Peer-to-peer	★		★	★	★★	★

communication problems in vehicular networks. Other external factors, like the existence of other vehicles or buildings are considered in realistic mobility patterns for VANET solutions [Naumov, Baumann, & Gross et al.2006].

The knowledge of both requirements and application allow us to efficiently identify the needs of each application. Thus, we use the applications introduced in the previous section to evaluate their networking requirements. This evaluation study is summarized in Table 1.

Communication Technologies

The usage of wireless communication technologies is continuously growing these days, with the aim of substituting typical wired connections and improving mobility. At the same time, the vehicular field is currently introducing into the telematics world, where informatics and telecommunications try to improve traffic security, efficiency and safety. In this frame, wireless communica-

tions are essential to connect the vehicle with the environment.

Bluetooth

Bluetooth is a wireless standard (IEEE 802.15.1) specially created for short range communications between devices usually connected by local ports. Thanks to Bluetooth it is possible to create a personal area network (PAN) where two or more devices can connect. It operates in the 2.4 GHz band and, due to the low power consumption features, enables communication in a range of tens of meters. Bluetooth terminals are grouped in *piconets*, which can also be interconnected by means of scatternets.

The properties of Bluetooth make it perfect for in-vehicle networks [Nolte, Hansson, & Lo Bello et al.2005]. Some researchers also advocate the usage of Bluetooth for V2V applications [Sugiura & Dermawan 2005]. However, this technology is limited by the necessary time to form piconets and scatternets (in the order of seconds) [Sawant, Tan, Yang, & Wang et al.2004] and, overall, the limited communication range.

WLAN and DSRC

Wireless Local Area Networks (WLAN) were created to cover connectivity requirements usually fulfilled by common LAN technologies, like Ethernet. The set of standards which deal with WLAN features are inside the 802.11x group, and consider a set of protocols which enable terminals to be connected to a base station, which is in charge of connecting computers to the rest of the wired network. Among these standards, 802.11a/b/g specifications are the most known. IEEE 802.11a was the first adopted WLAN technology, offering a maximum rate of 54 Mbps over distances of 100 meters. However, the used 5 GHz band is not available (mainly) in some European countries, and the 802.11b standard was finally accepted as the definitive WLAN technology. 802.11b implements the same core protocols than 802.11a, but uses the 2.4 GHz band, what decreases absorption problems due to walls and other obstacles. This way, the communication range is augmented until 140 meters, but data bandwidth is maintained under 11 Mbps. 802.11g overcome bandwidth limitations of 802.11b with a new modulation scheme over the 2.4 GHz, presenting the successor of 802.11b. Although the most used operation mode of 802.11 technologies is the infrastructure one, using a base station, these devices can also be configured to directly communicate with another terminal, using the ad-hoc mode. This one is preferred to enable vehicular communications. Many V2V works use WLAN technologies to test multitude of applications, such as cooperative collision avoidance using V2V communications between nearby vehicles [Ueki, Tasaka, Hatta, & Okada et al.2005, Ammoun, Nashashibi, & Laurgeau et al.2006], or multi-hop strategies [Biswas, Tatchikou, & Dion et al.2006]. However, common WLAN standards have some limitations

when critical information has to be transmitted in the vehicular environment [Yousefi, Bastani, &Fathy et al.2007]. For this reason, USA, Japan and Europe have allocated a specific band in the 5.8 and 5.9 GHz for vehicular transmissions, using Dedicated Short Range Communications (DSRC). A variation of the 802.11 standards, 802.11p, is being used as background in the DSRC research. This standard covers the requirements for communicating both periodic and critical information, which allows the deployment of a great variety of vehicular services, using both V2V [ElBatt, Goel, Holland, Krishnan, & Parikh et al.2006] and vehicle to roadside communications [Hattori, Ono, Nishiyama, & Horiuchi et al.2004].

Cellular Networks

Since initial analog technologies, such as the American AMPS, cellular networks have been gradually improved in terms not only of availability all around the world, but also in the quality of service offered. As a result of applying digital communications to cellular networks, the GSM (Global System for Mobile communications) technology achieved the purpose of spreading mobile phones around the world. Its wide adoption in Europe has led the expansion of GSM to other potential markets, like the Chinese one. Many people usually identify the GSM technology as the second generation (2G) of cellular networks, which substituted the first one, based on analog technologies. Although the main application field of cellular networks, until some years ago, was focused on telephony services, data connections are becoming more and more popular these days. GPRS (General Packet Radio Service) appeared with the aim of providing higher data rates than the 9.6 Kbps offered by the standard GSM. GPRS provides a maximum of 177/118 Kbps in the downlink/uplink channels, and it is understood as the intermediate step between 2G and 3G; hence, this is the reason why it is called 2.5G. Last years, the expansion of CDMA (Code Division

Multiple Access) communication technologies has lead to the appearance of the 3G cellular networks. CDMA2000 and UMTS (Universal Mobile Telecommunications System), this one as the evolution of GSM 2G, are two of the most extended 3G technologies. UMTS offers 384/128 Kbps, but the recent HSPA (High Speed Packet Access) improvements offer maximum data rates of 14.4/11.5 Mbps.

The introduction of cellular networks in the vehicular domain comes from several years ago, when GSM or GPRS data connections started to be used in tracking and monitoring systems. The appearance of GPRS also made possible the usage of cellular networks for providing traffic information or emergency warnings [Masini, Fontana, & Verdone et al.2004]. However, until the arrival of 3G technologies, low data rates had avoided the deployment of cellular networks in ITS [Adrisano, Verdone, et al.2000]. The advantages of the UMTS communication medium in mobility environments are defended by some authors, which use the UMTS aerial interface for direct V2V communications. The usage of the UMTS operator's infrastructure in bidirectional communications is present in the literature, as monitoring systems [Hoh, Gruteser, Xiong, & Alrabady et al.2006] for example, but its application for V2V communications is still a challenge, due to inherent delay problems. Another drawback of using data connections with cellular networks is the extra money which has to be paid for the usage of the operator's infrastructure. Current trend is paying a fixed quote per month, with an extra cost if the transmission rates fall out of the contract, but it is expected that the adoption of UMTS among the population and the vehicular field decreases the price of the final bill, by means of special agreements with operators ["3G/UMTS Evolution: towards a new generation of broadband mobile services"]. Apart of this, some people think that a general communication technology for the ITS domain is still needed, and cellular networks could be the solution [Kiess, Rybicki, & Mauve et al.2007].

WiMAX

WiMAX, or Worldwide Interoperability for Microwave Access, is a communication technology which try to fill the gap between 3G and WLAN standards, and it is the first implementation which appears to comply with the MAN(Metropolitan Area Network) concept, in a wireless manner. Two main standards are currently considered: 802.16d and 802.16e. The first one is used at fixed locations, and it is a perfect solution for connecting different buildings of a company at low cost, for example. This specification offers up to 48 Km of coverage and data rates of 70 Mbps. The 802.16e standard has been specifically designed for mobile users connected to a base station. The OFDM (Orthogonal Frequency Division Multiple access) technology is used in this specification to serve multiple users, and the final physical interface considered copes with mobility issues, such as interferences, multipath and delays. 802.16e is, hence, the most appropriate specification of WiMAX for the vehicular field. Tens of Mbps, mobility speed up to 100 Km/h, and 10 km of coverage to the base station, make 802.16e a good option for urban scenarios, where vehicles can be connected at a high data rate using a WiMAX deployment. Currently it is possible to obtain some Pre-WiMAX devices, but it is expected that, as soon as the final specifications are ready, the spectrum of vehicular services which could be deployed with WiMAX grow rapidly. In [Han, Moon, Lee, Jang, & Lee et al.2008] the authors analyze the performance of WiMAX in a subway, where the maximum speed is 90 Km/h. The results show that a mean of 2 Mbps and 5.3 Mbps can be obtained in real scenarios, with an average RTT of 100 ms. Venturi has designed an electrical vehicle which uses a pre-WiMAX interface for remote monitoring purposes, as a joint work between the vehicle manufacturer and Intel Corporation.

RDS and TMC

The Radio Data System (or RDS) was developed to carry digital data using the common FM radio band. This allows to multiplex additional information with the audio emission, such as the name of the radio station or the current song, but also it can include a data flag which indicates the receiver it has to pay attention to the broadcasting information because it is being transmitted a traffic bulletin. RDS offers a data rate of 1187.5 bps, and the transmission range offered by FM can reach locations at 80 kilometers far way the transmission station. The RDS version deployed in U.S. is called RBDS (Radio Broadcast Data System)and operates almost identically as RDS, however its usage is less common. A more suitable solution for traffic information dissemination is offered, however, by the Traffic Message Channel (TMC) system. With this system, information about traffic problems is broadcasted digitally, so an appropriate navigation device can warn the user and calculate an alternative route, for instance. The notifications reported by TMC include an event identifier and the location of the problem. TMC traffic is usually transmitted through RDS, and this is the reason why both technologies are usually put together.

Satellite

Satellite communication consists of three main entities: sender station, satellite system, and receiver devices. First of all, data is sent from the sender station to the satellite, which is in charge of forwarding the information to receiver devices.

Satellite communications offer a very wide coverage and great broadcast capabilities. It is suited to provide connectivity at remote places, such as mountain areas or islands, but also in developing countries. The data can be sent from an only sender to multiple receivers at the same time and using the same frequency. Thus, satellite communications are suitable for multimedia broadcasting, such as live video, movies and music.

Although sender stations and receiver devices are usually installed at fixed locations, the later ones can be mobile and equipped in vehicles. This kind of architecture is feasible for a unidirectional system providing an I2V service; however it must be taken into account the important delay that suffer data packets, due to the propagation distance to and from the satellites. The bandwidth obtained in a mobile terminal is between 300 and 500 kbps. A sender station is usually too big to be brought inside a vehicle, and it requires a precise orientation to the satellite used. The UniDirectional Link Routing (UDLR) [Duros, Dabbous, Izumiyama, Fujii, & Zhang et al.2001] has been standardized to emulate bidirectional communications with a satellite unidirectional link, where mobile terminals receive data using the satellite channel and transmit using other access technologies.

Synthesis

Connectivity necessities of vehicles can be divided in two main groups: vehicle to vehicle communications (V2V, VVC) or inter-vehicle communications (IVC), and communications with the infrastructure. In the literature, many authors use vehicle to infrastructure communications (V2I) to denote both data flow directions, however, according to the specific use of several technologies for one or the other communication pattern, it is more correct to distinguish between V2I and I2V (infrastructure to vehicle communications). It is important to consider this whole set of communication possibilities for vehicles because, depending on the application or service necessities, we will have to decide among one of the available wireless network technologies.

Apart from the communication pattern covered, wireless communication technologies can be divided into those which establish 1-to-1 physical links, and those which consider 1-to-n broadcast ones. In this last case, some kind of access point

Table 2. Properties of main vehicular communication technologies, and vehicular applicability (none-not possible, ★ possible, and ★★ suited)

Technology	Range	Link type	Data rate	Frequency band	Standard	Standard Vehicular applicability		
						V2V	V2I	I2V
Bluetooth	100 m	1-to-n	1 Mbps	2.4 Ghz	IEEE 802.15.1	★		
WLAN	200 m	1-to-1 1-to-n	10-50 Mbps	2.45 Ghz	IEEE 802.11a/b/g	★★	★	★
DSRC	1 Km	1-to-1	50 Mbps	5.9 Ghz	IEEE 802.11p	★★	★★	★★
WiMAX	10 Km	1-to-n	~20 Mbps	2.45 Ghz	IEEE 802.16e		★★	★★
Cellular	10 Km	1-to-n	~10 Mbps	700-2600 Mhz	n/a		★★	★★
RDS/TMC	80 Km	1-to-n	1187.5 bps	87.5-108.0 Mhz	CENELEC EN 50067 CEN ENV 12313			★★
Satellite	>10.000 Km	1-to-n	300-500 Kbps	950-1450 Mhz	n/a		★	★★

is in charge of sharing out the available bandwidth among the clients. This bandwidth, thus, could become insufficient when the number of served nodes increases inside the coverage area. Due to this, the tendency in short-range wireless technologies is taking advantage of the available bandwidth, sharing it among a small number of users because, anyway, the coverage is small. On the contrary, wide-range technologies must share the available bandwidth among much more users. However, short-range wireless media lack on stability, due to the small accessible area. It is also important to remark how V2V communications are obtained by means of 1-to-1 technologies, and communications with the infrastructure are commonly created using the 1-to-n ones.

A brief overview of main wireless technologies used in the vehicular domain is given in Table 2. For communications with the infrastructure, it is said that WLAN, DSRC, WiMAX, cellular and satellite are feasible. However it is important to remark the different application they cover in this domain. In the case of WLAN/DSRC, vehicles usually connect with local roadside units, what usually is called vehicle to road side communication. On the other hand, in the WiMAX/cellular case it is used a medium range 1-to-n network, and

in satellite communications a wide range 1-to-n model is applied. In the cellular and satellite cases the design of the network is even more fixed than in any other technology, because we have to use the operator's installations. This way, service providers usually consider the direct Internet connection offered by the operator, and there is no possibility to manage data traffic inside the operator's network.

Setting up the Communication Channel

In this section, the main network (level-three) technologies treated in standardization bodies for vehicular communications are described. NEMO, MANET and VANET are briefly described. Moreover, more specialized concepts, like Multihoming, Flow distribution, Route Optimization and MANEMO, are introduced. Fig. 1 shows a vehicular networking scheme where the most important technologies at level-three are included in an integral communication solution. Finally, an overlay architecture using cellular networks shows the feasibility of this technology to enable vehicular communications.

Figure 1. Overview of the application of network technologies in the vehicle domain

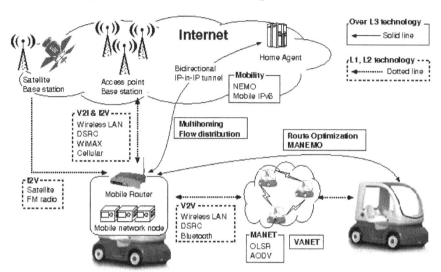

NEMO

The NEMO Basic Support [Devarapalli, Wakika-wa, Petrescu, & Thubert et al.2005] functionalities involve a router on the Internet to allow mobile computers to maintain a global connectivity to Internet. In the ITS field, the basic scheme is represented in Fig. 1, and is described as follows. A Mobile Router (MR) located in the vehicle acts as a gateway for the Mobile Network of the vehicle, and manages mobility on behalf of its Mobile Network Nodes (MNN). The MR and a fixed router in the Internet, called Home Agent (HA), establish a bi-directional tunnel which is used to transmit the packets between the MNN and their Correspondent Nodes (CN). In vehicular networks, this mechanism is often referred as a vehicle to infrastructure (V2I) communication pattern, because it involves the transmission of information through the fixed Internet.

Notice that in this scheme, the OBU can act as MR and the AU can be considered as a generic MNN. In the latter case, RSUs are attachment points either acting themselves as IPv6 access routers or as bridges directly connected to an access router.

Multihoming

MRs can be shipped with multiple network interfaces such as IEEE802.11a/b/g, WiMAX, GPRS/UMTS, etc. When a MR maintains these interfaces simultaneously up and has multiple paths to the Internet, it is said to be multihomed. In mobile environments, MRs often suffer from scarce bandwidth, frequent link failures and limited coverage. Multihoming comprises some benefits to alleviate these issues [Ernst, Montavont, Wakikawa, Ng, & Kuladinithi et al.2007]. The possible configurations offered by NEMO are classified in [Ng, Ernst, Paik, & Bagnulo, et al.2007], according to three parameters: (x) the number of MRs in the mobile network, (y) the number of HAs serving the mobile network, and (z) the number of MNPs (Mobile Network Prefixes) advertised in the mobile network. NEMO basic support has a "single MR, single HA and single MNP" configuration, referred to as (x; y; z) = (1; 1; 1). In this configuration, a tunnel is established between the HA address and a Care-of Address (CoA) of the MR in NEMO Basic Support, even if the MR is equipped with several interfaces. Multiple Care-of Addresses Registration (MCoA) [Wakikawa,

Ernst, Nagami, & Devarapalli et al.2008] is thus proposed as an extension of both Mobile IPv6 and NEMO Basic Support to establish multiple tunnels between MR and HA. Each tunnel is distinguished by its Binding Identification number (BID). In other words, NEMO Basic Support only realizes interface switching, while MCoA supports simultaneous use of multiple interfaces.

Flow distribution

To transfer data through multiple interfaces, a policy based flow distribution mechanism is necessary. The traffic can be distributed by multiple paths considering the source and destination addresses, source and destination ports, flow type, and so on. In NEMO basic support, traffic from the Internet to the mobile network is distributed by the HA, while the distribution in the opposite direction is carried out by the MR. This way, neither MR nor HA are able to change the complete round-trip path. Solving this drawback through policy rules can provoke, however, asymmetric paths that could not satisfy the user's demands. For this reason, a policy synchronization method between MR and HA is needed. Some proposals have been considered at the IETF [Soliman, Montavont, Fikouras, & Kuladinithi et al.2007, Larsson, Eriksson, Mitsuya, Tasaka, & Kuntz et al.2008].

Route Optimization

NEMO is one of the main level-three technologies of vehicle communication, however, some issues related to Route Optimization still remain unsolved in NEMO Basic Support, while they have already been covered in Mobile IPv6 [Johnson, Perkins, & Arkko et al.2004].

In NEMO, all the packets to and from MNNs must be encapsulated and sent by means of an IPs tunnel between the MR and the HA. Thus, all these packets between MNNs and CNs must go through the HA. This arises several performance issues.

Suboptimal routes are caused by the mandatory pass of packets through the HA. This leads to increased delays, undesirable for applications such as real-time multimedia streaming. Packet Encapsulation implies an additional head of 40-bytes, which can cause packet fragmentation. This also results in an increased processing delay at the generation and processing stages in both MR and HA, respectively. Bottlenecks in the HA are an important issue, because traffic to and from MNNs is aggregated at the HA, even when it supports several MRs acting as gateways for several MNNs. This may cause congestion at the HA, which could lead to additional packet delays, or even packet losses. Nested Mobile Networks is an issue that NEMO Basic Support raises. This permits a MR to host other MRs inside the mobile network. With nested mobile networks, the use of NEMO further amplifies the sub-optimality previously described. In IETF, route optimization issues of NEMO are addressed in [Ng, Thubert, Watari, & Zhao, et al.2007]. Requirements of route optimization in various scenarios are described for vehicular networks in [Baldessari, Festag, & Lenardi et al.2007], and for aeronautic environments in [Eddy, Ivancic, & Davis et al.2007].

MANEMO

Both MANET and NEMO have been designed independently as layer-three technologies. NEMO has been designed to provide global connectivity, and MANET to offer direct routing in localized networks. MANEMO comprises the usage of both concepts, MANET and NEMO, together, which could bring benefits for route optimization. Since direct routes are available in MANET, it can provide direct paths between vehicles, as Fig. 1 shows. These paths are optimized and tunnel-free, reducing overhead [Wakikawa, Okada, Koodli, Nilsson, & Murai et al.2005, J. Lorchat and K. Uehara 2006, Tsukada, Mehani, & Ernst et al.2008]. One possible topology configuration using MANEMO is described in [Wakikawa, Clausen, McCarthy,

& Petrescu et al.2007], and issues and requirements of such architectures are summarized in [Wakikawa, Thubert, Boot, Bound, & McCarthy et al.2007]. In addition, MANEMO is also used in vehicular communications; for example, VARON [Bernardos, Soto, Calder'on, Boavida, & Azcorra et al.2007] focuses on NEMO route optimization using MANET. It also provides the same level of security as the current Internet, even if the communication is done via the MANET route.

MANET and VANET

Mobile Ad hoc Networks (MANET) are suitable for wireless routing applications within dynamic topologies. This type of communication does not require any infrastructure. In order to route messages in these networks, each node is invited to participate in the message forwarding. Vehicular Ad hoc NETworks (VANET), a particular case of MANET, are characterized by a strong mobility of nodes, a high dynamic topology, a significant loss rate, and a very short duration of links. In these networks the node location is not stable, either locally or globally, and routing messages is a great challenge.

Many works have been done to design ad hoc routing algorithms to deal with the node's mobility: periodically updating routing tables by means of proactive algorithms (e.g. OLSR [Clausen et al.2001]); discovering routes under demand by means of reactive algorithms (.e.g AODV [Chakeres & Belding Royer 2004]); using geographical information to improve routing (e.g. GAMER, LBM [Maihöfer 2004], GPSR GPSR [Mauve, Widmer, & Hartenstein et al.2001]); detecting stable structures, or clusters [Jiang, Li, & Tay et al.2001]; using the node's movement for transporting messages [Zhao & Cao 2006]; following a broadcast approach for messages forwarding [Alshaer & Horlait 2005], etc. Some other protocols try to send packets only to a set of nodes located in a geographical zone (geocast), such as GeoGRID [Maihöfer 2004], for example.

Here, the geographic area is divided in 2D logical grids. In each grid, one node is elected as the gateway, and only this one is allowed to forward messages.

P2P Overlay Network over Cellular Networks

The usefulness of cellular networks in an architecture that enables communications between vehicles and with the infrastructure is presented in [Santa & Gomez- Skarmeta 2008]. The network architecture uses a P2P approach over the cellular network basis to enable vehicles to receive and send data packets.

Fig. 2 shows a general diagram of the proposed communication architecture. Traffic zones are organized in coverage areas, each one using different P2P communication groups. These zones are logical areas which do not have to fit in the cellular network cells. Information about the geometry of each area is maintained in the Group Server entity, and vehicles are able to move from one P2P group to another through a roaming process between coverage areas. This roaming is based on the vehicle location, provided by the GPS sensor. Information about areas is received from the Group Server using a TCP/IP link over UMTS. A local element called Environment Server manages special messages inside the area. These data packets are sent and received by service edges, located either at the vehicle or at the road side (Environment Servers). Messages are encapsulated in JXTA frames which are finally sent as UDP packets.

APPLICATIONS REQUIREMENTS ANALYSIS AND FUTURE RESEARCH DIRECTIONS

In this section, we analyze the previously presented vehicular applications requirements from the communication and network technologies

Figure 2. P2P/Cellular network overlay network for vehicular communications

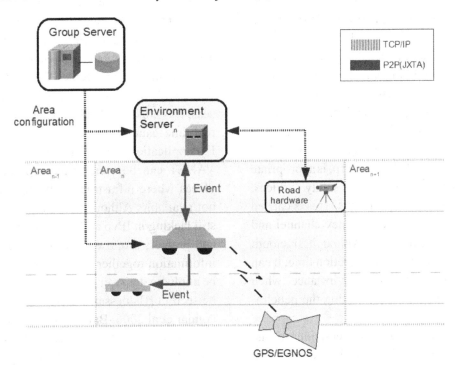

points of view. First, we start by explaining the contribution of layer-one/two technologies on applications requirements. Then, with the same aim, we discuss the layer-three technologies role.

Regarding wider range communication technologies, such as satellite, RDS, cellular and WiMAX, some common aspects can be found considering the application requirements they can fulfill. All of them can avoid penetration rate problems present in short range technologies (e.g. WLAN, Bluetooth and DSRC). This is solved by the necessary infrastructure, which provides the access to the network. An almost permanent access to the network can be available if the infrastructure deployment is good, supporting high degrees of mobility. However, the amount of users simultaneously connected to the network is limited by the available bandwidth in the case of WiMAX and cellular networks, which has to be shared among all users. RDS, however, does not present this problem, because it only transmits data

in the downlink channel, as it is also noticeable in most of satellite deployments. All wide-range technologies can simulate geocasting capabilities, by means of base station broadcasting. However, the performance of this method is limited by the size of coverage areas, which sometimes can be too large, as occurs in the extreme case of satellite communications. An overlay network like the one presented in [56] can solve this problem. Location functionalities are possible in cellular and WiMAX networks, following a detection mechanism at the base station. Cellular networks can take advantage of this method (overall) in urban environments, to provide a good approximation of the user position. Finally, it is important to treat the delay in these wide-range technologies. Real time services can also be considered using cellular and, overall, WiMAX. However, for the case of safety services, it is necessary to assure that the necessary infrastructure is available in the region of interest.

WLAN takes advantage of its two communication modes, infrastructure and ad hoc, to provide a permanent access under the lack of one of them. In the same way, it can help to reduce penetration rate drawbacks by combining these two communication modes. In infrastructure mode, access points can contribute to improve the location accuracy and offer geocast capabilities, as it is noticeable in the GeoNet Project [GeoNet Project]. DSRC, or more specifically IEEE 802.11p, is appropriate for critical applications such as safety services, considering real-time constraints. This is carried out by using a specific emergency channel and priority levels for data traffic. Although Bluetooth is limited by its range and connection time, it can be used in some situations; for instance, when vehicles are very close, alleviating the penetration rate problem.

Starting with level-three considerations, VANET protocols require a special mention. Due to vehicular network characteristics, specially high mobility and dynamicity, it is necessary to combine MANET concepts with new ones, for example the position of the vehicle. Many position-based routing protocols have been proposed integrating location information in the signaling messages (e.g. GPSR [Mauve, Widmer, & Hartenstein et al.2001], DREAM DREAM [Mauve, Widmer, & Hartenstein et al.2001]). Note that some of these works have been considered in standardization bodies (like ETSI [ETSIs. d.]]), vehicular consortiums (C2C-CC [Car-to-Car Communication Consortium]), and European projects (GeoNet). The geographical information about the vehicle could also be used to perform geocast routing, where messages are forwarded to a defined geographic area. As explained previously, V2V communications are highly dependent on the penetration rate. It is difficult to ensure a good communication under low and high load. To reduce this dependence, some solutions have been proposed. For example, under high load conditions, Geocast approaches can use the directed flooding approach, where the closer vehicle to the destination retransmits the message (e.g. LBM [Maihöfer 2004]). When the penetration is low, some solutions have been proposed, where messages progress towards the destination by means of node movements [Kosch 2002, Zhao & Cao 2006, Li & Rus 2000, Chatzigiannakis, Nikoletseas, & Spirakis et al.2001]. These solutions offer real-time features, by optimizing communications. For applications that require a permanent access, VANET can be seen as an important asset in places where infrastructure-based networks are not available. Although location information is still lacking in IPv6 and NEMO, many solutions and projects propose the usage of geographical information together with them. First, IPv6 can be implemented over geographical routing, as can be seen in [Baldessari,Festag, Matos, Santos, & Aguiar et al.2006, Baldessari, Festag, Zhang, & Le et al.2008, GeoNet Project. d.]. Other approach consists of extending IPv6 with geographical information [Chen, Steenstra, & K-S et al.2008, Vare, Syrjarinne, & Virtanen et al.2004].

The maintenance of multiple network interfaces (e.g. WLAN, WiMAX, GPRS/UMTS), thanks to multihoming, provides an extended permanent access to the network. For instance, WiMAX or cellular networks can be used when WLAN is not available, and vice versa. The traffic distribution into multiple paths increases the available bandwidth considerably and decrease the communication delay. Route optimization also improves the communication quality by reducing transmission delay. Moreover, the combination of NEMO and MANET takes advantage of both technologies, offering a continuous access to the network.

A summary about how applications requirements can be fulfilled by using communication and network technologies is summarized in Table 3. We can notice that VANET communication can provide location, time awareness and geocast capabilities. On the other hand, NEMO could enhance mobility and ensure a permanent Internet access. Due to this, we can notice that VANET

Table 3. Application requirements fulfilled with each technology

Technology/ App. Req.	Location Awareness	Geocast capability	Penetration rate dependence	Time Awareness	Permanent Access	Mobility
Layer 1/ 2						
Bluetooth	Possible		Sensitive		Help	O
WLAN	Possible	Help	Sensitive	Possible	Help	O
DSRC	Possible	Help	Sensitive	Possible	Help	O
WiMAX	Possible	Help			Help	O
Cellular	Possible	Help			Help	O
DS/TMC	X				Help	O
Satellite	X				Help	O
Layer3						
VANET	O	O	Sensitive	O	Help	O
NEMO					O	O
Multihoming					O	
Route optimization				O		
MANEMO				O	O	O

O = The technology fills the requirement (The requirement is the aim of the technology).
X = The technology cannot fill the requirement.
Possible = The technology can be used to fill the requirement with other technologies (The requirement cannot be filled by only the technology)
Sensitive = Penetration rate dependency sensitive
Help = The technology helps the requirement (The requirement cannot be filled by only the technology).

and NEMO are highly complementary in order to fill these requirements.

This analysis could be used as starting point for future research works. Thus, the main purpose of this study is to assist to choose the appropriate communication technologies. However, the performances of these technologies under real conditions must be considered before being applied on specific environments.

Take notice that, in our analysis study regarding networking requirements of vehicular applications, some research issues are still open,. Among these issues, geocasting feasibility with both short and wide-range technologies could be exhaustively studied. However, about the integration of geographical information in routing and addressing mechanisms, it is not clear which approach is suited for each application, and what is the expected performance of them. In this way,

additional studies are required. Security is one of the main issues in vehicular networks nowadays. All security hazards considered in other networks must be now considered in this field.

Although research activities are very important, standardization efforts are essential to accelerate the deployment of these applications. In this frame, considering application requirements is crucial. This, without forgotten the support of public administration to design novel vehicular services.

Although some communication architectures have been proposed, many of them are too dependent on technological viewpoints. Architectural modules need to be Interchangeable; for example 802.11b can be replaced by 802.11p in the future. Moreover, agreements between services providers and network operators to enable the deployment of telematics services with a lower communication cost are highly needed.

CONCLUSION

Many vehicular applications and services have been proposed at the beginning of this chapter. However, in order to achieve good performances, they should take into account the communication technology used. In this chapter we give an analysis of the available communication technologies, and study how they can fulfill the main networking requirements of ITS applications.

The initial overview of applications and services sorts them into three main families: safety, traffic management and monitoring, and comfort. Then, we describe three reference applications for each family that best represents them in the current literature. To assure the operation of these applications, new requirements, far away from the ones found in traditional services of fixed networks, appear in vehicular communications. To meet these demands, a number of communication technologies at level one/two are currently available. After explaining these, some of the most networking solutions at level three are described. Next, by means of an analysis which links applications, requirements and technologies, we give a vision of how each high level demand can be fulfilled by means of each technology. Since there is no any specific technology that can satisfy all the requirements, our opinion is that future vehicles will combine some of them in order to enable the deployment of different telematic applications.

Having the requirements and technologies in mind, vehicular network solutions can be designed by means of new communication architectures or integrating current ones. In this frame, our contribution should help in the design of both vehicular applications/services and technologies for tests scenarios, evaluations or commercial developments.

REFERENCES

Alexiou, A., Bouras, C., & Igglesis, V. (2004, November/ December). *Performance evaluation of tcp over umts transport channels.* Presented at the International symposium on communicationsinterworking. Ottawa, Canada.

Alshaer, H., & Horlait, E. (2005). *An optimized adaptive broadcast scheme for inter-vehicle communication.* Presented at the IEEE vehicular technology conference. Stockholm, Sweden.

Ammoun, S., Nashashibi, F., & Laurgeau, C. (2006, September). *Real-time crash avoidance system on crossroads based on 802.11 devices and GPS receivers.* Presented at the IEEE intelligent transportation systems conference. Toronto, Canada.

Baldessari, R., Festag, A., & Lenardi, M. (2007, July). C2c-c consortium requirements for nemo route optimization. *Manuel de logiciel* (IETF, draft-baldessari-c2ccc-nemoreq-01).

Baldessari, R., Festag, A., Matos, A., Santos, J., & Aguiar, R. (2006). Flexible connectivity management in vehicular communication networks. In *Proceedings of the WIT 2004.* Hamburg, Germany.

Baldessari, R., Festag, A., Zhang, W., & Le, L. (2008). A manetcentric solution for the application of nemo in vanet using geographic routing. In *Proceedings of the weedev.* Vienna, Austria.

Bernardos, C. J., Soto, I., Calder'on, M., Boavida, F., & Azcorra, A. (2007). Varon: Vehicular ad hoc route optimisation for nemo. *Computer Communications, 30*(8), 1765–1784. doi:10.1016/j.comcom.2007.02.011

Biswas, S., Tatchikou, R., & Dion, F. (2006, January). Vehicleto-vehicle wireless communication protocols for enhancing highway traffic safety. *IEEE Communications Magazine, 44*(1), 74–82. doi:10.1109/MCOM.2006.1580935

Boukerche, A., Oliveira, H., Nakamura, E., Jang, K., & Loureiro, A. (2008, July). Vehicular ad hoc networks: A new challenge for localization-based systems. *Computer Communications, 31*(12), 2838–2849. doi:10.1016/j.comcom.2007.12.004

Breitenberger, S., Grber, B., Neuherz, M., & Kates, R. (2004, July). Traffic information potential and necessary penetration rates. *Traffic engineering & control, 45*(11), 396–401.

Car-to-car. (n.d.). *Car-to-car communication consortium.* Retrieved from http://www.car-tocar.org

Chakeres, I., & Belding-Royer, M. (2004). AODV routing protocol implementation design. In *Proceedings of the international workshop on wireless ad hoc networking* (WWAN). Tokyo, Japan.

Chatzigiannakis, I., Nikoletseas, E., & Spirakis, P. (2001). *An efficient communication strategy for ad-hoc mobile networks.* Presented at the 15th international conference on distributed computing. London.

Chen, L., Steenstra, J., & K-S taylor. (2008, January). *Geolocation-based addressing method for ipv6 addresses* (Patent). San Diego, CA: Qualcomm Incorporated.

Clausen, T., Jacquet, P., Laouiti, A., Muhlethaler, P., Qayyum, A., & Viennot, L. (2001). Optimized link state routing protocol. In *Proceedings of IEEE international multitopic conference INMIC.* Islamabad, Pakistan.

Clifford Neuman, B. (1994). Scale in distributed systems. In *Readings in distributed computing systems* (pp. 463–489). IEEE Computer Society Press.

Devarapalli, V., Wakikawa, R., Petrescu, A., & Thubert, P. (2005, January). *Network mobility (NEMO) basic support protocol.* IETF RFC3963.

Duros, E., Dabbous, W., Izumiyama, H., Fujii, N., & Zhang, Y. (2001, March). *A link-layer tunneling mechanism for unidirectional links.* IETF RFC3077.

Eddy, W., Ivancic, W., & Davis, T. (2007, December). *Nemo route optimization requirements for operational use in aeronautics and space exploration mobile networks.* IETF, draft-ietf-mext-aero-reqs-00.

ElBatt, T., Goel, S., Holland, G., Krishnan, H., & Parikh, J. (2006, September). *Cooperative collision warning using dedicated short range wireless communications.* Presented at the International conference on mobile computing and networking, international workshop on vehicular ad hoc networks. Los Angeles.

Ernst, T., Montavont, N., Wakikawa, R., Ng, C., & Kuladinithi, K. (2007, July). *Motivations and scenarios for using multiple interfaces and global addresses,* Manuel de logiciel. IETF, draft-ietf-monami6-multihoming-motivation-scenario-02.

eSafety (n.d.). *The eSafety initiative.* Retrieved from http://www.esafetysupport.org/

European telecommunications (n.d.). *European telecommunications standards institute.* Retrieved from http://www.etsi.org

Geonet (n.d.). *Geonet project.* Retrieved from http://www.geonet-project.eu

Guo, M. M. H. A., & Zegura, E. W. (2005). V3: A vehicle to vehicle live video streaming architecture. In *Proceedings of IEEE Percom* (p. 171-180). Arlington, TX.

Han, M., Moon, S., Lee, Y., Jang, K., & Lee, D. (2008, April). *Evaluation of MoIP quality verWiBro.* Presented at the Passive and active measurement conference. Cleveland, OH.

Hattori, G., Ono, C., Nishiyama, S., & Horiuchi, H. (2004, January). *Implementation and evaluation of message delegation middleware for ITS application*. Presented at the International symposium on applications and the internet workshops. Tokyo, Japan.

Hoh, B., Gruteser, M., Xiong, H., & Alrabady, A. (2006, October-December). Enhancing security and privacy in traffic-monitoring systems. *IEEE Pervasive Computing / IEEE Computer Society [and] IEEE Communications Society, 5*(4), 38–46. doi:10.1109/MPRV.2006.69

Intelligent Transportation. (n.d.). *The Intelligent Transportation System*. Retrieved from http://www.its.dot.gov/its overview.htm

Jiang, M., Li, J., & Tay, Y. (2001). Cluster based routing protocol (CBRP) (Rapport technique). IETF. (Internet draft) Johnson, D., Perkins, C., & Arkko, J. (Eds.), Mobility support in ipv6, Manuel de logiciel. (IETF RFC 3775)

Khaled, Y., Ducourthial, B., & Shawky, M. (2005-Spring). IEEE 802.11 performances for inter-vehicle communication networks. In Proc. of th 61st IEEE semianual vehicular technology conference VTC. Stockholm, Sweden.

Khaled, Y., Ducourthial, B., & Shawky, M. (July, 2007). A usage oriented taxonomy of routing protocols in vanet. In *Proceedings of 1st ubiroads workshop with IEEE GIIS*. Marrakech, Morroco.

Kiess, W., Rybicki, J., & Mauve, M. (2007, February/March). *On the nature of inter-vehicle communications*. Presented at the Workshop on mobile ad-hoc networks. Bern, Switzerland.

King, T., Füßler, H., Transier, M., & Effelsberg, W. (2006, 03). Dead-Reckoning for Position-Based Forwarding on Highways. In *Proc. of the 3rd international workshop on intelligent transportation* (WIT 2006) (p. 199-204). Hamburg, Germany.

Kosch, T. (2002). *Technical concept and prerequisites of car to car communication (Rapport technique)*. Munich, Germany: BMW Group Research and Technology.

Landman, J., & Kritzinger, P. (2005). Delay analysis of downlink IP traffic on UMTS mobile networks. *Performance Evaluation, 62*(1-4), 68–82. doi:10.1016/j.peva.2005.07.007

Larsson, C., Eriksson, M., Mitsuya, K., Tasaka, K., & Kuntz, R. (2008, July). Flow distribution rule language for multi-access nodes. *Manuel de logiciel* (IETF, draft-larsson-mext-flowdistribution-rules-00)

Li, Q., & Rus, D. (2000). *Sending messages to mobile users in disconnected ad-hoc wireless networks*. Presented at the 6th annual international conference on mobile computing and networking (MOBICOM). Boston.

Lorchat, J., & Uehara, K. (2006, July). *Optimized Inter-Vehicle Communications Using NEMO and MANET* (Invited Paper). Presented at The Second International Workshop on Vehicle-to-Vehicle Communications 2006 (V2VCOM 2006). San Jose, CA.

Maihöfer, C. (2nd quarter 2004). A survey of geocast routing protocols. *IEEE Communications Surveys and Tutorials, 6*.

Masini, B., Fontana, C., & Verdone, R. (2004, October). *Provision of an emergency warning service through GPRS: Performance evaluation*. Presented at the IEEE intelligent transportation systems conference. Washington, DC.

Mauve, M., Widmer, J., & Hartenstein, H. (2001, November/December). A survey on position-based routing in mobile ad hoc networks. *IEEE Network Magazine*.

Meier, R., Hughes, B., Cunningham, R., & Cahill, V. (2005). Towards real-time middleware for applications of vehicular ad hoc networks. In IFIP WG 6.1 international conference, distributed applications and interoperable systems. Oslo, Norway.

Naumov, V., Baumann, R., & Gross, T. (2006, May). *An evaluation of inter-vehicle ad hoc networks based on realistic vehicular traces.* Presented at the ACM international symposium on mobile ad hoc networking and computing. Florence, Italia.

Ng, C., Ernst, T., Paik, E., & Bagnulo, M. (2007, October). *Analysis of multihoming in network mobility support* (IETF, RFC4980). Singapore: Panasonic Labs.

Ng, C., Thubert, P., Watari, M., & Zhao, F. (2007, July). *Network mobility route optimization problem statement* (IETF RFC4888). Singapore: Panasonic Labs.

Nolte, T., Hansson, H., & Lo Bello, L. (2005, September). *Automotive communications - past, current and future.* Presented at the IEEE international conference on emerging technologies and factory automation. Catania, Italy.

Qureshi, A., Carlisle, J., & Guttag, J. (2006, October). Tavarua: *Video streaming with WWAN striping.* Presented at Acm multimedia 2006. Santa Barbara, CA.

Santa, J., & Gomez-Skarmeta, A. (2008, July). Architecture and evaluation of a unified V2V and V2I communication system based on cellular networks. *Elsevier Computer Communications, 31*(12), 2850–2861.

Sawant, H., Tan, J., Yang, Q., & Wang, Q. (2004, October). *Using bluetooth and sensor networks for intelligent transportation systems.* Presented at the IEEE international conference on intelligent transportation systems. Washington DC.

Soliman, H., Montavont, N., Fikouras, N., & Kuladinithi, K. (2007, November). *Flow bindings in mobile ipv6 and nemo basic support*, Manuel de logiciel (IETF, draft-solimanmonami6-flow-binding-05). Germany: University of Bremen

Sugiura, A., & Dermawan, C. (2005, September). In traffic jam IVC-RVC system for ITS using bluetooth. *IEEE Transactions on Intelligent Transportation Systems, 6*(3), 302–313. doi:10.1109/TITS.2005.853704

Tsukada, M., Mehani, O., & Ernst, T. (2008, March 18). *Simultaneous usage of NEMO and MANET for vehicular communication.* Presented at WEEDEV 2008: 1st workshop on experimental evaluation and deployment experiences on vehicular networks in conjonction with TRIDENTCOM 2008. Innsbruck, Austria. Retrieved from http://hal.inria.fr/inria-00265652/

Ueki, J., Tasaka, S., Hatta, Y., & Okada, H. (2005). Vehicular collision avoidance support system (vcass) by inter-vehicle communications for advanced its. *IEICE Transactions on Fundamentals of Electronics, Communications and Computer Sciences. E (Norwalk, Conn.), 88-A*(7), 1816–1823.

3GUMTS. (2006, December). Evolution: towards a new generation of broadband mobile services, *Manuel de logiciel.* Adrisano, O., Verdone, R., & M, N. (2000, September). Intelligent transportation systems: The role of third-generation mobile radio networks. *IEEE Communications Magazine, 38*(9), 144–151.

Vare, J., Syrjarinne, J., & Virtanen, K.-S. (2004). Geographical positioning extension for IPv6. In *Proceedings of the ICN.* Guadeloupe, France.

Wakikawa, R., Clausen, T., McCarthy, B., & Petrescu, A. (2007, July). *Manemo topology and addressing architecture* IETF, draft-wakikawa-manemoarch-00. Kanagawa, Japan.

Wakikawa, R., Ernst, T., Nagami, K., & Devarapalli, V. (2008, January). *Multiple care-of addresses registration* IETF, draft-ietf-monami6-multiplecoa-05. Kanagawa, Japan.

Wakikawa, R., Okada, K., Koodli, R., Nilsson, A., & Murai, J. (2005, September). *Design of Vehicle Network: Mobile Gateway for MANET and NEMO Converged Communication*. Presented at The Second ACM International Workshop on Vehicular Ad Hoc Networks (VANET 2005) Philadelphia.

Wakikawa, R., Thubert, P., Boot, T., Bound, J., & McCarthy, B. (2007, July). *Problem statement and requirements for manemo*, Manuel de logiciel. IETF, draft-mccarthymanemo-configuration problems-01. Kanagawa, Japan.

Wewetzer, C., Caliskan, M., Meier, K., & Luebke, A. (2007, June). Experimental evaluation of umts and wireless lan for inter-vehicle communication. Presentd at the International conference its telecommunications. Sophia Antipolis, France.

Yousefi, S., Bastani, S., & Fathy, M. (2007, February). *On the performance of safety message dissemination in vehicular ad hoc networks*. Presented at the European conference on universal multiservice networks. Toulouse, France.

Zhao, J., & Cao, G. (2006). VADD: Vehicle-assisted data delivery in vehicular ad hoc networks. Presented at the 25th conference on computer communications INFOCOM). Barcelona, Spain.

Chapter 4
Safety and Commercial Applications

Samy El-Tawab
Old Dominion University, USA

Gongjun Yan
Old Dominion University, USA

ABSTRACT

Applications in Vehicular Networks are the main motive for all researchers and vehicle manufactures to design new protocols; technologies and implementations that allow a specific type of applications. The chapter starts with different classifications of Applications in Vehicular Ad-Hoc Network (VANET). Then, it gives a background on Applications in VANET. Then, it discusses different categories of applications in details starting with different types of safety application and commercial applications. It compares between communications in high and low safety application. Then, it describes in details monitoring, service applications and a view on entertainment applications. Finally, it will explain the requirements for real-time applications. At the end, the chapter gives some case studies for applications.

INTRODUCTION

Top vehicle manufactures are competing to the new technology of Vehicle-to-Vehicle communication (V2V) or Vehicle-to-Infrastructure (V2I) targeting the idea of improving their vehicles to improve the market. General Motors, Opel, Ford and Volvo are examples for manufactures that trying to improve themselves in this field. General Motors is focusing on 'Vehicle-to-X' communication system that is independent of the manufacturer or vehicle-type.

In June 2007, (*General Motors Website*) General Motors (GM) announced on its official website the start for a new era of vehicles by developing vehicles with a *Sixth Sense*. On the other hand, (*Ford Website*) Ford designing 'Smart Intersection' technology, which relies on GPS and wireless communication technologies to enable traffic lights and street signs to send warnings to approaching vehicles. Furthermore, Nissan and (*Volvo Website*) Volvo have confirmed similar systems.

There are many classifications for applications in Vehicular Networks. One of these classifications is using three categories for application depending

DOI: 10.4018/978-1-61520-913-2.ch004

Figure 1. Classification of VANET applications

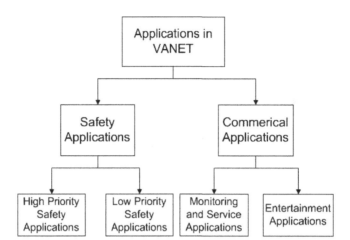

on the method of technology used for communications: *Santa, J., et al (2008)* used Vehicle-to-Vehicle, Vehicle-to-Infrastructure or a combination between both technologies. *Blum, J. et al (2004)* used another method which is to classify them to Safety Oriented, Convenience Oriented and Commercial Oriented. Our vision of classifications is a multi-level classification, level one: is to divide it into two categories of *Safety Applications* and *Commercial Applications*. Then, sublevel divides Safety Applications into two other categories of *Low Priority Safety Applications* and *High Priority Safety Applications*. On the other hand, Commercial Applications is divided into two other categories of *Monitoring & Service Applications* and *Entertainment Applications*. Figure 1 below shows this classification.

Safety and commercial applications are two different categories in Vehicular Ad Hoc Network (VANET). In general, real-time applications are a very challenging issue in Vehicular Networks. Commercial applications including entertainment applications, advertising applications, information guiding applications and shopping applications are less challenging than safety applications. Commercial applications – others *(Jordan, R. et al 2004)* call it Comfort Applications- can be defined as

a user application that requires a subscribing to receive specific type of data from specific locations. It includes the vehicle acceptance to generate data periodically or respond to some events. End-users or drivers may accept a delay or even a loss of data in commercial application for a specific margin. On the other hand, drivers will not accept the chance of risking their life or even relaying on applications that has a small margin of error. Safety application can also be categorized into two different types: High Priority Vehicle Safety and Low Priority Safety. First type includes the notifications of sudden problems that would result in a sudden accident or a vehicle, while the latter is more related to the passenger notifications of incident ahead or road weather predication can be called "*Advisory Message Delivery*" as mentioned by *Schagrin, M. (2008)*; which gives the driver the option to choose if he/she would prefer to continue driving or take another decision as taking a rest for a period of time.

Applications in VANET focus on a reliable communication that gives a guaranteed real-time message delivery. Different types of applications have been discussed recently by researchers: Emergency electronic Brake Light which is the first vehicle to vehicle cooperative active safety application that establishes EEBL messages. Cooperative Intersection Collision Avoidance Systems is another well known example which tries to alert drivers of intersection collisions. Other applications: parking location assistance; food drive through payment; road toll payment; download movies, games and mp3; and remote diagnostics for vehicle problems; have been introduced in recent research papers.

Real-time reliable communication is a great challenge to researcher and vehicle developers. A specific channel in the Dedicated Short-Range Communications (DSRC) is restricted to safety communication as mentioned in the *(DSRC Website)*. Other two channels are reserved for accident avoidance application and high power public safety communication usages. The rest of the DSRC channels are used for both safety and non safety applications. Also, IEEE has proposed standards for VANETs. It defines services and interfaces as well as message formats.

Security is the one of the main issues in all these application; sending false messages, forwarding un-secure messages which the goal of getting rid of vehicles on the road. Other famous attacks over the internet can be done in VANET such as denial of service (DoS). So, the main challenge here is to provide a secure system in VANET that can be trust.

BACKGROUND (APPLICATIONS IN VANET)

In VANET and vehicle communications, service requirements can be covered using two types of network topologies: communications between vehicle and infrastructure, and communications among vehicles. In the first case, on-board services require a connection with the infrastructure located at the road side. This kind of connectivity is usually named as Vehicle to Infrastructure (V2I) communication. An example of such technology can be found in electronic fee collection systems, where drivers are charged automatically, according to some road and vehicle parameters. The approach presented in *Santa, J. et al (2008)* that uses DSRC (Dedicated Short Range Communications) gantries to keep the path followed by a vehicle in order to calculate the associated cost. In V2I systems, the main technologies involved are DSRC, infrared, and wireless LAN. On the other hand, the second group of services with connectivity requirements is the vehicle to vehicle (V2V) solutions. In the current literature, several works for collision avoidance support, and warning mechanisms in general, can be found as in *Franz, W. et al (2001)*. For this type of services, the most extended technologies are based on ad hoc networks applied to the vehicle field (VANET or Vehicular ad hoc NETworks) as in *Bychkovsky, V. et al (2006)*. Also, *Santa, J. et al (2008)* gave an example on using Cellular and peer-to-peer (P2P) networks jointly to design a communication system based on coverage areas.

DSRC (DESIGNATED SHORT RANGE COMMUNICATIONS)

DSRC is allocated at the 5.9 GHz frequency band and is designed to support high vehicular velocities in a radio transmission range up to 1000m with a data rate up to 27Mbps per channel including two control channels and seven service channels as described in details in *(DSRC Website)*.

SAFETY APPLICATION

In safety applications, drivers cannot accept any kind of error in alerts provided by the vehicular network application. Moreover, they expect to depend on these features more often that might give the driver the reason to relax more while driving. Most current implemented or in the implementation phase safety applications depend on the sensing capabilities on the vehicle or surrounded infrastructure. Volvo (*Volvo Website*) has designed cars in 2009 that has what called *City Safety*; Volvo's in-house developed unique technology for avoiding low-speed collisions in city traffic. It allows Continental around the Closing Velocity (CV) sensor that reduces the risk of a rear-end collision. This is done through an infrared sensor supplies data for automatic brake application at city driving speeds to avoid rear-end collisions as announced in (*Volvo Website*). More details will be given on these types of systems later in the chapter.

The safety applications are divided into two sub categories: High priority Vehicle safety, in these types of applications the drivers must be alert or even the system should perform a task to avoid an accident or collision. The other type is low priority Vehicle safety, in these types of applications drivers are notified for their safety as there is a chance of an accident that occur if not alerted.

HIGH PRIORITY VEHICLE SAFETY

In High Priority Vehicle Safety application, applications may alert or in other cases take control of the braking system or other features in the vehicle to avoid a collision, below a list of some famous applications in high priority vehicle safety:

a. City Safety
b. Blind spot warning.
c. Precrash warning.
d. Highway collision warning.
e. Intersection collision Avoidance.

City Safety

Not only Volvo but also other manufacturing is doing lots of work in the field of sensing capability of the vehicles. BMW Parking Sensor is also one of the new technologies that help parking.

Most of these applications are working below the speed of 30 km/hr (18.6 miles/hr). The constant alternation between braking and accelerating in cities cause more than 75 percent of accidents. It is precisely at these speeds, in slow-moving or "stop and go" traffic, that this sensor system, developed and manufactured by *Continental around the Closing Velocity (CV) sensor*, reduces the risk of a rear-end collision as mentioned in *World Premiere of Continental Sensor System in the New Volvo XC60 (2008)*.

These types of sensors use three infrared beams to probe the road up to some six meters in front of the vehicle. The sensor picks up vehicles which are stationary or traveling in the same direction. If the gap is less than the distance which must be regarded as critical at the current speed, the system causes the brakes to be applied automatically as described in *(Volvo Website)*. Even if the braking system does not intervene automatically, Continental's CV sensor system can assist the driver. If the driver realizes that a rear-end collision is imminent and applies the brakes, the system will already have built up pressure as a precaution. The brake assist system will respond earlier, depending on how risky the situation is, shortening the stopping distance more effectively than would be possible without the CV sensor's warning.

In addition to this interface to the environmental sensors, the braking system also has a trailer stabilization function which detects if a trailer is beginning to "fishtail" and stabilizes the car-trailer combination by brake application to individual wheels (Trailer Stability Assist, TSA). A further driving safety feature is the roll-over protection function. As well as the usual *Electronic Stability Control* (ESC) sensors, the vehicle braking system has an additional sensor which records the vehicle body's rolling motion. If all the data it collects indicates that the vehicle is seriously at risk of overturning, the brakes are specifically applied to individual wheels. This roll sensor is built into the ESC cluster which, like the active

Figure 2. Infrared sensor supplies data for automatic brake

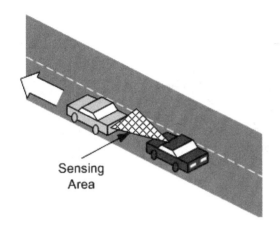

Sensing
Area

wheel speed sensors, the brake actuation unit and the new two-piston front axle. Wheel brakes are also supplied by Continental's Chassis & Safety Division.

Blind Spot Warning

In this type of application, the system adds some extra sensor that allows the vehicle to detect the present of a vehicle. Drivers giving a signal to turn right or left to the other lane will notice an alert of a vehicle existence. Some manufacturing is assuming to draw a small figure of these vehicles on the left and right mirrors of the vehicle in order to allow Smart Mirrors as mentioned in *Hecht, c. (2005)*. In trucks, the blind spot is larger than the small vehicles. Figure 3 below shows the Blind Spot in small vehicles.

Precrash Warning

It is a general case for the "Safety City" system, where the vehicle is surrounded with a bubble of sensing capabilities that allows the vehicle to sense any other object coming closer than usual and gives a warning signal to the driver. The same concept is sometimes called a "Smart Bubble", it is a 3-D sensing feature that allows the vehicle to

control any precrash situations. Figure 4 shows the vehicles surrounded with the eclipse shape which present the surrounding sensing area.

Highway Collision Warning

This application is concern with higher speed vehicles running on highways, with the increase of speed the distance required to stop the vehicle increases. So, application on highway takes in account the increase of safety distance and gives warning messages when the driver is getting close to vehicles that may lead to a collision. At 55 mph (≈88.5 kph), it will take about six seconds to stop and your vehicle will travel about 450 feet (≈137 meters) which is known as *Total Stopping Distance*. Whenever you double your speed, it takes about four times as much distance to stop and your vehicle will have four times the destructive power if it crashes. High speeds increase stopping distances greatly. By slowing down a little, you can gain a lot in reduced braking distance which is known as *The Effect of Speed on Stopping Distance*.

The stopping distance is given by:

$$d = \frac{v_0^2}{2\mu g}$$

Where d is the stopping distance, v_0 is the vehicle speed; μ is the coefficient of friction between the tires and the road and g is acceleration due to gravity. Also, note that this implies a stopping distance independent of vehicle mass, and in this case, driver reaction time. It also implies a quadrupling of stopping distance with a doubling of vehicle speed.

Intersection Collision Avoidance

As vehicles approach the intersection they must establish secure links with the Road Side Unit

Figure 3. Blind spot in the small vehicles

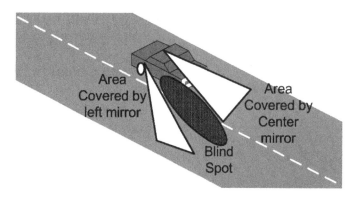

Figure 4. Smart bubbles around each vehicle

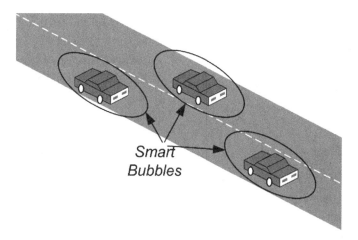

(RSU) via control channel by exchanging their digital certificates (Establishing secure links takes more time than exchanging normal messages). After that, vehicles start to interact with the RSU by sharing their data and receiving the intersection's condition messages from the RSU via service channel. If the traffic density and the arrival rate of the vehicles become high, the RSU might not be able to generate warning messages within the specified latency, and at the same time continue collecting information from all vehicles within the communication range. Moreover, the increase of vehicles' density results in increase of the packet loss. Hence, the challenge is to build a system that allows the RSU to offer safety services on time collect information from all vehicles within an allowable latency and reduce packet loss. *Rawashdeh, Z. et al (2008)* give an example of Intersection Collision Avoidance System Architecture where they study the analyses of parameters in the Intersection Collision Avoidance (ICA) system based on the radar sensors. The parameters include the positioning errors, the repeat period of the radar sensor, the conditions of potential collisions of two cross-path vehicles, etc. The analyses of the parameters can provide the requirements, limitations, or specifications of this ICA system. Figure 5 below shows an example of vehicle communicating with RSU.

Figure 5. Intersection warning

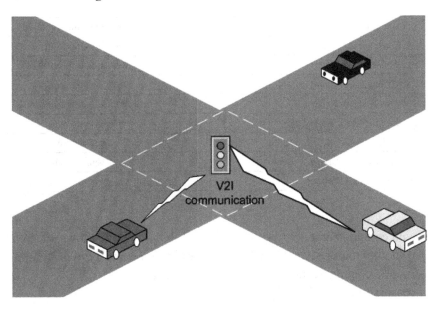

LOW PRIORITY SAFETY

In Low Priority Vehicle Safety application, applications will just notify the driver with critical situations (give a warning signal), it will not allow the vehicle to take control of the braking system or other features, below a list of some applications in low priority vehicle safety:

a. CSW: Curve Speed Warning
b. WZW: Work Zone Warning
c. WWW: Wrong Way Warning
d. LBW: Low Bridge Warning
e. EEBL: Emergency Electronic Brake Lights
f. MA: Merge Assistant
g. LCW: Lane Change Warning
h. DNPW: Do Not Pass Warning

Curve Speed Warning

In this type of applications, the vehicle will enter a curve through the highway; a notice will be sent the vehicles with certain speed to slow down for the curve. Usually Vehicle-to-Infrastructure communication is used in this case. If the vehicle is within the normal speed of the curve, no warning is sent.

Work Zone Warning

Similar to the Curve Speed warning system applications, the vehicle will enter a work zone through the highway; a notice will be sent the vehicles slow down for the work zone area. Usually a temporarily infrastructure is moved to the work zone. Vehicle-to-Infrastructure communication is used in this case.

Wrong Way Warning

In this case, vehicles entering wrong way will be detected and given a notification; Vehicle-to-Infrastructure communication is used in this case. Signal is kept alerting the driving until the vehicle return back to right direction.

Low Bridge Warning

In this type of applications, the vehicle will enter a bridge through the highway; a notice will be

Table 1. Warning type vs. communication required

Warning Type	Communication required
CSW: Curve Speed Warning	Vehicle-to-Infrastructure
ZW: Work Zone Warning	Vehicle-to-Infrastructure
WWW: Wrong Way Warning	Vehicle-to-Infrastructure
LBW: Low Bridge Warning	Vehicle-to-Infrastructure
EEBL: Emergency Electronic Brake Lights	Vehicle-to-Vehicle
MA: Merge Assistant	Vehicle itself
LCW: Lane Change Warning	Vehicle itself
DNPW: Do Not Pass Warning	Vehicle-to-Infrastructure

sent the vehicles with certain height not to enter the bridge and take another route or exit. Usually Vehicle-to-Infrastructure communication is used in this case with sensors to detect the height of the vehicles.

Emergency Electronic Brake Lights

This application will help the driver of following vehicles by giving an early notification of lead vehicle braking hard. This requires vehicle-to-vehicle communication.

Merge Assistant

When a signal is given to shift to another lane, a merge assistant will try to help you to merge safely.

Lane Change Warning

When lane change is happening inside a bridge or no signal is given or sudden lane change. A warning is issued by the vehicle to the driver.

DNPW: Do Not Pass Warning

When don't pass appear inside a tunnel or in a one way road, a warning message is given to all drivers or whom try to give a sign or change lanes.

Table 1 below shows the relation between warning type and type of communication used in each case.

COMMERCIAL APPLICATIONS

In commercial applications, the vehicle manufactures focus on how to increase the level of luxury in the vehicle or through the services provided to the vehicle. In fact, some vehicle manufactures are willing to pay extra money or join big food companies to provide some extra service. Drivers would like to be notified with weather condition through the road. Even parking, sometimes it requires a great effort; it would be great for an assistance to find an empty or closer spot. Not only drivers but also passengers wish to have more entertainment equipment in the vehicle as not to feel bored from the long travels.

Traffic monitoring is well known projects with Department of Transportation all over the world. The United States department of Transportation offers a Traffic Volume Trends which is a monthly report based on hourly traffic count data reported by the States. These data are collected at approximately 4,000 continuous traffic counting locations nationwide and are used to estimate the percent change in traffic for the current month compared with the same month in the previous year. Estimates are re-adjusted annually to match the vehicle miles of travel from the Highway Performance Monitoring System and are continually updated with additional data as mentioned in *Úbeda, B. et al (2004)*.

One of the most famous applications for the traffic management system is to determine the bad weather condition and notify drivers with it. Bad weather conditions include heavy rain, heavy snow, ice, black ice, fog and tornadoes. Also, automatic incident detections are one of top issues for traffic management systems. Lots of research has been done in weather conditions detection techniques that monitors the weather over the highways and inform drivers with bad weather condition. Moreover, it notifies drivers with incidents on the road.

In the United States, motor vehicle traffic crashes are the leading cause of death for all Americans between two and thirty four years of age as described in *Subramanian, R. (2007)*. In 2006, the National Highway Traffic Safety Administration reports that 42,642 people were killed in motor vehicle traffic crashes. Among all these accidents, each year, approximately 7,000 highway deaths and 800,000 injuries are associated with about 1.2 million weather-related accidents. *Traffic Safety Facts (2006)* estimated annual cost from these weather-related crashes (deaths, injuries and property) amounts to nearly $42 billion. Vehicular Network targets these problems. The main focus of researcher is to invent a new technology without expensive changes in the infrastructure to help notifying the drivers with bad weather conditions including rain, snow, sleet, fog, smoke, dust etc.

Below we give a list of most famous applications that goes under the category of Commercial Applications (Traffic Monitoring & service).

Traffic Monitoring & service Applications:

a. Road condition and Weather condition monitoring.
b. Parking location assistance.
c. Restaurant information and assistant, food drive through payment;

d. Road general services: road toll payment
e. Vehicle Services: remote diagnostics for vehicle problems

Road Condition and Weather Condition

Drivers need reliable and accurate information on weather and road conditions. Several systems have been introduced. Road Weather Information system (RWIS) – RWIS is a combination of technologies that collects, transmit, models, and disseminates weather and road condition information. The element of an RWIS that collects weather data is called the environmental sensor station (ESS) as mentioned in Weather *and Highways (2004)*. Road Weather Information System is a unique system consisting of several meteorological stations strategically located alongside the highway that allow the Department to make more informed decisions during winter storms. *Weather and Highways (2004)* mentioned that specialized equipment and computer programs monitor air and pavement temperature to make forecasts regarding how the winter storms impact the highways. This gives the Department opportunities to utilize alternate de-icing chemicals, make optimal use of materials and staff, and practice anti-icing techniques developed through years of research.

Meteorological Assimilation Data Ingest System (MADIS) is a framework for a national clearinghouse of RWIS data. Some State Departments of Transportation (DOTs) provide the information to be entered into the database, which can then be distributed to users of road weather information. Finally, Maintenance Decision support System (MDSS) is a project that takes road weather data and information and merges them into a computerized winter road maintenance program that can help to guide maintenance manager in making better road treatment decisions. Unfortunately most of these systems require some processing and does not allow real time information. Information is stored then processed then sent to

Figure 6. Example of road condition and weather condition notifications using v2v and v2i communication on highway

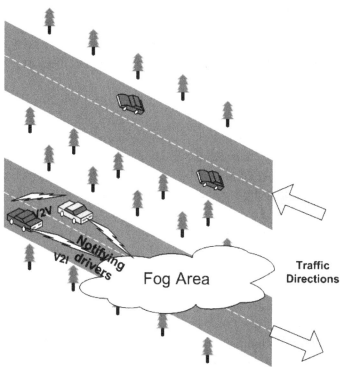

users. Highways are in a great need for a Real time Notification system for weather conditions.

As weather conditions get bad, sensors can collect information and process this information to leaders on the road that can notify drivers as early as possible with weather conditions.

Parking Location Assistance

"Smart Parking" as called in *Gongjun, Y. et al (2008)* is a common phrase known in the research in the field of Vehicular Network. *Kumar, R. et al (2007)* give a comparative study of different sensors for smart car park management, compare sensor data gathered from different varieties of Acoustic, light and Magnetic sensors. Even though mote sensors can cover larger fields and extract more substantial information about the scene than other sensors such as visual, and radar monitoring,

it is important to carefully evaluate the different modes of operation of these systems, in order to devise energy–aware resource management policies. The ultimate goal is to deliver adequate application–level performance (e.g., maximizes the probability of detecting events), yet maximally prolonging the system's operational lifetime.

Other research is done on smart and intelligent parking. Smart Parking is an intelligent parking service application as well as a novel security/privacy aware infrastructure. First, vehicles on the road can view and reserve a parking spot. The parking process can be an efficient and non-stop service. Second, privacy of the drivers is considered and protected by using the NOTICE infrastructure as called in *Abuelela, M. et al (2008)*. Finally, security of the information is protected by using the belt infrastructure and encryption/decryption approach. Simulation results proved that NOTICE results in high parking space utilization and fast parking spot finding time.

Restaurant Information and Assistant

Drivers would like to have some information about restaurants- also the prices and the availability or other services- over the highway or around the city. Other service such as food drive through payment would increase the service time on drive–thru restaurants. Also, the vehicle can be charged automatically through a smart system that allows the driver to pay the bill later online.

Road General Services: Road Toll Payment

A system for toll payment by electronic cash identifies an electronic purse and effects value transfer over a communication system without stopping the mobile (vehicle or person). *Cavoukian, A. (1998)* mention that Canada (Highway 407, Ontario), UK (Dartford Crossing, Mersey Tunnels and Severn Crossing) and Australia (Melbourne) have already implemented this system on one or more of its highways. Several large scale projects have either been developed or are under way in the United States, United Kingdom, Portugal, Italy, Finland, Sweden, Norway and Singapore. Ontario's 407 ETR represents a first globally — to date; it is the only highway of its kind that provides its customers with a way to travel their toll road without compromising their privacy.

The 407 ETR is a multi-lane toll highway, running 69 kilometers across the top of the Greater Toronto Area. What places it apart from other toll highways is its use of high-tech toll technology. It is the world's first completely electronic toll highway — a state-of-the-art transportation route that will move people and goods efficiently without any toll booths or plazas. *Cavoukian, A. (1998)* explain that Tolls are calculated based on time of day, day of the week, distance travelled,

and class/weight of vehicle, all collected using electronic technology.

ENTERTAINMENT APPLICATIONS

Entertainment Applications are another type of commercial applications where the focus is on both the passenger and the driver. Drivers wish to have some applications that allow them to download music while driving. Passengers would like more entertainment especially on long highway. Children wishes to have some games. This requires some peer-to-peer communications. The CarTel project as described by *Bychkovsky, V. et al (2006)* has explored stealing connections from open WiFi stations in Boston and Seattle.

Below we give a list of most famous applications that goes under the category of Commercial Applications (Entertainment Applications):

1. Download Multimedia (Movies and Music),
2. Playing games.
3. Chatting.
4. Shopping online.

CASE STUDY "MONITORING HIGHWAY TRAFFIC USING SENSORS"

In our case study, we discuss the idea of monitoring the highway to calculate the average speed and density in different periods of the day and week. This information would be very helpful for projects like MDSS. Maintenance Decision support System (MDSS) is a project that takes road weather data and information and merges them into a computerized winter road maintenance program that can help to guide maintenance manager in making better road treatment decisions. Also, it helps in taking critical decisions such as where to add a new lane, where and when to build new traffic signals.

Figure 7. Node on the highway to monitor vehicles

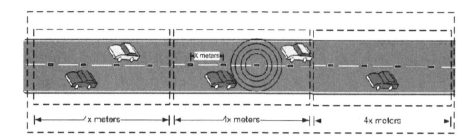

Monitoring the road means identifying the average speed, density with time and detecting an incident. Lots of work has been done in this area. *Abuelela, M. et al (2008)* proposed to build sensor belts in the road every specific interval while avoiding the heavy cost of optical fiber that has been used in Inductive loop detectors. They dig a belt on the road every couple of miles which will cost lots of money for maintaining the system. Also, they depend on vehicles to forward their message which cannot be done with sparse highway. Also, they cannot solve the problem of blocking incidents. On the other hand, *Wimmer, W. et al (2009)* are building a mapping system for the road constructions using sensors that is built above the road in a signal light or infrastructure beside the road. We describe detailed information about our system modes of operation, synchronization of nodes, scalability and applications

Cat's eyes – which are built in the road as reflectors that can help drivers to see the road in the fog condition or at night - can be used in the VANET technology. Our case study adds sensing capabilities to each node of Cat's eye in order to create an Ad-hoc Network that won't suffer from any network disconnection problem. As traffic incidents are considered one of the major factors leading to traffic jams; there is a crucial need to develop a system that helps reduces those road incidents. The proposed system will notify the drivers as early as possible of any risk or danger ahead. That gives the ability and the sufficient

data to make balanced and intelligent decision about these risks. Lots of architectures require an unrealistically expensive deployment and maintenance cost or cannot be converted to Highway. Therefore, our case study proposes a system for monitoring the highway and in the same time incident notifications.

Their goals are to monitor the road and to notify drivers if any accident occurs or bad weather conditions. The idea depends on the nodes placed on the road that allows forwarding data between clusters (a cluster is number of nodes) and by allowing cluster-to-cluster communication to forward our data where cluster is four nodes. They have three modes of operations. Mode of operation can be identifying from the mode bit. Normal mode (Mode bit =0): which can operate in normal situation of highways. Emergency mode (Mode bit= -1): Which the mode of evacuation or earth quakes. Night mode or closed mode. (Mode bit is +1): Which is the mode when the road is closed for ice conditions or road maintenance. Also, it is used at night in order to save power. Modes of operations are decided using the leader's analyzer.

In order to calculate the average speed in a sub cluster area, information is transferred between clusters to reach leaders. Leaders collect Vectors of data each contains time, syn, sensor number, and recorded values from different sensors. Assume a vehicle approaches sensor S1, values of sound, vibration and metal detection are recorded at time t1, these values are compared with values from the same cluster (same Syn number), to calculate speed. When the values are close and the difference doesn't exceed a threshold, speed can easily be calculated using the difference between time and distance between the two sensors.

CONCLUSION

Our chapter provided a complete discussion of application in Vehicular Networks. Our vision informs us that the Low Priority Safety Applications are more likely to be implemented more than the high Priority Safety Applications because of the high risk of the later one.

Also, it is more likely that new types of games will be developed in the coming years to fulfill the Entertainment Applications over the highways or in the cities for passengers beside or with the driver in the vehicle. The speed of these technologies gives us the guarantee that it will be implemented in the couple of years.

It requires lots of collaboration between vehicle manufacturing and the departments of transportation as it is not likely that every vehicle manufacture will build its own infrastructure.

REFERENCES

Abuelela, M., Olariu, S., & Weigle, M. C. (2008, May 11-14). NOTICE: An Architecture for the Notification of Traffic Incidents. In *Proceedings of the Vehicular Technology Conference, 2008.* (VTC Spring 2008). (pp. 3001-3005).

Blum, J. J., Eskandarian, A., & Hoffman, L. J. (2004). Challenges of intervehicle ad hoc networks. *IEEE Transactions on Intelligent Transportation Systems*, 5(4), 347–351. doi:10.1109/TITS.2004.838218

Bychkovsky, V., Hull, B., Miu, K., Balakrishnan, H., & Madden, S. (2006, September). *A Measurement Study of Vehicular Internet Access Using In Situ Wi-Fi Networks*. Presented at the 12th ACM MOBICOM Conf. Los Angeles.

Cavoukian, A. (1998, May). *Information and Privacy Commissioner Ontario 407 Express Toll Route: How You Can Travel the 407 Anonymously*. Ph.D. Commissioner.

Franz, W., Hartenstein, H., & Bochow, B. (2001, September). *Internet on the road via inter-vehicle communications*. Presented at the GI/OCG Annual Conference: Workshop on Mobile Communications over Wireless LAN: Research and Applications, Vienna, Austria.

Gongjun, Y., Olariu, S., Weigle, M., & Abuelela, M. (2008, October). SmartParking: A Secure and Intelligent Parking System Using NOTICE. In *Proceedings of the International IEEE Conference on Intelligent Transportation Systems* (pp. 569-574). Beijing, China.

Hecht, C., & Heinig, K. A. (2005). *Map based accident hot spot warning application Concept from the maps & adas vertical subproject of the 6FP integrated project PReVENT*. Germany: Institute of Transport, Road Engineering and Planning University of Hannover.

Jordan, R., Lucas, B., Randler, M., & Wilhelm, U. (2004, June 14-17). *Safety application specific requirements on the data processing of environmental sensors*. Presented at the 2004 IEEE Intelligent Vehicles Symposium University of Parma. Parma, Italy.

Kumar, R., Naveen, K., & Chilamkurti, B. S. (2007). *A Comparative Study of Different Sensors for Smart Car Park Management*. Presented at The 2007 International Conference on Intelligent Pervasive Computing (IPC 2007). Jeju Island, Korea

Rawashdeh, Z. Y., & Mahmud, S. M. (2008). Intersection Collision Avoidance System Architecture. In *Proceedings of the 5th IEEE Consumer Communications and Networking Conference 2008* (pp. 493-494).

Santa, J., & Gomez-Skarmeta, A. F. (2008). Architecture and evaluation of a unified V2V and V2I communication system based on cellular networks. *Computer Communications, 31*(12), 2850–2861. doi:10.1016/j.comcom.2007.12.008

Schagrin, M. (2008, January 16). *ITS Joint Program Office, Research and Innovative Technology Administration TRB 2008 Annual Meeting Session 415.*Palo Alto, CA: Dedicated Short Range Communications (DSRC) Home.

Ubeda, B., Toledo, R., Jordán, J., & Montes, S. (2004). A theoretical and practical analysis of GNSS based road pricing systems, considering the EGNOS/SISNeT contributions. Presented at NAVITEC 2004. Noordwijk, The Netherlands.

Wevers, K., & Blervaque, V. (2004, October). *MAPS&ADAS: Safety enhanced digital maps and standard interface to ADAS.* Presented at the 11th World Congress on ITS, (pp. 18-22), paper 2193. Nagoya, Japan.

Wimmer, W., & Flogel, D. (2009, March). Highly accurate mapping of road construction sites using laser scanner. In *Proceedings of the 6th International Workshop on Intelligent Transport* (pp. 33–38).

ADDITIONAL READING

Benson, J. P., O'Donovan, T., O'Sullivan, P., Roedig, U., & Sreenan, C. (2006). Car-park management using wireless sensor networks. In *Proceedings of 31st IEEE Conf. Local Computer Networks* (pp 588–595). Tampa, FL.

Bhawnani, P., Ruhe, G., Kudorfer, F., & Meyer, L. (2006). Problems in technology transfer from the industrial perspective. In *Proceedings of the 2006 international workshop on Software technology transfer in software engineering.*

Caliskan, M., Graupner, D., & Mauve, M. (2006). Decentralized discovery of free parking places. In *Proceedings of VANET '06: The 3rd international workshop on Vehicular ad hoc networks* (pp. 30–39). New York.

Funck, S., Mohler, N., & Oertel, W. (2004). Determining car-park occupancy from single images. In *Proceedings of International Symposium on Intelligent Vehicles* (IVS04) (pp. 325–328). Parma, Italy.

He, T., Krishnamurthy, S., Stankovic, J. A., Abdelzaher, T., Luo, L., Stoleru, R., et al. (2004). Energy-efficient surveillance system using wireless sensor networks. In *MobiSys '04: Proceedings of the 2nd international conference on Mobile systems, applications, and services* (pp. 270–283). New York.

Hubaux, J. P., Apkun, S. C., & Luo, J. (2004). The security and privacy of smart vehicles. *IEEE Security and Privacy, 2*(3), 49–55. doi:10.1109/MSP.2004.26

Karpiriski, M., Senart, A., & Cahill, V. (2006, March). *Sensor networks for smart roads.* Presented at the Fourth Annual IEEE International Conference on Pervasive Computing and Communications Workshops, 2006. (PerCom Workshops 2006) (pp. 5-310). Mannheim, Germany.

Mimbela, L. E. Y., & Klein, L. A. A. (2000, November). *Summary of vehicle detection and surveillance technologies used in intelligent transportation systems.* Washington, DC: U.S. Department of Transportation, FHWA

Musunuri, R., & Cobb, J. (2005, September). Hierarchical-battery aware routing in wireless sensor networks. In Vehicular Technology Conference, 2005. *VTC-2005-Fall. 2005 IEEE, 62*(4), 2311–2315.

NYCDCP. (2006, August-September). North America CBD Parking Rate Survey Highlights, New York City Department of City Planning. In *Proceedings of the North America CBD Parking Rate Survey Highlights*.

Olariu, S., & Weigle, M. C. (Eds.). (2009). *Vehicular Networks: From Theory to Practice*. Boca Raton, FL: CRC.

Panayappan, R., Trivedi, J. M., Studer, A., & Perrig, A. (2007). Vanet based approach for parking space availability. In *Proceedings of VANET '07: The fourth ACM international workshop on Vehicular ad hoc networks* (pp. 75–76). New York.

Takizawa, H., Yamada, K., & Ito, T. (2004). Vehicles detection using sensor fusion. In Proceedings of International Symposium on Intelligent Vehicles (IVS04) (pp. 238–243). Parma, Italy.

Tang, V., Zheng, Y., & Cao, J. (2006). An intelligent car park management system based on wireless sensor networks. *In Proceedings of the Int. Sym. Pervasive Computing and Applications* (pp. 65–70). UrumqiChina.

Van Greunen, J., & Rabaey, J. (2003). Lightweight time synchronization for sensor networks. In *Proceedings of WSNA '03: The 2nd ACM international conference on Wireless sensor networks and applications* (pp. 11–19). New York.

Weigle, M., & Olariu, S. (2007, April). Intelligent highway infrastructure for planned evacuations. In *Performance, Computing, and Communications Conference, 2007. IPCCC 2007. IEEE International*, (pp. 594–599).

Weigle, M., & Olariu, S. (2007, April). Intelligent highway infrastructure for planned evacuations. In *Proceedings of the First International Workshop on Research Challenges in Next Generation Networks for First Responders and Critical Infrastructures* (NetCri) (pp. 594–599). New Orleans, LA.

Wolff, J., Heuer, T., Gao, H., Weinmann, M., Voit, S., & Hartmann, U. (2006). Parking monitor system based on magnetic field sensors. In *Proceedings IEEE Conf. Intelligent Transportation Systems* (pp. 1275–1279). Toronto, CA.

WEB SITES

DSRC Website. http://www.leearmstrong.com/DSRC/DSRCHomeset.htm

Ford Website. http://www.ford.com/doc/sr07-ford-sustainability.pdf

General Motors Website. www.GM.com

National Highway Traffic Safety Administration. (2008). Traffic Safety Facts 2006. Report no. [Washington, DC: National Highway Traffic Safety Administration.]. *DOT HS, 810*, 818. Available online at: http://www-nrd.nhtsa.dot.gov/Pubs/TSF2006FE.PDF

Subramanian, R. 2007. Traffic Safety Facts Research Note: Motor vehicle traffic crashes as a leading cause of death in the United States, 2004. Report no. DOT HS 810 742. Washington, DC: National Highway Traffic Safety Administration. Available online at: http://www-nrd.nhtsa.dot.gov/Pubs/810742.PDF.

Volvo Website. http://www.volvocars.com/us/Pages/default.aspx

Weather and Highways: Highlights of a Policy Forum: American Meteorological Society, April 2004

World Premiere of Continental Sensor System in the New Volvo XC60 - Auto News from March 31, 2008 http://www.automotive.com/auto-news/02/35264/index.html

KEY TERMS AND DEFINITIONS

Blind Spot: Area behind and in the side of the vehicle where the driver cannot see it from the mirrors, it increases in the case of trucks.

Cat's Eyes: Built in the road as reflectors that can help drivers to see the road in the fog condition or at night

Closing Velocity (CV) Sensor: Sensor to detect close vehicles while moving.

Smart Bubble: Surrounding the vehicle with different types of sensors to build a bubble of sensing around the vehicle.

Smart Intersection: Where sensors can help in detecting any coming vehicles.

Smart Mirrors: A mirror that can notify the driver with the existence of a vehicle in the Blind Spot.

Smart Parking: To allow the vehicle to help you in parking, starting from sensors to camera.

Vehicle-to-X' Communication: A communication between the vehicle and any other thing may be another vehicle, an infrastructure or even other equipments.

Chapter 5
Information Sharing in VANETs

Marco Fiore
INSA Lyon, INRIA, France

Claudio Casetti
Politecnico di Torino, Italy

Carla-Fabiana Chiasserini
Politecnico di Torino, Italy

ABSTRACT

This chapter looks at a vehicular ad hoc network (VANET) as a peer-to-peer network, where mobile users may request information contents as well as provide them to other nodes, and it addresses the major technical issues that emerge when dealing with information sharing in VANETs. After briefly reviewing some proposals appeared in the literature on application and network protocols for data exchange in VANETs, the chapter focuses on a possible application for data sharing between vehicular users, which exploits the pull-based approach. It then highlights the main challenges in such a scenario and introduces some mechanisms that can be applied to solve two major issues in content sharing: content query propagation and content caching. A comparison among the schemes presented for query propagation, as well as between the mechanisms introduced for data caching, is shown through simulation results derived using the network simulator ns2. Finally, future challenges and emerging research topics for content sharing and dissemination in VANETs are outlined.

INTRODUCTION

Vehicular networking has established itself, in the short span of the last few years, as one of the most promising fields of research within the larger context of metropolitan-scale wireless networking. Enabling vehicle-to-vehicle (V2V) and vehicle-to-infrastructure (V2I) communication, a pervasive

DOI: 10.4018/978-1-61520-913-2.ch005

deployment of vehicular networking technologies would have an unprecedented impact on mass road transportation. As a matter of fact, potential applications encompass several facets of every-day private and public transportation, including road safety (e.g., warning of out-of-sight collisions), traffic monitoring and planning (e.g., prevention of vehicular congestion), driving assistance (e.g., quick automatic reactions to drivers' errors), priority traffic assistance (e.g., notification of ambulance approaching), and travel time reduction (e.g., real-time re-routing based on traffic conditions, advertisement of free parking slots). In addition, one can think of applications not directly related to road transportation, but targeted at infotainment, such as news updates, weather forecast, notification of nearby points of cultural or popular interest, advertisement and rating of local shops, hotels, restaurants.

Many of the applications listed above require that a user aboard a moving vehicle is able to retrieve a specific content, typically of small size, from a large set of items. Infrastructure-centric solutions may result impractical or costly: the high density of users (i.e., vehicles) with potentially heavy content request rate would require a pervasive deployment of Road Side Units (RSUs) that poses both feasibility problems (seamless high-throughput connectivity over large areas is still far from becoming a reality) as well as political and economic issues (which institution or company is going to provide the service, whom and how much it is going to charge for it).

On the other hand, the dense presence of collaborative users makes the scenario ideal for the pure ad-hoc networking paradigm adopted by Vehicular Ad-hoc Networks (VANET). The information, generated by few sparse RSUs, could be carried around and exchanged by swarming vehicles, and thus disseminated over the desired areas without any need for an ubiquitous infrastructure. Users aboard cars could then request and retrieve desired contents from other mobile users, in a pure peer-to-peer (P2P) fashion with no monetary cost implied.

However, VANETs are distributed, self-organizing communication networks built over traveling vehicles, and are thus characterized by nodes with very high speed and constrained movement patterns. Such specific features result in short-lived links and extremely fast network connectivity dynamics, that make it hard to organize the stable overlays that are traditionally employed in wired P2P networking. This requires that protocols for information sharing in VANETs are re-thought from their foundations, and that novel solutions are devised for key aspects such as the query propagation through the network and the content caching at peer nodes.

In this chapter, the problem of information sharing in VANETs is addressed. Different approaches can be used for information sharing, such as pull-based, push-based or epidemic techniques (Hauspie, 2004; Hayashi, 2006). Here, a pull-based approach is adopted, according to which nodes require information by issuing query messages. More specifically,

- First, it is shown that a data-centric approach can work well in the dynamic vehicular environment, by evaluating a data-centric P2P protocol for data retrieval in VANETs;
- Building on the above approach, the chapter then tackles the problem of the query propagation from requesting peers toward content providing peers, evaluating a number of schemes aimed at reducing the broadcast storms induced in the network by a trivial flooding approach;
- Finally, the problem of content caching is addressed, considering solutions that have been proposed in the literature to avoid that peer nodes swamp their storage capacity with needless information, reaching at a time an effective distribution of the different information items within the network.

The considered schemes and approaches are discussed considering realistic car mobility in urban vehicular environments. The aim of this chapter is to show that VANETs can be efficiently exploited for information sharing among vehicular users, given that dedicated techniques are adopted for the protocol design.

BACKGROUND

The growing attention of the networking research community towards the topic of information sharing in vehicular environments has led to a flurry of works proposing different approaches to the problem of disseminating and retrieving informative contents among mobile users.

A seminal work in this field is that by Frenkiel (2000), where small, high-data-rate communication islands over highway systems (Infostations) are proposed as an alternative to cellular coverage. The performance of Infostations are further investigated by Huyen (2003).

The technical challenges of delivering multimedia and safety information to cars forming an ad hoc network are outlined by Ghandeharizadeh (2004), who considers an in-vehicle entertainment system, through which users can download audio and video traffic. The problem addressed there concerns the availability of the information and how to predict such availability.

A cooperative strategy for content delivery and sharing is proposed by Das (2004) and Nandan (2005). The protocol by Das and Nandan, named SPAWN, addresses several issues: peer discovery, content selection, and content discovery. Peer discovery uses a centralized method as well as a distributed approach. The distributed technique leverages the broadcast nature of the wireless medium that allows nodes to overhear information about the content availability at neighbors. Content selection is determined by a proximity-driven piece selection strategy, where proximity estimation is based on hop count, while content discovery is implemented by making peers communicate which information they own to all their neighbors. A cooperative approach to provide data services in MANETs is proposed by Bottazzi (2004), where a context-aware group communication middleware is used to select collaborating partners and schedule messages. Information sharing and replication in VANETs is instead addressed in a work by Zhang (2009) where highly popular contents are cached by users that previously requested them, so as to create replicas and reduce the content access delay.

Several of the frameworks listed above assume the presence of a routing layer that manages the mobile network logical connectivity. It is worthwhile mentioning that several on-demand routing protocols for MANETs have been proposed: they distribute queries to network nodes and establish paths for unicast traffic (e.g., Perkins, 1999; Johnson, 2001); routing schemes dedicated to vehicular environment have also been proposed (e.g., Naumov, 2007).

Solutions have been proposed to reduce the routing overhead of on-demand protocols. For instance, Location Aided Routing (Ko, 2000) and Query Localization (Castaneda, 1999) limit the query flood by decreasing the number of nodes receiving route queries. The mechanism by Ko restricts the flooding of the query using the Global Positioning System (GPS), while Castaneda proposes that route requests are forwarded only in those areas where old paths existed. A fully distributed, data-centric peer-to-peer (P2P) approach, called Infoshare, is proposed by Fiore (2007), and it is discussed in details in this chapter.

Several studies have been also presented on service discovery protocols for large-scale MANETs (e.g., Kozat, 2003), which are based on the deployment of a virtual backbone of directories within the network. Chakraborty (2002) proposes a service discovery protocol aiming at an efficient usage of the network bandwidth. More specifically, the protocol involves the transmission of service advertisements by each node that hosts a service or knows that some of its neighbors is hosting it; also, nodes cache the received advertisements for a given time interval. Based on the cached advertisements, a node can know at which hop distance a service may be found, or the nodes to which the service request can be selectively sent. Techniques to improve the propagation of requests in mobile networks have been proposed by Naumov (2006) and Fiore (2009). The scheme by Naumov, named

Preferred Group Broadcasting (PGB), identifies the query forwarders depending on their estimated position with respect to the source of the request: only neighbors whose coverage areas do not overlap are selected as relayers, avoiding useless broadcasts that would not inform new nodes. Fiore introduces Eureka, which exploits local knowledge of the information density around nodes to drive queries towards areas of the network where the content is likely to be found.

Efficient caching in cooperative fashion and cache placement in wireless networks have been explored, among others, by Lu (2004), Yin (2006), Tang (2008), Hara (2001), Cao (2004) and Chow (2007). In particular, the work by Lu proposes a cooperative caching scheme that however requires the nodes to periodically broadcast their identity as well as their cache contents. Yin presents distributed caching strategies for ad hoc networks, according to which nodes may cache highly popular contents that pass by, or record the data path and use it to redirect future requests. The work by Tang presents both a centralized and a distributed solution to the cache placement problem of minimizing data access cost when network nodes have limited storage capacity. The distributed scheme, however, makes use of cache tables which, in mobile networks, need to be maintained in a similar vein as routing tables. Some approaches to eliminate information replicas among neighboring nodes are introduced by Hara: such schemes, however, require knowledge of the information access frequency and periodic transmission of control messages that allow nodes to coordinate their caching decisions. Cao observes that to improve data accessibility, mobile nodes should cache different data items than their neighbors. In particular, the solution presented by Cao aims at caching copies of the same content farther than a given number of hops, which again may be unsuitable for highly dynamic network topologies. The concept of caching different contents within a neighborhood is also exploited in the work by Chow (2007), where nodes with

similar interests and mobility patterns are grouped together to improve the cache hit rate. However, it is worth to point out that, there, caching management is based on instantaneous feedbacks from the neighboring nodes and does not involve any estimation of the content presence in the nodes' neighborhood. A solution that exploits the estimation of the information density (i.e., presence) in the network area to efficiently manage caches in VANETs is presented in (Fiore, 2009) and will be described in this chapter.

INFORMATION SHARING IN VANETs

Providing information to vehicular passengers is one of the most promising directions of the mobile infotainment business: infotainment devices are being deployed on new cars, and an on-board and roadside network infrastructure is expected to follow along. Unfortunately, information delivery to moving vehicles is also a most challenging task.

Beside transmission-related hurdles, several fundamental architectural and protocol issues are still being debated, among these:

- Which application should be implemented in vehicular communication nodes to enable content sharing in a peer-to-peer fashion between users;
- Which strategy should be adopted to retrieve a content in the network, in an efficient and low-overhead manner,
- What caching strategy is most appropriate in an environment where a cache-all-you-see approach is unfeasible but where the availability of popular information from nearby nodes is the key to success.

The rest of the chapter investigates how these issues can be solved in VANETs that operate either in a highway or an urban environment. For the sake of concreteness, consider a VANET where each vehicle is equipped with a radio interface and a data cache. Users on a vehicle wish to access information made available by fixed gateway nodes, located on the roadside, that are connected to the Internet and are broadcasting along the road. Furthermore, assume that N distinct pieces of information are available and may be requested by the users. Connectivity between vehicles and gateway nodes is, however, spotty and cooperation among vehicles is highly desirable. Finally, IEEE 802.11 is selected the wireless communication technology, since several experiments (Ebner, 2003; Singh, 2004; Singh, 2005; Bergamo, 2003) have shown that it is suitable for both inter-vehicular and infrastructure-to-vehicle communications.

In such a scenario, among all possible pull-based techniques for information sharing, the chapter focuses on the Infoshare application, which is described below.

Infoshare: A Data-Centric P2P Approach to Information Sharing in VANETs

The information sharing paradigm presented in this chapter has the following notable characteristics:

- It is data-centric, in that the informative content is at the center of the system. As an example, queries do not target specific nodes or topological areas in the network, but the actual data. Indeed, node- or network-centric approaches have to maintain state information on where the information is available, an extremely hard task in highly dynamic environments such as vehicular networks. However, a data-centric approach is more adaptive, and can also be load-efficient if smart techniques are employed for query propagation and content caching.

- It is based on a P2P-like cooperation among nodes, in order to avoid that the

whole information sharing process grinds on a limited amount of sparse RSUs. This allows to shorten the paths to the available contents and greatly reduce the network load, a crucial aspect in any resource-limited wireless network.

The next section details a possible implementation of a data-centric P2P system for vehicular ad-hoc networks.

Information Sharing Application

Infoshare is a lightweight application intended for a context in which multiple different small pieces of information with fast time dynamics are shared by vehicles moving along the road.

The general behavior of the Infoshare application is the following: a set of N different pieces of information is available for sharing, each type of information being identified by a unique id. A vehicle queries other vehicles for information pieces it does not have, with rate λ_i for information item i. Note that λ_i also represents the popularity level of a content. Queries are broadcast by the source vehicle and relayed by receiving nodes, so that the request is propagated in a multihop fashion until a vehicle carrying the desired data is reached. A flow chart detailing these operations is depicted in Figure 1. Once found, the information is returned to the query source through an application-driven, unicast path. Upon reception of the message containing the requested data, the query source vehicle caches the information for a certain time, after which the data is dropped and may be requested again [1].

The operations that follow the reception of an information message at a vehicle (either a source or a relay node) are illustrated in Figure 2. In the following paragraphs a detailed description of the Infoshare application functioning is provided.

Figure 1. Flow chart of operations following the reception of a query

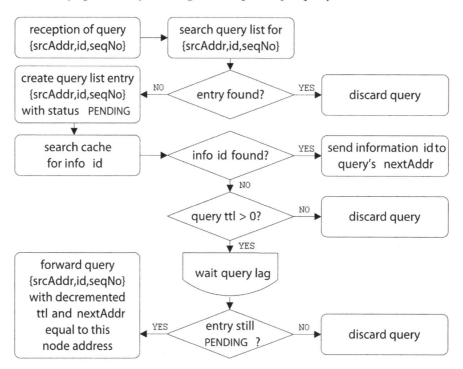

Figure 2. Flow chart of operations following the reception of an information message

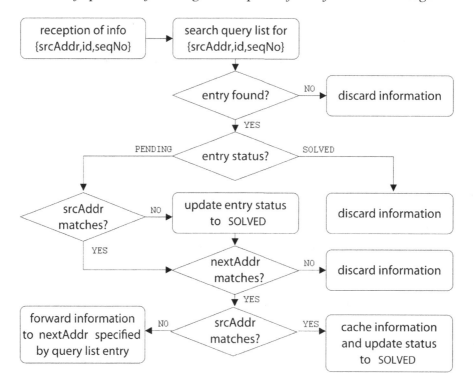

Query Message Format

A *query* message carries the following information:

- **Source Address** (*srcAddr*): the application-level address of the node that generated the query;
- **Information ID** (*id*): the identifier of the requested piece of information;
- **Sequence Number** (*seqNo*): the overall number of requests performed by this source. This value is incremented at the generation of a new query by the source vehicle;
- **Next Hop Address** (*nextAddr*): the address of the node that physically transmitted the query message. When the query is generated, this field matches the source address. On the other hand, since a multihop mechanism is employed by the application to spread the query, this address becomes different from the source one as the message is forwarded by intermediate nodes acting as relays;
- **Time To Live** (*TTL*): the remaining number of hops allowed for the current message. This field is decremented at each query forward by relaying vehicles.

Note that the {*srcAddr, id, seqNo*} triplet identifies the query in a unique way within the whole ad hoc network. Thus, it is possible for relay nodes to correctly forward new requests and discard those which are duplicate (i.e., already relayed) or out-of-date (i.e., queries for a piece of information for which a query from the same source and with a higher sequence number was already received and relayed). Also, the name of the *nextAddr* field may sound misleading, since it actually refers to the previous node in the forward path; however, it plays a crucial role in tracing the steps back to the query source, as discussed later, hence the "next hop" tag.

Query Transmission

The *query transmission* is performed by employing broadcast transmissions, and exploits a query list structure at each node to manage the relaying process.

The *query list* keeps track of the received queries, each list element containing the following fields:

- **Source Address:** the application-level address of the node that generated the query, obtained from the *srcAddr* field of the received query;
- **Information ID:** the identifier of the requested piece of information, obtained from the *id* field of the received query;
- **Sequence Number:** the overall number of requests performed by this source, obtained from the *seqNo* field of the received query;
- **Next Hop Address:** the address of the node that physically transmitted the query message. This is the address of the node from which the query was received, and is obtained from the *nextAddr* field of the received query;
- **Status:** the status of the request, either PENDING, i.e., waiting to be solved, or SOLVED, that is, already fulfilled. When a vehicle requests one piece of information, it broadcasts the new query message, but also adds an entry to its own query list. The status of the query added to the list is obviously set to PENDING. Note that, to avoid an uncontrolled growth of the list dimension, entries can be deleted after an expiration threshold, for which a suitable value can be 20 s.

As illustrated in Figure 1, each node receiving the query message first searches its query list for the same query. If the request is already present in the list, the message is discarded; otherwise, a new query list entry is created and the status of such a query list element is set to PENDING. Next, the node checks whether it owns the piece of information the source node is requesting. If the application does not have the requested information in its cache, and the *TTL* field in the query message is greater than zero, it acts as relay. However, before retransmitting the query, the node waits for a *query lag* interval of time, at the end of which it checks the query status: the query is only forwarded if the status is still PENDING. Such a procedure is then repeated at each hop, until a vehicle storing the requested information is found, or the *TTL* reaches zero. The introduction of the delay and of the *TTL* when relaying query messages limits query flooding; still, additional mechanisms must be implemented at the different layers of the protocol stack to reduce the overhead due to query traffic. A complete solution addressing this issue is described later in this chapter.

Some important remarks follow.

1. The next hop address fields stored at each forwarding application build up a multihop unicast "return path" to the source of the query.

2. The presence of a query list at each application and the control on the query sequence number prevent useless duplication of queries.

3. In spite of the *query lag* mechanism, query duplicates may still be generated in the network since all nodes receiving the query and not owning the requested information act as relays. Such redundancy has a twofold motivation. First, query spreading only relies on broadcast messages, which are by their nature unreliable[2]: the duplication of queries can be exploited to balance the unreliability of broadcast transmission. Secondly, the application should be kept as simple as possible, while limiting the number of forwarding nodes would imply a relay selection which

is usually based on the use of localization systems (e.g., GPS) complex computations.

Information Retrieval and Transmission

When the query is received by a node owning the desired piece of information, the application at such node immediately sends a unicast message containing the information to the vehicle it received the request from, which is then charged with the task of forwarding it towards the query source.

Typically, in mobile ad hoc networks unicast transmissions rely on a routing protocol. Infoshare instead does not require multihop capability at the network layer: the aforementioned "return path" is used at the application layer to transmit the information back to the vehicle that generated the request.

More specifically, the application header attached to the information payload replicates the structure of the query message, containing the {*srcAddr, id, seqNo*} triplet which enables the identification of the query the message replies to. Thus, a node receiving an information message can look up its query list for the corresponding query, update the status of such an entry to SOLVED, and retrieve the *nextAddr*, i.e., the address of the next hop in the application layer "return path". In other words, the application can indicate the next hop node to be used to feed the information back to the requesting vehicle, so that transmissions at the network layer are always single-hop ones. This mechanism is then iterated, as the next hop vehicle that receives the information message sets the status of the corresponding entry in the query list to SOLVED, and forwards in its turn the information to its next hop, until the source of the query is reached.

Note that, firstly, unicast reply messages via the return path ensure a reliable transmission of the information back to the source of the query, thanks to retransmissions at the MAC layer. Secondly, this application-driven routing feature of Infoshare can be leveraged jointly with the broadcast nature of wireless communications to improve the system performance. As a matter of fact, replies containing the information are unicast, which improves their reliability, but they can be sensed by other nodes within range, due to the nature of the wireless medium. Exploiting the *promiscuous* mode, which is implemented in 802.11 wireless LAN cards (Ethereal, 2009), also applications located at vehicles other than the intended destination can receive the information without penalty in terms of traffic load on the channel.

The drawbacks and advantages that can be identified in this solution are as follows.

Drawbacks:

- A slightly increased message size with respect to performing multihop routing at the network layer, since the additional *nextAddr* field in the application header is needed to identify the intended recipient of the information, and
- Additional processing effort by all applications located at nodes within transmission range, which are not the actual recipients of the message and must therefore discard it.

Advantages:

- There is no need for routing at the network layer, which could be very expensive in terms of both computational resources and channel overhead in the presence of dense, highly dynamic ad hoc networks, like VANETs;
- It is possible to exploit the fact that nodes not in the "return path" can receive the information message as well, to further reduce the number of useless transmissions. By listening to the channel, such nodes can learn that the data requested by a particular

query is on its way back to the query source and set to SOLVED the status of that query entry in their list. Thus, at nodes waiting to forward the query, when the query lag expires, the entry in the query list is found not to be PENDING anymore and the query is not rebroadcast. In practice, the query is not propagated any further than the first node having the requested information in cache, in each direction.

Information Caching

When the node that originated the query receives the information message, it updates the relative query list entry to a SOLVED status, and caches the data. After some time, the information is discarded and can be requested again with a new query. If the nodes cache is not large enough to store all the N pieces of information, a suitable drop time must be determined or proper content replacement policies must be designed to make room for newly received information when the cache is full.

Content Query Propagation Schemes

The propagation of content query is a fundamental process in information sharing, as it directly determines the network load associated to the content retrieval operation. In the following, several approaches to query propagation are described: Mitigated flooding, Location Aided Query Propagation and Eureka, and a possible add-on to query propagation mechanisms, called Preferred Group Broadcasting (PGB).

Mitigated Flooding

This technique spatially limits the propagation range of a request by forcing a Time To Live (*TTL*) for the query messages. Also, it avoids the rebroadcasting of already solved requests by means of a *query lag time*. That is, nodes forwarding a query message wait for a possible reply by an information holder prior to relaying the request. If during such waiting time, called query lag time, the nodes observe information messages in reply to the query, they avoid forwarding requests for already obtained chunks.

Location Aided Query Propagation

Location Aided Query Propagation (LAQP) exploits the basic idea below Location Aided Routing (LAR) for the propagation of queries in a mobile ad hoc network. LAR, a routing scheme proposed by Ko (2000), employs the location information provided by GPS or another absolute positioning system to route data through the network. Similarly, LAQP uses location information to propagate queries toward the last location where the information was seen to be cached. Targeting areas of the network where the requested information is more likely to be cached is a more efficient approach than targeting specific destination nodes in the highly dynamic MANET environment. In any case, LAQP requires that nodes are equipped with a GPS receiver; clearly, it is subject to GPS coverage blackouts, whose impact is especially relevant in indoor scenarios or urban canyons. Note that, in the absence of information position knowledge, LAQP degenerates to a mitigated flooding.

Eureka

Eureka (Fiore, 2009) extends mitigated flooding, by targeting queries towards areas of the network where the information is likely to be found. To this end, Eureka lets users estimate an information density for each information item, in a fully distributed manner. Then, it allows queries to be forwarded towards information-denser areas only, so that only potentially successful requests are propagated.

Eureka hinges on the concept of information density, i.e., the amount of information cached by nodes in a specific area. It estimates the local spatial density of information chunks cached at neighboring nodes and uses such estimate to steer queries toward areas where they are more likely to find the requested content. More specifically, a node generating a query adds to the query header its own density estimate for the requested information. A node receiving a query compares the information density estimate it computed against the one stored in the query message and checks the popularity of the requested content (i.e., it compares the value of its density estimate against the average density estimate computed over all information items the node is aware of). The node then acts according to the following three cases:

- If the queried information is popular and the receiver estimate is higher than that carried by the query, then the receiver re-broadcasts the query. The query thus has a chance to travel toward information-dense areas.
- If the queried information is popular and the receiver estimate is lower than that carried by the query, then the receiver refrains from broadcasting the query. Therefore, queries are unlikely to probe areas where information is scarce.
- If the queried information is unpopular, it is likely that information density values are unreliable. In this case, the receiver propagates the query with some probability, which is independent of the information density. The rebroadcast probability is set to the minimum between 1 and the ratio of the target number of forwarders to the current number of the receiver's neighbors. This mechanism, however, proves to be useless when unpopular information is requested in a scarcely connected network.

Information presence estimation is obtained, for each item i, through a locally distributed process, composed of two phases:

Figure 3. Simulation scenario. Dots represent gateways

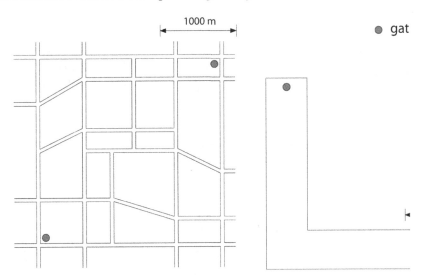

- A local phase, during which each node estimates the amount of content i cached in its surroundings. This is achieved by updating local counters every time the node replies to queries for item i, overhears information i messages passing by, or receives parts of information i it previously requested.
- A distributed phase, during which each node exchanges local estimates with its neighbors, and averages the received values with the locally computed one. This phase is performed with minimal overhead, by exploiting queries as carriers for local estimates, and leads to the final information density estimate.

Propagation Based on Preferred Group Broadcasting

Preferred Group Broadcasting (PGB) was introduced by Naumov (2006), as a solution to the broadcast storm problem in vehicular networks. PGB limits the network load through local, receiver-based decisions to rebroadcast a message. Intermediate nodes still wait for a lag time before rebroadcasting; however, its length depends on the value of the signal-to-noise ratio (SNR) associated

to the received message. By properly setting the SNR thresholds that discriminate among candidate forwarders, it is possible to select for rebroadcast only those nodes that experience good link quality, while providing fairly long distances between hops. In other words, the way PGB reduces the query propagation overhead involves a query lag time, whose duration is driven by distance-from-source estimation. Still, PGB limits the network load but does not specify how to find the desired information: indeed, PGB functionalities are orthogonal to those of the previous solutions, and can be integrated in the mitigated flooding, LAQP, and Eureka schemes.

Comparative Evaluation

The query propagation techniques presented above are compared in the vehicular environment in Figure 3. The figure represents a 6.25 km² road topology, where approx. 400 cars travel according to the Intelligent Driver Model with Intersection Management (IDM-IM), implemented in the VanetMobiSim simulator (Fiore, 2007). The IDM-IM takes into account car-to-car interactions, stop signs and traffic light presence, as well as drivers' activity patterns. Vehicles are assumed to

Figure 4. Query traffic generated by different propagation schemes

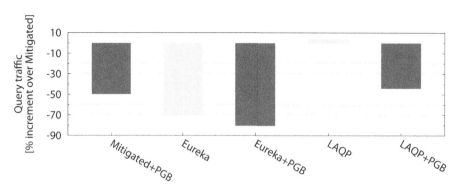

Figure 5. Queries solved by different propagation schemes

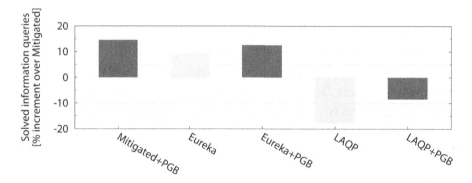

enter the scenario with an empty cache, and query other cars for information items. Also, in order to maintain contents availability in the scenario, two gateways, that are connected to the Internet and thus can provide the entire set of information, are deployed over the road topology. The data exchange is simulated using ns-2 (ns2, 2009).

The results, in Figure 4 and Figure 5, show the gain in performance brought by Eureka and LAQP, relatively to mitigated flooding, as well as the case where the PGB mechanism is used in combination with the various schemes. Comparing the basic schemes, i.e., without PGB, it can be observed that Eureka both reduces the query overhead (by 70 percent with respect to mitigated flooding) and increases the number of solved requests - an effect due to the high traffic load. On the contrary, LAQP does worse than the basic mitigated flooding as it cuts the number of

solved queries by 20 percent but keeps the query overhead to the same value.

The reason for this behavior is that, according to LAQP, a node seeking a content steers the query toward the location where it has last seen the information. Forwarding nodes have no active role in adjusting the target area but simply use the original location information inserted by the query generator to propagate the request. As it turns out, the original information on the content location may be outdated and uneven spatial distribution of contents dooms the LAQP strategy. In Eureka, instead, queries are steered toward the region where the information actually is, due to the active cooperation of all nodes that receive the query and propagate it based on their current estimation of the information density.

The introduction of PGB improves the performance of all schemes, as it reduces the query traffic, hence the congestion level, and increases the request solving rate. Specifically, in the case of Eureka, the use of PGB implies an improvement of 5 percent for both query traffic and number of solved queries; when compared directly against mitigated flooding, it can be obtained an increase of 15 percent in solved queries and over 80 percent of reduction in query traffic. However, notice that Eureka significantly outperforms all other schemes, even when they use PGB, as far as the query traffic is concerned. The reason is that PGB does help in reducing the number of query forwarders and, thus, the query overhead, but is unable to correctly choose a direction for query propagation.

With regard to the query solving time and the information traffic, it is worthwhile mentioning that Eureka significantly outperforms both flooding-based and GPS-aided schemes. Only when PGB is applied, do Eureka and mitigated flooding give similar results in terms of query solving time. However, such performance is achieved by Eureka with much less information traffic. Overall, the results obtained in the urban scenario show that, with respect to flooding-based schemes, a better outcome in terms of user satisfaction (i.e., high number of solved queries and lower query response time) is achieved through Eureka, despite the great reduction in the number of queries and, in turn, of reply messages. When compared against GPS-aided routing approaches, like LAQP, Eureka achieves comparable performance in scenarios where the information is evenly distributed over the network area, while it provides a significant gain in the case of inhomogeneous information density.

Content Caching Schemes

Consider a VANET where nodes implement the Infoshare application previously described. Also, assume that there are a number I of information items available to the users, each item divided into C chunks, small enough so that each chunk

fits an IP packet. Clearly, it can be assumed that vehicular nodes have sufficiently large caches to be able to store the desired contents without memory limitations. However, to avoid swamping their storage capacity with needless information picked up on the go, the network nodes have to efficiently manage their caches.

An efficient solution to this problem is provided by the Hamlet framework (Fiore, 2009), which allows vehicular users to take caching decisions on contents they have retrieved from the network.

Hamlet enables users to take caching decisions leveraging a node's local view of the information presence in its proximity. Indeed, by estimating the amount and kind of information items stored by users around it, a node can take caching decisions that favor a high content diversity in its surroundings, inherently easing the retrieval of data in the network.

The technique works on a per-item basis and its results apply to all chunks belonging to the same content. Also, it is fully distributed and does not introduce any signalling overhead, since it exploits the observation of query and information messages that are sent on the wireless channel as part of the operation of the content sharing application.

Note that, although the Infoshare application (and the information density estimation) requires the nodes to operate in promiscuous mode, only the node that issued the content query is entitled to cache a new copy of that content. A node that overhears an information message caches the content carried in the message only if this is an updated version of the chunks already owned by the node.

The main steps of the procedure are detailed below.

Let the reach range of a generic node n be the distance from node n to the farthest node that can receive a query generated by node n itself. The reach range obviously depends on the query *TTL* and is bounded by the product of *TTL* and the node radio range.

The generic node *n* uses the information captured within its reach range, during a generic estimation step *j* to compute the following quantities for each chunk *c* belonging to information item *i*.

- Provider counter: it accounts for the presence of new copies of information *i*'s chunk *c*, delivered by *n* to querying nodes within its reach range, during step *j*. Node *n* updates this quantity every time it acts as a provider node.

- Transit counter: it accounts for the presence of new copies of information *i*'s chunk *c*, transferred between two nodes within *n*'s reach range and received (or overheard) by *n*, during step *j*. Node *n* thus updates this quantity if it receives (or overhears) an information message and such message carries chunks belonging to the most recent content version it is aware of.

The provider and transit counters are updated through the hop count information that is included in the query and information message header.

Based on the above quantities, node *n* can compute a presence index of chunk *c* of information *i*, as observed during step *j* within node *n*'s reach range.

Let us refer to such value as $p_{ic}(n,j)$. The chunk presence estimate is then used to derive to an information presence. More specifically, node *n* composes the presence indices $p_{ic}(n,j)$ of all chunks of information *i* to an overall probability of information presence, on a per-information item basis. Finally, the information presence is used to determine a cache drop time after which the retrieved information items are removed from memory, with the goal of reducing the cache utilization without affecting the performance of the content distribution system.

The cache drop time for information *i* is derived in such a way that:

- In the extreme situation where the entire information i is estimated to be cached within node *n*'s reach range, i.e., $p_i(n,j)=1$, the caching time will be equal to a minimum caching time, typically set to zero. Clearly, if $p_i(n,j)=1$ and the minimum caching time is set to 0, the retrieved content is not stored by the node;

- On the contrary, when node *n* observes a complete lack of content *i* within its reach range, i.e., $p_i(n,j)=0$, the caching time will be equal to a maximum content caching time.

Comparative Evaluation

Here the performance of Hamlet is compared with the results obtained by using the well-known HybridCache scheme (Yin, 2006). According to HybridCache, a node, which requested a piece of information, always caches the received data. Instead, a node on the data path caches the information if its size is small, otherwise it caches the data path, provided that the content copy is not too far away. When the maximum cache size is exceeded, the less popular content is dropped.

Note that mitigated flooding is assumed to be used for query propagation under both schemes.

As a matter of fact, while deriving the results, it was observed that caching the data path leads to poor performance, due to node mobility; thus the HybridCache parameters are set so that (i) the size of the data never results in data path caching but always in information caching, and (ii) mitigated flooding is employed for query forwarding.

Consider a system in which nodes are provided with a large storage with respect to information size, but cooperative caching is required to use as few buffering resources as possible, since such storage room may be needed by other data, services and applications running at nodes.

Hamlet design allows it to cope with such a scenario without any calibration: nodes autono-

Figure 6. Solved queries ratio as functions of the node cache size. The performance of Hamlet and HybridCache are compared in an urban scenario for λ=0.003, 0.006

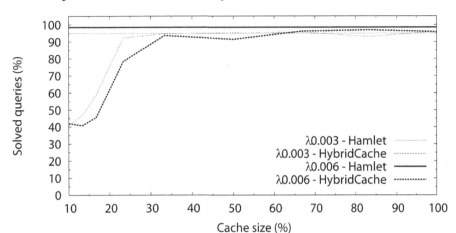

mously determine their storage needs, by estimating the right amount of buffering (if any) a given information item is worth spending at a certain time, from a cooperative caching perspective. Instead, the stricter storage policy in HybridCache requires a precise amount of caching that nodes must set aside for cooperative caching. Thus, simulations were performed limiting the cache size of HybridCache, and compared the resulting curves with reference values from a single simulation run with Hamlet, allowing it to self-adapt memory usage to its needs.

Simulations are run considering the same scenario as shown in Figure 3 and modeling vehicles movement is modeled with the Intelligent Driver Model with Intersection Management (IDM-IM) implemented in the VanetMobiSim simulator (Fiore, 2007).

Figure 6 and Figure 7 respectively present the solved queries ratio and the average cache occupancy as the cache size limit imposed to HybridCache varies, in an urban environment. Let both the cache occupancy and the cache size be expressed as a percentage of the amount of information items available to the users, and consider

results for two different values of information popularity level (namely, 0.003 and 0.006).

The plot in Figure 6 shows that, in the urban environment, a storage capacity as high as 35 percent of the available items is needed by HybridCache, if Hamlet performance in query solving is to be matched under any information popularity condition. Such cache size must therefore be set aside by all nodes performing cooperative caching since, as shown by the plot in Figure 7, HybridCache always uses up all the available storage room. Conversely, Hamlet never exceeds a 10 percent average cache usage, thus freeing more resources for other purposes. In addition, its performance is similar to that obtained by HybridCache even when nodes are allowed to store all the content. Clearly, Hamlet achieves a spatial distribution of information that does not require the residual caching room (representing 90 percent of the total).

FUTURE RESEARCH DIRECTIONS

The suitability of VANETs for applications that rely on P2P approaches for information exchange

Figure 7. Average cache occupancy as functions of the node cache size. The performance of Hamlet and HybridCache are compared in an urban scenario for λ=0.003, 0.006

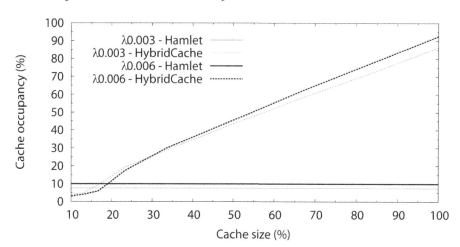

presents designers with several challenges. Indeed, not only do vehicular nodes require content delivery but they also act as content providers. Users are expected to offer data services in an effective manner, despite the scarcity of bandwidth and the intermittent connectivity due to the highly-dynamic nature of VANETs.

The sections below list some of the technical challenges in delivering information to vehicular users.

Bandwidth Constraints

The challenge of introducing P2P applications in vehicular networks is that P2P in the wired Internet rely on the IP routing infrastructure, which is resource rich especially in terms of bandwidth availability, VANETs are instead rather limited in bandwidth. Therefore, a high maintenance traffic, as it is used currently in structured overlay networks, will lead to scalability problems when legacy peer-to-peer services are used "as-is" in vehicular environments. One of the main issues is therefore how to efficiently provide the same kind of P2P services implemented in wired networks in VANETs.

Service Discovery

The propagation of query messages in the network is a critical aspect of the information sharing mechanism in a peer-to-peer system. There are two contrasting requirements that arise in VANETs. On the one hand, queries for information must be forwarded by relays until they reach nodes holding such information, and some redundancy in forwarding is necessary to compensate for the unreliable nature of broadcast transmission of queries (i.e., no acknowledgments). On the other hand, congestion deriving from excessive spreading of queries and reply duplication must be limited. The simplest solution for query propagation is, of course, plain flooding of requests, but this is hardly viable in tightly-meshed, bandwidth-hungry wireless networks where congestion is more than likely. Other, more refined approaches are needed.

Information Distribution and Survival

A final, critical issue pertains to achieving a desired distribution of the information within an area: regardless of how the information is distributed at the outset, the system should be able to identify where the information should be stored in the network area. In addition, a node storing the information acts as provider for that information; of course, this role may exact a high toll from nodal resources in terms of bandwidth or power consumption; it is advisable that the role of content provider be handed over to neighboring nodes quite frequently, without altering the information distribution. One or more nodes running out of power may affect the distribution of information and disrupt the peer-to-peer structure. Therefore, regardless of the initial information distribution, and of the density of nodes, information should never be allowed to die out. Related to the information survival is the evaluation of the minimum number of copies of a specific information that can satisfy users' needs (i.e., in terms of information retrieval time or response rate).

CONCLUSION

Recently, car manufacturers and the scientific community have put a significant effort in the development of an intelligent transportation system (ITS), with the aim to improve safety, efficiency, and easy of driving. Many technical challenges however have still to be solved. Beside reliable and high-speed inter-vehicle as well as vehicle-to-infrastructure communications, protocols and algorithms for the support of various applications and for data exchange are needed.

This chapter provided an overview of the main proposals that have appeared in the literature addressing the development of applications and network protocols for data exchange in vehicular networks. In particular, a solution was described for implementing data sharing in a vehicular network where each node can act either as a server or as a client, providing or requesting information contents in a peer-to-peer fashion. The chapter highlighted the main challenges in such a scenario and introduced techniques that can be applied to

solve some major issues, such as query propagation and content caching.

For query propagation, some efficient mechanisms were described, namely, Mitigated flooding, Location Aided Query Propagation, Eureka, and a scheme based on Preferred Group Broadcasting. These solutions specifically address the challenges posed by a vehicular environment, such as scarcity of bandwidth and a highly-dynamic network topology. They were compared by simulation; the results obtained in an urban scenario showed that, with respect to flooding-based schemes, a better outcome in terms of user satisfaction (i.e., high number of solved queries and lower query response time) is achieved through Eureka, despite the great reduction in the number of queries and, in turn, of reply messages. When compared against GPS-aided routing approaches, like LAQP, Eureka achieves comparable performance in scenarios where the information is evenly distributed over the network area, while it provides a significant gain in the case of inhomogeneous information density.

As for content caching, the chapter outlined Hamlet, one of the latest techniques presented in the literature, which is fully distributed and implies a low control overhead. The scheme allows each node, upon receiving a requested information, to determine the cache drop time of the information, depending on the perceived 'presence' of the content in the node's proximity. The comparison with a previously proposed solution, the so-called HybridCache, showed that Hamlet allows vehicular users to autonomously determine their storage needs, by estimating the right amount of buffering a given content is worth spending at a certain time. Instead, the stricter storage policy in HybridCache requires a precise amount of caching that nodes must set aside for cooperative caching.

In spite of the great deal of work that has been done on VANETs, several issues are still open. In particular, in the context of data sharing and dissemination, efficient and flexible solutions dealing with streaming traffic are still missing. Furthermore, schemes for content downloading involving an optimized interaction between roadside infrastructure and vehicles, as well as cooperation between vehicles, is an emerging, interesting subject of research.

REFERENCES

Bergamo, P., Cesana, M., Maniezzo, D., Pau, G., Yao, K., Whiteman, D., & Gerla, M. (2003). IEEE 802.11 Wireless network under aggressive mobility scenario. In *Proceedings of the International Telemetry Conference ITC/USA*, Las Vegas, NV.

Bottazzi, D., Corradi, A., & Montanari, R. (2004). Context-awareness for impromptu collaboration in MANETs. In *Proceedings of the IEEE International Symposium on Network Computing and Applications (NCA)*, (pp. 339–342). Cambridge, MA.

Cao, G., Yin, L., & Das, C. R. (2004). Cooperative cache-based data access in ad hoc networks. *IEEE Computer*, *37*(2), 32–39.

Castaneda, R., Das, S. R., & Marina, M. K. (1999). Query localization techniques for on-demand routing protocols in ad hoc networks. In *Proceedings of the ACM/IEEE International Conference on Mobile Computing and Networking (MobiCom)*, (pp. 186–194). Seattle, WA.

Chakraborty, D., & Joshi, A. (2002). GSD: A novel group-based service discovery protocol for MANETs. In *Proceedings of the IEEE Conference on Mobile and Wireless Communication Networks (MWCN)*. Stockholm, Sweden.

Chow, C.-Y., Leong, H. V., & Chan, A. T. S. (2007). GroCoca: Group-based peer-to-peer cooperative caching in mobile environment. *IEEE Journal on Selected Areas in Communications*, *25*(1), 179–191. doi:10.1109/JSAC.2007.070118

Das, S., Nandan, A., Pau, G., Sanadidi, M. Y., & Gerla, M. (2004). SPAWN: A swarming protocol for vehicular ad-hoc wireless networks. In *Proceedings of the First ACM Workshop on Vehicular Ad Hoc Networks (VANETs)*, (pp. 93–94). Philadelphia.

Ebner, A., Rohling, H., Wischhof, L., Halfmann, R., & Lott, M. (2003). Performance of UTRA TDD ad-hoc and IEEE 802.11b in vehicular environments. In *Proceedings of the IEEE 57th Vehicular Technology Conference Spring (VTC-Spring)*, (pp. 960–964). Jeju, South Korea.

Ethereal (n.d.). Ethereal WLAN cards. Retrieved May 29, 2009 from http://www.ethereal.com/

Fiore, M., Casetti, C., & Chiasserini, C. F. (2009). Information density estimation for content retrieval in MANETs. *IEEE Transactions on Mobile Computing*, *8*(3), 289–303. doi:10.1109/TMC.2008.110

Fiore, M., Casetti, C., Chiasserini, C.-F., & Garetto, M. (2007). Analysis and simulation of a content delivery application for vehicular wireless networks. *Elsevier Performance Evaluation*, *64*(5), 444–463. doi:10.1016/j.peva.2006.08.008

Fiore, M., Haerri, J., Filali, F., & Bonnet, C. (2007). Vehicular Mobility Simulation for VANETs. In *Proceedings of the IEEE Annual Simulation Symposium (ANSS)*, Norfolk, VA.

Fiore, M., Mininni, F., Casetti, C., & Chiasserini, C.-F. (in press). To cache or not to cache? In *Proceedings of IEEE International Conference on Computer Communications (INFOCOM)*.

Frenkiel, R. H., Badrinath, B. R., Borras, J., & Yates, R. D. (2000). The infostations challenge: Balancing cost and ubiquity in delivering wireless data. *IEEE Personal Communications Magazine*, *7*, 66–71. doi:10.1109/98.839333

Ghandeharizadeh, S., Kapadia, S., & Krishnamachari, B. (2004). PAVAN: A policy framework for content availability in vehicular ad-hoc networks. In *Proceedings of the First ACM Workshop on Vehicular Ad Hoc Networks (VANETs)*, (pp. 57–65). Philadelphia.

Ghandeharizadeh, S., & Krishnamachari, B. (2004). C2P2: Peer-to-peer network for on-demand automobile information services. In *Proceedings of the 15ᵗʰ International Workshop on Database and Expert Systems Applications (DEXA)*, (pp. 538–542). Zaragoza, Spain.

Hara, T. (2001). Effective replica allocation in ad hoc networks for improving data accessibility. In *Proceedings of the IEEE International Conference on Computer Communications (INFOCOM)*, Anchorage, AK.

Hauspie, M., Panier, A., & Simplot-Ryl, D. (2004). Localized probabilistic and dominating set based algorithm for efficient information dissemination in ad hoc networks. In *Proceedings of the IEEE International Conference on Mobile Ad-hoc and Sensor Systems* (MASS). Washington, DC.

Hayashi, H., Hara, T., & Nishio, S. (2006). On updated data dissemination exploiting an epidemic model in ad hoc networks. In *Proceedings of the 2nd International Workshop on Biologically Inspired Approaches to Advanced Information Technology* (BioADIT). Osaka, Japan.

Johnson, D. B., Maltz, D. A., & Broch, J. (2001). DSR: The dynamic source routing protocol for multi-hop wireless ad hoc networks. In Perkins, C. E. (Ed.), *Ad Hoc Networking* (pp. 139–172). Reading, MA: Addison-Wesley.

Ko, Y. B., & Vaidya, N. H. (2000). Location-aided routing (LAR) in mobile ad hoc networks. *Wireless Networks, 6*, 307–321. doi:10.1023/A:1019106118419

Kozat, U. C., & Tassiulas, L. (2003). Network layer support for service discovery in mobile ad hoc networks. In Proceedings of the *IEEE International Conference on Computer Communications (INFOCOM)*, (pp. 1965-1975). San Diego, CA

Lu, E. J. L., & Chen, C.-W. (2004). An enhanced EDCG replica allocation method in ad hoc networks. In *Proceedings of the 2004 IEEE International Conference on e-Technology, e-Commerce and e-Service.* (pp. 465 – 472). Washington, DC.

NS2. (n.d.). *The network simulator ns2.* Retrieved May 29, 2009 from http://www.isi.edu.nsam/ns/

Nandan, A., Das, S., Pau, G., Sanadidi, M. Y., & Gerla, M. (2005). Cooperative downloading in vehicular ad hoc networks. In *Proceedings of the IFIP Wireless On demand Networks, Systems and Services (WONS)*, (pp. 32–41). St. Moritz, Switzerland.

Naumov, V., Baumann, R., & Gross, T. (2006). An evaluation of inter-vehicle ad hoc networks based on realistic vehicular traces. In *Proceedings of the ACM International Symposium on Mobile Ad Hoc Networking and Computing (MobiHoc)*, Florence, Italy.

Naumov, V., & Gross, T. (2007). Connectivity-aware routing (CAR) in vehicular ad-hoc networks. In *Proceedings of the IEEE International Conference on Computer Communications (INFOCOM)*, (pp. 1919–1927). Anchorage, AK.

Perkins, C. E., & Royer, E. M. (1999). Ad hoc On-Demand Distance Vector Routing. In *Proceedings of the IEEE Workshop on Mobile Computing Systems and Applications*, (pp. 90-100). New Orleans, LA.

Singh, J. P., Bambos, N., Srinivasan, B., & Clawin, D. (2002). Wireless LAN performance under varied stress conditions in vehicular traffic scenarios. In *Proceedings of the IEEE 56th Vehicular Technology Conference Fall (VTC-Fall)*, (pp. 743–747). Vancouver, Canada.

Singh, J. P., Bambos, N., Srinivasan, B., Clawin, D., & Yan, Y. (2005). Empirical observations on wireless LAN performance in vehicular traffic scenarios and link connectivity based enhancements for multihop routing. In *Proceedings of the IEEE Wireless Communications and Networking Conference (WCNC)*, (pp. 1676–1682). New Orleans, LA.

Tang, B., Gupta, H., & Das, S. (2008). Benefit-based data caching in ad hoc networks. *Transactions on Mobile Computing*, *7*(3), 289–304. doi:10.1109/TMC.2007.70770

Yin, L., & Cao, G. (2006). Supporting cooperative caching in ad hoc networks. *IEEE Transactions on Mobile Computing*, *5*(1), 77–89. doi:10.1109/TMC.2006.15

Yuen, W. H., Yates, R. D., & Mau, S. C. (2003). Exploiting data diversity and multiuser diversity in non cooperative mobile infostation networks. In *Proceedings of the IEEE International Conference on Computer Communications (INFOCOM)*, (pp. 2218–2228). San Francisco.

Yuen, W. H., Yates, R. D., & Sung, C. W. (2003). Effect of node mobility on highway mobile infostation networks. In Proceedings of the *ACM/IEEE International Conference on Modeling, Analysis and Simulation of Wireless and Mobile Systems (MSWIM)*, (pp. 82–91). San Diego, CA.

Zhang, Y., Zhao, J., & Cao, G. (2009). Roadcast: a popularity aware content sharing scheme in VANETs. In *Proceedings of the IEEE International Conference on Distributed Computing Systems* (ICDCS). Montreal, Canada.

ADDITIONAL READING

Derhab, A., & Badache, N. (2009). Data replication protocols for mobile ad-hoc networks: A survey and taxonomy. *IEEE Communications Surveys & Tutorials*, *11*(2), 33–51. doi:10.1109/SURV.2009.090204

Fiore, M., Casetti, C., & Chiasserini, C. F. (2005). On-demand content delivery in vehicular wireless networks. *ACM/IEEE International Conference on Modeling, Analysis and Simulation of Wireless and Mobile Systems (MSWIM)* (pp. 87-94). Montreal, CA.

Luo, J., & Hubaux, J.-P. (2006). A survey of research in inter-vehicle communications. In Lemke, K., Paar, C., & Wolf, M. (Eds.), *Embedded Security in Cars* (*Vol. II*, pp. 111–122). Berlin Heidelberg, Germany: Springer-Verlag. doi:10.1007/3-540-28428-1_7

Tang, B., Gupta, H., & Das, S. (2008). Benefit-based data caching in ad hoc networks. *IEEE Transactions on Mobile Computing*, *7*(3), 289–304. doi:10.1109/TMC.2007.70770

Uzcátegui, R. A., & Acosta-Marum, G. (2009). WAVE: A tutorial. *IEEE Communications Magazine*, *47*(5), 126–133. doi:10.1109/MCOM.2009.4939288

Willke, T. L., Tientrakool, P., & Maxemchuk, N. F. (2009). A Survey of Inter-Vehicle Communication Protocols and Their Applications. *IEEE Communications Surveys & Tutorials*, *11*(2), 3–20. doi:10.1109/SURV.2009.090202

KEY TERMS AND DEFINITIONS

Ad Hoc Networks: Communication networks where nodes can communicate directly to each other, without the use of infrastructure

Content Caching: Storage in the communication nodes memory of information.

Content Dissemination: Delivery of information to users that required it

Information Sharing: Information exchange among network nodes communicating in ad hoc mode

Mobile Networks: Communication networks whose nodes are mobile and communicate via wireless

Query Propagation: Diffusion of queries for content retrieval

Vehicular Networks: communication networks where nodes are vehicles

ENDNOTE

1   Note that, according to the IEEE 802.11 MAC layer specifications, broadcast messages are not acknowledged by the receivers, and they are never retransmitted by the sender.

Section 3
Communication Protocols in VANETs

Chapter 6
Medium Access Protocols for Cooperative Collision Avoidance in Vehicular Ad–Hoc Networks

Md. Imrul Hassan
Swinburne University of Technology, Australia

Hai L. Vu
Swinburne University of Technology, Australia

Taka Sakurai
University of Melbourne, Australia

ABSTRACT

It is envisaged that supporting vehicle-to-vehicle and vehicle-to-infrastructure communications with a Vehicular Ad-Hoc Network (VANET) can improve road safety and increase transportation efficiency. Among the candidate applications of VANETs, cooperative collision avoidance (CCA) has attracted considerable interest as it can significantly improve road safety. Due to the ad hoc nature of these highly dynamic networks, no central coordination or handshaking protocol can be assumed and safety applications must broadcast information of interest to many surrounding cars by sharing a single channel in a distributed manner. This gives rise to one of the key challenges in vehicle-to-vehicle communication systems, namely, the development of an efficient and reliable medium access control (MAC) protocol for CCA. In this chapter, we provide an overview of proposed MAC protocols for VANETs and describe current standardization activities. We then focus on the performance of the IEEE 802.11 carrier sense multiple access (CSMA) based MAC protocol that is being standardized by the IEEE standards body for VANET applications. In particular, we review prominent existing analytical models and study their advantages, disadvantages and their suitability for performance evaluation of the MAC protocol for VANETs. After a discussion of the shortcomings of these models, we develop a new analytical model in the second half of the chapter. Explicit expressions are derived for the mean and standard deviation of the packet delay, as well as for the packet delivery ratio (PDR) at the MAC layer in an unsaturated network formed by moving vehicles on a highway. We validate the analytical results using extensive

DOI: 10.4018/978-1-61520-913-2.ch006

simulations and show that good accuracy can be achieved with the proposed model for a range of topologies and traffic load conditions. More importantly, using the model, we show that hidden terminals can have a severe, detrimental impact on the PDR, which may compromise the reliability required for safety applications.

INTRODUCTION

A Vehicular Ad-Hoc Network (VANET) supports vehicle-to-vehicle and vehicle-to-infrastructure communications and covers a wide range of applications based on smart information use to improve road safety and to increase transportation efficiency. Among the candidate applications, cooperative collision avoidance (CCA) has attracted considerable interest in the research community as it can significantly improve road safety. In CCA, moving cars form a network to wirelessly communicate and warn each other of changing conditions or dangers ahead on the road to avoid accidents.

While the aims of a VANET system are to both enhance road safety and to improve transportation efficiency, in this chapter, we only focus on the safety applications such as CCA. Road safety is supported by the transmission of routine status messages and event-driven emergency messages. Routine status messages are sent periodically to neighbouring vehicles to inform them of the current status of the originating vehicle (e.g. location speed, direction), whereby the receiving vehicles/drivers can then anticipate any potential hazards (e.g. traffic jam ahead) and take necessary action. Event-driven safety messages are triggered by rapid changes in vehicle behaviour such as a hard brake or an airbag explosion. To enable preventative action, it is essential that both types of safety messages are received correctly by surrounding vehicles in a timely fashion.

The likelihood of a rapidly changing VANET topology makes it difficult to rely on centrally coordinated communications. Therefore, decentralized broadcast is the natural choice of communication mode for safety messages in a VANET.

The broadcast could use multi-hop transmissions to enhance coverage, but recent studies suggest that a single-hop transmission is sufficient in most situations to reach all neighbouring vehicles in an accident's vicinity (Hartenstein & Laberteaux, 2008).

Ensuring reliable and timely packet delivery using decentralized broadcast is essential for CCA. For instance, according to (Biswas, Tatchikou, & Dion, 2006) the packet delay must be less than 400 ms in order to avoid chain collisions. Also, the VANET standard developed by the American Society for Testing and Materials (ASTM) (ASTM, 2003), requires that the communication devices should be capable of transferring safety messages with more than 90% reliability. One of the main difficulties to achieve those requirements is the loss of packets due to the presence of hidden terminals (Chen, Refai, & Ma, 2007). This occurs when a node is transmitting to a target node while a third node that is unaware of the transmitting node also starts its transmission and causes interference at the receiver. The hidden terminal problem can afflict all decentralized wireless networks, but is particularly severe in broadcast scenarios. In the broadcast case, there are multiple receivers for each message, scattered in the transmission range of the sender. Any node that is within sensing range of any receiver but outside the transmission range of the sender is a potential hidden terminal. Therefore, the potential hidden terminal region is significantly larger than that for unicast communication.

The distinctive demands of VANET applications, as well as the unique operating environment involving fast moving vehicles, mean that specifically tailored communication protocols are required for VANET systems. Particularly, the medium access control (MAC) protocol has an important role to play in ensuring timely packet delivery in CCA. Due to differences in performance requirements compared to other wireless networks, traditional MAC protocols must be carefully scrutinized before applying them in the VANET environment. In this book chapter, our objectives are two-fold: overview different MAC protocols and discuss their suitability for VANET safety applications, such as CCA; and provide performance evaluation for a class of contention-based MAC protocols in those applications.

The rest of the book chapter is organized as follows. In Section II, we provide an overview of proposed MAC protocols for VANET, and also present current VANET standardization activities. In Section III, we examine the existing models for performance analysis and present a new model with results and validations. Next in Section IV, we put forward a list of future research opportunities. Finally, in Section V, we summarize the chapter.

BACKGROUND

Overview of MAC Protocols

A medium access control (MAC) protocol enables multiple users to share a common physical medium and has a great impact on the feasibility and performance of safety applications being introduced in VANETs. Some MAC protocols have been evaluated in (Chen, Refai, & Ma, 2008; Menouar, Filali, & Lenardi, 2006) for their suitability in the VANET environment. The general conclusion is that an environment with fast moving vehicles and frequent topology changes will pose a major challenge to adapting existing MAC protocols for VANETs. Also, when the rigid constraints on delay and reliability for safety applications are considered, the choice of MAC protocol becomes more difficult. However, we can also take advantage of some of the nice features in VANETs, such as predictable directionality of relevant neighbour

nodes, since vehicles are often arrayed linearly on a road. And unlike some other ad hoc networks, resource limitations such as data storage and energy consumption are not major problems in VANETs. Furthermore, it is reasonable to assume that most of the vehicles would carry a GPS device, which can be used for acquiring position information and for providing time synchronization. The latter is only critical for certain protocols; it should be noted that such protocols should account for the fact that the GPS service may fail in urban environments, tunnels, etc.

Time Schedule-Based MAC Protocols

MAC protocols in ad-hoc networks can be classified according to how the channel is shared. Some of the proposed MAC protocols, such as ADHOC MAC (Borgonovo, Capone, Cesana, & Fratta, 2004), share the channel by defining frames with multiple time slots and scheduling transmissions by different nodes in different slots. The scheduling of the time slots in ADHOC MAC is based on the so-called Reliable R-ALOHA protocol (RR-ALOHA), which is an extension of the classical R-ALOHA protocol (Crowther, Rettberg, Waldem, Omstein, & Heart, 1973). In R-ALOHA, the time slots are classified as either RESERVED or AVAILABLE and a node can transmit in any of the AVAILABLE slots. If the transmission is successful, the slot is RESERVED for that node until its transmission finishes. However, the proper operation of the protocol requires a central repeater which conveys the slot information to every node. RR-ALOHA extends R-ALOHA to enable time scheduling in ad hoc networks by transmitting additional information, called frame information, to inform every node of the status of each slot.

The main benefit of ADHOC MAC is that the channel can be shared amongst vehicles with a reduced likelihood of collision. With proper operation of the protocol, hidden terminal and exposed terminal problems are also greatly reduced and high reliability can be achieved.

However, time schedule-based protocols are sensitive to mobility and topology changes and require significant reconfiguration time. Also, a central coordinator in VANETs is not realistic. Dynamic coordination requires knowledge of all neighbouring vehicles and it takes a few time cycles to agree on a stable schedule. As a result, the access delay in such a scenario is high.

Space Division Multiple Access (SDMA) Based MAC Protocols

Space division multiple access (SDMA) is proposed for VANETs in (Bana & Varaiya, 2001), where channel access is regulated by the physical location of the vehicles at any particular time. In SDMA, the coverage area is divided into smaller space divisions so that every division holds at most one vehicle. The bandwidth is also divided into time slots or frequency channels and each channel is uniquely mapped to a space division. It is assumed in (Bana & Varaiya, 2001) that each vehicle can accurately determine its position and that the mapping between the space division and bandwidth division is known by all vehicles. If these requirements are fulfilled, the SDMA protocol provides robust network organization and contention free channel access.

However, the basic SDMA protocol has poor bandwidth efficiency which linearly depends on the number of occupied space divisions. To alleviate this issue, an enhancement to SDMA was proposed, where a portion of the bandwidth is used according to SDMA to control the rest of the bandwidth. Nevertheless, there are other issues which make it difficult to realize SDMA in VANETs. For instance, it is hard to generate an optimum mapping function for all types of highways scenarios and also update/synchronize among all the vehicles whenever the road structure changes. Also, the SDMA frame structure cannot be dynamically tuned to specific scenarios, which will lead to more inefficiency. Imperfect position accuracy and time synchronization among

vehicles are some physical layer issues that can degrade SDMA performance in VANET. Also, these SDMA protocols generally require accurate power control to manage interference with other space divisions using the same channel.

A related protocol called the location-based channel access (LCA) protocol is proposed in (Katragadda, Ganesh Murthy, Ranga Rao, Mohan Kumar, & Sachin, 2003), where they make provisions for multiple vehicles in the same space division. Adaptive space division multiplexing (ASDM) is proposed in (Jeremy & Azim, 2007) to overcome the inefficiency associated with SDMA. The mapping function used in ASDM is also similar to SDMA, but vehicles can now utilize the unused time slots as well. There is an additional requirement, however, that a vehicle must know the location of its preceding vehicle to determine the unused slots. Both LCA and ASDM still suffer from the limitations of mapping function generation, position accuracy and time synchronization discussed for SDMA.

Cluster-Based MAC Protocols

There exist another group of MAC protocols (Su & Zhang, 2007; Zhang, Su, & Chen, 2006) which also relies on the geographic location of the vehicles. In those protocols, neighbouring vehicles are grouped in small geographic clusters and a vehicle is elected as a cluster-head. The cluster-head acts as a coordinator for the cluster and relay for safety messages across cluster boundaries. A schedule-based approach is used for intra-cluster communication and a contention-based approach is used for inter-cluster communication. However, to separate intra-cluster communication from inter-cluster communication, the protocol requires either multi-channel communication or partitioning of each time cycle. The complexities of the schedule-based approach are also present in this approach. Moreover, switching between intra-cluster and inter-cluster communications consumes a significant amount of the limited bandwidth available for VANET applications. The complexity of the protocol makes it less scalable in VANETs.

Directional Antenna-Based MAC Protocols

The use of directional antennas in wireless ad hoc networks can enhance performance by permitting multiple concurrent transmissions in the same neighbourhood (Ko, Shankarkumar, & Vaidya, 2000; Korakis, Jakllari, & Tassiulas, 2003; Yadumurthy, H., Sadashivaiah, & Makanaboyina, 2005), thereby increasing spatial reuse. A directional antenna can direct its transmission in any particular direction using a group of antenna elements. A number of non-overlapping beams can be formed to cover 360 degrees around the node. An additional omnidirectional antenna element can also be present to send control packets in all directions; otherwise omnidirectional transmission requires the use of all antenna elements at once.

In (Ko, et al., 2000), the D-MAC protocol is proposed to utilize directional antennas for unicast transmission. The authors assumed that the location of each receiver is known. The channel is reserved before each transmission by sending a directional Request to Send (RTS) frame and the receiver responds with an omnidirectional Clear to Send frame (CTS). Nodes hearing the RTS/CTS packets in any antenna element will refrain from transmitting any packet using that antenna element for the duration of the transmission. However, other antenna elements of those nodes can be used for concurrent transmission in the vicinity.

The basic scheme presented in (Ko, et al., 2000) has an high chance of control packet collisions due to directional RTS transmissions. As such, an alternative protocol is proposed in (Ko, et al., 2000) to use omnidirectional RTS packets. This is also useful when the location of the receiver is not known. However, use of an omnidirectional antenna reduces the possibilities of simultaneous transmissions. Also, it is difficult to coordinate

multiple simultaneous transmissions in practice. With high mobility in VANETs, antennas must be constantly tracked which further increases the system complexity.

A circular directional RTS is proposed in (Korakis, et al., 2003) to fully avoid omnidirectional transmissions. However, the proper operation of the protocol requires build-up of a neighbour's location table and continuous update of the table which can be hard to achieve for dynamic environments in VANETs. Additionally, the overhead in this case can be significantly higher as separate RTS packets are successively sent in each direction.

One of the major problems that can hinder D-MAC performance is the so-called "deafness" problem (Choudhury & Vaidya, 2004). Deafness is caused when a transmitter fails to communicate with its intended receiver because the receiver is beam-formed in a different direction. The degradation in performance due to deafness is also demonstrated in (Yadumurthy, et al., 2005), where a reliable D-MAC protocol for broadcast communication is proposed and evaluated. The performance is shown to be worse compared to a MAC using omnidirectional antennas due to this deafness problem.

CSMA-Based MAC Protocols

CSMA-based MAC protocols such as IEEE 802.11 DCF (IEEE Std 802.11-2007, 2007) have been widely used in wireless LANs and the technology has matured over the past decade. In CSMA-based protocols, a node must sense the channel for a period of time and transmit its data only if the channel is idle. To avoid collisions of data packets at the receiving nodes due to hidden terminals, some short signalling packets (RTS/CTS) are introduced in multiple access collision avoidance (MACA) (Karn, 1990) and multiple access collision avoidance for wireless lans (MACAW) (Bharghavan, Demers, Shenker, & Zhang, 1994) protocols. IEEE 802.11 DCF is based on CSMA with collision avoidance where two types of sensing are employed to avoid collision: physical carrier sensing and virtual carrier sensing. While physical carrier sensing mechanism is the same as other CSMA-based protocols, the virtual carrier sensing is achieved by setting a duration field to specify how long the sender expects to use the medium. Other nodes hearing the packet can defer their transmissions for that duration.

CSMA-based protocols do not require any reconfiguration upon a change in network environment. Also, the protocol works in a distributed manner without the need for a central coordinator. As a result, this is the preferred approach for most existing and emerging VANET standards such as the ASTM dedicated short range communication (DSRC) (ASTM, 2003) and the IEEE WAVE (IEEE P802.11p, 2008). Recent studies of CSMA-based protocols in VANETs suggest that the delay characteristic of such protocols under light to moderate load conditions meets the requirements for timely delivery of safety critical messages (Chen, et al., 2008).

Standardization Activities

In 1999, the U.S. Federal Communication Commission (FCC) allocated 75MHz of spectrum in the 5.9 GHz band for VANET use, which is often referred to as the DSRC band. The DSRC band is divided into seven 10 MHz wide channels, and a reserved 5 MHz channel. One of the 10 MHZ channels, called the control channel, is restricted to safety communications only, while the other channels are available for both safety and non-safety usage.

The initial effort at standardizing VANET radio technology took place in the ASTM 2313 working group (ASTM, 2003). Currently, the IEEE Wireless Access in Vehicular Environment (WAVE) project is developing specifications for the FCC DSRC band based on an OFDM air interface. IEEE WAVE encompasses the IEEE 802.11p standard (IEEE P802.11p, 2008) for the MAC and PHY,

and the IEEE 1609 family of standards, which define the higher layer protocols and the protocol architecture (Uzcategui, De Sucre, & Acosta-Marum, 2009). IEEE 802.11p (IEEE P802.11p, 2008) is based on IEEE 802.11a, but with modifications to support vehicular communications with low latency. The 802.11p MAC protocol, like other 802.11 variants, will use the distributed coordination function (DCF) for channel access. The standardization of a European Intelligent Transportation Systems (ITS) communication architecture is also underway, headed by ETSI (Kosch, et al., 2009).

Considering the suitability of CSMA-based protocols for VANETs as well as the standardization activities, we anticipate that CSMA-based protocols are currently the only foreseeable choice for VANET safety applications, and we will focus on the performance evaluation of those protocols in the rest of this book chapter.

PERFORMANCE ANALYSIS

IEEE 802.11 DCF Protocol

In the IEEE 802.11 DCF, nodes contend for the channel using a carrier sense multiple access mechanism with collision avoidance (CSMA/CA) as illustrated in Figure 1. When a node has a packet to send, the channel must be sensed idle for a guard period known as the distributed interframe space, DIFS. If during that period of time, the channel becomes busy, then the access is deferred until the channel becomes idle again and a backoff process is initiated. Backoff intervals are slotted, and stations are only permitted to commence transmissions at the beginning of slots. The discrete backoff time is uniformly distributed in the range [0, CW - 1], where CW is called the contention window. At the first transmission attempt, CW is set equal to W, the minimum contention window. The backoff time counter is decremented by one at the end of each idle slot. It is frozen when a

Figure 1. IEEE 802.11 DCF

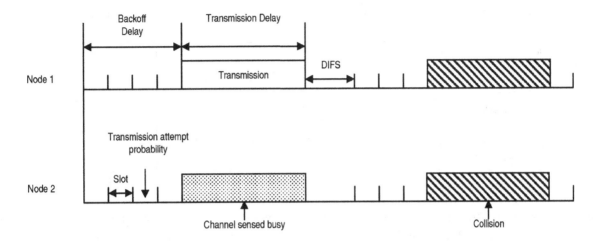

packet transmission is detected on the channel, and reactivated after the channel is sensed idle again for a guard period. The guard period is equal to a DIFS if the transmitted packet was error-free, and equal to the extended interframe space, EIFS, if the packet was in error. The station transmits when the backoff counter reaches zero. A collision occurs when the counters of two or more stations reach zero in the same slot. In the presence of hidden terminals, collision can also occur if a node starts its transmission while another node hidden from this node is already transmitting. After every successful data packet transmission, a station initiates a post-transmission random backoff. If the next packet was already enqueued when the previous packet was sent, its defer time will span the entire backoff period, whereas a packet that arrives at the MAC layer after the previous packet was sent would experience only part of the backoff period, or none at all if the backoff period has already elapsed.

Existing Analytical Models

The performance of CSMA/CA protocols, and the IEEE 802.11 DCF mechanism in particular, have been extensively studied in the wireless LAN environment. In this section, we present a short overview of some of the prominent analytical models that fall in two major different categories – unicast and broadcast communications, and discuss their viability for VANET. We can also classify models according to other attributes such as traffic conditions (saturated versus unsaturated networks) and the presence of hidden terminals. Table 1 summarizes the features considered in each of the analytical models presented here.

Models For Unicast Communication

The most influential analytical model for the IEEE 802.11 DCF was presented by Bianchi (Bianchi, 2000). In this model, the backoff process is modelled using a two dimensional Markov chain to accurately determine the saturation throughput in a fully connected network (i.e. there are no hidden terminals). The key enabling assumption in this work is that each packet collides with a constant and independent probability, and this has been adopted in most subsequent models from other researchers to simplify the analysis. Also, the model is based on renewal theory where it is sufficient to analyse a single renewal interval to derive the saturation throughput. However, the model is not applicable to networks with hidden terminals such as ad hoc networks. Further, the

Table 1. Comparison of our model with the existing models in the literature

Model	broadcast	hidden	unsaturated
(Bianchi, 2000)	X	X	X
(Malone, Duffy, & Leith, 2007)	X	X	√
(Tickoo & Sikdar, 2008)	X	X	√
(Tsertou & Laurenson, 2008)	X	√	X
(Rao, Kherani, & Mahanti, 2008)	√	X	√
(Chen, et al., 2007)	√	√	√
Proposed model (Section III.C of this chapter)	√	√	√

assumption of saturated traffic does not account for most typical network communications.

Malone et al (Malone, et al., 2007) extend the above model to the unsaturated case, but do not consider hidden terminals either. They introduce additional states in the two dimensional Markov chain to capture the post-backoff effect and the tagged node's idle state. To measure the degree of nonsaturation, additional model parameters are introduced, namely the channel idle probability and the buffer empty probability, and approximations are presented to calculate those parameters. A Poisson arrival process is assumed and the model yields the mean delay, throughput and conditional collision probability.

Tickoo and Sikdar (Tickoo & Sikdar, 2008) develop an alternative model that is not based on a Markov chain. In the model, they utilize the probability of an empty buffer to account for unsaturated conditions. Each station is modelled as a G/G/1 queue with arbitrary packet arrival and size. The analysis gives expressions for the probability generating functions of the queue length and the delay. However, the analytical results for the collision probabilities show a large mismatch with the simulation results.

All the above mentioned papers assume a fully connected network. Although there exists a wide body of literature analysing the hidden terminal problem, several limitations of those models are highlighted in (Tsertou & Laurenson, 2008) for the case of unicast communications. These limitations can be summarised as follows:

- One of the fundamental assumptions in Markov chain-based analytical models (Bianchi, 2000; Malone, et al., 2007) is the existence of a renewal point. In the presence of hidden terminals this assumption is not valid due to the desynchronization of the nodes.
- Another modelling approach (Alizadeh-Shabdiz & Subramaniam, 2004; Tickoo & Sikdar, 2008) for networks with hidden nodes is to assume independent and geometrically distributed transmission attempts instead of uniformly distributed attempts with an exponentially growing backoff window. Using that assumption, the probability of avoiding a packet collision due to hidden terminals is calculated by noting that a hidden node must not transmit for a number of successive slots during the vulnerable period (i.e. the time period when a transmission by a hidden node will cause a packet collision). However, the assumption may lead to inaccurate results for smaller values of backoff window when the collision probability due to hidden terminals is approaching one.

In order to fix the above problems, (Tsertou & Laurenson, 2008) proposed a new model based on the notion of a fixed slot length instead of a variable length slot and first order dependence of two successive channel states. However, the scope of this model is restricted to a particular network topology with two competing hidden nodes. Also, it is not straightforward to extend the model to the unsaturated case.

Models for Broadcast Communication

As we mentioned earlier, several applications envisioned for VANETs, especially safety related ones, rely on broadcast communications. Thus it is essential to consider the differences between broadcast and unicast communications. The key differences are due to the fact that request-response protocol handshaking cannot be supported in broadcast mode because it will lead to a "storm" of response messages. As a result, the broadcast mode cannot support positive acknowledgement and retransmission, nor can it have an RTS/CTS mechanism. Rao et al. develop an analytical model to determine the probability of packet collision in the broadcast scenario (Rao, et al., 2008). They analyse a bufferless MAC and a MAC with a finite buffer to calculate the transition probability and the buffer occupancy probability. They also provide a stability and sensitivity analysis for their model. However, they do not consider hidden terminals in their analysis.

The model in (Chen, et al., 2007) attempts to capture the characteristics of the VANET safety communications where broadcasting takes place in an unsaturated network with hidden terminals. However, the renewal theory based argument used in this model is not suitable for hidden terminal analysis, as pointed out in (Tsertou & Laurenson, 2008). Also, the IEEE 802.11 DCF protocol is not properly modelled in (Chen, et al., 2007) since the analysis assumes that a backoff is initiated for each

arriving packet at a node irrespective of whether the channel is idle or busy. In the next section we propose a model to address these shortcomings.

Proposed Model

In the following we develop a new analytical model to capture the behaviour of the IEEE 802.11 DCF protocol in unsaturated broadcast networks with and without hidden terminals. We will focus on the packet delay and the packet delivery ratio as the two main performance metrics of interest in our study. While we make necessary assumptions to keep the model simple, we will show via comparison with simulation that the results are accurate. We will also provide a comparison with results from the existing model in (Chen, et al., 2007) to demonstrate the superior accuracy of our model.

System Model

Let us consider a scenario of vehicle-to-vehicle communications for CCA applications on a highway as shown in Fig. 2. The highway consists of several lanes with vehicles moving in both directions. In our model we make the following assumptions: A.1 Vehicles on the highway can be represented as a collection of random and statistically identical stations in a one dimensional mobile ad-hoc network that are stationary during the communication interval; A.2 The transmission range and sensing range for each station are equal, deterministic and denoted by R; A.3 Data packets are generated at each station according to a Poisson process with rate λ (in packets per second); A.4 The collision probability experienced by a station is constant regardless of the state of the other nodes in the network; A.5 Channel conditions are ideal within the radius R, packet loss occurs solely as a result of packet collisions, and collisions lead to the loss of all collided packets.

Figure 2. Typical highway structure in DSRC environment. (S represents the sender, R the receiver and H the hidden terminal)

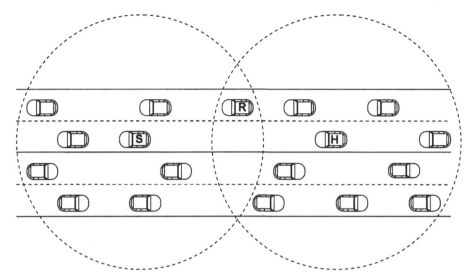

Assumption A.1 holds when the network topology does not change significantly during one packet transmission time, and the distance between lanes on the highway is negligible compared to the length of the network. Assumption A.2 implies that any vehicle in the range [R, 2R] and [-2R,-R] of a selected (tagged) vehicle is a potential hidden terminal. Let β be a vehicle density in vehicles per meter on the highway. The average number of vehicles in the transmission range of the tagged vehicle (N_{tr}) including the tagged station can be computed as

$$N_{tr}=1+2\beta R \tag{1}$$

and the average number of vehicles in the potential hidden terminal area (N_{ph}) can be expressed as

$$N_{ph}=2\beta R \tag{2}$$

Assumptions A.3, A.4 and A.5 are common in performance studies of the MAC protocol in mobile wireless ad-hoc networks (Chen, et al., 2007; Rao, et al., 2008) and help make the model analytically tractable, while still yielding meaningful indications of MAC performance. We only consider broadcasting with a single transmission attempt per packet in our work. Thus if a packet is collided, there is no subsequent retransmission and the packet is lost. Furthermore, the effect of the post backoff period (Tsertou & Laurenson, 2008) on packet delay is not considered in our model. This is because the probability of a packet arrival during the post backoff period is negligible in the safety message regime.

With the above assumptions, each vehicle can be modelled as an M/G/1 queue with an infinite buffer size, i.e. no packet loss due to buffer overflow. The assumption of an infinite buffer is obviously an idealisation, but may be reasonable in safety applications since there should not be many packets waiting to be broadcasted.. Our objective is to develop a fixed point approximation to compute the collision probability and the end-to-end packet delay experienced by the tagged vehicle. To this end, the fixed point approximation is established by combining the set of equations for the collision probability expressed in terms of the delay experienced by each packet sent by the tagged station, with an opposing set of equations for the delay expressed in terms of the collision probability. We derive the former set of equations in subsection III.C.b and the latter in subsection III.C.d.

Collision Probability

In this section, we derive the collision probability without accounting for hidden terminals (i.e. ``direct'' collisions only), and in the next section, we modify the result to allow for hidden terminals. To calculate the collision probability of safety messages, first we identify three sets of buffer and channel conditions that can confront a newly-generated packet in a vehicle operating in an unsaturated network. Firstly, a packet can arrive to an empty buffer and the channel can be sensed idle for a DIFS period. Secondly, a packet can arrive to an empty buffer and the channel can be sensed busy. Lastly, a packet can arrive to a non-empty buffer.

For the first case, the vehicle immediately sends the packet without performing a backoff (assuming post-backoff is negligible). In this case, a collision can occur only when another packet is generated at some other vehicle within the propagation delay. As the propagation delay in the studied transmission range is negligible, we can ignore any collisions of this type. As described before, we model each station as an $M/G/1/\infty$ queue and define ρ as the queue utilization expressed as

$$\rho = \lambda E[S] \qquad (3)$$

where $E[S]$ is the average packet service time, to be derived in subsection III.C.d. From standard $M/G/1/\infty$ queuing theory, the probability that the queue is empty is given by $1-\rho$. We also define P_{busy} as the probability that the channel is sensed busy when a new packet arrives. Therefore, the probability of finding an empty queue and sensing the channel idle is $(1-\rho)(1-P_{busy})$. The expression for P_{busy} will be derived later.

In the second case, the joint probability of a packet arrival to an empty buffer and the channel being busy due to transmission by other vehicles is $(1-\rho)P_{busy}$.

For the last case, the probability of a packet arrival to a non-empty buffer is ρ. Note that for the last two cases, the packet must undergo the backoff process before it is transmitted. After the backoff counter reaches zero, the tagged vehicle sends the packet in the following slot, and if another vehicle sends a packet at the same slot, a collision occurs and the packets are lost.

Let τ be the probability that a vehicle attempts to transmit in an arbitrary slot given that it has a packet in the queue. We approximate τ using a mean-value approach, where we assume that τ is the same for every slot and related to the reciprocal of the mean backoff period. Specifically, letting $\bar{W}$ be the average number of backoff slots preceding a transmission, we let

$$\tau = \frac{1}{\bar{W}+1}.$$

For any vehicle other than the tagged vehicle, the probability of transmitting in any arbitrary slot is $\rho\tau$. A collision occurs when any of the $N_{tr}-1$ vehicles transmit in the same slot as the tagged vehicle given that the tagged vehicle sees either of the last two cases. So, the collision probability is given by

$$p_c = (1-(1-\rho)(1-P_{busy}))(1-(1-\rho\tau)^{N_{tr}-1}), \qquad (4)$$

and the packet delivery ratio is

$$PDR = 1 - p_c \qquad (5)$$

Next, we express the probability that the channel is sensed busy when a new packet arrives, P_{busy}, as

$$P_{busy}=(N_{tr}-1)\lambda T(1-pc/2) \qquad (6)$$

where p_c is the conditional collision probability in (4) and T is the complete transmission time of a packet including the DIFS period. Equation (6) is based on quantifying the traffic load on the channel. As we have N_{tr}-1 vehicles other than the tagged vehicle transmitting λ packets per second, if there is no collision, then all the packet transmissions should take $(N_{tr}-1)\lambda T$ time each second. However, with a collision probability of pc $(Nt_{r-}1)$ λpc $_p$ackets will be involved in collisions. If we only consider collisions among two packets, the transmission time to send the collided packets would be $(Ntr_{-1})\lambda Tpc/2$. Adjusting for this collision period we get (6).

Hidden Terminal Case

In the previous section, we have calculated the collision probability assuming no hidden terminals. Now we present an approach to calculate the probability of collision when there are hidden terminals. We note that, two necessary conditions must be satisfied for there to be no collisions between packets from hidden terminals and the transmission of the tagged vehicle. Firstly, when the tagged vehicle starts its transmission, none of the hidden terminals can be in the transmitting state; we denote this event as H*1* Here, we define a hidden terminal to be in the transmitting state if it is either transmitting a packet or deferring for a DIFS period associated with an immediate packet transmission. Secondly, after the tagged vehicle starts its transmission assuming H*2* none of the hidden terminals should start transmitting until after the tagged vehicle is finished; we denote this event as H*2*

For event H_1, following a similar argument as (6), the probability of finding any hidden terminal in the non-transmitting state is expressed as

$$P(H)=1-N_{ph}\lambda T(1-pc/2) \qquad (7)$$

For event H_2, we need to calculate the probability that a packet is generated by the hidden terminal after the tagged vehicle starts its transmission. Note that in this case, packets generated in the last time portion of one DIFS period of the tagged vehicle's transmission will not collide because the actual transmission starts after a DIFS period. Thus, using the fact that the arrival process is Poisson, we can express the probability of H_2 as

$$P(H_2) = e^{-\lambda N_{ph}(t_{data}-t_{difs})}, \qquad (8)$$

where t_{data} is the actual transmission time of a packet and t_{difs} is the duration of DIFS period.

Considering the fact that direct collisions and collisions due to hidden terminals are independent of each other, we modify the collision probability (4) as follows:

$$p_h=1-(1-p_c)P(H_1)P(H_2) \qquad (9)$$

The associated packet delivery ratio is

$$PDR=1-p_h \qquad (10)$$

Expression for the Delay

In this section, we derive an expression for the packet delay using probabilistic arguments. The total delay (or sojourn time) experienced by a packet of a tagged vehicle includes the waiting time of the packet in the queue, the access delay and the complete time to transmit the packet. The access delay is defined as the time interval between the instant the packet reaches the head of the queue, to the instant when the packet transmission starts. We denote the total delay of the packet by D and write it as

$$D=Q+S=Q+A+T \qquad (11)$$

where Q and A are random variables (r.v.'s) representing the queuing delay and access delay. For each packet transmission, the channel is occupied for the duration of the actual packet transmission (t_{data}) and one DIFS. Recall that we define the complete transmission time T as the sum of the actual packet transmission time and one DIFS period. We also define the service time of the queue S as the sum of the access delay A and the transmission delay T.

To determine the access delay, we consider the following three possibilities:

- A packet arrives to an empty buffer and finds the channel idle. The access delay in this case is zero as the tagged vehicle transmits the packet without any backoff.
- A packet arrives to an empty buffer but finds the channel busy. The vehicle must wait until the ongoing transmission is finished and then perform a backoff before transmitting the packet.
- A packet arrives to a non-empty buffer and when it reaches the head of the queue, a backoff is performed before transmitting the packet.

Since, the probability of a non-empty buffer is ρ, and the probability of finding the channel busy is P_{busy}, we can express the access delay according to the above three cases as

$$
A = \begin{cases} 0 & \text{w.p.} \quad (1-\rho)(1-P_{busy}), \\ B + T_{Res} & \text{w.p.} \quad (1-\rho)P_{busy}, \\ B & \text{w.p.} \quad \rho. \end{cases} \tag{12}
$$

where T_{Res} is the residual lifetime of an ongoing packet transmission, B is the total backoff duration including periods when the backoff counter is suspended, and the notation 'w.p.' stands for 'with probability'.

During the backoff process, every slot can be interrupted by successful transmissions or collisions of packets transmitted by other vehicles.

During the interruption, the backoff counter is suspended and when the backoff counter is resumed, it starts from the beginning of the interrupted slot. For simplicity, we assume every backoff slot can be interrupted at most once. This simplification should not have a significant impact on accuracy, since the probability of multiple interruptions to the same slot is small. Thus, we can express B as a random sum

$$
B = \sum_{n=1}^{U} (\sigma + Y) \tag{13}
$$

where σ represents the duration of a backoff slot, Y is the interruption period, and U is the backoff counter value which is uniformly distributed in the range $[0, W\text{-}1]$ where W is the minimum contention window defined in Section III.A.

If no other vehicle transmits in a given slot, an interruption does not occur and Y equals zero. If one or more vehicles transmit in that slot, then the tagged vehicle will suspend its backoff process for the duration of the transmission. Therefore, we can write Y as

$$
Y = \begin{cases} 0 & \text{w.p.} \quad (1-p_b), \\ T & \text{w.p.} \quad p_b. \end{cases} \tag{14}
$$

where p_b is the probability that a slot is busy due to transmissions by other vehicles. Recall that the probability that a vehicle attempts to transmit in an arbitrary slot given that it has a packet in its buffer is given by τ and the probability that the buffer is non-empty is ρ. Therefore, the probability of a vehicle transmitting in an arbitrary slot is ρτ and a backoff slot of the tagged vehicle becomes busy when any of the other N_{tr}-1 vehicles transmit in that slot. Thus, we obtain

$$
p_b = 1 - (1 - \rho\tau)^{N_{tr}-1}. \tag{15}
$$

Mean and Standard Deviation

In this section, we determine the mean and standard deviation of the service time and the mean of the total delay. We express those using means and variances of the constituent random variables. From (11), we obtain

$$E[S]=E[A]+E[T] \tag{16}$$

$$\mathrm{StdDev}[S] = \sqrt{\mathrm{Var}[S]} = \sqrt{\mathrm{Var}[A] + \mathrm{Var}[T]}, \tag{17}$$

where $E[X]$, $\mathrm{StdDev}[X]$ and $\mathrm{Var}[X]$ denotes the mean, standard deviation and variance of the r.v. X.

In our study, we consider constant length packets for all vehicles. Thus for the mean and variance of the transmission time we have

$$E[T]=T \tag{18}$$

$$\mathrm{Var}[T]=0 \tag{19}$$

From (12), we observe that the distribution of A is a conditional distribution. The mean and variance of A can then be written as

$$E[A]=(1-\rho)P_{busy}(E[B]+E[T_{ReS}])+\rho E[B] \tag{20}$$

$$\begin{aligned}
\mathrm{Var}[A] &= (1-\rho)(1-P_{busy})\,\mathrm{E}[A]^2 \\
&\quad +(1-\rho)P_{busy}(\mathrm{Var}[B] + \mathrm{Var}[T_{Res}] + (\mathrm{E}[A] - \mathrm{E}[B] - \mathrm{E}[T_{Res}])^2) \\
&\quad +\rho(\mathrm{Var}[B] + (\mathrm{E}[A] - \mathrm{E}[B])^2).
\end{aligned} \tag{21}$$

To calculate the mean and variance of the residual lifetime of an ongoing transmission, T_{ReS}, we first determine the probability distribution function of T_{ReS}. Note that, inter-arrival time of packets generated at each vehicle follows a memoryless exponential distribution with rate λ. So, the interval between the starting time of ongoing transmission and arrival of a new packet at the tagged vehicle also follows an exponential distribution and we define it as $X{\sim}1-e^{-\lambda t}$. Therefore, we can represent the distribution of TR_{eS} as

the remaining transmission time, $X'=T-X$, conditioned on $X{\leq}T$.

Now, the probability distribution function of X' can be expressed as $F_{X'}(x') = 1 - F_X(T - x')$, where $F_Z(.)$ here represents the distribution function of r.v. Z. Applying the condition $X{\leq}T$, we get

$$F_{X'|X\leq T}(x') = 1 - F_{X|X\leq T}(T - x') = \frac{e^{-\lambda(T-x')} - e^{-\lambda T}}{1 - e^{-\lambda T}}. \tag{22}$$

Differentiating (22) we obtain the probability density function as

$$f_{X'|X\leq T}(x') = \frac{\lambda e^{-\lambda(T-x')}}{1 - e^{-\lambda T}}. \tag{23}$$

We can obtain the mean and variance of T_{ReS} from (23) as follows:

$$E[T_{Res}] = E[X' \mid X \leq T] = \frac{T}{1 - e^{-\lambda T}} - \frac{1}{\lambda}, \tag{24}$$

$$E[T_{Res}^2] = E[X'^2 \mid X \leq T] = \frac{T^2 - 2T/\lambda}{1 - e^{-\lambda T}} + \frac{2}{\lambda^2}, \tag{25}$$

$$\mathrm{Var}[T_{Res}] = E[T_{Res}^2] - E[T_{Res}]^2 = \frac{1}{\lambda^2} - \frac{T^2 e^{-\lambda T}}{(1 - e^{-\lambda T})^2}. \tag{26}$$

Using well-known identities for the mean and variance of a random sum (Feller, 1971), it follows from (13) that

$$E[B]=(\sigma+E[Y])E[U] \tag{27}$$

$$\mathrm{Var}[B]=\mathrm{Var}[Y]E[U]+(\sigma+E[Y])^2\mathrm{Var}[U] \tag{28}$$

As U is a r.v. which is uniformly distributed in the range [0, W-1], we have

Table 2. DSRC system parameters

Parameter	Value	Parameter	Value
W	16	Range, R	500 m
Slot size, σ	$16\,\mu s$	DIFS	$64\,\mu s$
PHY preamble	$32\,\mu s$	PLCP header	$8\,\mu s$
Vehicle density, β	0.01 - 0.2	Data rate, R_d	12, 24 Mbps
Packet arrival rate, λ	2, 10	Packet length, P	200, 400 bytes

$$\mathrm{E}[U] = \bar{W} = \frac{W-1}{2}, \tag{29}$$

$$\mathrm{Var}[U] = \frac{W^2 - 1}{12}. \tag{30}$$

For the interruption time Y, we can calculate the mean and variance from (14) as

$$\mathrm{E}[Y] = p_b T \tag{31}$$

$$\mathrm{Var}[Y] = p_b(1 - p_b)T^2 \tag{32}$$

Thus, based on (16)–(32), we can derive the mean and standard deviation of the service time in terms of P_{busy} and ρ. Now (3), (4), (6), and (16) constitute a non-linear system of equations that can be solved iteratively to calculate ρ, P_{busy}, p_c, and $\mathrm{E}[S]$. Using those computed values we can get the mean queuing delay, $\mathrm{E}[Q]$. Using the well-known result for the M/G/1 queue (Kleinrock, 1975), we obtain

$$\mathrm{E}[Q] = \frac{\lambda(\mathrm{Var}[S] + \mathrm{E}[S]^2)}{2(1 - \lambda\,\mathrm{E}[S])}, \tag{33}$$

from which we can find the mean total delay using

$$\mathrm{E}[D] = \mathrm{E}[Q] + \mathrm{E}[S] \tag{34}$$

Model Validation and Results Discussion

In this section, we present the simulation setup used to validate our analytical model. We used the ns-2 simulator (version 2.28) (ns-2.28, 2005) to simulate and obtain packet delay and PDR in a DSRC environment under various conditions. We adopted the patch for ns-2.28 provided in (Schmidt-Eisenlohr, Letamendia-Murua, Torrent-Moreno, & Hartenstein, 2006) where they fixed the following bug. According to IEEE802.11 specification (IEEE Std 802.11-2007, 2007), if the medium is sensed idle when a packet arrives at the MAC layer, the packet can be transmitted after an idle period of DIFS without any backoff. However, in the standard distribution of ns-2.28, a backoff is always started irrespective of whether the channel is idle or busy.

We use a ring topology in the simulation to obtain results presented later in this section where we place vehicles on a circle to avoid any unwanted effects of stations located at the edge of the network. The radius of the circle is kept significantly larger than the transmission range of each vehicle so that the highway scenario is actually simulated. The vehicles are placed randomly on the circle where the average inter-vehicle distance is a function of vehicle density, β. Each vehicle is setup to broadcast messages with fixed packet size, P and packet arrival rate, λ. We take into consideration additional headers for each packet which include the physical preamble and the physical layer convergence procedure (PLCP)

Figure 3. Total delay for direct collision using the following parameter set: (data rate, packet arrival rate, packet size)

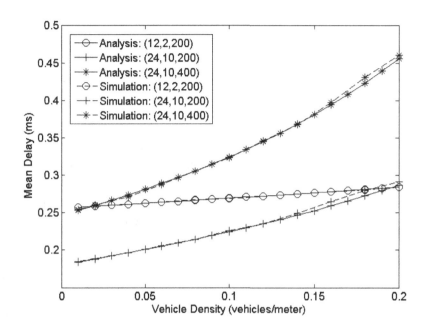

header. All the other DSRC related parameters are listed in Table 2.

In this section, we compare the numerical results with simulation to validate our model. We present results for the mean of the total delay, the standard deviation of the access delay, and the PDR. Another goal of our numerical experiments is to investigate the effect of different load conditions on the delay and PDR performance metrics.

We first present and discuss results for the direct collision case. In Fig. 3, we plot the mean of the total delay using (34) as a function of vehicle density, β, with different curves parameterised by the data rate R_d [Mbps], packet arrival rate λ [packets/sec], and packet size P [bytes]. Observe that our analytical model agrees well with the simulation results. In our plotted range, the mean delay increases almost linearly with the vehicle density, with the slope for the $\lambda=10$ case being larger compared to the $\lambda=2$ case. The largest mean delay observed is less than 0.5 ms which is well

below the maximum delay constraint of 400 ms for safety applications (Biswas, et al., 2006).

In Fig. 4, we study the accuracy of our model in terms of the standard deviation. Note that for the analytical results, we use the standard deviation of the service time in (17) as a proxy for the standard deviation of the total delay. We observe from the figure that the standard deviation for all cases is nearly zero for low vehicle densities. This is because the channel is mostly idle and no backoff is required by the vehicles. With increasing vehicle density, the standard deviation increases almost linearly. We note that the analytical results are always equal to or slightly less than the simulation results because we use (17) rather than the standard deviation of the total delay.

Next, we plot the packet delivery ratio for direct collisions in Fig. 5, where the analytical results are computed according to (5). The analysis slightly overestimates the number of packet collisions. For the $\lambda=2$ case, we see that the PDR is above 99% for all vehicle densities; however,

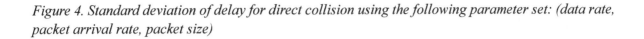

Figure 4. Standard deviation of delay for direct collision using the following parameter set: (data rate, packet arrival rate, packet size)

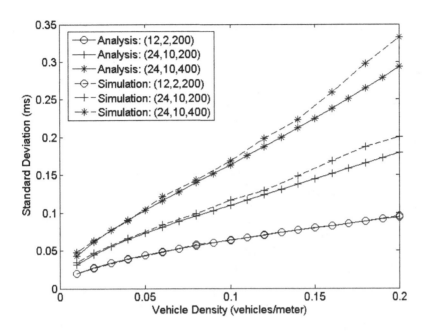

for the λ=10 case, the PDR drops with increasing vehicle density. Nevertheless, the PDR requirement of 90% stipulated by the ASTM (ASTM, 2003) is fulfilled.

For the hidden terminal case, the distribution of the packet delay is the same as for the direct collision case. This is because the presence of hidden terminals does not affect the backoff process of the tagged vehicle and there is no retransmission in broadcast communications. For this reason we omit the results for the mean and standard deviation of the delay when there are hidden terminals.

In Fig. 6, we plot results for the PDR according to (10) which accounts for hidden terminals and compare them with simulation. The PDR is above 90% for all cases under light load ($\beta \leq 0.02$) but drops linearly with increasing vehicle density. For higher vehicle densities, the PDR eventually drops below the reliability requirement of 90% for DSRC safety applications. We also observe that the PDRs for the λ=10 cases are much worse than that of the λ=2 case. To compare our analytical

model with the Chen's model, we plot the PDR for R_d=24 [Mbps], λ=10 [packets/sec], P=200 [bytes] case using both our model and the model proposed in (Chen, et al., 2007). Observe that our model is a much better match with the results obtained from the ns-2 simulation compared to the Chen's model.

From Fig. 5 and Fig. 6, we can compare the PDR values obtained for the hidden terminal case with that for the direct collision case. We fix our observation to the particular case with the parameters: R_d=24 [Mbps], P=200 [bytes] and β=0.1 [vehicles/m]. Our comparative results show that packet collision due to hidden terminals is the major source of collisions, and can reduce the PDR by up to 25% in the cases studied.

In summary, assuming that the packet delay will likely be within 3 standard deviations of the mean, which is 1.34 ms in our cases studied, there is no concern in meeting the delay constraint of 400 ms reported in (Biswas, et al., 2006). However, as shown in Fig. 6, the significant reduction

Figure 5. Packet delivery ratio for direct collision using the following parameter set: (data rate, packet arrival rate, packet size)

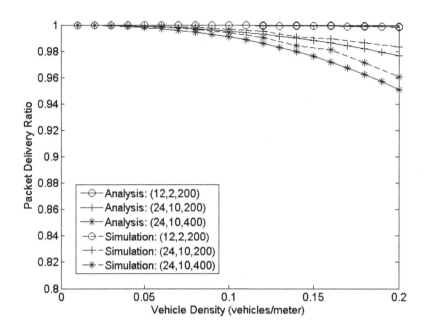

Figure 6. Packet delivery ratio in network with hidden terminals using the following parameter set: (data rate, packet arrival rate, packet size)

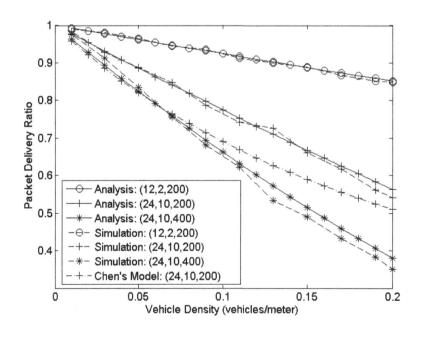

in PDR performance due to hidden terminals is indeed a real obstacle in using CSMA based MAC protocols for VANET safety applications.

FUTURE RESEARCH DIRECTIONS

The performance analysis presented in the previous section suggests that the 802.11 MAC protocol can only be deployed for safety applications in VANET under certain conditions where the PDR performance is still acceptable in the presence of hidden terminals. In the following, we discuss possible enhancements that can be made to improve the protocol and make it more suitable for safety applications.

- Repeated transmissions: A simple and obvious way to improve the reliability at the MAC layer is to send all safety messages multiple times repeatedly as proposed in (Jiang, Taliwal, Meier, Holfelder, & Herrtwich, 2006). Such a repetition scheme may increase PDR for the safety messages; however by repeating each packet excessively, the channel may become more congested and as a result the PDR performance may degrade. So, the number of repetitions needs to be optimized to benefit from repeated transmissions in various traffic load conditions.

- Out-of-band signalling: In addition to the data channel, a separate channel can be used to coordinate transmissions in a multihop network. In (Zhai, Wang, Chen, & Fang, 2006), the authors utilize a busy tone to reduce the effect of the hidden terminal problem in unicast communications. A contention tone is proposed in (Tantra & Foh, 2006) to avoid channel access collisions. Another use of out-of-band signalling is to separate control packets from data packets and send them using a separate channel (Zhai, et al., 2006). The

question of how to best utilize out-of-band signalling in broadcast communications is still an open problem.

- Priority: The IEEE 802.11p standard has provision for enhanced DCF (EDCF), which supports prioritization among different types of delay-sensitive data traffic. This mechanism could be applied to give emergency safety messages priority over routine safety messages. More research is needed to optimize the EDCF parameters so that increasing reliability for the higher priority packets does not starve the lower priority ones.

In addition to the above-mentioned enhancements, the incorporation of non-ideal channel conditions and mobility in the analytical model are possible future research directions. There are also some other enhancements proposed in the literatures to improve the performance for MAC protocols in VANETs which are mentioned in (Chen, et al., 2008; Zhai, et al., 2006). The model we proposed in Section III.C is flexible enough to be extended to study those enhancements.

CONCLUSION

In this chapter, we have provided an overview of different MAC protocols for vehicle-to-vehicle and vehicle-to-infrastructure communications using the DSRC standard. While both time-scheduled (TDMA) and contention based (CSMA) MAC protocols were described, it has been revealed that only the latter is being considered for safety applications in the DSRC environment. This is because the time schedule-based MAC protocols are sensitive to mobility and topology changes and require significant reconfiguration time. Focusing on the CSMA-based 802.11 MAC protocol, we have reviewed several key existing analytical models for its performance evaluation and highlighted their shortcomings when specific network and communication requirements are considered for safety applications in VANETs. For example, broadcast rather than unicast communication is recommended for CCA applications, which in turn extends the area of potential hidden terminals and aggravates the problem caused by them. We have developed in this chapter a new analytical model that studies those issues. Using our model, we have obtained expressions for the mean and standard deviation of the packet delay, as well as an expression for the packet delivery ratio at the MAC layer. The accuracy of our model has been validated by comparing the analytical results with simulation for a range of vehicle densities and traffic load conditions. The performance of vehicle-to-vehicle broadcasting communications using the 802.11 MAC protocol for safety communication has been discussed using the obtained performance metrics. We have shown that hidden terminals have a detrimental impact on the PDR which may compromise the reliability required for safety applications. On the other hand, the packet delay of safety messages was found to be well below the required threshold level. Therefore, there appears to be scope to modify the MAC protocol to trade the packet delay for the improved PDR.

REFERENCES

Alizadeh-Shabdiz, F., & Subramaniam, S. (2004). MAC layer performance analysis of multi-hop ad hoc networks. In *Proceedings of the IEEE Global Telecommunications Conference (GLOBECOM2004),* (Volume 5, 2781-2785). Dallas, TX.

ASTM. (2003). (n.d.). Standard specification for telecommunications and information exchange between roadside and vehicle systems - 5 GHz band Dedicated Short Range Communications (DSRC) Medium Access Control (MAC) and Physical Layer (PHY) specifications. *ASTM E,* 2213–0.

Bana, S. V., & Varaiya, P. (2001). Space Division Multiple Access (SDMA) for robust ad hoc vehicle communication networks. In *Proceedings of the 4th IEEE International Conference on ITS (ITSC2001)*, (pp, 962-967). Oakland, CA.

Bharghavan, V., Demers, A., Shenker, S., & Zhang, L. (1994). Macaw: a media access protocol for wireless lan's. In *SIGCOMM '94: Proceedings of the conference on Communications architectures, protocols and applications*, pages 212-225, New York: ACM.

Bianchi, G. (2000). Performance analysis of the IEEE 802.11 distributed coordination function. *IEEE Journal on Selected Areas in Communications, 18*(3), 535–547. doi:10.1109/49.840210

Biswas, S., Tatchikou, R., & Dion, F. (2006). Vehicle-to-vehicle wireless communication protocols for enhancing highway traffic safety. *IEEE Communications, 44*(1), 74–82. doi:10.1109/MCOM.2006.1580935

Borgonovo, F., Capone, A., Cesana, M., & Fratta, L. (2004). ADHOC MAC: new MAC architecture for ad hoc networks providing efficient and reliable point-to-point and broadcast services. *Wireless Networks, 10*(4), 359–366. doi:10.1023/B:WINE.0000028540.96160.8a

Chen, X., Refai, H. H., & Ma, X. (2007). A quantitative approach to evaluate DSRC highway inter-vehicle safety communication. In *Proceedings of the IEEE Global Telecommunications Conference (GLOBECOM2007)*, (pp.151-155). Washington, DC.

Chen, X., Refai, H. H., & Ma, X. (2008). On the enhancements to IEEE 802.11 MAC and their suitability for safety-critical applications in VANET, *Wireless Communications and Mobile Computing*. Retrieved from http://dx.doi.org/10.1002/wcm.674

Choudhury, R. R., & Vaidya, N. H. (2004). Deafness: a MAC problem in ad hoc networks when using directional antennas. In *Proceedings of the 12th IEEE International Conference on Network Protocols (ICNP2004)*, (pp. 283-292). Berlin, Germany.

Crowther, W., Rettberg, R., Waldem, D., Omstein, S., & Heart, F. (1973). A system for broadcast communications: Reservation ALOHA. In *Proceedings of the 6th Hawaii International Conference on System Sciences*, (pp. 596-603). Honolulu, HI.

Feller, W. (1971). *An Introduction to Probability Theory and Its Applications* (2nd ed., *Vol. 2*). New York: Wiley.

Hartenstein, H., & Laberteaux, K. P. (2008). Topics in ad hoc and sensor networks - A tutorial survey on vehicular ad hoc networks. *IEEE Communications*, *46*(6), 164–171. doi:10.1109/MCOM.2008.4539481

IEEE P802.11p (2008). Draft standard for information technology - Telecommunications and information exchange between systems - Local and metropolitan area networks-specific requirements - Part 11: Wireless LAN medium access control (MAC) and physical layer (PHY) specifications - Amendment 7: Wireless Access in Vehicular Environments.

Jeremy, J. B., & Azim, E. (2007). A reliable link-layer protocol for robust and scalable intervehicle communications. *IEEE Transactions on Intelligent Transportation Systems*, *8*(1), 4–13. doi:10.1109/TITS.2006.889441

Jiang, D., Taliwal, V., Meier, A., Holfelder, W., & Herrtwich, R. (2006). Design of 5.9 GHz DSRC-based vehicular safety communication. *IEEE Wireless Communications*, *13*(5), 36–43. doi:10.1109/WC-M.2006.250356

Karn, P. (1990). MACA a new channel access method for packet radio. In *Proceedings of the 9th Computer Networking Conference*, (pp. 134-140). Ontario, Canada.

Katragadda, S., Ganesh Murthy, C. N. S., Ranga Rao, M. S., Mohan Kumar, S., & Sachin, R. (2003). A decentralized location-based channel access protocol for inter-vehicle communication. In *Proceedings of the 57th IEEE Vehicular Technology Conference (VTC2003-Spring)*, (Volume 3, (pp. 1831-1835). Taipei, Taiwan.

Kleinrock, L. (1975). Theory: *Vol. 1. Queueing Systems*. New York: Wiley-Interscience.

Ko, Y. B., Shankarkumar, V., & Vaidya, N. H. (2000). Medium access control protocols using directional antennas in ad hoc networks. In *Proceedings of the 19th IEEE Conference on Computer and Communications (INFOCOM2000)*, (Volume 1, (pp. 13-21). Tel-Aviv · Israel.

Korakis, T., Jakllari, G., & Tassiulas, L. (2003). A MAC protocol for full exploitation of directional antennas in ad-hoc wireless networks. In *Proceedings of the 4th ACM International Symposium on Mobile Ad Hoc Networking & Computing (MobiHoc2003)*. Annapolis, MD.

Kosch, T., Kulp, I., Bechler, M., Strassberger, M., Weyl, B., & Lasowski, R. (2009). Communication Architecture for Cooperative Systems in Europe. *IEEE Communications*, *47*(5), 116–125. doi:10.1109/MCOM.2009.4939287

Malone, D., Duffy, K., & Leith, D. (2007). Modeling the 802.11 Distributed Coordination Function in Nonsaturated Heterogeneous Conditions. *IEEE/ACM Transactions on Networking*, *15*(1), 159-172.

Menouar, H., Filali, F., & Lenardi, M. (2006). A survey and qualitative analysis of mac protocols for vehicular ad hoc networks. *IEEE Wireless Communications*, *13*(5), 30–35. doi:10.1109/WC-M.2006.250355 ns-2.28 (2005). *The network simulator ns-2.28.* Retrieved from http://www.isi.edu/nsnam/ns/

Rao, A., Kherani, A. A., & Mahanti, A. (2008). Performance evaluation of 802.11 broadcasts for a single cell network with unsaturated nodes. In Das, A., Pung, H. K., Lee, F. B.-S., & Wong, L. W.-C. (Eds.), *Lecture Notes in Computer Science: Networking* (*Vol. 4982*, pp. 836–847). New York: Springer.

Schmidt-Eisenlohr, F., Letamendia-Murua, J., Torrent-Moreno, M., & Hartenstein, H. (2006). *Bug fixes on the IEEE 802.11 DCF module of the Network Simulator ns-2.28.* Germany: Department of Computer Science, University of Karlsruhe.

IEEE Std 802.11-2007 (2007). IEEE standard for information technology - Telecommunications and information exchange between systems - Local and metropolitan area networks-specific requirements - Part 11: Wireless LAN medium access control (MAC) and physical layer (PHY) specifications.

Su, H., & Zhang, X. (2007). Clustering-based multichannel MAC protocols for QoS provisionings over vehicular ad hoc networks. *IEEE Transactions on Vehicular Technology, 56*(6), 3309–3323. doi:10.1109/TVT.2007.907233

Tantra, J. W., & Foh, C. H. (2006). Achieving near maximum throughput in IEEE 802.11 WLANs with contention tone. *IEEE Communications Letters, 10*(9), 658–660. doi:10.1109/LCOMM.2006.1714536

Tickoo, O., & Sikdar, B. (2008). Modeling queueing and channel access delay in unsaturated IEEE 802.11 random access MAC based wireless networks. *IEEE/ACM Transactions on Networking, 16*(4), 878-891.

Tsertou, A., & Laurenson, D. I. (2008). Revisiting the hidden terminal problem in a CSMA/CA wireless network. *IEEE Transactions on Mobile Computing, 7*(7), 817–831. doi:10.1109/TMC.2007.70757

Uzcategui, R. A., De Sucre, A. J., & Acosta-Marum, G. (2009). Wave: a tutorial. *IEEE Communications, 47*(5), 126–133. doi:10.1109/MCOM.2009.4939288

Yadumurthy, R. M. H., A. C., Sadashivaiah, M., & Makanaboyina, R. (2005). Reliable MAC broadcast protocol in directional and omnidirectional transmissions for vehicular ad hoc networks. In *Proceedings of the 2nd ACM International Workshop on Vehicular Ad Hoc Networks (VANET2005)*, (pp. 10-19). Cologne, Germany.

Zhai, H., Wang, J., Chen, X., & Fang, Y. (2006). Medium access control in mobile ad hoc networks: challenges and solutions. *Wireless Communications & Mobile Computing, 6*(2), 151–170. doi:10.1002/wcm.376

Zhang, X., Su, H., & Chen, H.-H. (2006). Cluster-based multi-channel communications protocols in vehicle ad hoc networks. *IEEE Wireless Communications, 13*(5), 44–51. doi:10.1109/WCM.2006.250357

KEY TERMS AND DEFINITIONS

Cooperative Collision Avoidance (CCA): An application in VANET formed by moving vehicles to warn drivers of changing road conditions and danger ahead to avoid accident.

CSMA-based MAC Protocols: In Carrier Sense Multiple Access based protocols a node must sense the channel for a period of time and transmit its data only if the channel is idle.

Hidden Terminal: In a wireless network, hidden terminal refers to a station that is outside the transmission range of a tagged station but is within the receiving range of its receivers.

IEEE 802.11p: A draft standard for the MAC and physical layer in wireless LAN to support vehicular communications.

Medium Access Control (MAC): A protocol that provides a set of rules to govern medium access among several stations in the network.

Packet Delivery Ratio (PDR): Defined as the ratio of the number of packets successfully received by all the intended receivers to the total number of packets sent.

Vehicular Ad-Hoc Network (VANET): A non-infrastructure based network to provide wireless communications among nearby vehicles and between vehicles and nearby fixed equipment.

Chapter 7
Analyzing IEEE 802.11g and IEEE 802.16e Technologies for Single–Hop Inter–Vehicle Communication

Raúl Aquino-Santos
University of Colima, México

Víctor Rangel-Licea
National Autonomous University of México, México

Aldo L. Méndez-Pérez
Universidad Autónoma de Tamaulipas, México

Miguel A. Garcia-Ruiz
University of Colima, México

Arthur Edwards-Block
University of Colima, México

Eduardo Flores-Flores
University of Colima, México

ABSTRACT

This chapter analyzes two prominent technologies, IEEE 802.11g (WiFi) and IEEE 802.16e (WiMAX), for single-hop inter-vehicular communication (SIVC). We begin our analysis by comparing the physical and MAC layers of both standards. Following this, we simulate two scenarios, one with IEEE 802.11g and the other with IEEE 802.16e, in a single-hop inter-vehicular communication network. In both scenarios, the Location-Based Routing Algorithm with Cluster-Based Flooding (LORA-CBF) was employed to create a hierarchical vehicular organization that acts as a cluster-head with its corresponding member nodes. The simulation scenarios consist of five different node sizes of 20, 40, 60, 80 and 100 vehicles, respectively. We propose a novel simulation model that is suitable for mesh topologies in WiMAX networks and provide preliminary results in terms of delay, load and throughput for single-hop inter-vehicle communication.

DOI: 10.4018/978-1-61520-913-2.ch007

INTRODUCTION

Interest in inter-vehicular communication (IVC) and vehicle-to-roadside communication (VRC) has significantly increased over the last decade, in part, because of the proliferation of wireless networks. Most research in this area has concentrated on vehicle-to-roadside communication, also called beacon-vehicle communication (BVC) in which vehicles share the medium by accessing different time slots.

Some applications for vehicle-to-roadside communication, including Automatic Payment, Route Guidance, Cooperative Driving, and Parking Management have been developed to function within limited communication zones of less than 60 meters. However, the IEEE 802.11 Standard has led to increased research in the areas of wireless ad hoc networks and location-based routing algorithms, (Morris et. al., 2000), (Da Chen, Kung, & Vlah, 2001), (Füßler, et. al., 2003), (Lochert, et. al., 2003), (Kosh, Schwingenschlögl, & Ai, 2002). Applications for inter-vehicular communication include Intelligent Cruise Control, Intelligent Maneuvering Control, Lane Access, and Emergency Warning, among others. In (Morris et. al., 2000), the authors propose using Grid (Li, et. al., 2000), a geographic forwarding and scalable distributed location service, to route packets from car to car without flooding the network. The authors in (Da Chen, Kung, & Vlah, 2001) propose relaying messages in low traffic densities, based on a microscopic traffic simulator that produces accurate movement traces of vehicles traveling on a highway, and a network simulator to model the exchange of messages among the vehicles. Da Chen et. al., employ a straight bidirectional highway segment of one or more lanes. The messages are propagated greedily each time step by hopping to the neighbor closest to the destination. The authors in (Füßler, et. al., 2003) compare a topology-based approach and a location-based routing scheme. The authors chose Greedy Perimeter Stateless Routing (GPSR) (Karp & Kung,

2000) as the location-based routing scheme and Dynamic Source Routing (DSR) (Johnson, Maltz, & Hu, 2007) as the topology-based approach. The simulator used in (Füßler, et. al., 2003) is called FARSI, which is a macroscopic traffic model. In (Lochert, et. al., 2003), the authors compare two topology-based routing approaches, DSR and Ad Hoc On-Demand Distance Vector (AODV) (Perkins, Belding-Royer & Das, 2003), versus one position-based routing scheme, GPSR, in an urban environment. Finally, in (Kosh, Schwingenschlögl, & Ai, 2002), the authors employ a geocast routing protocol that is based on AODV.

In inter-vehicular communication, vehicles are equipped with on-board computers that function as nodes in a wireless network, allowing them to contact other similarity equipped vehicles in their vicinity. By exchanging information, vehicles can obtain information about local traffic conditions, which improves traffic control, lowers contamination caused by traffic jams and provides greater driver safety and comfort.

Future developments in automobile manufacturing will also include new communication, educational and entertainment technologies. The major goals are to provide increased automotive safety, achieve smoother traffic flow, and improve passenger convenience by providing information and entertainment. In order to avoid communication costs and guarantee the low delays required to exchange safety-related data between cars, inter-vehicular communication (IVC) systems, based on wireless ad hoc networks, represents a promising solution for future road communication scenarios. IVC allows vehicles to organize themselves locally in wireless ad hoc networks without any pre-installed infrastructure. Communication in future IVC systems will not be restricted to neighboring vehicles traveling within a specific radio transmission range. As in typical wireless scenarios, the IVC system will provide multi-hop communication capabilities by using "relay" vehicles that are traveling between the sender and receiver. Vehicles between the source-destination act as intermediate vehicles, relaying data to the receiver. As a result, the multi-hop capability of the IVC system significantly increases the virtual communication range, as it enables communication with more distant vehicles.

ORIGINS OF WIRELESS AD HOC NETWORKS

Historically, wireless ad hoc networks have primarily been used for tactical network-related applications to improve battlefield communications and survivability. The dynamic nature of military applications means it is not always possible to rely on access to a fixed pre-placed communication infrastructure on the battlefield. The Packet Radio Network (PRNET), under the sponsorship of the Defense Advanced Research Project Agency (DARPA), is considered the precursor of wireless ad hoc networks (MANET) (Toh, 2002).

PRNET was the first implementation of wireless ad hoc networks with mobile nodes, which was primarily inspired by the efficiency of packet switching technology, such as bandwidth sharing and store-and-forward routing and their possible application in wireless environments.

Survivable Radio Networks (SURANs) were deployed by DARPA in 1983 to address open issues in PRNET in the areas of network scalability, security, processing capability, and energy management. The main objectives of these efforts was to develop network algorithms to support networks that can scale to tens of thousands of nodes and can resist security attacks, as well as use small, low cost, low-power radio technology that can support more sophisticated packet radio protocols. This effort resulted in the design of Low-cost Packet Radio (LPR) technology in 1987, which featured a digitally controlled direct sequence spread spectrum (DSSS) radio with an integrated Intel 8086 microprocessor-based packet switch.

Although early MANET application and deployments were military oriented, non-military applications have grown substantially since then and have become the main focus today. This has been the case the last few years due to rapid advances in wireless ad hoc networks research. Wireless ad hoc networks have attracted considerable attention and interest from the commercial sector as well as the standards community. The introduction of new technologies such as IEEE 802.11g and IEEE 802.16e greatly facilitate the deployment of ad hoc technology outside of the military domain. As a result, many new ad hoc networking applications have since been conceived to help enable new commercial and personal communication beyond the tactical networks domain, including personal area networking, home networking, law enforcement operations, search-and-rescue operations, commercial and educational applications, sensor networks, and so on.

INTRODUCTION TO WIRELESS NETWORKS

The requirements of data communication, beyond the physical link, has resulted in the need for wireless networks (WNs), which have been fuelled by fabrication improvements of digital and radio frequency circuits, new large-scale circuit integration, and other miniaturization technologies that make portable radio equipment smaller, cheaper, and more reliable.

WNs represent flexible data communications systems that can be implemented as an extension to or as an alternative for, a wired Local Area Network (LAN). Using a form of electromagnetic radiation as the network medium, most commonly in the form of radio waves, wireless LANs transmit and receive data over air, minimizing the need for wired connections (cables). Thus, WNs combine data connectivity with user mobility. By combining mobile devices with wireless communications

Figure 1. Basic WLAN architectures: infrastructure and Ad hoc

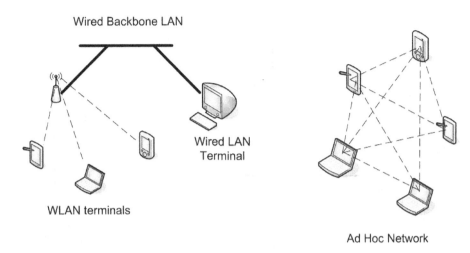

technologies, the vision of being connected at anytime and anywhere will soon become a reality.

Whereas today's expensive wireless infrastructure depends on centrally deployed hub and one-hop stations, wireless ad hoc networks consist of nodes that autonomously self-organize into networks. In wireless ad hoc networks, the nodes themselves and their intercommunicability comprise the network. This advantage permits seamless low cost communication in a self-organized fashion that can be easily deployed. The large degree of freedom and self-organizing capabilities of wireless ad hoc networks make them different from other networking solutions. For the first time, individuals have the opportunity to create their own networks, which can be deployed easily and inexpensively within the specified area determined by the specific needs and characteristics established by the user.

Ad hoc networks represent a key step in the evolution of wireless networks. However, they inherit many of the traditional problems of wireless and mobile communications such as bandwidth optimization, power control, and transmission quality enhancements. There are presently two standards that can be applied to single-hop inter-vehicular communications: IEEE 802.11g, and IEEE 802.16e.

IEEE 802.11 WLAN ARCHITECTURE

The IEEE 802.11 was the first international standard for WLANs (O'Hara, & Petrick, 1999). The basic service set (BSS) is the fundamental building block of the IEEE 802.11 architecture. A BSS is defined as a group of stations that are under the direct control of a single coordination function (e.g. Distribute Coordination Function (DCF) or Point Coordination Function (PCF)), which is defined below.

The geographical area covered by the BSS is known as the Basic Service Area (BSA), which is analogous to a cell in a cellular communication network. Conceptually, all stations in a BSS can communicate directly with all other stations in a BSS.

An ad hoc network is a defined group of stations that are organized into a single BSS for the purposes of inter-networked communications, without the aid of any additional network infrastructure. Figure 1 provides an illustration of a wireless infrastructure and independent BSS. The IEEE 802.11 Standard defines an ad hoc network as an independent BSS.

Any station can establish a direct communication session with any other station in the BSS in

Figure 2. IEEE 802.11 architecture

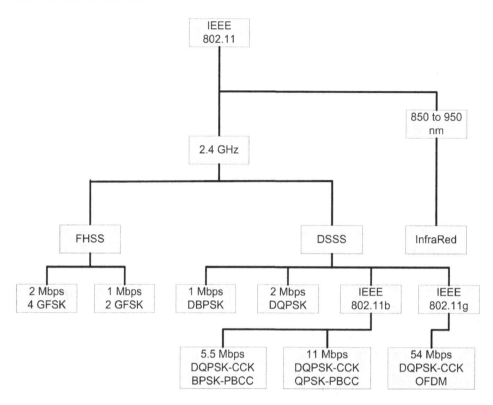

an ad hoc network, without having to channel all traffic through a centralized access point (AP).

PHYSICAL LAYER

The Institute of Electrical and Electronic Engineers (IEEE) specification calls for three different physical-layer implementations: Frequency Hopping Spread Spectrum (FHSS), Direct Sequence Spread Spectrum (DSSS), and Infrared. The FHSS utilizes the 2.4 GHz Industrial, Scientific, and Medical (ISM) band (e.g. 2.4- 2.4835 GHz). In the United States, a maximum of 79 channels are specified in the hopping set. The first channel has a central frequency of 2.402 GHz, and all subsequent channels are spaced at 1 MHz intervals. The 1 MHz separation is mandated by the Federal Communication Commission (FCC) for

the 2.4 GHz ISM band. The channel separation corresponds to 1 Mb/s of instantaneous bandwidth. Three different hopping sequence sets are established with 26 hopping sequences per set. Different hopping sequences enable multiple BSSs to coexist in the same geographical area, which may become necessary to alleviate congestion and maximize the total throughput of a single BSS. The minimum hop rate permitted is 2.5 hops/seconds. The basic access rate of 1 Mb/s uses two-level Gaussian frequency shift keying (GFSK). The enhanced access rate of 2 Mb/s uses four-level GFSK (Figure 2). The DSSS also uses the 2.4 GHz ISM frequency band, where the 1 Mb/s basic rate is encoded using differential binary phase shift keying (DBPSK), and a 2 Mb/s enhanced rate uses differential quadrature phase shift keying (DQPSK). The spreading is done by dividing the available bandwidth into 11 sub-channels, each 11

MHz wide, and using an 11-chip Barker sequence to spread each data symbol. The maximum channel capacity is therefore (11 chips/symbol)/ (11 MHz) = 1 Mb/s if DBPSK is used.

In October 1997, the IEEE 802 Executive Committee approved two extensions for higher data rate transmissions. The first extension, IEEE 802.11a, defines requirements for a PHY layer operating in the 5.0 GHz frequency and data rate transmission ranging from 6 Mbps to 54 Mbps. The second extension, IEEE 802.11b, defines a set of PHY layer specifications operating in the 2.4 GHz frequency band up to 11 Mbps. Both PHY layers are designed to operate with the existing MAC layer.

The IEEE 802.11a PHY is one of the physical layer extensions of IEEE 802.11 and is referred to as orthogonal frequency division multiplexing (OFDM) and the IEEE 802.11b is referred to as high rate direct sequence spread spectrum (HR/DSSS). The HR/DSSS PHY provides two functions. First, the HR/DSSS extends the packet service data unit (PSDU) data rates to 5.5 and 11 Mbps using an enhanced modulation technique, called Complementary Code Keying (CCK). Secondly, the HR/DSSS PHY provides a rate shift mechanism that allows 11 Mbps networks to fall back to 1 and 2 Mbps and interoperates with the legacy IEEE 802.11 standard. The most recent commercial standard is IEEE 802.11g, approved in June 2003, which we use in our simulation. The IEEE 802.11g standard provides optional data rates transmission of up to 54 Mbps, and requires compatibility with 802.11b devices to protect the substantial investments in today's WLAN installations. The 802.11g standard includes mandatory and optional components. It specifies OFDM and CCK as the mandatory modulation schemes with 24 Mbps as the maximum mandatory data rates, but it also provides for optional higher data rates of 36, 48 and 54 Mbps.

MEDIUM ACCESS CONTROL SUB-LAYER

The MAC sub-layer is responsible for channel allocation procedures, protocol data unit (PDU) addressing, frame formatting, error checking, and data fragmentation and reassembly.

The transmission medium can operate in the contention mode exclusively, requiring all stations to contend for access to the channel for each packet transmitted. The medium can also alternate between the contention mode, known as the contention period (CP) under the Distribute Coordination Function (DCF), and a contention-free period (CFP) under the Point Coordination Function (PCF). During the CFP, medium usage is controlled (or mediated) by the AP, thereby eliminating the need for stations to contend for channel access.

The DCF is the fundamental access method used to support asynchronous data transfer on a best effort basis. The DCF operates exclusively in ad hoc networks and is based on carrier sense multiple access with collision avoidance (CSMA/CA). In IEEE 802.11, carrier sensing is performed at both the air interface, referred to as physical carrier sensing and at the MAC sub-layer, also called virtual carrier sensing. Physical carrier sensing detects the presence of other IEEE 802.11 WLAN users by analyzing all detected packets and also detecting activity in the channel via relative signal strength from other sources.

A source station performs virtual carrier sensing by sending a MAC packet data unit (MPDU) duration information in the header of request-to-send (RTS), clear-to-send (CTS), and data frames. The duration field indicates the amount of time (in microseconds) after the end of the present frame. The channel will then be utilized to complete the successful transmission of the data or management frame. Stations in the BSS use the information in the duration field to adjust their network allocation vector (NAV), which indicates the amount of time that must elapse to complete a transmission session before the channel can be sampled again for idle status. The channel is marked busy if either the physical or virtual carrier sensing mechanisms indicates the channel is busy.

On the other hand, the PCF is an optional capability, which is connection-oriented, and provides contention-free (CF) frame transfer. The PCF relies on the point coordinator (PC) to perform polling, enabling polled stations to transmit without contending for the channel. The function of the PC is performed by the AP within each BSS.

PHYSICAL LAYER OF 802.11G

The 802.11g physical layer supports 4 modulation schemes (Vassis et al., 2005). Two of these schemes, extended rate PHY- orthogonal frequency division multiplexing (ERP-OFDM) and extended rate PHY- complementary code keying- direct sequence spread spectrum (ERP-CCK/DSSS), are mandatory and two, extended rate PHY-packet binary convolution coding (ERP-PBCC) and direct sequence spread spectrum-orthogonal frequency division multiplexing (DSSS-OFDM), are optional. Of the four schemes, only ERP-OFDM and DSSS-OFDM provide data rates of up to 54Mb/s using OFDM modulation schemes, while also providing explicit support for interoperating with 802.11b nodes. Such support is necessary as 802.11b nodes cannot detect or interpret OFDM modulated signals.

The ERP-OFDM scheme is a variant of the 802.11a PHY scheme modified for use in the 2.4 GHz band (Szczypiorski, and Lubacz, 2008). In this mode, all the data is sent by OFDM and can only be received by 802.11g stations. It is therefore known as 802.11g-only mode. The data rates are also 6, 9, 12, 18, 24, 36, 48, and 54 Mbps.

The ERP-CCK mode is used for compatibility with 802.11b stations. CCK stands for comple-

mentary code keying; the data rates supported are 5.5 and 11Mbit/s.

In the ERP-DSSS mode, data is transmitted using a technique called direct sequence spread spectrum (DSSS). ERP-DSSS provides backward compatibility with 802.11 stations supporting data rates of 1 and 2Mbit/s.

The ERP-PBCC mode is optional and rarely used. PBCC, or packet binary convolution coding, is used in conjunction with DSSS. The data rates achieved by ERP-PBCC are 5.5, 11, 22, and 33Mbit/s.

The DSSS-OFDM scheme is a hybrid modulation scheme that combines a DSSS and OFDM. DSSS is employed to transmit the header of a PHY frame. Doing so allows 802.11b devices to receive information and update their NAVs dynamically. Therefore, 802.11b stations and 802.11g stations can operate in the same network. The actual data is OFDM modulated and cannot be received by 802.11b stations. The data rates are 6, 9, 12, 18, 24, 36, 48, and 54Mbit/s.

PHY FRAMES

In order to transmit packets over the wireless link, the MAC frames are encapsulated into PHY frames. The format of the transmitted PHY protocol data unit (PPDU) consists of a physical layer convergence procedure (PLCP) preamble, a PLCP header and a packet service data unit (PSDU). Each PSDU consists of the MAC header, the frame body MAC service data unit (MSDU), and extra bits (Tail/Pad bits) (IEEE Std 802.11b, 1999).

Figure 3 shows the format of an ERP-OFDM PPDU, which is common to the 802.11g PHY standard. ERP-OFDM is the most often implemented PPDU in the 802.11g standard, and supports data rates of 6, 9, 12, 18, 24, 36, 48, and 54 Mbps. The ERP-OFDM PPDU has three parts: preamble, header, and data field. The PLCP preamble is carefully designed to enable synchronization. IEEE 802.11g typically uses the ERP-OFDM mode for

Figure 3. ERP-OFDM PPDU framing

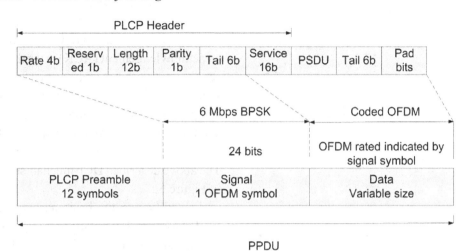

the PLCP format. With the ERP-OFDM preamble, it takes just 16μs to train the receiver after first detecting a signal on the radio frequency medium with respect to the 144μs for IEEE 802.11b. Failure in frame detection and/or synchronization results in a physical layer error. The ERP-OFDM header carries the essential information needed by the receiver to properly decode the rest of the frame. The data field consists of the service subfield, PSDU, tail subfield, and pad bits subfield. The service subfield consists of 16 bits, with the first 7 bits as zeros to synchronize the receiver descrambler. The remaining 9 bits are reserved for future use and set to all 0s. As part of the data field, the service subfield is transmitted at the rate specified in the signal field's rate subfield.

The 802.11g standard extends the use of the DSSS PHY by specifying an optional PPDU type consisting of the same DSSS preamble and header, but at the cost of accepting an ERP-OFDM PPDU as its PSDU. The IEEE calls this new PPDU type DSSS-OFDM. Both long and short preambles are supported with DSSS-OFDM, and no protection mechanisms are required by DSSS-OFDM stations when operating with DSSS stations present in the BSA. Figure 4 illustrates the construction of both long and short preamble formats for DSSS-OFDM

PPDUs. The preamble and header transmission rates apply to DSSS-OFDM as with DSSS.

MEDIUM ACCESS CONTROL OF 802.11G

The IEEE 802.11g standard builds on the MAC protocol specifications defined for legacy 802.11 networks (IEEE Std 802.11, 1999; IEEE Std 802.11a, 1999; IEEE Std 802.11b, 1999). In the 802.11 standard there are two different schemes that can be used in the medium control access.

When the Point Coordination Function (PCF) is employed, the access point controls access to the medium by assigning time slots to each station. The Distributed Coordination Function (DCF) on the other hand, needs no central coordinator. Because the PCF scheme is an optional access method of the 802.11 standard, only the functionality of the DCF will be described in this section. In addition, DCF defines a randomized access mechanism, which is based on the CSMA/CA (Carrier Sense Multiple Access/Collision Avoidance).

DCF constitutes the fundamental access mechanism of the original IEEE 802.11 standard. According to DCF, a wireless local area network

Figure 4. DSSS-OFDM PPDU framing, a) long preamble, b) short preamble

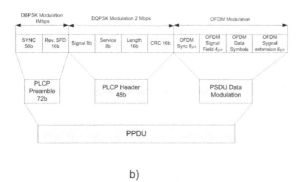

a)

b)

(WLAN) station must sense the medium before initiating the transmission of a packet. If the medium is sensed idle for a time interval greater than a distributed interframe space (DIFS), the station transmits the packet. Otherwise, the transmission is deferred and a backoff process begins. Specifically, the station initializes and begins decreasing a timer called a backoff counter. As soon as the backoff counter expires, the station is authorized to access the medium. The initial value of the backoff counter is defined as the backoff window, which is a random time interval uniformly distributed in the range of [0,CWmin − 1]. The parameter CWmin constitutes the minimum contention window and is doubled after each unsuccessful retransmission attempt up to a maximum value CWmax called the maximum contention window. Note that in the special case where the time elapsed between the last packet transmission and the current packet transmission is less than a DIFS, the station is obliged to execute the backoff process for the first transmission attempt. Given that collision detection is not possible in a WLAN environment, an acknowledgement (ACK) is used to notify the sending station that the transmitted frame has been successfully received. The transmission of the acknowledgement is initiated at a time interval equal to the short interframe space (SIFS) after the end of the reception of the transmitted frame. The above described DCF mechanism is depicted in Figure 5a.

In addition to the basic access mechanism, the IEEE 802.11 standard includes a protection mechanism for dealing with the hidden terminal problem (Kim et al., 2006). This mechanism is based on the exchange of two short control frames: a request-to-send (RTS) frame that is sent by a potential transmitter to the receiver and a clear-to-send (CTS) frame that is sent from the receiver in response to the RTS frame. The RTS and CTS frames include a duration field that specifies the time interval necessary to completely transmit the data frame and the related acknowledgement. Other stations can hear either the sender (RTS frame), or the receiver (CTS frame), in order to refrain from transmitting until the data frame transmission is completed. The effectiveness of the RTS/CTS mechanism depends upon the length of the packet being protected. Usually, a hybrid approach is used, where only packets with a size greater than a threshold called RTS Threshold are transmitted with the RTS/CTS mechanism. The operation of the RTS/CTS protection mechanism is depicted in Figure 5b. Moreover, this protection mechanism is used to improve the performance in 802.11b/g, and it communicates to 802.11g stations utilizing the CCK scheme. Another protection mechanism used in 802.11g is the CTS-to-self. In this protection mechanism, a station sends a CTS message when sends data, even though there is no RTS message received. Both of these mechanisms are designed to help reduce collisions.

Figure 5. Access mechanisms: a) basic, b) RTS/CTS

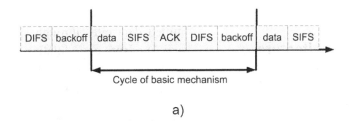

a)

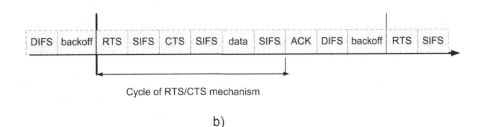

b)

Analysis of Throughput and Delay

Throughput is defined as the ratio of successfully transmitted payload from one node to another in a specified amount of time,

$$S = \frac{\text{successfully transmitted payload}}{\text{transmission time (delay)}}. \quad (1)$$

Taking into account the time diagram of the access mechanism (see Figure 5), we can derive the theoretical maximum achievable throughput (TMT) and minimum delay for IEEE 802.11g in both g-only and b/g modes. The following calculations assume ideal conditions for packet transmission, i.e., there is no packet loss.

In a scenario where the system is composed of both 802.11b and 802.11g stations (hybrid system), 802.11g can operate in an 802.11g ERP-OFDM scheme and ERP-CCK/DSSS (both mandatory). The 802.11b system, however, can only detect packets transmitted by ERP-CCK/DSSS, making it necessary to use a protection mechanism, such as that described previously. Therefore, the throughput is calculated as:

- ERP-CCK/DSS scheme:

$$S = \frac{MSDU_{size}}{T_{data} + T_{SIFS} + T_{ACK} + T_{DIFS} + T_{backoff}}, \quad (2)$$

and

- ERP-OFDM scheme:

$$S = \frac{MSDU_{size}}{T_{RTS} + T_{SIFS} + T_{CTS} + T_{SIFS} + T_{data} + T_{SIFS} + T_{ACK} + T_{DIFS} + T_{backoff}} \quad (3)$$

where:

TRTS is RTS time, TSIFS is SIFS time, TDIFS is DIFS time, Tdata is transmission time for the payload, TACK is ACK transmission time, and $T_{backoff} = \frac{CW_{min} T_{slot}}{2}$, where CWmin is the minimum backoff window size, and Tslot is a specified time slot.

If the system is composed only of 802.11g stations, it does not require the protection scheme.

Therefore, the throughput is calculated according to equation 2.

IEEE 802.16 WMAN Architecture

WiMAX (Worldwide Interoperability for Microwave Access) is an emerging wireless communication system that is expected to provide high data rate communications in metropolitan area networks (MANs). In the past few years, the IEEE 802.16 working group has developed a number of standards for WiMAX. The first standard was published in 2001, which supports communications in the 10-66 GHz frequency band. In 2003, IEEE 802.16a was introduced to provide additional physical layer specifications for the 2-11 GHz frequency band. These two standards were further revised in 2004 (IEEE 802.16-2004). Recently, IEEE 802.16e has also been approved as the official standard for mobile applications.

Physical Layer

In the physical layer, IEEE 802.16 supports four PHY specifications for the licensed bands. These four specifications are Wireless-MAN-SC (single carrier), -SCa, -OFDM, (orthogonal frequency – division multiplexing), and –OFDMA (orthogonal frequency – division multiple access). In addition, the standard also supports different PHY specifications (-SCa, -OFDM, and –OFDMA) for the unlicensed bands: wireless high-speed unlicensed MAN (WirelessHUMAN). Most PHYs are designed for non-line-of-sight (NLOS) operation in frequency bands below 11 GHz, except –SC, which is for operation in the 10-66 GHz frequency band. To support multiple subscribers, IEEE 802.16 supports both time-division duplex (TDD) and frequency-division duplex (FDD) operations.

The mobile version of IEEE 80.16 also supports the following features to enhance the performance of the wireless system: 1) multiple input, multiple output (MIMO) technique such as transmit/receive diversity multiplexing, 2)

multiple antennas schemes can also be used to increase the performance by increasing the transmitted data rates through spatial multiplexing, and 3) adaptive modulation and coding (AMC) is used to better match instantaneous channel and interference conditions.

Medium Access Control Sub-Layer

In the medium access control (MAC) layer, IEEE 802.16 supports two modes: point-to-multipoint (PMP) and mesh. The former organizes nodes into a cellular-like structure consisting of a base station (BS) and subscriber stations (SSs). The channels are divided into uplink (from SS to BS) and downlink (from BS to SS), and both uplink and downlink channels are shared among the SSs. PMP mode requires all SSs to be within the transmission range and clear line of sight (LOS) of the BS. On the other hand, in mesh mode, an ad hoc network can be formed with all nodes acting as relay routers in addition to their sender and receiver roles, although there may still be nodes that serve as BSs and provide backhaul connectivity.

In PMP, requests for resource allocations and data transmissions from SSs to the BS are carried in an uplink (UL) frame. Transmissions from the BS to SSs are carried by a downlink (DL) frame. A typical signaling frame for TDD includes a UL-frame (see Figure 6a) and a DL-frame (see Figure. 6b) using a single channel frequency as illustrated in Figure 6c. In FDD, these frames are transmitted at the same time using different channel frequencies as illustrated in Figure 6d.

The IEEE 802.16 MAC protocol regulates uplink (UL) channel access using time division multiple access (TDMA). Upon entering the broadband wireless access (BWA) network, each Subscriber Station (SS) has to go throughout the initialization process setup, described as follows:

Subscriber stations need to synchronize with a downlink channel and an uplink channel. When a SS has tuned to a downlink channel, it gets the

Figure 6. Frame structure for TDD and FDD access

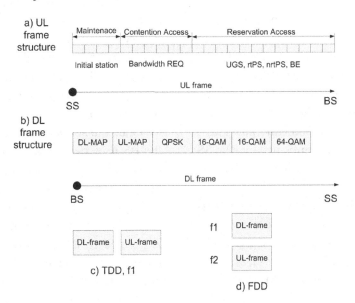

frame structure of the uplink channel, called a UL-MAP frame. Then a ranging procedure is performed, where the round-trip delay and power calibration are determined for each SS, so that SS transmissions are aligned to the correct mini-slot boundary. Following this, the SS negotiates basic capabilities with the BS. This is the phase where the SS and the BS exchange their supported parameters. Next, the SS should use the privacy key management (PKM) protocol to receive authentication from the BS. Then the SS performs the registration process by establishing a security association that allows the SS to enter the network. The next step is to establish IP connectivity. The BS uses the dynamic host configuration protocol (DHCP) mechanism to obtain an IP address for the SS and any other parameters needed to establish IP connectivity. Then, the SS establishes the time of the day, which is required for time-stamping logged events and key management. In the next step, the SS transfers control parameters via trivial file transfer protocol (TFTP), such as boot information, quality of service (QoS) parameters, fragmentation, and packing, among others. The last

step is to set up connections for pre-provisioned service flows belonging to the SS.

After the initialization process is completed, a SS can create one or more connections over which its data is transmitted to and from the BS. SSs contend for transmission opportunities using the contention access period (or contention block) of the current UL-frame. The BS collects these requests and determines the number of slots (grant size) that each SS will be allowed to transmit in the next UL-frame, using a UL_MAP sub-frame, as shown in Figure 6a. The UL-MAP frame contains Information Elements (IE), which describe the maintenance, contention or reservation access of the UL-frame. The UL-MAP is broadcasted in the DL channel by the BS in each DL-Frame. After receiving the UL-MAP, an SS can transmit data in the predefined reserved slots indicated in the IE. These reserved slots are transmission opportunities assigned by a scheduling algorithm using the following QoS service agreements.

Unsolicited Grant Service (UGS): This service supports real-time service flows that generate fixed-size data packets on a periodic basis (constant bit rate, CBR-like services), such as T1/

E1, voice over IP (VoIP) or videoconferencing. At the beginning of the connection setup, an SS provides the BS its service requirements, such as grant size, grant inter-arrival time, tolerated grant jitter and poll bit. The UGS service also includes Activity Detection (AD) to examine the flow state. If the state is inactive, then the UGS-AD service sets the poll bit to 1 and periodically provides a unicast transmission opportunity, in which an SS can request the BS reestablish its UGS service, thus saving bandwidth.

Real-Time Polling Service (rtPS): This service supports real-time service flows that generate variable size data packets on a periodic basis (variable bit rate, VBR-like services), such as moving picture expert group (MPEG) video streams. The rtPS service offers periodic transmission opportunity, which meets the flow's real-time needs and allows the SS to specify the size of the desired channel reservation. A SS should indicate its requirements to the BS at the beginning of the session, such as polling interval and tolerated poll jitter.

Non Real-Time Polling Service (nrtPS): This type of service is similar to rtPS. However, polling will typically occur at a much lower rate and may not necessarily be periodic. This applies to applications that have no requirement for a real time service but may need an assured high level of bandwidth. An example of this may be bulk data transfer (via file transfer protocol, FTP) or an Internet gaming application. The parameters required for this service are the polling interval, minimum and maximum sustained data rate.

Best Effort (BE): This kind of service is for standard Internet traffic, where no throughput or delay guarantees are provided.

The IEEE 802.16 MAC protocol can identify the type of service flow required by an SS using the following fields of the IEEE 802.16 protocol stack: source or destination MAC address, EtherType, source and destination IP address or network, IP protocol type, source or destination port number, IP type of service bits and any combination thereof.

A simple example of how a classification might be used would be to match VoIP traffic from a particular source IP address and user datagram protocol (UDP) port and to direct that traffic into a dynamically created service flow that has a QoS parameter set that provides a UGS mode of data transmission.

Once the service flows have been identified, the BS uses two modes of operation to allocate grants: 1) grants per connection (GPC) and grants per subscriber station (GPSS). In the first case, the BS grants bandwidth explicitly to each connection, whereas in the second case the bandwidth is granted to all the connections belonging to the SS. The latter case (GPSS) allows smaller uplink maps and allows more intelligent SSs to make last moment decisions and perhaps utilize the bandwidth differently than it was originally granted by the BS. This may be useful for real-time applications that require a faster response time from the system.

Analysis of Throughput and Delay for IEEE 802.16

This analysis only considers a best effort (BE) service. We start by describing the sequence of actions that takes place when a subscriber station (SS) makes use of a BE service for data transfer. When a SS is active, (let us say SS_x), it forms a continuous loop with the sequence of actions depicted in Figure 7. When a packet arrives from an upper layer protocol, the SS_x waits for the next UL-MAP containing a contention period. Then, the SS_x randomly chooses one of the available contention minislots and transmits a bandwidth request (REQ) indicating the packet length. If some other SS (let us say SS_y) selects the same contention minislot, a collision occurs and the subscriber stations (SS_x and SS_y) receive neither a grant nor an acknowledgement (ACK) in the following UL-MAP. Thus, the SS_x retransmits its REQ until it is successfully transmitted. Upon successful reception of a REQ from the SS_x, the BS converts the packet size to a number of minislots that should be reserved in subsequent UL-frames. In case the REQ from the SS_x does not fit in the next UL-frame, the BS sends a null grant to the SS_x in order to acknowledge the REQ.

Modeling of such events can be carried out by breaking down a single packet transmission into its delay components. Let us denote by i the time delay, measured in minislots, from the time a packet arrives from the upper layers until the beginning of the contention block where SS_x transmits its REQ. Let c represent the total time in minislots spent during contention, which starts with the beginning of the contention block where the SS_x transmits the first REQ, until SS_x receives an ACK (i.e., a null grant in the IEEE 802.16 protocol). Let us define by w the time in minislots that the scheduler takes in order to grant the REQ of the SS_x. This is measured from the ACK reception to the grant reception at the SS_x. At the BS, the scheduler serves REQs using a first input first output (FIFO) discipline. If the REQ from the SS_x cannot be granted in the next UL-frame, it waits until previous REQs from other SSs are served. Note that in case a REQ can be immediately served, instead of returning an ACK, the BS returns a grant indicating the number of minislots that were reserved. In this case, reception of such a grant also signals the end of the contention time c and therefore w is zero.

Finally, let us denote by x the delay component that represents the actual number of minislots spent during packet transmission from the SS_x. Figure 7 depicts the relation between the events described above and the delay components of the model. Therefore, the time to transmit a single packet (t) can be directly obtained by adding all delay components, i.e., $t=i+c+w+x$. By taking expectation on both sides of this equation we obtain:

$$\bar{t} = \bar{i} + \bar{c} + \bar{w} + \bar{x}. \tag{4}$$

Figure 7. Access delay components

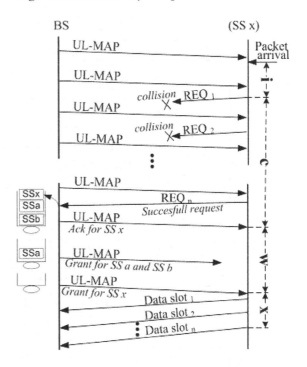

From these parameters, the normalized network throughput (γ) of the UL channel can be computed as the fraction of minislots actually spent in data transmission per station, scaled to the total number of SSs (N), thus:

$$\gamma = N\bar{x} / \bar{t} \tag{5}$$

The aim of this paper is to provide a method to compute this metric. The notation used in this derivation is presented in Table 1.

Regarding Eq. (5), it is necessary to compute $\bar{x}$ and $\bar{t}$. The mean delay for packet transmission in minislots (i.e. $\bar{x}$,) can be directly obtained from the packet size distribution, taking into consideration that minislots can be 2, 4, 8, 16, 32 or 64 bytes. Thus

$$\bar{x} - \left\lceil \frac{\bar{m} + MAC\_OV + PHY\_OV}{slot\_size} \right\rceil \tag{6}$$

Table 1. IEEE 802.16 MAC model notation

Symbol	Definition
C	Size of the contention block in a UL-frame
R	Size of the reservation period in a UL-frame
M	Total size of a UL-frame, $M=C+R$
i	Initial delay
c	Contention delay to transmit a REQ successfully
w	Time to grant a REQ for a SS
x	Time spent in a packet transmission
t	Total time in a transmission cycle, $t = i + c + w + x$
$\bar{i}$, $\bar{c}$, $\bar{w}$, $\bar{x}$, $\bar{t}$	Expectations of i, c, w, x, and t, respectively
P_{sc}	Probability of a successful contention in a UL-frame
n	Number of SSs contending in the current UL-frame
s	Number of SSs that transmitted a REQ successfully in the current UL-frame
$\bar{n}$, $\bar{s}$,	Expectations of n and s, respectively
$\bar{b}$	Expected number of contention periods per cycle, $\bar{t}$
N	Maximum number of active SSs
P_c	Probability that a SS contends in a contention period
P_s	Probability of a successful contention in a minislot
$\bar{d}$	Available transmission minislots for a SS per cycle
γ	System throughput

where $\bar{m}$ is the mean packet size at the logical link control (LLC) layer, *MAC_OV* is the MAC overhead of the IEEE 802.16 protocol (the default value for *MAC_OV* is 6 byes). The overhead at the physical layer, *PHY_OV,* depends on the coding techniques involved (see (IEEE 802.16-2004) Chapter 8, for further information on coding rates and modulation techniques).

Computation of $\bar{t}$ implies calculating other delay components as described below. Estimating the mean initial delay $\bar{i}$ has to consider the following three delay factors. First, packet arrival from an upper layer protocol may occur anywhere within the current UL-frame, thus the SS must wait for the next available contention block before transmitting a REQ. The mean value for this delay can be approximated by $M/2$ minislots, where M is

the total length of the UL-frame. Second, the SS has to wait a complete frame of size M minislots in order to transmit a REQ in the available contention block of the next UL-frame. Third, once the REQ is received, the BS may grant this REQ anywhere in the following UL-frame, which can also be approximately by $M/2$ minislots. Thus the initial delay, can be approximated as

$$\bar{i} \cong 2M. \tag{7}$$

Whereas computation of $\bar{x}$ and $\bar{i}$ is straightforward, computation of $\bar{c}$ and $\bar{w}$ is far more complicated. This procedure is described in the following sections.

Computation of the Contention Delay

For simplicity, we assume that the number of failed contentions that a SS needs to succeed follows a geometric distribution. Thus, given the probability of a successful contention in a contention block (P_{SC}), the mean number of minislots used for contention $\bar{c}$ would be given by

$$\bar{c} = C + M\frac{(1 - P_{SC})}{P_{SC}} \tag{8}$$

where C is the size of the contention block and M is the total length of a UL-frame (both measured in minislots).

Let $\bar{n}$ and $\bar{s}$ represent the expected number of the total and successful contenders in a contention block, respectively. It is clear that the probability P_{SC} can be estimated as

$$P_{SC} = \frac{\bar{s}}{\bar{n}} \tag{9}$$

Let us now turn our attention to the estimation of $\bar{n}$ and. $\bar{s}$ Let us denote by P_C the probability that a SS decides to contend in a contention block. Therefore, the expected number of contenders in a contention block is given by

$$\bar{n} = NP_C \tag{10}$$

and the number of successful contenders per contention block is

$$\bar{s} = \left(NP_C\right)P_{SC} \tag{11}$$

Note that there are $\bar{t}$ minislots per transmission cycle and one contention block every M minislots. Therefore, the mean number of contention blocks ($\bar{b}$) per transmission cycle is given by

$$\bar{b} = \frac{\bar{t}}{M} \tag{12}$$

Let us assume that the system is operating in steady state. Under this assumption, each active SS gets a chance to transmit every $\bar{t}$ minislots and parameter $\bar{s}$ can be estimated dividing the total number of SS among the mean number of contention blocks per transmission cycle as follows

$$\bar{s} = \frac{N}{\bar{b}} \tag{13}$$

Substituting (12) in (13) we obtain

$$\bar{s} = \frac{MN}{\bar{t}} \tag{14}$$

From (10) and (14) in (9) we can obtain

$$P_C = \frac{M}{P_{SC}\bar{t}} \tag{15}$$

Let us define the probability of successful contention in an arbitrary slot P_S as the probability that, from the mean number of contenders in a contention block $\bar{n}$, only *one* contends in a minislot (packet capture is not possible),

$$P_S = \binom{\bar{n}}{1}\frac{1}{C}\left(1 - \frac{1}{C}\right)^{\bar{n}-1} \tag{16}$$

Therefore, parameter $\bar{s}$ can be computed as

$$\bar{s} = CP_S \tag{17}$$

From (17) and (11) P_{SC} can be computed as

$$P_{SC} = \frac{CP_S}{NP_C} \tag{18}$$

Note that computation of $\bar{c}$ in (8) implies computation of P_{SC} which in turn depends on computation of P_C and P_S as indicated by (18). At this point, it is fair to mention that the authors in (Chite & Daigle, 2003) made use of these three probabilities in their analysis of IP-based services over general packet radio service (GPRS) networks. Although P_C and P_{SC} are computed here in the same way, the fact that we do not consider packet capture allows us to compute P_S in a fundamentally different way. Computation of this probability as defined by (16) is not equivalent to the method presented in (Chite & Daigle, 2003). This difference allows us to go one step further.

The authors in (Chite & Daigle, 2003) make use of the previously derived probabilities in order to iteratively compute P_{SC}. Although our model and theirs differ in several ways, we also make use of this procedure with good results. The procedure starts by assuming that $\bar{w}$ is known and providing an initial estimate for P_{SC}. Then, from (8), (4), (15) and (16) we compute P_C and P_S. These values are used in (18) in order to obtain the following value for P_{SC}. With this value the process can be repeated starting from (8). This loop can be ended when the difference between two consecutive values for P_{SC} is below a certain threshold. The final value for P_{SC} allows us to compute the value for the contention delay $\bar{c}$ using (8). Further adjustments on $\bar{w}$ would be needed if the assumed value for $\bar{w}$ does not satisfy all system conditions.

In what follows we derive the equation that represents the procedure just described. Let us identify with subindex n the n-th iteration. Thus, (8) and (4) become $\bar{c}_n = C + M\left(1 - P_{SC_n}/P_{SC_n}\right)$ and $\bar{t}_n = \bar{i} + \bar{c}_n + \bar{w} + \bar{x}$, respectively. From these equations, we derive

$$\bar{t}_n = \bar{i} + C + M\left(\frac{1 - P_{SC_n}}{P_{SC_n}}\right) + \bar{w} + \bar{x}. \qquad (19)$$

From (15) we know that $P_{Cn} = M\Big/\left(P_{SC_n}\bar{t}_n\right)$ which combined with (19) yields,

$$P_{Cn} = \frac{1}{\beta P_{SC_n} + 1} \qquad (20)$$

where $\beta = \left(\left(\bar{i} + C + \bar{w} + \bar{x}\right)\Big/M\right) - 1$

From (10) and (20) the estimated mean number of users at the n-th iteration is

$$\bar{n}_n = \frac{1}{\beta P_{SC_n} + 1}N. \qquad (21)$$

From (16) and (21) the estimated value of the probability of successful contention in an arbitrary slot at the n-th iteration is

$$P_{S_n} = \frac{N}{\beta P_{SC_n} + 1}\left(\frac{1}{C}\right)\left(1 - \frac{1}{C}\right)^{\frac{N}{\beta P_{SC_n} + 1} - 1}. \qquad (22)$$

Finally, from (20), (22) and (18) the difference equation that can be used to obtain the value of P_{SC} is

$$P_{SCn+1} = \left(1 - \frac{1}{C}\right)^{\frac{N}{\beta P_{SC_n} + 1} - 1}. \qquad (23)$$

In summary, given $\bar{w}$ and an initial estimate for P_{SC}, we iterate (23) until a consistent value for P_{SC} is obtained. With this value the contention delay $\bar{c}$ can be computed using (8). The algorithm implied by (23) is very easy to implement and it is much simpler than the one presented in [14].

Computation of the Waiting Delay

Recall that the value of $\bar{w}$ was assumed in the previously described procedure. It is necessary to determine whether this value needs to be adjusted or not. To this end, let us compute the mean number of available transmission minislots for each SS in an average transmission cycle. Let us denote this amount by $\bar{d}$. It is given by

$$\bar{d} = \frac{\bar{t} - C\bar{b}}{N}. \tag{24}$$

In addition, we know that the average number of transmission minislots required per SS is $\bar{x}$. Therefore, the minimum number of transmission minislots in a transmission cycle must be at least of $N\bar{x}$. If $\bar{d} < N\bar{x}$, we propose to increase $\bar{w}$ according to

$$\bar{w}_{m+1} = \bar{w}_m + 1. \tag{25}$$

and compute $\bar{c}$ again according to the procedure described in the previous section. If $\bar{d} \geq \bar{x}$, we can take the corresponding value of $\bar{w}$ and proceed to calculate the system throughput.

We could have updated $\bar{w}$ using larger steps as suggested in (Chite & Daigle, 2003), however increasing this value by one as shown in (25) provides good accuracy and the time to carry out this computations turns out to be negligible in a conventional computer.

Performance Analysis

The performance of the IEEE 802.16 system was analyzed using analytical and simulation models. A detailed simulation model of the IEEE 802.16 MAC protocol was implemented using OPNET Package v. 11 (Simulation software, 2009). For the simulation model, we used a network of 100 SSs distributed randomly in a cell with a radio of 5 km. Also, the minislot size was set to 16 bytes and the UL MAP describes M=450 minislots (=2ms) in the UL-frame. This corresponds to a 28.8 Mbps UL channel. All SSs used Best Effort technique for grant service. The traffic model

used by active SSs was Constant Bit Rate (CBR) service created from packets of 300 bytes at the MAC layer with a constant interarrival time of value $\bar{t}$. When these packets are coded at the physical layer of the IEEE 802.16 system, they become 21 minislots ($\bar{x}$ =21) using a codeword of 255 bytes, Reed Solomon parity of 10 bytes, preamble of 6 bytes and guard band of 4 bytes. In the simulation model, the size of the backoff window of the exponential backoff algorithm (EBA) was not allowed to grow. It was set at a fixed value according to the size of contention block used in the corresponding simulation (i.e., 30, 51, and 72 minislots). For the analytical model, we used an initial delay of $\bar{w}_0 = 1$ minislot and P_{SC0}=0.01.

We examined the throughput as a function of the number of active subscriber stations. Figure 8 shows the maximum system throughput as a function of the number of backlogged SSs. This figure includes the results of the analytical and simulation models with the number of contention minislots as a parameter.

For a small number of contention minislots per UL-frame, (i.e., $C = 30$ minislots), we observed that the maximum system throughput achieved with both models is approximately 52% of the channel capacity, which corresponds to a network with 40 SSs. This throughput is limited by the excessive number of collisions reported in each UL-frame. With 40 SSs, the average number of grants served per UL-frame was 11.6 of a total of $(M-C)/\bar{x}) = 21$ grants. The rest of the UL-frame was wasted, since just a few REQ could arrive to the BS due to collisions.

By increasing C to 51 minislots, the average number of grants served by a UL-frame increased considerably to 17, which nearly achieves 90% of system throughput when there are between 60 and 70 SSs. However, when there is a large number of SSs in the network, (i.e., more than 80 SSs) the system throughput cannot be maintained due to the large number of collisions reported.

Figure 8. Performance analysis of IEEE 802.16 based network

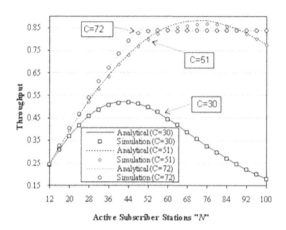

Figure 9. Initialization process of the mesh mode

With $C = 72$ minislots, the system throughput can be sustained even in very large networks. However, the maximum system throughput is just over 80% of channel capacity.

For the three values of C shown in Fig. 8, we observed that simulation results were in good agreement with analytical results. The maximum deviation from our simulation model was less than 3%.

Simulation Model for VANET

The initialization process at the mesh node carries out three principal phases: (1) the creation of the broadcast flow, (2) the neighbor discovery process and finally (3) the establishment of individual unicast flows for each of the neighbors, as show in Figure 9.

The generation of two broadcast flows, each with its corresponding connection identifier (CID), is one of the first processes carried out at the moment mesh nodes begin to interact. One of these flows is utilized to transmit the broadcast information generated in the upper layers of the mesh node (data), while the second flow is the control broadcast that sends information to the MAC layer. The discovery process and neighbor node localization is modeled by the simulator (software) which registers objects based on the

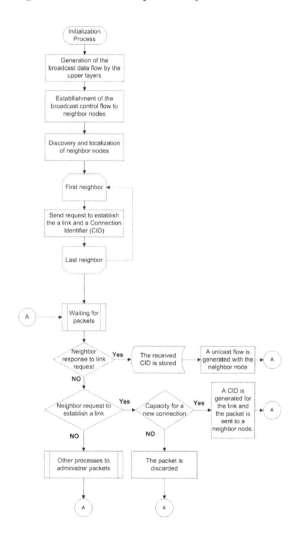

existing distances between each one of the nodes. For each neighbor node discovered, a unicast Hello message is sent to the upper data layers, which have the ability to administer the connection and accept the request, forwarding a response to the corresponding CID and establishing one of the points for the unicast flow connection. If the node responds affirmatively, it stores the request and establishes the other link point identified by a connection (CID) with the neighbor. In this way, it completes the other end point of the data flow. It is important to mention that, at some moment, the establishment of connections to the mesh node itself may be necessary. For this reason, mesh nodes should generate the identification and the connection and forward them, if possible, to the requesting node.

IEEE 802.11g (WiFi) and IEEE 802.16e (WiMAX) standards, respectively, include ad hoc and mesh topology in their specifications. However, to the best of our knowledge, there are no simulation results for vehicular ad hoc networks (VANETs) with mesh-WiMAX technology. In this work, we propose a new simulation model for VANETs with mesh architecture.

The advantage of our model is that it does not require a Base Station (BS), which is a compulsory element for point-to-multipoint architectures. Our simulation model has been implemented in OPNET Modeler (Simulation software, 2009). OPNET Modeler is an important network simulator that can be used to design and study communication networks, devices, protocols and applications. In addition, our simulation model is compatible with the PMP architecture.

The simulation model requires a new parameter to determine the direction of the communication. This is realized at the physical layer and is called a mesh link. The communication direction for the PMP architecture consists of a downlink and uplink; this is one important difference between mesh and the PMP architectures. Table 2, describes the main parameters utilized in the simulation model.

Simulation Scenarios

The simulation scenarios were implemented in OPNET Modeler. The scenarios simulate and compare two emerging wireless technologies, IEEE 802.11g and IEEE 802.16e, in a vehicular ad hoc network (VANET) of 20, 40, 60, 80 and 100 vehicular nodes uniformly distributed within a 200m x 200m area (Figure 10). We employed the Orthogonal Frequency Division Multiplexing (OFDM) at the physical layer and the Carrier Sense Multiple Access with Collision Avoidance (CSMA/CA) at the MAC layer for IEEE 802.11g (Scenario 1). Scenario 2 employs OFDM in the physical layer and Time Division Multiple Access (TDMA) in the MAC layer, as specified by IEEE 802.16e. Both scenarios consider one broadcast transmitter and 20, 40, 60, 80 and 100 broadcast receivers under a constant transmission range of 1000m. The simulation scenarios have a constant bit rate (CBR) for data flow and a uniform payload size of 512 bytes. The simulation parameters are listed in Tables 3 and 4.

The Location Based Routing Algorithm with Cluster-Based Flooding (LORA-CBF) was employed for single-hop inter-vehicle communications (Santos et al., 2005), (Santos et al., 2009).

Each vehicle detects neighboring vehicles to which it has a direct link. To accomplish this, each vehicle periodically broadcasts a Hello message containing its address and status. These control messages are transmitted in broadcast mode and are received by all one-hop neighbors. Data packets start at 100 seconds and are resent every second until the end of the simulation.

Results Obtained By Simulations

Figure 11 shows the delay for scenarios 1 and 2. IEEE 802.11g technology does not suffer any impact in delay because of the LORA CBF algorithm. However, IEEE 802.16e technology suffers a minimal impact in terms of delay; for 20 vehicles, the delay is almost 7.0 ms, for 40 vehicles 5.5 ms,

Table 2. Simulation parameters for the mesh WiMAX model

Parameters	Value
Antenna Gain (dBi)	-1 dB
Maximum Number of SS Nodes	10
Minimum Power Density (dBm/subchannel)	-90
Maximum Power Density (dBm/subchannel)	-60
CDMA Codes: Number of Initial Ranging Codes	8
CDMA Codes: Number of HO Ranging Codes	8
CDMA Codes: Number of Periodic Ranging Codes	8
CDMA Codes: Number of Bandwidth Request Codes	8
Back Off Parameters: Ranging Back Off Start	2
Back Off Parameters: Ranging Back Off End	4
Back Off Parameters: Bandwidth Request Back Off Start	2
Back Off Parameters: Bandwidth Request Back Off End	4
Neighbor Advertisement Interval (frames)	10
Neighborhood ID	0
Scanning Interval Definitions: Scanning Threshold (dB)	0.0
Scanning Interval Definitions: Scan Duration (N) (Frames)	5
Scanning Interval Definitions: Interleaving Interval (P) (Frames)	240
Scanning Interval Definitions: Scan Interaction (T)	10
Scanning Interval Definitions: Start Frame (M) (Frames)	5
Handover Parameters: Resource Retain Time (100 milliseconds)	2 (200 milliseconds)
Channel Quality Averaging Parameter	4/16
Distance Neighbors	1000 mts.
MAC Address	Auto Assigned
Maximum Transmission Power (W)	0.01
Mesh Role	Uncoordinated
PHY Profile	Wireless OFDMA 20 MHz
PHY Profile Type	OFDM
Multipath Chanel Model	ITU Pedestrian A
Path loss Model	Free Space
Terrain Type (Suburban Fixed)	Terrain Type A
Shadow Fading Standard Deviation	Disable Shadow fading
Ranging Power Step (mW)	0.25
Timers: T3 (ms)	50
Timers: T4 (ms)	10
Contention Ranging Retries	16

Figure 10. Simulation Scenario for WiFi and WiMAX models

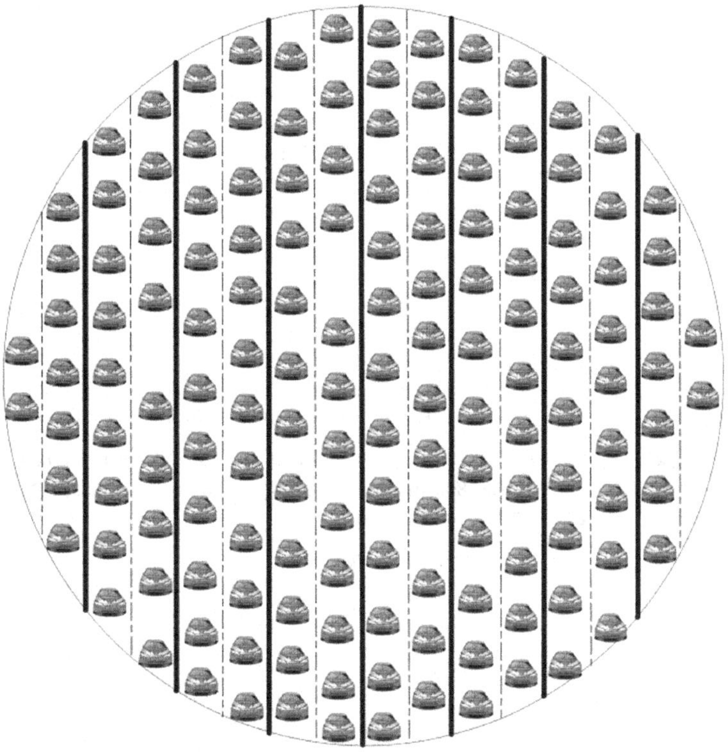

Table 3. Simulation parameters for scenario 1

Parameter	Value
Simulation area	200 m x 200 m
Total nodes	20, 40, 60, 80 and 100
Channel capacity	54 Mbps
MAC protocol	IEEE 802.11g
Packet flows	Constant bit rate (CBR)
Packet payload	512 bytes
Physical layer	OFDM
Simulation time	200 seconds
Frequency	2.4 GHz

Table 4. Simulation parameters for scenario 2

Parameter	Value
Simulation area	200 m x 200 m
Total nodes	20, 40, 60, 80 and 100
Channel capacity	54 Mbps
MAC protocol	IEEE 802.16e
Packet flows	Constant bit rate (CBR)
Packet payload	512 bytes
Physical layer	OFDM
Simulation time	200 seconds
Frequency	3.5 GHZ

for 60 vehicles 4.8 ms, for 80 vehicles 4.4, and for 100 vehicles 4.2 ms. The results of these two simulations permit us to infer that the delay for IEEE 802.16e technology is approximately 4 ms.

Figure 12 shows the load for scenarios 1 and 2. There is no impact in load for IEEE 802.11g

technology because of the LORA-CBF algorithm. However, for IEEE 802.16e technology, there is a significant impact in terms of load; for 20 vehicles, the load is almost 100,000 b/s, for 40 vehicles 230,000 b/s, for 60 vehicles 500,000 b/s, for 80 vehicles 900,000 b/s and for 100 vehicles 1.3 Mb

Figure 11. Delay for scenarios 1 and 2

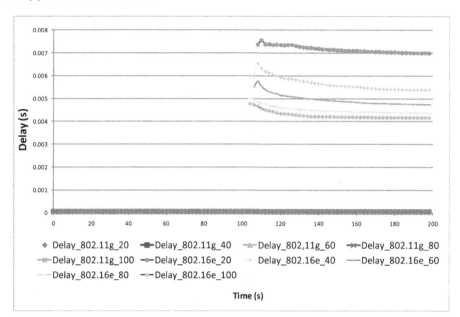

Figure 12. Load for scenarios 1 and 2

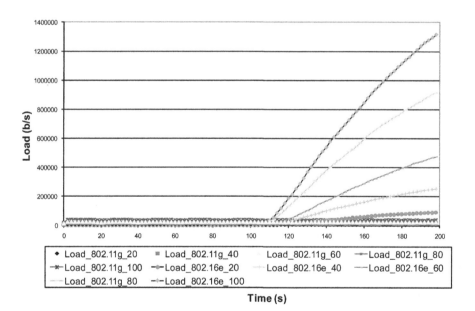

Figure 13 shows the throughput for scenarios 1 and 2. Again, there is no impact in throughput for IEEE 802.11g technology due to the LORA-CBF algorithm. However, for IEEE 802.16e technology, there is an impact in terms of throughput; for 20 vehicles the throughput is less than 5 Mb/s, for 40 vehicles is less than 10 Mb/s, for 60 vehicles is approximately 20 Mb/s, for 80 vehicles approximately 50 Mb/s and for 100 vehicles approximately 90 Mb/s.

Figure 13. Throughput for scenarios 1 and 2

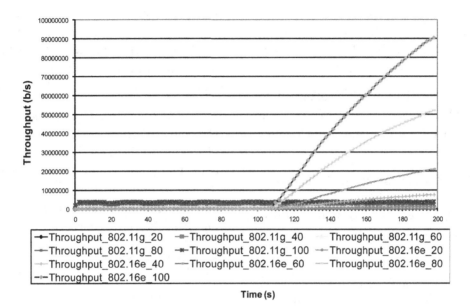

CONCLUSION

This chapter provided the results of two prominent technologies used for single-hop inter-vehicular communications (WiFi and WiMAX). We simulated similar scenarios employing both technologies and applied a Location Based Routing Algorithm with Cluster-Based Flooding (LORA-CBF) for broadcast data transmission. In addition, we considered a hierarchical vehicular organization that acts as a cluster-head with its corresponding member nodes. The simulation scenarios consisted of node sizes of 20, 40, 60, 80 and 100 vehicles, respectively. We provided preliminary results in terms of delay, load and throughput for single-hop inter-vehicle communications. Results show that WiMAX requires several processes before the node can begin transmitting data. These processes produce some delay, which impacts the previously mentioned metrics. However, WiMAX outperforms WiFi in terms of throughput. Finally, another important advantage is that the proposed model is suitable for a mesh topology in a WiMAX network and is compatible with the PMP architecture.

REFERENCES

Aquino-Santos, R., Rangel-Licea, V., García-Ruiz, M. A., González-Potes, A., Álvarez-Cárdenas, O., & Edwards-Block, A. (2009). Inter-vehicular Communications using Wireless Ad Hoc Networks. In Guo, H. (Ed.), *Automotive Informatics and Communicative Systems: Principals in Vehicular Networks and Data Exchange* (pp. 120–138). Hershey, PA: IGI Global.

Chite, V. A., & Daigle, J. N. (2003). Performance of IP-Based Services over GPRS. *IEEE Transactions on Computers, 52*(6), 727–741. doi:10.1109/TC.2003.1204829

Da Chen, Z., Kung, H. T., & Vlah, D. (2001, October). *Ad Hoc Relay Wireless Networks over Moving Vehicles on Highways*. Poster session presented at the Proceedings of the International Conference on Mobile Computing and Networking, Long Beach, CA (pp. 247-250). New York, NY, USA: ACM.

Füßler, H., Mauve, M., Hartenstein, H., Käsemann, M., & Vollmer, D. (2003). MobiCom Poster: Location-Based Routing for Vehicular Ad hoc Networks. *ACM SIGMOBILE Mobile Computing and Communication Review, 7*(1), 47–49.

IEEE802.16-2004 (2004). IEEE Standard for Local and Metropolitan Area Networks - Part 16: Air Interface for Fixed Broadband Wireless Access Systems.

Johnson, D., Maltz, D., & Hu, Y. C. (2007). *The Dynamic Source Routing Protocol (DSR) for Mobile Ad Hoc Networks for IPv4.* Retrieved from http://www.ietf.org/rfc/rfc4728.txt

Karp, B., & Kung, H. T. (2000, August). *GPSR:Greedy Perimeter Stateless Routing for Wireless Networks.* Paper presented at the Proceedings of the 6th ACM International Conference on Mobile Computing and Networking, Boston, Massachusetts (pp. 243-254). New York, NY, USA: ACM.

Kim, Y., Yu, J., Choi, S., & Jang, K. (2006). A novel hidden station detection mechanism in IEEE 802.11 WLAN. *IEEE Communications Letters, 10*(8), 608–610. doi:10.1109/LCOMM.2006.1665126

Kosh, T., Schwingenschlögl, C., & Ai, L. (2002, September). *Information Dissemination in Multihop Inter-vehicle Networks – Adapting the Ad hoc On-demand Distance Vector Routing Protocol (AODV).* Paper presented at the Proceedings in the 5th IEEE International Conference on Intelligent Transportation Systems, Singapore (pp. 685-690). USA: IEEE.

Li, J., Jannotti, J., De Couto, D., Karger, D., & Morris, R. (2000, August). *A Scalable Location Service for Geographic Ad Hoc Routing.* Paper presented at the Proceedings of the 6th ACM International Conference on Mobile Computing and Networking, Boston, Massachusetts (pp. 120-130). New York, NY, USA: ACM.

Lochert, C., Füßler, H., Hartenstein, H., Hermann, D., Tian, J., & Mauve, M. (2003, June). *A Routing Strategy for Vehicular Ad Hoc Networks in City Environments.* Paper presented at the Proceedings of the IEEE Intelligent Vehicles Symposium, Columbus, Ohio (pp. 156-161). USA: IEEE.

Morris, R., Jannotti, J., Kaashock, F., Li, J., & Decouto, D. (2000, September). *A Scalable Ad Hoc Wireless Network System.* Paper presented at the Proceedings of the 9th workshop on ACM SIGOPS European Workshop: beyond the PC: new challenges for the operating system, Kolding, Denmark (pp. 61-65). New York, NY: ACM.

O'Hara, B., & Petrick, A. (1999). *The IEEE 802.11 Handbook: A Designer's Companion.* Washington, DC: IEEE Press.

Perkins, C., Belding-Royer, E., & Das, S. (2003). *Ad hoc On-Demand Distance Vector (AODV) Routing.* Retrieved from http://www.ietf.org/rfc/rfc3561.txt

Santos, R. A., Edwards, A., Edwards, R. M., & Seed, N. L. (2005). Performance evaluation of routing protocols in vehicular ad hoc networks. *International Journal of Ad Hoc and Ubiquitous Computing, 1*(1/2), 80–91. doi:10.1504/IJA-HUC.2005.008022

Simulation software. (n.d.). Simulation software. Retrieved May 1, 2009, from http://www.opnet.com/solutions/network_rd/modeler.html

IEEE Std. 802.11. (1999). *Part 11: Wireless LAN Medium Access Control (MAC) and Physical Layer (PHY) Specifications.*

IEEE Std. 802.11a. (1999). Part *11*: Wireless LAN Medium Access Control (MAC) and Physical Layer (PHY) Specifications: High-speed Physical Layer in the 5GHz Band.

IEEEStd. 802.11b. (1999). Part 11: Wireless LAN Medium Access Control (MAC) and Physical Layer (PHY) Specifications: Higher-speed Physical Layer Extension in the 2.4GHz Band.

IEEEStd. 802.11g. (2003). Part 11: Wireless LAN Medium Access Control (MAC) and Physical Layer (PHY) Specifications- Amendment 4: Further Higher Data Rate Extension in the 2.4GHz Band.

Szczypiorski, K., & Lubacz, J. (2008). Saturation throughput analysis of IEEE 802.11g (ERP-OFDM) networks. *Telecommunication Systems*, *38*(1-2), 45–52. doi:10.1007/s11235-008-9090-4

Toh, C. K. (2002). *Ad Hoc Mobile Wireless Networks: Protocols and Systems*. Upper Saddle River, NJ: Prentice-Hall International, Inc.

Vassis, D., Kormentzas, G., Rouskas, A., & Maglogiannis, I. (2005). The 802.11g Standard for High Data Rate WLANs. *IEEE Network*, *19*(3), 21–26. doi:10.1109/MNET.2005.1453395

APPENDIX A: TABLE OF ACRONYMS

Table of Acronyms

ACK	Acknowledgement
AD	Activity Detection
AODV	Ad Hoc On-Demand Distance Vector
AMC	Adaptive Modulation and Coding
AP	Access Point
BE	Best Effort
BS	Base Station
BSA	Basic Service Area
BSS	Basic Service Set
BVC	Beacon-Vehicle Communication
BWA	Broadband Wireless Access
CBR	Constant Bit Rate
CCK	Complementary Code Keying
CFP	Contention-Free Period
CID	Connection Identifier
CP	Contention Period
CSMA/CA	Carrier Sense Multiple Access with Collision Avoidance
CTS	Clear-to-Send
DARPA	Defense Advanced Research Project Agency
DBPSK	Differential Binary Phase Shift Keying
DCF	Distribute Coordination Function
DHCP	Dynamic Host Configuration Protocol
DIFS	Distributed InterFrame Space
DL	Downlink
DQPSK	Differential Quadrature Phase Shift Keying
DSR	Dynamic Source Routing
DSSS	Direct Sequence Spread Spectrum
DSSS-OFDM	Direct Sequence Spread Spectrum-Orthogonal Frequency Division Multiplexing
EBA	Exponential Backoff Algorithm
ERP-CCK/DSSS	Extended Rate PHY- Complementary Code Keying- Direct Sequence Spread Spectrum
ERP-OFDM	Extended Rate PHY- Orthogonal Frequency Division Multiplexing
ERP-PBCC	Extended Rate PHY-Packet Binary Convolution Coding
FCC	Federal Communication Commission
FDD	Frequency-Division Duplex
FHSS	Frequency Hopping Spread Spectrum
FIFO	First Input First Output
FTP	File Transfer Protocol

continued on following page

GFSK	Gaussian Frequency Shift Keying
GPC	Grants per Connection
GPSS	Grants per Subscriber Station
HR/DSSS	High Rate Direct Sequence Spread Spectrum
IEEE	Institute of Electrical and Electronic Engineers
IE	Information Elements
IP	Internet Protocol
ISM	Industrial, Scientific, and Medical
IVC	Inter-Vehicular Communication
GPRS	General Packet Radio Service
GPSR	Greedy Perimeter Stateless Routing
LAN	Local Area Network
LLC	Logical Link Control
LORA-CBF	Location-based Routing Algorithm with Cluster-Based Flooding
LOS	Line Of Sight
LPR	Low-Cost Packet Radio
MAC	Medium Access Control
MANs	Metropolitan Area Networks
MANET	Mobile Ad hoc Network
MIMO	Multiple Input Multiple Output
MPDU	MAC Packet Data Unit
MPEG	Moving Picture Expert Group
MSDU	MAC Service Data Unit
NAV	Network Allocation Vector
NLOS	Non-Line-Of-Sight
nrtPS	Non Real-Time Polling Service
OFDM	Orthogonal Frequency Division Multiplexing
OFDMA	Orthogonal Frequency Division Multiple Access
PCF	Point Coordination Function
PDU	Protocol Data Unit
PKM	Privacy Key Management
PLCP	Physical Layer Convergence Procedure
PMP	Point-to-Multipoint
PPDU	PHY Protocol Data Unit
PRNET	Packet Radio Network
PSDU	Packet Service Data Unit
QoS	Quality of Service
REQ	Bandwidth Request
RTS	Request-to-Send
rtPS	Real Time Polling Service
SIFS	Short InterFrame Space
SIVC	Single-hop Inter-Vehicular Communication Network

continued on following page

SSs	Subscriber Stations
SURANs	Survivable Radio Networks
TDD	Time-Division Duplex
TDMA	Time Division Multiple Access
TFTP	Trivial File Transfer Protocol
UDP	User Datagram Protocol
UGS	Unsolicited Grant Service
UL	Uplink
VANETs	Vehicular Ad Hoc Networks
VBR	Variable Bit Rate
VoIP	Voice over IP
VRC	Vehicle-to-Roadside Communication
WiFi	Wireless Fidelity
WiMAX	Worldwide Interoperability for Microwave Access
WirelessHUMAN	Wireless High-speed Unlicensed MAN
WLAN	Wireless Local Area Network
WNs	Wireless Networks

Chapter 8
Survey of Routing Protocols in Vehicular Ad Hoc Networks

Kevin C. Lee
UCLA, USA

Uichin Lee
UCLA, USA

Mario Gerla
UCLA, USA

ABSTRACT

The chapter provides a survey of routing protocols in vehicular ad hoc networks. The routing protocols fall into two major categories of topology-based and position-based routing. The chapter discusses the advantages and disadvantages of these routing protocols, explores the motivation behind their design and trace the evolution of these routing protocols. Finally, it concludes the chapter by pointing out some open issues and possible direction of future research related to VANET routing.

INTRODUCTION

With the sharp increase of vehicles on roads in the recent years, driving has not stopped from being more challenging and dangerous. Roads are saturated, safety distance and reasonable speeds are hardly respected, and drivers often lack enough attention. Without a clear signal of improvement in the near future, leading car manufacturers decided to jointly work with national government agencies to develop solutions aimed at helping drivers on the roads by anticipating hazardous events or avoiding bad traffic areas. One of the outcomes has been a

novel type of wireless access called Wireless Access for Vehicular Environment (WAVE) dedicated to vehicle-to-vehicle and vehicle-to-roadside communications. While the major objective has clearly been to improve the overall safety of vehicular traffic, promising traffic management solutions and on-board entertainment applications are also expected by the different bodies (C2CCC[1], VII[2], CALM[3]) and projects (VICS[4] (Yamada, 1996), CarTALK 2000 (Reichardt D, 2002), NOW[5], CarNet (Morris R, 2000), FleetNet (Franz, 2001)) involved in this field.

When equipped with WAVE communication devices, cars and roadside units form a highly dynamic network called a Vehicular Ad Hoc Network (VANET), a special kind of Mobile Ad-Hoc

DOI: 10.4018/978-1-61520-913-2.ch008

Figure 1. Taxonomy of various routing protocols in VANET

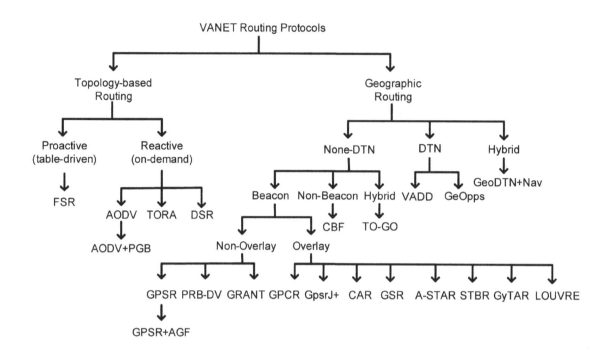

Networks (MANETs). While safety applications mostly need local broadcast connectivity, it is expected that some emerging scenarios (Lee, 2009) developed for intelligent transportation systems (ITS) would benefit from unicast communication over a multi-hop connectivity. Moreover, it is conceivable that applications that deliver contents and disseminate useful information can flourish with the support of multi-hop connectivity in VANETs.

Although countless numbers of routing protocols (Mauve, 2001; Mehran, 2004) have been developed in MANETs, many do not apply well to VANETs. VANETs represent a particularly challenging class of MANETs. They are distributed, self-organizing communication networks formed by moving vehicles, and are thus characterized by very high node mobility and limited degrees of freedom in mobility patterns.

As shown in Figure 1, there are two categories of routing protocols: topology-based and geographic routing. Topology-based routing uses the

information about links that exist in the network to perform packet forwarding. Geographic routing uses neighboring location information to perform packet forwarding. Since link information changes in a regular basis, topology-based routing suffers from routing route breaks.

Despite many surveys already published on routing protocols in MANETs (Mauve, 2001; Mehran, 2004Giordano, 2003; Stojemnovic, 2004), a survey of newly developed routing protocols specific to VANETs has long been overdue. Li et al. (2007) have made an effort to introduce VANET routing protocols, yet there is still deficiency in a thorough and comprehensive treatment on this subject. A discussion of VANET topics and applications is incomplete without detailed coverage of relevant routing protocols and their impact on overall VANET architecture. In this book chapter, we seek to provide the missing building blocks by detailing the advances in VANET routing protocols. Section III describes

Figure 2. Three categories of VANET network architecture

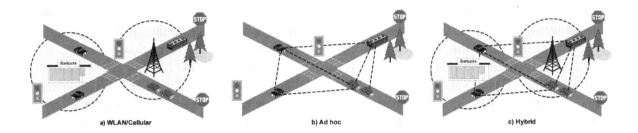

a) WLAN/Cellular   b) Ad hoc   c) Hybrid

the VANET architecture and its characteristics. Section IV presents a survey of these protocols experimented on or tailored to VANET and their advantages and disadvantages. It will explore the motivation behind their design and trace the evolution of these routing protocols. Finally, Section V will point out some open issues and possible direction of future research, and then conclude the book chapter.

NETWORK ARCHITECTURE AND CHARACTERISTICS

According to Figure 2, the architecture of VANETs falls within three categories: pure cellular/WLAN, pure ad hoc, and hybrid. In pure cellular/WLAN architecture, the network uses cellular gateways and WLAN access points to connect to the Internet and facilitate vehicular applications. Vehicles communicate with the Internet by driving by either a cellular tower or a wireless access point.

Since the infrastructure of cellular towers and wireless access points are not necessarily widely deployed due to costs or geographic limitations, nodes may only engage in communication with each other. Information collected from sensors on a vehicle can become valuable in notifying other vehicles about traffic condition and helping the police solve crimes (Lee, 2006). The infrastructure-less network architecture is in the pure ad hoc category where nodes perform vehicle-to-vehicle communication with each other.

When there are roadside communication units such as a cellular tower and an access point and vehicles are equipped with wireless networking devices, vehicles can take advantage of the infrastructure in communicating with each other. Various applications in areas of urban monitoring, safety, driving assistance, and entertainment (Lee, 2006) have used infrastructure communicating units to access dynamic and rich information outside their network context and share this information in a peer-to-peer fashion through ad hoc, infrastructureless communication. The hybrid architecture of cellular/WLAN and ad hoc approaches provides richer contents and greater flexibility in content sharing.

Similar to mobile ad hoc networks (MANETs), nodes in VANETs self-organize and self-manage information in a distributed fashion without a centralized authority or a server dictating the communication. In this type of network, nodes engage themselves as servers and/or clients, thereby exchanging and sharing information like peers. Moreover, nodes are mobile, thus making data transmission less reliable and suboptimal. Apart from these characteristics, VANETs possess a few distinguishing characteristics, presenting itself a particular challenging class of MANETs:

Highly dynamic topology. Since vehicles are moving at *high* speed, the topology formed by VANETs is *always* changing. On highways, vehicles are moving at the speed of 60 mph (25 m/sec). Suppose the radio range between two vehicles is 250 m. Then the link between the two vehicles lasts at most 10 sec.

Frequently disconnected network (Intermittent connectivity) The highly dynamic topology results in frequently disconnected network since the link between two vehicles can quickly disappear while the two nodes are transmitting information. The problem is further exacerbated by heterogeneous node density where frequently traveled roads have more cars than non-frequently traveled roads. Moreover, (non) rush hours only result in disparate node density, thus disconnectivity. A robust routing protocol needs to recognize the frequent disconnectivity and provides an alternative link quickly to ensure uninterrupted communication.

Patterned Mobility. Vehicles follow a certain mobility pattern that is a function of the underlying roads, the traffic lights, the speed limit, traffic condition, and drivers' driving behaviors. Because of the particular mobility pattern, evaluation of VANET routing protocols only makes sense from traces obtained from the pattern. There are various VANET mobility trace generators developed for the very purpose of testing VANET routing protocols in simulation. Realistic mobility traces gathered from vehicles (Jetcheva, 2003) have also been gathered for the same purpose.

Propagation Model. In VANETs, the propagation model is usually not assumed to be free space because of the presence of buildings, trees, and other vehicles. A VANET propagation model should well consider the effects of free standing objects as well as potential interference of wireless communication from other vehicles or widely deployed personal access points.

Unlimited Battery Power and Storage. Nodes in VANETs are not subject to power and storage limitation as in sensor networks, another class of ad hoc networks where nodes are mostly static. Nodes are assumed to have ample energy and computing power. Therefore, optimizing duty cycle is not as relevant as it is in sensor networks.

On-board Sensors. Nodes are assumed to be equipped with sensors to provide information useful for routing purposes. Many VANET routing protocols have assumed the availability of GPS unit from on-board Navigation system. Location information from GPS unit and speed from speedometer provides good examples for plethora of information that can possibly be obtained by sensors to be utilized to enhance routing decisions.

ROUTING PROTOCOLS

A routing protocol governs the way that two communication entities exchange information; it includes the procedure in establishing a route, decision in forwarding, and action in maintaining the route or recovering from routing failure. This section describes recent *unicast* routing protocols proposed in the literature where a single data packet is transported to the destination node without any duplication due to the overhead concern. Some of these routing protocols have been introduced in MANETs but have been used for comparison purposes or adapted to suit VANETs' unique characteristics. Because of the plethora of MANET routing protocols and surveys written on them, we will only restrict our attention to MANET routing protocols used in the VANET context. Figure 1 illustrates the taxonomy of these VANET routing protocols which can be classified as topology-based and geographic (position-based) in VANET.

Topology-Based Routing Protocols

These routing protocols use links' information that exists in the network to perform packet forwarding. They can further be divided into proactive (table-driven) and reactive (on-demand) routing.

Proactive (Table-Driven)

Proactive routing carries the distinct feature: the routing information such as the next forwarding

Figure 3. AODV route discovery

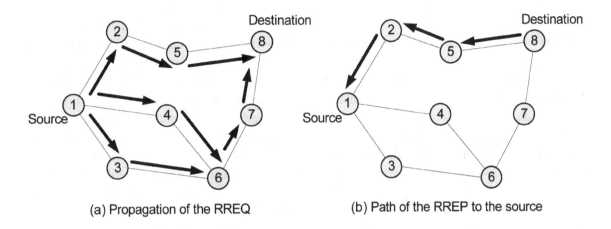

(a) Propagation of the RREQ

(b) Path of the RREP to the source

hop is maintained in the background regardless of communication requests. Control packets are constantly broadcast and flooded among nodes to maintain the paths or the link states between any pair of nodes even though some of paths are never used. A table is then constructed within a node such that each entry in the table indicates the next hop node toward a certain destination. The advantage of the proactive routing protocols is that there is no route discovery since route to the destination is maintained in the background and is always available upon lookup. Despite its good property of providing low latency for real-time applications, the maintenance of unused paths occupies a significant part of the available bandwidth, especially in highly mobile VANETs.

Fisheye State Routing (Iwata, 1999; Pei, 2000) is an efficient link state routing that maintains a topology map at each node and propagates link state updates with only immediate neighbors not the entire network. Furthermore, the link state information is broadcast in different frequencies for different entries depending on their hop distance to the current node. Entries that are further away are broadcast with lower frequency than ones that are closer. The reduction in broadcast overhead is traded for the imprecision in routing. However,

the imprecision gets corrected as packets approach progressively closer to the destination.

Reactive (On Demand)

Reactive routing opens a route only when it is necessary for a node to communicate with another node. It maintains only the routes that are currently in use, thereby reducing the burden on the network. Reactive routings typically have a route discovery phase where query packets are flooded into the network in search of a path. The phase completes when a route is found.

AODV – In Ad Hoc On Demand Distance Vector (AODV) (Perkins, 1999) routing, upon receipt of a broadcast query (RREQ), nodes record the address of the node sending the query in their routing table (Figure 3a). This procedure of recording its previous hop is called *backward learning*. Upon arriving at the destination, a reply packet (RREP) is then sent through the complete path obtained from backward learning to the source (Figure 3b). At each stop of the path, the node would record its previous hop, thus establishing the *forward* path from the source. The flooding of query and sending of reply establish a full duplex path. After the path has been established, it is maintained as long as the source uses it. A link failure will be reported recursively to the source and will in turn trigger another query-response procedure to find a new route.

AODV+PGB – Preferred Group Broadcasting (PGB) (Naumov, 2006) is a broadcasting mechanism that aims to reduce broadcast overhead associated with AODV's route discovery and to provide route stability especially important in VANETs where fast moving vehicles are used as wireless hosts. Based on the received signal of the broadcast, receivers can determine whether they are in the preferred group and which one in the group to broadcast. Since only one node is allowed to broadcast and since the preferred group is not necessarily the one that makes the most progress towards the destination, route discovery might take longer than before. Another drawback is that broadcast can discontinue if the group is found to be empty (possibly because of sparse networks). Packet duplication can happen as two nodes in the preferred group can broadcast at the *same* time. According to Naumov et al. (2006), the way to deal with broadcast duplication is to add packet's predecessors into the packet. This creates the same type of overhead in the packet as DSR.

DSR – Dynamic Source Routing (DSR) (Johnson, 1996) uses *source routing*, that is, the source indicates in a data packet's the sequence of intermediate nodes on the routing path. In DSR, the query packet copies in its header the IDs of the intermediate nodes that it has traversed. The destination then retrieves the entire path from the query packet (a la source routing), and uses it to respond to the source. As a result, the source can establish a path to the destination. If we allow the destination to send multiple route replies, the source node may receive and store multiple routes from the destination. An alternative route can be used when some link in the current route breaks. In a network with low mobility, this is advantageous over AODV since the alternative route can be tried before DSR initiates another flood for route discovery.

There are two major differences between AODV and DSR. The first is that in AODV data packets carry the destination address, whereas in DSR, data packets carry the full routing information. This means that DSR has potentially more routing overheads than AODV. Furthermore, as the network diameter increases, the amount of overhead in the data packet will continue to increase. The second difference is that in AODV, route reply packets carry the destination address and the sequence number, whereas, in DSR, route reply packets carry the address of each node along the route.

TORA – Temporally Ordered Routing Algorithm (TORA) (Park, 2007) routing belongs to a family of link reversal routing algorithms where a directed acyclic graph (DAG) toward the destination is built based on the height of the tree rooted at the source. The directed acyclic graph directs the flow of packets and ensures reachability to all nodes. When a node has a packet to send, it broadcasts the packet. Its neighbor only broadcasts the packet if it is the sending node's downward link based on the DAG.

A node would construct the directed graph by broadcasting a query packet. Upon receiving a query packet, if a node has a downward link to the destination, it will broadcast a reply packet; otherwise, it simply drops the packet. A node, upon receiving a reply packet, will update its height only if the height from the reply packet gives the minimum of all the heights from reply packets it has received so far. It then rebroadcasts the reply packet.

The advantages of TORA are that the execution of the algorithm gives a route to *all* the nodes in the network and that it has reduced far-reaching control messages to a set of neighboring nodes. However, because it provides a route to all the nodes in the network, maintenance of these routes can be overwhelmingly heavy, especially in highly dynamic VANETs.

Evaluation of the Topology-Based Routing

Jaap et al. (2005) has evaluated AODV, DSR, FSR, and TORA in city traffic scenarios on the network simulator ns-2. The city mobility model is based on a Manhattan-like road network of eight horizontal and vertical roads. The speed of the vehicles is determined based on the Intelligent-Driver Model (IDM) where a vehicle's speed is adjusted by other surrounding vehicles and road topology such as intersections (Helbing 2002). From their simulation, it is shown that AODV has the best performance and lowest control overhead. It is followed by FSR, DSR, and then TORA. DSR suffers from a very high delay because source routes change continuously due to high mobility. Its route overhead is comparable to FSR yet higher than AODV since DSR keeps route information within the packet header. The common characteristic among all four routing protocols is that performance degrades as network densities increase, indicating their scalability problem.

Lochert et al. (2003) conducted an evaluation study of Geographic Source Routing (See Section on GSR), AODV, and DSR in a small part of a map of Berlin. The movements of 955 vehicles are simulated by the traffic flow simulator Videlio (Kronjäger, et al., 1999) that incorporates a special lane changing model. The evaluation also considers a basic form of *obstacle modeling* in the propagation model. The obstacle modeling states that spaces between streets are assumed to be buildings and, therefore, radio waves cannot propagate through them. Simulation results have shown that AODV performs better than DSR for the same reason mentioned above because large packet overhead creates a significant bandwidth overload and mobility causes frequent route breakage. However, both of the topology-based reactive routing protocols do not perform as good as GSR.

Naumov et al. (2006) compared AODV, AODV+PGB, and GPSR (see later Section for the description of GPSR). The paper obtains its mobility trace of a 250 km x 260 km area of the city of Zurich, Switzerland from Multi-agent Traffic Simulator (MTS) developed by ETH Zurich. The propagation model is probabilistic Shadowing Model that considers the non-uniform non circular behavior of radio waves due to blockage. Results indicate that AODV+PGB performs better than AODV and GPSR in all node densities because of constant broadcast overhead. Comparing AODV and GPSR alone, as density of vehicles increases in both city and highway scenarios, the packet delivery ratio of AODV decreases and becomes worse than that of GPSR; and the overhead of AODV increases and becomes higher than that of GPSR. The problem of "the high administrative load" comes from frequent route breaks due to mobility and consequent route rediscovery through flooding.

Geographic (Position-Based) Routing

In geographic (position-based) routing, the forwarding decision by a node is primarily made based on the position of a packet's destination and the position of the node's one-hop neighbors. The position of the destination is stored in the header of the packet by the source. The position of the node's one-hop neighbors is obtained by the beacons sent periodically with random jitter (to prevent collision). Nodes that are within a node's radio range will become neighbors of the node. Geographic routing assumes each node knows its location, and the sending node knows the receiving node's location by the increasing popularity of Global Position System (GPS) unit from an onboard Navigation System and the recent research on location services (Flury, 2006; Li, 2000; Yu, 2004), respectively. Since geographic routing protocols do not exchange link state information and do not maintain established routes like proactive and reactive topology-based routings do, they are more robust and promising to the highly dynamic environments like VANETs.

In other words, route is determined based on the geographic location of neighboring nodes as the packet is forwarded. There is no need of link state exchange nor route setup.

Figure 1 sub-classifies Geographic routing into three categories of non-Delay Tolerant Network (non-DTN), Delay Tolerant Network (DTN), and hybrid. The non-DTN types of geographic routing protocols do not consider intermittent connectivity and are only practical in densely populated VANETs whereas DTN types of geographic routing protocols do consider disconnectivity. However, they are designed from the perspective that networks are disconnected by default. Hybrid types of geographic routing protocols combine the non-DTN and DTN routing protocols to exploit partial network connectivity. We describe these three sub-categories in the following:

Non-DTN – Overlay

The fundamental principle in the greedy approach is that a node forwards its packet to its neighbor that is closest to the destination. The forwarding strategy can fail if no neighbor is closer to the destination than the node itself. In this case, we say that the packet has reached the *local maximum* at the node since it has made the *maximum* local progress at the current node. The routing protocols in this category have their own recovery strategy to deal with such a failure.

GPSR – In Greedy Perimeter Stateless Routing (GPSR) (Karp, 2000), a node forwards a packet to an immediate neighbor which is geographically closer to the destination node. This mode of forwarding is termed *greedy mode*. When a packet reaches a local maximum, a recovery mode is used to forward a packet to a node that is closer to the destination than the node where the packet encountered the local maximum. The packet resumes forwarding in greedy mode when it reaches a node whose distance to the destination is closer than the node at the local maximum to the destination.

GPSR recovers from a local maximum using *perimeter mode* based on the right-hand rule shown in Figure 4. The rule states that when a node x first enters into the recovery mode, its next forwarding hop y is the node that is sequentially counterclockwise to the virtual edge formed by x and destination D. Afterwards, the next hop z is sequentially counterclockwise to the edge formed by y and its previous node x shown in Figure 4. While walking the face, however, if the edge yz formed by the current node and the next hop crosses the virtual edge xD and results in a point that is closer than the previous intersecting point x, perimeter mode will perform a *face change* in that the next hop w is chosen sequentially counterclockwise to the edge yz where the closer intersecting point was found. Such routing is called *face routing* because the packet traverses many faces formed by nodes in the network until it reaches a node closer to the destination than where the packet entered in the perimeter mode and where the face routing started.

Note that if the graph is not planar, that is, there are cross edges in the graph, routing loops may occur. Consider Figure 5, x tries to reach D in perimeter mode. The packet will eventually loop around face 3 with no intersecting point closer than p. Had the cross edge ut been removed, the packet would travel the exterior face u, s, x, v, t, and w to reach D. Given that perimeter mode must operate on planar graphs to avoid routing loops, GPSR provided two distributed algorithms that produce Relative Neighborhood Graph (RNG) (Toussaint, 1980) and Gabriel Graph (GG) (Gabriel, 1969) which are known to be planar. Both RNG and GG algorithms yield a connected planar graph so long as the connectivity between two nodes obeys the unit graph assumption: for any two vertices, they must be connected by an edge if the distance between them is less than or equal to some threshold distance d and must not be connected by an edge if the distance between them is greater than d. However, the unit graph assumption is not true in VANETs due to channel

Figure 4. Right-hand rule in GPSR's perimeter mode; packet performs face routing to route along Face 1, Face 2, and Face 3 toward destination D

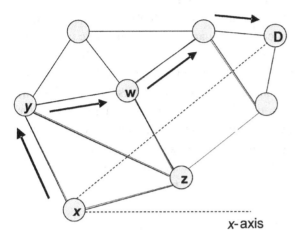

Figure 5. On the left, packet will loop around face 3; on the right, packet will eventually route to D through u, s, x, v, t, and w

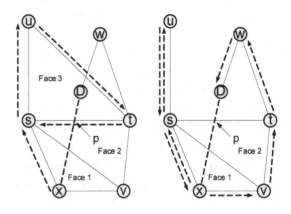

fading (obstacles and mobility). As a result, planar graphs are usually hard to achieve in VANETs.

F¨ußler in 2002 proposed a work to compare the results in packet delivery between GPSR and DSR in the highway scenario and showed that the successfully delivered packets for DSR diminish when the communication distance becomes larger. This is due to the fact that DSR needs to maintain a route from the sender. The maintenance becomes harder when the length of the route increases. GPSR packet delivery remains at close to 100% despite larger communication distance. The topology of highway favors GPSR since local maximum rarely happens on a highway. However, results of this work established GPSR to be used in a vehicular environment.

GPSR+AGF – Naumov et al. (2006) observed two problems with GPSR in VANETs. First, due to the mobile nature of VANETs, a node's neighbor table often contains outdated information of neighbors' position. The problem can be solved by increasing beacons' frequency, yet such a solution only increases congestion and brings in potential collisions. The second problem is that the destination's location within the packet is never updated despite the destination is moving. To ad-

dress these two problems, the authors proposed Advanced Greedy Forwarding (AGF) that incorporates the speed and direction of a node in the beacon packet and the total travel time, including the time to process the packet, up to the current forwarding node within the data packet. With the velocity vector, speed plus direction, each node can filter out outdated nodes in its neighbor table. With the total travel time, each forwarding node can better determine the deviation of the destination's original location and estimate its current location. Results have shown at least three times of improvement in packet delivery ratio to GPSR.

PRB-DV – Position-Based Routing with Distance Vector Recovery (PBR-DV) uses AODV-style recovery as packets fall into a local maximum. The node at the local maximum would broadcast a request packet in which is the node's position and destination's location. Upon receiving a request packet, a node would first check if it is closer to the destination than the node at the local maximum. If it is not, it records the node from which it receives the request packet (similar to backward learning) and rebroadcasts the request; otherwise, it sends a reply to the node from which it receives the request. As the reply packet travels back to the local maximum node, every intermediate node will record the previous node from which it receives the reply packet so that the local maximum node can maintain a route to a closer node than itself. The disadvantage of this scheme is that addition flooding is necessary to discover the non-greedy part of the route. There is no evaluation done comparing PRB-DV to GPSR nor AODV thus performance in packet delivery and overhead is inconclusive.

GRANT – Greedy Routing with Abstract Neighbor Table (GRANT) (Schnaufer, 2008) uses the concept of *extended greedy routing* where every node knows its *x* hop neighborhood. This gives every node a far sighted vision of the best route to take to avoid local maximum. The metric in selecting the next forwarding neighbor *E* is based on the multiplication of the distance between the node *N*, *x* hop away from *E* and the destination, the shortest path from *N* to *E*, and the charge per hop for multihop neighbors. The neighbor *E* that offers the smallest such metric will be chosen to be the next hop. Because transmitting *x*-hop neighbors in the beacon is too much overhead, GRANT separates the plane into areas and includes only one representative neighbor per area. Upon receiving a beacon, a node computes the area that the broadcasting node and its neighbors belong to, thus categorizing them into different hops from the current node.

The evaluation is based on snapshots of placement of cars from a uniform distribution. The propagation model is based on an important property of a city scenario that there are many radio obstacles such as buildings and trees. The model makes a simple assumption that nodes on different streets cannot hear each other because of radio obstacles. Results show that most of the routes in GRANT have shorter path length than traditional greedy routing. The number of times the packet is recovered per route is also less in GRANT than in traditional greedy routing. GRANT with Face routing as the recovery strategy is also compared to GRANT with Distance Vector-based recovery (similar to PRG-DV described above). The number of hops per recovery is way less in GRANT with

Distance Vector-based recovery than GRANT with Face routing. Despite the disadvantage of short-range flooding, Distance Vector recovery is robust to radio obstacles that plague Face routing[6]. Since the evaluation is done on static traces and the *x*-hop neighbors are assumed to be available, the beacon overhead and possible inaccuracy are not measured and well understood. In addition, although there are more paths that have smaller path length than traditional greedy routing on a normalized percentage basis, there is no absolute performance metric such as packet delivery ratio that can validate its true performance.

Overlay

An overlay routing has the characteristic that the routing protocol operates on a set of representative nodes *overlaid* on top of the existing network. In the urban environment, it is not hard to observe that decisions are made at junctions as these are the places where packets make turns onto a different road segment. Therefore, the overlaid routing protocols presented below have something to do with nodes at junction.

GPCR – Because nodes are highly mobile in VANETs, node planarization can become a cumbersome, inaccurate, and continuous process. In their work of Greedy Perimeter Coordinator Routing (GPCR), Lochert et al. (2005) have observed that urban street map naturally forms a planar graph such that node planarization can be completely eliminated. In this new representation of the planar graph using the underlying roads, nodes would forward as far as they can along roads in both greedy and perimeter mode and stop at junctions where decision about which next road segment to turn into can be determined. Figure 6 shows an example of GPCR forwarding where node *A* would forward packets to node *B* at a junction even though node *A*'s radio range covers node *C*.

GPCR not only eliminates the inaccuracy of node planarization, but also improves routing

Figure 6. GPCR routing along junctions

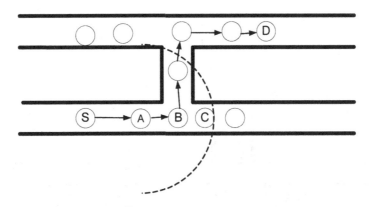

performance as packets travel shorter hops in the perimeter mode. Furthermore, the improved routing decision keeps packets from being routed to the wrong direction that often leads to higher delay. GPCR does not rely on a map to determine whether a node is located at a junction, but rather provides two heuristics to determine whether a node is a junction. The first heuristic uses beacon messages and determines a node x is located at a junction if it has two neighbors y and z that are within the range of each other but do not list each other as neighbors. The second heuristic is derived from a *correlation coefficient* that relates a node to its neighbors. A correlation coefficient close to 0 shows there is no linear relationship between the positions of the neighbors. This indicates the node is located at a junction. Their evaluation, based on a dedicated vehicular traffic simulator, has shown that packet delivery rate does increase over GPSR.

GpsrJ+ – GpsrJ+ (Lee, 2007) removes the unnecessary stop at a junction while keeping the efficient planarity of topological maps. It uses two-hop neighbor beaconing to predict which road segment its neighboring junction node will take. If the prediction indicates that its neighboring junction will forward the packet onto a road with a different direction, it forwards to the junction node; otherwise, it bypasses the junction and forwards the packet to its furthest neighboring

node. Figure 7 illustrates the advantage of prediction. The figure shows that GpsrJ+ can bypass the junction area and forward the packet to node E directly, yet GPCR forwards it to the junction node B, thus causing more transmissions. In the perimeter mode, GpsrJ+ uses the right-hand rule to determine the best direction (as opposed to final destination direction) and thereby the best forwarding node. That is, if the furthest node is in the same direction as the best direction, the best forwarding node is the furthest node; otherwise, the best forwarding node is a junction node. GpsrJ+ manages to increase packet delivery ratio of GPCR and reduces the number of hops in the recovery mode by 200% compared to GPSR.

CAR – Following their work on Preferred Group Broadcast (PGB) to minimize broadcast from AODV route discovery and Advanced Greedy Forwarding (AGF) to account for node mobility, Naumov et al. (2007) presented Connectivity-Aware Routing (CAR) in VANETs. CAR uses AODV-based path discovery to find routes with limited broadcast from PGB. However, nodes that form the route record neither their previous node from backward learning nor their previous node that forwards the path reply packet from the destination. Rather, *anchor points*, which are nodes near a crossing or road curve, are recorded in the path discovery packet. A node determines itself as an anchor point if its velocity vector is

Figure 7. Dashed arrows are GpsrJ+ and solid arrows are GPCR

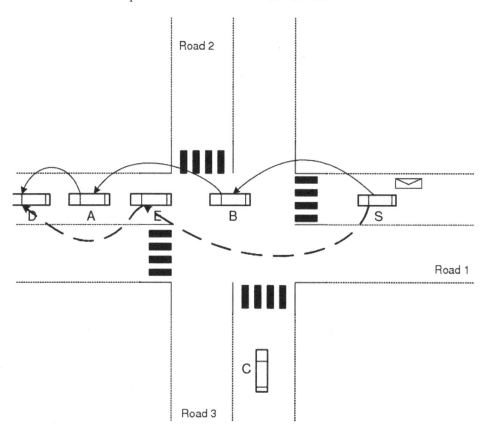

not parallel to the velocity vector of the previous node in the packet. The destination might receive multiple path discovery packets; it chooses the path that provides better connectivity and lower delays.

AGF is then used to forward the route reply back to the source via the recorded anchor points. When the source receives the route reply, it records the path to the destination and starts transmitting. Data packets are forwarded in a greedy manner toward the destination through the set of anchor points using AGF. In addition to handle mobility by AGF, CAR introduces "guards" to help to tack the current position of a destination. A guarding node can filter or redirect packets or adds information to a packet that will eventually deliver this information to the packet's destination.

The evaluation was done using a vehicular simulator and a probabilistic shadowing propagation model that uses a statistical approach to takes into account signal blockage. Results have shown CAR possesses higher packet delivery ratio (PDR) than GPSR and GPSR+AGF. The reason that CAR's PDR is higher than GPSR+AGF is that CAR guarantees to find the shortest connected path whereas GPSR+AGF may suffer from subopti- mality of greedy mode in terms of finding such a path. CAR's path discovery overhead is checked by PGB. The overhead of storing guard is not in the data packets but in the beacons. According to their finding, a node on average only broadcasts 2-3 guards during the simulation. Thus, the beacon overhead is not overwhelming.

GSR – Geographic Source Routing (GSR) (Lochert et al., 2003) relies on the availability of a map and computes a Dijkstra shortest path on the overlaid graph where the vertices are junction nodes and the edges are streets that connect those vertices. The sequence of junctions establishes the route to the destination. Packets are then forwarded greedily between junctions. GSR does not consider the connectivity between two junctions; therefore, the route might not be connected through. Recovery when such a case happens is greedy forwarding. The major difference between GSR and CAR is that CAR does not use a map and it uses proactive discovery of anchor points that indicate a turn at a junction.

As mentioned above, the movements of 955 vehicles are simulated by the traffic flow simulator Videlio (Kronjäger, 1999), that incorporates a special lane changing model. The evaluation also considers a basic form of *obstacle modeling* as the propagation model. Simulation results have shown that GSR performs better than AODV and DSR in packet delivery ratio. In a densely populated network, most roads are connected that GSR forwards most of the packets. Scalability is not a problem to GSR as to AODV and DSR. However, GSR is not compared with other position-based routing protocols. Its performance in sparse networks is not verified.

A-STAR – Anchor-Based Street and Traffic Aware Routing (A-STAR) (Seet, 2004) is similar to GSR in that packets are routed through anchor points of the overlay. However, A-STAR is traffic aware: the traffic on the road determines whether the anchor points of the road will be considered in the shortest path. A-STAR routes based on two kinds of overlaid maps: a statically rated map and a dynamically rated map. A statistically rated map is a graph that displays bus routes that typically imply stable amount of traffic. Dijkstra paths computed over the statistically rated map are in general connected because of the extra knowledge. A dynamically rated map is a map that is generated based on the real-time traffic condition on the roads. Road-side deployment units can monitor the city traffic condition and distribute this information to every vehicle. Thus, the difference between a statically rated map and a dynamically rated map is accuracy of road traffic; while a statically rated map is based on bus

routes that typically have high traffic volume, a dynamically rated map is based on the traffic monitored dynamically by road-side units.

A-STAR also proposes a different recovery algorithm when the packet gets stuck due to disconnectivity of the current path to the destination. The node will recompute a new anchor path and the road segment where the packet is currently located will be marked as "out of service" temporarily to prevent other packets from entering into the same problem. The notification of "out of service" is piggybacked in the recovered packets. Nodes that receive the recovered packets update their map and recomputed anchor paths accordingly.

The mobility model and propagation model are based on the M-Grid mobility model, a variant of the Manhattan model that considers not only the vehicular movement in a typical metropolis where streets are set out on a grid pattern but also the radio obstacles. A-STAR is compared to GSR and GPSR. Its packet delivery ratio is lower than GSR and GPSR with or without recovery as A-STAR can select paths with higher connectivity.

STBR – Street Topology Based Routing (STAR) (Forderer, 2005) went further than A-STAR by computing the road connectivity at junction nodes. One of the nodes at a junction is selected as a master that is responsible for checking if links to the next junctions are up or down. Within the broadcast from every master, there is also link information to all neighboring links. This is because every master will receive every other master's link information. Thus, every master contains a two-level junction neighbor table. The first level is through neighboring links to its direct junction nodes. The second level is its direct junction nodes through their neighboring links to their own junction nodes. In STBR, packets are routed based on their geographic distance to the street where the destination is on. This is different from GSR or A-STAR where routes are computed through Dijkstra shortest path.

GyTAR – Greedy Traffic Aware Routing protocol (GyTAR) (Jerbi, 2007) is an overlaid approach similar to the approaches mentioned above in that packets are forwarded greedily toward the next junction which will then determine the best junction to forward next. GyTAR assumes that the number of cars is given per each road from roadside units and determines the connectivity of roads. A score is given to each neighboring junction considering the *traffic density* and their *distance* to the destination. The weights to traffic density and their distance to the destination are configurable parameters. GyTAR tries to mimic the shortest path routing by taking into account the road connectivity.

Simulations are based on a 2500m x 2000m map of 100 to 300 nodes. The movement of cars is adapted to the mobility model from (Davis, et al., 2001). GSR is compared to GyTAR which shows better packet delivery ratio. However, since it is not compared to any other overlaid routing protocol in this category, it is hard to gauge its relative performance.

LOUVRE –Lee et al. (2008) has summarized geographic greedy overlay routing into two camps. The first camp is geo-reactive overlay routing where the next overlaid node is determined based on their neighboring nodes' distance to the destination (STBR) or a combination of it and traffic density (GyTAR). The second camp is geo-proactive overlay routing where the sequence of overlaid nodes is determined a-priori (GSR and A-STAR). Landmark Overlays for Urban Vehicular Routing Environments (LOUVRE) belongs to the second camp. It takes note of the fact that above a given vehicular density threshold, an overlay link remains connected regardless of the vehicular spatio-temporal distribution on the link. Thus, by only considering overlay links based on such density threshold when establishing overlay routes, most routes would partially use the same overlay links. With these considerations, geo-proactive overlay routing becomes attractive as it guarantees global route optimality and reduces the delay for establishing overlay routes. The drawback of this approach is obviously its scalability.

Figure 8 shows the procedure in which LOU-VRE obtains routes to nodes from node *S*. From the peer-to-peer density scheme, LOURVE first filters out roads that do not have density over the threshold, determined by the road length and radio range. Then the overlaid routes are built on top of roads whose density is above the threshold. This forms the graph the Dijkstra shortest path algorithm runs on. The algorithm automatically obtains the shortest path between *S* and its destination.

The novelty of LOUVRE is that road density which correlates to road connectivity is computed in a peer-to-peer fashion to remove reliance on deployment of roadside units. Thus, each node has the density of all the "connected" roads in the network. The Dijkstra shortest path is then built by roads with density above a certain density threshold, correlating closely to road connectivity. Simulation is conducted based on VanetMobisim (Härri, 2008), an open source and freely available realistic vehicular traffic generator for network simulators and simple road blocking propagation model. LOUVRE performs better than GPCR and GPSR due to LOUVRE's global knowledge of the density distribution on road segments and on local maxima, typical information that is not available to GPSR and GPCR. The hop count and delay are also significantly reduced as LOUVRE does rarely encounter local maxima and therefore mostly does not use a recovery mode.

CBF

Contention-Based Forwarding (CBF) (Fußler et al., 2004) is a geographic routing protocol that does not require proactive transmission of beacon messages. Data packets are broadcast to all direct neighbors and the neighbors decide if they should forward the packet. The actual forwarder is selected by a distributed timer-based contention process which allows the most-suitable node to forward the packet and to suppress other potential forwarders. Receivers of the broadcast data would compare their distance to the destination

Figure 8. Procedure in obtaining routes to nodes from S. Density threshold is 3 in the pictorial example

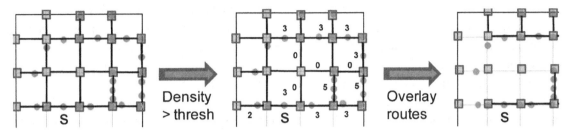

to the last hop's distance to the destination. The bigger the difference, the larger is the progress and shorter is the timer.

CBF is compared with GPSR with the perimeter mode disabled and with beacons of different intervals using realistic movement patterns of vehicles on a highway. With beacon interval of 0.25 seconds (the lowest set in the experiment), the packet delivery ratio (PDR) of GPSR is still not as good as that of CBF. As the beacon interval increases (up to 2 seconds), its PDR drops. (Please revise) Evaluation also shows that as the communication distance and thus the number of hops a packet has to travel increases, the load on the wireless medium increases more for GPSR than CBF due to GPSR's constant beaconing overhead.

Hybrid

Topology-assist Geo-Opportunistic Routing (TO-GO) (Lee et al., 2009) is a geographic routing protocol that exploits topology knowledge acquired via 2-hop beaconing to select the best target forwarder and incorporates opportunistic forwarding with the best chance to reach it. It is different from CBF in three main aspects. First, rather than picking the next forwarding node that makes the best progress to the destination, it picks the next forwarding node that makes the best progress to a target node. A target node is defined to be the node that greedy algorithm or recovery algorithm would normally pick except at the junction where optimization in choosing

the target node either beyond the junction or at the junction is based upon whether the routing is in greedy mode or recovery mode. The reason for choosing the target node instead of the destination as the frame of reference is to take care of the city topology where roads intersect and destination usually does not lie on the same street as the source as in the highway. Packets have to make multiple turns into different streets before arriving at the destination. The data is then broadcast to all direct neighbors. Whoever's distance is closer to the target node gets picked to be the next forwarding node.

The second difference is that unlike CBF, there is still the need of beacons, which are used for nodes to pick the target node. The fact that the data is broadcast and only the node that makes the furthest progress toward the target is chosen is to account for wireless channel errors and low packet delivery rate arising from multi-path fading, shadowing, and mobility – the furthest node (the target node) usually does not receive the data packet. Packets are therefore "opportunistically" making their best progress toward the target node and thus the destination. TO-GO uses a novel way to choose the forwarding set of nodes that are candidates for the next forwarding node. The set is chosen so that all nodes can hear one another (no hidden terminals) and make a progress toward the target node.

Lastly, TO-GO differs from CBF by providing routing decision for recovery. CBF on the highway works because the destination is always straight ahead. Thus, local maximum never occurs on the highway. Thus, the selection of the next forwarding node is always one that's closest to the destination. However, in city environments, streets cross each other and destination does not lie on the same street as the source. Thus, local maximum frequently occurs. TO-GO adapts the concept of CBF that packets are opportunistically sent to the target node, calculated by the routing decision in both the greedy and recovery mode.

Simulation results compare GPSR, GPCR, GpsrJ+, and TO-GO using mobility traces generated from VanetMobisim and road blocking propagation model. The first result shows TO-GO's performance comparable to GpsrJ+ while GPSR and GPCR lag behind in error-free channel scenario. In the error-prone channel scenario, as the channel error increases, TO-GO's packet delivery rate stays stably high while GpsrJ+'s decreases, showing the power of opportunistic forwarding.

DTN

There are vehicular routing protocols designed for VANETs which are treated as a form of Delay Tolerant Network (DTN). Since nodes are highly mobile, in this type of a network, they suffer from frequent disconnections. To overcome this, packet delivery is augmented by allowing nodes to store the packets when there is no contact with other nodes, to carry the packets for some distance until meeting with other nodes, and to forward based on some metric on nodes' neighbors (called carry-and-forward strategy). The notable DTN vehicular routing protocols are VADD and GeOpps described below.

VADD – Vehicle-Assisted Data Delivery (VADD) (Zhao et al., 2006) is a vehicular routing strategy aimed at improving routing in disconnected vehicular networks by the idea of carry-and-forward based on the use of predictable vehicle mobility. A vehicle makes a decision at a junction and selects the next forwarding *path* with the smallest packet delivery delay. A path

is simply a branched road from an intersection. The expected packet delivery delay of a path can be modeled and expressed by parameters such as road density, average vehicle velocity, and the road distance. The minimum delay can be solved by a set of linear system equations.

Zhao et. al. have introduced variations of VADD that chooses the next forwarding node after the next forwarding path has been determined. Location First Probe (L-VADD) would select a node closest to the next forwarding path even though such a node is going away from the forwarding path. Direction First Probe (D-VADD) would select a node which is going toward the forwarding path even though such a node might be further from the forwarding path than other nodes on the path. Multi-Path Direction First Probe (MD-VADD) would select multiple nodes going toward the forwarding path so as not to miss forwarding to a node that offers a shorter time to the destination. Finally, Hybrid Probe (H-VADD) combines L-VADD and D-VADD so the long packet delay from D-VADD is offset by L-VADD and routing loops from L-VADD are masked by D-VADD. Results comparing with GPSR plus buffer and various versions of VADD show that H-VADD has the best performance.

GeOpps – Geographical Opportunistic Routing (GeOpps) (Leontiadis, 2007) takes advantage of the suggested routes of vehicles' navigation system to select vehicles that are likely to move closer to the final destination of a packet. It calculates the shortest distance from packet's destination to the nearest point (NP) of vehicles' path, and estimates the arrival of time of a packet to destination. Figure 9 shows Node *A* in computing the NP of its neighbors *N1* and *N2*. Since N2 offers closer NP to the destination, Node *A* picks *N1* to forward its packets.

During the travel of vehicles, if there is another vehicle that has a shorter estimated arrival time, the packet will be forwarded to that vehicle. The process repeats until the packet reaches destination. The minimum delay used by VADD is indi-

Figure 9. Calculation of the Nearest Point (NP) from packet's Destination (D) for N1 and N2

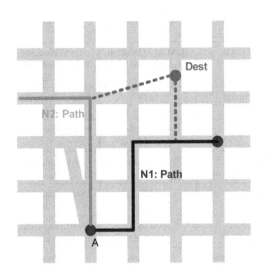

Figure 10. Virtual Navigation Interface

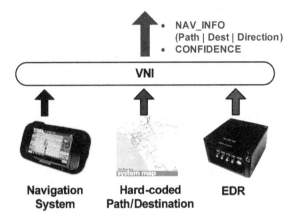

rectly obtained by selecting the next forwarding node whose path's nearest point is closest to the destination. GeOpps requires navigation information to be exposed to the network, thus, privacy such as vehicle's whereabouts might be an issue.

Hybrid

GeoDTN+Nav (Cheng et al., 2008) is a hybrid of non-DTN and DTN approach that includes the greedy mode, the perimeter mode, and the DTN mode. It switches from non-DTN mode to DTN mode by estimating the connectivity of the network based on the number of hops a packet has travelled so far, neighbor's delivery quality, and neighbor's direction with respect to the destination. The delivery quality of neighbors is obtained through *Virtual Navigation Interface* (VNI) which abstracts information from underlying hardware (e.g., Navigation System, EDR, etc.) shown in Figure 10 and provides necessary information for GeoDTN+Nav to determine its routing mode and forwarder. In addition to its hybrid approach, VNI offers users the option to protect their private

data and at the same time provides best-effort routing decision.

Cheng et al. compared GeoDTN+Nav with RandDTN, a *pure* DTN routing protocol that works as follows. At each beacon interval, a node forwards the packet that it is carrying with probability p. When $p = 0$, RandDTN is reduced to direct transmission scheme where packets reach the destination only when the source node meets the destination node. When $p = 1$, a node always considers its neighbors to forward the packet. To avoid the packet from being forwarded to any node, thus reducing progress towards the destination, a node would forward to its neighbor whose final destination is closest to the destination of the packet. If such a neighbor does not exist, the node would simply store and carry the packet waiting for the next beacon interval. The mobility trace is generated from VanetMobisim and the propagation model is road blocking model.

The result in a partitioned network shows that RandDTN achieves slightly better PDR and lower latency than GeoDTN+Nav. This illustrates the adaptive nature of GeoDTN+Nav in that it is able to recognize the partitioned network and quickly switch to DTN mode. RandDTN's slightly better PDR is due to the fact that GeoDTN+Nav tries to switch back to geographic routing whenever possible. However, in such a sparse network,

Table 1. Summary of VANET routing protocols

Routing Protocol	Type	Sub-Types	Overhead	Mobility Model	Propagation Model
FSR	Topology-based	Proactive	*All* link states	IDM on Manhattan Grid	Unknown
AODV	Topology-based	Reactive	Path states	IDM on Manhattan Grid, Videlio, MTS	Road blocking, Probabilistic shadowing
AODV+PGB	Topology-based	Reactive	Path states	MTS	Probabilistic shadowing
DSR	Topology-based	Reactive	Path states	IDM on Manhattan Grid, Videlio	Road blocking
TORA	Topology-based	Reactive	Path states	IDM on Manhattan Grid	Unknown
GPSR	Position-based	Non-DTN, Non-Overlay	Beacons	MTS	Probabilistic shadowing
GPSR+AGF	Position-based	Non-DTN, Non-Overlay	Beacons	MTS	Probabilistic shadowing
PRB-DV	Position-based	Non-DTN, Non-Overlay	Beacons and path states	Unknown	Unknown
GRANT	Position-based	Non-DTN, Non-Overlay	Two-hop beacons	Static trace from a uniform distribution	Road blocking
GPCR	Position-based	Non-DTN, Non-Overlay	Beacons	VanetMobisim	Road blocking
GpsrJ+	Position-based	Non-DTN, Overlay	Beacons	VanetMobisim	Road blocking
CAR	Position-based	Non-DTN, Overlay	Path states and beacons	MTS	Probabilistic shadowing
GSR	Position-based	Non-DTN, Overlay	Beacons	Videlio, M-Grid moblity	Road blocking
A-STAR	Position-based	Non-DTN, Overlay	Beacons	M-Grid mobility	Road blocking
STBR	Position-based	Non-DTN, Overlay	Beacons	Unknown	Unknown
GyTAR	Position-based	Non-DTN, Overlay	Beacons	Proprietory	Free space
LOUVRE	Position-based	Non-DTN, Overlay	Beacons	VanetMobisim	Road blocking
CBF	Position-based	Non-DTN, Non-Beacon	Data boradcast	Random way point	Two-Ray ground propagation model
TO-GO	Position-based	Non-DTN, Hybrid	Beacons and data broadcast	VanetMobisim	Road blocking
VADD	Position-based	DTN	Beacons	Unknown	Unknown
GeOpps	Position-based	DTN	Beacons	MTS	None
GeoDTN+Nav	Position-based	Hybrid	Beacons	VanetMobisim	Road blocking

GeoDTN+Nav is likely to fall back to DTN mode again. This increases the latency and also decreases the PDR. If the environment is tipped toward non-DTN network, however, GeoDTN+Nav will yield more favorable performance.

CONCLUSION

Table 1 summarizes the characteristics of representative routing protocols that have either been used or designed specifically for VANETs. The type and sub-types indicate whether they are topology-based or position-based and whether they are proactive/reactive, DTN or Non-DTN, overlay or not. The overhead describes the control packets associated with the successful operation of the protocols. Finally, the mobility model and propagation model present simulation settings used for protocol evaluation.

There is a plethora of VANET routing protocols. Most are designed to handle a special condition or a special problem. For example, GeOpps is designed for a special condition where VANET is assumed to be sparse and disconnected most of the time. CAR is designed for a specific problem where nodes obtain an inaccurate list of their neighbors and an inaccurate location of their destinations due to mobility. Some like TO-GO and GeoDTN+Nav address the special condition or problem by considering the hybrid approach. In TO-GO, for example, beacons are used to obtain the target node, and opportunistic forwarding is used to solve neighbor list inaccuracy. In GeoDTN+Nav, three types of modes are offered to enable nodes to determine the connectedness of the network and thus route packets in the timely manner by either the DTN or non-DTN mode.

Despite the special condition or problem that these routing protocols are considering or addressing, there is no agreed-upon standard or benchmark to validate their performance. The benchmark not only includes a standard routing protocol, but also a simulation environment. It is clear that GPSR is taken to be a widely-accepted benchmark. However, as position-based routing keeps advancing into many subareas (such as overlay, DTN, etc.) in VANETs, evaluation using GPSR is no longer a fair comparison. Furthermore, there is neither a widely-accepted mobility trace nor a propagation model used to evaluate these protocols[7]. Mobility traces can be either obtained from a close-to-reality traffic simulator or from actual traces. Because of the accessibility and limitation[8] of these traces, most evaluations use a mobility simulator. Yet, specifications about these simulator parameters are mostly non-standard. Because of the differences

in simulator implementation, some parameters cannot directly be translated over. The propagation model in urban environments has recently been caught with much attention. Most of the work thus far has based their propagation model on simple road blocking model or sophisticated analytical model. Because of the lack of understanding for the right values to plug in for these sophisticated models, most have shunned away from using them.

In summary, the open issue in VANET routing is then whether there is any benchmark tool for evaluating these protocols. The research direction is that as VANET routings are advancing and becoming mature, many of the underlying assumptions and technologies will need to become mature as well so that much validity can be given to the benefits of these routing protocols.

REFERENCES

Cheng, P. C., Weng, J. T., Tung, L. C., Lee, K. C., Gerla, M., & Härri, J. (2008). GeoDTN+NAV: A Hybrid Geographic and DTN Routing with Navigation Assistance in Urban Vehicular Networks. In *Proceedings of the 1st International Symposium on Vehicular Computing Systems* (ISVCS'08), Dublin, Ireland.

Davis, J., Fagg, A., & Levine, B. (2001). Wearable computers as packet transport mechanisms in highly-partitioned ad-hoc networks. In *Proceedings of the International Symposium on Wearable Computing*. Seoul, South Korea.

Flury, R., & Wattenhofer, R. (2006). MLS: an efficient location service for mobile ad hoc networks. In Proceedings of MobiHoc '06: The 7th ACM international symposium on Mobile ad hoc networking and computing, (pp. 226–237). New York.

Forderer, D. (2005, May). *Street-Topology Based Routing* (Master's thesis). Mannheim, Germany: University of Mannheim.

Franz, W., Eberhardt, R., & Luckenbach, T. (2001, October). FleetNet - Internet on the Road. In *Proceedings of the 8th World Congress on Intelligent Transportation Systems.* Sydney, Australia.

Füßler, H., Hannes, H., Jörg, W., Martin, M., & Wolfgang, E. (2004, March). Contention-Based Forwarding for Street Scenarios. In *Proceedings of the 1st International Workshop in Intelligent Transportation* (WIT 2004), (pp155–160). Hamburg, Germany.

Füßler, H., Mauve, M., Hartenstein, H., Käsemann, M., & Vollmer, D. (2002). Location-Based Routing for Vehicular Ad Hoc Networks. *Mobile Computing and Communication Review, 1*(2).

Gabriel, K. R., & Sokal, R. (1969). A new statistical approach to geographic variation analysis. *18. Systematic Zoology,* 231–268.

Giordano, S., et al. (2003, December). Position based routing algorithms for ad hoc networks: A taxonomy. In X. Cheng, X. Huang, & D. Z. Du (Eds.), Ad Hoc Wireless Networking. Boston: Kluwer.

Härri, J. (2008). *Vanet Mobisim project.* Retrieved from http://vanet.eurecom.fr

Helbing, D., Hennecke, A., Shvetsov, V., & Treiber, M. (2002). Micro- and Macrosimulation of Freeway Traffic. *Mathematical and Computer Modelling, 35*(5/6), 517–547. doi:10.1016/S0895-7177(02)80019-X

Iwata A. et al. (1999). Scalable Routing Strategies for Ad-hoc Wireless Networks. *IEEE JSAC, Aug*ust, 1369–1379.

Jaap, S., Bechler, M., & Wolf, L. (2005). Evaluation of Routing Protocols for Vehicular Ad Hoc Networks in City Traffic Scenarios. In Proceedings of the 5th International Conference on Intelligent Transportation Systems (ITS), *Telecommunications, June.*

Jerbi, M., Senouci, S. M., Meraihi, R., & Ghamri-Doudane, Y. (2007, June 24-28). An improved vehicular ad hoc routing protocol for city environments. In *Proceedings of the International Conference on Communications* (ICC '07), (pp. 3972–3979). Glasgow, Scotland

Jetcheva, J. G., & Hu, Y. C. PalChaudhuri, S., Saha, A. K., & Johnson, D. B. (2003, October 9-10). Design and evaluation of a metropolitan area multitier wireless ad hoc network architecture. In *Proceedings of the Fifth IEEE Workshop on Mobile Computing Systems and Applications,* (pp. 32-43). Monterey, CA.

Johnson, D. B., & Maltz, D. A. (1996). Dynamic Source Routing. In Imielinski, T., & Korth, H. (Eds.), *Mobile Computing Ad Hoc Wireless Networks* (pp. 153–181). Boston: Kluwer.

Karp, B., & Kung, H. T. (2000). GPSR: greedy perimeter stateless routing for wireless networks. In Proceedings of Mobile Computing and Networking, (pp243-254). Boston.

Kronjäger, W., & Hermann, D. (1999). Travel time estimation on the base of microscopic traffic flow simulation. In *Proceedings of ITS World Congress.* Toronto, Canada.

Lee, K., Le, M., Haerri, J., & Gerla, M. (2008). Louvre: Landmark overlays for urban vehicular routing environments. In *Proceedings of IEEE WiVeC.* Calgary, Canada.

Lee, K. C., Haerri, J., Lee, U., & Gerla, M. (2007, November 26-30). Enhanced perimeter routing for geographic forwarding protocols in urban vehicular scenarios. In *Proceedings of IEEE 2007 Globecom Workshops,* (pp. 1–10). Washington, DC.

Lee, K. C., Lee, U., & Gerla, M. (2009, February 2-4). TO-GO: TOpology-assist geo-opportunistic routing in urban vehicular grids. In *Proceedings of WONS 2009, The Sixth International Conference on Wireless On-Demand Network Systems and Services*, (pp.11-18). Snowbird, UT.

Lee, U., Cheung, R., & Gerla, M. (2009, March). 17). Emerging Vehicular Applications. In Olariu, S., & Weigle, M. C. (Eds.), *Vehicular Networks: From Theory to Practice*. Boca Raton, FL: Chapman & Hall/CRC Computer and Information Science Series.

Lee, U., Zhou, B., Gerla, M., Magistretti, E., Bellavista, P., & Corradi, A. (2006, October). Mobeyes: Smart mobs for urban monitoring with a vehicular sensor network. *IEEE Wireless Communications*, *13*(5), 52–57. doi:10.1109/WC-M.2006.250358

Leontiadis, I., & Mascolo, C. (2007). GeOpps: Geographical Opportunistic Routing for Vehicular Networks. In *Proceedings of WoWMoM 2007: The IEEE International Symposium on a World of Wireless, Mobile and Multimedia Networks*, (pp.1-6). Helsinki, Finland.

Li, F., & Wang, Y. (2007, June). Routing in vehicular ad hoc networks: A survey. *IEEE Vehicular Technology Magazine*, *2*(2), 12–22. doi:10.1109/MVT.2007.912927

Li, J., Jannotti, J., Couto, D. S. J. D., Karger, D. R., & Morris, R. (2000). A scalable location service for geographic ad hoc routing. In Proceedings of MobiCom '00: The 6th annual international conference on Mobile computing and networking, (pp.120–130). New York.

Lochert, C., Hartenstein, H., Tian, J., Fussler, H., Hermann, D., & Mauve, M. (2003, June 9-11). A routing strategy for vehicular ad hoc networks in city environments. In *Proceedings of the 2003 Intelligent Vehicles Symposium*, (pp. 156-161). Parma, Italy.

Lochert, C., Mauve, M., F¨ussler, H., & Hartenstein, H. (2005). Geographic routing in city scenarios. In []. Cologne, Germany.]. *Proceedings of the SIGMOBILE*, *9*(1), 69–72.

Mauve, et al. (2001). A survey on position-based routing in mobile ad hoc networks. *IEEE Network Magazine, November/December*, 30-39.

Mehran, A. (2004). A review of routing protocols for mobile ad hoc networks. *Ad Hoc Networks*, *2*, 1–22. doi:10.1016/S1570-8705(03)00043-X

Morris, R., Jannotti, J., Kaashoek, F., Li, J., & Decouto, D. (2000, September). CarNet: A scalable ad hoc wireless network system. In *Proceedings of the 9th ACM SIGOPS European Workshop*. Kolding, Denmark.

Naumov, V., Baumann, R., & Gross, T. (2006, May). An evaluation of Inter-Vehicle Ad Hoc Networks Based on Realistic Vehicular Traces. In *Proceedings of the ACM MobiHoc '06 Conference*. Florence, Italy.

Naumov, V., & Gross, T. R. (2007, May 6-12). Connectivity-Aware Routing (CAR) in Vehicular Ad-hoc Networks. In *Proceedings of INFOCOM 2007: The 26th IEEE International Conference on Computer Communications*, (pp.1919-1927). Anchorage, AK.

Park, V. D., & Corson, M. S. (1997, April 7-12). A highly adaptive distributed routing algorithm for mobile wireless networks. In *Proceedings of INFOCOM '97: The Sixteenth Annual Joint Conference of the IEEE Computer and Communications Societies*, (vol.3, pp.1405-1413). Kobe, Japan.

Pei, G., Gerla, M., & Chen, T. W. (2000, June). Fisheye State Routing: A Routing Scheme for Ad Hoc Wireless Networks. In [New Orleans, LA.]. *Proceedings, ICC*, 2000.

Perkins, C. E., & Royer, E. M. (1999, February). Ad-Hoc On-Demand Distance Vector Routing. In [New Orleans, LA.]. *Proceedings of the IEEE WMCSA*, *99*, 90–100.

Reichardt, D., Miglietta, M., Moretti, L., Morsink, P., & Schulz, W. (2002, June). CarTALK 2000 – safe and comfortable driving based upon inter-vehicle-communication. In. *Proceedings of the IEEE IV*, *02*, 545–550. Retrieved from http://www.cartalk2000.net.

Schnaufer, S., & Effelsberg, W. (2008, June 23-26). Position-based unicast routing for city scenarios. In Proceedings of the 2008 International Symposium on a World of Wireless, Mobile and Multimedia Networks, (WoWMoM 2008), (pp.1-8). Newport Beach, CA.

Seet, B.-C., Liu, G., Lee, B.-S., Foh, C.-H., Wong, K.-J., and Lee, K.-K. (2004). *A-STAR: A Mobile Ad Hoc Routing Strategy for Metropolis Vehicular Communications.*

Stojemnovic, I. (2004, July). Position-Based Routing in Ad Hoc Networks. *IEEE Communication Magazine.*

Toussaint, G. (1980). The relative neighborhood graph of a finite planar set. *Pattern Recognition*, *12*, 231–268. doi:10.1016/0031-3203(80)90066-7

Yamada, S. (1996). The strategy and deployment for VICS. *IEEE Communication*, *34*(10), 94–97. doi:10.1109/35.544328

Yu, Y., Lu, G. H., & Zhang, Z. L. (2004, October 25-27). Enhancing location service scalability with highgrade. In *Proceedings of 2004 IEEE International Conference on Mobile Ad-hoc and Sensor Systems*, (pp. 164–173). Ft. Lauderdale, FL.

Zhao, J., & Cao, G. (2006). VADD: Vehicle-Assisted Data Delivery in Vehicular Ad Hoc Networks. In *Proceedings of the 25th IEEE International Conference on Computer Communications*, (INFOCOM 2006), (pp.1-12). Barcelona, Spain.

ENDNOTES

[1] Car 2 Car Communication Consortium, http://www.car-to-car.org

[2] The Vehicle Infrastructure Integration (VII) Initiative, http://www.vehicle-infrastructure.org

[3] Continuous Air Interface for Long and Medium Interface (CALM), http://www.calm.hu

[4] Vehicle Information and Communication System

[5] Network On Wheels, www.network-on-wheels.de

[6] Radio obstacles produce asymmetric links as one node can hear the other node but the other node can hear the node. The graph produced by GG or RNG algorithm in the presence of radio obstacles is not planar.

[7] Two-ray fading model from the authors' opinion is a good model. Yet, it is not widely recognized and commonly used.

[8] The limitation of the realistic traces comes from the fact that roadside units are not widely populated and traces are collected from specific types of vehicles (like buses) following specific routes.

Chapter 9
Geographic Routing on Vehicular Ad Hoc Networks

Hirozumi Yamaguchi
Osaka University, Japan

Weihua Sun
Nara Institute of Science and Technology, Japan

Teruo Higashino
Osaka University, Japan

ABSTRACT

This chapter introduces geographic routing in vehicular ad hoc networks (VANETs). The aim of this chapter is to clarify the basic principle of geographic VANET routing protocols by stating their ideas. To this goal, we explain the common ideas behind the geographic routing protocols, and consider issues in applying those ideas to vehicular ad hoc networks. Then we summarize a wide variety of protocols; from ones in early design stages to understand the basic principle, to state-of-the-art ones to know recent research trends. After that, we give the detailed design of an example protocol to understand the design principle of VANET geographic routing protocols. Finally, we summarize the protocols introduced in this chapter and discuss future directions for possible research issues.

INTRODUCTION

VANETs are constituted of vehicles that are equipped with onboard units with GPS receivers. Therefore, it is natural to assume each vehicle knows its location. GPS provides position information with accuracy of 10m, and the differential GPS (DGPS) technology can complement it up to 1-3m (Navigation Center, U.S. Department of Homeland Security, 2009). Also technologies such as dead

reckoning and map matching using information from multiple sensors can enhance the accuracy. Also, other useful information on movement such as velocity and acceleration can be obtained. Using such information, *position-based routing* can be developed; we may let each vehicle transmit data packets to appropriate neighbors so as to maximize throughput and reliability or to minimize delay and traffic overhead. Furthermore, it is often difficult to know the destination vehicles' IDs in VANETs. Due to this nature, applications may want to deliver data to vehicles in a specific region (and in a certain

DOI: 10.4018/978-1-61520-913-2.ch009

Figure 1. Location-Aided Routing (LAR). (a) Scheme 1. (b) Scheme 2.

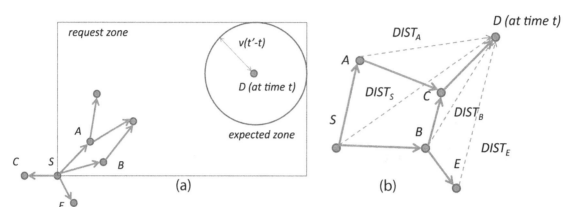

period of time). This suggests the necessity for *geocast* communication. In this chapter, we use the term "geographic routing" to indicate "geocast communication realized by position-based forwarding".

Principle of Position-Based Routing Protocols

Each node that joins a geographic routing protocol must know its location by GPS receivers or some positioning systems. As well as its own position, the source node must know the position of the destination node. This is achieved by some location services. The region where the destination node is expected to reside may be substituted for the exact position of the destination node in some approaches, since it is often difficult to obtain the timely position of remote nodes. We should note that many approaches assume that each node also knows its neighboring nodes' positions for choosing appropriate neighbors in forwarding messages. This is usually done by periodical broadcasting of positions to neighbors. Some others have nodes that receive the message determine whether they should forward the message or not (in the latter case, they drop it).

A well-known approach is Location-Aided Routing (LAR) (Ko & Vaidya, 1998). It assumes that the source node (node *S*) knows the position

of the destination node (node *D*) at time *t* but does not know its neighbors' positions. Now node *S* wants to establish a route to node *D* at time *t'* where $t \leq t'$. It introduces two schemes. The scheme 1 is "limited flooding" where messages are delivered within a given region determined by positions of nodes *S* and *D*. Node *S* calculates the *expected zone* of node *D*, the region in which node *S* expects to contain node *D*. This is a circle centered at the position of node *D* at time *t* with radius $v(t'-t)$, where *v* is the maximum speed of node *D*. Then, node *S* calculates the *request zone*, the smallest rectangle containing node *S* and the expected zone. This information is included in message *m* and each node determines whether it is in the request zone or not based on its position information. If in the request zone, the node forwards the message and discards it otherwise. Figure 1(a) shows how the LAR scheme 1 works. Nodes *A* and *B* are in the request zone and forward the message delivered by node *S*, while nodes *C* and *E* discard it. On the other hand, the scheme 2 considers distance from the destination. Each node *j* that receives a message from node *i* computes $\alpha \cdot DIST_j + \beta$ where α and β denote constant coefficients. If it is not larger than $DIST_i$, node *j* forwards the message and discards it otherwise. In Figure 1(b), the message transmitted by sender node *S* reaches nodes *A* and *B*. Here we assume $\alpha = 1$ and $\beta = 0$ for simplicity. Then both nodes forward the

Figure 2. DREAM protocol

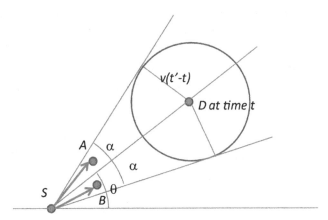

message since the distance from destination node D is shorter than the distance between S and D. Similarly, node C can forward the message from nodes A or B, but node E that receives the message from node B does not forward the message because D*ISTE* $_>$ D*ISTB* holds.

The DREAM protocol, which stands for Distance Routing Effect Algorithm for Mobility, was presented in the same year (Basagni, Chlamtac, Syrotiuk & Woodward, 1998). DREAM assumes that each node maintains a Location Table (LT) that contains the position of each other node and the last time when the position information was updated. Then DREAM mainly considers reducing overhead of control messages that deliver location information to the other nodes. Based on the observation that distant nodes' position information need not be updated frequently, DREAM introduces the lifetime of each message that indicates the maximum distance the message should be delivered from the message sender. Most messages have short lifetime and transmitted frequently, and long-lived messages are transmitted much less frequently but delivered over the network. This contributes to reduce the overhead without sacrificing the route discovery ratio. When source node S wants to transmit a message to destination node D, node S looks up LT and computes (D_θ, Dr) where Dθ and Dr are angle and distance from node S to node D, respectively.

Node S transmits the message to those nodes in the direction of $[\theta - \alpha, \theta + \alpha]$. α is determined based on the last time t when node D's position was updated and an expected speed v of node D. Concretely, $\alpha = \arcsin \dfrac{v(t'-t)}{r}$ as shown in Figure 2. If v is unknown but a probability function f(v) is known, we may determine α to guarantee a given probability p of containing node D.

The protocols explained above are in the family of a "*greedy forwarding*" strategy where the neighbors that are closer to the destination region are chosen. On the other hand, in a "*perimeter routing*" strategy, a "*polygon*" formed by the packet forwarder and its neighboring nodes is calculated based on the distance between them; if line a-b is shorter than a-c and b-c for any node c, we draw line a-b. As *a* result, a neighbor on the polygon is chosen as a next forwarder based on the "right-hand-rule" to detour the void or obstacle.

As an example of the perimeter routing protocols, we explain a well-known protocol, GPSR (Greedy Perimeter Stateless Routing) by Karp & Kung (2000). In GPSR, a source node knows the location of a destination node. The source node puts the location of the destination into a packet and transmits it to one of the neighbors. Each sender of the packet, including the source node, chooses the closest neighbor to the destination, among those closer to the destination than the sender.

Figure 3. GPSR packet forwarding strategy. (a) Greedy mode; sender A finds the closest neighbor to Dst among its neighbors closer to Dst than sender A. (b) Perimeter mode; since sender B cannot find a neighbor in greedy mode, perimeter mode is selected. Sender B finds node C, not closer to Dst than B but on the face B-C-D-E-F-I-K-L-M-B. The packet is traversed on this face based on the right-hand-rule until a sender finds a node in greedy mode. If a sender in perimeter mode cannot find a neighbor on the left-side of the face, the left-hand-rule is applied to find a neighbor, like node G's choice of node I

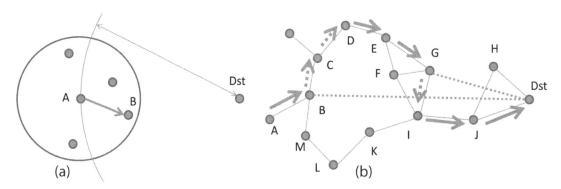

This forwarding mode is called gree*dy mode. An* example is shown in Figure 3(a) where sender A chooses node B. I*f* such a neighbor does not exist, the sender switches the mode from greedy mode to peri*meter mode. In* perimeter mode, each sender calculates a planar graph (like Gabriel graph or relative neighborhood graph) among its neighbors and finds the one on the "face" (i.e. *po*lygon), which is on the line between the source and destination. In finding such a neighbor, nodes follow the "right-hand-rule". Each node that receives a packet in perimeter mode continues the mode if it cannot find a node in greedy mode. An example is shown in Figure 3(b). In this figure, solid and dashed arrows represent packet transmission in greedy and perimeter modes, respectively. Nodes B an*d* C ar*e* in perimeter mode and node D sw*it*ches it to greedy mode. Node G sw*it*ches it to perimeter mode to find neighbor I. For the detailed descriptions, readers may refer to (Karp & Kung, 2000).

Aim of This Chapter

As shown by the above examples, geocast protocols have been thoroughly designed so far.

However, those for VANETs are very challenging due to their specific features. In this chapter, we address problems and challenges in designing geocast protocols and explain how existing approaches cope with them with unique and novel ideas. Among them, in order to exemplify how we incorporate position, movement and road structure information in VANET routing protocols, we introduce a QoS routing protocol which fully exploits such information for efficient discovery and maintenance of stable routes. We believe that this chapter promotes readers' good understanding of the principles of geocast protocols, challenges in VANET geocast design and the basic and state-of-the-art approaches.

We note that readers may also refer to existing surveys. For example, (Li & Wang, 2007) mainly aims at classifying existing approaches by many criteria. Also surveys on inter-vehicle communications are helpful to see the entire view of research categories (Luo & Hubaux, 2005; Sichitiu & Kihl, 2008; Willke, Tientrakool & Maxemchuk, 2008). In addition, recently published books (Guo, 2009; Moustafa & Zhang (Ed.), 2009; Olariu & Weigle (Ed.), 2009) are providing good introduction to vehicular networks.

PROBLEMS, CHALLENGES AND DESIGN ISSUES

Although a number of position-based routing and geocast protocols have been developed (Mauve, Widmer & Hartenstein, 2001; Stojmenovic, 2002; Maihöfer, 2004), those for VANETs need to be designed with very different design policies. The most fundamental factors that differentiate them from those for MANETs are the environmental factors such as geography, density of vehicles, equipment of vehicles and existence of infrastructure.

- *Geography*: vehicles move along roads, following traffic signals and rules. This indicates that we may only deal with one dimension if we consider routing on straight streets or highways. On the other hand, if we consider communication beyond a single street in city environment, we should also deal with a two-dimensional graph where nodes and edges represent intersections and roads between them, respectively. In this case, we need to design more complex routing strategies on such a graph.
- *Density of vehicles*: Usually on highways or in rural areas, there are no enough vehicles to maintain sufficient network connectivity for instantaneous multi-hop forwarding. That is, network topology is highly dynamic and partitions may occur frequently. Meanwhile, in city sections like crowded downtown area, the density of vehicles is likely to be high; there may be more than a hundred of vehicles within a few hundreds of meters from a single vehicle at an intersection of two multi-lane roads. In such situation, broadcast storm with hidden terminals' interference may easily occur.
- *Equipment of vehicles*: Most position-based routing protocols assume GPS receivers on vehicles. Recent approaches fully utilize road maps (and some assume traffic information). It is also natural to assume that the onboard sensors can provide more detailed information about movement like velocity and acceleration.
- *Infrastructure or infrastructure-less:* type of communication is either I2I (Infrastructure-to-Infrastructure), I2V (Infrastructure-to-Vehicle) or V2V (Vehicle-to-Vehicle). Here, the infrastructure usually means roadside units. Some V2V communication protocols assume the repeaters' assistance at intersections or roadside.

Routing protocols on vehicular ad-hoc networks should be tailored to these situations. For example, for highways with very few traffic, in which networks may be partitioned and vehicles are aligned along a line, we need to exploit a carry and forward strategy that is tolerant to temporary network disconnection. Meanwhile, in city environments, networks are well-connected but vehicles are not uniformly distributed. Due to road structure and building, there are a lot of "voids" where no vehicles exist. In such situation, we may need a strategy to detour these voids since it may interrupt a simple greedy forwarding.

Regarding the protocol design, an important issue is locality of information. We may assume that each vehicle can obtain mobility information about itself. However, it incurs some communication cost to obtain location of its neighboring or further vehicles. In general, the more information vehicles obtain, the more intelligent strategy they can take in route decision, sacrificing network bandwidth.

Finally, application requirements are wide-variety. Real-timeliness and reliability must be prioritized in safety applications, while information dissemination in wide area is usually delay-tolerant. I2V communication for Internet gateway needs continues connectivity, and information exchange between vehicles is realized by opportunistic communication. Accordingly, performance metrics deeply depend on these applications; delay, link/route lifetime, traffic overhead, throughput and path redundancy are typical ones.

ROUTING ON VANETS: CLASSIFICATION AND INTRODUCTION

Based on the above observation, we classify the existing approaches on VANET protocols, and introduce their behavior and characteristics.

Use of Position Information for Broadcast Optimization

There have been many approaches that use position and movement information not only for directional packet forwarding but also to optimize broadcast-based communication. The problem of redundant broadcast messages in a simple flooding strategy is known as the *broadcast storm* problem. This notion is presented by Ni, Tseng, Chen & Sheu (1999) and they propose several schemes including location-based scheme. After that, a number of papers like (Tseng, Ni & Shih, 2003) and (Fubler, Widmer, Kasemann, Mauve and Hartenstein, 2003) have dealt with this or related problems in Mobile Ad-hoc Networks (MANET). In addition, several VANET protocols deal with similar problems and adopt the location-based scheme to alleviate the overhead.

Briesemeister, Schäfers & Hommel (2000) provide a geocast protocol where packets are destined to "zone-of-relevance". They assume IEEE 802.11 and multi-hop transmission. The focused applications are safety critical applications like forward collision avoidance and hazard warning. For example, they suppose that a vehicle's sensor detects the dangerous situation and activates an emergency brake system. This information should be propagated immediately to the backward direction so as to avoid a pileup or other accidents. This

kind of warning system requires reliable and timely transmission of packets to the intended region.

The basic idea is to control retransmission timing in the MAC layer based on the location to avoid contention, and to prohibit duplicate transmission of the same message in the application layer. For the former one, they prioritize the vehicles closer to the border of the transmission circle of a packet sender in choosing the next sender(s). For this purpose, "waiting time" is defined such that vehicles having more distance from the sender have shorter waiting time to forward the message. For the latter one, they consider a simple solution where every vehicle has the message list that records the received messages. Since everybody joins this forwarding process, it may still suffer from broadcast inefficiency where hidden terminal problems may easily occur.

Figure 4 illustrates how a message is propagated among nodes in this approach. In Figure 4(a), node *A* sends a message containing the position of *A* to its neighbors. Nodes *B* and *C* receive the message and calculate their own waiting time. In this case node *C* is further than node *B* from node *A*, and thus obtains shorter waiting time. Node *C* sends the message earlier than node *B*, and node *B* refrains from the transmission of the message if it receives the message from node *C*. However, this easily causes collision since it generates the waiting time with respect to the distance from the sender. Accordingly, a hidden terminal problem may also occur as shown in Figure 4(b).

In the same year, *Role Based Multicast* (*RBM*) was presented by the same authors (Briesemeister & Hommel, 2000), for highly mobile but sparsely connected ad hoc networks. As the name suggests, a multicast group is defined by location, speed, driving direction and time in RBM. Let us consider an accident/hazard warning system as an example application. If the position and driving direction is known, each vehicle can determine if it is approaching to the accidental area or not. This can limit the multicast group to vehicles in one of the two directions and behind the hazardous

Figure 4. Message propagation in Briesemeister, Schäfers & Hommel (2000). (a) A message transmitted by node A is relayed by node C that is closer to the border of the radio area than node B. Node B refrains from relaying the same message. (b) A hidden terminal problem from two nodes near the border of node A's radio area

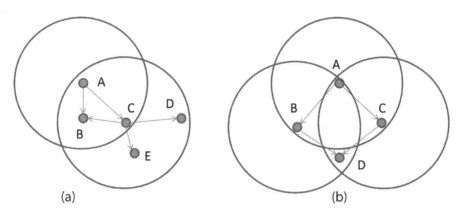

(a)   (b)

area. In a similar way, considering the minimum distance to stop a vehicle in emergency braking, the multicast group can further be limited to the vehicles that can stop before the area. Also, to cope with sparse connectivity, each vehicle maintains a list N of neighbors and a list S of senders of each message. Then it sends a message to the set $N\backslash S$ of neighbors according to the waiting time defined in the same way as their previous work (Briesemeister, Schäfers & Hommel, 2000).

Sun, Feng, Lai, Yamada, Okada & Fujimura (2000) present a location-based message broadcast system for V2V communication. This introduces the notion of mobility prediction, which is widely adopted in the recent approaches. The goal of this work is to broadcast a message to every vehicle. The approach consists of two fundamental protocols. First, the *TRADE* (*TRAcking DEtection*) protocol is presented. It assumes that each vehicle obtains the neighboring nodes' position information by periodical beaconing, and calculates their moving vectors. Based on them, each sender that received a message predicts the neighbors' directions and chooses the two furthest vehicles in its forward and backward directions on the same road and all vehicles on different roads as the next senders. The IDs of these vehicles are included

in the message. Because the size of the message headers is increased by the list of neighbors and periodical exchange of position information is required, this approach may consume a certain amount of bandwidth according to the density of nodes. Secondly, the *Distance Defer Transfer* (*DDT*) algorithm tries to alleviate this bandwidth consumption caused by transmission of position information and neighbor lists. The idea is similar with the one by Briesemeister, Schäfers & Hommel (2000) but DDT differs in the sense that it takes into account "coverage" by already relayed messages. Each sender includes its position in a message to be transmitted. Each neighbor of the sender receives the message and calculates the defer time, which is inversely proportional to the distance from the sender. During the defer time, it hears the messages forwarded by the others and knows their positions included in those messages. After the defer time, it calculates how much area is covered by those vehicles' precedent transmission. If there is a certain area where the message is not delivered in the vehicle's transmission circle, it transmits the message. Otherwise the message is discarded.

Figure 5 shows examples of TRADE and DDT. In Figure 5(a), the sender in the center of the

177

Figure 5. TRADE protocol and DDT protocol by Sun, Feng, Lai, Yamada, Okada & Fujimura (2000). (a) Selection of neighbors in TRADE. Vehicles A and B are selected as the furthest nodes on the same road as vehicle S. Since vehicles C, D and E are on the different road, they are also selected. (b) Vehicle D relays the message from S. In this case, vehicle A has little contribution to deliver the message to a new node that cannot hear from vehicles S and D, and thus refrains from relaying the message

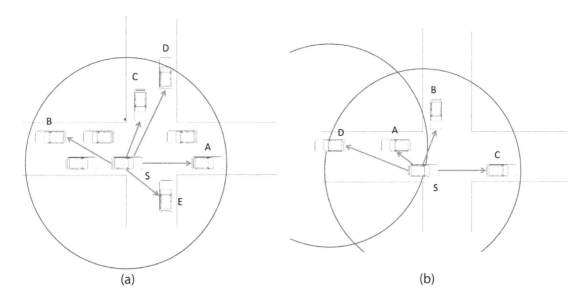

(a)   (b)

circle chooses the furthest vehicle *A* in its forward direction on the same road and *B* in the backward direction. Vehicles *C*, *D* and *E* are also selected since they are on the different road. Figure 5(b) shows how DDT works. A message that includes the position of *S* is received by vehicles *A*, *B*, *C* and *D*. Based on the distance from *S*, each node calculates the defer time. Let us assume that the defer time of *A*, *B*, *C* and *D* are 3, 2, 1 and 0, respectively, according to the distance. Then *D* first forwards the message and *A* can hear this message during its defer time. *A* calculates its transmission circle and knows that the most part of the circle is included in either *S*'s or *D*'s transmission circle. In this case, *A* discards the message.

Morris, Jannoti, Kaashoek, Li & De-couto (2000) present initial design of a routing scheme called *CarNet*. The goal of this work is to achieve scalable transmission in vehicular ad-hoc wireless networks with heterogeneous vehicle density. The two main issues are discussed in this scheme; lo-

cation service necessary to query the location of destination, and the management of sparse density. For the former one, CarNet introduces Grid Location Service (GLS). In GLS, all vehicles have the same hash-like function *f(i)* that encodes the ID of vehicle *i* to a set of locations. These locations indicate the "location servers" of vehicle *i*. As vehicle *i* moves, it sends update messages to these locations based on a geographic routing scheme, and the vehicles that are close to the locations act as the location servers that record the position of vehicle *i*. Using the location of the destination, each vehicle forwards the message in a greedy forwarding strategy, and obstacles or voids are detoured by the GPSR scheme.

A more recent approach is given by Naumov, Baumann & Gross (2006). They address two problems in choosing next hops in broadcast-based route discovery process. One is the hop-distance problem. Too short 1-hop distance results in a high number of hops in a discovered route, and too close to the maximum wireless range implies unstable links. Another problem is hidden terminal problem. Only the nodes within the receiving range from sender X and receiver Y are prohibited to transmit packets, and the other nodes may interfere with the reception at receiver Y depending on the signal strength from X.

Preferred Group Broadcasting (PGB) is presented to deal with the above two problems. It classifies nodes that receive broadcast packets into three groups. The received signal level (dBm) is compared to two values for this purpose; Inner Threshold (*IT*) and Outer Threshold (*OT*). Both thresholds have the following relation to the receiving threshold (*rxTh*), the power of a signal that corresponds to the maximum transmission range:

$$IT = rxTh + f_{IT}$$

$$OT = rxTh + f_{OT}$$

where f_{IT} and f_{OT} are positive integer system values (dB). If the sensed signal power is more than *IT*, the node is classified into the "IN" group, else if less than *OT*, the node falls into the "OUT" group, and in the preferred group otherwise. These groups can also be constructed together with the information about nodes' coordinates (if any). Nodes from the PG have the highest priority to be chosen as relays, those from the OUT group have the second, and those from the IN group have the lowest priority. According to these priorities, the *holding time* of each message is determined for each group so that a node from the higher priority group has the shorter holding time. For two nodes in the same group, their holding times are differentiated by the received signal strength compared to the baseline *OT,* as well as some system parameters.

We assume that node *A* wants to deliver a message to the other nodes. If node *B* from PG receives the message twice from two different nodes, it can drop it. This is because some other nodes have already forwarded the message. Also,

using the position information, node *B* verifies if node *C* from the same group that has already forwarded the message have the same predecessor with node *B*. If they have the same predecessor, say node *A*, and the height of the triangle *ABC* is less than a certain threshold, then node *C* refrains from forwarding the message.

Due to the space limitations, we omit other approaches such as the hybrid of the location-based and counter-based forwarding strategy by Oh, Kang & Gruteser (2006) and the opportunistic broadcast protocol by Li & Lou (2008).

Problem on Perimeter Routing Strategy in VANET

The above approaches have focused on the efficiency of message broadcast. Therefore, most of them consider single streets or highways. Besides these investigations, VANET routing protocols that utilize information about road structure have been presented. Therefore most of them focus on city scenarios.

Lochert, Hartenstein, Tian, Fuessler, Hermann & Mauve (2003) present the *Geographic Source Routing (GSR)*, a routing protocol for vehicular ad hoc networks in city environments. This work deals with issues on deploying GPSR on VANET in city sections. First, in such a situation, the lines of sights are sometimes blocked by buildings even though two vehicles are close to each other. Since GPSR assumes planarization based only on distance between nodes, this creates a problem such that senders cannot reach the next nodes due to shadowing problem. Second, if GPSR is in perimeter mode, a sender chooses the closest node as a next sender, while the furthest node is the best to reduce the number of hops. This increases the number of hops, which results in less reliability and larger delay. These are illustrated in Figure 7.

Their solution to these problems is following. First, the protocol obtains the location of the destination by reactive location service, which discovers on demand the location of the destina-

Figure 6. Preferred Group Broadcasting (PGB). (a) Holding time and received signal power. Node from PG group whose rxP is closer to OT has higher priority. (b) Location-based optimization. Node B does not forward a message considering relative positions of A, B and C

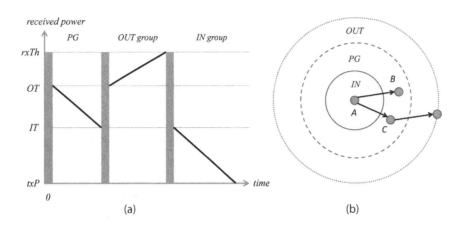

(a)   (b)

Figure 7. Problems of GPSR in VANETs stated by Lochert, Hartenstein, Tian, Fuessler, Hermann & Mauve (2003). (a) Planar graph. Vehicle B may be the best candidate of next node, but closer nodes are selected. A and C may not be reachable due to shadowing by buildings. (b) Short-range hop sequence problem in perimeter mode. Although vehicle A can reach vehicle C directly, vehicle B is chosen as a next sender in the planar graph

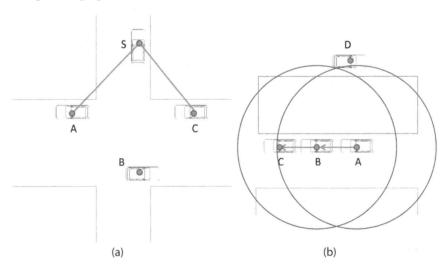

(a)   (b)

tion by broadcasting a query message. Using the destination's location information, the source node calculates a route on the map, which is represented as a sequence of intersections. We note that this calculation can be done by each intermediate node instead of the source node. In this case, there is a clear advantage that intermediate nodes can update the route dynamically if there is no node on the pre-calculated route. The shortest route can be calculated by the Dijkstra's algorithm. The work does not take dynamic road traffic information into account.

Figure 8. Inefficient path selection problem stated by Seet, Liu, Lee, Foh, Wong & Lee (2004) in GPSR perimeter mode. Vehicle S can reach Vehicle D through vehicles b1 and b2. However, vehicle S cannot know this fact. According to the right-hand-rule, vehicle S in perimeter mode finds vehicle a1 as a next sender

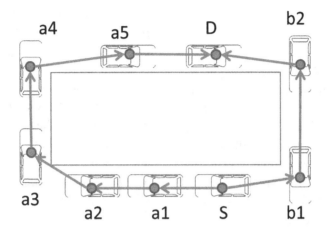

Seet, Liu, Lee, Foh, Wong & Lee (2004) proposed the *Anchor-based Street and Traffic Aware Routing (A-STAR)* algorithm. This is a position-based routing strategy on mobile ad hoc networks for metropolis vehicular communications since it utilizes the city bus route. This work also states a problem of GPSR in city sections as addressed by Lochert, Hartenstein, Tian, Fuessler, Hermann & Mauve (2003). In addition, they say that due to the right-hand-rule of GPSR and the lack of global knowledge about the future paths, the longer path may be chosen although shorter paths are available as shown in Figure 8.

A-STAR employs a source routing strategy that computes a sequence of intersections. This is a similar strategy with GSR by Lochert, Hartenstein, Tian, Fuessler, Hermann & Mauve (2003), but is different with respect to traffic awareness. A-STAR assumes that streets with bus lines are possibly major streets on which the presence of some vehicles can be expected. Accordingly, A-STAR weights streets depending on the number of bus lines. Then the "anchor-path" is computed using the Dijkstra's least-weight path algorithm.

GPCR, Greedy Perimeter Coordinator Routing by Lochert, Mauve, Füßler & Hartenstein (2005),

takes into account the fact that a road map that consists of nodes (intersections) and edges (streets) forms a planar graph in nature. Therefore it does not need a graph planarization algorithm. The key idea is to find a "coordinator", which is a node at a junction. A packet is forwarded along streets, if there is no coordinator. In this case, the node which has the largest distance from the sender toward the destination and is approximately on an extension of the line between the sender and its predecessor is selected. If coordinators are found, the packet should be forwarded to one of them. Coordinators can be found by their periodic advertisement. GPCR allows each vehicle to decide whether it is in a junction or not without a street map. For this goal, it provides two approaches. One is to let vehicles broadcast position information about itself and its neighbors. A node is a coordinator if it has two neighbors that are within a transmission range of each other but cannot hear each other. In this case, these neighbors are separated by obstacles such as buildings and only the coordinators can hear from both of the neighbors. Another is to compute the correlation coefficient of neighbors' x- and y-coordinates. It is defined as

$$\rho_{xy} = \left| \frac{\sigma_{xy}}{\sigma_x \sigma_y} \right| = \left| \frac{\sum_{i=1}^{n} (x_i - \overline{x})(y_i - \overline{y})}{\sqrt{\sum_{i=1}^{n} (x_i - \overline{x})^2 \sum_{i=1}^{n} (y_i - \overline{y})^2}} \right|$$

where x_i and y_i are the coordinates of neighbors and $\overline{x}$ and $\overline{y}$ denote means of the coordinates. The value of this coefficient is close to one if neighbors are on the same street, and is close to zero if neighbors are not aligned linearly. Finally, GPCR provides a repair strategy based on the perimeter routing strategy of GPSR. In the repair mode, if a coordinator cannot find the next node in greedy mode, the mode is switched to perimeter mode in which the packet is forwarded along a street to next coordinator by the right-hand-rule. If a coordinator receives the packet and can forward it in greedy mode, it switches the mode to greedy one. Otherwise it continues the right-hand-rule to find the next coordinator. In Figure 9, vehicles *B*, *D* and *F* are coordinators and vehicle *B* switches the mode to perimeter mode since no vehicle is found in greedy mode. Vehicle *D* is a coordinator and it switches the mode to greedy mode since it can find vehicle *E*.

Finally, Granelli, Boato, Kliazovich & Vernazza (2007) provide *GPSR-MA*, a movement-aware GPSR protocol. It briefly states how movement information is effective to enhance GPSR in VANETs. It uses speed and direction information to estimate the up-to-date location of neighbors. Also when a sender chooses a next sender, it chooses the one which has similar speed, is closer to the destination, and is moving toward the destination.

Routing Strategy in City Scenario

Not only the explicit route construction and maintenance protocols most of which are related with GPSR, new efficient data dissemination protocols have also been investigated. Different from those in the early stage (around 2000), the following approaches target data routing in city environments.

Korkmaz, Ekici, Ozguner, and Ozguner (2004) propose the *Urban Multi-hop Broadcast* (*UMB*) protocol. The main contributions of this work are two-fold. First, it introduces a handshake system to avoid hidden-terminal problem based on a location-based busy-tone mechanism. This also enables to select the furthest node as a forwarder of a message without the location information about neighbors. To increase the reliability, it also introduces ACK packets. Second, it utilizes repeaters at intersections to transmit the packet to all the directions.

The introduced handshake system is RTB/CTB, which stands for Request-To-Broadcast/Clear-To-Broadcast inspired by the RTS/CTS mechanism in IEEE802.11. A sender transmits an RTB packet which includes its position and an intended broadcast direction, as well as transmission duration like RTS. For transmission to more than one direction, RTB needs to be created for each direction. The receiver of this message computes distance *d* from the sender and sends an energy burst in time duration which is proportional to *d*. Actually, it is determined by the following formula where *R and SlotTime* denote the wireless transmission range and a unit length of time slot, respectively.

$$\left\lfloor \frac{d}{R} * N_{\max} \right\rfloor * SlotTime$$

We note that N_{max} is a protocol parameter explained later. Each vehicle listens to the channel after its burst, and is guaranteed to be (one of) the furthest vehicle(s) if the channel is empty. Then the vehicle sends CTB, a clear-to-broadcast packet. If there is more than one vehicle that has the same burst length, CTB packets will collide. Then the sender transmits RTB and only the

Figure 9. Repair mode in GPCR

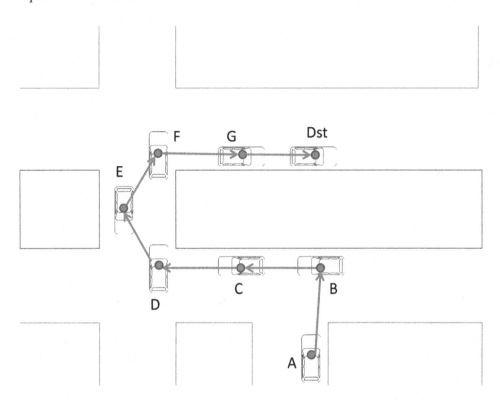

vehicles which have transmitted CTB will join the new selection process. In other words, these vehicles must be in the N_{max}-th segment, which is the furthest from the sender. The sender tries to divide this N_{max}-th segment into N_{max} sub-segments to distinguish them and find the furthest vehicle. The black-burst length for this purpose is given as follows where *Longest* and *W* denote the longest black-burst length and the length of the N_{max}-th segment, respectively.

$$\left\lfloor \left| \frac{d - Longest * W}{W} \right| * N_{max} \right\rfloor * SlotTime$$

By continuing this process, the sender finally determines only one vehicle. After that the sender transmits a data packet and the selected receiver sends ACK to notify the success of transmission.

We may remember that such a distance-based neighbor selection was proposed so far (see the protocol by Briesemeister, Schäfers & Hommel, 2000 and the TRADE protocol by Sun, Feng, Lai, Yamada, Okada & Fujimura, 2000), UMB gives detailed design for the case that bursts with similar length are overlapped in determining the furthest vehicle from a sender vehicle.

Another feature is the principle of broadcast at intersections. It relies on repeaters at intersections. Each vehicle inside the transmission range of a repeater sends the packet to the repeater by point-to-point communication of IEEE802.11.

Wu, Fujimoto, Guensler & Hunter (2004) present *MDDV, Mobility-centric Data Dissemination algorithm for Vehicular networks*. MDDV is designed to exploit vehicle mobility for data dissemination, and combines the idea of opportunistic forwarding, trajectory-based forwarding and geographical forwarding. In MDDV, each vehicle is equipped with GPS and a road map, and a destination is designated by a road segment. It does not assume the position information about neighbors. In the road map, the weighted distance of each road segment is calculated by its actual length and the number of lanes. A road is weighted more if it has less number of lanes or is longer than the others. Based on this weighted road map, a forwarding trajectory is calculated by the source vehicle.

Along this forwarding path, the vehicle which is moving toward and is closest to the destination becomes a *message head* and carries the message. However, since MDDV does not exploit neighbors' position information, each vehicle cannot know when it should be, or is no longer, the message head. To cope with this problem, MDDV introduces a notion of "group", which consists of the vehicles near the message head. To realize such a group by each vehicle's local operation, the message contains a "*message head pair*" (*l, t*)=(message head location, its generation time). This is inserted by each message head. Each node determines if it should be a message head candidate or a non-candidate, based on this information in the message and its current location and time. For example if a non-candidate holding the message with (*l, t*) passes recorded location *l* before time *t+T* where *T* is a short time, this message can be forwarded along the trajectory with high probability. On the other hand, a message head candidate is no longer the candidate if it moves away from the trajectory or it receives the message with pair (*l',t'*) where *l'* is the closer location than the current location. The message head pair is updated correspondingly if a message head candidate receives the same message with a newer pair.

A similar but recent approach is the delay-bounded routing in vehicular ad-hoc networks by Skordylis & Trigoni (2008). This is a protocol that delivers data to intended access points. The advantage of this method compared with MDDV is to allow intermediate vehicles to modify the route for smarter routing strategy.

GVGrid by Sun, Yamaguchi, Yukimasa & Kusumoto (2006) is a routing algorithm that constructs a route with long lifetime. It fully uses position, movement and map information to find such a route. A metric for longer route lifetime is presented. Another feature is to maintain a route. Once a route is found, such a route is maintained along the initial route. These ideas are later explained in details.

MORA, a *MOvement-based Routing Algorithm* is proposed by Granelli, Boato & Kliazovich (2006). It uses not only position information but also direction information. It considers the linear combination of the number of hops and a location- and direction-dependent metric. This is given as a function of distance between the sender and the destination and the moving direction toward the line between the source and the destination. The metric is larger if it is close to the destination and the moving angle is closer to the perpendicular of the line. In this context, the vehicles moving on the line between the source and the destination are most prioritized.

Finally, we explain *VADD, Vehicle-Assisted Data Delivery* by Zhao & Cao (2006). This takes a carry and forward approach to cope with the network partition problem in large-scale sparse vehicular networks. The key point that differentiates it from the existing work is to make use of the predicable vehicle mobility based on the road map and traffic patterns on it. It is done as follows. For each intersection *i*, the estimated delivery delay D_{ij} from intersection *i* to its neighboring intersection *j* is represented as follows in VADD;

$$D_{ij} = d_{ij} + \sum_{k \in N(j)} (P_{jk} \cdot D_{jk})$$

where d_{ij} is distance of street *i-j*, P_{jk} is a probability to choose street *j-k* from intersection *j*, and *N(j)* is a set of neighboring intersections of *j*. This equation can be solved in $\Theta(n^3)$ for a finite set of

n streets. By this computation, we get D_{ij} for the current intersection i. The packet holder can find the street with the smallest delay. Among all the vehicles within communication range, the packet holder will forward it to the one on the street with the smallest delay. If no such a vehicle is found, the street with the second smallest delay is chosen. Four forwarding strategies are provided based on the position and movement of neighboring nodes; L-VADD, D-VADD, MD-VADD and H-VADD, to maximize the chance to reach the destination. The details of these strategies are omitted here.

Recent Approaches

In recent years, more investigations with unique features have been published.

Maihöfer, Leinmüller & Schoch (2005) have presented the abiding geocast protocol, which provides time-stable geocast. This protocol aims at continuously sending data to vehicles inside a destination region within a certain period of time. To this goal, they give three different approaches. The first approach is the "server approach" where a server is used to store geocast messages. The messages are sent to this server by unicast and then sent by the server periodically or by explicit notification toward the destination. The second one is the "election approach" where a node in the destination region is elected to store geocast messages. In this case, message handover is necessary when this node leaves the destination region. The third one is the neighbor approach that assumes the knowledge about all neighbor nodes and their location. Each node stores all geocast packets destined for its location. If a node within the destination region detects a new neighbor, it passes the packet to the node. For these approaches, network load and delivery success ratios are analyzed.

Wisitpongphan, Bai, Mudalige, Sadekar & Tonguz (2007) have presented a routing strategy in sparse vehicular ad hoc wireless networks. The main contribution of this work is provision of the

vehicular model that characterizes inter-arrival time and inter-vehicle spacing between vehicles on freeways by using empirical data from a realistic traffic environment. Based on their analysis, they provide a store-and-carry routing strategy.

Utilizing movement information is still a hot topic. Taleb, Sakhaee, Jamalipour, Hashimoto, Kato & Nemoto (2007) have presented a stable routing protocol. Similar with the recent approaches, this approach also utilizes movement information on the position, speed, direction and road map. In order to achieve the goal to establish a stable route, it groups vehicles going to the same direction with similar speed and establishes routes on it. Mobility prediction-based routing protocols are also presented by Namboodiri & Gao (2007) as PBR (Prediction-Based Routing), by Feng, Hsu & Lu (2008) as VAR (Velocity-Assisted Routing). Border node-based Routing (BBR) has been presented by Zhang & Wolff (2008), which is an epidemic routing considering broadcast optimization as we have seen in the early part of this chapter. Ding, Wang & Xiao (2008) presented a static-node assisted adaptive routing protocol in vehicular networks. The basic idea is somehow similar with VADD, but it assumes an intelligent static node at each junction. Such a static node acts as a temporary holder of the message. If the static node finds appropriate vehicles that possibly move on an optimized forwarding path, then the message is sent to such vehicles.

RESILIENT GEOGRAPHIC ROUTING IN VANET

In this part, we present a resilient geographic routing protocol called *GVGrid* for VANETs (Sun, Yamaguchi, Yukimasa & Kusumoto, 2006). We present GVGrid in detail for the following reasons. First, it is designed based on many basic concepts in VANET routing protocols. For example, route discovery is performed using road map information and vehicles' position and movement information.

It also designs a novel route maintenance system, which attempts to avoid frequent reconstruction of routes. Second, it considers route lifetime, which is one of the most important performance metrics in VANET routing protocols.

GVGrid utilizes a route discovery strategy that finds a route from a stationary source (such as emergency vehicles and crashed cars at accident locations and roadside units) to vehicles that reside in or drive through a specified destination region. Each vehicle that forwards a route request message selects only appropriate neighbors that potentially are the constituents of routes. This helps to reduce message overhead, using digital maps and mobility information about neighbors. A route maintenance strategy reconstructs a route on the same location, using isolated segments of the broken route, which are expected to still be useful to constitute the new one.

Examples use cases are shown in Figure 10. In Figure 10(a), real-time information service about parking, local traffic jams, traffic accidents and shops/restaurants nearby is illustrated, and in Figure 10(b) an extension of Internet gateways at the roadside is shown.

Preliminaries

Hereafter, vehicles are referred to as nodes for simplicity. GVGrid assumes that each node is equipped with a short-range wireless device and has the same communication range r. GVGrid partitions the geographic region into squares of equal size called cells. The cell that includes node u (or point p, according to the context) is denoted as $G(u)$ (or $G(p)$). The side's length w of each cell is determined so that any node u can hear from every node v in the same cell or in one of the neighboring cells. Since the longest distance between u and v is $2\sqrt{2}w$ and since it must not be greater than the communication range r, w should not be greater than $\sqrt{2}r / 4$. This is illustrated in Figure 11. Also in GVGrid, each node needs to

identify the cell ID $G(p)$ from a given position p. For this purpose, $(0,0)$ is regarded as a reference point and for a position $p = (x, y)$, $G(p)=D*(x\ div\ y) + (y\ div\ w)$ where D is a constant value and is larger than the maximum value of y div w. Then knowing w, D and the reference point, $G(p)$ can be identified by p.

A road map is defined as an undirected graph *(V,E)* called a *road graph*, where V is a set of intersections and E is a set of *road segments*. Each road segment in E is a portion of a street fragmented by two adjacent intersections in V. Each road segment has a street ID to which the road segment belongs. Also, for each intersection, its geographic position information is attached. It is assumed that each node u has a digital road map as a road graph M and tracks its geographic position (denoted as $P(u)$) via GPS.

It is also assumed that position $P(u)$ of node u is associated with the corresponding position on the road graph M. This position is denoted by $P'(u)$. $P'(u)$ is represented by a pair of the road segment ID on which node u resides (denoted by $road(u)$) and the driving direction (denoted by $dir(u)$).

Route Discovery Process

A path on a network is called network route and a path on a road graph is called a driving route to avoid confusion. A network route is represented by a sequence of node IDs, and a driving route is represented by a sequence of road segment IDs. The source node s specifies a destination region as the location of a destination point d. GVGrid is a position-based routing protocol that finds a route from s to nodes in cell $G(d)$. GVGrid is designed for city environments where the density of vehicles is relatively high.

When source node s tries to find a network route to destination point d, s sets a region called *request zone* in which RREQ messages are transmitted. A request zone is specified as the minimum rectangle that includes $G(s)$ and $G(d)$.

Figure 10. Example use cases of GVGrid. (a) Sending traffic accident information to vehicles coming into a congested region. (b) Providing Internet access service to parking

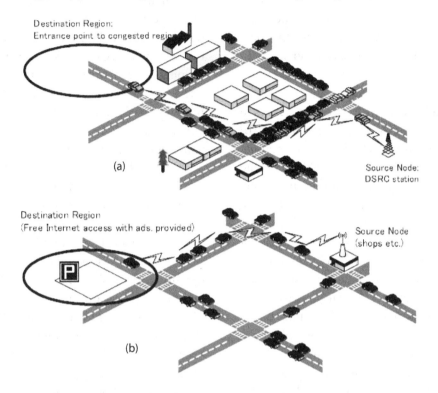

Figure 11. Communication range and cell size

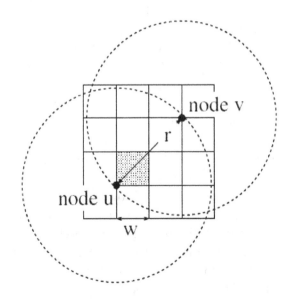

Like *LAR* (Ko & Vaidya, 1998), the size of the request zone can be enlarged considering the trade-off between the number of RREQ messages and the number of potential network routes found by the route discovery. Then source node *s* selects a node from each neighboring cell contained in the request zone and forwards an RREQ message to the node. A node, which received the RREQ message, selects its neighbors from the neighboring cells in the same way. This is a kind of selective forwarding like PLBR (Sisodia, Manoj & Murthy, 2002) and GPCR (Lochert, Mauve, Füßler & Hartenstein, 2005), where only limited and designated neighbors forward RREQ messages to avoid collision. If a node in a neighboring cell of *G(d)* receives an RREQ message, it designates the node (say node *d'*) with the smallest ID in cell *G(d)* and sends the RREQ message to the node. This node *d'* is called the representative node of the destination point *d*. Thus, multiple RREQ messages that have traversed different network routes may arrive at node d' if node d' waits for a while after it receives the first RREQ message. Node d' chooses the best network route (the route selection algorithm is given later), and sends an RREP (Route REPly) message to source node s on the chosen network route.

The goal of this route discovery process is to find a network route with a longer lifetime. To achieve this goal, it is best to find a network route on vehicles moving from s to d (or d to s) at the same speed, following the same driving route. To achieve this without knowledge about the current and future driving plan of each vehicle, GVGrid finds a network route along a driving route between s to d, which many vehicles may follow and in which a fewer number of streets and intersections is contained. It is usually expected that many vehicles are likely to keep their directions and speeds if the driving route contains a fewer number of streets, intersections and signals.

Figure 12 illustrates how RREQ and RREP messages are propagated. Each solid line represents a street, and each small square at a crossing point of streets represents an intersection. Also, the number attached to an arrow represents the number of RREQ messages transmitted. In Figure 12(a), starting from source node s, a node is selected from each neighboring cell contained in the request zone, and we can see that multiple RREQ messages (20 messages in this figure) arrive at node d', which is the representative node of cell $G(d)$. In response, an RREP message is returned as shown in Figure 12(b), updating the routing tables of the intermediate nodes.

A neighbor selection algorithm is used to select from a neighboring cell a neighbor to which an RREQ message is forwarded. This algorithm requires the list of neighbors and their position information. Node u selects a node on the same road segment $road(u)$ or an adjacent road segment of $road(u)$, from each neighboring cell (say g) of $G(u)$, which is in the request zone. Two road segments are said to be adjacent if they share an

intersection. The selection policy is given below. (1) A node on the road segment $road(u)$ or on the adjacent road segment (say e) is prioritized where $road(u)$ and e are on the same street. This is reasonable because node u can move while keeping a certain distance. If there is more than one node that is selected by the above policy, the following policy is applied: nodes moving toward the same direction as u are prioritized more than nodes moving in the opposite direction. Then the node that is the closest to a designated point (say point p) is prioritized. Point p is determined as follows. If g contains the intersection shared by $road(u)$ and e, this intersection is designated as p. Otherwise, the center of g is designated as p.

Determining p is based on the following idea. Usually in cities, the Line-of-Sight (LoS) is limited only to forward and backward directions. Therefore, in order to deliver an RREQ message to a crossing street with high probability, node u should select a node closest to an intersection. Such a node can relay the RREQ message to the crossing street. For example, in Figure 13(a), the selected neighbor y may have difficulty forwarding the received RREQ message to vertical directions because of obstacles at the corners, while it is easier for node x in Figure 13(b). If no node is selected in this policy (1), then policy (2) is applied. (2) A node on the other adjacent road segment (say e') of $road(u)$ is selected where $road(u)$ and e' are not on the same street. In this second policy, no direction information is used because there is no similarity of directions between two vehicles on different streets. If there are many of such nodes, then the node closest to a designated point p is selected. p is determined as follows. If g contains the intersection shared by $road(u)$ and e', this intersection is designated as p. Otherwise, the center of g is designated as p. If no node is selected in this policy, then no RREQ message is sent to this cell g from node u.

Figure 12(c) illustrates how this algorithm selects neighbors. Each line corresponds to a street. Node u in cell <11> selects node a from

Figure 12. Route discovery process examples

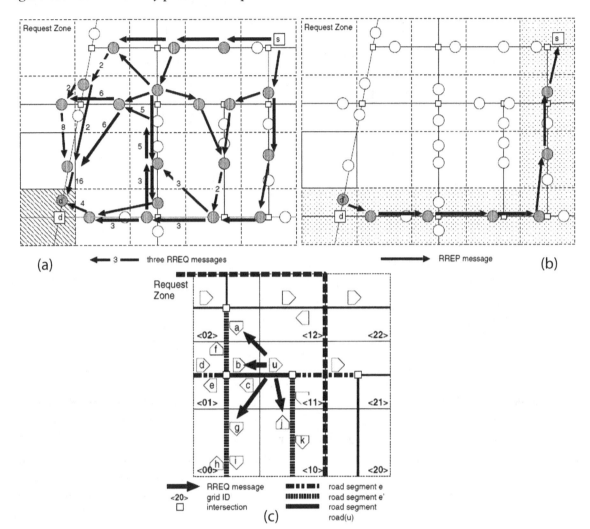

cell <02> and node g from cell <00> (if a signal from node u reaches them) according to policy (2). For both cells, their centers are specified as the point p because they do not contain the intersection shared with *road(u)*. Node b from cell <01> is selected according to policy (1). In cell <01>, nodes b and d are prioritized more than nodes c and e since their directions are the same as node u. Here, as with point p, the intersection shared with *road(u)* is designated. Thus node b, which is closer to p than node d, is selected. Cells <20>, <21> and <22> are outside of the request zone, and <12> has no adjacent road segment.

The algorithm requires each node u to know the following information for each neighbor v; geographic position $P(v)$ and position $P'(v)$ on the road graph (a pair of a road segment and a direction). One possible and ordinary implementation is using hello messages where each hello message sent from node u contains $P(u)$ and $P'(u)$. Here, a shorter interval of hello message transmissions may lead to higher interference, and a longer interval may lead to larger position errors. A possible solution in this case is to use a longer interval with compensation of position information using velocity. If each node may be

Figure 13. Effect of line-of-sight (LoS)

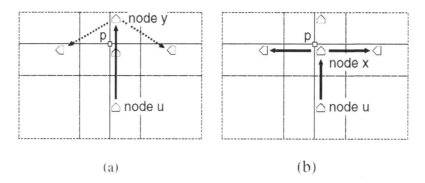

(a)   (b)

Figure 14. A network route

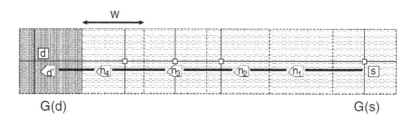

able to include the global time and velocity in addition to the position information in each hello message, the node that received the message can predict the current position using this information.

Another option is to use black-burst technique as it is done in UMB (Korkmaz, Ekici, Ozguner & Ozguner, 2004). Sender u of an RREQ message transmits a neighbor query message that includes the position information of node u. Each neighbor v, which hears this message immediately transmits a burst of noise for a period whose length is proportional to the Euclid distance between u and v. After the burst of noise, node v senses the channel, and transmits a reply to the neighbor query message only if the channel is empty, otherwise it becomes silent.

The impact of driving route characteristics on network route lifetime is an important issue. A route lifetime estimation algorithm is used by the representative node d' to choose the best route in the route discovery process. Since nodes on a

network route are in different cells, the average distance of two adjacent nodes on the network route is expected to be the side length w of the cell. As defined earlier, w is smaller than the communication range r. Therefore, a link between the two nodes will be maintained in a high probability if these two nodes move with similar speeds, in similar directions. As described in the neighbor selection algorithm, each node selects a neighboring node that moves in the same direction if such a node exists. Here, a network route is represented as s-n_1-...-n_k-d' as shown in Figure 14.

There are many factors that break the network route. (1) Since s is stationary, link (s, n_1) will be disconnected as n_1 moves. (2) The representative node d' in $G(d)$ will leave from $G(d)$. (3) (n_i, n_{i+1}) will be disconnected for the following three reasons. (a) Without loss of generality, we assume that n_{i+1} exists in front of n_i. If only n_i is stopped by a signal, the distance between n_i and n_{i+1} becomes longer as n_{i+1} moves. (b) At each intersection without a signal (i.e. nodes do not need to stop there), n_i may move in another direction going outside the cell sequence. (c) At each intersection with a signal, we have to mix the above two cases (3-a) and (3-b). During the green light, the number of disconnections per unit of time is obtained by (3-b). During the red light, it is obtained by (3-a).

Let V denote the average speed of nodes, C denote the interval of time when the light changes from green to red (i.e. the signal cycle), and ρ denote the ratio of the green light time in C (thus 1-ρ denotes the ratio of the red light time). Also, let θ denote the probability that a node stays on the road segment on the cell sequence after a node passes an intersection. Therefore, the node leaves the cell sequence with probability $1 - \theta$. The expected number of disconnections on the network route per unit of time is obtained as follows.

$$\frac{V}{r-w} + \frac{2V}{3w} + x^* \frac{V(1-\acute{A})}{C(r-w)} + y^* \frac{V(1-,)}{w}$$
$$+z^* \left\{ \frac{V(1-,)}{w} + \frac{V(1-,)(1-\acute{A})}{C(r-w)} \right\}$$

x, y and z denote the numbers of signals of type (3-a), intersections of type (3-b) and intersections of (3-c) on the driving route, respectively. Since x, y and z are recorded in every RREQ message, the representative node can determine the network route that will provide the longest lifetime, that is, the inverse of this disconnection ratio. The detailed analysis can be found in (Sun, Yamaguchi, Yukimasa & Kusumoto, 2006).

ROUTE MAINTENANCE PROCESS

The maintenance process is activated when a link of the network route is broken. The basic idea is that when a link is broken, the vehicles that are away from the recorded cell sequence are removed from the network route, and nodes on the cell sequence are found to recover the network route on the same cell sequence. It is possible because each node on the network route records the cell sequence in its routing table, and can determine whether the node is in one of the cells in the sequence or not. This idea is based on the observation that the driving route that is selected by the route selection algorithm is able to provide the best network route. Thus, another attempt of driving route discovery is not necessary.

Hereafter, let $f(u)$ and $b(u)$ denote the forward and backward neighbors of u on the network route, respectively. The basic procedure is as follows. If link (u, v) of the network route $(v = f(u))$ is broken, node u checks whether it is on the cell sequence or not. If not, node u tries to remove itself from the network route by disconnecting the link $(b(u), u)$. For this purpose, node u sends a LEAVE message. In response, node $b(u)$ does the same thing. As a result, node u and its upstream nodes that are away from the cell sequence are removed from the network route. Node v does the same thing towards the downstream. As a result, node v and its downstream nodes, which are away from the cell sequence, are removed from the network route. Then, the upstream node (say u') of u, which is still on the cell sequence, starts repairing the broken route, by selecting a new node u'' using the neighbor selection algorithm. This is done only from the neighboring cell of $G(u')$, which is in the cell sequence. If link (u', u'') is established, u' sends, as a Route Repair (RRPR) message, the cell sequence so that node u'' can find the forward neighbor. This is continued until a node with a route cache or a new representative node d'' of d is found. This means that route recovery is performed only on the cell sequence. Note that route cache is a routing table entry of the network route whose links are still active.

Figure 15. Route maintenance process

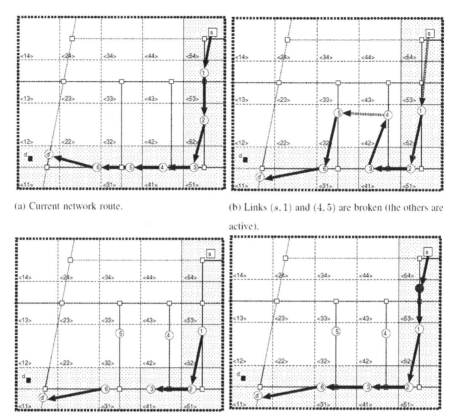

(a) Current network route.

(b) Links $(s, 1)$ and $(4, 5)$ are broken (the others are active).

(c) Nodes outside the grid sequence and associated links are removed from network route.

(d) Recovered route.

Therefore, if there is a node that has a network cache, such a node is searched for to utilize the fragmented network route. Such a node can immediately send a triggered hello message to let the neighbors know that it has a route cache. As an extra case, if representative node d' is away from a neighboring cell of $G(d)$, it immediately disconnects link $(b(d'), d')$ so that an alternative node can be found in $G(d)$.

Figure 15 illustrates how the route maintenance process works. The initial network route is shown in Figure 15(a). Then in Figure 15(b), links $(s, 1)$ and $(4, 5)$ are disconnected due to obstacles or distance. As a result, as shown in Figure 15(c), s and node 3 recognize that they need to find a new neighbor from the neighboring cell on the cell sequence, in order to recover the network route. Node s finds a new node, and the new node finds node 1, which has route cache. Also, node 3 finds node 6, which has route cache. The result is shown in Figure 15(d).

FUTURE RESEARCH DIRECTIONS

As we have seen in this chapter, recent routing protocols fully utilize position, movement and map information and are therefore expected to achieve higher performance in theory. They are very sophisticated based on unique and novel ideas. Therefore, further research on routing is required not in designing a new routing protocol, but for other issues. For example, vehicles' mobility analysis and real trace provision is desired

Table 1. Summary of VANET geographic routing protocols

	year	name	destination	communication style	design characteristics
Briesemeister & Hommel	2000	Role-based Multicast (RBM)	vehicles (by location, speed, driving direction and time)	broadcast	This mainly focuses on how to determine the multicast group
Sun, Feng, Lai, Yamada, Okada & Fujimura	2000	TRADE (TRacking DEtection) & DDT (Distance Defer Transfer)	every vehicle	broadcast	TRADE introduces the notion of mobility prediction. DDT is a delay-based control of retransmission
Morris, Jannoti, Kaashoek, Li & De-couto	2000	CarNet	vehicle (by position)	unicast	Location-service that tells the location of destination is desgined and heterogeneous vehicle density is considered for scalable commpnication
Lochert, Hartenstein, Tian, Fuessler, Hermann & Mauve	2003	Geographic Source Routing (GSR)	vehicle (by position)	unicast in city environment	Map-based route calculation at source is adopted
Seet, Liu, Lee, Foh, Wong & Lee	2004	Anchor-based Street and Traffic Aware Routing (A-STAR)	vehicle (by position)	unicast in city environment	This is similar with GSR, but A-STAR is traffic-aware
Korkmaz, Ekici, Ozguner, and Ozguner	2004	Urban Multi-hop Broadcast (UMB)	every vehicle	broadcast in city environment	Location-based busy tone is introduced
Wu, Fujimoto, Guensler & Hunter	2004	Mobility-centric Data Dissemination algorithm for Vehicular networks (MDDV)	vehicle group (by road segment)	store-and-carry in city environment	Forwarding path is calculated based on road map.
Lochert, Mauve, Füßler & Hartenstein	2005	Greedy Perimeter Coordinator Routing (GPCR)	vehicle (by position)	unicast in city environment	Coordinators at intersections are chosen to forward messages.
Maihöfer, Leinmüller & Schoch	2005	abiding geocast	vehicles (by region and time)	unicast	several schemes are considered to achieve time-dependent multicast
Sun, Yamaguchi, Yukimasa & Kusumoto	2006	GVGrid	vehicle group (by region)	unicast in city environment	Map and traffic-aware routing path is established for long-lived path
Granelli, Boato & Kliazovich	2006	MOvement-based Routing Algorithm (MORA)	vehicle (by position)	unicast in city environment	Appropriate forwarders are chosen based on source-destination line segment.
Zhao & Cao	2006	Vehicle-Assisted Data Delivery (VADD)	vehicle (by position)	store-and-carry	Traffic statistics and road map are used to determine the best forwarding direction.
Naumov, Baumann & Gross	2006	Preferred Group Broadcasting (PGM)	every vehicle	broadcast	broadcast optimization by signal strength (and position, if any)
Oh, Kang & Gruteser	2006	N/A	every vehicle	broadcast	hybrid forwarding strategy of location-based and counter-based ones is introduced to cope with very high density in VANETs.
Granelli, Boato, Kliazovich & Vernazza	2007	Movement-Aware GPSR (GPSR-MA)	vehicle (by position)	unicast in city environment	Speed and direction information is used to estimate the up-to-date location of neighbors and to choose apprpriate neighbors
Wisitpongphan, Bai, Mudalige, Sadekar & Tonguz	2007	N/A	vehicle (by position)	store-and-carry	Network connectivity is analyzed in empirical study and routing strategy is designed.

continued on following page

Table 1. continued

	year	name	destination	communication style	design characteristics
Taleb, Sakhaee, Jamalipour, Hashimoto, Kato & Nemoto	2007	stable routing protocol.	vehicle (by position)	unicast in city environment	Vehicles with similar mobility are grouped.
Namboodiri & Gao	2007	Prediction-Based Routing (PBR)	mobile gateway	unitcast in highway	Route lifetime is considered in the design.
Skordylis & Trigoni	2008	Delay-bounded Greedy Forwarding (D-Greedy) & Delay-bounded Min-Cost Forwarding (D-Min-Cost)	access point (by position)	store-and-carry	Forwarding path is calculated considering given delay-bound
Feng, Hsu & Lu	2008	Velocity-Assisted Routing (VAR)	vehicle (by position)	store-and-carry	Traffic patterns and road layout are fully utilized to choose the direction
Zhang & Wolff	2008	Border node-based Routing (BBR)	vehicle (by position) or every vehicle	store-and-carry	Routing in rural area is considered.
Ding, Wang & Xiao	2008	Static-node assisted Adaptive data Dissemination protocol for Vehicular networks (SADV)	vehicle	store-and-carry	Static nodes that assist to deliver messages are assumed at intersections
Li & Lou	2008	Opportunistic Broadcast Protocol (OBP)	every vehicle	broadcast	Two types of forwarders are introduced to guarantee time and minimum packet reception probability

for real development of routing protocols (Füßler, Torrent-Moreno, Transier, Krüger, Hartenstein & Effelsberg, 2005; Wisitpongphan, Bai, Mudalige, Sadekar & Tonguz, 2007). Analysis of link, route and topological characteristics under such realistic mobility models and traces or in real environments has been a hot topic (Chen, Kung & Vlah, 2001; Wang, 2004; Haerri, Filali & Bonnet, 2004; Naumov, Baumann & Gross, 2006; Fiore & Härri, 2008; Khabazian & Ali, 2008; Zhao, Arnold, Zhang & Cao, 2008; Huang & Fang, 2009). Design of data routing well-fit for domain-specific problems is a possible direction. In this case, not only safety applications but also non-emergency applications like communication assistance between drivers of merging vehicles (Wang, Kulik & Kotagiri, 2007) can be considered. New network architecture such as overlay networks (Lee, Le, Harri & Gerla, 2009) has recently been considered.

CONCLUSION

This chapter addresses several challenges for designing position-based routing protocols in VANETs. As we have shown, there are many factors to be considered in design. In VANETs, energy for computation and transmission is not limited and a variety of information can be obtained through each vehicle's GPS, sensors and digital maps. Information about neighbors can also be obtained through communication. Fully utilizing such rich information, the routing strategy should be intelligent, and many investigations have been done based on this observation. Furthermore, the routing strategies are very different from generic MANET routing because of VANETs' special features. We have introduced and classified existing approaches and stated their characteristics and novelty. We have summarized those protocols in Table 1 for convenience. We note that very recent publication (Bernsena, J. & Manivannan, D, 2009) provides comparison of unicast routing protocols, some of which are explained in this chapter. Interested readers may refer to the paper. We have also given a design reference of QoS routing on VANET. We believe that the chapter description will be informative for many readers who are engaged in VANET protocol research and development.

REFERENCES

Basagni, S., Chlamtac, I., Syrotiuk, V. R., & Woodward, B. A. (1998). A distance routing effect algorithm for mobility (DREAM). In *Proceedings of the 4th Annual ACM/IEEE International Conference on Mobile Computing and Networking* (MobiCom '98), (pp. 76–84). Dallas, TX.

Bernsena, J., & Manivannan, D. (2009). Unicast routing protocols for vehicular ad hoc networks: A critical comparison and classification. *Pervasive and Mobile Computing*, *5*(1), 1–18. doi:10.1016/j.pmcj.2008.09.001

Briesemeister, L., & Hommel, G. (2000). Role-based multicast in highly mobile but sparsely connected ad hoc networks. In *Proceedings of the 1st ACM International Symposium on Mobile Ad Hoc Networking and Computing* (MobiHoc'00), (pp. 45–50). Boston.

Briesemeister, L., Schäfers, L., & Hommel, G. (2000). Disseminating messages among highly mobile hosts based on inter-vehicle communication. In *Proceedings of the IEEE Intelligent Vehicles Symposium* (pp. 522-527). Dearborn, MI.

Chen, Z. D., Kung, H. T., & Vlah, D. (2001). Ad hoc relay wireless networks over moving vehicles on highways. In *Proceedings of 2nd ACM International Symposium on Mobile Ad Hoc Networking and Computing* (MobiHoc'01), (pp. 247-250). Long Beach, CA.

Ding, Y., Wang, C., & Xiao, L. (2008). A static-node assisted adaptive routing protocol in vehicular networks. In *Proceedings of the 5th ACM International Workshop on Vehicular Ad Hoc Networks* (VANET2008) (pp.59-68). San Francisco.

Feng, K. T., Hsu, C. H., & Lu, T. E. (2008). Velocity-assisted predictive mobility and location-aware routing protocols for mobile ad hoc networks. *IEEE Transactions on Vehicular Technology*, *57*(1), 448–464. doi:10.1109/TVT.2007.901897

Fiore, M., & Härri, J. (2008). The networking shape of vehicular mobility. In *Proceedings of the 9th ACM International Symposium on Mobile Ad Hoc Networking and Computing* (MobiHoc'08), (pp. 108–119). Hong Kong, China.

Fubler, H., Widmer, J., Kasemann, M., Mauve, M., & Hartenstein, H. (2003). Contention based forwarding for mobile ad-hoc networks. *Ad Hoc Networks (Elsevier)*, *1*(4), 351–369. doi:10.1016/S1570-8705(03)00038-6

Füßler, H., Torrent-Moreno, M., Transier, M., Krüger, R., Hartenstein, H., & Effelsberg, W. (2005). Studying vehicle movements on highways and their impact on adhoc connectivity. In *Proceedings of ACM International Conference on Mobile Computing and Networking* (Mobicom 2005). Cologne, Germany.

Granelli, F., Boato, G., & Kliazovich, D. (2006). MORA: a movement-based routing algorithm for vehicle ad hoc networks. In *Proceedings of the 1st IEEE Workshop on Automotive Networking and Applications* (AutoNet 2006). San Francisco.

Granelli, F., Boato, G., Kliazovich, D., & Vernazza, G. (2007). Enhanced GPSR routing in multi-hop vehicular communications through movement awareness. *IEEE Communications Letters*, *11*(10), 781–783. doi:10.1109/LCOMM.2007.070685

Guo, H. (2009). *Automotive informatics and communicative systems: principles in vehicular networks and data exchange*. Hershey, PA: IGI Global.

Haerri, J., Filali, F., & Bonnet, C. (n.d.). On meaningful parameters for routing in VANETs urban environments under realistic mobility patterns. In *Proceedings of 1st IEEE Workshop on Automotive Networking and Applications* (AutoNet 2006). San Francisco.

Huang, X., & Fang, Y. (2009). Performance study of node-disjoint multipath routing in vehicular ad hoc networks. *IEEE Transactions on Vehicular Technology*, *58*(4), 1942–1950. doi:10.1109/TVT.2008.2008094

Karp, B., & Kung, H. T. (2000). GPSR: greedy perimeter stateless routing for wireless networks. In *Proceedings of the ACM/IEEE International Conference on Mobile Computing and Networking* (MobiCom 2000). Boston.

Khabazian, M., & Ali, M. (2008). A Performance modeling of connectivity in vehicular ad hoc networks. *IEEE Transactions on Vehicular Technology*, *57*(4), 2440–2450. doi:10.1109/TVT.2007.912161

Ko, Y. B., & Vaidya, N. H. (1998). Location-aided routing (LAR) in mobile ad hoc networks. In *Proceedings of the ACM/IEEE International Conference on Mobile Computing and Networking* (MobiCom'98), (pp.66-75). Dallas, TX.

Korkmaz, G., Ekici, E., Ozguner, F., & Ozguner, U. (2004). Urban multi-hop broadcast protocol for inter-vehicle communication systems. In *Proceedings of the 1st ACM Workshop on Vehicular Ad Hoc Networks* (VANET 2004), (pp. 76-85). Philadelphia.

Lee, K. C., Le, M., Harri, J., & Gerla, M. (2009). Taking the LOUVRE approach. *IEEE Vehicular Technology Magazine*, *4*(1), 86–92. doi:10.1109/MVT.2009.931918

Li, F., & Wang, Y. (2007). Routing in vehicular ad hoc networks: a survey. *IEEE Vehicular Technology Magazine*, *2*(2), 12–22. doi:10.1109/MVT.2007.912927

Li, M., & Lou, W. (2008). Opportunistic broadcast of emergency messages in vehicular ad hoc networks with unreliable links. In *Proceedings of the 5th International ICST Conference on Heterogeneous Networking for Quality, Reliability, Security and Robustness* (pp. 1-7). Hong Kong, China.

Lochert, C., Hartenstein, H., Tian, J., Fuessler, H., Hermann, D., & Mauve, M. (2003). A routing strategy for vehicular ad hoc networks in city environments. In *Proceedings of the Intelligent Vehicles Symposium* (pp. 156-161). Parma, Italy.

Lochert, C., Mauve, M., Füßler, H., & Hartenstein, H. (2005). Geographic routing in city scenarios. *ACM Mobile Computation and Communication Review (MC2R)*, *9*(1), 69-72.

Luo, J., & Hubaux, J. P. (2005). *A survey of research in inter-vehicle communications, Embedded Security in Cars*. Berlin, Germany: Springer-Verlag.

Maihöfer, C. (2004). A survey of geocast routing protocols. *IEEE Communications Surveys & Tutorials*, *6*(2), 32–42. doi:10.1109/COMST.2004.5342238

Maihöfer, C., Leinmüller, T., & Schoch, E. (2005). Abiding geocast: time-stable geocast for ad hoc networks. In *Proceedings of the 2nd ACM International Workshop on Vehicular Ad Hoc Networks* (VANET '05), (pp. 20–29). Cologne, Germany.

Mauve, M., Widmer, A., & Hartenstein, H. (2001). A survey on position based routing in mobile ad hoc networks. *IEEE Network*, *15*(6), 30–39. doi:10.1109/65.967595

Morris, R., Jannoti, J., Kaashoek, F., Li, J., & De-couto, D. (2000, September). CarNet: a scalable ad hoc wireless network system. In *Proceedings of SIGOPS European Workshop*. Kolding, Denmark.

Moustafa, H., & Zhang, Y. (Eds.). (2009). *Vehicular networks: techniques, standards, and applications*. Boca Raton, FL: Auerbach Publications. doi:10.1201/9781420085723

Namboodiri, V., & Gao, L. (2007). Prediction-based routing for vehicular ad hoc networks. *IEEE Transactions on Vehicular Technology*, *56*(4), 2332–2345. doi:10.1109/TVT.2007.897656

Naumov, V., Baumann, R., & Gross, T. (2006). An evaluation of inter-vehicle ad hoc networks based on realistic vehicular traces. In *Proceedings of the 7th ACM International Symposium on Mobile Ad Hoc Networking and Computing* (MobiHoc'06), (pp. 108-119). Florence, Italy.

Navigation Center, U.S. Department of Homeland Security. (2009). *Differential Global Positioning System* (DGPS). Retrieved from http://www.navcen.uscg.gov/dgps/default.htm

Ni, S., Tseng, Y., Chen, Y., & Sheu, J. (1999). The broadcast storm problem in a mobile ad hoc network. In *Proceedings of the 5th Annual ACM/IEEE International Conference on Mobile Computing and Networking* (MobiCom '99), (pp. 151-162). Seattle, WA.

Oh, S., Kang, J., & Gruteser, M. (2006). Location-based flooding techniques for vehicular emergency messaging. In *Proceedings of the 2nd International Workshop on Vehicle-to-Vehicle Communications* (V2VCOM 2006), (pp. 1-9). San Jose, CA.

Olariu, S., & Weigle, M. C. (Eds.). (2009). *Vehicular networks: from theory to practice*. Boca Raton, FL: Chapman & Hall/CRC.

Seet, B. C., Liu, G., Lee, B. S., Foh, C. H., Wong, K. J., & Lee, K. K. (2004). A-STAR: A Mobile Ad Hoc Routing Strategy for Metropolis Vehicular Communications. In *Proceedings of IFIP Networking* (pp. 989-999). Athens, Greece.

Sichitiu, M. L., & Kihl, M. (2008). Inter-vehicle communication systems: a survey. *IEEE Communications Surveys & Tutorials*, *10*(2), 88–105. doi:10.1109/COMST.2008.4564481

Sisodia, R. S., Manoj, B. S., & Murthy, C. S. R. (2002). A preferred link based routing protocol for ad hoc wireless networks. *Journal of Communications and Networks*, *4*(1), 14–21.

Skordylis, A., & Trigoni, N. (2008). Delay-bounded routing in vehicular ad-hoc networks. In *Proceedings of the 9th ACM International Symposium on Mobile Ad Hoc Networking and Computing* (MobiHoc '08), (pp. 341-350). Hong Kong, China.

Stojmenovic, I. (2002). Position based routing in ad hoc wireless networks. *IEEE Communications Magazine*, *40*(7), 128–134. doi:10.1109/MCOM.2002.1018018

Sun, M. T., Feng, W. C., Lai, T. H., Yamada, K., Okada, H., & Fujimura, K. (2000). GPS-based message broadcasting for inter-vehicle communication. In *Proceedings of the 52nd Fall IEEE Vehicular Technology Conference* (Fall-VTC2000), (pp.2685-2692). Boston.

Sun, W., Yamaguchi, H., Yukimasa, K., & Kusumoto, S. (2006). GVGrid: a QoS routing protocol for vehicular ad hoc networks. In *Proceedings of the 14th IEEE International Workshop on Quality of Service* (IWQoS2006), (pp. 130-139). New Haven, CT.

Taleb, T., Sakhaee, E., Jamalipour, A., Hashimoto, K., Kato, N., & Nemoto, Y. (2007). A stable routing protocol to support ITS services in VANET networks. *IEEE Transactions on Vehicular Technology*, *56*(6), 3337–3347. doi:10.1109/TVT.2007.906873

Tseng, Y. C., Ni, S. Y., & Shih, E. Y. (2003). Adaptive approaches to relieving broadcast storms in a wireless multihop mobile ad hoc network. *IEEE Transactions on Computers*, *52*(5), 545–557. doi:10.1109/TC.2003.1197122

Wang, S. Y. (2004). On the intermittence of routing paths in vehicle-formed mobile ad hoc networks on highways. In *Proceedings of the IEEE International Conference on Intelligent Transportation Systems* (ITSC2004). Osaka, Japan.

Wang, Z., Kulik, L., & Kotagiri, R. (2007). Proactive traffic merging strategies for sensor-enabled cars. In *Proceedings of the 4th ACM International Workshop on Vehicular Ad Hoc Networks* (VANET2007), (pp. 39-48). Montreal, Canada.

Willke, T. L., Tientrakool, P., & Maxemchuk, N. F. (2008). A survey of inter-vehicle communication protocols and their applications. *IEEE Communications Surveys & Tutorials*, *11*(2), 3–20. doi:10.1109/SURV.2009.090202

Wisitpongphan, N., Bai, F., Mudalige, P., Sadekar, V., & Tonguz, O. (2007). Routing in sparse vehicular ad hoc wireless networks. *IEEE Journal on Selected Areas in Communications*, *25*(8), 1538–1556. doi:10.1109/JSAC.2007.071005

Wu, H., & Fujimoto, R. Guensler, R., & Hunter, M. (2004). MDDV: a mobility-centric data dissemination algorithm for vehicular networks. In *Proceedings of the 1st ACM Workshop on Vehicular Ad Hoc Networks* (VANET 2004), (pp. 47-56). Philadelphia.

Zhang, M., & Wolff, R. (2008). Routing protocols for vehicular ad hoc networks in rural areas. *IEEE Communications Magazine*, *46*(11), 126–131. doi:10.1109/MCOM.2008.4689255

Zhao, J., Arnold, T., Zhang, Y., & Cao, G. (2008). Extending drive-thru data access by vehicle-to-vehicle relay. In *Proceedings of the 5th ACM International Workshop on VehiculAr Inter-NETworking* (VANET 2008) (pp. 66-75). San Francisco.

Zhao, J., & Cao, G. (2006). VADD: vehicle-assisted data delivery in vehicular ad hoc networks. In *Proceedings of the 25th IEEE International Conference on Computer Communications* (Infocom'06), (pp. 1–12). Barcelona, Spain.

KEY TERMS AND DEFINITIONS

Geocast: Data transmission destined for some specific region. It usually employs position-based routing.

GPSR: Greedy Perimeter Stateless Routing.

Greedy Forwarding: A packet forwarding strategy where each packet forwarder chooses the neighbor node closest to the destination among the others and closer to the destination than the packet forwarder as a next forwarder.

Hidden Terminal Problem: Two nodes which cannot hear from each other interfere the reception by the same receiver.

LoS: Line of sight.

Perimeter Routing: A packet forwarding strategy where each packet is traversed on the perimeter of face in planar graph to detour obstacles, which cannot be detoured by greedy forwarding strategies.

Position-Based Routing: Routing where each node's position information is used in packet forwarding strategy.

Chapter 10
Reliable Routing Protocols in VANETs

Gongjun Yan
Old Dominion University, USA

Danda B. Rawat
Old Dominion University, USA

Samy El-Tawab
Old Dominion University, USA

ABSTRACT

One of the notoriously difficult problems in vehicular ad-hoc networks is to ensure that established paths do not break before the end of data transmission. This is a difficult problem because the network topology is changing constantly and the routing links are inherently unstable. This chapter reviews several routing protocols which are designed for vehicular network environment. Currently, there are five major types of routing protocols based on the metrics used for routing: 1) flooding based routing, 2) mobility based routing, 3) infrastructure based routing, 4) geographic position based routing, and 5) probability model based routing. We give a survey of each type of routing method. Since probability theory is an ideal tool to describe the dynamics of vehicles, we present one probability model based routing method as a detailed example.

INTRODUCTION

The impetus of VANET is that in the not-so-distant future vehicles equipped with computing, communication and sensing capabilities will be organized into a ubiquitous and pervasive network that can provide numerous services to travelers, ranging from improved driving safety and comfort, to delivering multimedia content on demand, and to other similar value-added service. Indeed, the fact of being networked together promotes car-to-car communications, even between cars that are tens of miles apart. Imagine, for example, a car that travels down an interstate and whose passengers are interested in viewing a particular movie. The various blocks of this movie happen to be available at various other cars on the interstate, often miles away. The task of collecting the blocks of the movie translates, at the network layer, into finding appropriate routes between the various sources (cars that are willing

DOI: 10.4018/978-1-61520-913-2.ch010

to share movie blocks) and the receiving car. Given the FCC-mandated short communication range, the routing paths between cars are usually multi-hop. In addition, cars in various lanes move at different speed, making the underlying network highly dynamic. In such a network, individual communication links are short-lived and the routing paths that rely on a multitude of such links are highly vulnerable to disconnection. A simple solution is flooding-based routing schemes. However, flooding-based routing methods occupy the whole network resources and each packet is repeatedly received by nodes between the sender and the receiver. Moreover, broadcasting storm will be resulted if the number of nodes is large. Therefore, there are some light-weighted routing methods are proposed. With the assistant of infrastructure, packets can be propagated among vehicles, even when the traffic is sparse. Infrastructures relay or even buffer packets until next vehicle is available. Geographic position is used to optimize the routing process. Vehicles knowing the geographic position of neighbors can select a greedy/efficient routing path to transmit packets. Both infrastructure based and geographic position based routing methods need extra device or information. The vehicle mobility is used to predict that if the link between two vehicles will break or not after a certain time interval, in mobility based methods. A probability model based routing method avoids using extra device or information. A probability model will be setup to model the wireless routing link which only involves two nodes. The durations of the routing links will be used as a major parameter, stability of a link. The probability based method selectively probes the routing links which compose a routing path, among possible links, to avoid brute-force flooding probing. There are two steps: selectively probing the possible links and selecting a reliable routing path which is composed by multiple routing links. We give a survey of each type of routing method. Since probability theory is an ideal tool to describe the dynamics of vehicles, we present

one probability model based routing method as a detailed example.

THE FLOODING BASED ROUTING

In flooding routing protocol, the basic idea is to broadcast packets on the whole network. Each node receiving a packet will rebroadcast it if the node is not the destination node. It is not an efficient routing protocol in terms of bandwidth and delay. If all nodes can be reached within the transmission range of transceiver, flooding method can be seen as an efficient routing scheme. However, in case of multi-hop communication, the performance of network will dramatically drop when the population of nodes increases. Flooding methods will encounter a lot of duplicates of packets, even causing broadcasting storm. In addition, the flooding methods scale badly beyond a few hundred nodes.

But it is a reliable routing in terms of availability, especially when the topology of network is constantly changing and the traffic density is not high. Since the pure flooding methods are costly in delay and bandwidth, enhanced flooding methods are proposed. The basic idea of the enhancement is to find a feasible routing path by broadcasting a control message or probe and then to send packets through the found routing path. For example, Namboodiri & Gao (2007) broadcast RREQ to find a routing path to gateway and a RREP is sent to acknowledge the routing path. Abedi et al. (2008); Li & Cuthbert (2004) use RREQ to explore routing path as well. These types of routing method are on the basis of AODV (Perkins et al. (2003)) which is initially proposed in MANET (Mobile Adhoc Network). AODV is a unicast on-demand routing protocol which includes two phases, route discovery process and route maintenance process. Four types of control packets are used: HELLO (a Hello message), RREQ (Route Request), RREP (Route Reply), and RERR (Route Error). Additionally, there are several other flooding based mechanisms used in MANET, for example DSR (Johnson et al. (2007)), DSDV (Perkins & Bhagwat (1994)).

Biswas et al. (2006) addressed a flooding routing method which extends the original flooding method by acknowledging the flooding message. When a node receives a packet, it rebroadcast the packet. This vehicle watches the packet from behind vehicles. If it receives the same message from behind, it infers that at least one vehicle in the back has received the packet and will retransmit the packet. Therefore, the event of receiving the same packet from behind vehicles is treated as a acknowledgment of flooding. If the vehicle does not receive the acknowledgment, it will periodically rebroadcast the packet until the acknowledgment is received.

THE MOBILITY BASED ROUTING

The Mobility Based Routing Mobility is one of the major differences between VANET and other network system, even MANET. In the wired networks, such as Ethernet and ACM, nodes are fixed in location. In the conventional wireless network, such as MANETs which is often used as network in a small region like airport, nodes often have slow mobility. In cellular networks, nodes can have fast mobility but the communications among nodes are often through infrastructure, i.e. base station. Nodes in VANET are often with high mobility, for example fast speed and frequently changing speed and directions. The high mobility makes many of the existing conventional routing algorithms not applicable to VANET. Mobility, therefore, is used as a key factor to select and maintain a routing path.

Li & Cuthbert (2004) and Taleb et al. (2007) present a routing method by grouping vehicles according to velocity. The basic idea of the method is to predict a possible link breakage event prior to its occurrence by computing from vehicle's speed.

Vehicles are grouped into four different groups based on their velocity vectors (speed with directions). If the directions of speeds of two vehicles are same, the link between the vehicles will stay longer than the link composed by two vehicles with different speed directions. The process of routing path searching is the following. Initially, the source node broadcasts a request packet: RREQ. This RREQ will be disseminated among nodes by rebroadcasting. The most suitable path is chosen when the RREQ is reached at the destination. The duration of the path is predicted by the vehicle's speed and the distance of the two vehicles. A new route discovery is always initiated prior duration of the routing path, i.e. the shortest link duration.

Abedi et al. (2008) present a enhanced routing protocol based on AODV to adapt the high mobility of vehicles, three mobility parameters: position, direction and speed. This method treats direction as most important parameter to select next hop because the nodes moving with the same directions will be more stable than nodes with opposite directions. Therefore, this method will select routing links composed by nodes with the same directions with source and/or destination nodes. Moreover, position is the second important parameter that is used for next hop selection.

Wedde et al. (2007) address a routing algorithm based on a rating value. The rating value is computed to evaluate the road conditions (actual traffic situation), based on the interdependencies of average vehicle speed, traffic density and the traffic quality (in terms of congestion). A routing link is incorporated into a routing path if the rating value satisfies a certain requirement, i.e. the rating value.

Niu et al. (2007) propose a new link reliability mathematical model which considers not only the impact of the link duration but also the traffic density. A purposed of this model is to find a route which is not only reliable but also compliant with delay requirements in multimedia application.

THE INFRASTRUCTURE BASED ROUTING

As a hybrid vehicular ad hoc networks (VANETs), roadside units (RSUs) which are stationary are combined to the on-board units (OBUs) equipped on vehicles to provide reliable routing and to provide differentiated applications (He et al. (2008)). This method proposes two notions, virtual equivalent node (VEN) and differentiated reliable path (DRP) to against link failures. The basic idea of this method is the following. RSUs are used to act as fixed reliable nodes. They are connected by backbone links with high bandwidth, low delay, and low bit error rates. Vehicles can directly communicate with each other by wireless links. If the routing path is broken, the roadside units (one or multiple) will act as VEN to provide connection for the broken clusters of vehicles. After a vehicle successfully connects with an RSU, its position information is synchronized to all related RSUs instantly.

Kim et al. (2008) address a novel routing protocol, called SARC, which can find the routing path and protect privacy in route discovery and data forwarding phase. The method adopts a street-based path calculation algorithm for route discovery. The identity, location, and route anonymity are defined and analyzed as well. Namboodiri & Gao (2007) connect Wireless LAN (WLAN) through roadside cellular stations. Accurate prediction of route lifetimes can significantly reduce the number of route failure packets. The lifetime of a link is defined as the duration of a link.

Kitani et al. (2008) proposed a information routing method that uses buses as message ferries which travel along regular routes. The motivation of this method is to monitor traffic conditions, like information of traffic jams and road construction places. These traffic condition information will be transmitted to drivers by FM broadcast and optical beacons on the roadside so that their car navigation systems can display congested areas/roads. Multiple special regions of a road are tagged as "areas". Each vehicle measures time consumption to pass an area. Traffic information statistics can be computed from the information received by cars in inter-vehicle communication. Buses are idea media to avoid losing traffic information statistics of areas which buses go along. In the proposed method, buses are assumed to have larger storage than other vehicles and hold traffic information statistics of all areas received from neighboring vehicles. Buses measure time to pass each area by themselves in order to provide traffic information on areas with only a few cars. In order to improve information propagation efficiency in low density areas, buses collect as much traffic in- formation as possible from cars in the communication region, and periodically disseminate the collected information to neighboring cars. Moreover, control packets with buses will be transmitted in advance to negotiate the type of information. The control messages can save wireless bandwidth by selecting the specified types of information, instead of sending all information.

THE GEOGRAPHIC POSITION BASED ROUTING

The Geographic Position Based Routing Position based routing protocols have been a great deal of attention in vehicular ad hoc networks. The routing protocols are very efficient in high mobility ad hoc network since the path to a destination can be projectively determined by location information of neighbor and destination nodes. The fundamental idea of geographic position based routing protocol is the following, as shown in Figure 1. The geographic position values of vehicles are used to partition the nodes into sub-sections of roads. The sub-sections can be dynamically created on the fly, shown in Figure 1, and they can be predefined and installed on each vehicle, shown in Figure 1. Therefore, vehicles in a sub-section become members in a group. Each group only has one or two vehicles functioning as gateways to

Figure 1. The fundamental idea of geographic position based routing

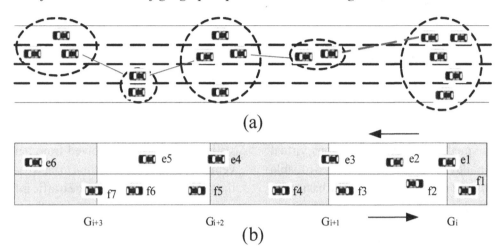

(a)

(b)

send/relay packets. Other members in the group keep silent and drop the packets. The advantage of this method is to reduce the duplicates of packets and therefore, to improve the delay and bandwidth utilization. But this method, especially for the routing method based on dynamical group creation, will introduce other issues like group management.

CarNet (Morris et al. (2000)) uses grid to propagate packets. The grid is defined on the basis of geographic position of nodes. A forwarding method based on geographic position and a scalable dissemination service based on location are designed to route packets from car to car without flooding the whole network. CarNet, as announced by authors, can sup- port many applications: IP connectivity, cooperative highway congestion monitoring, fleet tracking, and discovery of nearby points of interest. Kato et al. (2008) propose a method for constructing network groups according to lane position and evaluate the proposed method by simulation as well.

Bronsted & Kristensen (2006) present a zone flooding algorithm and a zone routing algorithm. A zone is defined as a geographic area, for example a section of a road, for example 500 meters of a road. If vehicles are in the zone, it allows to broadcast packets. Otherwise the received packets will be dropped. The effect of the zone is that packets are only delivered in a section of a road.

Gong et al. (2007); Lochert et al. (2003) present a greedy routing method on the basis of geographic positions of vehicles, as shown in Figure 1. The basic idea is the following. Each vehicle knows its own geographic position by the help of enlisted GPS receiver or some other methods, for example radio signal strength. Vehicles rebroadcast packets only at the nodes whose distance to the sender is the longest. The fact that vehicles transmit packets aggressively toward the destination gives the name "greedy". The directions of vehicles' movement are included into the geographic greedy routing. The direction of movement helps to select long duration links. But mere direction of movement does not help much. The mobility of vehicles are considered and the predictive directional greedy routing is proposed (Gong et al. (2007)).

Kihl et al. (2007) describe a routing protocol, called ROVER (RObust VEhicular Routing). The main idea of this method is the following. Zones are defined on the basis of positions of vehicles which are equipped with GPS receivers. ROVER broadcasts control packet, similar to AODV, among zones to find a routing path. Once the routing path is found, data packets are unicasted by the routing path to improve the performance of commu- nication. Similarly, Momeni & Fathy (2008) propose a reactive algorithm for mobile wireless ad-hoc networks, called Location Routing Algorithm with Directional Cluster-Based Flooding (LORA-DCBF). The LORA-DCBF uses zone-like group routing method. To reduce the number of Location Request (LREQ) packets and minimize duplicate retransmissions in the same region, the control traffic packets are selectively transmitted by the selected nodes, called gateways. All the members in the zone can read and process the packet, but do not retransmit the packets. Only gateway nodes retransmit packets between zones, i.e. gateway to gateway communication.

THE PROBABILITY BASED ROUTING

Because of high mobility, the topology of vehicles is changing constantly. Probability is an ideal metrics to find a routing path. In this section, we are going to discuss a promising method: the probability based routing methods. The basic idea of this type of routing methods is based on probability theory, for example the probability that a wireless link exists between two nodes at a certain time, or the probability that a wireless link stay connected after a certain time intervals. In literature, probability based routing methods are proposed by several researchers. We will give a short survey on these methods and present one of these methods as a representative in detail.

Jiang et al. (2008) present a routing method, called REAR, based on receipt probability of alarm messages of nodes. The proposed REAR can compute the receipt probability of alarm packets based on the real wireless channel in VANET. The selection of next hop is based on the receipt probability. The probability model is based on wireless signal strength and the loss of signal. The wireless signal loss is composed by two parts the path loss and the diffraction loss. The receipt probability is computed by using the relationship between packet loss rate and received signal strength. The receipt probability values of all neighboring nodes are estimated from the received signal strengths. The routing path with highest receipt probability value will be selected as the routing path.

Niu et al. (2007) dynamically create and maintain a robust route to provide QoS for multimedia application over VANETs. The routing methods are on two parameters: relia- bility and delay. The reliability is on the basis of probability function that can predict the future status of a wireless link. The probability function is introduced in litera- ture (Rubin & Liu (2003); Jiang et al. (2001)), defined as the probability that there is an active link between two nodes. The digital map and the GPS device are used to find the route with best reliability. The route is maintained by proactive communication among intermediate nodes. If a link is going to break, the route path will be rebuilt before the link breaks.

Yang et al. (2008) develop a new routing protocol called connectivity aware routing (CAR). The basis of this method is the connectivity prob- ability model of each road segment. A route with the highest probability of connectivity to forward packets will be selected. As acclaimed by Yang, the packet delivery ratio using the proposed method can be increased up to at least 90% and the delay is in the acceptable range as well. The connectiv- ity model is on the probability computation on a road which is partitioned into grids/cells. The unit of cell is the average length of a car, 5 meters. Then the probability to compute the connection between two nodes is to compute the probability that the distance between the two nodes is within a certain value (transmission range of wireless).

Sun et al. (2006) proposed an algorithm to find a reliable routing path that was compliant with delay requirements. The algorithm is based on several assumptions, namely (1) intermediate nodes are equally spaced, and (2) vehicle speed is normally distributed. Based on these assump- tions, they compute the probability of link lifetime as the reliability of a link. By querying possible links or paths, a path with high reliability and sufficiently small link delay will be selected as the routing path.

Yan & Olariu (2009a,b) proposed a ticket based routing method in VANET by using the expected duration of links. The expected link duration is computed by a probability model. A Ticket-Based Probing with Stability conStrained(TBP-SS) Routing method is also proposed in (Yan & Olariu (2009b)). The key parameter used to select a routing is based on the mean duration of a link (defined as stability) which is computed by the probability model. From the "divide and conquer" algorithm, each optimal routing link is selected and results an optimized routing path which is composed by each optimized link. Vehicles are equipped with a DSRC/IEEE 802-based wireless transceiver (e.g. IEEE 802.11p) and a GPS device.

Background of Yan's Method

TBP and TBP-SE

Chen & Nahrstedt (1999) have proposed Ticket-Based Probing (TBP) to detect paths that satisfy the delay or cost constrain. Toward the destination node (receiver) and starting from a sender, yellow tickets represent delay constrain and should be sent to the paths with low delay; and green tickets represent cost constrain and should be sent to the paths with low cost. In TBP-SE, Zhu et al. (June 19-21, 2006) extends TBP by importing stability and creating red tickets. Red tickets represent stability constrains and should be sent to the paths with high stability. The basic idea of TBP and TBP-SE is as follows:

- Node i keeps the up-to-date local state information of neighbors Ni: delay(linkij) and cost(linkij), j Ni;
- A probe is a control message which include a certain quota/permission of copies of the control packet. The distribution of the quota is determined by the sender.

- For a connection request, the sender generates a probe which includes a certain quota/permission of copies of the control packet. The quota is composed by three numbers: a certain number of yellow tickets (cost constrain), a certain number of blue tickets (stability constrain) and a certain number of green tickets (delay constrain).
- The number of tickets is the number of permissions needed to send a copy of the probe. As shown in Figure 2, the source node S generates a probe with 3 blue tickets based on the expected duration of links (i.e. stability). The 3 blue tickets mean that three duplicates of the tickets can be distributed among possible links. S has 6 links but only two links are selected. One link receives 2 ticket duplicates p2(2) reaching node *B* and the other link receives one duplicate p1(1) reaching node *A*. For the next link, the two ticket duplicates p2(2) are distributed in two links out of three possible links by node *B*. Each link receives one ticket, shown as p3(1) and p4(1). The duplicate p1(1) probes a successive link reaching node *C* with the same ticket p1(1). Each ticket records delay, cost and stability values of the past links.
- Each probe indicates a possible path, when the probe arrives at the destination node. Among them, the path with optimal parameter (for example smallest cost or biggest duration) is selected.

Limitations of TBP and TBP-SE

In TBP, a link is marked "transient" if it is just formed or "stationary" if it is unbroken for a while. Tickets are distributed only among stationary links whenever possible. However, this method is not sufficiently stable if the path contains transient links because of two reasons. First, both TBP and TBP-SE use distance-vector protocol to obtain the delay of packets (Chen & Nahrstedt (1999); Zhu et al. (June 19-21, 2006)). The distance-vector protocol must keep the other nodes' distance vectors which is the route to all the other nodes. But the distance-vector protocol is slow to update the route to other nodes. The slow update usually takes multiple rounds to update routing status. Therefore it is usually used in the stationary or slow mobility wireless networks (e.g. MANET). In VANET, vehicles move fast and the network topology is changed quickly. The distance-vector protocol is not applicable because the quickly changing topology of networks can cause network status exchange messages to be out-of-date. Moreover, two facts make the distance-vector protocol in VANET difficult and inaccurate. Fact one is that the population of nodes in VANET is big, often hundreds or thousands. Fact two is that the vehicles on a road are swapped in and out. The two factors plus the slow updates of distance-vector make the distance vector protocol impractical to estimate the state of metrics. In our proposal, instead of the distance-vector protocol, we use local/neighboring state to estimate the global state which is the state of metrics from source node to destination node. Second, TBP (Chen & Nahrstedt (1999)) bases the assumption that newly-formed links are more likely to be broken than links that have already existed for some time. This is certainly not always true. Indeed, it is often on the reverse case. Take highway as example, vehicles often catch up and stay at a certain distance to the previous vehicle. On the other hand, two vehicles staying relative stationary for a while often will move apart each other because of the dynamics of traffic. Therefore, most of the time, a new formed link will live longer than the link existing for a while. Second, no stability criteria are used to show the stable status of the link or path. A path with low-delay or low-cost does not mean a stable path. For example, a path A is composed of three links. All the nodes associated to the links are at the boundary of the transmission range. Another path B is composed by four or five links. All the nodes associated to the links are at the half of the

transmission range location. Although the cost or delay of path B is larger than that of path A, path B is more stable than path A. Third, the stability in (Zhu et al. (June 19-21, 2006)) is based on the wireless signal strength at the time to attempt a communication link. The stability can become weak very soon because no mobility is considered. In our proposal, the mobility is counted into stability definition.

Delay/Cost/Stability-Constrained QoS Routing

Delay of a routing path is defined as a time interval between sending and receiving a packet. The delay-constrained routing (Chen & Nahrstedt (1999); Zhu et al. (June 19-21, 2006)) means that the routing delay must be less than a certain delay threshold/requirement. Given the delay requirement is DLY, the goal of delay-constrained routing method is to detect a path, from source S to destination D, whose delay is not larger than DLY. Suppose the routing path includes n links, the delay of the routing path is the convolution of delays of all links,

$$delay(path) = \sum_{i=1}^{n} delaylink_i \quad DLY$$

where delay(path) is the delay of the routing path, delaylink_i is the delay associated with the i-th link. Cost of a routing path is defined as the number of links in the routing path. The cost-constrained routing means that the number of links must be less than a certain threshold NL,

$$cost(path) < NL$$

where cost(path) is the cost of the path, the total number of links. Stability of a routing path is defined as duration of time of the routing path.

Unlike wired network, even MANET, mobile nodes in VANET suffer more broken paths due to high mobility of vehicles and dynamic topology changes. Therefore, stability of a path outweighs the other criteria. The routing path is expected to survival as long as possible. The stability-constrained routing method, similarly, requires that the duration of routing path must be no less than the minimum duration requirement *STB*,

stab(path) = min{stab(0),stab(1),··?,stab(n)} STB

where stab(path) is the stability of the path, and, i [0,n], stab(i) is the duration of the i-th link.

Link Stability Specified by a Probabilistic Method

We define a term **stability** S as the duration of a link between nodes i and j. The derivations of all the claimed results will be found in (Yan & Olariu (2009a)). Two cases are discussed to compute the duration of link. Case 1 is that vehicle i is X apart from vehicle j at t0, where X is the distance between i and j and is log-normal distributed with parameter (μ,σ) (Yan & Olariu (2009a)). The two vehicles end up to be more than 300 meters apart, with the same sequence, and break the link at time t1, as shown in Figure 3. Case 2 is that the two vehicles end up to be more than 300 meters apart but vehicle i catches up and passes vehicle j, i.e. with a reverse sequence, and break the link at time t1, as shown in Figure 2.

Readers are referred to (Yan & Olariu (2009a)) for details. Let vr be the relative speed of j to i and ar be the relative acceleration of j to i. Both vr and ar take i as a relative stationary node and j as a relative mobile node. The expected duration of a link S can be computed by the following formula (Yan & Olariu (2009a)):

300 - e?2/2 S = Pr0,0 vr vr + 2ar(300 - e?2/2) - vr 2 + Pr0,1 ar 300 + e?2/2 + Pr1,0 vr vr + 2ar(300 + e?2/2) - vr 2 + Pr1,1, (1.1)

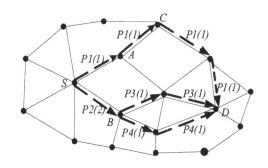

Figure 2. The Ticket-Based Probing. S: source node, D: destination node, P: probe packets, P(x): probes containing x tickets/quota

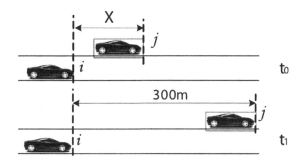

Figure 3. Case one: vehicle j moves away from vehicle i

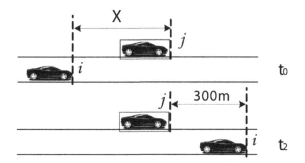

Figure 4. Case two: vehicle i catches up and passes vehicle j. The figure is not proportionally drawn

where $Pr0,0$ is the probability that the link is in Case 1 and $ac = 0$; $Pr0,1$ is the probability that the link is in Case 1 and $ac = 0$; $Pr1,0$ is the probability that the link is in Case 2 and $ac = 0$; $Pr1,1$ is the probability that the link is in Case 2 and $ac = 0$; similarly, $E(t0,0)$ means the link expectation in Case 1 and $ac = 0$; $E(t0,1)$ means the link expectation in Case 1 and $ac = 0$; $E(t1,0)$ means the link expectation in Case 2 and $ac = 0$; $E(t1,1)$ means the link expectation in Case 2 and $ac = 0$.

Imprecise State Model

The basic idea of TBP-SS is outlined below:

- Node i keeps the up-to-date local state information of neighbors N_i: link delay delay(linkij), link cost cost(linkij), and the link stability stabij, j Ni. The stabij is obtained by predicting based on formula 1.1. The mobility information such as relative speed vij and relative acceleration aij are updated between node i and j.
- Based on the imprecise state model, node i estimates the neighboring/local value of metrics (delay, cost and stability) and computes the estimation value of metrics of the whole routing path. Based on these estimations of metrics, the source node computes the initial number of tickets, red for stability, green for cost and yellow for delay. The guideline is that more tickets are issued for the links with tighter or more stringent requirements.
- The probe, a control packet which includes the number of colored tickets, is send out from the source node toward to the destination node in order to find the high stability, low-cost and low delay routing path.
- At each intermediate node, a probe with more than one ticket is allowed to be duplicated into multiple links. Each link will lead a different routing path. The total

number of probes is constrained by the initial number of tickets. Each intermediate node will duplicate the probe based on its own state estimation discussed in 6.1.
- Each probe indicates a possible path, when the probe arrives at the destination node. Among them, the path with optimal parameter (for example smallest cost or biggest duration) is selected.

The key problem of the proposed routing scheme, therefore, is an algorithm that determines the number of tickets and the number of duplicates of the probe. There are two main problems: 1) how to determine the initial number of tickets; 2) how to distribute the tickets among links. The basic rule of determining the number of tickets is that more tickets are issued for the links with tighter requirements to increase the chances to find an optimal routing path.

Initial Number of Tickets

The initial number of tickets N0 is the sum of the number of each colored tickets, i.e. $N0 = R0 + G0 + Y0$ where $R0,G0,Y0$ are the number of red, green and yellow tickets respectively. The basic idea is to use more green tickets to find low-cost possible paths and more yellow tickets to find low-delay possible paths. But use red tickets as a backup to ensure to find a feasible path that satisfies stability requirement, with a high likelihood. Therefore, stability is our fundamental metrics and all initial number of tickets is determined by the estimation of stability of the routing path. For each of colored tickets, we determine the initial number in the following way.

Red Tickets

If ES Max(i) where *ES* is the estimation of stability of the whole routing path and *Max(i)* is the upper bound of the threshold stability, then $R0 = 0$. If

Figure 5. The number of red tickets as a function of stability requirement

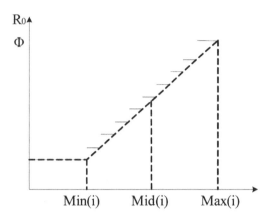

Figure 6. Computing green tickets as a function of the stability requirement

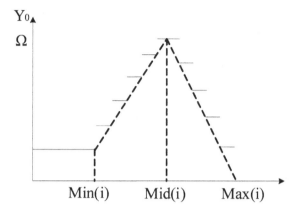

the stability require- ment is too stringent to be satisfied, then no ticket is issued and the connection request is rejected. If *Min(i) ES < Max(i)*, then R0 = ?Max(i)-Min(i) ? where Φis *ES-Min(i)* a system parameter specifying the maximum allowable number of red tickets and *Min(i)* is the lower bound of the threshold stability. Because the stability requirement is larger than *Min(i)*, the stability requirement is considered not sufficiently low and the main aim is to detect enough feasible paths as backups. If *ES < Min(i)*, then *R0 = ?1* where θ is another system parameter which is a threshold specifying a enough big range for the stability requirement, for example θ[1,5]. Because the stability requirement is sufficiently low, one red ticket suffices to detect a feasible path with high stability. The above rules are illustrated in Figure 5.

Green and Yellow Tickets

The initial number *G0* and *Y0* are determined in the same way. Therefore, we use *T0* represents the number of initial number of the two tickets, i.e. T0 = G0 = Y0. If *ES Max(i)*, then T0 = 0. If the stability requirement *ES* is too stringent to be satisfied, then no tickets are issued and the connection request is rejected. If *Max(i) > ES*

Mid(i), then T0 = ?Max(i)-Mid(i) ?. Because the stability requirement is larger than the ES-Mid(i) Mid(i) but less than Max(i), some links can satisfy the requirement. So the main objective is to detect feasible paths by red tickets. Therefore, we reduce the number of green tickets and yellow tickets to give more chance to red tickets to find feasible paths as backups. If Mid(i) > ES Min(i), then T0 = ?Max(i)-Min(i) ES-Min(i) ?. Because more stable links exist, the stability requirement is not stringent and the main objective is to detect better paths which have low-delay or low-cost. If ES < Min(i), then T0 = ?1. Because the stability requirement is sufficiently low, one ticket is sufficiently to find a feasible path. The above rules are illustrated in Figure 6.

Distributing the Probes

Candidate Neighbors
If the probe proceeds a new link (i,j), the candidate neighbors are a set of neighbors satisfying the following constrains: i) stab(i,j) > Sr for stability, where Sr is the stability requirement and stab(i,j) is the stability prediction of link (i,j). Since the stability is defined as expected duration of links, each routing link must survival longer time than requirement of duration Sr. ii) The sum of delays

of all links must be less than the delay requirement D, i.e. delay(p) + Edelay(i,j) < D where delay(p) is the accumulative delay of routing path, Edelay(i,j) is the estimation of delay from node i to the destination node. The estimation of delay can be determined by 1.6.1. Initially, delay(p) = 0. For each previous link (m,n) < (i,j), delay(p) = delay(p) + delay(m,n) where delay(m,n) is real delay of link (m,n). iii) The sum of cost of all links must be less than the cost requirement C, i.e. cost(p) + Ecost(i,j) < C where cost(p) is the accumulative delay of routing path, Ecost(i,j) is the estimation of delay from node i to the destination node. Initially, cost(p) = 0. For each previous link (m,n) < (i,j), cost(p) = cost(p) + cost(m,n) where cost(m,n) is real cost of link (m,n).

Distributing Tickets among Candidates

A ticket is a permission of a probe. If the number of tickets is more than one, the scheme to distribute the tickets among candidate links is the following. If the probe proceeds a new link (i,j), 1) the number of red tickets of link (i,j) is assigned as R(pj), stab(i,j) R(pj) = ?stab(p) (1.2) Ti k=1 stab(i,k) Ti R(pj) must be integer (either R(pj) or R(pj)) and satisfies j =1 R(pj) = stab(p). 2) the number of yellow tickets of link (i,j) is assigned as Y (pj), Ti j =1 delay(p) + delay(i,k) Y (pj) = ?delay(p) (1.3) delay(p) + delay(i,j) Ti Y (pj) must be integer (either Y (pj) or Y (pj)), and satisfies k=1 Y (pk) = delay(p). 3) the number of green tickets of link (i,j) is assigned as G(pj), Ti k=1 cost(p) + cost(i,k) G(pj) = ?cost(p) (1.4) cost(p) + cost(i,j) Ti G(pj) must be integer (either G(pj) or G(pj)), and satisfies k=1 G(pk) = cost(p).

Termination and Path Selection

The routing process is terminated when all probes have either reached or dropped. Timeout is used to handle the problem of ticket losses that may result from network partition, buffer overflow, channel errors, etc. If time is not critical, the best path can be selected among all the received probes after the timeout has expired. If time is critical, we need to select a path before the timeout expires. This problem can be mapped to the classic probability problem: secretary problem (Ferguson (1989)). The probability to select the best path is about 36.8%. Once the primary path is selected, a confirmation message is sent back along the path to the source and reserves resources along the way. The cost of selecting a delay optimized routing path is trivial because the first arrived probe (a control message) contains the least delay routing path which is the delay optimized routing. The cost of selecting stability and cost optimized routing discussed later, is depended on the number of tickets (quotas of the probe copies). But no matter what routing paths elected, the paths are stable enough because all the path selection are based on stability.

CONCLUSION

In this chapter, we present a survey of routing protocols in VANET. Five types of current routing protocols are introduced and compared. Probability theory is often used in dynamical systems. We prefer the probability-based routing protocols because of the dynamics of VANET caused by the high mobility of vehicles. As a concrete example, we address a routing protocol based on probability values

REFERENCES

Abedi, O., Fathy, M., & Taghiloo, J. (2008). Enhancing aodv routing protocol using mobility parameters in vanet. In *Proceedings of AICCSA '08: The 2008 IEEE/ACS International Conference on Computer Systems and Applications*, (pp. 229-235). Washington, DC.

Biswas, S., Tatchikou, R., & Dion, F. (2006). Vehicle-to-vehicle wireless communication protocols for enhancing highway traffic safety. *Communications Magazine, IEEE, 44*(1), 74–82. doi:10.1109/MCOM.2006.1580935

Bronsted, J., & Kristensen, L. M. (2006). Specification and performance evaluation of two zone dissemination protocols for vehicular ad-hoc networks. In *ANSS '06: Proceedings of the 39th annual Symposium on Simulation*, (pp. 68-79), Washington, DC.

Chen, S., & Nahrstedt, K. (1999). Distributed quality-of-service routing in ad-hoc networks. *IEEE Journal on Selected Areas in Communications, 17*(8), 1488{1505.

Ferguson, T. S. (1989). Who solved the secretary problem? *Statistical Science, 4*(1), 282–296. doi:10.1214/ss/1177012493

Gong, J., Xu, C. Z., & Holle, J. (2007). Predictive directional greedy routing in vehicular ad hoc networks. In *Proceedings of ICDCSW '07: The 27th International Conference on Distributed Computing Systems Workshops*, (p. 2). Washington, DC.

He, R., Rutagemwa, H., & Shen, X. (2008). Differentiated reliable routing in hybrid vehicular ad-hoc networks. (pp. 2353-2358).

Jiang, H., Guo, H., & Chen, L. (2008). Reliable and efficient alarm message routing in vanet. In *Proceedings of ICDCSW '08: The 2008 The 28th International Conference on Distributed Computing Systems Workshops*, (pp. 186{191). Washington, DC.

Jiang, S., He, D., & Rao, J. (2001). A prediction-based link availability estimation for mobile ad hoc networks. (vol. 3, pp. 1745-1752).

Johnson, D. B., Maltz, D. A., & Hu, Y. C. (2007). *The dynamic source routing protocol for mobile ad hoc networks (Tech. rep.)*. IETF MANET Working Group.

Kato, T., Kadowaki, K., Koita, T., & Sato, K. (2008). Routing and address assignment using lane/position information in a vehicular ad hoc network. In *Proceedings of APSCC '08: The 2008 IEEE Asia-Paci_c Services Computing Conference*, (pp.1600-1605). Washington, DC.

Kihl, M., Sichitiu, M., Ekeroth, T., & Rozenberg, M. (2007). *Reliable Geographical Multicast Routing in Vehicular Ad-Hoc Networks*. Berlin, Germany: Springer.

Kim, H., Paik, J., Lee, B., & Lee, D. (2008). Sarc: A street-based anonymous vehicular ad hoc routing protocol for city environment. In *Proceedings of EUC '08: The 2008 IEEE/IFIP International Conference on Embedded and Ubiquitous Computing*, (pp. 324-329). Washington, DC.

Kitani, T., Shinkawa, T., Shibata, N., Yasumoto, K., Ito, M., & Higashino, T. (2008). Efficient vanet-based traffic information sharing using buses on regular routes. (pp. 3031-3036).

Li, X., & Cuthbert, L. (2004). On-demand node-disjoint multipath routing in wireless ad hoc network. In Proceedings of LCN '04: The 29th Annual IEEE International Conference on Local Computer Networks, (pp. 419-420). Washington, DC.

Lochert, C., Hartenstein, H., Tian, J., Fussler, H., Hermann, D., & Mauve, M. (2003). A routing strategy for vehicular ad hoc networks in city environments. (pp. 156-561).

Momeni, S., & Fathy, M. (2008). Vanet's communication. (pp. 608-612).

Morris, R., Jannotti, J., Kaashoek, F., Li, J., & Decouto, D. (2000). Carnet: A scalable ad hoc wireless network system. In *Proceedings of the 9th ACM SIGOPS European workshop: Beyond the PC: New Challenges for the Operating System*, (pp. 61?5). New York: ACM Press.

Namboodiri, V., & Gao, L. (2007). Prediction-based routing for vehicular ad hoc networks. Vehicular Technology. *IEEE Transactions on, 56*(4), 2332–2345.

Niu, Z., Yao, W., Ni, Q., & Song, Y. (2007). Dereq: a qos routing algorithm for multimedia communications in vehicular ad hoc networks. In *Proceedings of IWCMC '07: The 2007 international conference on Wireless communications and mobile computing*, (pp. 393-398). New York.

Perkins, C. E., Belding-Royer, E. M., & Das, S. R. (2003). *Ad hoc on-demand distance vector (aodv) routing*, RFC Experimental 3561. Retrieved from http://rfc.net/rfc3561.txt

Perkins, C. E., & Bhagwat, P. (1994). Highly dynamic destination-sequenced distance-vector routing (dsdv) for mobile computers. *SIGCOMM Comput. Commun. Rev., 24*(4), 234–244. doi:10.1145/190809.190336

Rubin, I., & Liu, Y. C. (2003). *Link stability models for qos ad hoc routing algorithms.* (vol. 5, pp. 3084-3088).

Sun, W., Yamaguchi, H., & Yukimasa, K. (2006). Gvgrid: A qos routing protocol for vehicular ad hoc networks. In *Proceedings of the Fourteenth IEEE International Workshop on Quality of Service* (IWQoS 2006), (pp. 130-139). New Haven, CT: Yale University.

Taleb, T., Sakhaee, E., Jamalipour, A., Hashimoto, K., Kato, N., & Nemoto, Y. (2007). A stable routing protocol to support its services in vanet networks. *IEEE Transactions on Vehicular Technology, 56*(6), 3337–3347. doi:10.1109/TVT.2007.906873

Wedde, H. F., Lehnhoff, S., & van Bonn, B. (2007). Highly dynamic and scalable vanet routing for avoiding traffic congestions. In *Proceedings of VANET '07: The fourth ACM international workshop on Vehicular ad hoc networks*, (pp. 81-82). New York.

Yan, G., & Olariu, S. (2009a). *A probabilistic analysis of path stability in vehicular ad hoc networks (Technique Report in Computer Science).* Norfolk, VA: Old Dominion University.

Yan, G., & Olariu, S. (2009b). *A reliable routing in vehicular ad hoc networks using probabilistic analysis of path stability (Technique Report in Computer Science).* Norfolk, VA: Old Dominion University.

Yang, Q., Lim, A., & Agrawal, P. (2008). Connectivity aware routing in vehicular networks. (pp. 2218-2223).

Zhu, W., Song, M., & Olariu, S. (2006, June 19-21). Integrating stability estimation into quality of service routing in mobile ad-hoc networks. In *Proceedings of the Fourteenth IEEE International Workshop on Quality of Service* (IWQoS 2006). New Haven, CT: Yale University.

Chapter 11
Mobility and Traffic Model Analysis for Vehicular Ad-Hoc Networks

Shrirang Ambaji Kulkarni
Gogte Institute of Technology, India

G. Raghavendra Rao
NIE Institute of Technology, India

ABSTRACT

Vehicular Ad Hoc Networks represent a specialized application of Mobile Ad Hoc Networks. Here the mobile nodes move in lanes and their mobility can be modeled based on realistic traffic scenarios. To meet the above challenge the goal of defining the mobility model for vehicular ad hoc network along with a realistic traffic pattern is an important research area. Vehicular mobility is characterized by acceleration, deceleration, possibility of different lanes and intelligent driving patterns. Also a modeling of traffic is necessary to evaluate a vehicular ad hoc network in a highway environment. The traffic model has to take into account the driver behavior in order to take decisions of when to overtake, change lanes, accelerate and decelerate. To overcome the limitation of traditional mobility models and mimic traffic models, many traffic model based simulators like CORSIM, PARAMICS and MOVE have been proposed. In this chapter we provide taxonomy of mobility models and analyze their implications. To study the impact of mobility model on routing protocol for vehicular motion of nodes we analyze the performance of mobility models with suitable metrics and study their correlation with routing protocol. We also discuss the fundamentals of traffic engineering and provide an insight into traffic dynamics with the Intelligent Driver Model along with its lane changing behavior.

INTRODUCTION

Traffic Management is a huge problem in large cities. Absence of technological support to complement road safety measures results in loss of precious human lives and severe implications to our environment. According to National Highway Traffic Safety administration (Fatal Car Accidents, 2005), around 43,000 people were killed in accidents, millions of people were injured and the economic consequences of these accidents were $230 billion. The traditional safety measures like seat belts, airbags alone cannot

DOI: 10.4018/978-1-61520-913-2.ch011

eliminate the problem. It is also required that the driver has the ability to foresee the developing situation on highways ahead of time (Ebner & Rohling, 2001). The usage of sensors, computer and wireless communication leads to the prediction of speed and generate warning messages frequently (Glathe, Karlsson, Brusaglino & Calandrino, 1990). Thus the wireless communication in ubiquitous fashion is achievable through Mobile Ad-Hoc Networks (MANETs). Vehicular Ad-Hoc Networks (VANETs) is one of a rapidly emerging and challenging class of MANETs (Fiore, Harri, Filali & Bonnet, 2007). In VANET nodes represent vehicles moving at a high speed and vehicle traffic determined by regularity (Takano, Okada & Mase, 2007). VANET allows for communication between vehicles and nearby road-side infrastructure (Csilla & Yuliya). With the inception of VANET, the commercial and research based interests in intelligent transport systems, accident control, traffic jams and weather updates have increased. VANETS are being studied for applications where nodes or vehicles can communicate with each other in urban streets and highways (Mahajan, Potinis, Gopalan and Wang An I-A, 2005). The cost of testing VANETs in realistic scenarios is very high and time consuming. Also the complexities involved in theoretical analysis of these dynamic vehicles with ever changing topologies are not feasible. An automated simulation tool can imitate VANETs and yields a similar result to that of real world (Hassan, 2009). To support the goal of realistic VANET simulation it is important to generate a realistic mobility model. The usage of mobility models will have a direct reflection on the protocol being used by VANETs. To explore the area of mobility models further we classify them and analyze their performance. Traffic Engineering provides a lot of useful insights into vehicular distribution and traffic jams. We discuss the basics of traffic engineering and also the traffic based motivation for mobility models. Finally we analyze the Intelligent Driver Model

and future research in the area of mobility models and traffic engineering for VANETs.

MOBILITY MODELS FOR VANET: A BACKGROUND

Mobility models attempt to mimic the movements of real mobile nodes. The mobility scenario thus generated can then be integrated into a network simulator to perform tasks between the nodes. A mobility model for VANET poses challenges in terms of visualizing its separation at Macroscopic and Microscopic level (Fiore M et al. 2007). The node mobility that considers streets lights, roads, building, etc. are classified as Macroscopic. The movement of vehicles and their behavior is called as Microscopic. Another way to visualize mobility model for VANET is to consider it as a constituent of two blocks: Motion Constraints and Traffic Generator. (Harri, Filali & Bonnet, 2005). Motion constraints describe how each vehicle moves and which is obtained from a topological map. Traffic generator, generates different kinds of cars and deals with interactions with cars. Traffic regulations and traffic sign considerations.

If we consider globally, the development of modern vehicular mobility models can be clustered into four different classes like the synthetic model, traffic simulator based model, survey based models and finally trace-based model (Harri J, Filali F & Bonnet C, 2007). This is illustrated in Figure 1.

The above classification is as described in the following sections

Synthetic Models

The basic mobility models were the first to evolve from the synthetic class models. The classification of Synthetic models according to Fiore (Fiore M 2006, 2009) is divided into five classes. Stochastic Models, Traffic Stream Models, Car following Models, Queue Models and Behavioral Models.

Figure 1. Global taxonomy of VANET mobility models

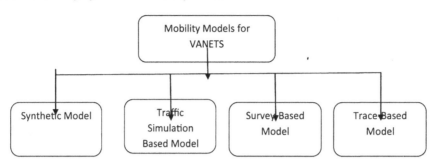

Stochastic Models

Stochastic models are the ones which constrain random movements of nodes on a graph. The graphs usually represent road topologies and nodes are found to be traveling at randomly chosen speeds. The models that belong to this category are City section model, Freeway mobility model and Manhattan Grid Mobility Model (Davies V, 2000), (Bai, Sadagopan & Helmy, 2003),(BonnMotion, 2005) and (PalChaudhuri, Boudec, & Vojnovic, 2006). The City Section model constraints node movements on a grid road topology, where all edges are considered bi-directional, single-lane roads. Vehicles randomly select one of the intersections as their destination over the grid and move in that direction with consistent speed. In this model car-to-car intersections are ignored, since all adjacent vehicle travel at same speed.

The Freeway Mobility (FW) (Bai et.al, 2003) model uses a map representing several bi-directional multi-lane freeways. Here each mobile node is restricted to its lane on freeway. The velocity of mobile node is temporally dependent on its previous velocity. The model also takes cases of minimum safety requirements between vehicles. The Manhattan Grid Mobility Model uses a grid topology and was introduced in (ETSI, 1998). Manhattan mobility model is popular example of geographic restricted mobility model where motion of vehicles is restricted by freeways or local streets in urban areas. The Manhattan model employs a probabilistic approach in selection of

node movements. Thus it differs from the Freeway model in giving the node some freedom to change its direction. The Freeway and Manhattan models have simple car interaction rules and do not reproduce a realistic driver behavior.

Saha and Johnson (Saha & Johnson, 2004) at Rice University modeled mobility of vehicles obtained from the TIGER database (TIGER, 2003), extracted from the maps of US Census Bureau. They constrained vehicle mobility to street boundaries and did not enforce any traffic rules. The model presented in Saha (Saha et.al, 2004) is closest to City Section model. But the difference was City Section Model allowed streets to be related by users which is only as realistic as the user's imagination.

Analysis of Stochastic Models

A performance analysis of two models namely Manhattan Grid Model and City Section Model is carried out. Mobility model exhibit certain important characteristics and it is necessary to quantify them with appropriate metrics to study their impact on routing protocols. In our analysis of mobility models we use the metrics provided by (Bai, Sadagopan & Helmy, 2003)., which are as follows

Average Link Duration: This metric specifies the longest interval of time [t1, t2] for nodes i and j forming the link (i, j). This is then averaged for all node pairs for all existing links specifying the equation written as

$$LD' = \frac{\sum_{t1=0}^{T} \sum_{i=1}^{M} \sum_{j=i+1}^{M} LD(i,j,t1)}{P}$$

where P is no of tuples $(i, j, t1)$ and $LD(i, j, t1) \neq 0$

Average Relative Speed: Relative speed is given by equation written as

$$RST(i,j,t) = |Vi(t) - Vj(t)|$$

where $Vi(t)$ and $Vj(t)$ is the velocity vector of

node i and j at time t. The average value of $RST(i, j, t)$ is given by equation

$$RST' = \frac{\sum_{i=1}^{M} \sum_{j=1}^{M} \sum_{t=1}^{T} RST(i,j,t)}{P}$$

where P is no of tuples $(i, j, t1)$ and $RST(i, j, t1) \neq 0$

Average degree of spatial dependence: It is a measure of the extent of similarity of velocities of given two nodes not so far apart, given by Ds(i, j, t) and averaged over pair of nodes and time instants and formalized by the equation written as.

$$Ds' = \frac{\sum_{t=1}^{T} \sum_{i=1}^{M} \sum_{j=i+1}^{M} Ds(i,j,t1)}{P}$$

where P is no of tuples $(i, j, t1)$ and $Ds'(i, j, t1) \neq 0$

The performance analysis of the Manhattan, and City Section is analyzed using a analysis tool (Bai, Sadagopan & Helmy, 2005) and the results are illustrated as shown

In Figure 2 (a) we observe that City Section Mobility Model slightly outperforms Manhattan Mobility Model for average link duration metric. But in overall scenario both mobility models have a low average link duration mainly because of the opposite direction of motion of nodes

In Figure 2(b) we observe that City Section model exhibits slightly higher average relative speed as compared to Manhattan Mobility Model.

In Figure 2 (c) we observe that City Section Mobility model exhibits slightly higher average degree of spatial dependence as compared to Manhattan Mobility model. But if we consider the overall scenario, the use of lanes in opposite direction in maps, the positive degree of spatial dependence cancel the negative degree of spatial dependence which move in opposite direction

We use AODV (Perkins & Royer, 1999) protocol for analysis to study its performance under Manhattan (Bonnmotion, 2005) and City Section Model (Random Trip Mobility Model). AODV is not only suitable under high mobility and offered load but also when traffic diversity increases (Roberto Beraldi, Roberto Baldoni, 2003). NS-2 ver. 2.29 (The NS-2 Simulator, 2005) simulator is used and the performance measures packet delivery ratio versus number of nodes and number of Constant Bit Rate (CBR) traffic sources. The packet delivery ratio measures the ratio between the number of packets originated by the application layer to those delivered to the final destination. Thus the packet delivery ratio is an important metric in terms of robustness of a routing protocol. The results are as shown in Figure 3(a) and 3(b) as illustrated.

In Figure 3(a) we observe the performance of AODV by measuring its packet delivery ratio by varying the number of cars on Manhattan Grid and City Section Mobility Model. From the Figure 3(a) it is clear that AODV on City section slightly outperforms the Manhattan model. The reason is also that City Section Mobility model exhibits good link duration and spatial dependence metric In case of Figure 3(b) we measure the performance by varying the number of traffic sources. Here we observe that the packet delivery ratio of AODV is more or less same for both the models and AODV on City Section Mobility model slightly

Figure 2. (a) Average link duration of city section and Manhattan mobility model. (b) Average relative speed for city section and Manhattan mobility model (c) Average degree of spatial dependency for city section and Manhattan mobility model

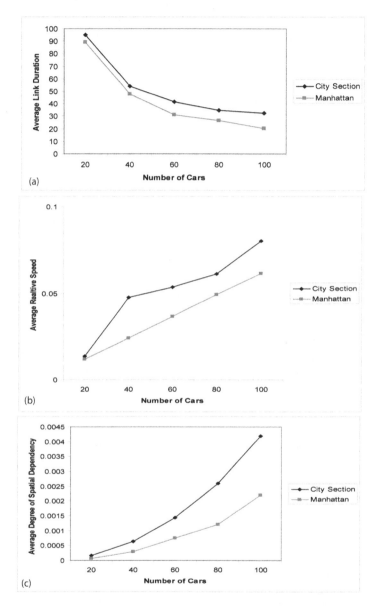

(a)

(b)

(c)

outperforms as compared to AODV on Manhattan Mobility Model. Thus the mobility metrics provide a useful insight on the performance of routing protocols for vehicular based traffic.

Traffic Stream Models

A look at traffic flow from a very long distance reveals that heavy traffic flows as a stream of fluid. Thus a macroscopic theory can be developed with the help of hydrodynamic theory of fluids as an effective one-dimensional compressible fluid.

Figure 3. (a) Manhattan and city section model with varying number of cars. (b) Manhattan and city section model with varying number of CBR sources

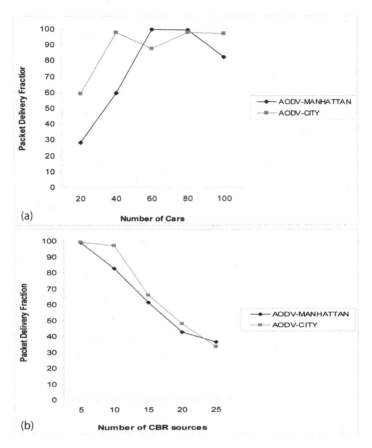

(a)

(b)

The basic equation derives from the idea of law of conservation of number of vehicles on the road. Assuming vehicles are moving from left to right, the continuity equation can be written as

$$\frac{\partial k(x,t)}{\partial t} + \frac{\partial q(x,t)}{\partial x} = 0$$

where x denotes spatial coordinate in the direction of traffic flow, t is the time, k is the density and q denotes the flow. We write two equations from the two regimes of flow i.e. before and after a bottleneck. Thus the flow rate before and after will be same.

$k1v1=k2v2$

From this shockwave velocity can be derived as

$$v(to)p = \frac{q2 - q1}{k2 - k1}$$

v(to)p = propagation velocity of shock wave (miles/hour)

q2 = flow prior to change in conditions (vehicles/hour)

q1 = flow after change in conditions (vehicles/hour)

k2 = traffic density prior to change in conditions (vehicles/mile)

k1 = traffic density after change in conditions (vehicles/mile)

This is referenced to as Stocks Shockwave formula. Traffic Stream models can handle large quantities of vehicles. This makes them interesting for high-level analytical studies of traffic behavior. Chandler (Chandler, Herman & Montroll 1958) studied the analytical distributions of vehicular traffic theory on realistic traffic scenarios and determined the duration of connections between traveling vehicles and fixed gateway along the highway. They also analyzed the dynamics of topological changes that are caused by vehicles joining or leaving communication and detection radii and observed that in cases of high traffic densities and high relative velocities the probability of the topology remains stable in nearly 60%

Car Following Models

Car following models describe the behavior of each driver with respect to the vehicle ahead. They regard vehicles as independent entities and are categorized as microscopic. The general form of the car-following model is

$$response(t) = sensitivity(t - \tau_n) * stimulus(t - \tau_n)$$

Where t= time of observation

$\tau_n = reaction\ time\ for\ driver\ n$
$response(t) = acceleration\ applied\ at\ time\ t$

The various car-following models proposed to substantiate microscopic modeling are discussed. Chandler (Chandler et.al, 1958) was the first to propose the car-following model as a simple linear model. Here a driver response is proportional to the stimulus he perceives. A major limitation of this model is the assumption of constant sensitivity for all simulations. Later in 1961 the car following model developed by Gazis (Gazis, Herman, & Rothrey, 1961) was known as the General Motors Nonlinear Model. The advantage of this model was it was one of the most general models.

One of the limitations of this model was that no rigorous framework for estimating the model was provided. Leutzbach (Leutzbach, & Wiedemeann, 1986) proposed a model that considered psycho-physical aspects of driving behavior. This model addressed two limitations of the car-following models from behavioral aspects. First drivers do not follow their leader's at large spacing and second drivers cannot perceive small differences in front relative speeds, which is generally considered as stimulus and sensitivity. The disadvantage of Leutzbach model was that it lacked mathematical formulation or any direction of how perceptual threshold (a relative speed threshold as a function of space headway) is estimated. Gipps (Gipps, 1981) proposed a model that was on common sense assumptions about driving behavior such acceleration; deceleration and maximum speed. This model is widely preferred for simulation purposes. The cellular automaton model (Nagel & Schrekenberg 1992) discretize the roads in cells, each containing at most one vehicle. Rules are applied to determine the speed of each car according to nearby cell status i.e. availability of vehicle in the cell and if so it current speed. The advantage of this model is that it allows for simulation of a large number of interacting vehicles even with limited processing power. However the cellular automaton models lack the accuracy of time-continuous models. The Newell Model (Newell, 2002) was a simple model based on the concept of the driver following vehicles drives as a shifted space trajectory of the vehicle ahead. It was stated the space trajectory of the following vehicle is same as that of the vehicle ahead except for a translation in space and time. The advantage of the Newell model is advantage of integrability to obtain different macroscopic speed-flow-density relationships. The limitation is that there was no quantitative result to validate the model.

Analysis of the Car-Following Models

In their work Ranjitkar (Ranjitkar, Nakatsuji & Kawamua, 2005) a performance benchmarking

Table 1. Link analysis of INVENT mobility scenarios for 50,100, 150 and 200 cars

Number of Cars	Average Link Duration	Average Relative Speed	Average Degree of Spatial Dependency
50	350.771393	2.210663	0.001105
100	113.875946	7.892879	0.003181
150	34.626072	17.668259	0.006702
200	20.918547	21.679150	0.008510

of the above mentioned models was carried out to evaluate their capabilities in representing real driving behavior. Data precision was achieved using Real Time Kinematics (RTK) GPS. The RTK GPS makes it possible to acquire high resolution vehicular movement data with great amount of accuracy. The models likes Chandler, CGM, Cellular Automata, Newell, Leutzbach and Gipps were optimized for their performance applying Genetic Algorithms (GA). The simulation based results suggested Chandler Model and Generalized GM Model performed well, by producing lower percentile of errors for speed and acceleration predictions. Cellular Automata performed better compared to other models in terms of prediction for spacing. The Gipps model performed well behind the leading, models for spacing, speed prediction while its percentile error was high. Newell model had a competitive percentile error values for spacing prediction, but the speed and acceleration was relatively higher. The percentile error was for Leutzbach model was generally higher. It was observed that interpersonal variations are influential particularly in case of speed predictions.

In our analysis of a car-following model we first consider the analysis of mobility scenario models of microscopic vehicular traffic generator called as INVENT (INVENT). The vehicular traffic generator is based on the car-following models and lane-changing model proposed by Gipps. (Gipps 1981, 1986). The ability of this model is that it allows vehicles to ply at maximum speed, but by avoiding collision. The traffic generator

produces scenario that includes traffic lights at road intersections, bidirectional lanes and multi line traffic. The city map is derived from TIGER/ line database. We include the scenario files which are compliant for NS-2 simulator and are generated for 50, 100, 150, and 200 cars. The analysis results are as illustrated in Table 1

From Table 1 we observe that the spatial dependency is very low for the INVENT Mobility Model scenarios and increases slightly when the car density increases. Also as the number of vehicles are increasing the relative speed is increasing and the corresponding link duration is decreasing. This affects the packet delivery ratio of the underlying routing protocol, when tested for vehicular traffic.

We consider the AODV routing protocol and ran the simulation for 300 sec for CBR traffic of 15 sources on a 5000 x 5000 topology. We measure the results for packet delivery fraction as it indicates the robustness of the underlying protocol. The simulation results are as depicted in Figure 4.

In the Figure 4 we observe that the packet delivery fraction (pdf) drops when the car density is less, this is because of network partitions which become prevalent in the large topology area. Also at this point in time the spatial dependency is very low. At medium and high density the shortest paths among the nodes become prevalent and the spatial dependency increases slightly thus the performance of AODV in terms of pdf increases slightly. From the above discussion we can observe that a routing protocol which is more relevant to realistic traffic scenarios needs to be developed.

Figure 4. Packet delivery fraction for AODV using **INVENT** *traffic generator*

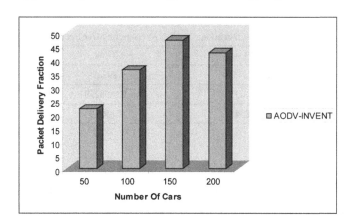

Queue Based Models

Queue Models were applied by Gawron (Gawron, 1998) to model fast vehicular oriented traffic flow. Here every link in a road network has a capacity which corresponds to the number of cars which can pass the link in a unit time. The Queue builds up when the number of car increases. The link is represented by a priority queue. Each link is characterized by capacity q (maximum flow), length l & the number of lanes. A travel time t_{travel} is calculated from the current number n of cars on a link and the desired velocity Vo of the vehicle. The vehicle is then placed on the priority queue. Queue models describe each independent vehicle in a minimal way. They allow us to model large road topologies with large number of vehicles, but lack the precision which can be obtained from other models.

Behavioral Model

In Behavioral Models the human mobility modeling is considered for modeling vehicular traffic. In their work Legendre (Legendre, Borrel, Dias & Dida, 2006) presented a new class of mobility models namely Behavioral Mobility Models (BM), which classifies mobility into simple atomic individual behaviors. They demonstrated the power of behavioral models by their capacity to revisit the way models can be designed to gain a better understanding of mobility in various contexts.

Trace-Based Models

A Trace-Based Model extracts a Generic Mobility pattern from movement traces. It involves complex mathematics to predict mobility patterns available in the traces. It can only be applied to particular class of vehicles and cannot be extended to other class. This approach prompted agencies to start collect mobility traces like MIT Reality Mining (MIT Media Lab) and USC Mobilib (MobiLib), Yoon (Yoon, Noble & Liu, 2006) in their work analyzed a trace-driven framework capable of building realistic mobility models from simulation based studies. Their framework combined coarse-gained wireless traces to an actual map of the space from which traces where derived. They modeled user movement as a second order Markov chain. They applied the scheme to a college campus. The framework provided useful technique to generate a statistical mobility model and helped gaining statistical information of user densities on the roads, buildings and transition probabilities at road intersections. However their study lacked the emphasis on correlation between nodes. Kim (Kim M, Kotz & Kim, 2006) also emphasized in their work on extracting mobility model from real user traces. They developed a method to collect wireless network data set at Dartmouth College. They observed that speed and pause time follow a log normal distribution and direction of movements is nearer to that direction of movements on roads and walkways. Their validation results proved that synthetic tracks match real tracks with a medium relative error of 17%.

Thus the realistic traces analyzed by various researchers helped in extracting real world traces in mobility models and model the speed and pause time distributions.

Survey Based Models

Modeling day to day urban-life and its impact on vehicular movements on road usage has a great deal of significance. One way to achieve this is to collect realistic social data as collected by US Department of Labor. The UDel Mobility Model (UDEL) is one of the examples for this. The mobility simulator is based on surveys from US Department of Labor and Statistics on time used by business community, pedestrians, and vehicle mobility studies by urban planning and traffic engineering communities. Thus it simulates arrival times to work, lunch time, breaks, pedestrian dynamics and workday time usage. Vehicle traffic data is realized by the data collected from state and local governments which helps in modeling vehicle dynamics and street usage. Agenda Based Model (Zheng, Liu, 2006) takes in account not only geographical movements but also human's social role. The authors use a constructive modeling approach to allow the model to conform to real world and study the impact of network routing performance on their model. They used the US National Household Travel Survey data to obtain activity distribution, occupation, distribution and dwell time distribution.

Traffic Simulator Based Models

The experience gained by refining synthetic models, real traces, behaviors and survey based models, lead the research teams and companies to develop realistic simulators like CORSIM (CORSIM, 2009), TRANSIM (TRANSIM), MOVE (Karnadi, Hand & Lan 2007)., PARAMICS(PARAMICS, 2008), VISSIM (VISSIM, 2009). TSIS-CORSIM is an effective tool to perform traffic operations analysis and to evaluate new ITS Technologies. CORSIM is a microscopic simulation model that is designed to simulate highways and surface streets. CORSIM has the ability to model complicated geometry conditions (Owen, Zhang, Rao & McHale, 2000). It has the ability to model different traffic conditions. The output of CORSIM is a MOE (Measure of Effectiveness) file. CORSIM as a tool enables to reach high level of precision in VANET Simulation (Marfia, Pau, Giordano, Sena & Gerla M. 2007). In case of TRANSIMS realistic mobility traces are drawn, which enable the motion of nodes through urban grid. However the simulator could not be used directly for simulation and they had to be tied up with network simulators raising issues of compatibility. MOVE allowed users to rapidly generate realistic mobility models for VANET simulation. It also provided interfacing with real world databases like TIGER (TIGER, 2003) and Google Earth. The output of MOVE was a trace file compatible with popular simulators like NS-2 and Qualnet (Qualnet Network Simulator). The results obtained from MOVE where promising and significantly different than the ones used from Random Waypoint model. PARAMICS [39] is developed by Quadstone Ltd. It provides a set of high-performance microsimulation software tools. It is the state of art parallel microscopic traffic simulator. PARAMICS can simulate intersections, highways. Urban areas, work zones and so on. VISSIM is a commercial microscopic simulator developed by PTV America. VISSIM is implemented on multithreading making it faster on multiprocessors and multicore computers. User can work with 3D modeling and 3D animations on it. It operates on Windows operating system like CORSIM and PARAMICS.

TRAFFIC FLOW THEORY

Traffic system represents a complex system, where millions of vehicles ply with their drivers to reach their destination safely. Traffic researchers say that 15% of United States Gross National Product (GNP) is spent on transportation (Nagel & Schreckenberg, 1992). In the year 2005, 29.6 percent of all reported crashes where due to rear end collisions (National Highway Traffic Safety Administration 2007). as reported by National Highway Traffic Safety Administration US. So the designers and researchers are always planning to develop better strategies to improve the system with tremendous economic advantages. The underlying management of traffic includes considering driver behavior, traffic instabilities and individual motorized traffic. To achieve these goals we analyze the traffic models that help us achieve the Intelligent Transportation System (ITS).

Parameters Involved in Traffic Flow Theory

Traffic Flow is a difficult phenomenon. To get a clear picture we explain it with the following parameters.

Speed (v)

The speed (v) is defined as the rate of motion, as distance per unit of time. It is obvious that each vehicle on the roadway will have a speed that is somewhat different from those around. Thus in transports engineering two types of speeds are defined: time mean speed (TMS) and space mean speed (SMS). Time mean speed (vt) is given as the arithmetic mean of speed of all vehicles passing a point on the road.

$$\overline{vt} = \sum_{i=1}^{n} \frac{vi}{N}$$

where v is the speed of ith vehicle, n is the number of vehicles. The space mean speed (vs) is defined as the harmonic mean of speeds passing a point during a period of time.

$$\overline{vs} = \frac{N}{\sum_{i=1}^{n} vi}$$

where v is the speed of ith the vehicle and N is the number of vehicles.

Density (k)

Density refers to the number of vehicle present on a given length of roadway. Normally density is given in terms of vehicles per kilometer. High densities indicate that individual vehicles are close to each other, while low densities suggest greater distances between vehicles. In a measurement interval for a certain point in time t_1, k can be calculated over a road section of length (L) as

$$k = \frac{N}{L}$$

where N is the number of vehicles passing a point in roadway at t_1 sec and k is the density.

Flow Rate (q)

Flow signifies one of the most common traffic parameters. Flow is the rate at which vehicles pass a given point on the roadway and is normally given as vehicles per hour.

$$q = \frac{3600\,N}{tm}$$

N = Number of vehicles per hour
tm = time measured in a specific interval.

Speed-Flow-Density Relationship

Speed, flow and density are all related to each other. Under uninterrupted flow conditions, speed, density and flow are related by the following equation (Khisty & Lall, 2003).

q=k*v

where q = Flow (vehicles/hour)

v = Speed (kilometers/hour)
k = Density (vehicles/kilometers)

The above equation 11.9 has some interesting points. The flow is minimal when either speed or density is low. Two common traffic conditions illustrate these points. First condition is the traffic jam, where traffic density is high and speed is low. The combination results in a low flow. The second condition is when traffic density is very low and drivers obtain free flow speed. The extremely low density compensates for high speed and the resulting flow is very low.

Analysis of Traffic Models

In order to analyze the effects of traffic models, we need to consider the underlying road models, the types of vehicles plying the road, the traffic conditions, the driver behavior and the traffic models.

Road Models

In Vehicular Ad Hoc Networks (VANETs) nodes move along streets which are modeled as road models. The nodes move in lanes according to the rules of well established traffic models. The road models are as illustrated in Figure 5 below.

The basic models popularly categorize the straight highway and the road grid (Khil & Sichitiu, 2009). The straight highway as shown in Figure 5 (a) is considered as models for highways outside cities. Vehicles ply in lanes either one or two directions. Here the vehicles communicate via messages in single dimensions. One of the special cases of highway is the circular road model as shown in Figure 5(b) where vehicles move in single or multiple lanes forming a closed loop. The road grid represents the urban roads as shown in Figure 5(c). It incorporates traffic lights, intersections where the traffic moves in two or three dimensions. The road grid is a complicated model. An alternative to road grid are real road maps as shown in Figure 5 (d), where realism is infused in traffic and road modeling.

Vehicle Classes

The classification of traffic with respect to types of vehicles (like buses, car and trucks) is very important. The Federal Highway Administration (FHWA) US has defined the following classes

- Motorcycles
- Passenger Cars
- Pick Up Trucks, Vans
- Buses
- Single-Unit Trucks
- Tractor Trailers.

Vehicle classification has a significant role in transport engineering as it determines the design of bridges, roads and traffic flow.

Traffic Conditions

The traffic conditions on the roadways affect the lives of human beings and the economies of the nation. According to the Urban mobility report (Schrank & Lomax, 2007), estimate Americans

Figure 5 (a) Straight highway. (b) Circular ring road. (c) Road grid. (d) Real road map (from Philipp Sommer(available at http://gmsf.hypert.net/. with permission)

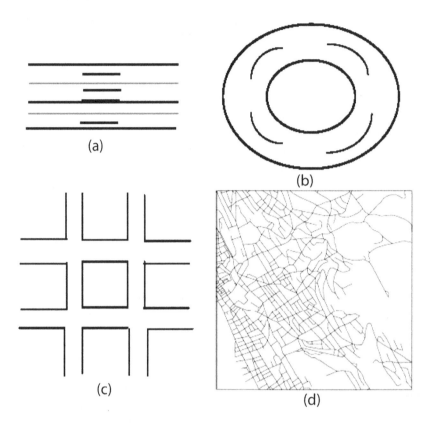

(a)

(b)

(c)

(d)

spent 4.2 billion hours and 2.9 billion gallons of gasoline during congestion. Congestion is classified into two broad categories (Fontaine, 2009), recurring and non-recurring congestion. Recurring congestion is a phenomenon because of increase in traffic of capacity constrained roadways. Non-recurring congestion occurs because of accident, road construction, weather or any other such condition affecting traffic on roadways. Traveler can mitigate recurring congestion by travel planning whereas non-recurring congestion are very difficult to predict.

Driver Behavior

An important parameter of traffic modeling is the driver behavior. The driver action in different situations determines the traffic throughput. Sometime

a driver may decide to change lanes, accelerate, slowdown or overtake another vehicle. Thus this behavior has an impact on the performance of VANET. A study in (Dastrup, Less, Dawson, Lee & Rizzo, 2009) was carried out to investigate the car following behavior of younger and old drivers. The drivers were informed to maintain two car lengths from a virtual lead vehicle (Lv). It was found that old drivers were less able to match changes in lead vehicle velocity. The younger drivers were willing to follow lead vehicle at shorter distances because they felt more comfortable with the risk and task demands. Also the older drivers followed further behind lead vehicle a potential compensatory strategy to avoid collisions.

Modeling Traffic

The initial mathematical modeling and fundamental relations of traffic flow, velocity and density was conducted by Greenshields (Greenshields.D, 1959). At present there exist many models for modeling traffic. Two of the major approaches like Macroscopic and Microscopic are discussed in Section 2.1.2. In this section we discuss the Intelligent Driver Model (IDM) (Treiber, Hennecke & Helbing, 2000). The IDM belongs to the class of deterministic follow the leader model. It has the following advantages like; it behaves accident free because of the dependence on relative velocity. Due to it metastabilty it shows self organized characteristics. Its model parameters have good interpretation and it allows a fast numerical simulation. The IDM acceleration function is given by [Treiber & Kesting, 2009].

$$\frac{dva}{dt} = a_{mic}(Sa, Va, \Delta a) = \left[1 - \left(\frac{va}{vo}\right) - \left(\frac{s*(va, \Delta Va)}{Sa}\right)^2\right]$$

where $V\alpha$ is velocity of vehicle α

$S\alpha$ is the gap of vehicle α
$\Delta V\alpha$ is the velocity difference
$a_{mic}(Sa, Va, \Delta a)$ is the IDM acceleration.

The deceleration depends on the ratio between the effective desired gap and the actual gap Sa.

$$S*(u, \Delta v) = So + vT + \frac{u\Delta v}{2\sqrt{ab}}$$

where So is the minimum distance

vT is following the leading vehicle with a constant desired gap T
$\Delta v \neq 0$ implements the intelligent driver behavior.
b is the comfortable deceleration
a is the maximum acceleration.

The dynamic properties of IDM are controlled by maximum acceleration and comfortable deceleration. In their experiments in (Treiber et.al, 2000) they did not explore congested traffic for multilane and heterogeneous traffics.

Intelligent Driver Model and Traffic Scenario Analysis

To demonstrate the behavior of Intelligent Driver Model (IDM) and the effect of traffic conditions we use the Microscopic Traffic Model (Treiber). The applet simulates the Intelligent Driver Model (Dastrup et.al, 2009) and the MOBIL lane changes (Kesting, Treiber & Helbing, 2007) in six scenarios. Two types of road topologies are supported like ring (circular) road and an oval shape road. Vehicles supported are truck and cars. For our analyze we use two scenarios

- Oval-Shaped Road Topology
- Ring Road with Lane changes

The parameters set are given in the Table 2 and Table 3.

The Figure 6(a) and 6(b) illustrate the scenarios in Tables 2 and 3.

In Figure 6(a) we observe that the system is inhomogeneous and on-ramp is acting as a bottleneck. We also observe that with high density of vehicles lead to a traffic jam quickly. In Figure 6(b) we introduce Lane changes to Ring Road. The traffic here consists of cars only. We observe that this scenarios lead to some bottlenecks inducing some amount of traffic jam. The above observations provide various useful insights into the reason for traffic congestion by simulation based studies.

CONCLUSION AND FUTURE SCOPE

In this chapter we discussed the concept of mobility models associated with Vehicular Ad Hoc Network. We also provided a detailed taxonomy

Table 2. Oval shaped road topology with an on-ramp

Main inflow	3300 Vehicles/h
Ramp inflow	400 vehicles/h
Ramp P-Factor	0.0
a-bias. On ramp	-2.0
Time Wrap Factor	6.9 times

Table 3. Ring road with lane changes

Politeness Factor	0.25
Changing Threshold	0.1 m/s2
Time Wrap Factor	6.9 times

Figure 6. (a) Oval road topology with on –ramp. (b) Ring road with lane changes (from Treiber M, Microsimulation of road traffic, available http://www.trafficsimulation.de/. with permission)

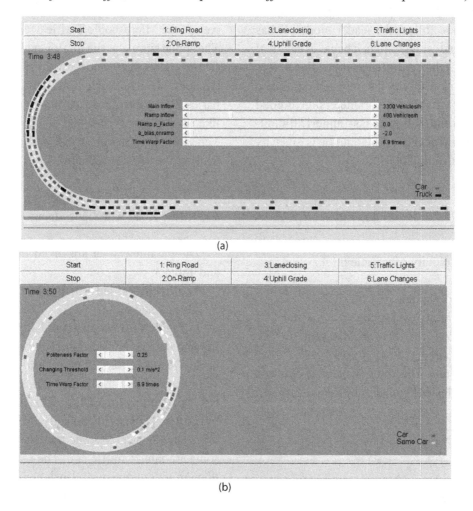

(a)

(b)

of various mobility models namely the synthetic based, traffic simulation based, survey based and trace based, by giving the popular models that follow under them and their latest developments We

also analyzed mobility models with appropriate mobility metrics and the role they play in affecting the underlying routing protocols. We introduced the traffic engineering fundamentals required for traffic modeling. Here we considered an Intelligent driver model as an example and simulated its behavior under lane changing conditions. A lot of work has to be still done to introduce more realism by correlating mathematical models, real time traffic traces, and social network pattern of commuters with appropriate traffic simulator models that simulate large number of vehicle to vehicle communication, thus contributing to safe and efficient transportation.

REFERENCES

Bai, F., Sadagopan, N., & Helmy, A. (2003). The IMPORTANT framework for analyzing the Impact of Mobility on Performance of RouTing protocols for Adhoc NeTworks. *Elsevier Ad Hoc Networks, 1*, 383–403.

Bai, F., Sadagopan, N., & Helmy, A. (2005). *Software: Mobility Simulation and Analysis Tools*, Retrieved from http://nile.cise.ufl.edu/important/software.htm

Beraldi, R., & Baldoni, R. (2003). Unicast Routing Techniques for Mobile Ad Hoc Networks. In Ilyas, M. (Ed.), *The Handbook of Ad Hoc Wireless Networks*. CRC Press.

Chandler, R. E., Herman, R. & Montroll, E. W. (1958). Traffic Dynamics: Studies in Car Following, Operations Research 6. *Operations Research Society of America*, 165-184.

Community-wide Library. (n.d.). *Community-wide Library of mobility and Wireless Networks Measurements*. Retrieved from http://nile.usc.edu/MobiLib

CORSIM. Microscopic Traffic Simulation Model (2009). *CORSIM: Microscopic Traffic Simulation Model* Retrieved from http://www-mctrans.ce.ufl.edu/featured/TSIS/Versio5/corsim.htm

Csilla, Y. K. (n.d.). Application Level Protocol for Accident Reconstruction in VANETs. Retrieved from http://www.cse.sc.edu/research/isl/docs/Preliminary_Proposal_813.pdf

Dastrup, E., Less, M. L., Dawson, J. D., Lee, J. D., & Rizzo, M. (2009, June 22-25). Differences in Simulated Car Following Behavior of Younger and Older Drivers. In *Proceedings of the Fifth International Driving Symposium on Human Factors in Driver Assessment, Training and Vehicle Design*. Big Sky, MT.

Davies, V. (2000). *Evaluating Mobility Models within an Ad Hoc Network* (MS thesis). Golden, CO: Colorado school of Mines.

Ebner, A., & Rohling, H. (2001). A self-organized radio network for automotive applications. In *Proceedings of ITS 2001, 8th World Congress on Intelligent Transportation Systems*. Sydney, Australia.

ETSI, Universal Mobile Telecommunications System (UMTS). (1998). *Selection procedures for choice of radio transmission technologies of the UMTS* (UMTS 30.03 Version 3.2.0). Retrieved from http://www.3gpp.org/ftp/specs/html-info/3003u.htm

Fatal Car Accidents. (2005). *Fatal Car Accidents*. Retrieved from http://www.car-accidents.com/pages/fatal-accident-statistics.html

Fiore, M. (2006). *Mobility Models in Inter Vehicle Communications Literature (Technical Report)*. Politecnico di Torino.

Fiore, M. (2009). Vehicular Mobility Models. In S Olariu, M C Weigle (Ed.), Vehicular Networks From Theory to Practise, (pp 12-2 to 12-15).Boca Raton, FL: CRC Press.

Fiore, M., Harri, J., Filali, F., & Bonnet, C. (2007). *Vehicular Mobility Simulation for VANETs Simulation*. Presented at ANSS '07, 40th Annual In Simulation Symposium, (pp. 301-309).

Fontaine, M. D. (2009). Traffic Monitoring. In Olariu, I. S., & Weigle, M. C. (Eds.), *Vehicular Networks form Theory to Practice* (pp. 1-2–1-4). Boca Raton, FL: CRC Press.

Gawron, C. (1998). An iterative algorithm to determine the dynamic user equilibrium in a traffic simulation model. *International Journal of Modern Physics C*, *9*(3), 393–407.

Gazis, D. C., Herman, R., & Rothrey, R. W. (1961). Non Linear Follow the Leader Models of Traffic Flow. *Operations Research*, *9*(4), 545–567.

Generic Mobility Simulation Framework (GMSF). (2007). *Generic Mobility Simulation Framework*. Retrieved from http://gmsf.hypert.net/

Gipps, P. G. (1981). A Behavioral Car Following Model for Computer Simulation. *Transportation Research Part B: Methodological*, *15*, 105–111.

Gipps, P. G. (1986). A model for the structure of lane-changing decisions. *Transportation Research Board*, *20*(5), 403–414.

Glathe, H. P., Karlsson, K., Brusaglino, G. P., & Calandrino, L. (1990, May). The Prometheus Programme – Objectives, Concepts and Technology for future Road Traffic. *XXIII Fisita Congress*, 477-484.

Greenshields, D. (1959). A study of Traffic Capacity. In *Proceedings of the Highway Research Board*, (Vol. 14, pp 228-477). Washington, DC: Highway Research Board, Harri, J., Filali, F., & Bonnet, C. (2005). A Framework for Mobility Models Generation and its Application to Inter-Vehicular Networks (Research Report RR-05-137). Sophia-Antipolis, France: Department of Mobile Communication.

Harri, J., Filali, F., & Bonnet, C. (2007). *Mobility Models for Vehicular Ad Hoc Networks: A survey and Taxonomy* (Research Report RR-06-168). Antipolis, France: Institute of EURECOM.

Hassan, A. (2009). *VANET Simulation Technical Report*, IDE 0948.

INVENT. (n.d.). *INVENT*. Retrieved from http://www.njit.edu/~borcea/invent/invent-vehicular-traffic-generator.tar.gz

Karnadi, F. K., Mo, Z. H., & Lan, K. (2007). Rapid Generation of Realistic Mobility Models for VANET. In *Proceedings of the IEEE Wireless Communication and Networking Conference* (WCNC '07). Hong Kong, China.

Kesting, A., Treiber, M., & Helbing, D. (2007). MOBIL: General lane changing model for car following models, Transportation Research Record. *Journal of the Transportation Research Board*, 86-94.

Khil, M., & Sichitiu, M. L. (2009). Performance Issues in Vehicular Ad Hoc Networks. In Boukerche, A. (Ed.), *Algorithms and Protocols for Wireless and Mobile Ad Hoc Networks* (pp. 447–450). New York: John Wiley and Sons.

Khisty, C. J., & Lall, B. K. (2003). *Transport Engineering An Introduction*. Upper Saddle River, NJ: Prentice Hall.

Kim, M., Kotz, D., & Kim, S. (2006). Extracting a Mobility Model from Real User Traces. In *Proceedings of the 26th Annual IEEE Conference on Computer Communications* (INFOCOM '06), Barcelona, Spain.

Legendre, F., Borrel, V., Dias de Amorim, M., & Dida, S. F. (2006). *Reconsidering Microscopic Mobility Modeling for Self Organizing Networks*. IEEE Network Magazine.

Leutzbach, W., & Wiedemeann, R. (1986, May). Development and Application of Traffic Simulation Models at Karlsruhe Institute fur VerKehrwesen. *Traffic Engineering and Control*, 270-278.

Mahajan, A., Potinis, N., Gopalan, K., & Wang, A. I.-A. (2005). *Evaluation of Mobility Models for Vehicular Ad Hoc Network Simulations*. (Technical Report N.051220). Tallahassee, FL: Florida State University.

Marfia, G., Pau, G., Giordano, E., Sena, E. D., & Gerla, M. (2007). VANET: On Mobility Scenarios and Urban Infrastructure. A Case Study. In *Proceedings of the International Workshop on Vehicular Networks* and *The International Conference on Computer Communications* (INFOCOM 2007), Anchorage, AK.

Media Lab, M. I. T. (n.d.). *MIT Media Lab: Reality Mining*. Retrieved from http://reality.media.mit.edu

Motion, B. (2005). *A mobility scenario generation and analysis tool*. Retrieved from http://web.informatik.uni-bonn.de/iv/mitarbeiter/decvaal/bonnmotion

Nagel, K., & Schreckenberg, M. (1992). A cellular automaton model for freeway traffic. *Journal de Physique. I, 2,* 2221.

Nagel, K., & Schrekenberg, M. (1992). A Cellular Automaton Model for Physics, *France, 12,* 2221-2229.

National Highway Traffic Safety Administration. (2007). *Traffic Safety facts annual report*. Washington, DC: Department of Transportation.

Newell, G. F. (2002). A Simplified Car Following Theory: A lower Order Model. *Transportation Research Part B: Methodological, 36,* 195–205.

NS-2. (2005). *The NS-2 Simulator*. Retrieved from http://www.isi.edu/nsnam/ns

Owen, L. E., Zhang, Y., Rao, L., & McHale, G. (2000). Traffic Flow Simulation using CORSIM. In *Proceedings of 2000 Winter Simulation Conference*, J A Joines, R R Barton, K Kang and P A Fishwick (eds), (pp. 1143-1147). Orlando, FL.

PalChaudhuri. S., Boudec, J.-Y. L., & Vojnovic, M. (2005). Perfect Simulations for Random Trip Mobility Models. In *Proceedings of the 38th Annual Simulation Symposium*, San Diego, CA.

PARAMICS. (2008). *PARAMICS*. Retrieved from http://www.paramics-online.com/

Perkins, E., & Royer, M. (1999). Ad-Hoc On-Demand Distance Vector Routing. In *proceedings of 2nd IEEE Workshop on Mobile Computing Systems and Applications*. New Orleans, LA.

Qualnet (n.d.). *Qualnet Network Simulator*. Retrieved from http://www.scalable-networks.com/

Random Trip Mobility Model. (n.d.). *Random Trip Mobility Model*. Retrieved from http://monarch.cs.rice.edu/~santa/research /mobility/code.tar.gz

Ranjitkar, P., Nakatsuji, T., & Kawamua, A. (2005). Car-Following Models: An Experiment Based Benchmarking. *Journal of the Eastern Asia Society for Transportation Studies, 6,* 1582–1596.

Saha, A. K., & Johnson, D. B. (2004). *Modeling Mobility for Vehicular Ad Hoc Networks*. VANET.

Schrank, D., & Lomax, T. (2007). *The 2007 Urban Mobility Report*. College Station, TX: Texas Transportation Institute.

Takano, A., Okada, H., & Mase, K. (2007). Performance Comparison of a Position Based Routing Protocol for VANET In *Proceedings of Mobile Adhoc and Sensor Systems*, (MASS 2007), (pp. 1-6). Pisa, Italy.

TIGER. (2003). *TIGER (Topologically Integrated Geographic Encoding and Referencing)*. Retrieved from http://www.census.gov/geo/www/tiger/tiger2003/tgr2003.html

TRANSIM (n.d.). *TRANSIM*. Retrieved from transims.tsas.lanl.gov

Treiber, M. (n.d.). *Microsimulation of road traffic*. Retrieved from http://www.trafficsimulation.de/

Treiber, M., Hennecke, A., & Helbing, D. (2000). Congested traffic states in empirical observations and microscopic simulations. *Physical Review E: Statistical Physics, Plasmas, Fluids, and Related Interdisciplinary Topics*, *62*, 1805–1824.

Treiber, M., & Kesting, A. (2009). Models for Traffic Flow and Vehicle Motion. In Olariu, S., & Weigle, M. C. (Eds.), *Vehicular Networks From Theory to Practice* (pp. 26–28). Boca Raton, FL: CRC Press.

UDEL. (n.d.). *Models for Simulation of Urban Mobile Wireless Networks*. Retrieved from http://udelmodels.eecis.udel.edu/

VISSIM. (2009). *VISSIM*. Retrieved from http://www.tomfotherby.com/Websites/VISSIM/index.htm

Yoon, J., Noble, B. D., & Liu, M. (2006). Building Realistic Mobility Models from Coarse-Grained Traces. In *Proceedings of the ACM International Conference on Mobile Systems, Applications and Services* (Mobisys '06), (177-190). Uppsala, Sweden.

Zheng, Q., & Liu, X. H. J. (April 2006). An Agenda-based Mobility Model. In *Proceedings of the 39th IEEE Annual Simulation Symposium* (ANSS-39-2006). Huntsville, AL.

Chapter 12
Probabilistic Information Dissemination in Vehicular Ad Hoc Networks

Mylonas Y.
University of Cyprus, Cyprus

Lestas M.
University of Cyprus, Cyprus

Pitsillides A.
University of Cyprus, Cyprus

Xeros A.
Open University of Cyprus, Cyprus

Andreou M.
Open University of Cyprus, Cyprus

Ioannou P.
University of Southern California, USA

ABSTRACT

Many of the applications in VANETs, especially the safety related ones, set up requirements for information dissemination which are different from conventional networks and are thus difficult to fulfill with existing strategies. In this chapter, we review recently proposed data dissemination schemes in VANETs and we present novel solutions and analytical evaluation tools. We focus on the use of probabilistic methods as these are known to provide effective solutions and at the same time address the highly stochastic nature of many of the processes involved in VANETs. We present a short range multi-hop broadcast scheme which employs speed adaptive probabilistic flooding to overcome the broadcast storm problem in the case of high traffic density, a hovering scheme which employs probabilistic flooding to overcome the intermittently connected nature of the network within the hovering area and finally, we establish analytically lower bounds on the probability of information propagation at an intersection taking into account the vehicle speeds and the traffic density which is reflected in the vehicle arrival rate.

DOI: 10.4018/978-1-61520-913-2.ch012

INTRODUCTION

Intelligent Vehicle Systems (IVSs) employing vehicle to vehicle (V2V) and vehicle to infrastructure (V2I) communications harness the potential of information and communication technologies (ICTs) to create a safer, smarter and more efficient transportation network. The rapid growth in transportation needs and car ownership has led to a severe increase in road traffic which has generated a number of social and economic problems: congestion of road transportation networks, environmental hazards and above all traffic accidents. On an average day in Europe (U.S.), vehicle collisions kill more than 100 (116) people and injure 4600 (7900). Government agencies and automotive industries are responding by investing billions of dollars in an effort to reduce these terrifying numbers. Intelligent Transportation Systems (ITS) are considered central cornerstones of this effort and vehicular ad hoc networks (VANETs) are emerging as the preferred network design for ITS technologies. The recently published 802.11p standard supports both vehicle-to-vehicle and vehicle-to-infrastructure communications allowing the formation of vehicular ad hoc networks which are envisioned to accommodate the new generation of cooperative safety applications. The range of applications of VANETs goes beyond the safety related ones to include traffic monitoring, platooning, text messaging, distributed passenger teleconferencing, music downloading, roadside e-advertisements etc.

Many of the aforementioned applications in VANETs, especially the safety related ones, set up requirements for information dissemination which are different from conventional networks and are thus difficult to fulfil with existing strategies. Safety applications pose stringent delay requirements on emergency message delivery and address geographical areas in which data needs to be cooperatively collected, distributed and maintained. Design challenges are then posed by the variable node density along the transportation network, the high mobility, the confined but often unpredictable movement and the unreliable radio channel. Variations in traffic density are of particular importance as low traffic densities cause the network to become intermittently connected whereas high traffic densities lead to excessive contention. These phenomena significantly degrade the performance of data dissemination strategies whether these are routing protocols or broadcast based schemes. In this chapter, we review recently proposed data dissemination schemes and we present novel solutions and analytical evaluation tools which address the aforementioned problems. We focus on the use of probabilistic methods as these are known to provide effective solutions and at the same time address the highly stochastic nature of many of the processes involved in VANETs. We present a short range multi-hop broadcast scheme which employs speed adaptive probabilistic flooding to overcome the broadcast storm problem in the case of high traffic density, a hovering scheme which employs probabilistic flooding to overcome the intermittently connected nature of the network within the hovering area and finally, we establish analytically lower bounds on the probability of information propagation at an intersection taking into account the vehicle speeds and the traffic density which is reflected in the vehicle arrival rate. Simulation results which are outlined in the Chapter validate our analytical findings and indicate that the proposed protocols satisfy to a very good extent the posed design objectives.

The chapter is organized as follows. In section 2 we review recently proposed data dissemination schemes, in section 3 we present the Speed Adaptive Probabilistic Flooding scheme, in section 4 we demonstrate the effectiveness of Gaussian like Probabilistic Flooding for information hovering, in section 5 we derive a formula which calculates lower bounds on the probability of message propagation on intersections and finally in section 6 we offer our conclusions and future research directions.

BACKROUND

Data dissemination schemes in VANETs can have fundamentally different characteristics and design objectives. Consider, for example a cooperative warning application which upon detection of an unexpected event such as a traffic accident, causes vehicles to generate warning messages which contain critical information regarding the unexpected event. A short range multi-hop broadcast scheme may be used to disseminate the emergency warning message to all neighboring vehicles warning them of the imminent danger. A routing protocol can also be employed to facilitate the transfer of the warning message over long distances to emergency services such as hospitals and police stations. Finally, a hovering scheme can be used to maintain the message in a confined geographical area for a specific period of time, notifying all vehicles entering the area of the unexpected event. In this chapter, we address major challenges in the design of such information protocols and we propose novel solutions and analytical evaluation tools.

The simplest protocol which can serve as a short-range multi-hop broadcast scheme, is blind flooding (Tseng, 2002), a scheme which involves each vehicle rebroadcasting the message whenever it receives it for the first time. However, blind flooding is known to generate a large number of redundant messages leading to contention, unnecessary collisions and thus high latency of message delivery. This phenomenon is better known in literature as the Broadcast Storm Problem (Tseng, 2002) and significantly degrades the performance of time sensitive applications such as the ones accommodated in VANETs. Several techniques have been proposed in literature to alleviate the problem [Alzoubi, 2002; Calinescu, 2001; Lim, 2001; Peng, 2000; Ni, 2001; Hu, 2003; Laouiti, 2001; Korkmaz, 2004; Korkmaz, 2006). The main idea has been to reduce the number of nodes rebroadcasting the message without affecting the achieved reachability. In VANETs the most popu-

lar and effective approach to reduce the number of vehicles rebroadcasting the message has been to choose vehicles which lie on the boundary of the transmission range of the vehicle transmitting the message (Chiasserini, 2005; Tonquz, 2007; Alshaer, 2005; Sasson, 2003). However, this method requires a positioning system, such as GPS, which may not always be available. In this chapter we describe an alternative solution (Mylonas, 2008) which employs adaptive probabilistic flooding to create a protocol which does not require any positioning system and is shown to work effectively.

Information Hovering is a relatively new information dissemination paradigm in mobile ad hoc networks (Serugendo, 2007) in general and VANETs in particular. Hovering allows decoupling information from its host and promotes coupling this information with a specific geographical location. The information hovers from one mobile device to another, in a quest to remain in the vicinity of its anchoring geographical location, and be available to users that are entering or present in this geographical location. The main requirement of a single piece of hovering information is to keep itself attached to its location and to its vicinity area (anchor area), despite the unreliability of the mobile device on which it is stored (Villalba 2008; Konstantas 2006).

Many solutions can be developed and applied. However, the solution space should be limited to the ones using minimum resources such as processing power, bandwidth, storage, etc and at the same time, achieving high message reachability to all vehicles residing or entering the hovering area throughout the lifetime of the hovering information. As in the case of a short-range multi-hop broadcast scheme the simplest solution to consider is blind flooding (Tseng, 2002). This method ensures the highest reachability possible at the expense, however, of an enormous number of exchanged messages. To reduce the number of exchanged messages one might consider vehicles exchanging information when both reside in the hovering area. However, the problem with this approach is that it may also reduce the achieved reachability in the case of low traffic densities within the hovering area. Low traffic densities may cause the vehicular network to become intermittently connected. In such a case, sections of the network which are partitioned from the information sources cannot receive the information message thus leading to low reachability. In this chapter, we overcome this problem by applying probabilistic flooding outside the hovering area. The rationale behind this design choice is that informed vehicles outside the area can serve as information bridges towards partitioned uninformed sub areas, thus increasing message reachability. In addition, since blind flooding outside the hovering area is avoided, the number of exchanged messages is also reduced.

In cases where information needs to propagate over large distances, various routing protocols have been proposed, see a syrvey paper of Li and Wang (Li, 2007). The Mobility-Centric Data Dissemination Algorithm (MDDV) (Wu, 2004) is one of the few that provides a complete architecture for vehicular routing. It combines the ideas of opportunistic, trajectory-based and geographical forwarding. The protocol disseminates data to intended receivers, while maintaining design demands such as high delivery ratio, low delay and low memory occupancy. The Geographic Source Routing (GSR) protocol proposed by Lochert in (Lochert, 2003) addresses the problem of base-line position-based routing in two-dimensional urban scenarios. GSR combines position-based routing with topological information. In (Lee, 2004) Lee et.al., present an Anchor based Street and Traffic Aware Routing scheme. They use information on city bus routes to identify an anchor path with high connectivity for packet delivery. In addition, distributed protocols for decentralized network organization have been proposed in (Chrisalita, 2004). The protocols require the receivers to analyze the exchanged messages so that they can infer whether they are the intended destinations.

None of the above approaches, however, considers the problem of finding optimal routes which maximize the message delivery probability when the latter has to be done in a specific amount of time. This problem is of particular interest in VANETs since safety messages in such networks are often characterized by a finite lifetime period. In this chapter, we present a preliminary result (Xeros, 2007), which can be utilized by routing algorithms to generate message propagation routes which guaranty that the message will be delivered on time with high probability. In (Xeros, 2007) we provide a lower bound on the information propagation probability among vehicles traveling on intersecting roads. This result when combined with the average message propagation speed on a road provided by Wu et. al. in (Wu, 2004) can yield a powerful tool for the development of a new routing protocol with analytically verifiable properties.

SPEED ADAPTIVE PROBABILISTIC FLOODING

In this section, we propose Speed Adaptive Probabilistic Flooding (SAPF), a new short range multi-hop broadcast scheme which can facilitate the fast and reliable distribution of emergency warning messages in case of an unexpected event. The protocol provides an effective solution in highway settings and enjoys a number of benefits relative to other approaches: it is simple to implement, it does not introduce additional communication burden as it requires local information only, it does not rely on the existence of a positioning system which may not always be available and above all, mitigates the effect of the broadcast storm problem, typical when utilizing blind flooding. Our results indicate that the proposed algorithm outperforms blind flooding, especially in cases of heavy congestion. The SAPF algorithm achieves high reachability and unlike blind flooding, maintains low latency as the density of vehicles in the road network increases.

Design Rationale and Methodology

Our primary objective has been to design a decentralized, simple to implement short range multi-hop broadcast scheme which achieves low latency of message delivery and high reachability. The broadcast storm problem poses the most significant challenges to the fulfillment of the above objectives and SAPF solves the problem by employing probabilistic flooding. A unique feature of the protocol is that the rebroadcast probability is regulated adaptively based on the vehicle speed which can be obtained locally. The rationale behind this design choice is that low vehicle speeds in a highway setting imply large vehicle densities which in turn imply that lower rebroadcast probability values are sufficient to achieve high reachability with low latency.

A major challenge in the design of the SAPF protocol has been the derivation of the rebroadcast probability function which maps the speed of the vehicle to the rebroadcast probability value in case of an emergency warning message being received for the first time. In a highway setting, the speed of the vehicle is sufficient to provide information regarding the vehicle density by means of speed-density curves which can be readily obtained from field data (Wang, 2006). This implies that the problem of deriving a function which maps the speed of the vehicle to the rebroadcast probability can be reduced to the problem of deriving a function which maps the density of the vehicles to the rebroadcast probability. The question that arises is then the following: for a particular vehicle density, what is the rebroadcast probability which achieves the highest possible reachability with the minimum possible latency? In this work, for each vehicle density we obtain such rebroadcast probability values by taking advantage of phase transition phenomena observed when relating the reachability with the rebroadcast probability

(Krishnamachari, 2001). For a particular vehicle density, there exists a critical rebroadcast probability beyond which all vehicles receive the message with high probability thus achieving high reachability (Erdos, 1960, Frank, 1995). This critical probability is the desired rebroadcast probability value for the vehicle density under consideration. So, in order to derive the desired rebroadcast probability function we adopt the following methodology: we first choose a suitable set of vehicle density values; for each vehicle density we conduct simulation experiments which we use to obtain rebroadcast probability vs. reachability curves; on these curves we identify the critical probability value at the onset of the phase transition; we then use the obtained data to construct the probability vs. density curve and finally we combine the latter with the speed-density curve to obtain the desired rebroadcast probability function. Below we provide details regarding the adopted procedure and the results obtained.

All the simulation experiments were conducted using an integrated platform combining two simulators, VISSIM, a traffic simulator, and OPNET Modeler, a network simulator. The topology of the reference simulation model is a two lane highway spanning a distance of 6km and the assumed scenario involves an unexpected event occurring on the highway at a predetermined time and location. A vehicle upon detecting the unexpected event becomes an abnormal vehicle (AV) and instantly transmits an early warning message (EWM) to warn approaching vehicles of the imminent danger. Any vehicle that receives the EWM for the first time decides to rebroadcast the message with probability p, and not to rebroadcast the message with probability 1-p. Specifications of the 802.11b standard were used for the network communication with the transmission range set to 300m for all vehicles. The main metrics of interest are the latency of message delivery and the message reachability. The former is defined as the time interval between the instant the message is transmitted by the vehicle detecting the road

Figure 1. Message reachability vs. probability

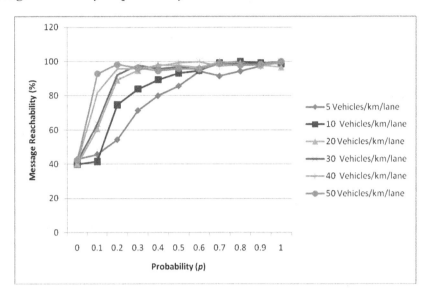

hazard and the instant that the last vehicle in the area of interest receives the message. The latter is defined as the number of vehicles that have received the EWM in the area of interest over all vehicles which reside in this area.

As mentioned above, the first step in this design procedure is to choose a set of vehicle density values. The values chosen were 5, 10, 20, 30, 40, and 50 measured in vehicles per kilometer per lane. In the simulation experiments that we conducted, the vehicle density was set by appropriately setting the vehicle penetration rate in the test site under consideration. For each vehicle density value, reachability vs. rebroadcast probability graph was obtained. Rebroadcast probabilities in the range 0 to 1 in steps of 0.1 were considered. All values obtained are averages over 10 simulation experiments. Figure 1 shows the reachability values obtained as we varied the rebroadcast probability for the vehicle density values under consideration. For a particular density it is evident that there exists a critical threshold probability beyond which the number of vehicles receiving the message suddenly increases and stays almost constant. This sudden change is compatible with phase transition phenomena observed in

the literature of random graphs and percolation theory (Frank, 1995). This critical probability is the desired rebroadcast probability for the corresponding vehicle density. The reason for this is that among all rebroadcast probability values which achieve almost 100% reachability, this is the one which minimizes the latency, the number of rebroadcasts and the contention. This is a result of these quantities relating to the rebroadcast probability through strictly increasing functions (Mylonas, 2008).

Having obtained the desired rebroadcast probability values for each of the considered vehicle density values, their relationship is depicted graphically in Figure 2(a). We observe an almost linear decrease of the critical probability as the penetration rate increases up to a saturation point (50 per kilometer per lane) after which the critical probability stays constant. This saturation is due to the fact that after some value of the penetration rate the vehicle density remains almost constant since the capacity of the particular road has been reached. For a particular section of the road there is a maximum number of vehicles which can be present simultaneously in that section.

Figure 2. Critical probability vs. density and vehicle speed

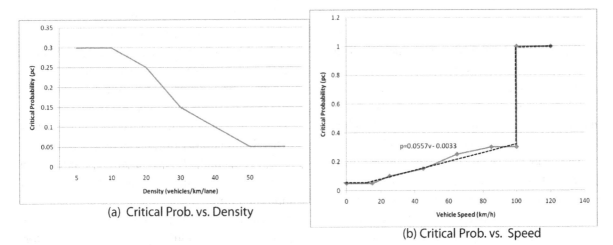

(a) Critical Prob. vs. Density

(b) Critical Prob. vs. Speed

The final step is to combine the obtained re-broadcast probability vs. density function with the speed vs. density curve (Mylonas, 2008), obtained using field data, to derive the desired rebroadcast probability vs. speed function. This is shown in Figure 2(b). We consider a linear approximation of the obtained graph whose equation which is given by:

$$p = 0.0557v - 0.003 \qquad (1)$$

where p denotes the rebroadcast probability and v the velocity of the vehicles. In addition, for speeds above 100km/h (speed limit) we set the rebroadcast probability equal to 1. The reason is that beyond such speeds it is impossible to estimate the density based on speed information only and so, we adopt a rather aggressive rebroadcast policy in order to ensure message delivery to all vehicles. On the other hand for speed values below 15km/h, we assume that the network has almost reached its capacity and so we consider a constant rebroadcast probability of 0.05. The resulting rebroadcast probability vs. speed function used in the proposed SAPF scheme is shown in Figure 2(b).

Based on the function of Figure 2(b), the speed adaptive probabilistic flooding algorithm is as follows:

Speed Adaptive Probabilistic Flooding Algorithm

1. upon reception of EWM s at node n:
2. if EWM received first time and it is not the originator of message s and TTL > 0 then
    a. if(veh. speed >= 15km/h && veh. speed <= 100km/h) then broadcast EWM **s** with probability **p** = 0.0557v-0.0033
    b. else if (veh. speed < 15km/h) then broadcast EWM **s** with probability **p** = 0.05
    c. else if (veh. speed > 100km/h) then broadcast EWM **s** with probability **p** = 1
3. *end if*

For the implementation of the SAFP algorithm we used the OPNET Modeler simulation engine by making appropriate modifications to the 802.11 WLAN station model which excludes implementations of layers above the MAC layers such as TCP/IP.

Performance Evaluation

In this section, we evaluate the performance of the SAPF algorithm using an integrated platform combining two simulators, the traffic simulator VISSIM and OPNET Modeler. We have used VISSIM to generate traces of the vehicles involved in our scenarios, which were then furnished into the OPNET Modeler simulation model.

The topology of the simulation model used in our study is based on a section of the Nicosia-Limassol highway in Cyprus. The chosen test site is a two lane highway which spans a distance of 6Km. Our objective has been to evaluate the performance of the SAPF algorithm with respect to chosen performance metrics and compare it with the Blind Flooding (BF) algorithm. The performance metrics considered were the percentage of nodes receiving the transmitted emergency message i.e. message reachability, and the latency of message delivery. We conducted a number of experiments, in order to evaluate the performance of the SAPF scheme in scenarios reflecting three types of congestion: light congestion, regular congestion and heavy congestion. We emulated the different congestion levels in the chosen topology as follows: the vehicles in the considered two-lane freeway propagate were ariginally abiding to a speed limit in the range 90-120km/h. In order to generate congestion, at the 3rd kilometer of the freeway we suddenly changed the speed limit to lie in the range 30-60km/h. We then created different levels of congestion by varying the penetration rate. We considered three penetration rate values, 2000veh/hour, 5000veh/hour and 50000veh/hour reflecting light, regular and heavy congestion conditions respectively. The traffic accident takes place at the 5th kilometer of the Nicosia-Limassol highway, where a vehicle transmits an emergency warning message.

The network is confined within a 10m x 6000m area, where each vehicle has a constant transmission range of 300m. The latter is ensured by setting the transmission power equal to 0.00043w.

Each vehicle uses 802.11b MAC layer protocol and operates in ad hoc mode. The vehicles are configured to operate in broadcast mode with no ACK/CTS/RTS mechanisms. The TTL value is set to 2 in order to guarantee a maximum of 3-hop transmission. This creates a multi-hop transmission range of approximately 900m. The data size of each packet is set to a constant value of 1024 bytes. In all simulations, the early warning message is generated 400 seconds after the simulation start time. All simulations run for 1 hour network simulated time.

Below we present the results obtained and we extract useful conclusions regarding the performance of the SAPF algorithm comparing it with the BF algorithm under light, regular and heavy congested traffic. Our results indicate that the SAPF algorithm outperform blind flooding as it maintains high reachability and low latency of message delivery at all congestion levels. Figure 3(a) shows the percentage of vehicles receiving the emergency warning message for the three penetration rates under consideration. It is evident, that both algorithms in all cases perform equally well achieving reachability values higher than 92%. The SAPF algorithm in fact achieves reachability values greater than 97% which is more than satisfactory.

In Figure 3(b) we show plots of the message latency. This graph highlights the true superiority of the SAPF scheme compared to the BF algorithm. As the congestion becomes heavier, the BF algorithm takes more time to deliver the message to all vehicles. The SAPF algorithm, on the other hand, manages to maintain almost constant latency values at all congestion conditions. In the heavy congestion case for example we observe that blind flooding reports a delay of approximately 60ms while the SAPF reports a delay of approximately 10ms. This significant reduction in the delay is of great importance in the considered applications as it gives the drivers or the automatic controller additional time to respond effectively.

Figure 3. Message reachability and latency of blind flooding and SAPF in each of the considered congestion levels

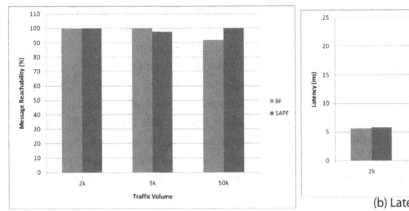

(a) Message Reachability vs. Traffic Vol

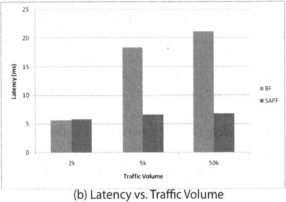

(b) Latency vs. Traffic Volume

INFORMATION HOVERING

In this section we consider the information hovering problem in VANETs and we investigate the use of probabilistic flooding as an effective solution which can lead to high reachability values within the hovering area and at the same time achieve low number of exchanged messages. We investigate a number of hovering protocols which we evaluate through simulations. Our results indicate that probabilistic flooding with a Gaussian like probability function outperforms other approaches by satisfying to the greatest extent the posed design objectives.

Information Hovering Protocols

We first provide a formal definition of the information hovering problem in VANETs and we present the protocols which we consider in this work as candidate solutions.

We consider a bounded geographical area which we refer to as the hovering area in which there exists at least one node which stores or generates information messages useful to all vehicles in the area. We refer to such vehicles as information sources. All equipped vehicles employ wireless communication to form a vehicular ad hoc network which may also communicate with fixed infrastructure present in the region. The main objective is then for the information sources to utilize the vehicular ad-hoc network to persistently disseminate the useful messages to all vehicles in the hovering area. Persistent dissemination implies that the property of all vehicles receiving the message is not instantaneously achieved, but holds for an arbitrary time interval, during which vehicles dynamically enter and leave the hovering area.

A number of solutions can be developed to solve the problem as described above. However, the solution space can be refined by choosing solutions which make efficient use of the available resources such as storage, power, bandwidth etc. Towards this goal we pose the additional objective of minimizing the number of exchanged messages. Few numbers of exchanged messages imply less storage requirements, less power consumption, less bandwidth use and above all smaller latency of information delivery since phenomena like severe congestion and contention which lead to collisions are avoided. The problem can thus be defined as follows.

Problem Definition

Given a road map area which we refer to as the Hovering Area and a single message information data, it is required to find an Information Dissemination Protocol in VANETs so that when applied, a high percentage of Vehicles that exist in the area receive the message, with a small number of messages exchanged

We investigate the relative performance of seven information dissemination protocols in order to infer which one satisfies, to the greatest extent, the objectives posed in the problem definition. The evaluation method has been simulative and the performance metrics used were the number of messages exchanged and the percentage of informed vehicles in the hovering area. The results indicate that probabilistic flooding with a Gaussian like probability function exhibits superior performance as it achieves high reachability and relatively low number of messages exchanged. Below, we describe in detail and discuss the relative merits of the considered information dissemination protocols.

- *Blind flooding:* Blind flooding is a simple to implement and popular solution for many information dissemination problems. It involves each vehicle rebroadcasting the message whenever it identifies an uninformed neighbor. Message exchange is independent of the vehicles' distance from the hovering area. Such a scheme can be useful in special cases where the hovering area is unbounded which means that the useful message must be delivered as far as the network connectivity allows. It can also prove to be handy in cases where the information source is distant from the hovering area. In such cases blind flooding can be used both as a routing protocol, to facilitate the transfer of the message from the source to the hovering area and as a hovering protocol to facilitate

persistent message dissemination to all vehicles within the hovering area. The main advantage of the protocol is that it guarantees the highest possible reachability as it unravels all possible routes to any given destination. However, this comes at the expense of a huge number of exchanged messages many of which are redundant. It is well known, that blind flooding leads to increased contention which causes collisions. Such collisions lead to retransmissions and significantly increase the observed latency of message delivery. This phenomenon is known in literature as the broadcast storm problem. Many techniques have been proposed to alleviate the problem. The main idea has been to reduce the number of neighboring nodes rebroadcasting each message, without affecting the total number of nodes receiving the message. Probabilistic flooding belongs to this class of protocols.

- *Exchange messages if and only if both the sender and the receiver lie in the hovering area:* This method can be considered as a geographically confined blind flooding scheme. Its main advantage is that it drastically decreases the number of exchanged messages thus making more efficient use of the available resources. However, it has a number of disadvantages. When the information sources are outside the hovering area it cannot facilitate the transfer of the information from the sources to the hovering area. In such a case, a separate routing protocol must be invoked to facilitate the transfer, before the hovering scheme disseminates the message to all vehicles within the hovering area. However, the greatest disadvantage of the protocol is that it may lead to low percentage of informed vehicles. In cases of low traffic density, the network may become intermittently connected. When the partitioned areas of the network do not accommodate any of the information carriers, the vehicles within these areas cannot receive the useful information thus degrading performance in terms of the reachability achieved. In a worst case scenario, where all the information carriers lie on the boundary of the hovering area it is possible that they all move outside the hovering area thus endangering the survivability of the information. When this happens the system can only recover if an information carrier moves back to the hovering area.

- *Exchange messages if and only if the receiver is in the Hovering Area (Receiver in Area):* This method attempts to alleviate the problem of low reachability in case of low traffic densities, by allowing vehicles which lie within one transmission range from the hovering area to retransmit the received messages. Vehicles lying outside the hovering area can serve as information bridges between informed and uninformed areas thus increasing the percentage of informed vehicles. They can also help in improving the survivability of the information by providing an alternative way with which the information can return to the hovering area in case all information carriers move outside.

- *Probabilistic Flooding:* In a way similar to the previous protocol this scheme allows messages to be exchanged when the receiver lies within the hovering area. However, in order to further improve the achieved reachability, even in the case that the receiver lies outside the hovering area, the scheme offers the opportunity of retransmission by applying probabilistic flooding. Probabilistic flooding works as follows. When an informed vehicle identifies an uninformed neighbor and the neighbor lies outside the hovering area, the sender decides to transmit the message

with probability p and decides not to retransmit the message with probability 1-p. The probability p is calculated based on a probability function *f*. The function can have several input variables such as the distance from the hovering area, the traffic conditions, the priority of the message, etc., however, in this work we focus on a single input variable which is the distance from the hovering area. We consider strictly decreasing functions which cause the retransmission probability to decrease as the distance of the vehicle from the hovering area increases. The reasoning behind this design choice is that since the information is logically attached to a geographical area its usefulness decreases as the distance from the hovering area increases. We thus take advantage of this decrease in usefulness to decrease the number of exchanged messages by decreasing the retransmission probability. In this work we investigate the performance of four probability functions which are described below. In the equations that follow, *d* is the distance between the receiver and the hovering area and *r* is the vehicle's transmission range.

○ *Step probabilistic flooding:*

$$p = \begin{cases} 0.8 & if\ d \le (r\ /\ 4) \\ 0.6 & if\ (r\ /\ 4) < d \le (r\ /\ 2) \\ 0.4 & if\ (r\ /\ 2) < d \le (r*\ 3\ /\ 4) \\ 0.2 & if\ (r*\ 3\ /\ 4) < d \le r \\ 0 & if\ d > r \end{cases}$$

○ *Gaussian probabilistic flooding:*

$$p = e^{\frac{-d^2}{2(2r)^2}}$$

The above equation is obtained by considering a normal curve

$$p = \frac{1}{2r\sqrt{2\pi}} e^{-\frac{d^2}{2(2r)^2}}$$

with the mean equal to 0 and the standard deviation equal to *2r*, which is then multiplied by a factor $2r\sqrt{2\pi}$. The latter is necessary to ensure that the transmission probability on the boundary of the hovering area is equal to 1.

- *Linear probabilistic flooding:*

p = 1- d/r (d<r)

p = 0 (d>r)

- *Exponential probabilistic flooding:*

$$p = e^{-\frac{3d}{r}}$$

Performance Evaluation

The performance evaluation method has been simulative. We attempt a comparative study to show that probabilistic flooding enjoys a number of benefits as it achieves high reachability, similar to the one reported by blind flooding, and at the same time significantly reduces the number of exchanged messages thus making more efficient use of the available resources. We conduct our simulation experiments using the VISSIM microscopic simulation tool. The reference model used is drawn from a sample traffic setup of the simulator. It represents a section of the transportation network in the cities of Bellevue and Redmond in Washington.

We conduct each simulation experiment with a different seed number. The duration time of all simulations is set to 1000sec which is more than enough for the system to converge to its equilibrium state. The output of each simulation experiment is a text file which contains records for a number of fields such as the vehicle's id, the simulation step, the coordinates of each vehicle at every step, etc. The simulation step is set to 200ms. Once the system has converged to its equilibrium state, we processed data for 10 minutes in order to evaluate the performance of the consider protocols.

In order to simulate the information hovering schemes presented in the previous section we have developed an application in C++ which processes the text files generated by the VISSIM simulator. The application takes a number of input parameters:

- *Vehicle Transmission Range*: Each vehicle selects its transmission range in a min-max interval according to a uniform distribution. The selected transmission range for each vehicle remains constant throughout the simulation. The min and max values are the input parameters.
- *Hovering Area*: The hovering area is assumed circular in which case the input parameters are the coordinates of the center and the radius of the circle.
- *Successful transmission probability*: In order to model problems in the communication channel which may lead to messages being lost, every transmission is characterized by a constant probability of successful delivery. This is an input parameter whose value depends on the quality of the hardware being used, the weather conditions, the structures present in the area, the ground morphology, the transmission frequency, the multiple access method used and other possible sources of communication interference. Even though this probability depends on the distance between sender and receiver, we use a constant value since it also depends on the factors mentioned above, making it complex and difficult to model.
- *Market Penetration Rate of equipped vehicles (MPR):* This parameter is defined as the percentage of appropriately equipped

Figure 4. Number of exchanged messages and reachability in hovering area B with the market penetration rate being equal to 2.2%

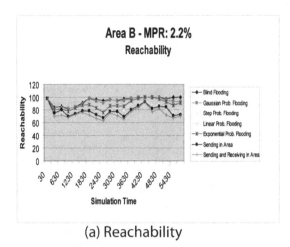

(a) Reachability

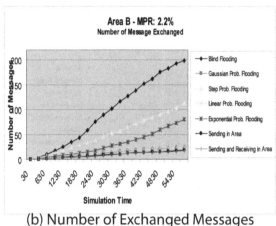

(b) Number of Exchanged Messages

vehicles to participate in VANETs over all vehicles driving in the city.

- *Scanning Frequency*: Vehicles periodically exchange beacon messages which allow them to discover which of their neighbors are uninformed. This parameter indicates the frequency with which each vehicle sends its beacon message.

In all simulation experiments the above parameters, except the market penetration rate, are kept constant to render the comparative study meaningful. Their values are as follows: Transmission Range: 140-220m, Successful Transmission Probability 0.8, Frequency of Scanning: 1 second, Radius of Hovering Area R = 500m. In all simulations we also assume that the system has undergone an initialization procedure so that at its initial state, all vehicles within the hovering area possess the useful message.

We consider 2 different hovering areas within the transportation network which reflect two different congestion levels: area 'A' which is congested with heavy traffic reported within its boundaries area and area 'B' which is a medium/light traffic area.

Our first simulation scenario considers area B which, as mentioned above, represents an area of medium to low traffic density. We consider an MPR value equal to 2.2%. In Figure 4(a) we show the time evolution of the percentage of informed vehicles within the hovering area whereas in figure 4(b) we show the time evolution of the number of exchanged messages for each of the considered hovering protocols. The 100% reachability value at time 0 reflects the fact that at the initial stage of the simulation all vehicles residing in the hovering area are already informed. As the simulation time increases, the reachability is shown to decrease. This reveals the problem of uninformed partitioned areas in the case of low traffic densities. As new cars enter the hovering area some of them are located at positions which are beyond the transmission range of the informed vehicles and can thus not be informed. This causes the percentage of informed vehicles to decrease. This behavior is common to all protocols. However, their subsequent behavior differs. Blind flooding, after some time, is successful in disseminating the useful message to almost all uninformed vehicles. This is highlighted in Figure 4(a) which shows that the percentage of informed vehicles, after some initial drop, gradually increases to values

Figure 5. number of exchanged messages and reachability in hovering area B with the market penetration rate being equal to 1.3%

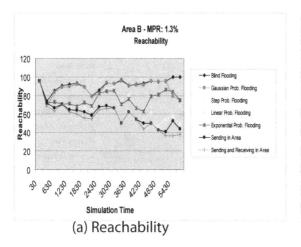

(a) Reachability

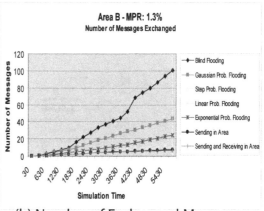

(b) Number of Exchanged Messages

close to 100%. Similar behavior is exhibited by the Gaussian probabilistic flooding scheme. All the other protocols fail to recover from the original decrease, persistently reporting smaller reachability values and most of them eventually converging to reachability values close to 80%.

Figure 4(b) reveals the main disadvantage of the blind flooding scheme. Blind flooding reports the greatest number of messages exchanged. Gaussian probabilistic flooding on the other hand, manages to achieve a significant decrease in the number of exchanged messages, while at the same time maintain reachability values comparable to the ones reported by blind flooding. The other protocols also achieve a decrease in the number of exchanged messages, at the expense, however, of lower reachability. The above indicate that Gaussian probabilistic flooding is the protocol of choice for the considered scenario.

In order to investigate the performance of the considered protocols in the case of fewer vehicles being appropriately equipped to participate in VANETs, we repeat the same experiment with a market penetration rate equal to 1.3%. The results are shown in Figure 5. We observe that the system behavior is very similar to the one reported in the previous experiment. The major difference is that

the protocols which were consistently reporting relatively low reachability, report even smaller values. The reason is that lower market penetration rate values imply less vehicles participating in the network thus creating a larger number of partitioned areas which exemplify the low reachability problem. Both blind flooding and Gaussian probabilistic flooding are shown to successfully alleviate the problem by converging to reachability values close to 100%. In addition, Gaussian probabilistic flooding is still the protocol of choice as it continues to reduce the number of exchanged messages by more than a factor of 2.

Our final simulation experiment considers area A which is characterized by heavy traffic. We consider an MPR value equal to 1.1%. Larger MPR values lead to high reachability values at all times for all the considered protocols due to the large number of equipped vehicles rendering the vehicular network almost fully connected. When the MPR value is set to 1.1% the results are shown in Fig 6. They exhibit similar behavior to the ones obtained in previous experiments. The intermittently connected nature of the ad hoc network causes the percentage of informed vehicles to experience a sudden drop at the initial stages of the simulation experiment. Blind flooding and

Figure 6. Number of exchanged messages and reachability in hovering area A with the market penetration rate being equal to 1.1%

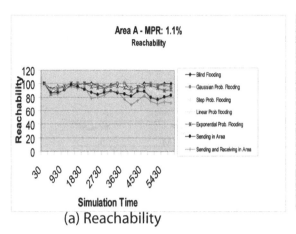

(a) Reachability

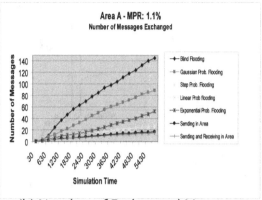

(b) Number of Exchanged Messages

Gaussian probabilistic flooding are then successful in alleviating the problem, by slowly increasing the reachability to values which are close to 100%. The rest of the protocols report smaller values, with the Sending and Receiving in the Area scheme exhibiting the worse performance. Figure 6 (b) then indicates that blind flooding does not only achieve high reachability values but also reduces to a significant extent the number of exchanged messages, making it the protocol of choice for this scenario as well.

INFORMATION PROPAGATION PROBABILITY ON INTERSECTIONS

In this section, we address the problem of finding the probability of information propagation along vehicles traveling on intersecting roads in a certain amount of time when there is no static infrastructure, such as repeaters. The motivation for the study of this problem originates from the potential use of such a result in the design of a new routing protocol whose objective is to maximize the probability of message delivery from source to destination. Our result can be combined with the findings in (Wu et. al. 2004) to calculate the latter probability.

Our main contribution is the derivation of a formula which calculates lower bounds on the desired information propagation probability. The formula indicates that the probability is highly dependent on the traffic conditions of the target road, such as the distribution of vehicle speeds and the traffic density. We validate our analytical findings using simulations. Good agreement is observed between the theoretical and the simulation results.

Problem Formulation

In this paragraph we formulate the considered problem mathematically and we introduce the basic notations, definitions and assumptions utilized throughout the section. We model the roadway network as a set of straight line roads which connect a set of intersections. We denote by $I=\{I_1, I_2, \ldots, I_w\}$ the set of intersections, where I_j denotes the jth intersection and w the cardinality of the set. Without loss of generality we assume one-way traffic along the roads. We denote by h_{jk} the road segment connecting intersection I_j to intersection I_k with the traffic flow moving from I_j to I_k.

For all vehicles we assume the following: a) the speed is constant and selected uniformly and

Figure 7. An ordinary intersection in a road network. Illustration of the basic notation

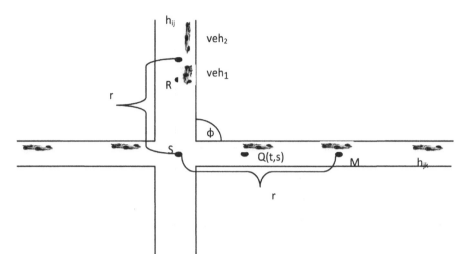

independently from the interval $[v_{min}(h_{jk}), v_{max}(h_{jk})]$, where $v_{min}(h_{jk})$ and $v_{max}(h_{jk})$ denote the minimum and the maximum allowable velocities in road h_{jk} respectively, b) vehicles move independently at their chosen velocity, c) the number of vehicles entering road h_{jk} is a random variable modeled as a Poisson stochastic process. Several experiments have shown that the outcomes of such a model are in good agreement with real measurements obtained in practice see (Pakoz, 2002). The probability density function of the arrival process at road h_{jk} is thus given by the following formula:

$$P_z^{h_{jk}}(t) = \frac{(\lambda_{jk}t)^z}{z!} e^{-(\lambda_{jk}t)},\qquad(2)$$

where λ_{jk} denotes the mean arrival rate at road h_{jk} and z denotes the number of arrivals in the time interval 0 to t. The equation corresponds to the probability of seeing exactly z arrivals in that period of time.

Without loss of generality, in the remaining of our analysis we consider a segment of the roadway network with two intersecting roads, h_{ij} and h_{jk}, as shown in Figure 7. The figure introduces additional notation which is defined as follows: φis

the angle formed between the intersecting roads, R is the point on h_{ij} that is r apart from intersection I_j and M the corresponding point on road h_{jk}. veh_1 is the *head of the information*, meaning that there are no other informed vehicles ahead of it on road h_{ij}. Its velocity is denoted by V_1.

In our analysis, time zero, i.e., $t=0$, represents the time that the information head, i.e., veh_1, is at distance less than r from intersection I_j. After time zero, veh_1 can propagate the information to vehicles on road h_{jk} either by transmitting it to a vehicle on h_{jk} while still on h_{ij} (we refer to this way as *transmitting way*), or by conveying it by itself after it crosses the intersection and enters h_{jk} (we call this way the *driving way*).

Theoretical Analysis of Message Propagation Probability on Intersections

I In this paragraph we provide a lower bound on the probability to propagate information from an informed vehicle on road h_{ij} to a vehicle on road h_{jk}, when these two vehicles are close to intersection I_j. The calculation of the actual probability is inherently complex, as it involves a large number of propagation scenarios that are dependent on a variety of parameters. For example the number of intersecting roads, the number of lanes, multiple traveling directions and various structures of complex intersections complicate the analysis.

To render the problem tractable, in this work we focus on the two basic propagation scenarios described above i.e., transmitting way and driving way. We denote the probabilities of successful information propagation of the corresponding scenarios by $p_{tr}^{h_{ij}h_{jk}}$ and $p_{dr}^{h_{ij}h_{jk}}$. The probability of information propagation along the intersection is thus given by:

$$p_{h_{ij}h_{jk}} = p_{tr}^{h_{ij}h_{jk}} + (1 - p_{tr}^{h_{ij}h_{jk}}) * p_{dr}^{h_{ij}h_{jk}}. \qquad (3)$$

In the following subsections we derive the formulas which calculate the probabilities $p_{tr}^{h_{ij}h_{jk}}$ and $p_{dr}^{h_{ij}h_{jk}}$.

The Transmission Way

Here, we study two different scenarios for information propagation from the head vehicle, veh_1, traveling on road h_{ij} to vehicles on road h_{jk} in a certain amount of time y (under the assumption that there are no buildings or other obstacles that block signal transmission). The two cases differ on the state of veh_1 when this passes from point R: in the first case veh_1 already possesses the information while in the second case the information is transmitted to veh_1 by a preceding vehicle on h_{ij}, while it is travelling from point R to intersection I_j. Note that time $y \leq \dfrac{r}{V_{max}(h_{ij})}$, where the latter is the time needed by the fastest moving vehicle on h_{ij} to travel distance r. It is easily seen that veh_1 will cover a distance less or equal to r by that time.

For each different case we need to consider two possible ways with which the information can be transmitted to vehicles on road h_{jk}. The first way is to have a vehicle entering h_{jk} during the time interval $[0, y]$. This vehicle will definitely receive

the information from veh_1 since it is going to be located at a distance smaller than r from veh_1. The second way is to have veh_1's transmission range to embrace a vehicle that has entered h_{jk} before $t=0$, during the interval $[0,y]$. This second way may occur when the vehicles that have entered h_{jk}, are moving slow enough so that, at some point, the transmission range of veh_1 (which must be moving fast enough) embraces them. We call the probability of the first way, *probability of entering* and denote it by p_e, and the probability of the second way *probability of catching up* and denote it by p_c. We proceed with a theoretical analysis of these probabilities.

Case 1. veh_1, has the information when it passes from point R.

We start with the calculation of the entering probability p_e. This probability is equal to the probability of vehicles entering road h_{jk} (from intersection I_j) during the time interval $[0,y]$, since they are definitely going to receive the information from veh_1. Thus, $P_e = 1 - P_0^{h_{jk}}(y)$, where $P_0^{h_{jk}}(y)$ is the probability of having zero vehicles entering h_{jk} during period y as defined in equation (2).

Now we proceed with the calculation of the *probability of catching up* (p_c). We define $d(t)$ as the furthest away point from intersection I_j, on road h_{jk}, which lies in the transmission range of veh_1 at time t. It can be easily seen, that any vehicle between I_j and $d(t)$ is going to receive the message. Using basic trigonometric rules we provide the relation between $d(t)$, the transmission range r, the angle φ and V_1, which is given by

$$d(t) = (r - V_1 t)\cos\varphi + \sqrt{r^2 - (r - V_1 t)^2 \sin^2\varphi}$$

. In the case that the intersecting roads are perpendicular, $d(t) = \sqrt{r^2 - (r - V_1 t)^2}$.

We also define $X(t)$ as the distance of the closest vehicle to I_j at time t on road h_{jk}, over all vehicles that have entered h_{jk} before $t=0$. So,

$$X(t) = \min(V_i' * (t - T_i)), i = 1, 2, ..., Z(\gamma)$$

where V_i' is the speed that vehicle i has on road h_{jk}, uniformly distributed in the range $[v_{min}(h_{jk}), v_{max}(h_{jk})]$, T_i is the time when vehicle i passed intersection point I_j, T_i<0, γ is the amount of time prior to t=0 which must elapse so that vehicles entering h_{jk} lie within the transmission range of veh_1. This amount of time is equal to $\dfrac{r}{v_{min}(h_{jk})}$, which is the time that the slowest vehicle moving on h_{jk} needs to cover distance r. Finally, $Z(\gamma)$ is the number of vehicles that have entered h_{jk} during period [-γ,0]. The function distribution of $X(t)$ is given by the equation:

$$F_{X(t)}(d(t)) = \sum_{z=0}^{\infty} P[X(t) < d(t) \mid Z(\gamma) = z] * P[Z(\gamma) = z]$$

The points of time T_i at which $Z(\gamma)$ vehicles have entered road h_{jk}, are considered as random variables and are distributed independently and uniformly in the interval [-γ,0].

Since $T_1, T_2, ..., T_z$ and $V'_1, V'_2, ...V'_z$ are independent and identically distributed (i.i.d), we can remove the subscripts. From equation (2),
$$P[X(t) \leq d(t) \mid Z(\gamma) = z] =$$
it follows that $1 - P[X(t) > d(t) \mid Z(\gamma) = z] =$
$$1 - P[V'^* (t - T) > d(t)]^z.$$

Finally, the probability of transmitting the information in the catching up scenario is given by: $p_c = \displaystyle\int_0^y F_{X(t)}(d(t))dt$

Case 2. veh_1 received the information while it was traveling between point R and intersection I_j.

This case is more complicated than *Case1*. Here, t=0 when veh_1 receives the information from a preceding vehicle on h_{ij} before it reaches intersection I_j. We denote by S the position of veh_1 at time t=0 and by s the distance that point S has from R. Let us proceed to examine what happens when the time needed by veh_1 to reach I_j, which is $\dfrac{r-s}{V_1}$, is greater than or equal to y or less than y. When $\dfrac{r-s}{V_1} \leq y$ then the scenario is very similar to *Case1*. However, we need to consider

the possibility that vehicle veh_2 which travels with speed V_2, following veh_1 on h_{ij}, will pass point R by time $t = \dfrac{r-s}{V_1}$. If veh_2 passes from R before veh_1 passes from intersection I_j, then it can also transmit the information to vehicles entering road h_{jk} until time y expires. In order not to have an informed vehicle in RI_j during some time in period [0,y] the following must hold: 1) veh_1 passed point R without having the information and veh_2 transmits the information to veh_1 at time t=0. 2) at $t = \dfrac{r-s}{V_1}$, which is the time needed by veh_1 to pass from intersection I_j, veh_2 is still before point R. In order for this to happen V_1 must be greater than V_2. We can thus conclude that veh_1 either entered h_{ij} before veh_2 or passed veh_2 at some time just before passing from point R. In the former case, since the distance between the two vehicles remained smaller than r, all the way from the time they entered the road until the end, it is highly unlikely that their distance became greater than r just before veh_1 exited road h_{ij}. In the latter case, since veh_1 passed from veh_2 and at that time neither of the vehicles was informed, it follows that veh_2 got the information from the preceding vehicles just after the passing of veh_1 and before the distance of the two vehicles became greater than r. The only way that no informed vehicles were present between R and I_j during period [0,y], is in the extreme case which involves veh_1 being very close to intersection I_j at time zero. Then, the time needed by veh_1 to exit road h_{ij} should not be enough for veh_2 to cover the distance from R. Thus, the circumstances under which there are no informed vehicles in the area RI_j during the period [0,y] are extremely rare to occur. We therefore assume that there is at least one informed vehicle in the area RI_j to propagate the information to any vehicle entering road h_{jk} during the period [0,y]. Thus the *probability of entering* is given by the same formula as in *Case1*.

We now need to calculate the *probability of catching up* (p_c). Our analysis will be a generalization of the previous one. Let us denote by $Q(t,s)$ the furthest away point, from I_j, on h_{jk} which at time t lies in the transmission range of veh_1, which was at position S at time zero. $Q(t,s)$ is a random variable depending on time and the initial value of s, given that s is uniformly distributed along RI_j. It is given by

$$Q(t,s) = (r - s - V_1 t)\cos\varphi + \sqrt{r^2 - (r - s - V_1 t)^2 \sin^2\varphi}.$$

In the case that φ forms a right angle then, $Q(t,s) = \sqrt{r^2 - (r - s - V_1 t)^2}$. The function distribution that we are interested in is given by $F_{X(t)-Q(t,s)}(0)$. So,

$$F_{X(t)-Q(t,s)}(0) = \int_0^r \sum_{z=0}^{\infty} P[X(t) - Q(t,s) < 0 \mid Z(\gamma) = z] * P[Z(\gamma) = z] * f_s(s) ds.$$

Finally, same as in *Case1*, we want to see if during period $[0,y]$, $Q(t,s)$ becomes greater than $X(t)$. So, the *probability of catching up* is given by the following equation: $p_c = \int_0^y F_{X(t)-Q(t,s)}(0) dt$.

Now that we know the probability to transmit the information for both cases we need to combine them in order to calculate the overall probability $p_{tr}^{h_{ij}h_{jk}}$ to transmit the information from road h_{ij} to road h_{jk}. To do so, we need to find the probability for each case to happen separately.

In order for *Case1* to occur, veh_1 must pass point R carrying the information, without any other vehicle in RI_j to transmit it. Let us denote by τ the time gap between two consecutive vehicles. Then their distance, $dist_{veh_1,veh_3}$ is equal to $\tau * V_1$. Rudack et. al. in (Rudack, 2002) show that the time gaps between vehicles are distributed according to the following pdf and PDF, $p_\tau(\tau) = \lambda e^{-\lambda\tau}$ and $P_\tau(\tau > T) = e^{-\lambda T}$, respectively. So, the probability that *Case1* happens is:

$$P_{cs_1} = P_\tau(\tau > \frac{r}{V_1}) = e^{-\lambda\frac{r}{V_1}}.$$

Regarding *Case2*, it is sufficient to see that it is the compliment of *Case1* since either veh_1 is in the road segment RI_j when it gets the information or, it passes R and enters RI_j with the information. So, $P_{cs_2} = 1 - P_{cs_1}$.

So, the overall probability to have the information transmitted to road h_{jk} from road h_{ij} during a period of time y is given by:

$$p_{tr}^{h_{ij}h_{jk}} = P_{cs_1} * (p_e^{cs_1} + (1 - p_e^{cs_1}) * p_c^{cs_1}) + P_{cs_2} * (p_e^{cs_2} + (1 - p_e^{cs_2}) * p_c^{cs_2})$$

(4)

Driving Way

In this paragraph we derive the probability $p_{dr}^{h_{ij}h_{jk}}$, defined as the probability that vehicle veh_1 chooses to turn on road h_{jk} once it reaches intersection I_j. $p_{dr}^{h_{jk}}$ is strongly related to the structure of the intersection we are studying, since we need to consider all possible roads that a vehicle approaching intersection h_{jk} may choose. On intersection I_j of Figure 7 we only need to consider two choices: veh_1 going straight or turn left. However, in general cases with more complicated intersections the driver has more roads to choose from. The general equation covering all cases is: $p_{dr}^{h_{ij}h_{jk}} = \dfrac{\lambda(h_{jk})}{\sum \lambda(h_{jb})}$, for all b such that road h_{jb} exists.

Now, we have everything needed to calculate all the terms of equation (3), which gives the lower bound on the probability of information propagation $p_{h_{ij}h_{jk}}$, from an informed vehicle on road h_{ij} to uninformed vehicles on road h_{jk}.

Simulative Validation

The analysis presented in the previous section indicates that the most interesting case when studying the probability of information propagation on intersections is when an informed vehicle on one road transmits the information to an uninformed vehicle on another road (the transmission way).

Figure 8. Theoretical transmission probability as a function of time for different arrival rates

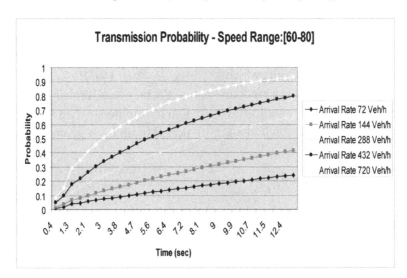

Figure 9. Theoretical vs. simulation results of the transmission probability

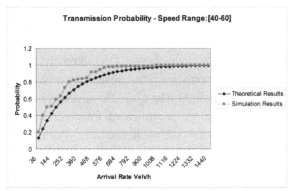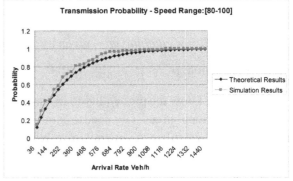

This is the case we consider in all our simulation experiments. We have conducted a number of simulation experiments using the microscopic simulation tool VISSIM in order to validate equation (4). The topology we consider is the one shown in Figure 7, with φ-90°. Since, the information propagation probability in the transmission way ($p_{tr}^{h_{ij}h_{jk}}$) depends on the traffic characteristics of the road intended to receive the information, the setup parameters of our simulations are the vehicle arrival rates on road h_{jk}, the range of speeds attained by the vehicles on road h_{jk} and the speed of veh_l moving on road h_{ij} and driving towards intersection I_j. We set the transmission range of

each vehicle to 250m and the simulation step to be 100 ms. The output of each simulation experiment is a text file which we process using a C++ application, that we have developed. For each set of parameters we repeat the simulation 100 times and we calculate the frequency with which the information is successfully transmitted. The probability of information transmission is estimated by dividing the number of successes by the number of times we have repeated the simulation.

In order to gain insights on the behavior of equation (4) as this was obtained analytically in the previous section, we first plot probability values as a function of y (the time window available for veh_l to transmit the information to h_{jk}), for different vehicle arrival rates on road h_{jk}. The graphs are depicted in Figure 8. The speed range of the vehicles traveling on that road is kept constant in the interval 60-80 Km/h. As expected, the probability increases in a concave fashion with increasing time window. In addition, as the arrival rate increases so does the probability.

The next step is to validate our theoretical findings with simulation results. Due to lack of space, here we only show a few of the results that we obtained. For a more comprehensive study you may refer to [Xeros 2007]. In Figure 9 we show plots of the theoretical probability and the frequency values obtained using simulations as a function of the arrival rate at road h_{jk}. The time window is fixed and is equal to the time needed by a vehicle with speed 65Km/h to cover a distance r.

The figures indicate that our theoretical findings are in good agreement with the obtained simulation results thus demonstrating the validity of our theoretical work. It is interesting to observe that for high arrival rates (1100 Veh/h, i.e., 1 vehicle every 3 seconds) the transmission probability is very close to 1. The reason for this is that for such high arrival rate values, it is highly likely that, at least one vehicle has entered road h_{ij} after 14 seconds. Even if the arrival rate is half of the above value i.e. 500 Veh/h (1 vehicle every 7 seconds) the information transmission probability is still high after 14 seconds reporting a value of 0.8.

CONCLUSION

In this chapter we examine the design of data dissemination schemes in VANETs and we propose a number of novel solutions and analytical evaluation tools. We focus on the use of probabilistic methods as these are known to provide effective solutions and at the same time address the highly stochastic nature of many of the processes involved in VANETs. We demonstrate that probabilistic flooding can be successfully used as a baseline to develop new information hovering and short-range broadcast schemes which are shown through simulations to work effectively. In addition we derive a formula which provides lower bounds on the probability of information propagation at an intersection. Such bounds can be used in the design of routing protocols in VANETs and will be the topic of future research. Moreover, we aim at proposing enhancements to the proposed data dissemination schemes and further evaluate their performance using analysis and simulations and practical implementation. The chapter reveals many of the challenges in the design of information dissemination schemes in VANETs and demonstrates the effectiveness of probabilistic methods to provide effective solutions.

REFERENCES

Alshaer, H., & Horlait, E. (2005). An optimized adaptive broadcast scheme for Inter-vehicle communication. In []. Stockholm, Sweden.]. *Proceedings of the Vehicular Technology Conference, 5,* 2840–2844.

Alzoubi, K. M., Wan, P. J., & Frieder, O. (2002). New Distributed Algorithm for Connected Dominating Set in Wireless Ad Hoc Networks. In *Proceedings of the 35th Annual Hawaii International Conference on System Sciences,* (pp. 297). Big Island, HI.

Calinescu, G., Mandoiu, I., Wan, P. J., & Zelikovsky, A. (2001). Selecting Forwarding Neighbors in Wireless Ad Hoc Networks. In *Proceedings of the ACM Int'l Workshop Discrete Algorithms and Methods for Mobile Computing,* (pp. 34-43).

Chiasserini, C. F., Fasolo, E., Furiato, R., Gaeta, R., Garetto, M., Gribaudo, M., et al. (2005). Smart Broadcast of Warning Messages in Vehicular Ad Hoc Networks. In *Proceedings of the Workshop Interno Progetto NEWCOM.* Turin, Italy.

Chisalita, I., & Shahmehri, N. (2004). A context based vehicular communication protocol. In *Proceedings of the IEEE Personal, Indoor and Mobile Radio Communication Symposium*. Barcelona, Spain.

Erdos, P., & Renyi, A. (1960). On the evolution of random graphs. *Mathematical Institute of the Hungarian Academy of Sciences, 5*, 17–61.

Frank, J., & Martel, C. U. (1995). Phase transitions in the properties of random graphs. In *Principles and Practice of Constraint Programming (CP-95)*. Cambridge, MA: MIT Press.

Hu, C., Hong, Y., & Hou, J. (2003). On mitigating the broadcast storm problem with directional antennas. *In Proceedings of the IEEE International Conference, on Communications, 1*, 104-110. San Francisco.

Konstantas, D., & Villalba, A. C. (2006). Towards hovering information. *In Proceedings of the First European Conference on Smart Sensing and Context*, (EuroSSC), (pp. 161-166). University of Twente, The Netherlands.

Korkmaz, G., & Ekici, E. (2004). Urban Multi-Hop Broadcast for Inter-Vehicle Communication Systems. *In Proceedings of ACM VANET*. (pp. 76-85). Philadelphia.

Korkmaz, G., & Ekici, E. (2006). An Efficient Fully Ad-Hoc Multi-Hop Broadcast Protocol for Inter-Vehicular Communication Systems. *In Proceedings of IEEE International Conference on Communications* (Vol. 1. pp. 104-110). Istanbul, Turkey.

Krishnamachari, B., Wickery, S., & Bejarx, R. (2001). Phase Transition Phenomena in Wireless Ad Hoc Networks. In []. San Antonio, TX.]. *Proceedings of IEEE GLOBECOM, 5*, 2921–2925.

Laouiti, A., Qayyum, A., & Viennot, L. (2001). Multipoint relaying: An efficient technique for flooding in mobile wireless network. In *Proceedings of the IEEE 35th Annual Hawaii International Conference on System Sciences* (pp. 3866-3875). Big Island, HI.

Lee, B. S., Seet, B. C., Liu, G. P., Foh, C. H., & Wong, K. J. (2004). A Routing Strategy for Metropolis Vehicular Communications. *In Proceedings of the International Conference on Information Networking* (ICOIN'04), (vol. 2, pp 533-542). South Korea.

Li, F., & Wang, Y. (2007). Routing in Vehicular Ad Hoc Networks: A Survey. *IEEE Vehicular Technology Magazine, 2*(2), 12–22. doi:10.1109/MVT.2007.912927

Lim, H., & Kim, C. (2001). Flooding in Wireless Ad Hoc Networks. *Computer Communications, 24*(3-4), 353–363. doi:10.1016/S0140-3664(00)00233-4

Lochert, C. (2003). A Routing Strategy for Vehicular Ad Hoc Networks in City Environments. In *Proceedings of the Intelligent Vehicles Symposium, IV*, Ohio, USA.

Mylonas, Y., Lestas, M., & Pitsillides, A. (2008). Speed Adaptive Probabilistic Flooding in Cooperative Emergency Warning. *In The First International Workshop on Wireless Vehicular Networking Technology*. Vancouver, Canada.

Ni, S., Tseng, Y., & Shih, E. Y. (2001). Adaptive approaches to relieving broadcast storms in a wireless multihop mobile Ad Hoc network. In *Proceedings IEEE 21st International Conference on Distributed Computing Systems*. (pp. 481-488). Phoenix, AZ.

Peng, W., & Lu, X. C. (2000). On the Reduction of Broadcast Redundancy in Mobile Ad Hoc Networks. In *Proceedings of the 1st ACM international symposium on Mobile ad hoc networking & computing*. (pp. 129-130).

Perkins, C., & Royer, E. M. (1999). Ad-Hoc On-Demand Distance Vector Routing. In *Proceedings of the Second IEEE Workshop Mobile Computing Systems and Applications* (pp. 90-100). New Orleans, LA.

Qayyum, A., Viennot, L., & Laouiti, A. (2002). Multipoint Relaying for Flooding Broadcast Message in Mobile Wireless Networks. In *Proceedings of the 35th Annual Hawaii International Conference on System Sciences* (pp. 3866-3875). Big Island, HI

Sasson, Y., Cavin, D., & Schiper, A. (2003). Probabilistic Broadcast for Flooding in Wireless Mobile Ad Hoc Networks. In []. New Orleans, LA.]. *Proceedings of IEEE Wireless Communications and Networking Conference, 2*, 1124–1130.

Serugendo, C., Villalba, A. G. D. M., & Konstantas, D. (2007). Dependable Requirements for Hovering Information. *In Supplementary Proceedings of the 37th Annual IEEE/IFIP International Conference on Dependable Systems and Networks* (DSN'07). (pp. 36–39). Edinburgh, UK.

Stojmenovic, I., Seddigh, S., & Zunic, J. (2002). Dominating Sets and Neighbor Elimination Based Broadcasting Algorithms in Wireless Networks. *IEEE Transactions on Parallel and Distributed Systems, 13*(1), 14–25. doi:10.1109/71.980024

Tonquz, O., Wisitpongphan, N., Bai, F., Mudalige, P., & Sadekar, V. (2007). Broadcasting in VANET. In *Proceedings of 2007 Mobile Networking for Vehicular Environments* (pp. 7-12). Anchorage, AK.

Tseng, Y.-C., Ni, S.-Y., Chen, Y.-S., & Sheu, J.-P. (2002). The broadcast storm problem in a mobile Ad Hoc network. In *Proceedings of the 5th annual ACM/IEEE international conference on Mobile computing and networking* []. Atlanta, GA.]. *Wireless Networks, 8*, 153–167. doi:10.1023/A:1013763825347

Villalba, A. C., Serugendo, G. D. M., & Konstantas, D. (2008). Hovering Information - Self-Organising Information that Finds its own Storage. In *Proceedings of the International IEEE Conference on Sensor Networks, Ubiquitous and Trustworthy Computing* (pp. 193-200). Taichung, Taiwan.

Wang, Y., & Ioannou, P. (2006). Real-time Parallel Parameter Estimators for a Second-order Macroscopic Traffic flow Model. In *Proceedings of the IEEE Intelligent Transportation Systems Conference.* (pp. 1466-1470). Toronto, Canada.

Wu, H., Fujimoto, R., Guensler, R., & Hunter, M. (2004). MDDV: A Mobility-Centric Data Dissemination Algorithm for Vehicular Networks. In *Proceedings of the 1st ACM Workshop on Vehicular Ad Hoc Networks.* Philadephia.

Wu, H., Fujimoto, R., & Riley, G. (2004). Analytical Models for Information Propagation in Vehicle-to-Vehicle Networks. In *Proceedings of the IEEE Vehicular Technology Conference.* Los Angeles.

Xeros, A., Andreou, M., Pitsillides, A., & Lestas, M. (2007). Information Propagation Probability in VANETS. In Proceedings of Vehicle to Vehicle Communication workshop, (V2Vcom). Istanbul, Turkey.

Section 4
General Research Challenges in VANETs

Chapter 13
Clustering, Connectivity, and Monitoring Challenges in Vehicular Ad Hoc Networks

Ameneh Daeinabi
Sahand University of Technology, Iran

Akbar Ghaffarpour Rahbar
Sahand University of Technology, Iran

ABSTRACT

Vehicular Ad Hoc Networks (VANETs) are appropriate networks that can be applied for intelligent transportation systems. Three important challenges in VANETs are studied in this chapter. The first challenge is to defend against attackers. Because of the lack of a coordination unit in a VANET, vehicles should cooperate together and monitor each other in order to enhance security performance of the VANET. As the second challenge in VANETs, scalability is a critical issue for a network designer. Clustering is one solution for the scalability problem and is vital for efficient resource consumption and load balancing in large scale VANETs. On the other hand, due to the high-rate topology changes and high variability in vehicles density, transmission range of a vehicle is an important issue for forwarding and receiving messages. In this chapter, we study the clustering algorithms, the solutions appropriate to increase connectivity, and the algorithms that can detect attackers in a VANET.

INTRODUCTION

Communications among vehicles is an important field of study for transportation systems. Vehicular Ad Hoc Networks (VANETs) are appropriate networks that can be applied to intelligent transportation systems (Nadeem, 2006). VANET is based on short-range wireless communications among vehicles and is built on-the-fly and do not need any

investment, except the wireless network interfaces that will be a standard feature in the next generation of vehicles. The Federal Communications Commission (US FCC) has allocated 75 MHz of spectrum in the 5.9 GHz band for the Dedicated Short Range Communication standard (DSRC) for VANET communications (Abdulhamid, 2007). The purpose of DSRC is to enhance bandwidth and to reduce latency for vehicle-to-vehicle and vehicle-to-infrastructure communications (Abdulhamid, 2007).

DOI: 10.4018/978-1-61520-913-2.ch013

Using car to car communications, VANET does not entirely rely on a fixed infrastructure, but it can harness the fixed infrastructure for improved performance and functionality. VANETs are distinguished from other kinds of ad hoc networks by their hybrid network architectures, vehicle movement characteristics, and new application scenarios. Therefore, they are facing many unique networking challenges such as high mobility, scalability, connectivity, security, and privacy.

Scalability is a critical issue among many challenges running for the VANET technology. In practice, when a flat-topology network contains a large number of vehicles, a large percentage of limited wireless bandwidth should be used for the control of overhead (e.g., routing packets). One solution for this problem is to group vehicles into a number of clusters. Clustering is vital for efficient resource consumption and load balancing in large scale networks.

In a VANET, messages should be generated and forwarded correctly. However, the messages may be damaged by attacker vehicles. A successful attack to a VANET might have disastrous results, such as the loss of lives. Therefore, making a vehicular communication network secure is not an extension but a primary concern. Note that security at the routing level is very important because protocol layers on top of the network layer would not work properly when routing fails. For this purpose, several algorithms have been suggested to detect attackers and to isolate them from network.

One of the most important criteria for organizing a VANET is network connectivity (Lee, 2008). When the inter-vehicle network has low interconnection, it must ensure that information is disseminated to and within a targeted area (Adler, 2006). This means that connectivity shows the probability that a vehicle can make a connection and then exchange information with another vehicle. The transmission range of a vehicle is an important factor to maintain connectivity. A vehicle receives messages if other vehicles are located within its transmission range. In a VANET, transmission ranges are usually considered static based on the DSRC standard (Abdulhamid, 2007). For example, transmission range for vehicles is set to 300m and remains constant during communication. However, due to the high rate of topology changes and the high variability in vehicles density, it is better to adaptively determine the transmission range in VANETs.

BACKGROUND

In this section, we shall provide an introduction to challenges and solutions for scalability, connectivity, and attack problems in VANETs.

Attackers

It is essential to correctly forward messages in a VANET on time. However, the messages may be damaged by attacker vehicles, where attackers are vehicles that disobey the common protocols adopted for vehicular networking. In other words, any vehicle that deviates from the legitimate vehicular network protocol is defined as misbehaving vehicles or attackers. On the other hand, when a vehicle forwards messages correctly or generates right messages, it has a normal behavior. Attackers may perform in several ways with different objectives (Picconi, 2006) such as eavesdropping the communication between vehicles, dropping, changing, or injecting packets to the network. Therefore, with respect to the lack of a coordination unit or a centralized infrastructure in a VANET, vehicles should cooperate together to enhance security performance of the VANET. In this section, we shall review different kinds of attackers and then describe the techniques that have been suggested to detect attackers in VANETs.

Attackers may perform in several ways with different objectives. Therefore, the attackers can be classified according to their capacities or targets.

If attackers are classified based on their capacities, four categories can be defined as follows:

1. **Active and Passive (Raya, 2005):** Active attacks involve injecting, altering, or blocking packets. Examples include: Denial of Service (DoS), message omission, spoofing, and bogus information attacks. A passive attack focuses on eavesdropping to the communication between two vehicles such as tracking a given car or profiling its driver.
2. **Insider and Outsider (Raya, 2005):** If an attacker is an authenticated member of the network in such a way that it can communicate with other members, it is called insider attacker. When the network members consider that an attacker is an intruder, then the attacker is limited in the diversity of attacks. This attack is called outsider attack.
3. **Malicious and Rational (Raya, 2005):** A malicious attacker has no personal profits from its attacks and its main purpose is to damage members or network functions. On the other hand, a rational attacker has personal profits, and therefore, it is more predictable in terms of attack means and attack target.
4. **Local and Extended (Raya, 2006):** A local attacker can control several vehicles or base stations which are located in its range. On the other hand, an extended attacker controls several entities that are distributed across the network, thus extending its range.

One can also classify security threats into three groups based on their applications and targets as:

1. **Attacks on safety-related applications (Raya & Hubaux, 2005):** This type of attacks affect on safety-related (Raya, 2006) applications and can lead to terrible occurrences such as accidents and loss of lives.
2. **Attacks on payment-based applications (Raya & Hubaux, 2005):** In a payment

system such as a financial transaction, attackers can create a set of corresponding financial deceits and leverage on these systems.
3. **Attack on privacy (Raya & Hubaux, 2005):** Privacy is an important factor for security of a VANET. However, it is possible that an attacker tracks drivers when vehicles communicate with each other. Moreover, the big brother phenomenon (Raya & Hubaux, 2005) may be created over a large scale network such as VANET, where the big brother phenomenon is described as the ID disclosure of other vehicles.

Detecting attackers that affect on messages is very vital for VANETs because forwarding wrong messages can lead to terrible events. For this purpose, we illustrate examples of attacks which influence on messages:

1. **Bogus information attack (Raya & Hubaux, 2005):** In this case, an attacker propagates wrong information within the network and causes other vehicles to make wrong decisions. In fact, attackers inject information that does not correspond to real events or observations. For example, an attacker can propagate false information about congestion, and then other vehicles may alter their routes in order to avoid the congestion. Therefore, the attacker can go faster.
2. **Cheating with identity, speed, or positioning information (Raya & Hubaux, 2005):** It is possible that an attacker attempts to cheat other vehicles by sending wrong information of their location, speed or direction at a given time. For instant, a vehicle which is responsible of an accident propagates wrong information about its position at a certain time in order to clear of any blame.
3. **Disruption of network operation (Raya & Hubaux, 2005):** An attacker causes a VANET not to be able to correctly perform

its safety-related functions. For example, an attacker may inject dummy messages which can lead to incorrect results. In addition, channel jamming is another instant of this case, called Denial of Service (DOS). DOS can interrupt all communications both safety-related and payment-based applications.

4. **ID disclosure of other vehicles (Raya & Hubaux, 2005):** This case of attack can be considered as an example for passive attacks. An attacker can use the data that can be obtained from monitoring of the trajectories of target entities. Then, the attacker will be able to affect on other entities which are located around its target. This attack is called the Big Brother attack.

Finally, we state some examples of attackers which generally happen in VANETs. They can be combinations or details of aforementioned attackers:

1. **Hidden vehicle (Raya, 2006):** In order to reduce congestion on wireless channels, vehicle v broadcasts a warning message. When v assures that at least one neighbor has listened its message and has a better position for warning other vehicles, v stops its broadcasting. Now, if a position cheating attacker pretends that it has a better position than v, then v entrusts to the attacker its responsibility of broadcasting the message and stops its broadcasting. Then, the attacker quiets and hides v by this manner. Therefore, the warning message is not forwarded in time and may lead to terrible events.
2. **Tunnel (Raya, 2006):** In a jammed area such as a tunnel or a place that an attacker can block it, the GPS signal cannot be received by a vehicle until the vehicle leaves the jammed area. Therefore, the attacker can propagate false information in jammed areas.

3. **Wormhole (Raya, 2006):** If an attacker is located between at least two entities which are remote from each other, the attacker can control these entities and the high speed communication link between them; in such a way that the attacker can hide their broadcast packets and then propagate wrong messages within a certain area.
4. **Bush Telegraph (Raya, 2006):** In this case, an attacker can control several entities over several wireless hops. Therefore, the attacker can inject errors to the information at each hop. These errors are small at the beginning such that the neighbors accept the information, but finally small errors can lead to the bogus information at the last hop.

Scalability

Scalability is a critical issue among many challenges running for the VANET technology. In practice, when a flat-topology network contains a large number of vehicles, a large percentage of limited wireless bandwidth should be used for the control of overhead such as routing packets. One solution for this problem is to divide vehicles into a number of clusters, by which efficient resource consumption and load balancing in large scale networks can be achieved. Routing based on clustering is appropriate for vehicular networks because vehicles may be formed as clusters in a road.

In unicast routing protocols, AODV (Ad hoc On Demand Distance Vector) based protocols and cluster–based protocols are two common routing protocols that are useful for fixed addressing applications. In fixed addressing, each node has a fixed address assigned by some mechanism at the moment it joins the network (Sichitiu, 2008). AODV-based protocols are designed for demand unicast routing. In other words, routs are not maintained unless they are needed. Therefore, this type of protocols can reduce overhead within the network. When a route is needed to send a packet from a source to a destination, the source broadcasts a route request (RREQ) message for the intended destination across the network. Each node that receives an RREQ updates its routing tables and then rebroadcasts the RREQ. When the destination node receives the RREQ, it sends a route reply (RREP) to the source thought the reverse path of the RREQ that has been stored at intermediate nodes. After arriving the RREP at the source, a path is set up and data is transferred to the destination. However, the route discovery mechanism cannot set up reliable routes in rapidly changing vehicular networks. Moreover, it is suitable for small networks since the route discovery phase may cause network congestion in large networks. In (Wei, 2008), simulation results show that the AODV is unsuitable for VANET scenarios in terms of packet delivery ratio, routing load, and end-to-end delay. Therefore, AODV needs to be modified (such as using gateway) in order to be used in vehicular networks (Wakikawa, 2005). In this technique, a predefined maximum number of hops is determined that shows the required maximum number of hops that a vehicle needs to reach its gateway. The RREQ is only flooded up to maximum number of hops. If the intended destination is not associated with the same gateway as the source, the gateway will forward the RREQ to other gateways.

On the other hand, cluster-based routing protocols are suitable for VANETs because vehicles driving on a highway may naturally form clusters. Vehicles in a VANET move within the constraints of traffic flow and communicate with each other through wireless links. Due to the lack of routers or other dedicated communication hardware, a possible method to optimize communication within the network is to develop a hierarchical clustering system within the network. The advantages of clustering (Liu, 2007) can be summarized as follows:

1. Clustering facilitates the reuse of resources and then improves the capacity of system.
2. Clustering decreases the amount of information that is used to store the network state.
3. The amount of routing information propagated in the network is reduced under cluster-based routing.
4. A cluster-head (CH) will gather the status of its members and build an overview of its cluster condition.
5. Distant vehicles outside of a cluster usually do not need to know the details of specific events occurring inside the cluster. Therefore, an overview of the cluster's status is sufficient for those far-away vehicles to make control decisions.

In clustering, vehicles are located inside clusters, where each cluster has one cluster-head, and one or more members (see Figure 1). Vehicles that form a cluster are coordinated by its cluster-head (CH). Vehicles in one cluster communicate together directly, but vehicles that are located in two different clusters communicate together via cluster-heads. Each vehicle can play three roles: cluster-head, gateway, and member. If one vehicle is located within two or more clusters, it is called a gateway. Cluster-heads maintain information about their members and gateways. In this approach, data and control packets are sent via cluster-heads and gateways. In order to prevent from interference among inter and intra clustering transmission, each cluster-head communicates with two different frequencies. One frequency is used for communication among cluster-heads and another frequency is allocated for communication between a cluster-head and its members (Liu, 2007).

When a vehicle moves out of its cluster, it will firstly check whether it can be a member of another cluster. If such a cluster exists, it will separate itself from the current cluster and join to

Figure 1. An example of clustering within the network

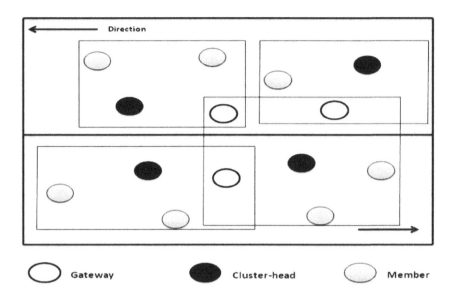

the new one. The process of joining to a new cluster is known as re-affiliation (Wang, 2007). One disadvantage of common clustering algorithms is high re-affiliation frequency, where network topology changes very fast. High frequency of re-affiliation will increase re-calculations of determining cluster-heads, and consequently will increase the communication overhead in network (Wang, 2007). Thus, reducing the volume of re-affiliation is necessary in VANET.

Connectivity in VANET

Network connectivity is an important criterion for organizing a VANET (Lee, 2008). When the inter-vehicle network has low interconnection, it must ensure that information is disseminated to and within a targeted area (Adler, 2006). It means that connectivity shows the probability that a vehicle can make a connection to exchange information with another vehicle. However, vehicles may even leave a certain area without having met another network vehicle to communicate with each other. Therefore, developing a routing protocol for connectivity in VANETs is a challenging task

due to potentially large network sizes, rapidly changing topology and frequent network disconnections. There are factors that affect the network connectivity such as the density of vehicles, the distribution of vehicle positions, the geographical characteristics, and the transmission range (Lee, 2008). Several approaches have been suggested to solve these problems as follows.

The (Naumov, 2007) has suggested a connectivity-aware routing (CAR) that is a position-based routing protocol. In this scheme, a path is auto-adjusted between a source and a destination immediately without using another discovery process. Moreover, they have introduced the concept of a guard to track the current position of the destination and to keep the state information such as velocity, position, and geographical area. The guard is located in the periodic hello messages and each node records the time of receiving the guards. An adaptive connectivity aware routing (ACAR) protocol has been proposed in (Yang, 2008) that can choose the best network transmission quality based on statistical and real-time density data. It means that ACAR first computes a route based on its statistical density data, then puts the route information into packet headers and transmits packets along this selected route. While forwarding packets to their destination, network densities of all road segments along this path are collected simultaneously (Yang, 2008). The obtained density information is called real-time density. In this technique, each road is split into segments and the most efficient multi-hop path is selected in each road segment. Their results show that ACAR can improve data delivery ratio, throughput and data packet delay. In other words, this protocol chooses the route with the best transmission quality, increases the data delivery ratio and decreases the transmission delay. Another algorithm has been suggested in (Yousefi, 2007), where some publicly available statistical data and realistic traffic patterns are used to obtain optimum values for the number of base-stations and their transmission ranges in order to achieve the intended degree of connectivity.

In the above techniques, transmission range is static, however, the transmission range is a very critical factor for the connectivity in ad hoc networks and VANETs. The influence of transmission range on connectivity has been studied in (Lee, 2008), where the results show that the transmission range, having the great impact on the connectivity, can obtain up to 70% connectivity on the common parameter values (Lee, 2008, pp.1304). However, in VANET, a static transmission range cannot maintain the network's connectivity because of the non-uniform distribution of vehicles and rapid change of traffic conditions (Artimy, 2007). Therefore, a dynamic transmission range is required to maintain a good connectivity in non-uniform networks.

TECHNIQUES TO DETECT ATTACKERS IN VANET

Due to the significant information that may be broadcast inside a VANET, it is necessary to make sure that the information cannot be inserted or modified by an attacker. Therefore, security mechanisms, facilities, and protocols are needed to diminish and to eliminate the attacker's effect. Several algorithms have been proposed to monitor and detect attackers in VANETs reviewed in this section.

VANET Techniques

The effectiveness of using MANET techniques in a VANET has been illustrated in (Fonseca, 2006) based on scalability, packet overhead, topology changes and security mechanisms. The security mechanisms have been classified and compared based on the security objectives, and their performances. However, we aim to explain the approaches that can be applied to secure a VANET.

Eviction of Misbehaving and Faulty Vehicles

The (Raya& Papadimitratos, 2007) has introduced a technique to identify, to detect, and to evict misbehaving vehicles. In this scheme, there are three basic components: (1) the centralized revocation of a vehicle by the certificate authority (*CA*); (2) the local detection of misbehavior performed individually by each vehicle; and (3) a distributed and localized protocol for the eviction of attackers by its neighboring vehicles. The overview of this scheme is showed in Figure 2. In this technique, there are two assumptions: (1) each vehicle has a Trusted Component (*TC*) which stores all cryptographic material and performs all cryptographic operations; and (2) there is an honest majority in an attacker's neighborhood.

In this technique, two kinds of misbehaviors are considered:

1. **Known misbehaviors:** this kind of misbehavior can be identified by monitoring specific parameters of a vehicle or network behavior.

Figure 2. The Overview of the Detection and Eviction Scheme (Raya & Papadimitratos, 2007)

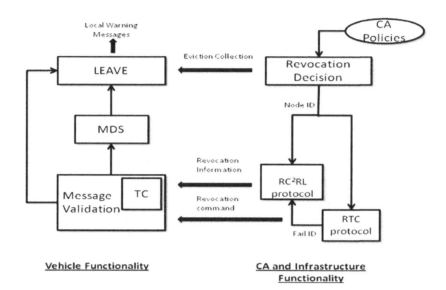

2. **Data anomalies:** when an attacker changes or injects safety messages to network, we cannot detect these misbehaviors based on a known pattern.

Two revocation protocols are used in this technique: RTC (Revocation of the Trusted Component) and RC²RL (Revocation using Compressed Certificate Revocation Lists). In order to revoke vehicle *v* by the certificate authority (*CA*), the RTC protocol is used in the first step. Each *CA* is a trusted third party that manages identities, cryptography keys, and credentials of vehicles. For this purpose, the *CA* generates a revocation message to aware the TC_v and related Road-Side Units (RSU) from revoking decision. The message format is:

$$CA \rightarrow TC_V: E_{PuKv}(V), T, Sig_{CA}[E_{PuKv}(V), T],$$

where P_uK_v and *T* are *v*'s public key and a time-stamp, respectively. The parameter *E* shows the encryption operator and Sig_{CA} represents the message that is signed by the *CA*. Then, the *CA* sends the signed revocation message to TC_v through

related *RSU*s. When TC_v receives the revocation message, it instantly removes the cryptography keys and stops signing messages. Then, TC_v sends a message back to the *CA* with the following format:

$$TC_V \rightarrow CA: ACK, T, Sig_{PrKv}[ACK, T],$$

where *ACK* is acknowledge, *T* is timestamp, and *Sig* represents the message that is signed by the TC_v. If vehicle *v* is an attacker and blocks the received message, the *CA* will receive no *ACK*. Therefore, we need another protocol to remove the failure of RTC protocol as RC²RL. The RC²RL uses Bloom filters (Bloom, 1970). The Bloom filters provide a probabilistic data structure to ensure that the CA can efficiently revoke all targeted vehicles.

One of the objectives of the proposed algorithm is to isolate misbehaving vehicles before their information becomes available. To design a robust and efficient system, (Raya & Papadimitratos, 2007) has proposed to use Misbehavior Detection System (MDS) and Local Eviction of Attackers by Voting Evaluators (LEAVE). The Misbehavior MDS enables the neighbors of a misbehaving or faulty vehicle to detect its deviation from normal behaviors. To detect a misbehaving vehicle, the MDS should rely on both the data that vehicles provide and the probability density function which is obtained in MDS. In vehicular networks, there may be many attacks that do not follow any known pattern, and therefore, we cannot detect them by only monitoring the specific metrics and fitting on a given model. Consequently, in order to compare between anomalous and normal behaviors of a vehicle, (Raya& Papadimitratos, 2007) uses entropy which is a typical measurement of information and an effective and efficient solution. Every vehicle can classify the safety messages received from another vehicle based on its sensory input, messages received from its neighbors, and a set of evaluation rules. Then, the messages that are received beyond their expected area of propagations or outdated messages are determined as false messages. Moreover, the senders of false messages are tagged as misbehaving vehicles. The MDS can only detect the vehicles that are in its current neighborhood.

In order to temporarily evict a misbehaving vehicle by its neighbors, the LEAVE protocol has been proposed, run in two phases as:

1. Neighbor Warning System: In this phase, the warning system relies on gathering information from a vehicle's neighborhood and a weighted sum. If vehicle v is accused by other participants, the accusation message which is issued by v has a low weight. To detect the accused vehicle u, if the sum of weighted accusation against the vehicle u goes over a defined threshold, u is locally evicted by LEAVE. This mechanism is a simple system because it needs no setup overhead, no interactive mechanisms, and therefore, reputation system requires no long period of observation. Warned vehicle is a vehicle that gathers enough accusations against an attacker to reach the eviction threshold. Moreover, a warned vehicle that disregards all bogus messages from the

attacker is called initially warned vehicle. With respect to the above definitions, we can introduce evaluators as vehicles that have enough information about a suspect and can evaluate whether it is misbehaving or not.

2. Definition of the attacker's neighborhood: In this phase, for each suspected vehicle, a suspect's neighborhood N is defined; $N(s, e)$ is defined to be the intersection of the coverage areas of both the suspected vehicle s and the evaluator e. All vehicles can receive messages from the suspect and accuse the suspected vehicle when they enter within N. Note that a neighborhood of vehicle v refers to a subset of the attacker and all one-hop neighbors of vehicle v that run MDS. When enough evidence is collected against an attacker, then the *CA* can revoke the keys of the attacker by initiating one of the described revocation protocols.

Detecting and Correcting Malicious Data in VANETs

The approach in (Gelle, 2004) is based on sensors in which vehicles can detect incorrect information and identify the sources of this incorrect information with a high probability. There are four assumptions in this technique: (1) a vehicle can bind observations of its local environment with the communication it receives; (2) a vehicle can talk its neighbors independent of the interference of other vehicles; (3) the network is sufficiently dense; and (4) after sufficiently coming in close contact, vehicles can authenticate their communication to one another. Considering these assumptions, now we describe the proposed model. Firstly, the notations of the model are defined as follows:

P: Euclidian space
$\|P_1 - P_2\|$: Euclidian distance from point P_1 to P_2.
E: an event.
D: data associated with the event.

f: locator function that is a continuous function $f: T \rightarrow P$ and indicates the location of the event over the lifetime of the event.

T: lifetime of an event. Note that the lifetime of an event may be a single point in time $T = \{t\}$ or an interval of time $T = [t_0, t_1]$.

N: an integer number that uniquely identifies the vehicle.

β: the observation radius.

K: global database of all assertions contributed by all vehicles.

In this model, event *E* is defined by a pair $E = (D, f)$ and a vehicle is shown by a triplet (N, f, β). Vehicles can observe each event which occurs within their observation radius. The observed event is called assertion and denoted by $\langle (D, f) \rangle_{O_i}$, where vehicle O_i is the witness of event (D, f). Note that vehicle (O_i, f_i, β_i) can record the assertion $\langle (D, f) \rangle_{O_i}$ if *T* is a subset of T_i and for all $t \in T$ we have $\| f(t) - f_i(t) \| \leq \beta_i$. Then, the recorded assertion by a vehicle is immediately universally available to all other vehicles.

Moreover, in this approach, the set of all sets of events *ε* is considered based on statistical properties or rules. The model of the VANET is a function $M: \varepsilon \rightarrow \{valid, invalid\}$. A set of events $\{E_1, ..., E_n\} \in \varepsilon$ is called consistent with the model of the VANET if $M(E_1, ..., E_n) = valid$ and inconsistent if $M(E_1, ..., E_n) = invalid$. After determining explanations set of correct and malicious events, the score is allocated to the explanations. This score is determined by statistical method such as Occam's razor. Then, the explanations are ordered based on their scores. After ordering the models, each vehicle accepts the data that exists in the model sets. Otherwise, the data will be refused.

Detection and Localization of Sybil Vehicles in VANETs

Sybil attacker is an example of cheating attacks in which a malicious vehicle creates delusion traffic congestion by claiming multiple identities. Not only this does create an illusion, it has the potential to inject false information into the networks via a number of fabricated non-existing vehicles.

The (Xiao, 2006) has suggested a static algorithm to detect whether a vehicle honestly claims its position or not. In this technique, each vehicle is defined by triplet (N, f, f_1), where *N* is the vehicle's ID, *f* is a continuous function $f: T \rightarrow P$ which indicates to the claimed position of the vehicle over lifetime *T*, and *P* represents the Euclidian space and equals to $\| P_1 - P_2 \|$ (Euclidian distance from point P_1 to P_2). Moreover, f_1 is another continuous function $f_1: T \rightarrow P$ which indicates the estimated position over lifetime *T*. Note that the estimated position is computed based on the signal strength measurements.

In this algorithm, there are five steps to detect Sybil vehicles:

- **Step 1:** vehicle *v* periodically broadcasts beacon messages and receives beacon messages from its neighboring vehicles.

- **Step 2:** vehicle *v* stores corresponding signal strength measured for each received beacon message in its memory.

- **Step 3:** when vehicle *v* collects enough signal strength measurements for a neighboring vehicle, then vehicle *v* executes a static algorithm. In this algorithm, time is divided into several distinct times as t_0, t_1, ..., t_n. Claimed positions and estimated positions of normal vehicle *v* are computed in t_0, t_1, ..., t_n. Then, the difference $d_i = f_1(t_i) - f(t_i)$ is calculated. Note that the standard normal distribution is assumed for d_i with mean $\mu_d = 0$ and variance σ_0^2. Since an estimated position usually has an error, therefore, the estimated position should follow the normal distribution.

- **Step 4:** using the mean and variance of the samples (i.e., positions in t_0, t_1, ..., t_n) and also mean and variance of the d_i distribution, two test static values and two critical values are obtained in vehicle *v*, where the critical values are critical value of the standard normal distribution $N(0, 1)$. One static value (z) is related to the mean of samples and another static value (x) is related to the variance of samples. The parameters z and x are obtained based on the values of mean and variance of the d_i distribution, number of samples (n), and mean and variance of the standard normal distribution.

- **Step 5:** vehicle v can check the test static values with the critical values for its neighbors and then can detect Sybil vehicles. If z becomes lower than the critical value of the normal distribution and also x becomes lower than or equal to the critical value of the distribution, then the algorithm finds that its neighbor vehicle u honestly claims its position. Otherwise, vehicle u is detected as a Sybil vehicle.

CLUSTERING ALGORITHMS

Considering the influence of clustering on solving scalability challenges, a number of clustering algorithms have been suggested. However, some characteristics of VANET cause that the traditional approaches proposed for MANETs cannot be appropriate for clustering in VANETs. For example, high dynamic mobility of vehicles and high change of network topology in VANET reduce the stability of cluster formation when using MANET approaches. In the following, clustering algorithms appropriate for VANET are studied.

MANET Clustering Algorithms

In this part, we first review three algorithms which have been mainly proposed for MANETs. Then, we describe the VANET clustering algorithms in Section 4.2, where some of them are improved versions of these MANET algorithms.

The Highest-Degree Heuristic Algorithm (Lin, 1997; Baker, 1981)

The Highest-degree algorithm (HD) chooses a cluster-head based on a vehicle degree, where the vehicle degree means the number of vehicle neighbors. Therefore, the vehicle with maximum number of neighbors is selected as a cluster-head and other neighbor vehicles are considered as members of the cluster. Experiments show that the system has a low rate of cluster-head change, but the throughput is low. This especially happens when the numbers of vehicles increases because in this approach there is no upper bound on the number of members in each cluster. When a large number of members exist in a cluster, the cluster-head cannot manage the cluster operation well and then the throughput of the network reduces.

The Lowest-ID Algorithm (Lin, 1997; Gerla, 1995)

The Lowest-ID (LID) algorithm uses a unique ID for each vehicle (i.e., a number which is assigned to each vehicle), and then orders vehicles based on their ID values and chooses the vehicle with the minimum ID as a cluster-head. For this purpose, each vehicle within the network broadcasts its ID to all other reachable vehicles during the clustering stage. Each vehicle, in turn, chooses as its cluster-head the vehicle with the lowest ID. The main advantage of this algorithm is the maintenance of connectivity in situations where other clustering algorithms cannot maintain connectivity. Moreover, clusters can be overlapping in this approach. The Lowest-ID is better than the Highest Degree heuristic in terms of throughput. The drawback is its bias towards vehicles with smaller IDs, which leads to the battery drainage of certain vehicles in wireless networks.

The Weighted Clustering Algorithm (WCA)

In this section, we briefly illustrate the WCA (Chatterjee, 2002). When vehicle *v* has obtained enough information and created its neighbor list, the WCA calculates a weighted sum of vehicle *v* using Eq.(1)

$$W_v = w_1\Delta_v + w_2 J_v + w_3 M_v + w_4 P_v , \qquad (1)$$

where Δ_v is the degree-difference between the number of members of vehicle *v* and the number of vehicles that it can manage under ideal condition, J_v is the sum of the distances of the members to vehicle *v*, M_v is the average speed of the vehicle *v*, and P_v is the accumulative time of vehicle *v* being a cluster-head. The parameters w_1, w_2, w_3, and w_4 (with the condition of $w_1 + w_2 + w_3 + w_4 = 1$) are the corresponding weight factors. The vehicle within the minimum W_v is chosen as the cluster-head.

Experimental results in (Chatterjee, 2002) show that the WCA can perform obviously better than both of the Highest Degree and the Lowest Degree heuristics in several important parameters such as the number of cluster-heads, and the number of re-affiliations (i.e., updates in the clusters where some vehicles could join another clusters).

However, the algorithms that are useful for MANET cannot be practical for VANETs since important parameters of VANETs are mainly different from MANETs. The vehicles cannot randomly move within the physical space because the vehicles should follow the limitations that exist in roads and network topology (Fonseca, 2006). For example, vehicles generally travel in a single direction and are constrained to travel within a two-dimensional movement. Moreover, each vehicle is constrained by the movements of surrounding vehicles and traffic constraints. Consequently, current MANETs clustering techniques are unstable in vehicular networks because of high dynamic mobility of vehicles and high change of network topology. The clusters created by these techniques are too short-lived to provide scalability with low communications overhead. Therefore, it is necessary to design more intelligent clustering techniques for VANET environments through movement restrictions and the knowledge of position, velocity, and acceleration which are obtained from on-board vehicle systems and Global Position System (GPS).

VANET Clustering Algorithms

With respect to the differences between MANETs and VANETs, we stated that the algorithms that are useful for a MANET are usually unstable in vehicular networks because of high dynamic mobility of vehicles and high change of network topology. Therefore, we review algorithms which are suggested for VANETs based on VANET's characteristics.

Improvement of HD and LID (Fan & Haran, 2005)

The two clustering methods are suggested to improve stability of the Degree and Lowest-ID algorithms in order to be useful for vehicular networks. Firstly, two parameters are defined:

1. **Closest Position to Average**: A vehicle selects its cluster-head based on the ordering of the absolute difference of candidate's position to the average position of all proximal vehicles. This means that the average position of all proximal vehicles that are firstly located within the same broadcast range is computed. Then, the difference between the calculated average position and the position of each vehicle is considered as a parameter of a weighted function.

2. **Closest Velocity to Average**: A vehicle chooses its cluster-head based on the

ordering of the absolute difference of candidate's velocity to the average velocity of all proximal vehicles.

According to these parameters, the following process is executed based on the weighted function and one of the above defined parameters:

1. Each vehicle can determine the vehicles within a range by polling the local broadcast message and tracking the candidate cluster-head set S_CH. All vehicles within the broadcast range are considered as candidate cluster-heads.

2. Using S_CH and the state information received by broadcasting, each candidate cluster-head is evaluated using the weighted function.

3. The cluster-head is chosen in a decreasing order of a weighted function. The weighed function is a weighted algorithm that uses a weighting scheme of 85% weighting to the Lowest-ID or Highest-Degree logic, and 15% weighting to the traffic specific information of position or velocity. The request for cluster membership is broadcast to the candidate vehicle. If the candidate vehicle denies the request, then the vehicle with the next highest utility is selected and this step is repeated. For example, it is possible that a candidate vehicle denies the selection if either it has reached its maximum limit of cluster members or the candidate vehicle has already decided to join another cluster-head (Fan & Haran, 2005, pp.37).

Clustering for Open Inter-Vehicle communication Networks

The (Blum, 2003) has proposed a Clustering for Open Inter vehicle communication Networks (COIN) algorithm. Cluster-head election is based on vehicular dynamics and driver intentions, instead of ID or relative mobility as in classical clustering methods. This algorithm also accommodates the oscillatory nature of inter-vehicle distances. It is showed that COIN can produce much more stable structures in VANETs while introducing a little additional overhead. The COIN algorithm is as follows:

- **Step 1:** vehicle v checks whether the cluster-head is in its neighborhood. If there is no cluster-head, v declares itself as a cluster-head. Note that vehicle v selects itself as a cluster-head, if v has the highest weight within all unaffiliated nearby vehicles. The cluster-head of vehicle v and vehicle v itself should be located within their broadcasting range. If vehicle v loses radio contact with its cluster-head, vehicle v is called an unaffiliated vehicle.

- **Step 2:** the distance between two cluster-heads should be greater than IC_{min}. Otherwise, the cluster-head with the smaller weight should be abdicated. The parameter IC_{min} is the minimum distance between two cluster-heads and should be less than or equal to the radio range. Moreover, the cluster-head weight is proportional to the amount of time it will remain on the current road, and thus, it captures a driver's intentions.

- **Step 3:** if vehicle v disconnects from its cluster-head, it will connect to a new cluster-head that has the highest association weight. Note that association weight $W_{v \to u}$ is the suitability of vehicle u to be the cluster-head for vehicle v at time t and is conversely proportional to the distance between vehicles v and u.

Location-Based Routing Algorithm with Cluster-Based Flooding

The (Santos, 2005) has presented a reactive location based routing algorithm that uses cluster-based flooding for VANETs called Location-Based

Routing Algorithm with Cluster-Based Flooding (LORA_CBF). Each cluster-head has a cluster table which contains the addresses and geographic locations of other members. In reality, the cluster-head maintains information about its members and gateways. Packets are sent from a source to destination X by a protocol similar to the greedy routing (Karp, 2000). The source will forward the location request (LREQ) packets, if the location of the destination is not available. When other cluster-heads receive a location request, they check whether the destination is a member of their cluster. If one cluster-head finds destination X, it returns a Location Reply (LREP) packet to the sender using the geographic routing (i.e., any routing that performs based on geographic information such as GPS information), because each vehicle knows the position of the source and the closest neighbor based on the information from the received LREQ. Once the source receives the location of destination X, it recovers the data packet from its buffer and sends it to the closest neighbor toward destination X.

Clustered Gathering Protocol

In (Salhi, 2009), a road is divided into several virtual segments with the same length. In each segment, a cluster-head should be elected by executing the following algorithm:

- **Step 1:** after ending a selection period ($t_{selection}$), each vehicle computes its qualification using Eq.(2):

Posision $(i, t+t_{selection}) >$ seg_end $\rightarrow i \neq$ CH,   (2)

where *seg_end* means the segment end position, *Pos(i, t)* is the position of vehicle i at time instant t, and $t_{selection}$ is the cluster-head selection duration.

- **Step 2:** each vehicle remains cluster-head until receiving a CH_ANNOUNCE

message from another vehicle or until ending the cluster-head election period. Note that the CH_ANNOUNCE message includes the ID of sender and its position.

- **Step 3:** when vehicle i receives a CH_ANNOUNCE message from vehicle j which shows vehicle j has a better position than vehicle i, vehicle i cancels its CH_ANNOUNCE.
- **Step 4:** finally, with respect to CH_ANNOUNCE messages which are exchanged among vehicles, the eligible vehicle that is the closest vehicle to the segment end will be selected as a cluster-head.
- **Step 5:** then, the cluster-head computes a back-off time to announce its neighbors using Eq.(3):

$T_{backoff}(i)=rand(0, t_{collect})+Priority(Pos(i,t), seg\_end)$ (3)

where $T_{backoff}(i)$ is the back-off time of vehicle i, and *Rand(x,y)* is a function that returns a uniform distributed random integer number bounded between x and y. Moreover, *Priority(x, Seg_end)* is a function that returns a period correlated with the distance between the node and the segment end position. Thus, the closer is the node to the segment end; the shorter will be the period. The parameter $t_{collect}$ represents the duration time that is necessary for gathering important information in order to form clusters (Salhi, 2009).

- **Step 6:** After waiting a random bounded back-off time, a member that wants to send data, first should send a request message to its cluster-head. When the vehicle receives a reply message from its cluster-head, then the vehicle sends its data to the cluster-head.

A Direction Based Clustering (Fan & Mohamadian, 2007)

In this technique, a new distributed algorithm has been proposed in which a cluster-head can be selected based on the moving direction of vehicles, leadership duration of cluster-heads, and membership duration of cluster members. Note that the leadership duration is the time period during which a cluster-head (CH) remains in its cluster-head role. The algorithm is executed as follows:

- **Step 1:** each vehicle can claim that it is a CH. Then, it broadcasts a beacon containing its ID and position to other vehicles. Moreover, each vehicle *v* receives beacons from its neighbors.
- **Step 2:** each vehicle provides a "candidate pool" list which is formed by all its neighboring CH vehicles with the same moving direction as well as having a lower ID than its ID.
- **Step 3:** if *u* the sender of a beacon has the same direction with vehicle *v*, then *v* checks whether *u* is a CH. If *u* is a CH, then *v* checks its CH's leadership duration.
- **Step 4:** if the CH's leadership duration of *v* becomes lower than the CH's leadership of *u,* and the ID of *u* becomes smaller, then *v* changes its old CH to *u.*
- **Step 5:** after identifying the CH by *v*, vehicle *v* should receive CH's beacon within a predefined period of time. If *v* does not receive any CH's beacon, it means that *v* has lost its CH and immediately should find a new CH from existing CHs based on the above explained conditions. If its neighbors cannot satisfy above conditions, *v* would claim itself as a CH.

TECHNIQUES TO IMPROVE CONNECTIVITY

With respect to the non-uniform distribution of vehicles and rapid change of traffic conditions in a VANET, a static transmission range cannot maintain the network's connectivity well, as mentioned in Section 2.3. In this section, we review several techniques have been suggested to obtain optimum transmission range of vehicles based on network conditions.

Fair Power Adjustment for Vehicular (FPAV) Environments

The (Monero, 2005) has proposed a power control algorithm to find the optimum transmission range of every vehicle. The FPAV algorithm is run in two stages: (1) in the first stage, the minimum transmission range for all vehicles is maximized in a synchronized approach; (2) in the second stage, a maximum transmission range is achieved for all vehicles individually, while satisfying the condition of keeping the channel load under a certain limit.

In this technique, there are several assumptions and definitions which we firstly explain them. A set of vehicles $V = \{v_1,..., v_n\}$ is assumed to move along a road. Moreover, the road is modeled as a one dimensional line of unit length. Notice a normalized coordination is considered for each vehicle, where vehicles can be modeled as points in $R = [0, 1]$. For a given set of vehicles $V = \{v_1,..., v_n\}$, a power assignment PA is introduced that is a function to assign a ratio $PA(i) \in [0, 1]$ to every network vehicle v_i, with $i = 1,..., n$. The power used by vehicle v_i to send the beacon is $PA(i) \times P_{max}$. Note that P_{max} is the maximum transmission power. In addition, there is a threshold value called Max Beaconing Load (MBL) that represents a limit where safety protocols can achieve a reasonable performance. The interference range of v_i under *PA*, *IR(i, PA)*, is defined as the intersection between the carrier sense (*CS*) range of vehicle v_i at power $PA(i) \times P_{max}$ and the operation region *R*. Interference (x, PA) is the number of vehicles which have point x in their *CS* range under *PA*. Finally, the beaconing network load under *PA* is defined as $BL(PA) = max\{$ *Interference*(x, PA) $\}$ (for $x \in [0,1]$). Now, the FPAV is executed in two phases as:

- **Phase 1:** An optimal solution to Beaconing Max-Min Power Problem (BMMTxP) is calculated, and then this solution augments into a per-vehicle maximal power assignment.
    - every vehicle starts with the minimum transmission power.
    - each vehicle increases its power assignment by adding ε to its current power assignment, where $\varepsilon > 0$.
    - the increase is continued as long as the network load remains below the beaconing threshold *MBL*.
    - when the network load becomes beyond the beaconing threshold *MBL*, the power assignment should be decreased by an amount of ε.
- **Phase 2:** The power assignment computed by stage one of FPAV (which is increased by amount ε) is an approximation of the optimal solution to BMMTxP. Since step size ε is an arbitrarily small constant, the solution computed by BMMTxP can be regarded as optimal for all practical purposes. To find the per-vehicle maximal power assignment, the following procedure is executed.
    - each vehicle sequentially increases its transmission power by $\varepsilon \times P_{max}$ (only one step) if the condition $BL(PA) \leq$ *MBL* is not violated.
    - this sequence is repeated after all vehicles have been given a chance and

until no vehicle is able to increase without violating the condition on the beaconing network load. It ensures that any vehicle will increase its transmission power by a maximum amount of $\varepsilon \times P_{max}$ before letting others try it. Therefore, per-vehicle maximal power assignment can be obtained by this algorithm.

Dynamic Transmission Range Assignment (DTRA)

The Dynamic Transmission Range Assignment (DTRA) (Artimy, 2007) algorithm adjusts a vehicle's transmission range according to local traffic conditions. The DTRA algorithm requires no external information (such as vehicle position) and no communication overhead because the algorithm uses only the vehicle's internal state to determine the transmission range. In DTRA, the value of f_s = T_s/T_t is first computed, where f_s is the average fraction of stopped vehicles (including vehicles that are stopped due to traffic conditions, but not parked vehicles), and T_s represents the stopping time of a test vehicle circulating in a network during a trip time T_t. Now,

- If f_s is equal to zero, it means that the free-flow traffic condition is considered. Then, transmission range is set to the maximum transmission range of *MR*. The maximum range *MR* depends on the available transmitter power and the specifications of the physical layer.
- if f_s is not equal to zero (i.e., congested traffic condition), then the following parameters are calculated:

$$\lambda_1 = \frac{\lambda}{u_{max} \times k_{jam}} \qquad (4)$$

$$K = \frac{1}{[1 + \frac{1 - f_s}{\lambda_1}]} \qquad (5)$$

$$t_1 = MR \times (1-K) \tag{6}$$

$$t_2 = \alpha \times MR + \sqrt{\frac{MR \times \log(MR)}{K}} \tag{7}$$

where k_{jam} denotes the maximum vehicle density at the traffic jam and u_{max} is the maximum speed among vehicles. Moreover, λ measures the sensitivity of the vehicle interaction, and α is a constant value set to 0.25 in the DTRA evaluation. Then, with respect to the obtained parameters, the minimum value between t_1 and t_2 is selected as transmission range.

Adaptive Allocation of Transmission Range

An Adaptive Allocation of Transmission Range (AATR) technique is closely related to topology control algorithm that has been proposed in (DaeiNabi, 2009), where hello messages and density of traffic around vehicles are used to adaptively adjust the transmission range among vehicles. Therefore, if there is no neighbor around a vehicle, the vehicle can adaptively increase its transmission range and can find its neighbors. In this approach, three steps are executed.

- **Step 1:** each vehicle determines its minimum and maximum transmission ranges. Then, every vehicle periodically broadcasts a hello message. The minimum range is obtained based on a threshold value as:
  - If the number of vehicles around vehicle v becomes greater than the threshold value, the minimum transmission value is set to 100m.
  - Otherwise, the minimum value is considered equal to 300m.
  - The maximum transmission range is set to 1000m for all vehicles (based on the DSRC standard).

- **Step 2:** when vehicle v wants to send a message, it first seeks its neighborhood table. If there is no neighbor in its list, vehicle v sends a request message in the current transmission range. If vehicle v receives a reply message from neighbor u, vehicle v checks the correction of the received reply message from u and then sends its messages to vehicle u. However, if vehicle v does not receive any reply message after elapsing a timeout, it increases its transmission range and repeats its requests. When vehicle v finds a neighbor, it stops increasing its transmission range. Note that increasing transmission range is continued until R_{max}. If vehicle v cannot find any neighbor after reaching to R_{max}, vehicle v may save messages based on their contents for future forwarding.

- **Step 3:** increasing transmission range is executed based on normalized traffic density. If the normalized traffic belongs to [0, 0.8), then the increase is done by an exponential function. Otherwise, for normalized traffic belongs to [0.8, 1.0], a linear function is used. Moreover, in order to avoid message collision, the transmission range can be decreased when the traffic density increases. Similar to the increase of the transmission range, the decrease of the transmission range can be performed using (1) a linear function for normalized traffic that belongs to [0, 0.2), and (2) an exponential function for normalized traffic in range [0.2, 1.0].

PERFORMANCE COMPARISION

To insight on the performance of clustering, monitoring and connectivity schemes, in this section, we compare the algorithms that have been suggested to solve the challenges of scalability, connectivity and attack in VANETs. For all illustrated algorithms, results have been obtained from their relevant references.

Performance of Algorithms to Detect Attackers

A scheme to detect malicious data in a VANET has been introduced in (Gelle, 2004), where the same event is observed by multiple entities. This is not often true because of high speed of vehicles and high variation of network topology. Moreover, this scheme does not have any details on possible tests.

In (Raya& Papadimitratos, 2007), the immediate revocation of certificates of misbehaving vehicles is combined with a detection system in; where timestamp, trusted components, and signed messages (i.e., the messages that are signed when they are sent between CA and TC_V as mentioned in Section 3.1.1) are used in the network. Results of this scheme show that this technique can robustly and efficiently isolate misbehaving and faulty vehicles within acceptable delays. However, it is assumed that there is always an honest majority to evaluate the behavior of vehicles (Raya& Papadimitratos, 2007).

The technique described in (Xiao, 2006) can be resistant to spoof attackers (malicious nodes that contribute invalid or incorrect data) because this technique implies signal strength distribution and it is difficult for a malicious physical vehicle that changes its signal strength distribution. However, this scheme cannot detect subtle small-scale attacks because of the limited accuracy of the signal-strength-based approach.

Performance of Clustering Algorithms

A number of clustering algorithms has been suggested to solve the scalability challenges in section 4. In this section, we show some comparison results among them. Table 1 depicts the effect of varying the transmission range on the average number of cluster-head changes, in which the simple HD

method has the poorest performance, i.e., the largest cluster-head change. Clearly, the addition of traffic-specific information (e.g., position or average velocity) to the HD clustering enables more stable clusters. The three LID algorithms show very similar performances. Table 2 illustrates the effect of varying the maximum speed on the average number of cluster-head changes with a fixed transmission range of 150m. Simulation results show that the speed limits are only useful in heavy traffic situations. Note that data is readily available in (Fan & Haran, 2005, pp.39-40).

Comparing average cluster-head lifetime and re-affiliation frequency metrics, Table 3 shows that the COIN has improved the stability compared to the Lowest-ID. The cluster maintenance can be achieved through stable cluster[1] architecture that helps to reduce the re-affiliation rate and minimizes re-clustering situations. Note that the average cluster-head lifetime is the most direct measurement of the stability of cluster-head elections. Note that cluster lifetime shows a duration in which a cluster-head remains as a cluster-head. Moreover, the re-affiliation frequency, i.e., the process in which a given vehicle joins to the cluster, represents the stability of a cluster membership.

Table 4 shows that the number of CHs of the Direction based algorithm (Fan&Mohamadian, 2007) that remains almost unchanged as the number of vehicles increases. It means that this algorithm is very scalable for vehicular networks. Moreover, the CH leadership duration has been compared to evaluate the stability. Table 5 illustrates that the performance of Direction based clustering algorithms is a clear improvement. Note that all these data are obtained from (Fan&Mohamadian, 2007, pp.15-16).

The LORA-CBF is a hierarchical architecture, and therefore, it needs a smaller route discovery time and a lower delivery ratio. However, LORA-CBF increases routing overhead, general overhead and routing load (Santos, 2005, pp.2291).

Table 1. Average cluster-head Changes vs. Transmission Range (Fan & Haran, 2005, pp.39)

Transmission Range (meters) Algorithm	25m	50m	100m	150m	200m	250m	300m
HD	0.36	0.38	0.41	0.41	0.44	0.42	0.47
HD with Ave. velocity	0.325	0.36	0.35	0.335	0.35	0.365	0.3
HD with Position	0.3	0.28	0.3	0.25	0.3	0.275	0.23
LID	0.06	0.18	0.09	0.065	0.07	0.075	0.065
LID with Position	0.07	0.15	0.075	0.06	0.05	0.055	0.065
LID with Ave. velocity	0.07	0.13	0.095	0.065	0.055	0.075	0.065

Table 2. Average cluster-head Changes vs. Max. Speed (Fan & Haran, 2005, pp.40)

Max. speed (Km/h) Algorithm Range (m)	40 Km/h	80 Km/h	100 Km/h	120 Km/h	140 Km/h
HD	0.425	0.43	0.41	0.43	0.435
HD with Ave. velocity	0.03	0.27	0.35	0.28	0.3
HD with Position	0.28	0.26	0.3	0.265	0.29
LID	0.085	0.08	0.08	0.06	0.06
LID with Position	0.08	0.085	0.09	0.065	0.06
LID with Ave. velocity	0.06	0.065	0.075	0.06	0.06

Table 3. Stability of Clustering Algorithms (Blum, 2003, pp.154)

	Cluster lifetime	Re-affiliation frequency
Lowest ID	4.2	35.5
COIN	112.8	241.7

Performance of Connectivity Algorithms

In Section 5, we mentioned three algorithms that can determine transmission range dynamically. These algorithms can be divided into two mechanisms: power control and topology control. In this section, we illustrate some advantages and disadvantage of mentioned connectivity algorithms.

The power control mechanisms can improve throughput of network and maintain the quality and reliability of wireless links because the bit error rate is controlled at any receiver. In general, there is a tradeoff between the quality of information and the cost or required overhead. Therefore, the designer of a power control protocol should consider some factors such as fully distributed and asynchronous implementation, and should also use local information if he wants to have a protocol that can carefully maintain connectivity. The Fair Power Adjustment for Vehicular (FPAV) algorithm (Monero, 2005) is a power control algorithm to find the optimum transmission range of every vehicle in which the minimum transmission range for all vehicles is maximized in a synchronized approach. Then, a maximum transmission range is achieved for all vehicles individually, while satisfying the condition of keeping the channel load under a certain threshold (Monero, 2005). Moreover, vehicles forward

Table 4. Number of CHs vs. number of vehicles(Fan & Mohamadian, 2007)

No. of Vehicles Algorithm	50	100	150	200	250
LID	17	34	46	48	56
HD	13	17	20	23	28
Direction based	10	12	14	16	17

Table 5. Average CH duration vs. number of vehicles (Fan & Mohamadian, 2007)

No. of Vehicles Algorithm	50	100	150	200	250
LID	1	0.9	0.7	0.6	0.5
HD	0.6	0.4	0.5	0.4	0.4
Direction based	7.8	6.7	6.6	6.5	6.2

beacon messages (including velocity, direction, etc.) periodically to inform other vehicles about safety conditions. Note that the current version of FPAV is centralized and it requires synchronization among nodes. To remove the synchronization, an approach should be developed that depends on the accuracy of the knowledge about the state of other vehicles, and the complete knowledge of the environment. Therefore, their scheme has a tradeoff between computing an optimal solution with global knowledge.

The Dynamic Transmission-Range-Assignment (DTRA) (Artimy, 2007) is closely related to a class of topology control algorithms that control a vehicle's degree by adjusting the transmission power. The experimental results show that DTRA is effective to keep a high degree of connectivity in highway configurations, where the VANET topology varies rapidly (Artimy, 2007, pp.411). This algorithm depends on the mobility of vehicles and local density is estimated locally. In addition, it does not require communication overhead involved since the algorithm uses only the vehicle's internal state to determine the transmission range.

The Adaptive Allocation of Transmission Range (AATR) (DaeiNabi, 2009) technique is closely related to the topology control algorithm and dynamically determines transmission range based on the received hello messages and the density of traffic around vehicles. Compared to the static transmission range, AATR can guarantee connectivity and ensure other vehicles in network to receive messages. Similar to DTRA, AATR is also adaptable to traffic conditions. Moreover, AATR uses hello messages (with vehicle's ID, velocity, direction, etc.) which are periodically sent by vehicles to inform other vehicles about itself and environment's conditions therefore. In order to avoid collision under high vehicle density, the transmission range is reduced adaptively.

FUTURE RESEARCH DIRECTIONS

With respect to the existent challenges in VANETs and their solutions, the following works can be proposed for future research:

* work on a vehicular clustering algorithm based on weighted clustering algorithm (WCA) that considers important parameters of VANET.

- work on new clustering algorithms to improve stability, connectivity, and security, and reduce overhead in VANET communications.
- work on a monitoring algorithm to detect malicious vehicles and to isolate them from honest vehicles, where each vehicle can be monitored by some of its trustier neighbors.

CONCLUSION

In this chapter, we have explained three challenges and solutions for VANETs: attacks, scalability, and connectivity. After clarifying attacks, the algorithms that have been proposed to detect attackers have been reviewed.

We have also described that one solution for the scalability problem is to group vehicles into a number of clusters. Clustering is vital for efficient resource consumption and load balancing in large scale networks. Then, we have reviewed several clustering algorithms that have been suggested for VANETs.

Focusing on the transmission range as the critical factor to the connectivity between two adjacent vehicles, the connectivity problem has been explained in VANETs. The algorithms that can determine optimum transmission range for vehicles have been studied as the solutions for the third challenge in VANETs.

REFERENCES

Abdulhamid, K., & Abdel-Raheem, E. (2007). Performance of DSRC systems using conventional channel estimation at high velocities. *International Journal of Electronics and Communication, 61*(8), 556–561. doi:10.1016/j.aeue.2006.10.005

Adler, C. J. (2006, April). *Information Dissemination in Vehicular Ad Hoc Networks* (Thesis). Munich, Germany: Der Ludwig- Maximilians- University at Munchen.

Artimy, M. (2007, September). Local Density Estimation and Dynamic transmission-Range Assignment in Vehicular Ad Hoc Networks. *IEEE Transactions on Intelligent Transportation Systems, 8*(3), 400–412. doi:10.1109/TITS.2007.895290

Baker, D. J., & Ephremides, A. (1981, April). A distributed algorithm for organizing mobile radio telecommunication networks. In *Proceedings of the 2nd International Conference on Distributed Computer Systems*. Paris.

Bloom, B. (1970). Space/time trade-offs in hash coding with allowable errors. *Communications of the ACM, 13*(7), 422–426. doi:10.1145/362686.362692

Blum, J., Eskandarian, A., & Hoffman, L. (2003). Mobility management in IVC networks. In *Proceedings of the IEEE Intelligent Vehicles Symposium* (150-155). Columbus, OH.

Chatterjee, M., Das, S. K., & Turgut, D. (2002). WCA: A weighted clustering algorithm for mobile ad hoc networks. *Cluster Computing, 5*(2), 193–204. doi:10.1023/A:1013941929408

DaeiNabi. A., Ghaffarpour Rahbar, A., & Khademzadeh, A. (2009. May). Adaptive Allocation of Transmission Range in Vehicular Ad-Hoc Networks. In *Proceedings of the 17th Iranian Conference on Electrical Engineering* (*ICEE*2009), Tehran, Iran.

Fan, P., Harran, G. J., Dillenburg, J., & Nelson, P. C. (2005). Cluster-Based Framework in Vehicular Ad-Hoc Networks (ADHOC-NOW 2005, LNCS 3738), (32–42). New York: Springer.

Fan, P. A., Nelson, P., Haran, J., & Dillenburg, J. (2007). A Novel Direction-Based Clustering Algorithm in Vehicular Ad Hoc Networks. In *Proceedings of the Transportation Research Board 86ʰ Annual Meeting*, Washington DC

Fonseca, E., & Festag, A. (2006, March). *A Survey of Existing Approaches for Secure Ad Hoc Routing and Their Applicability to VANETS* (Technical Report NLE-PR). Heidelberg, Germany: NEC Network Laboratories.

Gelle, P., Grren, D., & Staddon, J. (2004). Detection and Correcting Malicious Data in VANETs. In [Philadelphia.]. *Proceedings of VANETS, 04*, 29–37.

Gerla, M., & Tsai, J. (1995). Multicluster, mobile, multimedia radio network. *Wireless Networks, 1*(3), 255–265. doi:10.1007/BF01200845

Karp, B., & Kung, H. T. (2000). GPSR: Greedy Perimeter Stateless Routing for Wireless Networks. In *Proceedings of the 6ᵗʰ Annual ACM/IEEE International Conference on Mobile Computing and Networking*. Boston.

Lee, J. (2008). Measurement of transmission range effect to the connectivity of vehicular telematics networks. In *Proceedings of the 23ʳᵈ International Technical Conference on Circuits/Systems, Computers and Communications* (1301-1304). Japan.

Lin, C. R., & Gerla, M. (1997, September). Adaptive Clustering for Mobile Networks. *IEEE Journal on Selected Areas in Communications, 15*(7), 1265–1275. doi:10.1109/49.622910

Liu, X., Fang, Zh., & Shi, L. (2007, July). Securing Vehicular Ad Hoc Networks. In *Proceedings of the 2ⁿᵈ conference on International Pervasive Computing and Applications* (424-429). Birmingham, UK

Monero, M. T., Santi, P., & Hartenstein, H. (2005. September). Fair Sharing of Bandwidth in VANETs. In *Proceedings of VANET'05*, Cologne, Germany.

Nadeem, T., & Shankar, P. (2006, July). A Comparative Study of Data Dissemination Models for VANETs. In *Proceedings of IEEE Mobile and Ubiquitous Systems: Networking & Services*, (1 – 10). San Jose, CA.

Naumov, V., & Gross, T. R. (2007, May). Connectivity - Aware Routing (CAR) in Vehicular Ad Hoc Networks. In *Proceedings of IEEE International Conference on Computer Communications* (INFOCOM'07), (1919-1927). Anchorage, AK.

Picconi, F., Ravi, N., Gruteser, M., & Iftode, L. (2006). Probabilistic Validation of Aggregated data in Vehicular Ad Hoc Networks. In *Proceedings of the International Conference on Mobile Computing and Networking*, (76-85). Los Angeles.

Raya, M., & Hubaux, J. P. (2005, November). The Security of Vehicular Ad Hoc Networks. In *Proceedings of the Third ACM Workshop on Security of Ad Hoc and Sensor Networks* (*SASN 2005*), Alexandria, VA.

Raya, M., & Hubaux, J. P. (2005.March). Security Aspects of Inter-Vehicle Communications. In *Proceedings of the 5ᵗʰ Swiss Transport Research Conference,* Monte Verità, Ascona.

Raya, M., & Hubaux, J. P. (2007). Securing vehicular ad hoc networks. *Journal of Computer Security, 15*(1), 39–68.

Raya, M., Papadimitratos, P., Aad, I., Jungels, D., & Hubaux, J. P. (2007). October). Eviction of Misbehaving and Faulty Vehicles in Vehicular Networks. *IEEE Journal on Selected Areas in Communications, 25*(8), 1557–1568. doi:10.1109/JSAC.2007.071006

Salhi, I., Cherif, M., & Senouc, S. M. (2009, June). A New Framework for Data Collection in Vehicular Networks. In *Proceedings of IEEE ICC'09*. Dresden, Germany.

Santos, R. A., Edwards, A., Edwards, R., & Seed, L. (2005). Performance evaluation of routing protocols in vehicular ad hoc networks. *The International Journal of Ad Hoc and Ubiquitous Computing, 1*(1/2), 80–91. doi:10.1504/IJAHUC.2005.008022

Sichitiu, M. L., & Kihl, M. (2008). Inter-Vehicle Communication System: A Survey. IEEE Communications Surveys & Tutorials, 2nd Quarter 2008, 88-105.

Wakikawa, R., & Sahasrabudhe, M. (2005). Gateway Management for Vehicle to Vehicle Communication. In *Proceedings of the 1ˢᵗ Int'l. Workshop on Vehicle-to-Vehicle Communications*. Philadelphia.

Wang, Y. X., & Bao, F. Sh. (2007). An Entropy-based Weighted Clustering Algorithm and Its Optimization for Ad hoc Networks. In *Proceedings of the 3ʳᵈ IEEE International Conference on Wireless and Mobile Computing, Networking and Communications (WiMob2007)*. White Plains, NY.

Wei, X., & Qing-Quan, L. (2008). Performance evolution of data dissemination for vehicular ad hoc networks in highway scenarios. *The International Archives of the Photogrammetry, Remote Sensing and Spatial Information Sciences. XXXVII (B1)*. Beijing, China.

Xiao, B., Yu, B., & Gao, Ch. (2006, September). Detection and Localization of Sybil Vehicles in VANETs. In *Proceedings of DIWANS'06*, Los Angeles.

Yang, Q., Lim, A., Li, Sh., Fang, J., & Agrawal, P. (2008, August). ACAR: Adaptive Connectivity Aware Routing Protocol for Vehicular Ad Hoc Networks. In *Proceedings of the 17ᵗʰ International Conference on Computer Communications and Networks (ICCCN'08)*. St. Thomas, US Virgin Islands.

Yusefi, S., Altman, E., El-Azouzi, R., & Fathy, M. (2007, June). Connectivity in vehicular ad hoc networks in presence of wireless mobile base-stations. In *Proceedings of the 7ᵗʰ International Conference on ITS*. Sophia Antipolis, France.

ADDITIONAL READING

Artimy, M. M., Robertson, W., & Phillips, W. J. (2006). Minimum transmission range in vehicular ad hoc networks over uninterrupted highways. In *Proceedings of IEEE ITSC* (1400–1405). Toronto, Canada.

Baldessari, R., Festag, A., Matos, A., Santos, J., & Aguiar, R. (2006, March). Flexible Connectivity Management in Vehicular Communication Networks. In *Proceedings of the 3ʳᵈ International Workshop on Intelligent Transportation*, (211-216). Hamburg, Germany.

Baumann, R. (2004). *Vehicular Ad hoc Network* (Master's Thesis). Zurich, Switzerland.

Bernsen, J., & Manivannan, D. (2009). Unicast routing protocols for vehicular ad hoc networks: A critical comparison and classification. *Pervasive and Mobile Computing, 5*(1), 1–18. doi:10.1016/j.pmcj.2008.09.001

Depienne, F., Noubir, G., & Wang, Y. (2006, December). A Platform for Heterogeneous Vehicular Communications and Applications. In *Proceedings of the 1ˢᵗ IEEE Workshop on Automotive Networking and Applications (AutoNet 2006) Co-located with IEEE Globecom 2006*. San Francisco.

Dikaiakos, M. D., Florides, A., Nadeem, T., & Iftode, L. (2007). Location-aware Services over Vehicular Ad-HocNetworks using Car-to-Car Communication. *IEEE Journal on Selected Areas in Communications, 25*(8), 1590–1602. doi:10.1109/JSAC.2007.071008

Farivar, M., Mehrdad, B., & Ashtiani, F.(2008). Two Dimensional Connectivity for Vehicular Ad-Hoc Networks.

Fonseca, E., Festag, A., Baldessari, R., & Aguiar, R. (2007, March). Support of Anonymity in VANETs Putting Pseudonymity into Practice. In *Proceedings of IEEE Wireless Communications and Networking Conference,* Hong Kong, China.

Guo, J., Baugh, J. P., & Wang, Sh. (2007, May). A Group Signature Based Secure and Privacy-preserving Vehicular Communication Framework. In Proceedings of Mobile Networking for Vehicular Environments, (103-108). Anchorage, AK.

Ho, Y. H., Ho, A. H., & Hua, K. A. (2008). Routing protocols for inter-vehicular networks: A comparative study in high-mobility and large obstacles environments. *Computer Communications, 31*(12), 2767–2780. doi:10.1016/j.comcom.2007.11.001

Huaqun, G. (Ed.). (2009). *Automotive Informatics and Communicative Systems: Principals in Vehicular Networks and Data Exchange.* Hershey, PA: IGI Global.

Jaap, S., Bechler, M., & Wolf, L. (2005, July). Evaluation of Routing Protocols for Vehicular Ad hoc Network. In *Proceedings of the 11ᵗʰ Open European Summer School EUNICE 2005,* Colmenarejo, Spain.

Kafsi, M., & Papadimitratos, P. Doussey, O., Alpcanz, T. & Hubaux, J. P. (2008, December). VANET Connectivity Analysis. *Proceedings of IEEE Workshop on Automotive Networking and Applications Autonet,* New Orleans, LA.

Khakbaz, S., & Fathy, M. (2008). A Reliable Method for Disseminating Safety Information in Vehicular Ad hoc Networks Considering Fragmentation problem. In *Proceedings of the 4ᵗʰ International Conference on Wireless and Mobile Communications.* Athens, Greece.

Kihl, M., Sichitiu, M., Ekeroth, T., & Rozenberg, M. (2007). Reliable Geographical Multicast Routing in Vehicular Ad-Hoc Networks. In [Coimbra, Portugal.]. *Proceedings of WWIC, 2007,* 315–325.

Laurendeau, Ch., & Barbeau, M. (2007). Secure Anonymous Broadcasting in Vehicular Networks. In *Proceedings of 32ⁿᵈ IEEE Conference on Local Computer Networks.* Dublin, Ireland.

Lin, X., Zhang, Ch., Sun, X., Ho, P. H., & Shen, X. (2007). Performance Enhancement for Secure Vehicular Communication. In [Washington, DC.]. *Proceedings of IEEE GLOBECOM, 2007,* 480–485.

Lochert, Ch., Hartenstein, H., Tian, J., Füßler, H., Hermann, D., & Mauve, M. (2003). A Routing Strategy for Vehicular Ad Hoc Networks in City Environments. In *Proceedings of IEEE Intelligent Vehicles Symposium.* Columbus, OH.

Moustafa, H., & Zhang, Y. (Eds.). (2009). *Vehicular Networks: Techniques, Standards, and Applications.* Boca Raton, FL: Auerbach Publications. doi:10.1201/9781420085723

Olariu, S., & Weigle, M. C. (Eds.). (2009). *Vehicular Networks: From Theory to Practice.* Boca Raton, FL: Chapman & Hall/CRC.

Varadharajan, V., Shankaran, R., & Hitchens, M. (2004). Security for cluster based ad hoc networks. *Computer Communications, 27*(5), 488–501. doi:10.1016/j.comcom.2003.10.005

Wang, N. W., Hauang, Y. M., & Chen, W. M. (2008, July 30). A novel secure communication scheme in vehicular ad hoc networks. *Computer Communications, 31*(12), 2827–2837. doi:10.1016/j.comcom.2007.12.003

Wang, Z., & Chigan, C. (2007). Countermeasure Uncooperative Behaviors with Dynamic Trust-Token in VANETs. [Glasgow, Scotland.]. *Proceeding of IEEE ICC, 2007,* 3959–3964.

Wang, Z., & Chigan, C. (2007). Cooperation Enhancement for Message Transmission in VANETs. *Wireless Personal Communications, 43*(1), 141–156. doi:10.1007/s11277-006-9235-2

Yan, G., Olariu, S., & Weigle, M. C. (2008, July). Providing VANET security through active position detection. *Computer Communications, 31*(12), 2883–2897. doi:10.1016/j.comcom.2008.01.009

Zhau, T., Choudhury, R. R., Ning, P., & Chakrabarty, K. (2007.August). Privacy-Preserving Detection of Sybil Attacks in Vehicular Ad Hoc Networks. In *Proceedings of 4ᵗʰ Annual International Conference on Mobile and Ubiquitous Systems: Networking & Services*. Philadelphia.

KEY TERMS AND DEFINITIONS

Attackers: Attackers are vehicles that disobey the common protocols of vehicular networking.

Clustering: Grouping of vehicles within clusters is called "clustering".

Connectivity: Connectivity shows the probability that a vehicle can make a connection to exchange information with another vehicle.

Monitoring: Verifying the behavior of vehicles in order to specify the type of their behavior.

Scalability: The ability to manage both vehicles and road side units with the number of information objects that have to be transmitted, without suffering a considerable loss of performance or increase in complexity.

Transmission range: A vehicle can receive messages from other vehicles when they are located within their communication range. This certain range is called transmission range.

Vehicular Ad Hoc Network: VANETs are networks that can be applied to intelligent transportation systems.

ENDNOTE

[1] A VANET cluster is stable when it can maintain its cluster-head and members over the longest possible time period.

Chapter 14
Opportunistic Networking in Delay Tolerant Vehicular Ad Hoc Networks

Ashish Agarwal
Boston University, USA

Thomas D.C. Little
Boston University, USA

ABSTRACT

Vehicular Area Networking (VANET) is an emerging technology to support a class of applications involving communications between vehicles, and vehicles and the environment. Activity in this area includes development of the Dedicated Short Range Communication (DSRC) protocol aimed at enabling vehicles to exchange safety information to enhance awareness of the vehicle beyond the line of sight, and to enhance safety features such as active braking and collision warning. While safety is the primary driver for development, additional applications emerge as potential users of this technology that are more general in nature. Real-time traffic and route updates, traffic monitoring, remote diagnostics, general purpose Internet access and in-car entertainment are examples that require data collection and dissemination analogous to the wired Internet. However, DSRC and related short-range communications technology would appear to be insufficient for these scenarios. In this chapter, we describe, how and under what conditions it is feasible, and in fact desirable, to use short range communications. We describe a network formed over moving vehicles implemented by short-range communication and thereby analyze factors that affect the design and performance. Observations reveal intermittent connectivity between vehicles traveling on the roadway in opposite directions that hinders applications. Techniques adapted from related research in computer networks provide solutions for enabling networking in a fragmented network of moving vehicles. We elaborate and demonstrate analytically the application of techniques that enable networking through short-range communication.

DOI: 10.4018/978-1-61520-913-2.ch014

INTRODUCTION

Vehicles are an integral part of urban and suburban life. Mobility of humans, to a large extent, is served by vehicles on land, sea and air. Vehicles serve as instruments in the quest for mobility, cultural exchange and social interaction. As people travel each day, they come into interaction with unique individuals. Vehicles, too, have an opportunity to interact with other unique vehicles. The mobility patterns are often random leading to opportunistic interaction with unique sets of individuals. It has been shown in related work that the opportunistic interaction between different sets can often span the entire network with the passage of time, as is the case with the epidemic spread of news or disease viruses in the human population. Thus, vehicles can be modeled as unique nodes of a network that interact opportunistically, and with sufficient passage of time, span the network.

Our vision for vehicles of the future involves adding communications to all vehicles and connecting them to the larger Internet. Vehicles equipped with communication capability will exchange safety and state information that will allow reactive and proactive systems to warn of potential hazards or mitigate the severity of a collision. Ongoing work exists to develop protocols and standards to allow autonomous communication between vehicles and between vehicles and infrastructure. The US FCC has allocated spectrum in the 5.9 GHz range Dedicated Short Range Communications (DSRC) to allow vehicle-to-vehicle and vehicle-to-infrastructure communication. Our vision for networked automobiles is to enable autonomous control through coordination thereby achieving environmental, economic and societal challenges.

Ad hoc networks formed over moving vehicles, VANETs (vehicular area networks), are a subset of Mobile Ad hoc Networks (MANETs). The network is characterized by fast-paced nodes traveling on constrained paths (roadways) with potentially short-lived connectivity. Vehicles traveling on the vast network of roadways potentially come into contact with many unique vehicles as they cross each other on the roadway. The nature of vehicular mobility presents an interesting challenge to exploit the spatial-temporal correlation of vehicles traveling on the roadway. Vehicles collect statistical travel data as they traverse the roadway. The data are shared with vehicles in the vicinity. The collected data are aggregated and processed to be shared with servers or vehicles outside the immediate neighboring area. The nature of applications in the VANET space has contrasting requirements. Safety-critical applications exist that require very low latency and high reliability. Non-safety-critical, and traffic warning applications have relatively relaxed constraints. Internet access and general purpose data exchange require connectivity to the backbone network that is strongly hierarchical and is a high latency network model.

In this chapter we explore applications that are short-range enabled by multihop communication that exploit the localized nature of information generation and consumption. Observations and analysis highlight the fragmented nature of vehicular connectivity and the potential challenges in enabling vehicular networking. We describe some of the proposed solutions for applications that are localized in nature, especially those where data are generated and consumed in a neighborhood of vehicles connected by multiple hops. We demonstrate that opportunistic contacts in vehicular networks can very well be used to instantiate and sustain certain applications with reasonable assumptions. We summarize the novel concepts of delay tolerant networking (DTN), a connectionless messaging paradigm utilizing opportunistic contacts and intermittent connectivity to forward data.

State of the Art

Core objectives of several organizations such as the NHTSA (National Highway Traffic Safety

Administration) are to reduce road fatalities by improving road awareness of the traveler, reducing driver error and increasing reaction time. Research in vehicular technology deals with developing new means of improving safety of travelers on city and highway roads. Chief among these efforts is the development of safety norms in design of vehicles to protect occupants and fellow travelers in the event of an impact – a reactive approach (Car 2 Car Communication Consortium). A more recent approach to enhance safety – the proactive one – is to equip vehicles with sensors that warn drivers to prevent impacts. Examples of such technologies under development include proximity sensors that aid the braking process by maintaining a safe distance and speed with respect to the vehicle in front. Other technologies under development include visual aids in the form of cameras and in-car display systems to aid viewing in difficult corners of the vehicles. Developments in the area of vehicular safety seek also to network vehicles to enable them to share data from neighboring vehicles to assist the vehicle control systems proactively prevent accidents. Notable are the efforts by consortium comprising of government organizations, universities and industrial groups leading efforts to develop standards for inter-vehicle communication. DSRC or Dedicated Short Range Communications is one such body formed to develop protocols for inter-vehicle communication (Xu, Mak, Sengupta, & Ko, 2004). There is a rush to develop vehicular communications and networking applications. The IEEE WAVE (Wireless Access for Vehicular Environments) is an effort to develop standards and protocols for inter-vehicle communication (Berger, 2007). The consortium combines the efforts of government organizations, universities and industrial groups towards the development of dedicated short-range communications band at 5.9 GHz. The primary motivation is safety messaging. The DARPA Urban Challenge is a research and development program with the goal of developing technology that will enable autonomous ground vehicles maneuvering in a mock city environment, executing simulated military supply missions (Grossman, 2008). The vehicles are expected to perform actions such as merging into moving traffic, navigating traffic circles, negotiating busy intersections, and avoiding obstacles. The challenge showcases developments in robotics and vehicle control systems that will eventually be incorporated in production vehicles.

VEHICULAR NETWORKING ENVIRONMENT

The large expanses of the roadway network and vehicle population present a challenge to enable networking. Several models and architectures have been presented in related research for interconnecting vehicles. We focus on models that are implemented by short-range localized communication and study factors such as vehicular mobility, vehicular traffic density, communication range and the nature and scope of data exchange that influence the performance of messaging in the context of opportunistic and ad hoc communication.

Application Scenario: Nature and Scope of Data Exchange

Applications in the vehicular networking space are broadly classified into three categories on the basis of their operation characteristics and scope (Agarwal & Little, Prospects for Networked Vehicles of the Future, 2007). First, applications that actively or proactively enhance safety of vehicles are classified as *safety messaging*. These applications are near-space applications where vehicles in close proximity, of the order of few hundred meters, exchange status information to increase awareness and safety. The goal for data exchange is to enable vehicles with enhanced safety systems to react timely to emergency conditions and avert accidents. A requirement of such applications is strict latency constraints, of the order of few

Figure 1. Three classifications of data exchange in vehicular networks

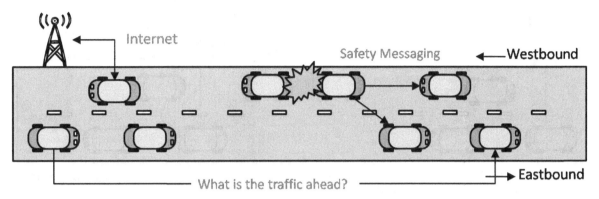

milliseconds, due to the time-critical nature of data. An example is active braking in the car-following model on the roadway. When a vehicle applies brakes due to an emergency condition, the information is broadcast to vehicles that are following (Figure 1). The vehicles are able to react proactively and avoid a collision. The broadcast information should be received faster than the human reaction time to visualize the condition and apply brakes manually for such a system to be productive.

Second, *traffic and congestion monitoring* require collecting information from many vehicles that span multiple kilometers. The goal of applications is to collect data from multiple sources on the roadway to estimate the traffic behavior. While the data are essential for trip planning, the latency requirements are relatively relaxed and the applications can be characterized as 'delay tolerant'. Such applications are *spatio-temporal* in nature. Data, such as traffic statistics, are collected over a section of the roadway and are useful to vehicles that are approaching that roadway but are some distance, say 5 miles, away at the time. The data are valid for a limited time interval, i.e. the data expire and new data collected are shared. For example, notification of heavy traffic on a certain section of the roadway is relevant only to vehicles approaching that section and valid only until the traffic situation eases. Thus, it is possible

to exploit the space-time relationship of vehicles and data to enable data forwarding in the network.

Finally, the third type of data is general purpose *Internet access* in which vehicles are connected to a backbone network. Applications such as Internet access, video streaming, and voice based applications that require constant connectivity to the network are classified into this category. The three broad classifications are illustrated in Figure 1.

Network Architecture

There are three primary models for interconnecting vehicles (we do not consider a satellite-based model here). One architecture is an infrastructure-based solution in which vehicles connect to a centralized server or a backbone network such as the Internet, with the help of road-side infrastructure such as cell-phone towers, WiMax, or 802.11 access points, as illustrated in Figure 2. The infrastructure is able to 'manage' the network and provides connectivity to the backbone network (Internet). However, the roundtrip delays for data are potentially high, of mixed reliability and therefore, unsuitable for safety applications. Connectivity in this model is subject to availability of infrastructure and often such solutions are cost intensive.

Another solution proposes to exploit multihop connectivity and form an ad hoc network over mov-

Figure 2. An infrastructure-based solution for data dissemination

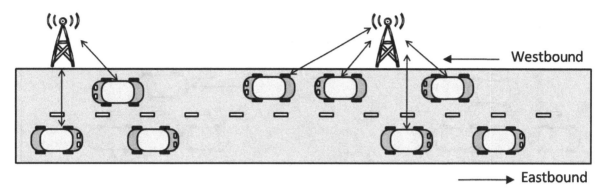

Figure 3. An illustration depicting an ad hoc model with multihop connectivity

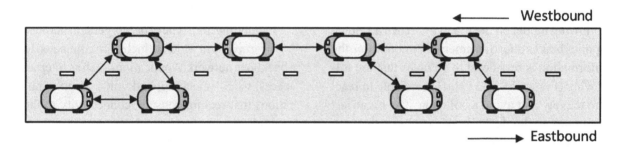

ing vehicles, illustrated in Figure 3. The vehicle-to-vehicle communication at a short space can have minimal delay and this architecture is well suited for safety applications. However, connectivity in this model is subject to prevailing traffic conditions under the assumption of short-range radio communication. Daytime traffic is likely to be sufficiently dense while night-time traffic is likely to be sparse. Furthermore, vehicular mobility can be difficult to predict. Individual vehicles may leave or join a highway at random. Thus, end-to-end connectivity is hard to achieve for low density and random departure scenarios. For short-range communication, the connectivity in this model is subject to prevailing traffic conditions.. Complex solutions are required to manage the network in the absence of a centralized authority.

The third architectural solution is a hybrid network that proposes to use a combination of the two schemes. Vehicles connect to roadside infrastructure directly when in range and exploit multihop connectivity otherwise. The infrastructure is assumed to be placed intermittently in the network such that vehicles are not always connected directly. However, the vehicles are able to exploit multihop communication and achieve connectivity. The infrastructure is assumed connected to the backbone network (Internet), thereby providing suitable connectivity for applications.

Mobility Scenarios

There are two predominant models used for modeling vehicular mobility and conducting analysis for network connectivity and application testing. The first is the *highway model* characterized by bidirectional linear roadway on which vehicles are assumed to consistently travel for long periods.

Figure 4. Vehicles in an urban grid ("Manhattan model")

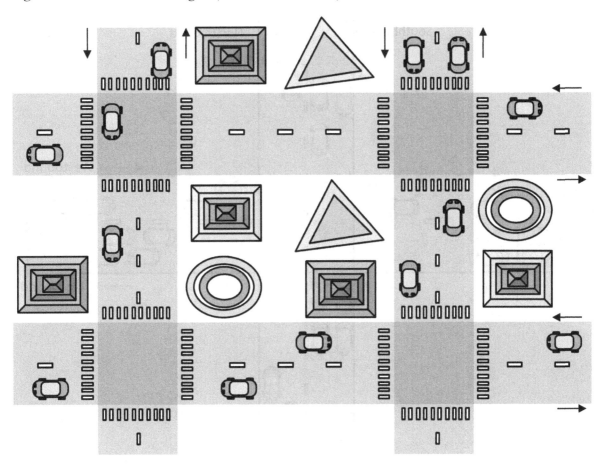

Vehicle mobility rates are often assumed to be as high as 20 m/s, road and traffic conditions permitting. The other popular model is the "***Manhattan model***" of mobility, (Bai, Sadagopan, & Helmy, 2003) in which vehicles exist in an urban setting comprised of a grid, illustrated in Figure 4. Vehicular motion is relatively slow and often random considering turns and one-way streets. Vehicular traffic density is high due to higher population density. In contrast, the highway model, Figure 5, is relatively sparse with higher mobility rates and fewer intersecting routes. The mobility patterns of the two models are somewhat different and influence the connectivity, node mobility and hence, the design of routing models, protocols and application functionality. Recent work has focused on developing map-based models for simulating vehicular mobility and traffic conditions (Mangharam, Weller, Stencil, Rajkumar, & Parekh, 2005). The model projects mobile nodes on a realistic roadway map of a region and enables model validation for protocols. While the model provides an accurate projection of a geographic area, it is difficult to develop generalized concepts for connectivity analysis and routing models.

Vehicular Traffic Density

Vehicle traffic has been studied in great detail in road traffic analysis. Microscopic studies involve behavioral analysis of each vehicle. However, from a computer network perspective the micro-

Figure 5. Vehicles traveling on intersecting highways

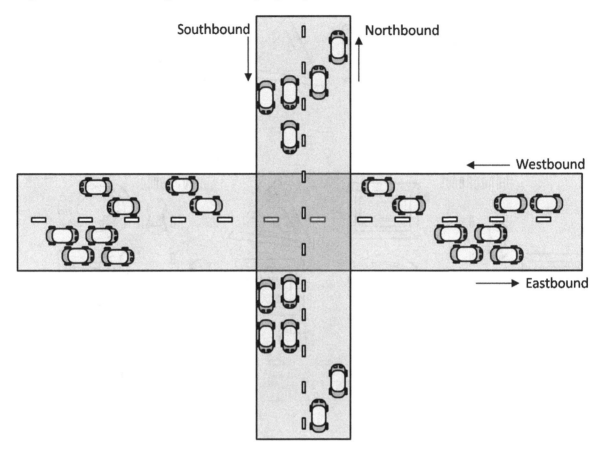

scopic models of vehicle traffic are less relevant. The transmission range for radio connectivity is of the order of a few 100 meters. Microscopic changes in vehicle position of the order of a few meters are less significant when considering radio connectivity. At a macroscopic level, vehicular traffic is interesting in that it varies significantly in quantity depending upon the time of the day and the location. Mornings and evenings are usually times of heavy traffic density ("rush hour") and can have congestion. At off-peak times (e.g., night-time), roadways can be empty. Urban areas yield high density scenarios of slow moving traffic while rural areas have relatively sparse population of vehicles. A network formed

over moving vehicles is a function of the vehicle traffic density and the physical radio model. The node density of a network is an important property that determines several characteristics such as connectivity that ultimately determines the performance of the network. Crucially, in a vehicular networking environment, the density is a varying quantity and not necessarily consistent throughout the network of roadways. As the traffic density varies from extremes of sparse to dense conditions, the requirement is of a messaging paradigm that enables functionality irrespective. Through the remaining sections, it will be evident that density plays a significant role in the design of an efficient network model.

OPPORTUNISTIC NETWORKING

Interconnecting vehicles with communications technology ("networking" vehicles) presents new challenges. Based on aforementioned scenarios, we characterize the network conditions mathematically. Vehicles travel at speeds ranging from 30 km/h to 120 km/h. Considering short range communication capability for vehicles traveling on the roadway in a highway setting, the connectivity graph of the network changes at a fast rate, compared to MANET models such as human mobility in urban environments. Here, the connectivity graph is described as a graph where the vehicles form vertices and the paths are defined by the short-range communication. We analyze connectivity over time with snapshots of the graph. A time-varying traffic density implies a scenario in which there is lack of end-to-end connectivity between vehicles on the highway. Thus, in networking terminology, the network becomes partitioned. As vehicles traverse on a bidirectional roadway, vehicles come in contact for a short duration with other vehicles traveling in opposite, or sometimes perpendicular directions. This short-lived, opportunistic connectivity can be utilized to exchange data. Thus, the partitioning in the network is time varying in nature as vehicles traverse the road network and come in intermittent contact with other vehicles. This time-varying partitioning is called network *fragmentation* (Little & Agarwal, 2005).

We demonstrate that the opportunistic connectivity offered by vehicles traveling in different directions is sufficient to bridge the partitions that exist in the network, under certain conditions. Importantly, we characterize the performance of messaging in a *fragmented* network under the assumption of delay tolerant networking, radio characteristics and vehicular traffic. Finally, we describe solutions based on opportunistic networking that exploit opportunistic connectivity and enable messaging in a *fragmented* environment.

Vehicle Density, Connectivity and Fragmentation

Vehicle density is a time-varying quantity that is inconsistent through the network of roadways. A macroscopic observation of density shows that it varies with time of day and location. Traffic can be congested (high), medium or sparse ranging from more than 100 vehicles/km to 40–60 vehicles/km to less than 25 vehicles/km, respectively. Typically, mornings and evenings experience heavy traffic volume while at the other extreme during night-time, traffic is extremely sparse. Under a simple model of exponential distribution of traffic, each node traveling on a roadway passes other unique vehicles on the other side of the roadway. The number of unique nodes encountered by a stationary observer on the highway can be computed using Little's Law, (Bertsekas & Gallager, 1987), as follows:

$$N = \lambda T,$$

where N is the number of vehicles, λ is the arrival rate and T is the time spent on the roadway. Thus, the number of potential encounters increases linearly with time and traffic density.

Connectivity in a VANET can be characterized by a time-varying graph model. Under the assumption of a fixed radius model for the radio, vehicles traveling in the same direction are connected to each other given their separation is less than radio range R. Assuming exponentially distributed inter-vehicle distances, we can show that vehicles traveling in the same direction are likely to be disconnected. The probability that two consecutive vehicles are disconnected is given by:

$$P\{X > R\} e^{-\lambda R} \neq 0$$

where X is the inter-vehicle distance, λ is the distribution parameter and R is the radio range. The probability of connectivity is, thus, a function of the vehicle traffic density (λ) and the radio range

Figure 6. Probability of node connectivity varies as the vehicle traffic density, for various values of communication range

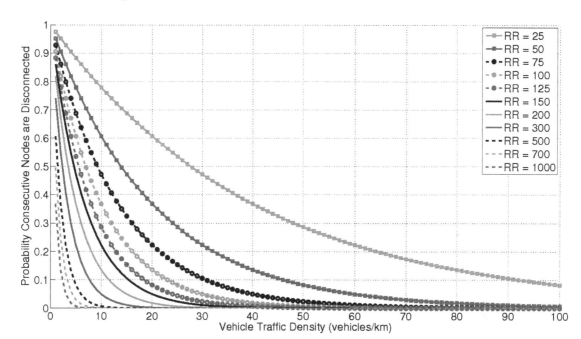

Figure 7. Vehicles form disconnected sub-nets on the roadway

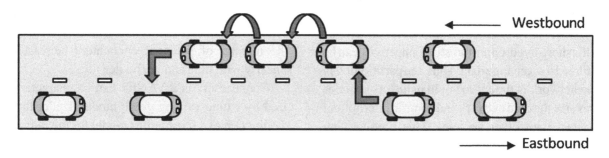

(*R*). Figure 6 shows the progression of connectivity as the density ranges from 0 vehicle/km to a 100 vehicles/km, for different values radio range parameter (*R*). It is evident from the graph that as the vehicle traffic density increases the probability that nodes are disconnected decreases. Similarly, for the same value of vehicle traffic, it is intuitive that nodes are disconnected with increasing probability as the radio range decreases. However, it is significant to note that there is always a non-zero

probability that nodes are disconnected. A routing scheme that relies on a path formation strategy will likely fail due to the absence of end-to-end path connectivity. Thus, it is important to consider these factors when considering design of a routing mechanism as the source-destination pairs are potentially separated by large distances.

It has been shown in related work by statistical observation of vehicles traveling on the highway that vehicles are partitioned (Naumov, Baumann,

& Gross, 2006), (Fussler, Mauve, Hartenstein, Vollmer, & Kasemann, 2003). A time-series snapshot of the highway demonstrates that vehicles tend to travel in small clusters that are disconnected in terms of radio connectivity. This is a classic fragmentation that in network terminology would be deemed a highly partitioned network. The connectivity graph formed by vehicles can be described as a partition yielding multiple disconnected subnets, as illustrated in Figure 7.

Formation of an end-to-end path over large distances is difficult if not impossible. Thus, MANET (Mobile Ad hoc Network) routing schemes that rely on path-formation strategies are a poor solution. If nodes traveling in opposing direction are used in path formation, the resulting paths are short-lived, leading to considerable overhead in path formation and route maintenance.

The clusters formed in one direction of the highway come in intermittent contact with clusters of vehicles traveling in the opposite direction. Thus, the partitioning in the network is time varying as vehicle mobility leads to changing topologies. The opportunistic contacts can be exploited to bridge the partitioning that exists between clusters traveling in the same direction of the roadway.

Delay Tolerant Networking

End-to-end connectivity is hard to achieve for large distances as time varying topology and partitioning lead to a fragmented network. A store-carry-forward approach based on Delay Tolerant Networking (DTN) (Fall, 2003) has been proposed to exploit intermittent connectivity to enable data propagation. A DTN is a connection-less messaging paradigm where instantaneous end-to-end connectivity is assumed unavailable. The common assumption is that data are cached within a node's memory, when nodes are disconnected, until transient connectivity to the next hop is available. Delay tolerant networking has been explored for application in inter-satellite space

communications, wildlife sensor networks and cellular networks.

In the VANET context, we apply the concepts of delay tolerant networking to facilitate data propagation through intermittent contacts. Messages are propagated multi-hop when connectivity is available. In the absence of connectivity, messages are buffered in the nodes until connectivity is achieved. A routing algorithm and protocol has been proposed in related work, (Little & Agarwal, 2005). The protocol is essentially a geographic routing protocol that uses attributed data and the spatial-temporal relationship to achieve directed propagation over nodes traveling in orthogonal directions. The protocol is able to exploit the paths that exist in a short space for a limited time to opportunistically forward data over several subnets.

Figure 8 illustrates scenario in which two nodes are disconnected at a time instant. As the network topology changes with vehicular mobility, an opportunistic path exists between previously disconnected nodes. Data are forwarded in a greedy manner to exploit the short-lived path. This model can be repeated over multiple subnets that exist through the network to achieve data propagation. It is possible that a routing scheme based on path formation would fail due to the absence of an end-to-end path between source and destination pairs that are located in distant subnets. The protocol described in reference (Little & Agarwal, 2005) utilizes a combination of space and time limits to achieve directed, yet constrained dissemination of data.

A delay in message propagation is introduced at each hop when instantaneous connectivity to the next hop is unavailable. The data propagation rate is computed as an average over time. It is essential to characterize the time period for which data are buffered in a node. The time period until connectivity is achieved can be expressed as the classical *pattern-matching* problem, (Ross, 2004). The pattern-matching problem is defined as finding the expected number of trials until n consecutive occurrences are observed, given that

Figure 8. Vehicles communicate when connectivity is achieved

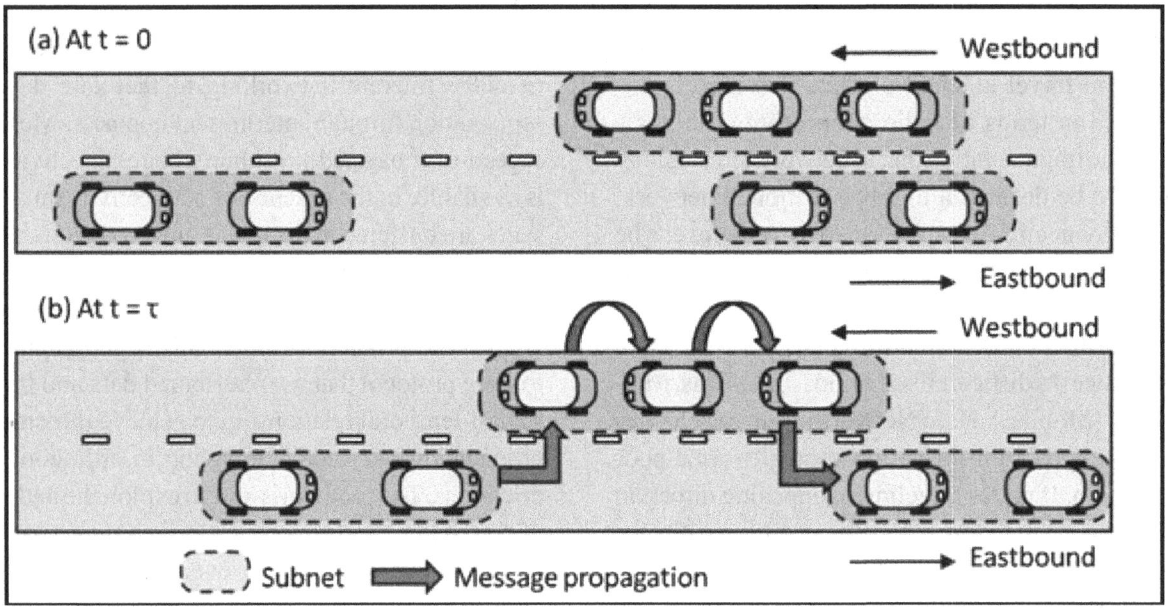

each occurrence has probability p. For example, a coin toss yields *heads* or *tails* each with probability 1/2. The pattern matching would define the task of finding the number of coin tosses required to observe n consecutive heads. Mathematically, the expected number of trials (N) until n consecutive events are observed is expressed as:

$$E[N] = \frac{1 - p^n}{(1 - p)p^n}$$

where p is the probability of success for a single event. For bridging network partitions in VANETs, we apply pattern matching to compute the expected distance traversed until a connected subnet is observed in the opposite direction that is sufficient to bridge the partition. It is important here to note that the traffic in the opposing direction is also likely to be partitioned and hence, may not sufficiently connect always. Thus, the data are buffered until the connectivity is achieved. The time delay until connectivity and the distance traversed are required to compute the performance

of the messaging. We utilize the analogy to find an approximation on the time and distance until partition between consecutive subnets is bridged under the assumption of bidirectional traffic, constant vehicle speed and radio range (R).

Message Propagation Rate

Analytical bounds for message propagation rate have been derived in previous work (Agarwal, Starobinski, & Little, Exploiting Downstream Mobility to Achieve Fast Upstream Propagation, 2007), (Agarwal, Starobinski, & Little, Analytical Model for Message Propagation in Vehicular Ad Hoc Networks, 2008). The message propagation rate is defined as the physical distance covered by the message in unit time similar to vehicle speed. This is logical as the source-destination pairs in the network are spatially distributed. The analytical computation is a function of vehicle traffic density, vehicle speed and physical radio characteristics. The message propagation takes place in two distinct phases. In phase 1 of the message propagation, two consecutive nodes are

Figure 9. Comparing average message propagation rates of end-to-end connectivity scheme with that of a delay tolerant network model for a fixed distance of 12.5 km

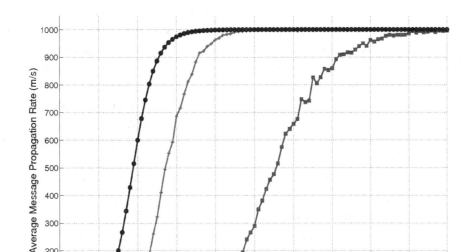

disconnected. The data are buffered in a node's memory, and the vehicle traverses a physical distance. The vehicle speed (v) is assumed to be constant for the highway, equivalent to 20 m/s. In phase 2 of the message propagation, the previously disconnected nodes are opportunistically connected multi-hop by traffic in the opposing direction. Hence, once connectivity is achieved the messages are able to propagate over connected clusters at a very fast rate as defined by the radio. We define this as the radio speed (v_{radio}). In our analysis, we assume the radio speed equivalent to 1000 m/s. It is approximated as the distance covered in a single hop, equal to the radio range (R), divided by the time taken including delays. Thus, as the messages propagate over nodes of a network with time varying connectivity, the messaging rate alternates between the two distinct phases. We analytically compute the expected time spent in each of the two phases of transmission. The message propagation is described as an *alternating renewal process*, (Ross, 2004), and

the resultant is a function of time spent in the two phases. Analytically,

$$V_{eff} = \frac{E[T_1]v + E[T_2]v_{radio}}{E[T_1] + E[T_2]}$$

where V_{eff} is the effective message propagation rate, $E[T_1]$, $E[T_2]$ are the times spent in phase 1 and phase 2 respectively, 'v' is the vehicle speed and 'v_{radio}' is the propagation rate over each hop as defined by the radio.

We compare the performance of the proposed mechanism with the performance of routing schemes based on end-to-end connectivity. End-to-end connectivity is achieved either over one direction of traffic or over bidirectional traffic. The results presented in Figure 9 compare the effective propagation rate as the vehicle traffic density increases for a source-destination pair 12.5 km apart. The propagation rate is equivalent to vehicle speed (20 m/s) for low densities as the network is largely disconnected and no gains are achieved from multihop. However, as densities increase, the network is increasingly connected, on average, and messages are propagated multihop, at radio speed (1000 m/s) as defined by the physical radio characteristics. The results indicate that for the message propagation rate, a phase transition phenomenon is observed, where the network is mostly disconnected for low density scenarios and is, almost surely, fully connected for high density scenarios. The interesting aspect of this result is the density at which these phenomena are observed. For end-to-end connectivity over unidirectional traffic, the network, on average, achieves maximum rate at density value 90 vehicles/km. For bidirectional connectivity, the requirement is for a lower density value of 45 vehicles/km as traffic on either side of the roadway is utilized for connectivity. The DTN scheme, however, shows the same performance for a much lower density value of 30 vehicles/km as it exploits the short-lived contacts for

message propagation. This demonstrates that we are able to exploit the opportunistic contacts between nodes in traveling in opposing direction to bridge partitions and enable message propagation. Moreover, the opportunistic networking is able to achieve the maximum performance even when the network is not fully connected, by virtue of the time-varying partitioning.

Significantly, these density requirements remain the same as the distance between the source-destination pair increases to 30 Km, as shown in Figure 10. While the end-to-end connectivity based schemes require considerably larger node densities, the DTN scheme performance is the same irrespective of the source-destination separation. This proves our hypothesis that end-to-end connectivity schemes perform poorly over large spatial separations of source-destination pairs in the VANET context. Thus, our routing mechanism that exploits opportunistic connectivity between nodes is a solution that performs well for low, medium and high-density scenarios.

Figure 10. Comparing average message propagation rates of end-to-end connectivity scheme with that of a delay tolerant network model for a fixed distance of 30 km

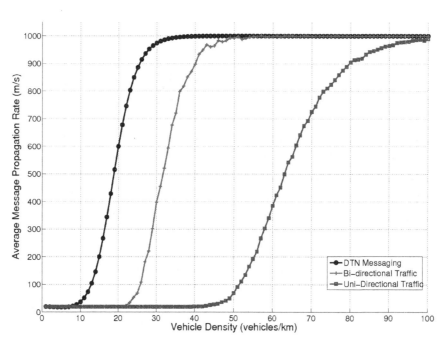

In Figure 11, we show the effect of increased vehicle speed on the performance of messaging. We consider a hypothetical scenario where vehicle speed increases from 0 m/s to 100 m/s and observe the performance at a fixed density. The results show that increased vehicle speed actually aids in messaging performance. At a density of 15 vehicles/km an increase in vehicle speed from 0 m/s to 20 m/s yields an order of magnitude in messaging performance from 0 m/s to 200 m/s. This is contrary to the expectation that increased mobility increases the rate of topology change and hence, decreases the messaging performance. Here, we observe that increased mobility rate significantly increases the rate at which the partitioning is bridged and thus, achieves higher message propagation rates. This further supports our claim to exploit the opportunistic connectivity between nodes traveling in orthogonal directions to aid message propagation in vehicular networks. This resultant is consistent with related work in delay tolerant networks which claim that a partitioned network is connected by exploiting the space-time paths in the network as density and mobility in the network as time progresses, (Merugu, Ammar, & Zegura, 2004). This behavior is also observed in epidemic models for routing data, spread of diseases, news, etc. In our result, we are able to exploit the high rate of mobility of vehicles to further the message propagation goal.

APPLICATION SCENARIOS

We classified the nature of applications broadly in our introduction to the vehicular networking environment. We highlighted the spatial temporal correlation of data in the network formed over moving vehicles and finally demonstrated the ability to exploit opportunistic connectivity between nodes to enable message propagation. We now describe the role of opportunistic connectivity in each of the application scenarios.

Figure 11. Impact of increasing vehicular traffic density on effective propagation rate for various values of vehicular speed

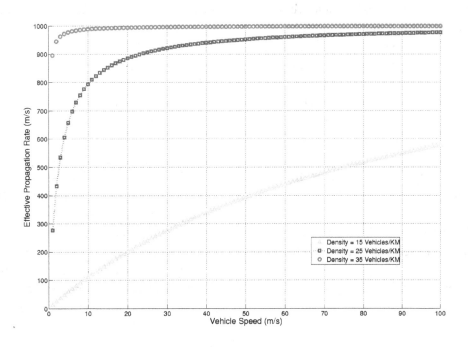

Information Warning Functions

The most important application of enabling inter-vehicle communication is to provide greater safety for travelers on roads. The goal is to share information amongst neighboring vehicles such that the traveler is aware of conditions prevailing in regions beyond the line of sight. An example is the case where "pile-ups" occur on highways. It is often observed that accidents occurring on roads have a ripple effect on approaching vehicles. Such situations can be averted by disseminating vehicle speed and braking information to vehicles in pursuit. A vehicle approaching a point of accident can be alerted earlier and approach the region with caution and at safe speeds.

Vehicles are increasingly equipped with advanced sensors that can detect various road conditions. Range sensors that use radar technology are used to warn vehicles of close proximity to the vehicle in front. These are coupled with active braking systems and pre-tensioner seat belts to avoid collisions and improve passenger safety in the event of a crash. Technologies under development include lane departure warnings that detect a vehicle drifting outside its current traveling lane and into the path of other vehicles. Although these technologies are working on a single element of the system, i.e., an individual vehicle, safety of the surrounding environment can be sufficiently enhanced by sharing this information with surrounding vehicles. Highlighted below are instances where exchanging safety critical information is important –

- Lane merging/ lane change at highway intersections.
- Blind spots in vehicles.
- Hidden driveway collision warning.
- Adaptive cruise control and co-operative driving.
- Roadway condition awareness.

In the event that an accident occurs, the task for the network is to alert the approaching vehicles of the accident. At the same time, the vehicles are expected to pass the accident event to the nearest police and ambulance to aid the victims of the accident. The timely reaction of medical team is crucial to saving lives. In the event of a catastrophe such as hurricanes, floods or fires, the same network can be used to co-ordinate and control evacuation procedures. It is important to note that the vehicles that interact in these scenarios connect to each other opportunistically and potentially in ad hoc manner.

Traffic Information Services

Traffic related information is essential to compute travel time estimates. Efforts to provide traffic related information in recent times include web-cameras that help determine traffic situations on major highways or in urban areas. Magnetic loop installations have been used to determine the traffic rates and densities on roads. Traffic control centers monitor and control traffic with the help of web cameras. However, the systems described are latent and do not relay active information to the traveler on the road. A distributed automated system can be devised with networked vehicles and traffic lights that is more efficient and proactive than a centralized control system. With the help of inter-vehicle communication, active systems can potentially be developed to relay updated and accurate information on travel estimates. Coupled with GPS systems, the traveler can get information about traffic on specific routes, occurrence of accidents, tolls, road works, etc. Armed with this information, alternate routes can be planned thereby saving travel time. Savings could be further extrapolated to fuel and emissions saved in idling vehicles stuck in traffic. Certain highways use large sign-boards to warn travelers of heavy traffic, but such information cannot be fully exploited unless an alternate route is proposed.

That is where the map-based GPS systems can be employed to map alternate routes and determine travel time on those routes to save time. Often sections of roadways are under repair thereby increasing travel time. Additionally, detour paths can be guided by wireless beacons where map-based information is not available to the road user.

The vast distributed network of vehicles equipped with sensors provides real-time data for transportation research applications. Data collected from roadside observation can be an automated task that reveals traffic flow characteristics and road usage data. Lane charging or fee-based usage of special high-speed lanes on highways is a concept proposed to ease congestion and generate revenue to support highways. Toll collection and booth management are applications aimed at easing congestion on sections of the highways and ensuring smooth travel.

Smart Traveler Services

Vehicles in the network are highly mobile elements that traverse predictable paths and can be exploited as 'messengers' in the network. An interesting application would be 'hailing taxi cabs'. The general norm is to flag one down as it passes and hope that it is empty. At the same time, taxi cab drivers drive around a city hoping to find customers. In the process, precious fuel is wasted while people hoping to find a cab often have to wait long to find a cab sometimes in harsh weather. A clever application is the ability to raise a flag on one's mobile phone indicating the requirement for a taxi. The request could be forwarded by networked vehicles in the region and the taxi-cab nearest can respond to the request. This application could be extended to public transport such as buses and subways where people can know the time interval until the next arrival, while the Mass Transit Authorities can be alerted of traffic on various routes. It can be used to devise efficient means of allocating resources such as buses on busy routes.

A great application proposed in (Basu & Little, 2004) is the development of smart parking meters to determine the availability of parking spots in an urban setting. Parking meters can be networked with vehicles to relay information about available spaces to approaching cars which in turn would save time and fuel for the traveler. At the same time it would be a useful tool for securing revenue for the city as the meter can monitor the precise time for which the parking space was utilized.

A legacy wireless radio standard called the Citizens Band Radio has been popular in North America. It is a voice band protocol in the unlicensed spectrum that allows open channel communication between people in a short range (kilometers). It has been used by fleet companies to facilitate inter-vehicle communications. Such voice applications could also be supported on vehicular networks. With networking capability, fleet management and cargo services can be extended to increase efficiency and service. Vehicles are being made smarter in that they are able to predict and warn users of mechanical faults and service-check requirements. In the event that a vehicle breaks down on an isolated road, the networked-vehicle can self-diagnose the problem, call for assistance from the nearest mechanic with right spare parts to fix the fault.

Providing general Internet access to networked vehicle has several benefits. GPS systems already provide information about gas stations, ATMs, stores etc. However, the information provided is pre-stored and not updated regularly. With Internet access updated information including enhanced details such as timings, phone numbers and special offers from stores could be provided. This would allow stores to execute road-side marketing campaigns to promote business. An example is food outlets on highways can market special packages for off-peak hours, thereby attracting customer traffic. Internet access is also a very useful distraction for fellow passengers especially children. The ability to access Internet while on the move is very desirable for young netizens and the Internet offers several activities such as movies, social networking, music, chatting, etc.

CONCLUSION

Vehicular area networking is an emerging and exciting field of research that presents unique challenges. In this chapter, we provide an overview of various solutions to enable networking among vehicles on the roadway. We have described the contrasting scenarios that exist with respect to the physical conditions in the network, such as time varying vehicular traffic densities and the absence of deployed infrastructure. We concentrate our efforts on a solution based on short-range communications and demonstrate that under reasonable assumptions it is feasible to exploit the time varying partitioning in the network to forward data opportunistically. We describe techniques such as delay tolerant networking and attributed routing that enable message propagation. The message propagation rate shows a continuous phase transition behavior with respect to vehicular traffic density. The critical density for phase transition is lower under the delay tolerant networking assumption. This result strengthens our argument that exploiting opportunistic paths achieves better performance under assumptions of traffic density. Finally, we describe application scenarios that are able to exploit this opportunistic connectivity. An extension of this work is a model for placement of road-side infrastructure that supports vehicular networking. The goal for is to optimize the placement of access points on the roadway and exploit multihop connectivity over vehicles while maintaining quality of service.

ACKNOWLEDGMENT

This material is based upon work supported by the National Science Foundation under Grant Nos. CNS-0721884 and EEC-0812056. Any opinions, findings and conclusions or recommendations expressed in this material are those of the author(s) and do not necessarily reflect the views of the National Science Foundation (NSF).

REFERENCES

Agarwal, A., & Little, T. D. (2007). Prospects for Networked Vehicles of the Future. In *Proceedings of the Smart Transportation Workshop in IEEE Real-Time Embedded Technology and Applications Symposium (RTAS)*. Bellevue, WA: IEEE Press.

Agarwal, A., Starobinski, D., & Little, T. D. (2007). Exploiting Downstream Mobility to Achieve Fast Upstream Propagation. In *Proceedings of Mobile Networking for Vehicular Environments (MOVE) at IEEE INFOCOM '07*. AK: Anchorage.

Agarwal, A., Starobinski, D., & Little, T. D. (2008). Analytical Model for Message Propagation in Vehicular Ad Hoc Networks. In *Proceedings of the IEEE Vehicualr Technology Conference (VTC-Spring '08)*. Singapore: IEEE Press.

Basu, P., & Little, T. D. (2004). *Wireless Ad Hoc Discovery of Parking Spaces*. Boston, MA: MobiSys.

Berger, I. (2007, March). Standards for Car Talk. *The Institute*.

Bertsekas, D., & Gallager, R. (1987). *Data Networks*. Upper Saddle River, NJ: Prentice Hall Inc.

Briesemeister, L., & Hommel, G. (2000). Role-based Multicast in Highly Mobile But Sparsely Connected Ad Hoc Netwokrs. In *Proceedings of the First ACM International Symposium on Mobile Ad hoc Networking and Computing (MobiHoc '00)* (pp. 45-50). Boston, MA: IEEE Press.

Car 2 Car (n.d.). *Car 2 Car Communication Consortium*. Retrieved September 2007, from http://www.car-2-car.org

Fall, K. (2003). A Delay Tolerant Network Architecture for Challenged Internets. In [New York: ACM Press.]. *Proceedings of SIGCOMM, 03*, 27–34.

Fussler, H., Mauve, M., Hartenstein, H., Vollmer, D., & Kasemann, M. (2003). *Location Based Routing for Vehicular Ad Hoc Networks. ACM SIGMOBILE Mobile computing and Communication Review* (pp. 47–49). New York: ACM.

Grossman, L. (n.d.). *Building the Best Driverless Robot Car*. Retrieved March 2008, from http://www.time.com/time/magazine/article/0,9171,1684543,00.html

Little, T. D., & Agarwal, A. (2005). An Information Propagation Scheme for Vehicular Networks. In *Proceedings of IEEE Intelligent Transportation Systems Conference (ITSC)* (pp. 155-160). Vienna, Austria: IEEE.

Mangharam, R., Weller, D. S., Stencil, D. D., Rajkumar, R., & Parekh, J. S. (2005). GROOVESIM: A Topography-Accurate Simulator for Geographic Routing in Vehicular Networks. In *Proceedings of the Second ACM International Workshop on Vehicular Ad Hoc Networks (VANET '05)* (pp. 59-68). New York: ACM Press.

Merugu, S., Ammar, M., & Zegura, E. (2004). *Space-Time Routing in Wireless Networks with Preictable Mobility*. College of Computing, Georgia Institute of Technology, Technical (Report GIT-CC-04-07). Atlanta, GA.

Naumov, V., Baumann, R., & Gross, T. (2006). An Evaluation of Inter-Vehicle Ad Hoc Networks Based on Realistic Vehicular Traces. In *Proceedings of the Seventh ACM International Symposium on Mobile Ad Hoc Netowkring and Computing (MobiHoc '06)* (pp. 108-119). Florence, Italy.

Ross, S. M. (2004). *Introduction to Probability Models*. New York: Academic Press.

Xu, Q., Mak, T., Sengupta, R., & Ko, J. (2004). Vehicle-to-Vehicle Safety Messaging in DSRC. In *Proceedings of the First Workshop on Vehicular Ad Hoc Networks* (pp. 19-28). New York: ACM Press.

Zhao, W., & Ammar, M. H. (2003). Message Ferrying: Proactive Routing in Highly-Partitioned Wireless Ad Hoc Networks. In *Proceedings of the Ninth IEEE Workshop on Future Trends of Distributed Computing Systems (FTDCS '03)* (pp. 308-314). San Juan, Puerto Rico.

ADDITIONAL READING

Bai, F., Sadagopan, N., & Helmy, A. (2003, November). The IMPORTANT framework for analyzing the Impact of Mobility on Performance Of RouTing protocols for Adhoc NeTworks. *Ad Hoc Networks, 1*(4), 383–403. doi:10.1016/S1570-8705(03)00040-4

Farkas, K. I. (2006). Vehicular Communication. [IEEE Press.]. *IEEE Pervasive Computing / IEEE Computer Society [and] IEEE Communications Society*, 55–62. doi:10.1109/MPRV.2006.90

Information Superhighway Hits The Road. (2007, February). *Information Superhighway Hits The Road*. Retrieved February 2007, from http://www.boston.com/cars/news/articles/2007/02/18/information superhighway hits the road

Little, T. D., & Agarwal, A. (2008). Connecting Vehicles to 'The Grid'. *Proc. NITRD National Workshop on High-Confidence Automotive Cyber-Physical Systems*. Detroit, MI.

Nadeem, T., Shankar, P., & Iftode, L. (2006). A Comparative Study of Data Dissemination Models for VANETs. *Third Annual International Conferece on Mobile and Ubiquitous Systems (MOBIQUITOUS '06)*, (pp. 1-10). San Jose, CA.

National Highway Traffic Safety Administration. (n.d.). *National Highway Traffic Safety Administration*. Retrieved February 2007, from http://www.nhtsa.dot.gov

Wu, H., Fujimoto, R., Guensler, R., & Hunter, M. (2004). MDDV: A Mobility-Centric Data Dissemination Algorithm for Vehicular Networks. *Proceedings of the First ACM International Workshop on Vehicular Ad Hoc Networks (VANET '04)*, (pp. 47-56). New York: ACM Press.

Chapter 15
Adaptive Solutions in Multihop Communication Protocols for Vehicular Ad Hoc Networks

Carlos Caloca
CICESE Research Center, Mexico, and University of Lille-North of France, France

Thierry Delot
University of Lille-North of France, France

J. Antonio Garcia Macias
CICESE Research Center, Mexico

ABSTRACT

The potential for vehicular applications is rapidly increasing. However this variety also demands a flexible multihop communication protocol supporting different communications needs and adapting to the network environment and to context elements specified by the application itself. We think that adaptive solutions, recently starting to be applied to VANET routing and dissemination protocols, have a great potential for solving the problems stated above. The objective of this chapter is to introduce the reader to these kinds of solutions, show their benefits and also mention the challenges involved. Because one important aspect of adaptive solutions (in this case a common communication protocol for all applications), is having in-depth knowledge of the problem to solve, we first review these different vehicular applications and their classification, followed by their communication needs.

INTRODUCTION

Starting with the idea of providing safer driving by using inter-vehicle communication, the concept of vehicular ad hoc networks (VANETs) has been extended to support various applications, which can benefit from wireless short range communication (e.g. IEEE 802.11 standards) between vehicles.

Today, VANET applications range from simple exchanges of data describing the vehicle status, to highly complex, large-scale traffic management including the integration of fixed infrastructure. This diversity goes from active safety applications that are necessary life-saving applications like local danger and emergency braking warnings, to traf-

DOI: 10.4018/978-1-61520-913-2.ch015

fic and parking applications that are less critical but can add value to a future installed VANET. In their core functionality, all these applications have one thing in common: the need for a communication (routing or dissemination) protocol to deliver relevant information (e.g., available parking space, traffic conditions, etc.) to potentially interested drivers.

Together, all these potential applications will help promote the adoption of a real world VANET technology. However, this is not an easy task due to the diversity of communications needs by the applications, and, also the very dynamic network conditions specific to VANET environments complicate the design of adequate multihop solutions. This is why we strongly suggest that, for a Network Layer communication protocol for VANET applications dealing with the requirements stated above, important modules of the protocol has to support adaptive solutions or adaptable characteristics.

The goal of this chapter is to explore more in depth the use of adaptive solutions in the design of a communication protocol for VANETs. More precisely, we aim to introduce the reader to the benefits of choosing adaptive proposals and talk about the advantages and challenges of choosing an adaptive solution, and suggest further steps to design such adaptive protocols.

The rest of this chapter is organized as follows. In section 2, we introduce some applications relying on VANETs and discuss different classifications which have been proposed. In section 3, we describe the wide variety of communications protocols used by the applications introduced in section 2. In section 4, we motivate the need of adaptation in the construction of communication protocols to bring VANET applications to the real world. Then, in section 5, we introduce adaptive solutions and show the state of the art of these solutions in dynamic networks like VANETs, after we highlight the challenges to address to design such an adaptive protocol supporting the constraints

imposed by the VANET environment. Section 6 ends the chapter with some concluding remarks.

VEHICULAR NETWORKS APPLICATIONS AND DIFFERENT CLASSIFICATIONS

A major requirement in order to propose good adaptive solutions is first to know the environment in which the adaptation will occur. In the case of multihop communication protocols for VANETs, it is imperative to have a general view of all the applications that will use the protocol in the upper layer, know their characteristics and synthesize their communications needs. That is why as a first step, this section illustrates the vehicular applications envisioned by the research community.

The original motivation behind vehicular communications was to improve safety on the roads, as many lives have been lost and much more injuries have been incurred due to car crashes. A driver seeing the brake lights on the car in front of her has only a few seconds to react. Moreover, even if she responded in time, cars behind her could also crash since they were not warned of what was happening in front of them. This has motivated one of the first applications for vehicular communications, namely cooperative collision warning, which relies on vehicle-to-vehicle (V2V) communication[1]. From here on, other safety applications emerged more recently, such as applications that aim at providing drivers with real-time information about traffic conditions.

To better contrast the differences and similarities between the applications envisioned in this kind of networks, instead of listing all these applications specifically one by one, a better approach is to illustrate how they are classified in the literature and how this classification is evolving with the introduction of more potential applications.

Figure 1. Early VANET application classification

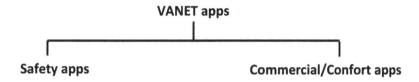

Overview of the Evolution of VANET Applications Classification

There have been efforts in grouping VANET applications into categories, and there are now several categories proposed in the literature. Some classifications (Abdalla et al., 2006; Yousefi et al., 2006) consider only two categories (see Figure 1):

- *Safety applications* whose purpose revolves around the passenger safety and augmenting the network traffic efficiency. These types of applications are of social interest and could be funded by governments. Some examples of such applications concern automatic traffic lights control, work and dangerous road warnings, notifications about accidents provided to emergency vehicles, emergency brake announcement, etc.
- *Commercial (or comfort) applications* whose main purpose is to offer services that make driving easier or more comfortable, by simply using the wireless link to interact with external systems. These applications of interest for the industry could offer immediate incentive to the final user to install wireless equipments in the vehicle. Some examples of this type of applications concern the location of available parking spaces, downloading touristic information and maps for restaurants and gas stations, navigation and route guidance, payment at tolls roads, Internet access.

Although safety applications are important and supported by government funding programs (e.g. the NOW[2], Fleenet[3], CarTALK[4] projects), thus originating the allocation of radio spectrum (DSRC standard) specifically for wireless vehicular communications, non-safety applications are also as important for the vehicular network service for three reasons (Matheus et al., 2004):

- Vehicular network systems rely on specific equipments that should be installed in every car and should be widely available to the users. However, it is unlikely that individuals can afford such expensive equipment.
- Safety applications generally require limited bandwidth for short intervals of time. Since bandwidth efficiency is an important factor, non-safety applications are important to increase bandwidth efficiency.
- The availability of roadside units (RSU) provides an infrastructure that can be used to provide a lot of services with only little increase in cost.

Other authors, like the ones of the prominent NoW project, divide VANET applications into three categories (Festag et al., 2008): safety, traffic efficiency and infotainment applications. This classification (see Figure 2) is similar to the one previously mentioned, only that it is more fine grained, by separating traffic efficiency applications that have a more distributed global nature, from safety applications that require more dissemination of information and have greater

Figure 2. A latter finer grained VANET application classification

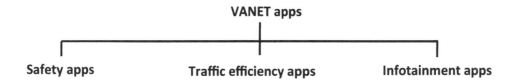

Figure 3. Schoch et al. newer VANET application classification

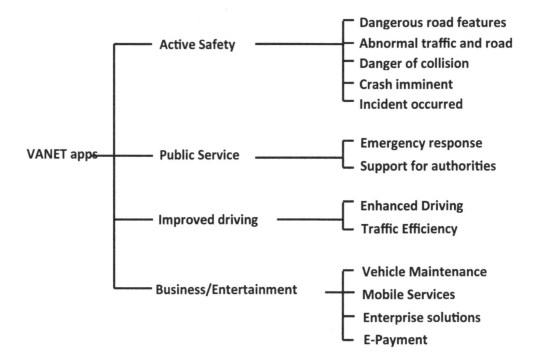

time constraints. The infotainment category is essentially the same as the commercial category from the previous classification, however there is a distinction made by the authors about a bigger dependency in session establishment, unicast routing and bidirectional communication requirements by infotainment applications.

Recently, Schoch et al. (2008) proposed an even more fine grained classification of VANET applications (see Figure 3); the authors also compiled a more complete list of possible applications, categorizing them into 4 main groups:

Active safety Applications: Typical and most useful group of applications for VANETs with a direct impact on road safety. For example, such applications may concern warnings about a potential danger (curve speed, violated traffic lights or stop signal), abnormal traffic or danger of collision (lane change, emergency brake lights), warnings about incidents occurred (post-crash, breakdown lights), etc.

• *Public service:* Vehicular networks are also intended to support public service applications like police or emergency recovery units (e.g., warnings about an emergency vehicle approaching or stolen vehicle tracking service).

- *Improved Driving:* This category includes applications that try to improve or simplify driving. The idea comprises microscopic scenarios in the immediate surroundings of a vehicle as well as macroscopic optimization of traffic efficiency. (e.g., cooperative cruise control, enhanced route guidance and navigation, parking spot locator, etc.).

- *Mobile Business and Entertainment*: A large block of applications can be comprised under the terms business and entertainment. Here, the focus is on delivering services to customers, automation of vehicle-related tasks or payment applications. (e.g., vehicle maintenance applications (wireless diagnostics, software updates), mobile services (Internet service providing, video/voice/text communication with surrounding vehicles, point of interest notification), enterprise solutions applications (fleet management, vehicle tracking).

As we can see, most authors group VANET applications by their user benefits and how they impact the driver. Safety applications have the most crucial impact to the driver because they can save his life, but the driver only appreciates it when an accident occurs. Improved driving applications have a more global impact, as they mostly improve some aspects of the driving experience, but this impact is not usually a matter of life or death. The application category with less impact is mobile business and entertainment, where the impact to the driver could be considered an optional service.

The evolution of these classifications is probably due to the constant introduction of new applications as VANET research is progressing; this fact reaffirms even more the potential utility of the deployment of this type of networks. From this view of VANETs applications, one starts to realize that the communications needs of all ap-

plications are not the same. In the next section we present the different communications needs identified for VANET applications.

The Intelligent Transportation System (ITS) project webpage[5] constitutes a great source for potential VANET applications; Abdalla et al. (2006) also provide a good list of VANET applications extracted from the ITS. Schoch et al. (2008) also compile a good list of possible VANET applications separated by their classification.

COMMUNICATION REQUIREMENTS FOR VANET APPLICATIONS

After analyzing the similarities and differences of potential VANET applications, our focus now turns to proposing a network design perspective, taking into account the identification of the different multihop communication technologies that applications will need in their design (e.g. unicast, geocast). In this section we will mention some alternatives of multihop communication modes presented in the literature.

In the beginning, two communications modes were clearly distinguished for inter-vehicle applications. The first one, called vehicle-to-vehicle communication (V2V) relies on direct information exchanges between vehicles; the second one, called vehicle-to-infrastructure communication (V2I), uses a communication infrastructure to deliver information to vehicles, or for vehicles to communicate information to the fixed network (e.g., in fleet tracking applications). The majority of projects focus on V2V communications as a viable communication solution. However recent works are starting to realize the importance of V2I communications as a means for augmenting the connectivity in vehicular networks dealing with sparse conditions, and also to provide some services that are not easy to address with only V2V communication (e.g., Internet access (Otto et al., 2004)).

In the NOW project, (Festag et al. (2008), a distinction of communications requirements is made between the different categories of vehicular applications. Safety applications typically disseminate information about events or other vehicles in the local vicinity (periodic, short, status-awareness messages) or a certain geographical region (event-based messages). In contrast, infotainment applications typically establish sessions and exchange unicast data packets in greater numbers, bidirectional and over multiple hops. Based on these communications assumptions, the NOW project proposed a loosely coupled dual stack communication protocol architecture, where essentially two broad communication modes are supported for VANET applications to use:

- Standard TCP/IP unicast communication supported by one half of the stack that has TCP and Mobile IP layers. This type of communication is mostly to be used for infotainment applications and Internet access.
- Multihop Geocast or one-hop broadcast communication, supported by the other half of the stack, that has custom NOW transport and network layers. These types of communications are mostly intended to be used by safety applications. The concept of Geocast in the NOW Network layer supports the following communication modes which are considered within the scope of most applications requirements:
  - GeoBroadcast for flooding-like distribution of data packets in a geographical region,
  - GeoAnycast to address any single node inside a geographical region,
  - GeoUnicast for packet transport between two nodes via multiple wireless hops,
  - Topologically-scoped broadcast (TSB) to broadcast a packet to all nodes in an n-hop neighborhood.

Schoch et al. (2008) also and analyze the communications approaches in the literature contrasting with possible VANET applications. Their main contribution is noticing that in virtually all applications the communication can be grouped into a small set of "communication patterns". The authors state that these recurring patterns with multiple, similar characteristics, will form a generic base for the design of VANET communication systems.

Because their concept of "communication pattern" seems prudent and not ambiguous, adopting the concept and using it as a building block for identifying these communications requirements seems prudent and worth explaining in detail. Aiming to refine these patterns, we add the Carry and Forward pattern. Another change to the patterns is the redefinition of the Geobroadcast pattern into the Geocast pattern, that in a way is a broader definition of the Geobroadcast concept and distinctive from the Advance Information Dissemination pattern. We now present and illustrate these different communication patterns.

Beaconing

This pattern allows the continuous update of information among neighboring nodes, using periodic broadcast (or in some occasions by an external trigger). This pattern is also of very common use in protocols with other communication patterns (e.g., a proactive unicast routing protocol). Some applications which use this pattern are: warning of dangerous road features like curve speed, lane change assistant, emergency electronic brakes, emergency vehicle approaching warning, or just-in-time repair notification.

Geocast

This pattern deals with the distribution of information using multihop dissemination within a geographical destination region defined by the sender of the message. The message has to be retained inside the dissemination area, working around the movement of the vehicles that enter or exit the target area. Such a communication solution is used to advertise incidents, like traffic congestions on highways, where the destination area should then be set, so that drivers can be warned far enough from the event to find an exit on the highway and avoid encountering it. A more advanced scenario of this pattern consists in disseminating information to a target area in which the sender is not in, so the message needs to be first relayed to the target area using unicast communication (in order to avoid overloading the network) and only after arriving to the target area a dissemination begins, e.g. GeoGRID (Liao et al, 2000). This communication pattern may be used in different applications such as work zone warning, cooperative cruise control, incident occurred (post-crash, breakdown warning), suspicious vehicle warning, emergency vehicle approaching warning and distributed parking spot locator.

Some works that use these communication patterns are: LMB (Kon et al., 1999), GeoGRID (Liao et al., 2000) and Stored Geocast (Maihöfer et al., 2003) dealing with the retention of the message inside the destination area for some specified time.

Advance Information Dissemination

This pattern uses broadcast and considers various parameters to determine whether a message should be resent or not, in order to avoid flooding. Here, the sender of the message does not explicitly specifies a destination (it depends on the contextual relevance), and it is adapted to bandwidth constraints. Some authors (Cenerario et al., 2008; Adler et al., 2006) have enhanced this definition to also consider geographical input to drive the spread of the dissemination. Such a communication pattern allows adapting the delivery of the information to the type of information carried. For example, a message about traffic congestion should be only delivered to the vehicles that could encounter it, whereas a message indicating an available parking space should be broadcast to all the vehicles in the vicinity of the resource. Some example applications that need such a pattern are: Intelligent traffic flow, efficiency-enhanced route guidance and navigation, post-crash warning, point of interest notification, distributed parking spot locator service. Examples in this type of communication pattern are the works of Cenerario et al. (2008), Adler et al (2006), and Eichler et al. (2006).

Unicast Routing

Although this communication pattern is common in traditional network protocols, it is difficult to implement in VANETs. The purpose of this pattern is to transport data through the ad hoc network to a destination (vehicle or RSU). As opposed to the other ones, this communication pattern is the only one that fully supports bidirectional communication (connection-oriented). Some types of applications using this solution include the delivery of information about road surface conditions to traffic authority centers, or video/voice/text communication with surrounding vehicles. This pattern is needed to deploy applications such as electronic license plate and driver's license request by authority, map download/update, centralized parking spot locator service, road surface conditions to traffic authority center, Internet service providing, video/voice/text communication with surrounding vehicles. Some unicast proposals examples are OLSR[6] as a proactive routing protocol, AODV[7] as a reactive routing protocol, and GPSR (Karp et al., 2000) as a position-based routing.

Information Aggregation

This pattern is very different from the others because it is information-oriented rather than message-oriented. Data here is not simply forwarded, but also processed and merged by nodes. The central component is a knowledge base, augmented with local information and remote data collected by vehicles. The benefits consist in a reduction of the network load when multiple vehicles detect an event and a better quality of the information. However, this pattern is not appropriate for time-sensitive applications. Some applications that could use this pattern are: abnormal traffic and road conditions warnings, intelligent traffic flow control, parking spot locator service, post-crash warnings, work zone warning. Some information aggregation proposals are giving by Defude et al. (2008), Tian et al. (2005) and Wischhof et al. (2005).

Carry and Forward

This pattern aims at relying on the mobility and direction of vehicles to diffuse a message in the network. Therefore, a moving vehicle carries the packet until it reaches the target area where the information should be delivered or until it reaches a new vehicle interested in carrying the packet. Here, the vehicle is considered as a data mule in charge of the transportation of the information. Carry and forward can help to better route in sparse and partitioned networks. Predicted mobility/destination with road layout can improve this pattern greatly (i.e. by knowing the regular paths the drivers take every day, since we all generally tend to take only a limited number of usual paths), or knowing their middle/final destination from their navigation system, by knowing where the road leads, or even explicitly by the driver. Some example applications that could use this pattern are: SOS service to aide center, stolen vehicle tracking service, incident occurred (post-crash, breakdown warning), vehicle tracking.

Some works using the carry and forward solution are: VADD (Zhao et al., 2008) takes advantage of the predicable vehicle mobility, limited by the traffic pattern and road layout; KioskNet (Guo et al., 2007), utilizes buses and cars as "mechanical backhaul" devices to carry data between rural village kiosks and internet gateways. Chen et al. (2001) test the hypothesis that the motion

of vehicles on a highway can contribute to successful message delivery, provided that they use a carry and forward solution to relay messages. To better highlight the differences between these communications patterns, we present a table (see Table 1) explaining a set of characteristics for each pattern. These characteristics are extracted also from Schoch et al. (2008), in part resuming their explanation on these patterns plus adding the Carry and Forward pattern.

NEED FOR ADAPTIVITY IN THE DESIGN OF A COMMUNICATION PROTOCOL FOR VANETS

In this section we will highlight several reasons to use adaptive solutions in the design of a multihop communication protocol for VANET.

First, as explained previously, VANET applications require distinct communications solutions (or in other words communication patterns). This has originated that most existing multihop communications protocol proposals in the literature (for routing or dissemination of information) are tailored for a particular type of application; therefore they may be very efficient for one kind of applications but offer very poor performance for others. For example, applications like post-crash or breakdown warnings are adequate to use the advance dissemination pattern, because the information to transfer has to be delivered as quickly as possible to a subset of surrounding vehicles. On the contrary, applications like Internet service providing and road surface conditions to traffic authority center are not well suited for this communication pattern, because the destination of the message is of great importance and one on one communication is desired; in this case, using unicast routing pattern seems more adequate. Ideally, the standard multihop communication protocol of future vehicles needs to be wide/comprehensive enough to support multiple unique modes, and additionally be simple and compact, offering a

Table 1. Classification of the different communications patterns according to certain characteristics

Communication pattern	Communication Mechanism	Trigger	Characteristics			Purpose
			Direction	Data	Quality of service	
Beaconing	Single hop link layer broadcast	Mostly periodically (sometimes by external trigger)	Unidirectional	Generated by the sender, usually local sensor data	Many applications have mid-range latency requirements	Continuous update of information among all neighboring nodes
Geocast	Multihop dissemination within a geographical destination region. Attention in retaining dissemination in geographical area	Typically sent upon a certain event	Unidirectional	The sender determines destination region and retain time, they are attach to message. Typically small messages	Often require very low latency, some applications may need best possible delivery success	Dissemination of information in a target area, for a specific period of time
Unicast Routing	Single-multi hop route messages towards destination (single node or destination region)	Mostly sent upon system internal events or manual user interaction	Uni- or bidirectional (connection-oriented comm.)	Support for reliable transport of data of multiple packets. Packets carry arbitrary data, set by sender	Priority of lower than safety apps. Some apps can tolerate high delays and retransmissions (reliability)	Transport data through ad hoc network to a destination (vehicle or RSU)
Advance Information Dissemination	Uses broadcast. Sender doesn't specify a destination (spread) and message resending depends on contextual relevance	Based on events or discovered information	Unidirectional	Content and meta data of a message created by source is never changed. Meta data to determine the relevance of message may be attached	Widespread and time-stable dissemination of messages are more important than a low latency. Prioritization is implicitly included	Dissemination of information among vehicles enduring a certain time, capable to bridge network partitions and prioritizing information
Information Aggregation	The central component is a knowledge base, augmented with local information and remote data collected and processed by vehicles	Information shared with others when detected or periodically	Not clearly distinguished anymore	Deals with information rather than messages (Containing aggregated information from multiple sources over time)	Cannot be used for messages with very time sensitive applications	Data processed and merged by nodes not simply forwarded. Reduce overhead when event detection by multiple vehicles. Improve information quality
Carry and Forward	Multihop routing of messages to destination. Node retains message and forward decision based on the vehicle mobility, driver navigation information	Similar to unicast routing, event based or manual user interaction	Unidirectional	Sender define destination of message. Not altered by routing. Meta-data to forward packet could be geographical or road layout	Not for time sensitive applications, dependency of human factor. Great for delay tolerant apps	Transport of connectionless oriented data though vehicle network in sparse conditions

minimal set of modes. Adaptive solutions can be of great help in reducing the number of proposed modes, either by joining similar modes or by generalizing a mode to support various situations solved in other similar protocols.

Second, all the previously mentioned VANET applications will surely help the driver accept this new technology, and as a result accelerate the deployment of dense vehicular networks in the following years. Nevertheless, for this to work, each application needs to offer good service performance individually and in interaction with the other applications running concurrently in the same network. Thus, the multihop communication protocol has to act as the administrator of the network resources by means of prioritizing application information traveling between vehicles, Adaptive solutions that prioritize the sending of messages between applications for the local and neighboring benefit (as proposed in Adler et al. (2006) and Eichler et al. (2006)) are worth exploring more in-depth. Here the different categories of applications play an important role in the assignment of the network resources, because it is important that the communication protocol gives priority of network usage to applications critical to human safety. For example, the communication protocol will need to give more network resources to the dissemination of messages related to safety (life-saving) applications, like emergency braking announcement, than to the dissemination of messages for parking spot applications.

Third, VANET applications can be potentially very complex and may need to use various communication patterns to enhance message delivery. For example, the post-crash announcement application, where the vehicle uses a geocast pattern to inform nearby vehicles, could provide a more complete solution if the vehicle also used the unicast pattern to send a message to the emergency call center. Moreover, the applications also need to adapt to the network and application characteristics in order to maintain a good quality of service. Thus, changing the communication pattern used by the same application may sometimes be necessary due to a change in the network context. To illustrate, let us consider the dissemination of information related to an "accident" event. When the number of vehicles driving in the direction of the accident is high, a standard dissemination protocol will efficiently relay the message to interested drivers. On the contrary, when the number of vehicles is low (e.g., the accident happened during the night), the message cannot be relayed far enough. A carry-and-forward strategy, considering the use of the vehicles driving in the opposite direction as message carriers (Zhao et al., 2008; Adler et al., 2006; Costa et al., 2006), would then lead to better results in terms of message delivery.

Lastly, in general a multihop communication protocol for VANETs has to be tolerant with some network factors that are not taken into account in other related networks like MANETs or Ad hoc networks. Here again, adaptive solutions could help in dealing with these factors in order to maintain the application performance. These network factors include vehicle-to-infrastructure communication (V2I) and the extreme dynamicity of some networks characteristics; we will talk about them in the next subsections.

V2I Integration in Communication Protocols

At the early period of VANET research, even though vehicle to vehicle (V2V) and vehicle to infrastructure (V2I) communication were envisioned, most proposals were mostly focused on pure V2V communication. However, in recent proposals, some authors (Lochert et al., 2007) indicate that pure V2V communications are not sufficient to offer good network performance in low density scenarios, and thus propose routing protocols that use a backbone infrastructure (V2I) to improve performance (so called hybrid routing protocols). One important issue that arises when integrating V2I communication consists in defining the optimum amount of infrastructure (RSU nodes) that a network needs. Indeed, this greatly depends on the number of wireless-enabled vehicles that are in the system (i.e. it depends on the penetration rate of the technology). A good scalable communication protocol for VANET should work independently of the amount of vehicle-to-infrastructure communication used.

RSUs can either be isolated or attached to a larger structured network. In the first case, their function is to distribute information (e.g. dangerous curve, construction site ahead) or simply to extend the vehicle communication range by acting as forwarding entities. In the latter case, RSUs distribute information towards or from a remote entity (e.g. control center). They can also interconnect the vehicular network to an infrastructure network and the Internet.

Here again an adaptive solution can be implemented to take advantage of V2I communication when present (especially in low density scenarios), possibly taking advantage of the stationary characteristics of RSUs and maybe their bigger transmission range. Also, for the geocast multihop mode, the presence of an RSU inside the area of dissemination can greatly reduce the problem of maintaining the message circulating in the area for a long period of time, in spite of the movement of vehicles, so adapting to this situation is worth exploring. Finally, the presence of RSUs attached to an infrastructure network (e.g. RSUs interconnected by a WAN or 3G network) could be exploited by an adaptive solution to enhance performance, by means of relaying the message in the assumingly more interconnected, reliable or faster network than the V2V network, when the situation demands it (e.g. low density scenario, V2V network is saturated, route message to a distant place).

Extreme Dynamic Network Characteristics

Although VANETs are ad-hoc networks, there are several network characteristics that make them dif-

ferent from other types of ad-hoc networks, such as MANETs. The difficulty of dealing with these characteristics is that they are very dynamic and can have extremely opposite values in the course of the application's lifetime, thus making more necessary the use of adaptive solutions. If these network characteristics are not managed and the proposed protocol does not work satisfactorily for these extremes values, future VANET applications are going to be disappointing for users due to their recurrent poor performance. Let us now review some network characteristics specific to VANETs (Schoch et al., 2008).

Node Velocity

Node velocity may range from zero for stationary RSUs, or when vehicles are stuck in a traffic jam, to over 130 kmph on highways. These two extremes pose a special challenge to the communication system. With a high node velocity, the mutual wireless communication window is very short due to a small transmission range of one or several hundred meters. On the other extreme, with almost no mobility, the network topology is much more stable; however, slow movements in the vehicular domain also usually mean a very high vehicle density, which results in high interference, medium access problems, etc.

Movement Patterns

Vehicles do not move around arbitrarily, but use predefined roads, usually in two directions. Unpredictable changes in the direction of vehicles usually occur only at intersections of roads. We distinguish three types of roads: dense city road network, where the road density is relatively high, there are many intersections, and buildings limit wireless communication; rural roads where intersections are rare and few vehicles are on the road; and lastly highways, where there are multilane roads, movements are quasi one-dimensional and vehicles usually keep their direction towards another city.

Node Density

It is not hard to imagine that vehicles in mutual radio range may vary from zero to dozens or even hundreds. If we assume a traffic jam on a highway with 4 lanes, one vehicle at every 20 meters and a radiofrequency range of 300m, each node theoretically has 120 vehicles within its transmission range. In addition, node density is not only correlated to the type of road, but also to time (high density during the daytime, low density at night). In the case of very low density, immediate message forwarding gets impossible. In this case, more sophisticated information dissemination is necessary, for instance, a type of dissemination which can store and forward selected information when vehicles encounter each other. In high-density situations, the opposite must be achieved. Here, only selected nodes should repeat a message, because otherwise this may lead to an overloaded channel.

Node Heterogeneity

Among the nodes participating in the envisioned applications, we find numerous different types. First, a basic distinction can be made between vehicles and infrastructural units, often called road side units (RSU). As discussed previously, these nodes may simply emit data to the network or have a complete ad hoc functionality. Moreover, infrastructural nodes may provide access to background networks, and these nodes are stationary. Vehicles can be further categorized into private vehicles, authority vehicles, road construction and maintenance vehicles and so on. Each category may have additional functionality not present in normal vehicles (e.g. private vehicles like busses surely know their destination, authority vehicles like ambulances or policy cars may have priority to send in the network or additional security

privileges to get information like license plate from normal vehicles, etc). Although a GPS module is becoming standard in vehicles, there may some vehicles that don't have the communication module with GPS (or the GPS is not working properly), forcing the multihop communication protocol to adapt to this situation. In the case of other optional modules like a navigation system, there will surely be more vehicles that are not equipped with such device; an adaptive solution that takes advantage of those vehicles that do have them will generate additional communication performance.

Beside the network characteristics (seen as context elements) of the vehicle, variable application context could also change the way the message is communicated in the network, for example:

- With the advance dissemination multihop communication mode, the area of relevance of a message depends on the type of information carried (as we mentioned earlier), but also on the context. For instance, when available parking spaces are disseminated, the area that should be considered also depends on the number of neighboring vehicles searching for a parking space. If this number is high, it is not useful to broadcast the information far away since that would lead to wasted bandwidth and provide obsolete information to drivers.
- The amount of data to be transferred can greatly influence the multihop communication protocol in use (e.g., does the message contain multimedia data like an audio description or a picture attached to the event?).

DESIGN OF ADAPTIVE COMMUNICATION PROTOCOLS AND CHALLENGES

Throughout the previous section, we have shown the strong need for adaptability as a design feature of a VANET communication protocol; this way it would be flexible enough to offer applications multiple communications patterns and maintain efficiency when dealing with the frequently changing networks conditions.

In the broader sense of the term, adaptive solutions are defined as those that change the behavior of the executing system at runtime. In Ad hoc networks, Hadzic et al. (1999) have defined adaptive solutions or protocols as those that automatically adjust their behavior to runtime phenomena such as traffic or link characteristics.

The importance of proposing adaptive solutions in communication protocols is starting to be addressed for dynamic networks like Ad hoc, MANET and VANET. In this section we present the state of the art in adaptive solutions in communication protocols proposals. Then, we will talk present a decomposition of adaptive solutions into sub concepts that can help classify the adaptive solutions presented and others. To conclude, we present a comparative analysis between adaptive solutions from the point of view of how they implement the metric, mechanism and policy concepts. Finally, we present some problems to consider and challenges faced when using adaptation in the construction of a VANET communication protocol.

Adaptive Solutions in Communications Protocols Proposals

Adaptive solutions have been implicitly integrated in communication protocols in other networks besides VANETs and have shown their efficiency in dealing with changing environments. Traditional network protocol architectures have used adaptive solutions to deal with dynamic characteristics, such as TCP/IP's congestion-control algorithms, which adapt to the available throughput. The measurable parameters it uses to detect IP packet loss are checksums, sequence numbers and timers. The "congestion window" size reflects a policy decision in response to these phenomena.

Adaptive solutions have also appeared in order to enhance routing protocols performance in ad hoc networks. A first approach to adapt unicast routing protocols is to combine proactive and reactive strategies. SHARP (Ramasubramanian et al., 2003) is a routing protocol that automatically finds the balance point between proactive dissemination and reactive discovery of routing information, in such a way that it can dynamically adapt to changing network characteristics and traffic behavior.

The adaptive behavior can also be achieved by tuning the parameters of the routing protocol at runtime. The adaptive zone routing protocol (AZRP) (Giannoulis et al., 2004) is an example of a protocol that uses variable zone radius and controllable route update interval.

An adaptive routing framework is proposed by Zhao et al. (2006), this framework allows the introduction of adjustable parameters and programmable routing modules. The solution supports three adaptive mechanisms: Selecting routing module, tuning routing algorithm parameters and adjusting routing metric. Control information is disseminated to exchange state variables; a global distributed policy manager is responsible for the adaptive operations at nodes of the network. The authors mention that while switching routing protocols and routing metrics results in extra overhead and service discontinuity, an integrated adaptive algorithm to a particular routing element such as routing metric is a more practical alternative.

In the realm of VANETs adaptive solutions are starting to be exploited. For example, Adler et al. (Adler, 2006; Adler et al., 2006) stated various requirements for a good dissemination protocol for Local Danger Warning (LDW) applications. They also propose a recipient-based framework that can quickly adapt the dissemination area, message time, message prioritization depending on a number of custom network and applications context variables. These adaptations in each recipient maximize the relevance parameter tied to the performance of the application, each LDW application having its own relevance parameter. The interesting conclusion is that by exploiting the adaptability property it is possible to have a protocol that is general enough to work well with different applications and in different contexts.

Cenerario et al. (2008) proposed a variant of this kind of adaptive dissemination protocol for LDW messages, designed to optimize the "encounter probability" parameter. They go farther by proposing a more detailed framework to adapt the dissemination area and message lifetime for static/mobile and direction-dependent/non direction-dependent events. The authors show good results in terms of information dissemination in the vehicular network considering different context conditions, and also demonstrate the feasibility and value of these kinds of adaptive protocols.

Bako et al. (2007) proposed an adaptive gossiping (lightweight dissemination) protocol for VANET highway scenarios; this protocol can adapt the forwarding probability dynamically to different network topologies and node densities based on position information from beacon messages.

In the Traffic-Adaptive Packet Relaying protocol (TAPR) for VANETs (Abuelela et al., 2007), each car uses a strategy to decide whether it should use co-directional (running on the same direction as the packet direction) or oncoming traffic based on local traffic conditions. TAPR makes adaptive packet relaying decisions by switching between carry and forward and routing according to current traffic conditions. TAPR chooses carry and forward whenever there is no connection to the next oncoming cluster on the road.

For adaptive solutions to prioritize the sending of message between applications, Eichler et al. (2006) proposed an altruistic communication scheme which differentiates data traffic according to the benefit it is likely to provide to potential recipients. This approach is able to take into account individual driver's interest to determine message importance and benefit. Network nodes apply a mechanism to evaluate the benefit the current messages in the send queue may provide to potential recipients and prioritize message packets accordingly. Based on this value, the strategy follows two main concepts. First, a local order among the messages within the send queue of each vehicle is computed. Then, the medium access strategy is adapted accordingly, favoring packets with a higher expected benefit.

How to Analyze Adaptive Solutions

From the adaptive solutions presented in the previous section, it can be noticed that each of them performs the adaptation in different ways and also aims at adapting to different characteristics. This diversity of adaptive solutions can make it difficult to review or classify them. In addition, if we try to analyze the problem entirely, it can become cumbersome, that is why it is important to decompose the adaptation concept into subconcepts that render more manageable the entire adaptive solution. The decomposition can be done by separating the concepts of a metric, mechanism and policy. In this section we will explain the origin and meaning of these concepts in an adaptive solution.

Origin of Metric, Mechanism and Policy Concepts in Adaptive Solutions

These concepts originated from various works proposing adaptive solutions; works from Hadzic et al. (1999) and Boleng et al. (2002) are essential starting points towards a better comprehension of adaptive solutions.

One first separation of an adaptive solution is given by the policy and mechanism concepts. TCP/IP's algorithms provide illustrative examples of policy and mechanism separation. For example, to detect IP packet loss, the TCP protocol uses measurable parameters such as checksums, sequence numbers and timers (these being the mechanism to adapt). The "congestion window" size reflects a policy decision in response to these

Figure 4. Separation of an adaptive solution into three sub-concepts

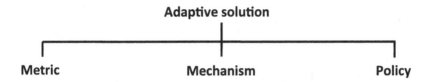

phenomena. Hadzig et al. (1999) also separated an adaptive solution in policy and mechanism concepts, they stated that an adaptive protocol architecture can be effectively designed using a policy/mechanism separation, The authors used as example of a mechanism the FEC (Forward Error Correction) and using a simple threshold policy the targeted application was the TCP/IP throughput improvement in a noisy environment.

Parallel from the policy and mechanism concepts, Boleng et al. (2002) mention the importance of the metric concept in an adaptive solution, the authors proposed a mobility metric (link duration) that can be used to develop an adaptive ad hoc network protocol. They investigate the suitability for enabling adaptive ad hoc network protocols of several previously proposed popular metrics, but none meets all the requirements, only link duration.

Metric, Mechanism and Policy Concepts

Combining the knowledge of the previous research, we can go one step forward and define the decomposition of an adaptive solution into three sub-concepts (see Figure 4): the metrics, the mechanism and the policies used in an adaptive solution. Below we explain more in detail the meaning of these three sub-concepts.

Metric: We can define a metric of the adaptive solution define as the parameters that the entity using the adaptive solution supervises in order to make the proper modifications to increase the overall benefit of the application. To state it simply, defining a possible metric for an adaptive solu-

tion involves answering the question: how does it detect that it needs to adapt? Some possible metrics for communication protocols for VANETS could be the dynamic network characteristics mention in a previous section. For example from previously cited adaptive solutions, Cenerario et al. (2008) use as metric the vehicle and event direction/mobility vector; the TCP congestion algorithm uses checksums, sequence numbers and timers as metrics; Bako et al. (2007) use network topologies and node densities as metric for the adaptive solution. In another manner, the election of a good metric is a problem by itself, because not all possible metrics are appropriate to be used in an adaptable protocol. Boleng et al. (2002) highlights this problem and defined a set of requirements that metrics must met in order to enable adaptive MANET protocols, these requirements can be extrapolated to VANETs.

Mechanism: A mechanism can be defined as the element that will be modified (or maybe added or removed) in order to make the adaptation possible in the solution. To put in a simple way, defining a mechanism for an adaptive solution involves answering the question: how does it adapt? From some previously cited adaptive solutions we can extract the mechanism they use in order to adapt: Cenerario et al. (2006) used the dissemination area and time; Adler (2006) apart of using dissemination area and time, proposed also message prioritization; the TAPR protocol (Abuelela et al., 2007) use a change between carry and forward and unicast routing protocols; Ramasubramanian et al. (2003) for their adaptation solution propose as mechanism the change between reactive or proactive unicast protocols; Zhao et al. (2006) propose using change of protocols, protocols parameters or routing metrics. Some others mechanisms not explored in previous works are modulation of transmission power, use of carry and forward routing or use of backbone infrastructure.

Policy: A policy can be defined as the decisions or logic taken by the adaptive solution in order to determine in which conditions it should adapt, or to manage the mechanism in order to accomplish the desired behavior. Simply stated, defining a policy for an adaptive solution involves answering the question: when does it know, and how much does it need to adapt? Some examples of policies used in previously mentioned adaptive solutions are the congestion window of TCP/IP's congestion-control algorithms, the encounter probability of Cenerario et al. (2008) and the relevance of Adler et al. (2006). The policy sub-concept is noted by Hadzic et al. (1999) as the major challenge for any adaptation scheme, these authors also stated some factors in which depends the performance of an adaptive protocol when choosing policies. A policy can be as simple as a threshold decision to a policy of very complicated logic based upon various metrics.

To give a quick example, imagine an adaptive solution for a VANET application which goal is to achieve acceptable performance in low and high traffic scenarios. A separation of metric, mechanism and policy could be like this:

- *Metric:* Some examples of possible variables to detect high/low traffic conditions could be node density, type of road/hour of day or shared medium contention, but there could be many others.
- *Mechanism:* Possible ways to maintain performance in spite the traffic condition could be to limit the information sent, adapt dissemination area or control the dependency on vehicle-to-infrastructure network to forward information. There could

be other possible mechanisms, and finding the best mechanism is a problem in itself.
- *Policy:* Here a possible complex policy could be a relevance function that takes into account one or many metrics or even activate various mechanisms in responds. To give an concrete example, one of the most simple policies could be a conditional statement (threshold) like the one showed below:

```
If local_node_density is greater
than 6
Limit_information_sent by 50%
Else
100% information_sent
```

Comparative Analysis between Adaptive Solutions

In order to better understand the differences between the examined adaptive solutions, below we will present a comparative table (Table 2) of the adaptive solutions based their elections in metrics, mechanisms and policies.

Challenges and Problems to Consider

We have discussed throughout this chapter the benefits of using adaptive solutions to deal with varying network environments and applications needs. However, before beginning to integrate these types of solutions, we need to first address some challenges associated with a complex environment such as a VANET. In this section we will give an overview about the problems to consider and challenges faced when using adaptive solutions.

Throughout this chapter we have mentioned some important examples of adaptive solutions found in the literature. However, there exist many

Table 2. Comparative analysis of adaptive solutions presented in this chapter

Adaptive solutions	Field of research	Metrics used	Mechanisms used	Policy used
Adler et al. (2006)	VANETs	No specific metrics, general approach by relevance parameters	Area of dissemination, time of dissemination, priority to send message	Message relevance function defined by authors
Cenerario et al. (2008)	VANETs	Mobility and direction vector of event and vehicle	Area of dissemination, time of dissemination	Encounter probability function defined by authors
SHARP	MANETs	Perceived packet overhead, packet loss rate and jitter between neighbor	Zone radius of each destination, i.e. area of node in which it routes proactively	Three heuristics to calculate each perceive metric, then modified the zone radius when reach certain threshold
TCP congestion window	Wired networks, Transport layer	IP packet loss based on inspecting checksums, sequence numbers and timers	Congestion window size	Congestion window heuristic
AZRP	Ad Hoc networks	Routing failure and number of nodes in zone	Zone radius and route update interval	Decision to modify radius zone if result is outsize of threshold
Zhao et al. (2006)	Ad Hoc networks	Architecture doesn't not have specific metrics, only gives examples like degree to which channel is busy	Selecting routing module, tuning routing algorithm parameters and adjusting routing metric	Architecture doesn't have specific policies, gives examples of threshold policies
Bako et al. (2007)	VANETs	Neighbor message direction through position information	Forwarding probability and neighborhood relationship	Maintenance of a parent-sibling-child relationship from beacon messages of neighbors
TAPR	VANETs	Local traffic conditions	Switch between mulling of routing	By detecting presence of path to next oncoming cluster on the road, doesn't explain well how
Eichler et al. (2006)	VANETs	No specific metrics, general approach by context parameters	Priority to send message	Message benefit function define by authors

others proposals that implicitly include adaptation but it only becomes evident when seen from the points of view analyzed in this chapter. As we said earlier, some adaptive solutions in the literature are not easy to spot, as many of them are not presented as "adaptive", but rather use some other related terms like policy, dynamic, context-aware, etc. One has to analyze them carefully and extract the adaptive contribution of the work. This is where the decomposition of the adaptive solution in metric, mechanism and policy will help enormously in better analyzing the whole solution.

There are also some other topics in computer science that center on the idea of adaptation. Further reading in these subjects will be of great help mostly in identifying different policy methods for adaptive solutions, particularly since Hadzig et al. (1999) noted that the major challenge for any adaptation solution is the policy decision. For example, the idea of computational reflection, referring to the capability of a system to reason about and act upon itself, originated proposals of reflective middleware. Dynamic aspect oriented programming middleware, policy middleware, and autonomic computing also center around the idea of adaptation.

Another issue that we will most surely encounter is the need to select between multiple adaptive solutions that tackle the same problem. This issue involves a difficult decision because they will probably use different metrics, mechanisms or policies, and thus we need to select the best combination. A broad evaluation is also needed to test the final adaptive solution in all operating conditions of the communication protocol where it is implemented.

Adaptive solutions that are distributed (i.e. involving various participants) have additional challenges to take into account. Because VANETs have a distributed nature, adaptive changes potentially involve all vehicles in the network; these considerations need to be taken into account when proposing an adaptive solution. The challenges of distributed adaptive solutions are:

- *Consensus:* When multiple vehicles are involved, the adaptation operation sometimes needs to be agreed upon by all the participants; it could be the case that the adaptive decision involves the knowledge of a group of vehicles or even all the network. Even if only one vehicle could make the adaptation operation without prior agreement, there is also the problem of informing and scheduling the adaptation operation to all participants.
- *Consistency:* Special care is needed when doing multiple adaptation operations (there could be entirely different adaptive operations); they are not supposed to conflict with each other rendering unexpected results. This is specially truth in VANETs because the network is a shared resource.

To illustrate the challenge of consensus, we will take as example the adaptive proposal of Zhao et al. (2006). This proposal includes a mechanism to change the routing protocol at runtime when needed; however, the distributed problems emerge because the change of protocol needs to be done in all the nodes in the network. The adaptive framework previously referenced defines a global distributed policy manager responsible for detecting the need to change and informing all network nodes to change the protocol. In this work it can be noticed that the definition of the global distributed policy manager is an important part of the proposal.

CONCLUSION

As seen in the first half of the chapter, potential VANET applications are very diverse, each having different communications needs (dissemination, unicast, aggregation, etc). We have evidenced these needs in the form of multihop communication modes and presented their differences. Even supporting all these multihop modes, the communications needs of vehicular applications are not static, as they change depending on the dynamic networks characteristics and the application context. In section 4 we talk about these dynamic characteristics and about the context that can make the application change its behavior; the focus is oriented towards highlighting the need of a VANET communication protocol (in the Network Layer of the OSI model) of being adaptable to all these varying conditions.

Having highlighted the need for adaptation, section 5 finalizes this chapter by introducing the reader to the state of the art in adaptive solutions in VANETs and similar dynamic networks; we then present a classification of adaptive solutions to make it more manageable and have a better understanding of them. Lastly, we talk about the challenges faced when adopting this approach in the solution.

As we have shown in this chapter, adaptation is an essential tool in the construction of a communication protocol for VANET. Interoperability of the shared network between applications, merging communications patterns and making them dynamic to network conditions are all problems that could benefit from adaptive solutions. The adaptive solutions presented here represent a good sample of what is currently found in the literature, although being a dynamic research field the reader may find others of recent appearance.

Adaptive solutions are not something new, as they have been proposed before in other areas of computer science, like computational reflection, autonomic computing, etc.; adaptation is a very recurrent mechanism when dealing with dynamic conditions. The objective of this chapter, in a nutshell, is to evidence the need for adaptation in a communication protocol and provide a starting point for the interested the reader to pursue a more in-depth exploration of adaptive solutions.

REFERENCES

Abdalla, G., Abu-Rgheff, M., & Senouci, S. (2006). Current Trends in Vehicular Ad Hoc Networks. In *Proceedings of the 6th International Conference on In ITS Telecommunications,* (pp. 761-766). Chegdu, China.

Abuelela, M., & Olariu, S. (2007). Traffic-adaptive packet relaying in VANET. In *Proceedings of the fourth ACM international workshop on Vehicular ad hoc networks (VANET '07).* Pages 77-78. Montreal, Canada

Adler, C. (2006). *Information Dissemination in Vehicular Ad Hoc Networks* (PhD thesis). University of Munchen, Germany

Adler, C., Eichler, S., Kosch, T., Schroth, C., & Strassberger, M. (2006, September). Self-organized and Context-Adaptive Information Diffusion in Vehicular Ad Hoc Networks. In *Proceedings of the 3rd International Symposium on Wireless Communication Systems (ISWCS '06),* (pp. 307-311). Valencia, Spain.

Bako, B., Rikanovic, I., Kargl, F., & Schoch, E. (2007). Adaptive Topology Based Gossiping in VANETs Using Position Information. [). New York: Springer.]. *Lecture Notes in Computer Science, 4864,* 66–78. doi:10.1007/978-3-540-77024-4_8

Boleng, J., Navidi, W., & Camp, T. (2002). Metrics to Enable Adaptive Protocols for Mobile Ad Hoc Networks. In [Las Vegas, NV.]. *Proceedings of the International Conference on Wireless Networks ICWN, 02,* 293–298.

Cenerario, N., Delot, T., & Ilarri, S. (2008, June). Dissemination of information in inter-vehicle ad hoc networks". In [Eindhoven, The Netherlands.]. *Proceedings of the IEEE Intelligent Vehicles Symposium, 2008,* 763–768.

Chen, Z., Kung, H., & Vlah, D. (2001). Ad Hoc Relay Wireless Networks over Moving Vehicles on Highways. In *Proceedings of ACM Mobihoc.* Long Beach, CA.

Costa, P., Frey, D., Migliavacca, M., & Mottola, L. (2006). Towards lightweight information dissemination in inter-vehicular networks. *In Proceedings of the 3rd international workshop on Vehicular ad hoc networks* (VANET'06), (pp. 20-29). Los Angeles.

Defude, B., Delot, T., & Ilarri, S. Zechinelli, Martini, J. -L., & Cenerario, N. (2008, July). Data aggregation in VANETs: the VESPA approach. In *Proceedings of Mobiquitous '08 - 1st International Workshop on Computational Transportation Science IWCTS'08.* Dublin, Ireland: ACM Digital Library.

Eichler, S., Schroth, C., Kosch, T., & Strassberger, M. (2006, July). Strategies for context-adaptive message dissemination in vehicular ad hoc networks. In *Proceedings of the Second International Workshop on Vehicle-to Vehicle Communications* (V2VCOM), (pp. 1-9). San Jose, CA.

Festag, A., Noecker, G., Strassberger, M., Lübke, A., & Bochow, B. (2008, March). NoW – Network on Wheels: Project Objectives, Technology and Achievements. In *Proceedings of the 5th International Workshop on Intelligent Transportation (WIT).* (pp. 211-216). Hamburg, Germany.

Giannoulis, S., Katsanos, C., Koubias, S., & Papadopoulos, G. (2004, September). A hybrid adaptive routing protocol for ad hoc wireless networks. In *Proceedings of IEEE International Workshop on Factory Communication Systems WFCS'04.* (pp. 287-290). Vienna, Austria.

Guo, S., & Falaki, M. H. Oliver, Rahman, S., Seth, A., Zaharia, M., Ismail, U., & Keshav, S. (2007). Design and implementation of the kiosknet system. In *Proceedings of the International Conference on Information and Communication Technologies and Development* (ICTD 2007), (pp. 300–309). Bangalore, India.

Hadzic, I., Marcus, W., & Smith, J. (1999, January). *Policy and Mechanism in Adaptive Protocols* (Technical report no. MS-CIS-01-03). Philadelphia: Department of Computer & Information Science University of Pennsylvannia and Bellcore.

Karp, B., & Kung, H. (2000). GPSR: greedy perimeter stateless routing for wireless networks. In *Proceedings of the 6th annual international conference on Mobile computing and networking* (MobiCom '00), (pp. 243-254). New York: ACM Press.

Ko, Y., & Vaidya, N. (1999). Geocasting in mobile ad hoc networks: Location-based multicast algorithms. In *Proceedings of the Second IEEE Workshop on Mobile Computer Systems and Applications,* (WMCSA). Washington, DC.

Kon, F., Costa, F., Blair, G., & Campbell, R. (2002, June). The case for reflective middleware. *Communications of the ACM, 45*(6), 33–38. doi:10.1145/508448.508470

Liao, W., Tseng, Y., Lo, K., & Sheu, J. (2000). GeoGRID: A geocasting protocol for mobile ad hoc networks based on GRID. *Journal of Internet Technology, 1,* 23–32.

Lochert, C., Scheuermann, B., Caliskan, M., & Mauve, M. (2007, January). The feasibility of information dissemination in vehicular ad-hoc networks. *Fourth Annual Conference on Wireless on Demand Network Systems and Services* (WONS '07), (pp. 92-99). Obergurgl, Austria.

Maihöfer, C., Franz, W., & Eberhardt, R. (2003, February). Stored geocast. In *Proceedings of the 13 Fachtagung Kommunikation in Verteilten Systemen (KiVS) Informatik Aktuell* (pp. 257–268). Leipzig, Germany.

Matheus, K., Morich, R., & Lübke, A. (2004). *Economic background of CAR-to-Car Communications*. Retrieved from http://www.network-on-wheels.de/documents.html

Otto, J., & Kutscher, D. (2004, March). Drive thru internet: IEEE 802.11 for automobile users. In *Proceedings of the 23rd Conf. on Computer Communications* (INFOCOM'04), (pp. 365-373). Hong Kong, China.

Ramasubramanian, V., Haas, Z., & Sirer, E. (2003, June). SHARP: a hybrid adaptive routing protocol for mobile ad hoc networks. In *Proceedings of the ACM International Symposium on Mobile Ad Hoc Networking and Computing* (MobiHoc'03), (pp. 303-314). Annapolis, MD.

Schoch, E., Karg, F., Leimüller, T., & Weber, M. (2008, November). Communication Patterns in VANETs. *IEEE Communications Magazine*, *46*(11), 119–125. doi:10.1109/MCOM.2008.4689254

Tian, J., Marrón, P., & Rothermel, K. (2005, February). Location-Based Hierarchical Data Aggregation in Vehicular Ad Hoc Networks, In *Proceedings of the 14 ITG/GI-Fachtagung Kommunikation in Verteilten Systemen* (KiVS'05), (pp. 166-177). Kaiserslautern, Germany.

Wischhof, L., Ebner, A., & Rohling, H. (2005, March). Information Dissemination in Self-organizing Intervehicle Networks. *IEEE Transactions on Intelligent Transportation Systems*, *6*(1), 90–101. doi:10.1109/TITS.2004.842407

Yousefi, S., Mousavi, M., & Fathy, M. (2006). Vehicular Ad Hoc Networks (VANETs): Challenges and Perspectives. In *Proceedings of the 6th International Conference on ITS Telecommunications*. (pp. 761-766). Chegdu, China.

Zhao, J., & Cao, G. (2008, May). VADD: Vehicle-Assisted Data Delivery in Vehicular Ad Hoc Networks. *IEEE Transactions on Vehicular Technology*, *57*(3), 1910–1922. doi:10.1109/TVT.2007.901869

Zhao, S., & Raychaudhuri, D. (2006, March). Policy-Based Adaptive Routing in Mobile Ad Hoc Wireless Networks. In *Proceeding of the IEEE 2006 Snarnoff Symposium*. (pp. 1-4). Princeton, NJ.

KEY TERMS AND DEFINITIONS

Adaptation: In computer science, adaptation refers to the changing of behavior of an executing system at runtime in order to achieve more performance.

Broadcast: Refers to the network operation of transmitting to every receiving station in the communication range.

Context: The circumstances or events that form the environment within which something exists or takes place.

Multihop: Multihop refers when the communication between two nodes is done by passing by other nodes of the network.

Network Layer: The Network Layer is layer three of the seven-layer OSI model of computer networking, this layer is responsible for end-to-end (source to destination) message delivery including passing through intermediate hosts, whereas the Data Link Layer is responsible for node-to-node message delivery on the same link.

Pattern: A form or model proposed for a general reusable solution imitation. Anything proposed for imitation; an archetype; an exemplar; that which is to be, or is worthy to be, copied or imitated;

Policy: A policy is a set of considerations designed to guide decisions on courses of actions.

Protocol: In computer network, a protocol is a common language (set of formal rules) that allows nodes to communicate between them. In its simplest form, a protocol can be defined as the rules governing the syntax, semantics, and synchronization of communication.

VANET: A Vehicular Ad-Hoc Network, or VANET, is a form of Mobile ad-hoc network, to provide communications among nearby vehicles and between vehicles and nearby fixed equipment, usually described as roadside equipment.

ENDNOTES

[1] http://www.itsoverview.its.dot.gov/. This website provides an overview of the applications addressed by the Federal Intelligent Transportation Systems (ITS) program and contains links to various information resources that will be useful in the planning and deployment of ITS.

[2] http://www.network-on-wheels.de. Network on Wheels was a German research project carried out by major car manufacturers, suppliers, research institutes and universities, and supported by the German government.

[3] http://www.et2.tu-harburg.de/fleetnet/index.html. FleetNet - Internet on the Road was set up by a consortium of car companies and universities and partly funded by the German Bundesministerium für Bildung und Forschung. FleetNet started on September 2000 and ended on December 2003.

[4] http://www.cartalk2000.net (link not working anymore). CARTALK was an advanced driver support system based on vehicle to vehicle communication technologies as a first step in the development of future co-operative systems for road safety. This European project was comprised of 7 partners, including a car manufacturer, a parts supplier, research institutes and universities.

[5] http://www.itsoverview.its.dot.gov/. This website provides an overview of the applications addressed by the Federal Intelligent Transportation Systems (ITS) program and contains links to various information resources that will be useful in the planning and deployment of ITS.

[6] http://www.ietf.org/rfc/rfc3626.txt. OLSR IETF Standard RFC specification.

[7] http://www.ietf.org/rfc/rfc3561.txt. AODV IETF Standard RFC specification.

Compilation of References

3GUMTS. (2006, December). Evolution: towards a new generation of broadband mobile services, *Manuel de logiciel.* Adrisano, O., Verdone, R., & M, N. (2000, September). Intelligent transportation systems: The role of third-generation mobile radio networks. *IEEE Communications Magazine, 38*(9), 144–151.

Abdalla, G., Abu-Rgheff, M., & Senouci, S. (2006). Current Trends in Vehicular Ad Hoc Networks. In *Proceedings of the 6th International Conference on In ITS Telecommunications,* (pp. 761-766). Chegdu, China.

Abdulhamid, K., & Abdel-Raheem, E. (2007). Performance of DSRC systems using conventional channel estimation at high velocities. *International Journal of Electronics and Communication, 61*(8), 556–561. doi:10.1016/j.aeue.2006.10.005

Abedi, O., Fathy, M., & Taghiloo, J. (2008). Enhancing aodv routing protocol using mobility parameters in vanet. In *Proceedings of AICCSA '08: The 2008 IEEE/ACS International Conference on Computer Systems and Applications,* (pp. 229-235). Washington, DC.

Abuelela, M., & Olariu, S. (2007). Traffic-adaptive packet relaying in VANET. In *Proceedings of the fourth ACM international workshop on Vehicular ad hoc networks (VANET '07).* Pages 77-78. Montreal, Canada

Abuelela, M., Olariu, S., & Weigle, M. C. (2008). *NOTICE: An Architecture for the Notification of Traffic Incidents.* Paper presented at the VTC Spring 2008. *IEEE Vehicular Technology Conference,* 2008.

Adler, C. (2006). *Information Dissemination in Vehicular Ad Hoc Networks* (PhD thesis). University of Munchen, Germany

Adler, C., Eichler, S., Kosch, T., Schroth, C., & Strassberger, M. (2006, September). Self-organized and Context-Adaptive Information Diffusion in Vehicular Ad Hoc Networks. In *Proceedings of the 3rd International Symposium on Wireless Communication Systems (ISWCS '06),* (pp. 307-311). Valencia, Spain.

Agarwal, A., & Little, T. D. (2007). Prospects for Networked Vehicles of the Future. In *Proceedings of the Smart Transportation Workshop in IEEE Real-Time Embedded Technology and Applications Symposium (RTAS).* Bellevue, WA: IEEE Press.

Agarwal, A., Starobinski, D., & Little, T. D. (2007). Exploiting Downstream Mobility to Achieve Fast Upstream Propagation . In *Proceedings of Mobile Networking for Vehicular Environments (MOVE) at IEEE INFOCOM '07.* AK: Anchorage.

Agarwal, A., Starobinski, D., & Little, T. D. (2008). Analytical Model for Message Propagation in Vehicular Ad Hoc Networks. In *Proceedings of the IEEE Vehicualr Technology Conference (VTC-Spring '08).* Singapore: IEEE Press.

Alexiou, A., Bouras, C., & Igglesis, V. (2004, November/December). *Performance evaluation of tcp over umts transport channels.* Presented at the International symposium on communications interworking. Ottawa, Canada.

Alizadeh-Shabdiz, F., & Subramaniam, S. (2004). MAC layer performance analysis of multi-hop ad hoc networks. In *Proceedings of the IEEE Global Telecommunications Conference (GLOBECOM2004),* (Volume 5, 2781-2785). Dallas, TX.

Alshaer, H., & Horlait, E. (2005). An optimized adaptive broadcast scheme for Inter-vehicle communication. In []. Stockholm, Sweden.]. *Proceedings of the Vehicular Technology Conference, 5,* 2840–2844.

Alvarez, L., & Horowitz, R. (1997). *Safe Platooning In Automated Highway Systems.*

Alzoubi, K. M., Wan, P. J., & Frieder, O. (2002). New Distributed Algorithm for Connected Dominating Set in Wireless Ad Hoc Networks. In *Proceedings of the 35th Annual Hawaii International Conference on System Sciences,* (pp. 297). Big Island, HI.

Ammoun, S., Nashashibi, F., & Laurgeau, C. (2006, September). *Real-time crash avoidance system on crossroads based on 802.11 devices and GPS receivers.* Presented at the IEEE intelligent transportation systems conference. Toronto, Canada.

Aquino-Santos, R., Rangel-Licea, V., García-Ruiz, M. A., González-Potes, A., Álvarez-Cárdenas, O., & Edwards-Block, A. (2009). Inter-vehicular Communications using Wireless Ad Hoc Networks. In Guo, H. (Ed.), *Automotive Informatics and Communicative Systems: Principals in Vehicular Networks and Data Exchange* (pp. 120–138). Hershey, PA: IGI Global.

Artimy, M. (2007, September). Local Density Estimation and Dynamic transmission-Range Assignment in Vehicular Ad Hoc Networks. *IEEE Transactions on Intelligent Transportation Systems, 8*(3), 400–412. doi:10.1109/TITS.2007.895290

Artimy, M. M., Robertson, W., & Phillips, W. J. (2004, May). Connectivity in inter-vehicle ad hoc networks. In *Proceedings of the Engineering Canadian Conference on Electrical and Computer* (pg. 293-298).

Bai, F., Sadagopan, N., & Helmy, A. (2003). The IMPORTANT framework for analyzing the Impact of Mobility on Performance of RouTing protocols for Adhoc NeTworks. *Elsevier Ad Hoc Networks, 1,* 383–403.

Bai, F., Sadagopan, N., & Helmy, A. (2005). *Software: Mobility Simulation and Analysis Tools,* Retrieved from http://nile.cise.ufl.edu/important/software.htm

Baker, D. J., & Ephremides, A. (1981, April). A distributed algorithm for organizing mobile radio telecommunication networks. In *Proceedings of the 2nd International Conference on Distributed Computer Systems.* Paris.

Bako, B., Rikanovic, I., Kargl, F., & Schoch, E. (2007). Adaptive Topology Based Gossiping in VANETs Using Position Information. []. New York: Springer.]. *Lecture Notes in Computer Science, 4864,* 66–78. doi:10.1007/978-3-540-77024-4_8

Baldessari, R., Festag, A., & Lenardi, M. (2007, July). C2c-c consortium requirements for nemo route optimization. *Manuel de logiciel* (IETF, draft-baldessari-c2ccc-nemoreq-01).

Baldessari, R., Festag, A., Matos, A., Santos, J., & Aguiar, R. (2006). Flexible connectivity management in vehicular communication networks. In *Proceedings of the WIT 2004.* Hamburg, Germany.

Baldessari, R., Festag, A., Zhang, W., & Le, L. (2008). A manetcentric solution for the application of nemo in vanet using geographic routing. In *Proceedings of the weedev.* Vienna, Austria.

Bana, S. V., & Varaiya, P. (2001). Space Division Multiple Access (SDMA) for robust ad hoc vehicle communication networks. In *Proceedings of the 4th IEEE International Conference on ITS (ITSC2001),* (pp. 962-967). Oakland, CA.

Basagni, S., Chlamtac, I., Syrotiuk, V. R., & Woodward, B. A. (1998). A distance routing effect algorithm for mobility (DREAM). In *Proceedings of the 4th Annual ACM/IEEE International Conference on Mobile Computing and Networking* (MobiCom '98), (pp. 76–84). Dallas, TX.

Basu, P., & Little, T. D. (2004). *Wireless Ad Hoc Discovery of Parking Spaces*. Boston, MA: MobiSys.

Beraldi, R., & Baldoni, R. (2003). Unicast Routing Techniques for Mobile Ad Hoc Networks . In Ilyas, M. (Ed.), *The Handbook of Ad Hoc Wireless Networks*. CRC Press.

Bergamo, P., Cesana, M., Maniezzo, D., Pau, G., Yao, K., Whiteman, D., & Gerla, M. (2003). IEEE 802.11 Wireless network under aggressive mobility scenario. In *Proceedings of the International Telemetry Conference ITC/USA*, Las Vegas, NV.

Berger, I. (2007, March). Standards for Car Talk. *The Institute*.

Bernardos, C. J., Soto, I., Calder'on, M., Boavida, F., & Azcorra, A. (2007). Varon: Vehicular ad hoc route optimisation for nemo. *Computer Communications*, *30*(8), 1765–1784. doi:10.1016/j.comcom.2007.02.011

Bernsena, J., & Manivannan, D. (2009). Unicast routing protocols for vehicular ad hoc networks: A critical comparison and classification. *Pervasive and Mobile Computing*, *5*(1), 1–18. doi:10.1016/j.pmcj.2008.09.001

Bertsekas, D., & Gallager, R. (1987). *Data Networks*. Upper Saddle River, NJ: Prentice Hall Inc.

Bharghavan, V., Demers, A., Shenker, S., & Zhang, L. (1994). Macaw: a media access protocol for wireless lan's. In *SIGCOMM '94: Proceedings of the conference on Communications architectures, protocols and applications*, pages 212-225, New York: ACM.

Bianchi, G. (2000). Performance analysis of the IEEE 802.11 distributed coordination function. *IEEE Journal on Selected Areas in Communications*, *18*(3), 535–547. doi:10.1109/49.840210

Bianchi, G., Campbell, A. T., & Liao, R. R. F. (1998, May). On utility-fair adaptive services in wireless networks. In *Proceedings of the. 6th International Workshop on Quality of Service (IEEE/IFIP IWQOS'98)*. Napa Valley, CA.

Biswas, S., Tatchikou, R., & Dion, F. (2006). Vehicle-to-vehicle wireless communication protocols for enhancing highway traffic safety. *Communications Magazine, IEEE*, *44*(1), 74–82. doi:10.1109/MCOM.2006.1580935

Bloom, B. (1970). Space/time trade-offs in hash coding with allowable errors. *Communications of the ACM*, *13*(7), 422–426. doi:10.1145/362686.362692

Blum, J. J., Eskandarian, A., & Hoffman, L. J. (2004). Challenges of intervehicle ad hoc networks. *IEEE Transactions on Intelligent Transportation Systems*, *5*(4), 347–351. doi:10.1109/TITS.2004.838218

Blum, J., Eskandarian, A., & Hoffman, L. (2003). Mobility management in IVC networks. In *Proceedings of the IEEE Intelligent Vehicles Symposium* (150-155). Columbus, OH.

Blum, J., Eskandarian, A., & Hoffman, L. (2003). Performance Characteristics of Inter- Vehicle Ad Hoc Networks". *The IEEE 6th International Conference on Intelligent Transportation Systems,* Shanghai, China, page 114-119, 2003.

Boleng, J., Navidi, W., & Camp, T. (2002). Metrics to Enable Adaptive Protocols for Mobile Ad Hoc Networks. In [Las Vegas, NV.]. *Proceedings of the International Conference on Wireless Networks ICWN*, *02*, 293–298.

Borgonovo, F., Capone, A., Cesana, M., & Fratta, L. (2004). ADHOC MAC: new MAC architecture for ad hoc networks providing efficient and reliable point-to-point and broadcast services. *Wireless Networks*, *10*(4), 359–366. doi:10.1023/B:WINE.0000028540.96160.8a

Bottazzi, D., Corradi, A., & Montanari, R. (2004). Context-awareness for impromptu collaboration in MANETs. In *Proceedings of the IEEE International Symposium on Network Computing and Applications (NCA)*, (pp. 339–342). Cambridge, MA.

Boukerche, A., Oliveira, H., Nakamura, E., Jang, K., & Loureiro, A. (2008, July). Vehicular ad hoc networks: A new challenge for localization-based systems. *Computer Communications*, *31*(12), 2838–2849. doi:10.1016/j.comcom.2007.12.004

Breitenberger, S., Grber, B., Neuherz, M., & Kates, R. (2004, July). Traffic information potential and necessary penetration rates. *Traffic engineering & control*, *45*(11), 396–401.

Briesemeister, L., & Hommel, G. (2000). Role-based Multicast in Highly Mobile But Sparsely Connected Ad Hoc Netwokrs. In *Proceedings of the First ACM International Symposium on Mobile Ad hoc Networkingand Computing (MobiHoc '00)* (pp. 45-50). Boston, MA: IEEE Press.

Briesemeister, L., Schäfers, L., & Hommel, G. (2000). Disseminating messages among highly mobile hosts based on inter-vehicle communication. In *Proceedings of the IEEE Intelligent Vehicles Symposium* (pp. 522-527). Dearborn, MI.

Bronsted, J., & Kristensen, L. M. (2006). Specification and performance evaluation of two zone dissemination protocols for vehicular ad-hoc networks. In *ANSS '06: Proceedings of the 39th annual Symposium on Simulation*, (pp. 68-79), Washington, DC.

Bychkovsky, V., Hull, B., Miu, K., Balakrishnan, H., & Madden, S. (2006, September). *A Measurement Study of Vehicular Internet Access Using In Situ Wi-Fi Networks*. Presented at the 12th ACM MOBICOM Conf. Los Angeles.

Calinescu, G., Mandoiu, I., Wan, P. J., & Zelikovsky, A. (2001). Selecting Forwarding Neighbors in Wireless Ad Hoc Networks. In *Proceedings of the ACM Int'l Workshop Discrete Algorithms and Methods for Mobile Computing*, (pp. 34-43).

Cao, G., Yin, L., & Das, C. R. (2004). Cooperative cache-based data access in ad hoc networks. *IEEE Computer*, *37*(2), 32–39.

Car2Car (n.d.). *Car2Car Communication Consortium*. Retrieved from http://www.carto-car.org/

Castaneda, R., Das, S. R., & Marina, M. K. (1999). Query localization techniques for on-demand routing protocols in ad hoc networks. In *Proceedings of the ACM/IEEE International Conference on Mobile Computing and Networking (MobiCom)*, (pp. 186–194). Seattle, WA.

Cavoukian, A. (1998, May). *Information and Privacy Commissioner Ontario 407 Express Toll Route: How You Can Travel the 407 Anonymously*. Ph.D. Commissioner.

Cenerario, N., Delot, T., & Ilarri, S. (2008, June). Dissemination of information in inter-vehicle ad hoc networks". In [Eindhoven, The Netherlands.]. *Proceedings of the IEEE Intelligent Vehicles Symposium*, *2008*, 763–768.

Chakeres, I., & Belding-Royer, M. (2004). AODV routing protocol implementation design. In *Proceedings of the internationalworkshop on wireless ad hoc networking (WWAN)*.Tokyo, Japan.

Chakraborty, D., & Joshi, A. (2002). GSD: A novel group-based service discovery protocol for MANETs. In *Proceedings of the IEEE Conference on Mobile and Wireless Communication Networks (MWCN)*.Stockholm, Sweden.

Chandler, R. E., Herman, R. & Montroll, E. W. (1958). Traffic Dynamics: Studies in Car Following, Operations Research 6. *Operations Research Society of America*, 165-184.

Chatterjee, M., Das, S. K., & Turgut, D. (2002). WCA: A weighted clustering algorithm for mobile ad hoc networks. *Cluster Computing*, *5*(2), 193–204. doi:10.1023/A:1013941929408

Chatzigiannakis, I., Nikoletseas, E., & Spirakis, P. (2001). *An efficient communication strategy for ad-hoc mobile networks*. Presented at the 15th international conference on distributed computing. London.

Chen, L., Steenstra, J., & K-S taylor. (2008, January). *Geolocation-based addressing method for ipv6 addresses* (Patent). San Diego, CA: Qualcomm Incorporated.

Chen, S., & Nahrstedt, K. (1999). Distributed quality-of-service routing in ad-hoc networks. *IEEE Journal on Selected Areas in Communications*, *17*(8), 1488{1505.

Chen, X., Refai, H. H., & Ma, X. (2007). A quantitative approach to evaluate DSRC highway inter-vehicle safety communication. In *Proceedings of the IEEE Global Telecommunications Conference (GLOBECOM2007)*, (pp.151-155). Washington, DC.

Chen, X., Refai, H. H., & Ma, X. (2008). On the enhancements to IEEE 802.11 MAC and their suitability for safety-critical applications in VANET, *Wireless Communications and Mobile Computing*. Retrieved from http://dx.doi.org/10.1002/wcm.674

Chen, Z. D., Kung, H. T., & Vlah, D. (2001). Ad hoc relay wireless networks over moving vehicles on highways. In *Proceedings of 2nd ACM International Symposium on Mobile Ad Hoc Networking and Computing* (MobiHoc'01), (pp. 247-250). Long Beach, CA.

Cheng, P. C., Weng, J. T., Tung, L. C., Lee, K. C., Gerla, M., & Härri, J. (2008). GeoDTN+NAV: A Hybrid Geographic and DTN Routing with Navigation Assistance in Urban Vehicular Networks. In *Proceedings of the 1st International Symposium on Vehicular Computing Systems* (ISVCS'08), Dublin, Ireland.

Chiasserini, C. F., Fasolo, E., Furiato, R., Gaeta, R., Garetto, M., Gribaudo, M., et al. (2005). Smart Broadcast of Warning Messages in Vehicular Ad Hoc Networks. In *Proceedings of the Workshop Interno Progetto NEWCOM*. Turin, Italy.

Chisalita, I., & Shahmehri, N. (2004). A context based vehicular communication protocol. In *Proceedings of the IEEE Personal, Indoor and Mobile Radio Communication Symposium*. Barcelona, Spain.

Chite, V. A., & Daigle, J. N. (2003). Performance of IP-Based Services over GPRS. *IEEE Transactions on Computers*, *52*(6), 727–741. doi:10.1109/TC.2003.1204829

Choudhury, R. R., & Vaidya, N. H. (2004). Deafness: a MAC problem in ad hoc networks when using directional antennas. In *Proceedings of the 12th IEEE International Conference on Network Protocols (ICNP2004)*, (pp. 283-292). Berlin, Germany.

Chow, C.-Y., Leong, H. V., & Chan, A. T. S. (2007). GroCoca: Group-based peer-to-peer cooperative caching in mobile environment. *IEEE Journal on Selected Areas in Communications*, *25*(1), 179–191. doi:10.1109/JSAC.2007.070118

Clausen, T., Jacquet, P., Laouiti, A., Muhlethaler, P., Qayyum, A., & Viennot, L. (2001). Optimized link state routing protocol. In *Proceedings of IEEE international multitopic conference INMIC*. Islamabad, Pakistan.

Clifford Neuman, B. (1994). Scale in distributed systems . In *Readings in distributed computing systems* (pp. 463–489). IEEE Computer Society Press.

Community-wide Library. (n.d.). *Community-wide Library of mobility and Wireless Networks Measurements*. Retrieved from http://nile.usc.edu/MobiLib

Costa, P., Frey, D., Migliavacca, M., & Mottola, L. (2006). Towards lightweight information dissemination in inter-vehicular networks. *In Proceedings of the 3rd international workshop on Vehicular ad hoc networks* (VANET'06), (pp. 20-29). Los Angeles.

Crowther, W., Rettberg, R., Waldem, D., Omstein, S., & Heart, F. (1973). A system for broadcast communications: Reservation ALOHA. In *Proceedings of the 6th Hawaii International Conference on System Sciences*, (pp. 596-603). Honolulu, HI.

Csilla, Y. K. (n.d.). Application Level Protocol for Accident Reconstruction in VANETs. Retrieved from http://www.cse.sc.edu/research/isl/docs/Preliminary_Proposal_813.pdf

Da Chen, Z., Kung, H. T., & Vlah, D. (2001, October). *Ad Hoc Relay Wireless Networks over Moving Vehicles on Highways*. Poster session presented at the Proceedings of the International Conference on Mobile Computing and Networking, Long Beach, CA (pp. 247-250). New York, NY, USA: ACM.

DaeiNabi. A., Ghaffarpour Rahbar, A., & Khademzadeh, A. (2009. May). Adaptive Allocation of Transmission Range in Vehicular Ad-Hoc Networks. In *Proceedings of the 17th Iranian Conference on Electrical Engineering (ICEE2009)*, Tehran, Iran.

Das, S., Nandan, A., Pau, G., Sanadidi, M. Y., & Gerla, M. (2004). SPAWN: A swarming protocol for vehicular ad-hoc wireless networks. In *Proceedings of the First ACM Workshop on Vehicular Ad Hoc Networks (VANETs)*, (pp. 93–94). Philadelphia.

Dastrup, E., Less, M. L., Dawson, J. D., Lee, J. D., & Rizzo, M. (2009, June 22-25). Differences in Simulated Car Following Behavior of Younger and Older Drivers. In *Proceedings of the Fifth International Driving Symposium on Human Factors in Driver Assessment, Training and Vehicle Design.* Big Sky, MT.

Davies, V. (2000). *Evaluating Mobility Models within an Ad Hoc Network* (MS thesis). Golden, CO: Colorado school of Mines.

Davis, J., Fagg, A., & Levine, B. (2001). Wearable computers as packet transport mechanisms in highly-partitioned ad-hoc networks. In *Proceedings of the International Symposium on Wearable* Computing. Seoul, South Korea.

Defude, B., Delot, T., & Ilarri, S. Zechinelli, Martini, J. -L., & Cenerario, N. (2008, July). Data aggregation in VANETs: the VESPA approach. In *Proceedings of Mobiquitous'08 - 1st International Workshop on Computational Transportation Science IWCTS'08.* Dublin, Ireland: ACM Digital Library.

Devarapalli, V., Wakikawa, R., Petrescu, A., & Thubert, P. (2005, January). *Network mobility (NEMO) basic support protocol.* IETF RFC3963.

Ding, Y., Wang, C., & Xiao, L. (2008). A static-node assisted adaptive routing protocol in vehicular networks. In *Proceedings of the 5th ACM International Workshop on Vehicular Ad Hoc Networks* (VANET2008) (pp.59-68). San Francisco.

Duros, E., Dabbous, W., Izumiyama, H., Fujii, N., & Zhang, Y. (2001, March). *A link-layer tunneling mechanism for unidirectional links.* IETF RFC3077.

Ebner, A., & Rohling, H. (2001). A self-organized radio network for automotive applications. In *Proceedings of ITS 2001, 8th World Congress on Intelligent Transportation Systems.* Sydney, Australia.

Ebner, A., Rohling, H., Wischhof, L., Halfmann, R., & Lott, M. (2003). Performance of UTRA TDD ad-hoc and IEEE 802.11b in vehicular environments. In *Proceedings of the IEEE 57th Vehicular Technology Conference Spring (VTC-Spring),* (pp. 960–964). Jeju, South Korea.

Eddy, W., Ivancic, W., & Davis, T. (2007, December). *Nemo route optimization requirements for operational use in aeronautics and space exploration mobile networks.* IETF, draft-ietf-mext-aero-reqs-00.

Eichler, S., Schroth, C., Kosch, T., & Strassberger, M. (2006, July). Strategies for context-adaptive message dissemination in vehicular ad hoc networks. In *Proceedings of the Second International Workshop on Vehicle-toVehicle Communications* (V2VCOM), (pp. 1-9). San Jose, CA.

ElBatt, T., Goel, S., Holland, G., Krishnan, H., & Parikh, J. (2006, September). *Cooperative collision warning using dedicated short range wireless communications.* Presented at the International conference on mobile computing and networking, international workshop on vehicular ad hoc networks. Los Angeles.

Erdos, P., & Renyi, A. (1960). On the evolution of random graphs. *Mathematical Institute of the Hungarian Academy of Sciences, 5*, 17–61.

Ernst, T., Montavont, N., Wakikawa, R., Ng, C., & Kuladinithi, K. (2007, July). *Motivations and scenarios for using multiple interfaces and global addresses,* Manuel de logiciel. IETF, draft-ietf-monami6-multihoming-motivation-scenario-02.

eSafety (n.d.). *The eSafety initiative.* Retrieved from http://www.esafetysupport.org/

Ethereal (n.d.). Ethereal WLAN cards. Retrieved May 29, 2009 from http://www.ethereal.com/

ETSI, Universal Mobile Telecommunications System (UMTS). (1998). *Selection procedures for choice of radio transmission technologies of the UMTS* (UMTS 30.03 Version 3.2.0). Retrieved from http://www.3gpp.org/ftp/specs/html-info/3003u.htm

European telecommunications (n.d.). *European telecommunications standards institute.* Retrieved from http://www.etsi.org

F¨ußler, H., Hannes, H., J¨org, W., Martin, M., & Wolfgang, E. (2004, March). Contention-Based Forwarding for Street Scenarios. In *Proceedings of the 1st International Workshop in Intelligent Transportation* (WIT 2004), (pp155–160). Hamburg, Germany.

F¨ußler, H., Mauve, M., Hartenstein, H., Käsemann, M., & Vollmer, D. (2002). Location-Based Routing for Vehicular Ad Hoc Networks. *Mobile Computing and Communication Review, 1*(2).

Fall, K. (2003). A Delay Tolerant Network Architecture for Challenged Internets. In [New York: ACM Press.]. *Proceedings of SIGCOMM, 03,* 27–34.

Fan, P. A., Nelson, P., Haran, J., & Dillenburg, J. (2007). A Novel Direction-Based Clustering Algorithm in Vehicular Ad Hoc Networks. In *Proceedings of the Transportation Research Board 86ᵗʰ Annual Meeting,* Washington DC

Fan, P., Harran, G. J., Dillenburg, J., & Nelson, P. C. (2005). Cluster-Based Framework in Vehicular Ad-Hoc Networks (ADHOC-NOW 2005, LNCS 3738), (32–42). New York: Springer.

Fatal Car Accidents. (2005). *Fatal Car Accidents.* Retrieved from http://www.car-accidents.com/pages/fatal-accident-statistics.html

Feller, W. (1971). *An Introduction to Probability Theory and Its Applications* (2nd ed., *Vol. 2*). New York: Wiley.

Feng, K. T., Hsu, C. H., & Lu, T. E. (2008). Velocity-assisted predictive mobility and location-aware routing protocols for mobile ad hoc networks. *IEEE Transactions on Vehicular Technology, 57*(1), 448–464. doi:10.1109/TVT.2007.901897

Ferguson, T. S. (1989). Who solved the secretary problem? *Statistical Science, 4*(1), 282–296. doi:10.1214/ss/1177012493

Festag, A., Noecker, G., Strassberger, M., Lübke, A., Bochow, B., Torrent-Moreno, M., et al. (2008). *'NoW – Network on Wheels': Project Objectives, Technology and Achievements.* Paper presented at the 5rd International Workshop on Intelligent Transportation (WIT).

Fiore, M. (2006). *Mobility Models in Inter Vehicle Communications Literature (Technical Report).* Politecnico di Torino.

Fiore, M. (2009). Vehicular Mobility Models. In S Olariu, M C Weigle (Ed.), Vehicular Networks From Theory to Practise, (pp 12-2 to 12-15).Boca Raton, FL: CRC Press.

Fiore, M., & Härri, J. (2008). The networking shape of vehicular mobility. In *Proceedings of the 9th ACM International Symposium on Mobile Ad Hoc Networking and Computing* (MobiHoc'08), (pp. 108–119). Hong Kong, China.

Fiore, M., Casetti, C., & Chiasserini, C. F. (2009). Information density estimation for content retrieval in MANETs. *IEEE Transactions on Mobile Computing, 8*(3), 289–303. doi:10.1109/TMC.2008.110

Fiore, M., Casetti, C., Chiasserini, C.-F., & Garetto, M. (2007). Analysis and simulation of a content delivery application for vehicular wireless networks. *Elsevier Performance Evaluation, 64*(5), 444–463. doi:10.1016/j.peva.2006.08.008

Fiore, M., Haerri, J., Filali, F., & Bonnet, C. (2007). Vehicular Mobility Simulation for VANETs. In *Proceedings of the IEEE Annual Simulation Symposium (ANSS),* Norfolk, VA.

Fiore, M., Mininni, F., Casetti, C., & Chiasserini, C.-F. (in press). To cache or not to cache? In *Proceedings of IEEE International Conference on Computer Communications (INFOCOM).*

FleetNet. (n.d.). *The FleetNet Project.* Retrieved from http://www.fleetnet.de

Flury, R., & Wattenhofer, R. (2006). MLS: an efficient location service for mobile ad hoc networks. In Proceedings of MobiHoc '06: The 7th ACM international symposium on Mobile ad hoc networking and computing, (pp. 226–237). New York.

Fonseca, E., & Festag, A. (2006, March). *A Survey of Existing Approaches for Secure Ad Hoc Routing and Their Applicability to VANETS* (Technical Report NLE-PR). Heidelberg, Germany: NEC Network Laboratories.

Fontaine, M. D. (2009). Traffic Monitoring. In Olariu, I. S., & Weigle, M. C. (Eds.), *Vehicular Networks form Theory to Practice* (pp. 1-2–1-4). Boca Raton, FL: CRC Press.

Forderer, D. (2005, May). *Street-Topology Based Routing* (Master's thesis). Mannheim, Germany: University of Mannheim.

Frank, J., & Martel, C. U. (1995). Phase transitions in the properties of random graphs. In *Principles and Practice of Constraint Programming (CP-95)*. Cambridge, MA: MIT Press.

Franz, W., Eberhardt, R., & Luckenbach, T. (2001, October). FleetNet - Internet on the Road. In *Proceedings of the 8th World Congress on Intelligent Transportation Systems*. Sydney, Australia.

Franz, W., Hartenstein, H., & Bochow, B. (2001, September). *Internet on the road via inter-vehicle communications*. Presented at the GI/OCG Annual Conference: Workshop on Mobile Communications over Wireless LAN: Research and Applications, Vienna, Austria.

Franz, W., Wagner, C., Maihofer, C., & Hartenstein, H. (2004). *Fleetnet: Platform for inter-vehicle communications*. Paper presented at the 1st Intl. Workshop on Intelligent Transportation.

Frenkiel, R. H., Badrinath, B. R., Borras, J., & Yates, R. D. (2000). The infostations challenge: Balancing cost and ubiquity in delivering wireless data. *IEEE Personal Communications Magazine, 7*, 66–71. doi:10.1109/98.839333

Füßler, H., Mauve, M., Hartenstein, H., Käsemann, M., & Vollmer, D. (2003). MobiCom Poster: Location-Based Routing for Vehicular Ad hoc Networks. *ACM SIGMOBILE Mobile Computing and Communication Review, 7*(1), 47–49.

Füßler, H., Torrent-Moreno, M., Transier, M., Krüger, R., Hartenstein, H., & Effelsberg, W. (2005). Studying vehicle movements on highways and their impact on adhoc connectivity. In *Proceedings of ACM International Conference on Mobile Computing and Networking* (Mobicom 2005). Cologne, Germany.

Gabriel, K. R., & Sokal, R. (1969). A new statistical approach to geographic variation analysis. *18. Systematic Zoology*, 231–268.

Gawron, C. (1998). An iterative algorithm to determine the dynamic user equilibrium in a traffic simulation model. *International Journal of Modern Physics C, 9*(3), 393–407.

Gazis, D. C., Herman, R., & Rothrey, R. W. (1961). Non Linear Follow the Leader Models of Traffic Flow. *Operations Research, 9*(4), 545–567.

Gelle, P., Grren, D., & Staddon, J. (2004). Detection and Correcting Malicious Data in VANETs. In [Philadelphia.]. *Proceedings of VANETS, 04*, 29–37.

Generic Mobility Simulation Framework (GMSF). (2007). *Generic Mobility Simulation Framework*. Retrieved from http://gmsf.hypert.net/

Geonet (n.d.). *Geonet project*. Retrieved from http://www.geonet-project.eu

Gerla, M., & Tsai, J. (1995). Multicluster, mobile, multimedia radio network. *Wireless Networks, 1*(3), 255–265. doi:10.1007/BF01200845

Ghandeharizadeh, S., & Krishnamachari, B. (2004). C2P2: Peer-to-peer network for on-demand automobile information services. In *Proceedings of the 15th International Workshop on Database and Expert Systems Applications (DEXA)*, (pp. 538–542). Zaragoza, Spain.

Ghandeharizadeh, S., Kapadia, S., & Krishnamachari, B. (2004). PAVAN: A policy framework for content availability in vehicular ad-hoc networks. In *Proceedings of the First ACM Workshop on Vehicular Ad Hoc Networks (VANETs)*, (pp. 57–65). Philadelphia.

Giannoulis, S., Katsanos, C., Koubias, S., & Papadopoulos, G. (2004, September). A hybrid adaptive routing protocol for ad hoc wireless networks. In *Proceedings of IEEE International Workshop on Factory Communication Systems WFCS'04*. (pp. 287-290). Vienna, Austria.

Giordano, S., et al. (2003, December). Position based routing algorithms for ad hoc networks: A taxonomy. In X. Cheng, X. Huang, & D. Z. Du (Eds.), Ad Hoc Wireless Networking. Boston: Kluwer.

Gipps, P. G. (1981). A Behavioral Car Following Model for Computer Simulation. *Transportation Research Part B: Methodological, 15*, 105–111.

Gipps, P. G. (1986). A model for the structure of lane-changing decisions. *Transportation Research Board, 20*(5), 403–414.

Glathe, H. P., Karlsson, K., Brusaglino, G. P., & Calandrino, L. (1990, May). The Prometheus Programme – Objectives, Concepts and Technology for future Road Traffic. *XXIII Fisita Congress*, 477-484.

Gong, J., Xu, C. Z., & Holle, J. (2007). Predictive directional greedy routing in vehicular ad hoc networks. In *Proceedings of ICDCSW '07: The 27th International Conference on Distributed Computing Systems Workshops*, (p. 2). Washington, DC.

Gongjun, Y., Olariu, S., Weigle, M., & Abuelela, M. (2008, October). SmartParking: A Secure and Intelligent Parking System Using NOTICE. In *Proceedings of the International IEEE Conference on Intelligent Transportation Systems* (pp. 569-574). Beijing, China.

Granelli, F., Boato, G., & Kliazovich, D. (2006). MORA: a movement-based routing algorithm for vehicle ad hoc networks. In *Proceedings of the 1st IEEE Workshop on Automotive Networking and Applications* (AutoNet 2006). San Francisco.

Granelli, F., Boato, G., Kliazovich, D., & Vernazza, G. (2007). Enhanced GPSR routing in multi-hop vehicular communications through movement awareness. *IEEE Communications Letters, 11*(10), 781–783. doi:10.1109/LCOMM.2007.070685

Greenshields, D. (1959). A study of Traffic Capacity. In *Proceedings of the Highway Research Board*, (Vol. 14, pp 228-477). Washington, DC: Highway Research Board, Harri, J., Filali, F., & Bonnet, C. (2005). A Framework for Mobility Models Generation and its Application to Inter-Vehicular Networks (Research Report RR-05-137). Sophia-Antipolis, France: Department of Mobile Communication.

Grossman, L. (n.d.). *Building the Best Driverless Robot Car.* Retrieved March 2008, from http://www.time.com/time/magazine/article/0,9171,1684543,00.html

Guo, H. (2009). *Automotive informatics and communicative systems: principles in vehicular networks and data exchange.* Hershey, PA: IGI Global.

Guo, M. M. H. A., & Zegura, E. W. (2005). V3: A vehicle to vehicle live video streaming architecture. In *Proceedings of IEEE Percom* (p. 171-180). Arlington, TX.

Guo, S., & Falaki, M. H. Oliver, Rahman, S., Seth, A., Zaharia, M., Ismail, U., & Keshav, S. (2007). Design and implementation of the kiosknet system. In *Proceedings of the International Conference on Information and Communication Technologies and Development* (ICTD 2007), (pp. 300–309). Bangalore, India.

Hadzic, I., Marcus, W., & Smith, J. (1999, January). *Policy and Mechanism in Adaptive Protocols* (Technical report no. MS-CIS-01-03). Philadelphia: Department of Computer & Information Science University of Pennsylvannia and Bellcore.

Haerri, J., Filali, F., & Bonnet, C. (n.d.). On meaningful parameters for routing in VANETs urban environments under realistic mobility patterns. In *Proceedings of 1st IEEE Workshop on Automotive Networking and Applications* (AutoNet 2006). San Francisco.

Han, M., Moon, S., Lee, Y., Jang, K., & Lee, D. (2008, April). *Evaluation of MoIP quality verWiBro.* Presented at the Passive and active measurement conference. Cleveland, OH.

Hara, T. (2001). Effective replica allocation in ad hoc networks for improving data accessibility. In *Proceedings of the IEEE International Conference on Computer Communications (INFOCOM),* Anchorage, AK.

Härri, J. (2008). *VanetMobisim project.* Retrieved from http://vanet.eurecom.fr

Harri, J., Filali, F., & Bonnet, C. (2007). *Mobility Models for Vehicular Ad Hoc Networks: A survey and Taxonomy* (Research Report RR-06-168). Antipolis, France: Institute of EURECOM.

Hartenstein, H., & Laberteaux, K. P. (2008). Topics in ad hoc and sensor networks - A tutorial survey on vehicular ad hoc networks. *IEEE Communications, 46*(6), 164–171. doi:10.1109/MCOM.2008.4539481

Hartenstein, H., & Laberteaux, K. P. (2008, June). A tutorial survey on vehicular ad hoc networks. *IEEE Communications Magazine, 46*(6), 164–171. doi:10.1109/MCOM.2008.4539481

Hassan, A. (2009). *VANET Simulation Technical Report,* IDE 0948.

Hattori, G., Ono, C., Nishiyama, S., & Horiuchi, H. (2004, January). *Implementation and evaluation of message delegation middleware for ITS application.* Presented at the International symposium on applications and the internet workshops. Tokyo, Japan.

Hauspie, M., Panier, A., & Simplot-Ryl, D. (2004). Localized probabilistic and dominating set based algorithm for efficient information dissemination in ad hoc networks. In *Proceedings of the IEEE International Conference on Mobile Ad-hoc and Sensor Systems* (MASS). Washington, DC.

Hayashi, H., Hara, T., & Nishio, S. (2006). On updated data dissemination exploiting an epidemic model in ad hoc networks. In *Proceedings of the 2nd International Workshop on Biologically Inspired Approaches to Advanced Information Technology* (BioADIT). Osaka, Japan.

He, R., Rutagemwa, H., & Shen, X. (2008). Differentiated reliable routing in hybrid vehicular ad-hoc networks. (pp. 2353-2358).

Hecht, C., & Heinig, K. A. (2005). *Map based accident hot spot warning application Concept from the maps & adas vertical subproject of the 6FP integrated project PReVENT.* Germany: Institute of Transport, Road Engineering and Planning University of Hannover.

Helbing, D., Hennecke, A., Shvetsov, V., & Treiber, M. (2002). Micro- and Macrosimulation of Freeway Traffic. *Mathematical and Computer Modelling, 35*(5/6), 517–547. doi:10.1016/S0895-7177(02)80019-X

Hoh, B., Gruteser, M., Xiong, H., & Alrabady, A. (2006, October-December). Enhancing security and privacy in traffic-monitoring systems. *IEEE Pervasive Computing / IEEE Computer Society [and] IEEE Communications Society, 5*(4), 38–46. doi:10.1109/MPRV.2006.69

Hu, C., Hong, Y., & Hou, J. (2003). On mitigating the broadcast storm problem with directional antennas. *In Proceedings of the IEEE International Conference, on Communications, 1,* 104-110. San Francisco.

Huang, X., & Fang, Y. (2009). Performance study of node-disjoint multipath routing in vehicular ad hoc networks. *IEEE Transactions on Vehicular Technology, 58*(4), 1942–1950. doi:10.1109/TVT.2008.2008094

IEEE P802.11p (2008). Draft standard for information technology - Telecommunications and information exchange between systems - Local and metropolitan area networks-specific requirements - Part 11: Wireless LAN medium access control (MAC) and physical layer (PHY) specifications - Amendment 7: Wireless Access in Vehicular Environments.

IEEE Std 802.11-2007 (2007). IEEE standard for information technology - Telecommunications and information exchange between systems - Local and metropolitan area networks-specific requirements - Part 11: Wireless LAN medium access control (MAC) and physical layer (PHY) specifications.

IEEE. (n.d.). *IEEE 802.11p Task Group.* Retrieved from http://grouper.ieee.org/-groups/scc32/dsrc/index.html

IEEE802.16-2004 (2004). IEEE Standard for Local and Metropolitan Area Networks - Part 16: Air Interface for Fixed Broadband Wireless Access Systems.

IEEEStd. 802.11a. (1999). Part *11*: Wireless LAN Medium Access Control (MAC) and Physical Layer (PHY) Specifications: High-speed Physical Layer in the 5GHz Band.

IEEEStd. 802.11b. (1999). Part 11: Wireless LAN Medium Access Control (MAC) and Physical Layer (PHY) Specifications: Higher-speed Physical Layer Extension in the 2.4GHz Band.

IEEEStd. 802.11g. (2003). Part 11: Wireless LAN Medium Access Control (MAC) and Physical Layer (PHY) Specifications- Amendment 4: Further Higher Data Rate Extension in the 2.4GHz Band.

Intelligent Transportation. (n.d.). *The Intelligent Transportation System.* Retrieved from http://www.its.dot.gov/its overview.htm

Internet, I. T. S. (n.d.). *Internet ITS.* Retrieved from http://www.internetits.org

Iwata A. et al. (1999). Scalable Routing Strategies for Ad-hoc Wireless Networks. *IEEE JSAC, Aug*ust, 1369–1379.

Jaap, S., Bechler, M., & Wolf, L. (2005). Evaluation of Routing Protocols for Vehicular Ad Hoc Networks in City Traffic Scenarios. In Proceedings of the 5th International Conference on Intelligent Transportation Systems (ITS), *Telecommunications, June.*

Jakubiak, J., & Koucheryavy, Y. (2008, January 10-12). State of the Art and Research Challenges for VANETs. Presented at the*5th IEEE Consumer Communications and Networking Conference, 2008. CCNC 2008* (pp.912-916).

Jerbi, M., & Senouci, S. M. (2008, April). Characterizing Multi-Hop Communication in Vehicular Networks.*IEEE Wireless Communications and Networking Conference, 2008. WCNC 2008* (pp.3309 – 3313).

Jerbi, M., Senouci, S. M., Doudane, Y. G., & Beylot, A. (2008, October 24). Geo-localized virtual infrastructure for urban vehicular networks. Presented at the *8th International Conference on ITS Telecommunications, 2008. ITST'08* (pp.305-310).

Jerbi, M., Senouci, S. M., Meraihi, R., & Ghamri-Doudane, Y. (2007, June 24-28). An improved vehicular ad hoc routing protocol for city environments. In *Proceedings of the International Conference on Communications* (ICC '07), (pp. 3972–3979). Glasgow, Scotland

Jeremy, J. B., & Azim, E. (2007). A reliable link-layer protocol for robust and scalable intervehicle communications. *IEEE Transactions on Intelligent Transportation Systems, 8*(1), 4–13. doi:10.1109/TITS.2006.889441

Jetcheva, J. G., & Hu, Y. C. PalChaudhuri, S., Saha, A. K., & Johnson, D. B. (2003, October 9-10). Design and evaluation of a metropolitan area multitier wireless ad hoc network architecture. In *Proceedings of the Fifth IEEE Workshop on Mobile Computing Systems and Applications*, (pp. 32-43). Monterey, CA.

Jiang, D., & Delgrossi, L. (2008). *IEEE 802.11p: Towards an International Standard for Wireless Access in Vehicular Environments.* Paper presented at the IEEE Vehicular Technology Conference, 2008. VTC Spring 2008.

Jiang, D., Taliwal, V., Meier, A., Holfelder, W., & Herrtwich, R. (2006). Design of 5.9 GHz DSRC-based vehicular safety communication. *IEEE Wireless Communications, 13*(5), 36–43. doi:10.1109/WC-M.2006.250356

Jiang, H., Guo, H., & Chen, L. (2008). Reliable and efficient alarm message routing in vanet. In *Proceedings of ICDCSW '08: The 2008 The 28th International Conference on Distributed Computing Systems Workshops*, (pp. 186{191). Washington, DC.

Jiang, M., Li, J., & Tay, Y. (2001). Cluster based routing protocol (CBRP) (Rapport technique). IETF. (Internet draft) Johnson, D., Perkins, C., & Arkko, J. (Eds.), Mobility support in ipv6, Manuel de logiciel. (IETF RFC 3775)

Jiang, S., He, D., & Rao, J. (2001). A prediction-based link availability estimation for mobile ad hoc networks. (vol. 3, pp. 1745-1752).

Johnson, D. B., & Maltz, D. A. (1996). Dynamic Source Routing . In Imielinski, T., & Korth, H. (Eds.), *Mobile Computing Ad Hoc Wireless Networks* (pp. 153–181). Boston: Kluwer.

Johnson, D. B., Maltz, D. A., & Broch, J. (2001). DSR: The dynamic source routing protocol for multi-hop wireless ad hoc networks . In Perkins, C. E. (Ed.), *Ad Hoc Networking* (pp. 139–172). Reading, MA: Addison-Wesley.

Johnson, D. B., Maltz, D. A., & Hu, Y. C. (2007). *The dynamic source routing protocol for mobile ad hoc networks (Tech. rep.)*. IETF MANET Working Group.

Jordan, R., Lucas, B., Randler, M., & Wilhelm, U. (2004, June 14-17). *Safety application specific requirements on the data processing of environmental sensors*. Presented at the 2004 IEEE Intelligent Vehicles Symposium University of Parma. Parma, Italy.

Kapadia, S., Krishnamachari, B., & Ghandeharizadeh, S. (2004, October). PAVAN: A Policy Framework for Availability in Vehicular Ad-Hoc Networks. Presented at the *First ACM Workshop on Vehicular Ad Hoc Networks (VANET 2004), Held in conjunction with ACM MobiCom*, Philadelphia, PA.

Karn, P. (1990). MACA a new channel access method for packet radio. In *Proceedings of the 9th Computer Networking Conference*, (pp. 134-140). Ontario, Canada.

Karnadi, F. K., Mo, Z. H., & Lan, K. (2007). Rapid Generation of Realistic Mobility Models for VANET. In *Proceedings of the IEEE Wireless Communication and Networking Conference* (WCNC '07). Hong Kong, China.

Karp, B., & Kung, H. (2000). GPSR: greedy perimeter stateless routing for wireless networks. In *Proceedings of the 6th annual international conference on Mobile computing and networking* (MobiCom '00), (pp. 243-254). New York: ACM Press.

Karpiriski, M., Senart, A., & Cahill, V. (2006). *Sensor Networks for Smart Roads*. Paper presented at the PerCom Workshops 2006 - Fourth Annual IEEE International Conference on Pervasive Computing and Communications Workshops, 2006.

Kato, T., Kadowaki, K., Koita, T., & Sato, K. (2008). Routing and address assignment using lane/position information in a vehicular ad hoc network. In *Proceedings of APSCC '08: The 2008 IEEE Asia-Paci_c Services Computing Conference*, (pp.1600-1605). Washington, DC.

Katragadda, S., Ganesh Murthy, C. N. S., Ranga Rao, M. S., Mohan Kumar, S., & Sachin, R. (2003). A decentralized location-based channel access protocol for inter-vehicle communication. In *Proceedings of the 57th IEEE Vehicular Technology Conference (VTC2003-Spring)*, (Volume 3, (pp. 1831-1835). Taipei, Taiwan.

Kchiche, A., Kamoun, F., Makram, S. A., & Gunes, M. (2008, September 29-October 4). A Traffic-Aware Infrastructure-Based Architecture for Inter-vehicles File Sharing. Presented at *The Second International Conference on Mobile Ubiquitous Computing, Systems, Services and Technologies, 2008. UBICOMM '08* (pp.44-49).

Kesting, A., Treiber, M., & Helbing, D. (2007). MOBIL: General lane changing model for car following models, Transportation Research Record. *Journal of the Transportation Research Board*, 86-94.

Khabazian, M., & Ali, M. (2008). A Performance modeling of connectivity in vehicular ad hoc networks. *IEEE Transactions on Vehicular Technology, 57*(4), 2440–2450. doi:10.1109/TVT.2007.912161

Khaled, Y., Ducourthial, B., & Shawky, M. (2005-Spring). IEEE 802.11 performances for inter-vehicle communication networks. In Proc. of th 61st IEEE semianual vehicular technology conference VTC. Stockholm, Sweden.

Khaled, Y., Ducourthial, B., & Shawky, M. (July, 2007). A usage oriented taxonomy of routing protocols in vanet. In *Proceedings of 1st ubiroads workshop with IEEE GIIS*. Marrakech, Morroco.

Khil, M., & Sichitiu, M. L. (2009). Performance Issues in Vehicular Ad Hoc Networks . In Boukerche, A. (Ed.), *Algorithms and Protocols for Wireless and Mobile Ad Hoc Networks* (pp. 447–450). New York: John Wiley and Sons.

Khisty, C. J., & Lall, B. K. (2003). *Transport Engineering An Introduction*. Upper Saddle River, NJ: Prentice Hall.

Kiess, W., Rybicki, J., & Mauve, M. (2007, February/March). *On the nature of inter-vehicle communications*. Presented at the Workshop on mobile ad-hoc networks. Bern, Switzerland.

Kihl, M., Sichitiu, M., Ekeroth, T., & Rozenberg, M. (2007). *Reliable Geographical Multicast Routing in Vehicular Ad-Hoc Networks.* Berlin, Germany: Springer.

Kim, H., Paik, J., Lee, B., & Lee, D. (2008). Sarc: A street-based anonymous vehicular ad hoc routing protocol for city environment. In *Proceedings of EUC '08: The 2008 IEEE/IFIP International Conference on Embedded and Ubiquitous Computing,* (pp. 324-329). Washington, DC.

Kim, M., Kotz, D., & Kim, S. (2006). Extracting a Mobility Model from Real User Traces. In *Proceedings of the 26th Annual IEEE Conference on Computer Communications* (INFOCOM '06), Barcelona, Spain.

Kim, Y., Yu, J., Choi, S., & Jang, K. (2006). A novel hidden station detection mechanism in IEEE 802.11 WLAN. *IEEE Communications Letters, 10*(8), 608–610. doi:10.1109/LCOMM.2006.1665126

King, T., Füßler, H., Transier, M., & Effelsberg, W. (2006, 03). Dead-Reckoning for Position-Based Forwarding on Highways. In *Proc. of the 3rd international workshop on intelligent transportation* (WIT 2006) (p. 199-204). Hamburg, Germany.

Kitani, T., Shinkawa, T., Shibata, N., Yasumoto, K., Ito, M., & Higashino, T. (2008). Efficient vanet-based traffic information sharing using buses on regular routes. (pp. 3031-3036).

Kleinrock, L. (1975). Theory: *Vol. 1. Queueing Systems.* New York: Wiley-Interscience.

Ko, Y. B., & Vaidya, N. H. (2000). Location-aided routing (LAR) in mobile ad hoc networks. *Wireless Networks, 6*, 307–321. doi:10.1023/A:1019106118419

Ko, Y. B., Shankarkumar, V., & Vaidya, N. H. (2000). Medium access control protocols using directional antennas in ad hoc networks. In *Proceedings of the 19th IEEE Conference on Computer and Communications (INFOCOM2000),* (Volume 1, (pp. 13-21). Tel-Aviv · Israel.

Ko, Y., & Vaidya, N. (1999). Geocasting in mobile ad hoc networks: Location-based multicast algorithms. In *Proceedings of the Second IEEE Workshop on Mobile Computer Systems and Applications,* (WMCSA). Washington, DC.

Kon, F., Costa, F., Blair, G., & Campbell, R. (2002, June). The case for reflective middleware. *Communications of the ACM, 45*(6), 33–38. doi:10.1145/508448.508470

Konstantas, D., & Villalba, A. C. (2006). Towards hovering information. *In Proceedings of the First European Conference on Smart Sensing and Context,* (EuroSSC), (pp. 161-166). University of Twente, The Netherlands.

Korakis, T., Jakllari, G., & Tassiulas, L. (2003). A MAC protocol for full exploitation of directional antennas in ad-hoc wireless networks. In *Proceedings of the 4th ACM International Symposium on Mobile Ad Hoc Networking & Computing (MobiHoc2003).* Annapolis, MD.

Korkmaz, G., & Ekici, E. (2004). Urban Multi-Hop Broadcast for Inter-Vehicle Communication Systems. *In Proceedings of ACM VANET.* (pp. 76-85). Philadelphia.

Korkmaz, G., & Ekici, E. (2006). An Efficient Fully Ad-Hoc Multi-Hop Broadcast Protocol for Inter-Vehicular Communication Systems. *In Proceedings of IEEE International Conference on Communications* (Vol. 1. pp. 104-110). Istanbul, Turkey.

Kosch, T. (2002). *Technical concept and prerequisites of car to car communication (Rapport technique).* Munich, Germany: BMW Group Research and Technology.

Kosch, T., Kulp, I., Bechler, M., Strassberger, M., Weyl, B., & Lasowski, R. (2009). Communication Architecture for Cooperative Systems in Europe. *IEEE Communications, 47*(5), 116–125. doi:10.1109/MCOM.2009.4939287

Kosh, T., Schwingenschlögl, C., & Ai, L. (2002, September). *Information Dissemination in Multihop Inter-vehicle Networks – Adapting the Ad hoc On-demand Distance Vector Routing Protocol (AODV).* Paper presented at the Proceedings in the 5th IEEE International Conference on Intelligent Transportation Systems, Singapore (pp. 685-690). USA: IEEE.

Kozat, U. C., & Tassiulas, L. (2003). Network layer support for service discovery in mobile ad hoc networks. In Proceedings of the *IEEE International Conference on Computer Communications (INFOCOM)*, (pp. 1965-1975). San Diego, CA

Krishnamachari, B., Wickery, S., & Bejarx, R. (2001). Phase Transition Phenomena in Wireless Ad Hoc Networks. In []. San Antonio, TX.]. *Proceedings of IEEE GLOBECOM*, *5*, 2921–2925.

Kronjäger, W., & Hermann, D. (1999). Travel time estimation on the base of microscopic traffic flow simulation. In *Proceedings of ITS World Congress*. Toronto, Canada.

Kumar, R., Naveen, K., & Chilamkurti, B. S. (2007). *A Comparative Study of Different Sensors for Smart Car Park Management*. Presented at The 2007 International Conference on Intelligent Pervasive Computing (IPC 2007). Jeju Island, Korea

Landman, J., & Kritzinger, P. (2005). Delay analysis of downlink IP traffic on UMTS mobile networks. *Performance Evaluation*, *62*(1-4), 68–82. doi:10.1016/j.peva.2005.07.007

Laouiti, A., Qayyum, A., & Viennot, L. (2001). Multipoint relaying: An efficient technique for flooding in mobile wireless network. In *Proceedings of the IEEE 35th Annual Hawaii International Conference on System Sciences* (pp. 3866-3875). Big Island, HI.

Larsson, C., Eriksson, M., Mitsuya, K., Tasaka, K., & Kuntz, R. (2008, July). Flow distribution rule language for multi-access nodes. *Manuel de logiciel* (IETF, draft-larsson-mext-flowdistribution-rules-00)

Lee, B. S., Seet, B. C., Liu, G. P., Foh, C. H., & Wong, K. J. (2004). A Routing Strategy for Metropolis Vehicular Communications. *In Proceedings of the International Conference on Information Networking* (ICOIN'04), (vol. 2, pp 533-542). South Korea.

Lee, J. (2008). Measurement of transmission range effect to the connectivity of vehicular telematics networks. In *Proceedings of the 23rd International Technical Conference on Circuits/Systems, Computers and Communications* (1301-1304). Japan.

Lee, K. C., Haerri, J., Lee, U., & Gerla, M. (2007, November 26-30). Enhanced perimeter routing for geographic forwarding protocols in urban vehicular scenarios. In *Proceedings of IEEE 2007 Globecom Workshops*, (pp. 1–10). Washington, DC.

Lee, K. C., Le, M., Harri, J., & Gerla, M. (2009). Taking the LOUVRE approach. *IEEE Vehicular Technology Magazine*, *4*(1), 86–92. doi:10.1109/MVT.2009.931918

Lee, K. C., Lee, U., & Gerla, M. (2009, February 2-4). TO-GO: TOpology-assist geo-opportunistic routing in urban vehicular grids. In *Proceedings of WONS 2009, The Sixth International Conference on Wireless On-Demand Network Systems and Services*, (pp.11-18). Snowbird, UT.

Lee, K., Le, M., Haerri, J., & Gerla, M. (2008). Louvre: Landmark overlays for urban vehicular routing environments. In *Proceedings of IEEE WiVeC*. Calgary, Canada.

Lee, U., Cheung, R., & Gerla, M. (2009, March). 17). Emerging Vehicular Applications . In Olariu, S., & Weigle, M. C. (Eds.), *Vehicular Networks: From Theory to Practice*. Boca Raton, FL: Chapman & Hall/CRC Computer and Information Science Series.

Lee, U., Zhou, B., Gerla, M., Magistretti, E., Bellavista, P., & Corradi, A. (2006, October). Mobeyes: Smart mobs for urban monitoring with a vehicular sensor network. *IEEE Wireless Communications*, *13*(5), 52–57. doi:10.1109/WC-M.2006.250358

Legendre, F., Borrel, V., Dias de Amorim, M., & Dida, S. F. (2006). *Reconsidering Microscopic Mobility Modeling for Self Organizing Networks*. IEEE Network Magazine.

Leontiadis, I., & Mascolo, C. (2007). GeOpps: Geographical Opportunistic Routing for Vehicular Networks. In *Proceedings of WoWMoM 2007: The IEEE International Symposium on a World of Wireless, Mobile and Multimedia Networks*, (pp.1-6). Helsinki, Finland.

Leutzbach, W., & Wiedemeann, R. (1986, May). Development and Application of Traffic Simulation Models at Karlsruche Institute fur VerKehrwesen. *Traffic Engineering and Control*, 270-278.

Li, F., & Wang, Y. (2007, June). Routing in vehicular ad hoc networks: A survey. *IEEE Vehicular Technology Magazine, 2*(2), 12–22. doi:10.1109/MVT.2007.912927

Li, J., Jannotti, J., Couto, D. S. J. D., Karger, D. R., & Morris, R. (2000). A scalable location service for geographic ad hoc routing. In Proceedings of MobiCom '00: The 6th annual international conference on Mobile computing and networking, (pp.120–130). New York.

Li, M., & Lou, W. (2008). Opportunistic broadcast of emergency messages in vehicular ad hoc networks with unreliable links. In *Proceedings of the 5th International ICST Conference on Heterogeneous Networking for Quality, Reliability, Security and Robustness* (pp. 1-7). Hong Kong, China.

Li, Q., & Rus, D. (2000). *Sending messages to mobile users in disconnected ad-hoc wireless networks.* Presented at the 6th annual international conference on mobile computing and networking (MOBICOM). Boston.

Li, X., & Cuthbert, L. (2004). On-demand node-disjoint multipath routing in wireless ad hoc network. In Proceedings of LCN '04: The 29th Annual IEEE International Conference on Local Computer Networks, (pp. 419-420). Washington, DC.

Liao, W., Tseng, Y., Lo, K., & Sheu, J. (2000). GeoGRID: A geocasting protocol for mobile ad hoc networks based on GRID. *Journal of Internet Technology, 1*, 23–32.

Lim, H., & Kim, C. (2001). Flooding in Wireless Ad Hoc Networks. *Computer Communications, 24*(3-4), 353–363. doi:10.1016/S0140-3664(00)00233-4

Lin, C. R., & Gerla, M. (1997, September). Adaptive Clustering for Mobile Networks. *IEEE Journal on Selected Areas in Communications, 15*(7), 1265–1275. doi:10.1109/49.622910

Lin, X., Lu, R., Zhang, C., Zhu, H., Ho, P.-H., & Shen, X. (2008). 2008). Security in Vehicular ad hoc . *Networks, 46*(4), 88–95.

Little, T. D., & Agarwal, A. (2005). An Information Propagation Scheme for Vehicular Networks. In *Proceedings of IEEE Intelligent Transportation Systems Conference (ITSC)* (pp. 155-160). Vienna, Austria: IEEE.

Liu, X., Fang, Zh., & Shi, L. (2007, July). Securing Vehicular Ad Hoc Networks. In *Proceedings of the 2ⁿᵈ conference on International Pervasive Computing and Applications* (424-429). Birmingham, UK

Lochert, C. (2003). A Routing Strategy for Vehicular Ad Hoc Networks in City Environments. In *Proceedings of theIntelligent Vehicles Symposium, IV*, Ohio, USA.

Lochert, C., Füßler, H., Hartenstein, H., Hermann, D., Tian, J., & Mauve, M. (2003, June). *A Routing Strategy for Vehicular Ad Hoc Networks in City Environments.* Paper presented at the Proceedings of the IEEE Intelligent Vehicles Symposium, Columbus, Ohio (pp. 156-161). USA: IEEE.

Lochert, C., Hartenstein, H., Tian, J., Fuessler, H., Hermann, D., & Mauve, M. (2003). A routing strategy for vehicular ad hoc networks in city environments. In *Proceedings of the Intelligent Vehicles Symposium* (pp. 156-161). Parma, Italy.

Lochert, C., Mauve, M., Füßler, H., & Hartenstein, H. (2005). Geographic routing in city scenarios. *ACM Mobile Computation and Communication Review (MC2R), 9*(1), 69-72.

Lochert, C., Scheuermann, B., Caliskan, M., & Mauve, M. (2007, January). The feasibility of information dissemination in vehicular ad-hoc networks. *Fourth Annual Conference on Wireless on Demand Network Systems and Services* (WONS '07), (pp. 92-99). Obergurgl, Austria.

Lorchat, J., & Uehara, K. (2006, July). *Optimized Inter-Vehicle Communications Using NEMO and MANET* (Invited Paper). Presented at The Second International Workshop on Vehicle-to-Vehicle Communications 2006 (V2VCOM 2006). San Jose, CA.

Luo, J., & Hubaux, J. P. (2005). *A survey of research in inter-vehicle communications, Embedded Security in Cars.* Berlin, Germany: Springer-Verlag.

Mahajan, A., Potinis, N., Gopalan, K., & Wang, A. I.-A. (2005). *Evaluation of Mobility Models for Vehicular Ad Hoc Network Simulations.* (Technical Report N.051220). Tallahassee, FL: Florida State University.

Maihöfer, C. (2004). A survey of geocast routing protocols. *IEEE Communications Surveys & Tutorials, 6*(2), 32–42. doi:10.1109/COMST.2004.5342238

Maihöfer, C., Franz, W., & Eberhardt, R. (2003, February). Stored geocast. In *Proceedings of the 13 Fachtagung Kommunikation in Verteilten Systemen (KiVS) Informatik Aktuell* (pp. 257–268). Leipzig, Germany.

Maihöfer, C., Leinmüller, T., & Schoch, E. (2005). Abiding geocast: time-stable geocast for ad hoc networks. In *Proceedings of the 2nd ACM International Workshop on Vehicular Ad Hoc Networks* (VANET '05), (pp. 20–29). Cologne, Germany.

Malone, D., Duffy, K., & Leith, D. (2007). Modeling the 802.11 Distributed Coordination Function in Nonsaturated Heterogeneous Conditions. *IEEE/ACM Transactions on Networking, 15*(1), 159-172.

Mangharam, R., Weller, D. S., Stencil, D. D., Rajkumar, R., & Parekh, J. S. (2005). GROOVESIM: A Topography-Accurate Simulator for Geographic Routing in Vehicular Networks. In *Proceedings of the Second ACM International Workshop on Vehicular Ad Hoc Networks (VANET '05)* (pp. 59-68). New York: ACM Press.

Marfia, G., Pau, G., Giordano, E., De Sena, E., & Geria, M. (2007, May 11). On Mobility Scenarios and Urban Infrastructure . In *Proceedings of A Case Study 2007 Mobile Networking for Vehicular Environments* (pp. 31–36). VANET.

Masini, B., Fontana, C., & Verdone, R. (2004, October). *Provision of an emergency warning service through GPRS: Performance evaluation.* Presented at the IEEE intelligent transportation systems conference. Washington, DC.

Matheus, K., Morich, R., & Lübke, A. (2004). *Economic background of CAR-to-Car Communications.* Retrieved from http://www.network-on-wheels.de/documents.html

Mauve, M., Widmer, A., & Hartenstein, H. (2001). A survey on position based routing in mobile ad hoc networks. *IEEE Network, 15*(6), 30–39. doi:10.1109/65.967595

Media Lab, M. I. T. (n.d.). *MIT Media Lab: Reality Mining.* Retrieved from http://reality.media.mit.edu

Mehran, A. (2004). A review of routing protocols for mobile ad hoc networks. *Ad Hoc Networks, 2*, 1–22. doi:10.1016/S1570-8705(03)00043-X

Meier, R., Hughes, B., Cunningham, R., & Cahill, V. (2005). Towards real-time middleware for applications of vehicular ad hoc networks. In IFIP WG 6.1 international conference, distributed applications and interoperable systems. Oslo, Norway.

Menouar, H., Filali, F., & Lenardi, M. (2006). A survey and qualitative analysis of mac protocols for vehicular ad hoc networks. *IEEE Wireless Communications, 13*(5), 30–35. doi:10.1109/WC-M.2006.250355

Merugu, S., Ammar, M., & Zegura, E. (2004). *Space-Time Routing in Wireless Networks with Preictable Mobility.* College of Computing, Georgia Institute of Technology, Technical (Report GIT-CC-04-07). Atlanta, GA.

Momeni, S., & Fathy, M. (2008). Vanet's communication. (pp. 608-612).

Monero, M. T., Santi, P., & Hartenstein, H. (2005. September). Fair Sharing of Bandwidth in VANETs. In *Proceedings of VANET'05,* Cologne, Germany.

Morris, R., Jannoti, J., Kaashoek, F., Li, J., & De-couto, D. (2000, September). CarNet: a scalable ad hoc wireless network system. In *Proceedings of SIGOPS European Workshop.* Kolding, Denmark.

Motion, B. (2005). *A mobility scenario generation and analysis tool.* Retrieved from http://web.informatik.uni-bonn.de/iv/mitarbeiter/decvaal/bonnmotion

Moustafa, H., & Zhang, Y. (Eds.). (2009). *Vehicular networks: techniques, standards, and applications.* Boca Raton, FL: Auerbach Publications. doi:10.1201/9781420085723

Murray, T., Cojocari, M., & Fu, H. (2008). *Measuring the Performance of IEEE 802.11p Using ns-2 Simulator for Vehicular Networks.* Paper presented at the IEEE International Conference on Electro/Information Technology, 2008. EIT 2008.

Mylonas, Y., Lestas, M., & Pitsillides, A. (2008). Speed Adaptive Probabilistic Flooding in Cooperative Emergency Warning. *In The First International Workshop on Wireless Vehicular Networking Technology.* Vancouver, Canada.

Nadeem, T., & Shankar, P. (2006, July). A Comparative Study of Data Dissemination Models for VANETs. In *Proceedings of IEEE Mobile and Ubiquitous Systems: Networking & Services,* (1 – 10). San Jose, CA.

Nagel, K., & Schreckenberg, M. (1992). A cellular automaton model for freeway traffic . *Journal de Physique. I, 2,* 2221.

Namboodiri, V., & Gao, L. (2007). Prediction-based routing for vehicular ad hoc networks. *IEEE Transactions on Vehicular Technology, 56*(4), 2332–2345. doi:10.1109/TVT.2007.897656

Namboodiri, V., Agarwal, M., & Gao, L. (2004, October). A study on the feasibility of mobile gateways for vehicular ad-hoc networks. In *Proceedings of the first ACM workshop on Vehicular ad hoc networks* (pp. 66-75). Philadelphia.

Nandan, A., Das, S., Pau, G., Sanadidi, M. Y., & Gerla, M. (2005). Cooperative downloading in vehicular ad hoc networks. In *Proceedings of the IFIP Wireless On demand Networks, Systems and Services (WONS),* (pp. 32–41). St. Moritz, Switzerland.

National Highway Traffic Safety Administration. (2007). *Traffic Safety facts annual report.* Washington, DC: Department of Transportation.

Naumov, V., & Gross, T. (2007). Connectivity-aware routing (CAR) in vehicular ad-hoc networks. In *Proceedings of the IEEE International Conference on Computer Communications (INFOCOM),* (pp. 1919–1927). Anchorage, AK.

Naumov, V., Baumann, R., & Gross, T. (2006). An Evaluation of Inter-Vehicle Ad Hoc Networks Based on Realistic Vehicular Traces. In *Proceedings of the Seventh ACM International Symposium on Mobile Ad Hoc Netowkring and Computing (MobiHoc '06)* (pp. 108-119). Florence, Italy.

Navigation Center, U.S. Department of Homeland Security. (2009). *Differential Global Positioning System (DGPS).* Retrieved from http://www.navcen.uscg.gov/dgps/default.htm

Nekoui, M., Eslami, A., & Pishro-Nik, H. (2008, April). The capacity of Vehicular Ad Hoc Networks with infrastructure. Presented at the *6th International Symposium on Modeling and Optimization in Mobile, Ad Hoc, and Wireless Networks and Workshops, 2008. WiOPT 2008* (pp. 267-272).

Network-on-Wheels. (n.d.). *The Network-on-Wheels Project.* Retrieved from http://www.networkon-wheels.de

Newell, G. F. (2002). A Simplified Car Following Theory: A lower Order Model . *Transportation Research Part B: Methodological, 36,* 195–205.

Ng, C., Ernst, T., Paik, E., & Bagnulo, M. (2007, October). *Analysis of multihoming in network mobility support* (IETF, RFC4980). Singapore: Panasonic Labs.

Ng, C., Thubert, P., Watari, M., & Zhao, F. (2007, July). *Network mobility route optimization problem statement* (IETF RFC4888). Singapore: Panasonic Labs.

Ni, S., Tseng, Y., & Shih, E. Y. (2001). Adaptive approaches to relieving broadcast storms in a wireless multihop mobile Ad Hoc network. In *Proceedings IEEE 21st International Conference on Distributed Computing Systems.* (pp. 481-488). Phoenix, AZ.

Ni, S., Tseng, Y., Chen, Y., & Sheu, J. (1999). The broadcast storm problem in a mobile ad hoc network. In *Proceedings of the 5th Annual ACM/IEEE International Conference on Mobile Computing and Networking* (MobiCom '99), (pp. 151-162). Seattle, WA.

Niu, Z., Yao, W., Ni, Q., & Song, Y. (2007). Dereq: a qos routing algorithm for multimedia communications in vehicular ad hoc networks. In *Proceedings of IWCMC '07: The 2007 international conference on Wireless communications and mobile computing*, (pp. 393-398). New York.

Nolte, T., Hansson, H., & Lo Bello, L. (2005, September). *Automotive communications - past, current and future.* Presented at the IEEE international conference on emerging technologies and factory automation. Catania, Italy.

O'Hara, B., & Petrick, A. (1999). *The IEEE 802.11 Handbook: A Designer's Companion.* Washington, DC: IEEE Press.

Oh, S., Kang, J., & Gruteser, M. (2006). Location-based flooding techniques for vehicular emergency messaging. In *Proceedings of the 2nd International Workshop on Vehicle-to-Vehicle Communications* (V2VCOM 2006), (pp. 1-9). San Jose, CA.

Olariu, S., & Weigle, M. C. (Eds.). (2009). *Vehicular networks: from theory to practice.* Boca Raton, FL: Chapman & Hall/CRC.

Otto, J., & Kutscher, D. (2004, March). Drive thru internet: IEEE 802.11 for automobile users. In *Proceedings of the 23rd Conf. on Computer Communications* (INFO-COM'04), (pp. 365-373). Hong Kong, China.

Owen, L. E., Zhang, Y., Rao, L., & McHale, G. (2000). Traffic Flow Simulation using CORSIM. In *Proceedings of 2000 Winter Simulation Conference*, J A Joines, R R Barton, K Kang and P A Fishwick (eds), (pp. 1143-1147). Orlando, FL.

PalChaudhuri. S., Boudec, J.-Y. L., & Vojnovic, M. (2005). Perfect Simulations for Random Trip Mobility Models. In *Proceedings of the 38th Annual Simulation Symposium*, San Diego, CA.

Park, S., & Zou, C. C. (2008, April 28-30). Reliable Traffic Information Propagation in Vehicular Ad-Hoc Networks, *IEEE Sarnoff Symposium 2008* (pp. 16).

Park, V. D., & Corson, M. S. (1997, April 7-12). A highly adaptive distributed routing algorithm for mobile wireless networks. In *Proceedings of INFOCOM '97: The Sixteenth Annual Joint Conference of the IEEE Computer and Communications Societies*, (vol.3, pp.1405-1413). Kobe, Japan.

Parno, B., & Perrig, A. (2005). *Challenges in securing vehicular networks.* Paper presented at the Fourth Workshop on Hot Topics in Networks (HotNets-IV).

PATH. (n.d.). *The PATH Project.* Retrieved from http://www.path.berkeley.edu

Pei, G., Gerla, M., & Chen, T. W. (2000, June). Fisheye State Routing: A Routing Scheme for Ad Hoc Wireless Networks. In [New Orleans, LA.]. *Proceedings, ICC*, 2000.

Peng, W., & Lu, X. C. (2000). On the Reduction of Broadcast Redundancy in Mobile Ad Hoc Networks. In *Proceedings of the 1st ACM international symposium on Mobile ad hoc networking & computing.* (pp. 129-130).

Perkins, C. E., & Bhagwat, P. (1994). Highly dynamic destination-sequenced distance-vector routing (dsdv) for mobile computers. *SIGCOMM Comput. Commun. Rev.*, 24(4), 234–244. doi:10.1145/190809.190336

Perkins, C. E., & Royer, E. M. (1999). Ad hoc On-Demand Distance Vector Routing. In *Proceedings of the IEEE Workshop on Mobile Computing Systems and Applications*, (pp. 90-100). New Orleans, LA.

Petit, B., Ammar, M., & Fujimoto, R. (2006, April). Protocols for Roadside-to-Roadside Data Relaying over Vehicular Networks, *In Proc. of IEEE WCNC.*

Picconi, F., Ravi, N., Gruteser, M., & Iftode, L. (2006). Probabilistic Validation of Aggregated data in Vehicular Ad Hoc Networks. In *Proceedings of the International Conference on Mobile Computing and Networking*, (76-85). Los Angeles.

PReVENT. (n.d.). *The PReVENT Project.* Retrieved from http://www.prevent-ip.org

Qayyum, A., Viennot, L., & Laouiti, A. (2002). Multipoint Relaying for Flooding Broadcast Message in Mobile Wireless Networks. In *Proceedings of the 35th Annual Hawaii International Conference on System Sciences* (pp. 3866-3875). Big Island, HI

Qualnet (n.d.). *Qualnet Network Simulator.* Retrieved from http://www.scalable-networks.com/

Qureshi, A., Carlisle, J., & Guttag, J. (2006, October). Tavarua: *Video streaming with WWAN striping.* Presented at Acm multimedia 2006. Santa Barbara, CA.

Ramasubramanian, V., Haas, Z., & Sirer, E. (2003, June). SHARP: a hybrid adaptive routing protocol for mobile ad hoc networks. In *Proceedings of the ACM International Symposium on Mobile Ad Hoc Networking and Computing* (MobiHoc'03), (pp. 303-314). Annapolis, MD.

Random Trip Mobility Model. (n.d.). *Random Trip Mobility Model.* Retrieved from http://monarch.cs.rice.edu/~santa/research /mobility/code.tar.gz

Ranjitkar, P., Nakatsuji, T., & Kawamua, A. (2005). Car-Following Models: An Experiment Based Benchmarking. *Journal of the Eastern Asia Society for Transportation Studies, 6*, 1582–1596.

Rao, A., Kherani, A. A., & Mahanti, A. (2008). Performance evaluation of 802.11 broadcasts for a single cell network with unsaturated nodes . In Das, A., Pung, H. K., Lee, F. B.-S., & Wong, L. W.-C. (Eds.), *Lecture Notes in Computer Science: Networking* (*Vol. 4982*, pp. 836–847). New York: Springer.

Rawashdeh, Z. Y., & Mahmud, S. M. (2008). Intersection Collision Avoidance System Architecture. In *Proceedings of the 5th IEEE Consumer Communications and Networking Conference 2008* (pp. 493-494).

Rawat, D. B., Treeumnuk, D., Popescu, D., Abuelela, M., & Olariu, S. (2008). *Challenges and Perspectives in the Implementation of NOTICE Architecture for Vehicular Communications.* Paper presented at the MASS 2008. 5th IEEE International Conference on Mobile Ad Hoc and Sensor Systems, 2008.

Rawat, D. B., Yan, G., Popescu, D., Weigle, M., & Olariu, S. (2009). *Dynamic Adaptation of Joint Transmission Power and Contention Window in VANET.* Paper presented at the IEEE Vehicular Technology Conference 2009 - Fall'09.

Raya, M., & Hubaux, J. P. (2005, November). The Security of Vehicular Ad Hoc Networks. In *Proceedings of the Third ACM Workshop on Security of Ad Hoc and Sensor Networks* (*SASN* 2005), Alexandria, VA.

Raya, M., & Hubaux, J. P. (2005.March). Security Aspects of Inter-Vehicle Communications. In *Proceedings of the 5th Swiss Transport Research Conference,* Monte Verità, Ascona.

Raya, M., Papadimitratos, P., Aad, I., Jungels, D., & Hubaux, J. P. (2007). October). Eviction of Misbehaving and Faulty Vehicles in Vehicular Networks. *IEEE Journal on Selected Areas in Communications, 25*(8), 1557–1568. doi:10.1109/JSAC.2007.071006

Reichardt, D., Miglietta, M., Moretti, L., Morsink, P., & Schulz, W. (2002, June). CarTALK 2000 – safe and comfortable driving based upon inter-vehicle-communication. In . *Proceedings of the IEEE IV, 02*, 545–550. Retrieved from http://www.cartalk2000.net.

Rosi, U. T. Chowdhury, S. H., & Tai-hoon, K, A. (2008). Novel Approach for Infrastructure Deployment for VANET. *Future Generation Communication and Networking,* vol. *1*, 234-238. Presented at the 2nd International Conference on Future Generation Communication and Networking, 2008.

Rosi, U. T., Hyder, C. S., & Kim, T. (2008). *A Novel Approach for Infrastructure Deployment for VANET.* Paper presented at the FGCN '08. Second International Conference on Future Generation Communication and Networking, 2008.

Ross, S. M. (2004). *Introduction to Probability Models.* New York: Academic Press.

Rubin, I., & Liu, Y. C. (2003). *Link stability models for qos ad hoc routing algorithms.* (vol. 5, pp. 3084-3088).

Saha, A. K., & Johnson, D. B. (2004). *Modeling Mobility for Vehicular Ad Hoc Networks*. VANET.

Salhi, I., Cherif, M., & Senouc, S. M. (2009, June). A New Framework for Data Collection in Vehicular Networks. In *Proceedings of IEEE ICC'09*. Dresden, Germany.

Santa, J., & Gomez-Skarmeta, A. F. (2008). Architecture and evaluation of a unified V2V and V2I communication system based on cellular networks. *Computer Communications, 31*(12), 2850–2861. doi:10.1016/j.comcom.2007.12.008

Santa, J., Moragon, A., & Gomez-Skarmeta, A. F. (2008). *Experimental Evaluation of a Novel Vehicular Communication Paradigm Based on Cellular Networks*. Paper presented at the IEEE Intelligent Vehicles Symposium 2008.

Santos, R. A., Edwards, A., Edwards, R., & Seed, L. (2005). Performance evaluation of routing protocols in vehicular ad hoc networks. *The International Journal of Ad Hoc and Ubiquitous Computing, 1*(1/2), 80–91. doi:10.1504/IJAHUC.2005.008022

Sasson, Y., Cavin, D., & Schiper, A. (2003). Probabilistic Broadcast for Flooding in Wireless Mobile Ad Hoc Networks. In []. New Orleans, LA.]. *Proceedings of IEEE Wireless Communications and Networking Conference, 2*, 1124–1130.

Sawant, H., Tan, J., Yang, Q., & Wang, Q. (2004, October). *Using bluetooth and sensor networks for intelligent transportation systems*. Presented at the IEEE international conference on intelligent transportation systems. Washington DC.

Schagrin, M. (2008, January 16). *ITS Joint Program Office, Research and Innovative Technology Administration TRB 2008 Annual Meeting Session 415*.Palo Alto, CA: Dedicated Short Range Communications (DSRC) Home.

Schmidt-Eisenlohr, F., Letamendia-Murua, J., Torrent-Moreno, M., & Hartenstein, H. (2006). *Bug fixes on the IEEE 802.11 DCF module of the Network Simulator ns-2.28*. Germany: Department of Computer Science, University of Karlsruhe.

Schnaufer, S., & Effelsberg, W. (2008, June 23-26). Position-based unicast routing for city scenarios. In Proceedings of the 2008 International Symposium on a World of Wireless, Mobile and Multimedia Networks, (WoWMoM 2008), (pp.1-8). Newport Beach, CA.

Schoch, E., Karg, F., Leimüller, T., & Weber, M. (2008, November). Communication Patterns in VANETs. *IEEE Communications Magazine, 46*(11), 119–125. doi:10.1109/MCOM.2008.4689254

Schrank, D., & Lomax, T. (2007). *The 2007 Urban Mobility Report*. College Station, TX: Texas Transportation Institute.

Seet, B. C., Liu, G., Lee, B. S., Foh, C. H., Wong, K. J., & Lee, K. K. (2004). A-STAR: A Mobile Ad Hoc Routing Strategy for Metropolis Vehicular Communications. In *Proceedings of IFIP Networking* (pp. 989-999). Athens, Greece.

Serugendo, C., Villalba, A. G. D. M., & Konstantas, D. (2007). Dependable Requirements for Hovering Information. *In Supplementary Proceedings of the 37th Annual IEEE/IFIP International Conference on Dependable Systems and Networks* (DSN'07). (pp. 36–39). Edinburgh, UK.

Shankar, P., Alam, M. T., Musharoff, S., Ravi, N., Prados, C. V., Gradinescu, V., et al. (2005). *Outdoor Experience with the TrafficView Application*.

Sichitiu, M. L., & Kihl, M. (2008). Inter-vehicle communication systems: a survey. *IEEE Communications Surveys & Tutorials, 10*(2), 88–105. doi:10.1109/COMST.2008.4564481

Simulation software. (n.d.). Simulation software. Retrieved May 1, 2009, from http://www.opnet.com/solutions/network_rd/modeler.html

Singh, J. P., Bambos, N., Srinivasan, B., & Clawin, D. (2002). Wireless LAN performance under varied stress conditions in vehicular traffic scenarios. In *Proceedings of the IEEE 56th Vehicular Technology Conference Fall (VTC-Fall)*, (pp. 743–747). Vancouver, Canada.

Singh, J. P., Bambos, N., Srinivasan, B., Clawin, D., & Yan, Y. (2005). Empirical observations on wireless LAN performance in vehicular traffic scenarios and link connectivity based enhancements for multihop routing. In *Proceedings of the IEEE Wireless Communications and Networking Conference (WCNC)*, (pp. 1676–1682). New Orleans, LA.

Sisodia, R. S., Manoj, B. S., & Murthy, C. S. R. (2002). A preferred link based routing protocol for ad hoc wireless networks. *Journal of Communications and Networks*, *4*(1), 14–21.

Skordylis, A., & Trigoni, N. (2008). Delay-bounded routing in vehicular ad-hoc networks. In *Proceedings of the 9th ACM International Symposium on Mobile Ad Hoc Networking and Computing* (MobiHoc '08), (pp. 341-350). Hong Kong, China.

Soliman, H., Montavont, N., Fikouras, N., & Kuladinithi, K. (2007, November). *Flow bindings in mobile ipv6 and nemo basic support*, Manuel de logiciel (IETF, draft-solimanmonami6-flow-binding-05). Germany: University of Bremen

Stojemnovic, I. (2004, July). Position-Based Routing in Ad Hoc Networks. *IEEE Communication Magazine*.

Stojmenovic, I. (2002). Position based routing in ad hoc wireless networks. *IEEE Communications Magazine*, *40*(7), 128–134. doi:10.1109/MCOM.2002.1018018

Stojmenovic, I., Seddigh, S., & Zunic, J. (2002). Dominating Sets and Neighbor Elimination Based Broadcasting Algorithms in Wireless Networks. *IEEE Transactions on Parallel and Distributed Systems*, *13*(1), 14–25. doi:10.1109/71.980024

Su, H., & Zhang, X. (2007). Clustering-based multichannel MAC protocols for QoS provisionings over vehicular ad hoc networks. *IEEE Transactions on Vehicular Technology*, *56*(6), 3309–3323. doi:10.1109/TVT.2007.907233

Sugiura, A., & Dermawan, C. (2005, September). In traffic jam IVC-RVC system for ITS using bluetooth. *IEEE Transactions on Intelligent Transportation Systems*, *6*(3), 302–313. doi:10.1109/TITS.2005.853704

Sun, M. T., Feng, W. C., Lai, T. H., Yamada, K., Okada, H., & Fujimura, K. (2000). GPS-based message broadcasting for inter-vehicle communication. In *Proceedings of the 52nd Fall IEEE Vehicular Technology Conference (Fall-VTC2000)*, (pp.2685-2692). Boston.

Sun, W., Yamaguchi, H., & Yukimasa, K. (2006). Gvgrid: A qos routing protocol for vehicular ad hoc networks. In *Proceedings of the Fourteenth IEEE International Workshop on Quality of Service* (IWQoS 2006), (pp. 130-139). New Haven, CT: Yale University.

Szczypiorski, K., & Lubacz, J. (2008). Saturation throughput analysis of IEEE 802.11g (ERP-OFDM) networks. *Telecommunication Systems*, *38*(1-2), 45–52. doi:10.1007/s11235-008-9090-4

Takano, A., Okada, H., & Mase, K. (2007). Performance Comparison of a Position Based Routing Protocol for VANET In *Proceedings of Mobile Adhoc and Sensor Systems*, (MASS 2007), (pp. 1-6). Pisa, Italy.

Taleb, T., Sakhaee, E., Jamalipour, A., Hashimoto, K., Kato, N., & Nemoto, Y. (2007). A stable routing protocol to support its services in vanet networks. *IEEE Transactions on Vehicular Technology*, *56*(6), 3337–3347. doi:10.1109/TVT.2007.906873

Tang, B., Gupta, H., & Das, S. (2008). Benefit-based data caching in ad hoc networks. *Transactions on Mobile Computing*, *7*(3), 289–304. doi:10.1109/TMC.2007.70770

Tantra, J. W., & Foh, C. H. (2006). Achieving near maximum throughput in IEEE 802.11 WLANs with contention tone. *IEEE Communications Letters*, *10*(9), 658–660. doi:10.1109/LCOMM.2006.1714536

Tian, J., Marrón, P., & Rothermel, K. (2005, February). Location-Based Hierarchical Data Aggregation in Vehicular Ad Hoc Networks, In *Proceedings of the 14 ITG/GI-Fachtagung Kommunikation in Verteilten Systemen* (KiVS'05), (pp. 166-177). Kaiserslautern, Germany.

Tickoo, O., & Sikdar, B. (2008). Modeling queueing and channel access delay in unsaturated IEEE 802.11 random access MAC based wireless networks. *IEEE/ACM Transactions on Networking, 16*(4), 878-891.

Toh, C. K. (2002). *Ad Hoc Mobile Wireless Networks: Protocols and Systems.* Upper Saddle River, NJ: Prentice-Hall International, Inc.

Tonquz, O., Wisitpongphan, N., Bai, F., Mudalige, P., & Sadekar, V. (2007). Broadcasting in VANET. In *Proceedings of 2007 Mobile Networking for Vehicular Environments* (pp. 7-12). Anchorage, AK.

Toussaint, G. (1980). The relative neighborhood graph of a finite planar set. *Pattern Recognition, 12,* 231–268. doi:10.1016/0031-3203(80)90066-7

Treiber, M., & Kesting, A. (2009). Models for Traffic Flow and Vehicle Motion . In Olariu, S., & Weigle, M. C. (Eds.), *Vehicular Networks From Theory to Practice* (pp. 26–28). Boca Raton, FL: CRC Press.

Treiber, M., Hennecke, A., & Helbing, D. (2000). Congested traffic states in empirical observations and microscopic simulations. *Physical Review E: Statistical Physics, Plasmas, Fluids, and Related Interdisciplinary Topics, 62,* 1805–1824.

Tseng, Y. C., Ni, S. Y., & Shih, E. Y. (2003). Adaptive approaches to relieving broadcast storms in a wireless multihop mobile ad hoc network. *IEEE Transactions on Computers, 52*(5), 545–557. doi:10.1109/TC.2003.1197122

Tseng, Y.-C., Ni, S.-Y., Chen, Y.-S., & Sheu, J.-P. (2002). The broadcast storm problem in a mobile Ad Hoc network. In *Proceedings of the 5th annual ACM/ IEEE international conference on Mobile computing and networking* []. Atlanta, GA.]. *Wireless Networks, 8,* 153–167. doi:10.1023/A:1013763825347

Tsertou, A., & Laurenson, D. I. (2008). Revisiting the hidden terminal problem in a CSMA/CA wireless network. *IEEE Transactions on Mobile Computing, 7*(7), 817–831. doi:10.1109/TMC.2007.70757

Tsukada, M., Mehani, O., & Ernst, T. (2008, March 18). *Simultaneous usage of NEMO and MANET for vehicular communication.* Presented at WEEDEV 2008: 1st workshop on experimental evaluation and deployment experiences on vehicular networks in conjonction with TRIDENTCOM 2008. Innsbruck, Austria. Retrieved from http://hal.inria.fr/inria-00265652/

Ubeda, B., Toledo, R., Jordán, J., & Montes, S. (2004). A theoretical and practical analysis of GNSS based road pricing systems, considering the EGNOS/SISNeT contributions. Presented at NAVITEC 2004. Noordwijk, The Netherlands.

UDEL. (n.d.). *Models for Simulation of Urban Mobile Wireless Networks.* Retrieved from http://udelmodels.eecis.udel.edu/

Ueki, J., Tasaka, S., Hatta, Y., & Okada, H. (2005). Vehicular collision avoidance support system (vcass) by inter-vehicle communications for advanced its. *IEICE Transactions on Fundamentals of Electronics, Communications and Computer Sciences . E (Norwalk, Conn.), 88-A*(7), 1816–1823.

Uzcategui, R. A., De Sucre, A. J., & Acosta-Marum, G. (2009). Wave: a tutorial. *IEEE Communications, 47*(5), 126–133. doi:10.1109/MCOM.2009.4939288

Valldorf, U., & Gessner, W. (Eds.). (2005). *Advanced Microsystems for Automotive Applications 2005.* Springer Berlin Heidelberg. doi:10.1007/b139105

Vare, J., Syrjarinne, J., & Virtanen, K.-S. (2004). Geographical positioning extension for IPv6. In *Proceedings of the ICN.* Guadeloupe, France.

Vassis, D., Kormentzas, G., Rouskas, A., & Maglogiannis, I. (2005). The 802.11g Standard for High Data Rate WLANs. *IEEE Network, 19*(3), 21–26. doi:10.1109/MNET.2005.1453395

Verma, M., & Huang, D. (2009, January 10-13). SeGCom: Secure Group Communication in VANETs. Presented at the *6th IEEE Consumer Communications and Networking Conference,* 2009. (pp. 1-5).

Villalba, A. C., Serugendo, G. D. M., & Konstantas, D. (2008). Hovering Information - Self-Organising Information that Finds its own Storage. In *Proceedings of the International IEEE Conference on Sensor Networks, Ubiquitous and Trustworthy Computing* (pp. 193-200). Taichung, Taiwan.

VISSIM. (2009). *VISSIM.* Retrieved from http://www.tomfotherby.com/Websites/ VISSIM/index.htm

Wakikawa, R., & Sahasrabudhe, M. (2005). Gateway Management for Vehicle to Vehicle Communication. In *Proceedings of the 1ˢᵗ Int'l. Workshop on Vehicle-to-Vehicle Communications.* Philadelphia.

Wakikawa, R., Clausen, T., McCarthy, B., & Petrescu, A. (2007, July). *Manemo topology and addressing architecture* IETF, draft-wakikawa-manemoarch-00. Kanagawa, Japan.

Wakikawa, R., Ernst, T., Nagami, K., & Devarapalli, V. (2008, January). *Multiple care-of addresses registration* IETF, draft-ietf-monami6-multiplecoa-05. Kanagawa, Japan.

Wakikawa, R., Okada, K., Koodli, R., Nilsson, A., & Murai, J. (2005, September). *Design of Vehicle Network: Mobile Gateway for MANET and NEMO Converged Communication.* Presented at The Second ACM International Workshop on Vehicular Ad Hoc Networks (VANET 2005) Philadelphia.

Wakikawa, R., Thubert, P., Boot, T., Bound, J., & McCarthy, B. (2007, July). *Problem statement and requirements for manemo*, Manuel de logiciel. IETF, draft-mccarthymanemo-configuration problems-01. Kanagawa, Japan.

Wang, S. Y. (2004). On the intermittence of routing paths in vehicle-formed mobile ad hoc networks on highways. In *Proceedings of the IEEE International Conference on Intelligent Transportation Systems* (ITSC2004). Osaka, Japan.

Wang, Y. X., & Bao, F. Sh. (2007). An Entropy-based Weighted Clustering Algorithm and Its Optimization for Ad hoc Networks. In *Proceedings of the 3ʳᵈ IEEE International Conference on Wireless and Mobile Computing, Networking and Communications (WiMob2007).* White Plains, NY.

Wang, Y., & Ioannou, P. (2006). Real-time Parallel Parameter Estimators for a Second-order Macroscopic Traffic flow Model. In *Proceedings of the IEEE Intelligent Transportation Systems Conference.* (pp. 1466-1470). Toronto, Canada.

Wang, Y., Ahmed, A., Krishnamachari, B., & Psounis, K. (2008). *IEEE 802.11p Performance Evaluation and Protocol Enhancement.* Paper presented at the IEEE International Conference on Vehicular Electronics and Safety.

Wang, Z., Kulik, L., & Kotagiri, R. (2007). Proactive traffic merging strategies for sensor-enabled cars. In *Proceedings of the 4th ACM International Workshop on Vehicular Ad Hoc Networks* (VANET 2007), (pp. 39-48). Montreal, Canada.

Wedde, H. F., Lehnhoff, S., & van Bonn, B. (2007). Highly dynamic and scalable vanet routing for avoiding traffic congestions. In *Proceedings of VANET '07: The fourth ACM international workshop on Vehicular ad hoc networks*, (pp. 81-82). New York.

Wegener, A., Hellbruck, H., Wewetzer, C., & Lubke, A. (2008, November 30-December 4). VANET Simulation Environment with Feedback Loop and its Application to Traffic Light Assistance. In Proceedings of the IEEE GLOBECOM Workshops, 2008 (pp. 1-7).

Wei, X., & Qing-Quan, L. (2008). Performance evolution of data dissemination for vehicular ad hoc networks in highway scenarios. *The International Archives of the Photogrammetry, Remote Sensing and Spatial Information Sciences. XXXVII (B1).* Beijing, China.

Wevers, K., & Blervaque, V. (2004, October). *MAPS&ADAS: Safety enhanced digital maps and standard interface to ADAS.* Presented at the 11th World Congress on ITS, (pp. 18-22), paper 2193. Nagoya, Japan.

Wewetzer, C., Caliskan, M., Meier, K., & Luebke, A. (2007). *Experimental Evaluation of UMTS and Wireless LAN for Inter-Vehicle Communication.* Paper presented at the ITST '07. 7th International Conference on ITS Telecommunications, 2007. ADDITIONAL READINGS Ghandeharizadeh, S., & Krishnamachari, B. (2004). C2P2: A Peer-to-Peer Network for On-Demand Automobile Information Services. *In First International Workshop on Grid and Peer-to-Peer Computing Impacts on Large Scale Heterogeneous Distributed Database Systems (Globe'04).*

Willke, T. L., Tientrakool, P., & Maxemchuk, N. F. (2008). A survey of inter-vehicle communication protocols and their applications. *IEEE Communications Surveys & Tutorials, 11*(2), 3–20. doi:10.1109/SURV.2009.090202

Wimmer, W., & Flogel, D. (2009, March). Highly accurate mapping of road construction sites using laser scanner. In *Proceedings of the 6th International Workshop on Intelligent Transport* (pp. 33–38).

Wischhof, L., Ebner, A., & Rohling, H. (2005, March). Information Dissemination in Self-organizing Inter-vehicle Networks. *IEEE Transactions on Intelligent Transportation Systems, 6*(1), 90–101. doi:10.1109/TITS.2004.842407

Wischhof, L., Ebner, A., Rohling, H., Lott, M., & Halfmann, R. (2003, April). SOTIS –a self-organizing traffic information system. In *Proceedings of the 57th IEEE Semiannual Vehicular Technology Conference* (pp. 2442-2446). Jeju, South Korea.

Wisitpongphan, N., Bai, F., Mudalige, P., Sadekar, V., & Tonguz, O. (2007). Routing in sparse vehicular ad hoc wireless networks. *IEEE Journal on Selected Areas in Communications, 25*(8), 1538–1556. doi:10.1109/JSAC.2007.071005

Wu, H., & Fujimoto, R. Guensler, R., & Hunter, M. (2004). MDDV: a mobility-centric data dissemination algorithm for vehicular networks. In *Proceedings of the 1st ACM Workshop on Vehicular Ad Hoc Networks* (VANET 2004), (pp. 47-56). Philadelphia.

Wu, H., Fujimoto, R., & Riley, G. (2004). Analytical Models for Information Propagation in Vehicle-to-Vehicle Networks. In *Proceedings of the IEEE Vehicular Technology Conference*. Los Angeles.

Xeros, A., Andreou, M., Pitsillides, A., & Lestas, M. (2007). Information Propagation Probability in VANETS. In Proceedings of Vehicle to Vehicle Communication workshop, (V2Vcom). Istanbul, Turkey.

Xiao, B., Yu, B., & Gao, Ch. (2006, September). Detection and Localization of Sybil Vehicles in VANETs. In *Proceedings of DIWANS'06*, Los Angeles.

Xu, Q., Mak, T., & Sengupta, R. (2004). *Vehicle-to-Vehicle Safety Messaging in DSRC*. ACM VANET, Oct 2004.

Xu, Q., Mak, T., Sengupta, R., & Ko, J. (2004). Vehicle-to-Vehicle Safety Messaging in DSRC. In *Proceedings of the First Workshop on Vehicular Ad Hoc Networks* (pp. 19-28). New York: ACM Press.

Yadumurthy, R. M. H., A. C., Sadashivaiah, M., & Makanaboyina, R. (2005). Reliable MAC broadcast protocol in directional and omni-directional transmissions for vehicular ad hoc networks. In *Proceedings of the 2nd ACM International Workshop on Vehicular Ad Hoc Networks (VANET2005)*, (pp. 10-19). Cologne, Germany.

Yamada, S. (1996). The strategy and deployment for VICS. *IEEE Communication, 34*(10), 94–97. doi:10.1109/35.544328

Yan, G., & Olariu, S. (2009). *A probabilistic analysis of path stability in vehicular ad hoc networks (Technique Report in Computer Science)*. Norfolk, VA: Old Dominion University.

Yan, G., & Olariu, S. (2009). *A reliable routing in vehicular ad hoc networks using probabilistic analysis of path stability (Technique Report in Computer Science)*. Norfolk, VA: Old Dominion University.

Yang, Q., Lim, A., & Agrawal, P. (2008). Connectivity aware routing in vehicular networks. (pp. 2218-2223).

Yang, Q., Lim, A., Li, Sh., Fang, J., & Agrawal, P. (2008, August). ACAR: Adaptive Connectivity Aware Routing Protocol for Vehicular Ad Hoc Networks. In *Proceedings of the 17th International Conference on Computer Communications and Networks (ICCCN'08)*. St. Thomas, US Virgin Islands.

Yin, L., & Cao, G. (2006). Supporting cooperative caching in ad hoc networks. *IEEE Transactions on Mobile Computing, 5*(1), 77–89. doi:10.1109/TMC.2006.15

Yoon, J., Noble, B. D., & Liu, M. (2006). Building Realistic Mobility Models from Coarse-Grained Traces. In *Proceedings of the ACM International Conference on Mobile Systems, Applications and Services* (Mobisys '06), (177-190). Uppsala, Sweden.

Yousefi, S., Bastani, S., & Fathy, M. (2007, February). *On the performance of safety message dissemination in vehicular ad hoc networks*. Presented at the European conference on universal multiservice networks. Toulouse, France.

Yousefi, S., Mousavi, M. S., & Fathy, M. (2006). Vehicular Ad Hoc Networks (VANETs): Challenges and Perspectives, In *Proceeding of ITS Telecommunications s, 2006 6th International Conference on June 2006* (pp. 761-766).

Yu, Y., Lu, G. H., & Zhang, Z. L. (2004, October 25-27). Enhancing location service scalability with highgrade. In *Proceedings of 2004 IEEE International Conference on Mobile Ad-hoc and Sensor Systems*, (pp. 164–173). Ft. Lauderdale, FL.

Yuen, W. H., Yates, R. D., & Mau, S. C. (2003). Exploiting data diversity and multiuser diversity in non cooperative mobile infostation networks. In *Proceedings of the IEEE International Conference on Computer Communications (INFOCOM)*, (pp. 2218–2228). San Francisco.

Yuen, W. H., Yates, R. D., & Sung, C. W. (2003). Effect of node mobility on highway mobile infostation networks. In Proceedings of the *ACM/IEEE International Conference on Modeling, Analysis and Simulation of Wireless and Mobile Systems (MSWIM)*, (pp. 82–91). San Diego, CA.

Yuen, W. H., Yates, R. D., & Sung, C. W. (2003). Performance evaluation of highway mobile infostation network. Presented at theIEEE GLOBECOM 2003 at San Francisco, December, 2003.

Yusefi, S., Altman, E., El-Azouzi, R., & Fathy, M. (2007, June). Connectivity in vehicular ad hoc networks in presence of wireless mobile base-stations. In *Proceedings of the 7ᵗʰ International Conference on ITS*. Sophia Antipolis, France.

Zhai, H., Wang, J., Chen, X., & Fang, Y. (2006). Medium access control in mobile ad hoc networks: challenges and solutions. *Wireless Communications & Mobile Computing, 6*(2), 151–170. doi:10.1002/wcm.376

Zhang, M., & Wolff, R. (2008). Routing protocols for vehicular ad hoc networks in rural areas. *IEEE Communications Magazine, 46*(11), 126–131. doi:10.1109/MCOM.2008.4689255

Zhang, X., Su, H., & Chen, H.-H. (2006). Cluster-based multi-channel communications protocols in vehicle ad hoc networks. *IEEE Wireless Communications, 13*(5), 44–51. doi:10.1109/WC-M.2006.250357

Zhang, Y., Zhao, J., & Cao, G. (2009). Roadcast: a popularity aware content sharing scheme in VANETs. In *Proceedings of the IEEE International Conference on Distributed Computing Systems* (ICDCS). Montreal, Canada.

Zhao, J., & Cao, G. (2006). VADD: vehicle-assisted data delivery in vehicular ad hoc networks. In *Proceedings of the 25th IEEE International Conference on Computer Communications* (Infocom'06), (pp. 1–12). Barcelona, Spain.

Zhao, J., Arnold, T., Zhang, Y., & Cao, G. (2008). Extending drive-thru data access by vehicle-to-vehicle relay. In *Proceedings of the 5th ACM International Workshop on VehiculAr Inter-NETworking* (VANET 2008) (pp. 66-75). San Francisco.

Zhao, S., & Raychaudhuri, D. (2006, March). Policy-Based Adaptive Routing in Mobile Ad Hoc Wireless Networks. In *Proceeding of the IEEE 2006 Snarnoff Symposium*. (pp. 1-4). Princeton, NJ.

Zhao, W., & Ammar, M. H. (2003). Message Ferrying: Proactive Routing in Highly-Partitioned Wireless Ad Hoc Networks. In *Proceedings of the Ninth IEEE Workshop on Future Trends of Distributed Computing Systems (FTDCS '03)* (pp. 308-314). San Juan, Puerto Rico.

Zheng, Q., & Liu, X. H. J. (April 2006). An Agenda-based Mobility Model. In *Proceedings of the 39ᵗʰ IEEE Annual Simulation Symposium* (ANSS-39-2006). Huntsville, AL.

Zhu, J., & Roy, S. (2003, December). MAC for dedicated short range communicatins in intelligent transport system. *IEEE Communications Magazine, 41*.

Zhu, W., Song, M., & Olariu, S. (2006, June 19-21). Integrating stability estimation into quality of service routing in mobile ad-hoc networks. In *Proceedings of the Fourteenth IEEE International Workshop on Quality of Service* (IWQoS 2006). New Haven, CT: Yale University.

About the Contributors

Mohamed Khalil Watfa is currently in the college of Computer Science and Engineering at the University of Wollongong in Dubai. Before that he was at the Computer Science department at the American University of Beirut (AUB). He received his Ph.D. from the School of Electrical and Computer Engineering at the University of Oklahoma in Norman, OK, USA in 2006. He was one of the youngest PhD holders to graduate from his university at the age of 23. He has been given a number of prestigious awards including a recent Research Excellence Award in 2009. His research interests include wireless sensor networks, intelligent systems, Vehicular Ad-hoc Networks, wireless networking, resource management, energy issues, tracking, routing, and performance measures. He has more than 40 journal and conference publications. For more info about Prof. Watfa, check out his personal website at: http://mohamedwatfa.synthasite.com/

***

Ashish Agarwal is currently working towards his PhD degree, at the Electrical and Computer Engineering Department at Boston University, Boston, MA. He received his MS degree in Computer Systems Engineering from Boston University, Boston, MA in 2007 and BE degree from Delhi Institute of Technology, University of Delhi, New Delhi, India in 2003, (now Netaji Subhas Institute of Technology, (NSIT)). His research interests include semantic routing with application towards wireless, mobile and ad hoc networks (MANETs) including sensor networks and vehicular networks (VANETs). He is also interested in message dissemination schemes for intermittently connected and delay tolerant networks (DTN).

Maria Andreou is a tutor on the MSc programme "Information Systems", and a researcher at the Open University of Cyprus. She holds a Ph.D. in Theoretical Computer Science (2004) and a BSc in Computer Science (CS), both from the University of Patras. Previously she was a lecturer at the Electrical & Computer Engineering Department of the University of Cyprus and at the Computer Science Department of the University of Nicosia. She has a number of published papers in various international refereed journals and conferences. Currently, she is working at the projects Revitalizing Small Remote Schools for LifeLong Distance e-Learning (REVIT) and Emergency Message Dissemination for Safety Applications in Vehicular ad hoc Networks (eVANETs). Her main research interests are graph theory, algorithmic engineering, information systems, VANETs.

Avijit Bhattacharyya has done Bachelor of Engineering (Electrical) and Master of Engineering (Production, specializing in Automation & Robotics) both from Jadavpur University, Kolkata, India. He was awarded the *University Gold Medal* for standing First Class First in the Master of Engineering program. He is currently employed in Tata consultancy Services India for last 19 years. He is experienced in directing high valued, enterprise-level IT projects for international and Indian clients in both the public and private sectors. He has been involved in multiple strategic projects in the career till date, including projects in the automotive sector. His recent engagement is as Head SAP Centre of Excellence – Manufacturing Industry Solution Unit. He is also a Certified Quality Analyst (CQA), awarded by Quality Assurance Institute, USA and SAP Certified Consultant.

Debika Bhattacharyya has done B.Tech and M.Tech in Radiophysics and Electronics from Calcutta University. She has done Ph.D (Engg.) in wireless communication from Jadavpur University. She has secured National Scholarship twice in her career. She has more than twenty National and International publication in wireless communication. She has more than five years of valuable industry experience. She is currently serving as a Professor and Head of The Department of Computer Science & Engineering in Institute of Engineering & Management. She is the Principal Investigator (PI) of a All India Council for Technical Education (AICTE) sponsored national level project. She is in the advisory board of many AICTE sponsored projects. Currently her area of research includes Mobile Ad hoc Network (MANET), WiMax, VANET, Network Security etc.

Carlos Caloca's main research interests are network protocols, distributed systems and ubiquitous computing. He received his Masters Degree in 2007 at CICESE research center in Mexico, working in the security aspects of Wireless Sensor Networks. He is currently doing his PhD at the University of Valenciennes in conjunction with CICESE research center, having for research theme Vehicular Ad Hoc Networks (mainly network layer aspects). Carlos Caloca is part of the VESPA (Vehicular Event Sharing with a mobile P2P Architecture) group, a system designed to share different types of events in inter-vehicle ad hoc networks.

Claudio Casetti graduated in Electrical Engineering from Politecnico di Torino in 1992 and received his PhD in Electronic Engineering from the same institution in 1997. In 1995, he was a visiting scholar with the Networks Group of the University of Massachusetts, Amherst. In 2000, he was a visiting scholar with the Networking Group at UCLA. He is an Assistant Professor at the Dipartimento di Elettronica of Politecnico di Torino. He has coauthored more than 80 journal and conference papers in the fields of networking and holds three patents. His interests focus on performance evaluation of TCP/IP networks and wireless communications.

Carla-Fabiana Chiasserini graduated in Electrical Engineering from the University of Florence in 1996 and received her PhD in Electronic Engineering from Politecnico di Torino, Italy, in 2000. Since then she has been with the Department of Electrical Engineering at Politecnico di Torino, where she is currently an Associate Professor. From 1999 to 2003, she has worked as a visiting researcher at the University of California at San Diego. She has coauthored more than 150 papers, forty of which on international journals. She has been TPC co-chair of several prestigious conferences and general chair of ACM/IEEE MSWiM 2006 and 2007. She has edited several special issues of international journals and she is a member of the editorial board of the Ad Hoc Networks Journal (Elsevier), Computer Communications (Elsevier), and the IEEE Communications Letters.

Ameneh Daeinabi received her B.Sc. degree in electrical engineering from Karaj Branch Islamic Azad University, Tehran, Iran in 2005. She received her M.Sc. degree in communication engineering from Sahand University of technology, Tabriz, Iran in 2008. Her main research interests are: Ad Hoc Networks; VANET; and security.

Thierry Delot's main research interests are in database systems, distributed systems, and mobile/pervasive computing. He received his Masters Degree in 1998 and his PhD in Computer Science in 2001 at the University of Versailles. He is currently assistant professor at the University of Valenciennes and works in the Distributed Information System Group at LAMIH laboratory (UMR UVHC-CNRS 8530). His recent research work concerns mobile P2P networks. In this context, Thierry Delot works on VESPA (Vehicular Event Sharing with a mobile P2P Architecture), a system designed to share different types of events in inter-vehicle ad hoc networks. Thierry Delot participated in numerous conferences as organization chair, program committee member or tutorial presenter. He also coordinated and participated in several research projects in cooperation with French institutions and industrial partners.

Arthur Edwards received his masters degree in Education from the University ofHouston in 1985. He has been a researcher-professor at the University of Colimasince 1985, where he has served in various capacities. He has been with theSchool of Telematics since 1998. His primary areas of research are ComputerAssisted Language Learning (CALL), distance learning, collaborative learning,multimodal leaning and mobile learning. The primary focus of his research ispresently in the area of mobile collaborative learning.

Samy El-Tawab obtained his B.Sc. in Computer Science from the College of Engineering, Alexandria University, Egypt in 2002. After joining the Unilever Mashreq Company for couple of months as an application developer, he was appointed as a teaching assistant in the Mathematic and Engineering Physic Department at Alexandria University. In 2006, Samy obtained his M.S. degree in Computer Science from Alexandria University in the field of Networks. He worked on the U.S. - EGYPT JOINT BOARD ON SCIENTIFIC AND TECHNOLOGICAL COOPERATION on the project of "Redundant Traffic Encoding and Marking Scheme for Voice-Over-IP Quality of Service", 2004. In the fall of 2006, Samy started his Ph.D. program at Old Dominion University in Computer Science under the supervision of his advisor, Professor Stephan Olariu. Recently, one of his papers was awarded a prize for Excellence in Scholarship in "The College of William and Mary's Eighth Annual Graduate Research Symposium".

Thierry Ernst holds a Ph.D. obtained from University Joseph Fourier(Grenoble, France) in October 2001 and prepared jointly at INRIA (Grenoble) and MOTOROLA Labs (Paris) in France. His dissertation on "Network Mobility Support in IPv6" has served as the foundation of the research work on this new topic and led to standardization activities. As such, he setup and chaired the NEMO Working Group and the MONAMI6 Working Group at the IETF and is involved in the ISO Technical Committee 204 Working Group 16 developing a communication architecture for ITS (Intelligent Transportation Systems) based on IPv6.

Marco Fiore received MS degrees in Computer Science from the University of Illinois at Chicago, in 2003, and from Politecnico of Torino, in 2004. He received his PhD degree from Politecnico di Torino on 2008. He is currently a Post-Doc fellow at Politecnico di Torino. He visited the Networks Group led by Prof. Edward Knightly at Rice University in 2006, and the Computer Networking Group led by Prof. Jorge Garcia Vidal at Universitat Politecnica de Catalunya in 2008. He is currently associate professor at INSA-Lyon, France. His research interests include mobility modeling, information sharing, and security in vehicular networks, routing and handover mechanisms in wireless LANs and wireless mesh networks.

Eduardo Flores graduated from the University of Colima with a BE in Communications and Electronic Engineering and MSc degree in Computer Science. He has been member of the technical staff of Telecommunications department at University of Colima since 2002. Cisco Certificate Advanced Instructor (CCAI) in 2006. Where, he is currently lecturer for Computer Science courses and instructor for the program Cisco Networking Academy to teachers at University of Colima.

Miguel A. Garcia-Ruiz graduated in Computer Systems engineering and obtained his MSc in Computer Science from the University of Colima, Mexico. He received his PhD in Computer Science and Artificial Intelligence from the School of Cognitive and Computing Sciences, University of Sussex, England. He took a virtual reality course at Salford University, England and a graphics techniques internship at the Madrid Polytechnic University, Spain. Miguel has been a visiting professor at the University Of Ontario Institute Of Technology, Canada. He has been teaching Computer Science courses, and doing research mainly on virtual reality and multimodal interfaces at the University of Colima. Miguel has published various scientific papers in major journals and a book, and has directed a video documentary about an introduction to virtual reality.

Mario Gerla is a Professor in the Computer Science at UCLA. He holds an Engineering degree from Politecnico di Milano, Italy and the Ph.D. degree from UCLA. He became IEEE Fellow in 2002. At UCLA, he was part of the team that developed the early ARPANET protocols under the guidance of Prof. Leonard Kleinrock. At Network Analysis Corporation, New York, from 1973 to 1976, he helped transfer ARPANET technology to Government and Commercial Networks. He joined the UCLA Faculty in 1976. At UCLA he has designed and implemented network protocols including ad hoc wireless clustering, multicast (ODMRP and CODECast) and Internet transport (TCP Westwood). He has lead the $12M, 6 year ONR MINUTEMAN project, designing the next generation scalable airborne Internet for tactical and homeland defense scenarios. He is now leading two advanced wireless network projects under ARMY and IBM funding. His team is developing a Vehicular Testbed for safe navigation, urban sensing and intelligent transport. A parallel research activity explores personal communications for cooperative, networked medical monitoring (see www.cs.ucla.edu/NRL for recent publications).

Imrul Hassan is currently a PhD candidate at Swinburne University of Technology under supervision of Assoc.-Prof. Dr. Hai L. Vu. Imrul received his BSc in Electrical and Electronic Engineering from the Islamic University of Technology, Bangladesh (2003), a PGDip in Information and Communication Technology from the Bangladesh University of Technology (2005) and an MSc in Radio Engineering from Kyung Hee University, South Korea (2008). From 2004 to 2006 he was a Lecturer in the Department of Electrical and Electronic Engineering at the Islamic University of Technology. His research interest includes wireless communication, the design of MAC protocols, cognitive radio and RoF links.

Teruo Higashino received his B.S., M.S. and Ph.D. degree in Engineering from Osaka University, Japan in 1979, 1981 and 1984, respectively. He joined the faculty of Osaka University in 1984. Since 2002, he has been a Professor in Graduate School of Information Science and Technology at Osaka University. His current research interests include design and analysis of distributed systems, communication protocol and mobile computing. He is a senior member of IEEE, a fellow of Information Processing Society of Japan (IPSJ), and a member of ACM and IEICE of Japan.

Petros Ioannou joined the Department of Electrical Engineering-Systems, University of Southern California, in 1982 where he became full Professor and the Director of the Center of Advanced Transportation Technologies which he founded. In addition he was one of the founders of the University Transportation Center METRANS funded by the US Department of Transportation. His research interests are in the areas of Intelligent Transportation Systems, Control and Dynamics, Marine transportation, aircraft control, automation and robotics, vehicle dyanmics and control and safety analysis, vehicle routing and optimization etc. He was a visiting Professor at the University of Newcastle, Australia and the Australian National University in Canberra during parts of Fall of 1988, the Technical University of Crete in summer of 1992 and Fall of 2001 and served as the Dean of the School of Pure and Applied Science at the University of Cyprus in 1995 where he pioneered the establishment of the School of Engineering. He was a recipient of the Outstanding Transactions Paper Award by the Control System Society of IEEE and the recipient of a Presidential Young Investigator Award for his research by the White House. In 2009 he was the recipient of the IEEE Intelligent Transportation Systems Society Best Practice Award. He was also the recipient of the IET Achievement Medal Award for his research by the Institute of Engineering Technology (IET) former IEE. He held consulting positions with Ford, General Motors, Rockwell International, Lockheed, ACORN Technologies, Textron, Dynamic Systems, General Electric and others. His center was one of the founders of ITS America. Dr. Ioannou is a Fellow of IEEE and of the International Federation of Automatic Control (IFAC) and the author/co-author of 8 books and over 200 research papers in the area of controls, neural networks, nonlinear dynamical systems, communication networks and intelligent transportation systems.

Yacine Khaled received his B.Eng. degree in computer science from the University of Technology of Algiers (USTHB), Algeria, in 2003, M.Sc and PhD degrees in mobile network in 2004 and 2007 from University de Technologie de Compiegne (UTC), Compiene, Currently, he is occupying post-doctoral position at IMARA project team (INRIA), France. His research interests are in the areas of ad hoc networks, vehicular ad hoc networks, medium access, geographical addressing and routing and IPv6.

Shrirang Ambaji Kulkarni Is currently working as Assistant Professor in the Department of Computer Science and Engineering, Gogte Institute of Technology, Belgaum. He received his B.E. in Computer Science and Engineering from Karnataka University Dharwar, in the year 2000 and his M.Tech. in Computer Network Engineering from VTU Belgaum, in the year 2004. He is currently pursuing Ph.D. in the area of ad hoc networks. He has published several papers in International Conferences and Journals. His current research interest includes Reinforcement Learning Algorithms, Mobile Ad Hoc Networks and Vehicular Ad Hoc Networks .He is a life member of CSI, CSTA and ISTE.

Kevin C. Lee is currently a Ph.D. student in the Computer Science Department at the University of California, Los Angeles. He received his B.S. in Computer Science Engineering and B.A. in Mathematics at the University of Pennsylvania in 2002. He also received M.S. in Computer Science at the Carnegie Mellon University in 2004. Kevin has published numerous papers in the fields of vehicular ad hoc networks ranging from developing and running a peer-to-peer application on the real vehicular testbed, designing an optimized geographic routing protocol in urban scenarios, developing a light-weight loop-free geographic routing protocol, and proposing novel link-state routing routing based on density. He has also written technical reports in network process migration in the area of network system programming and in classification in the area of artificial intelligence. His current research interests include vehicular ad hoc network routing, theoretical analysis of computer networks, WiMax networks, QoS, and mobile applications for vehicular ad hoc networks.

Uichin Lee received the B.S. in computer engineering from Chonbuk National University in 2001, the M.S. degree in computer science from Korea Advanced Institute of Science and Technology (KAIST) in 2003, and the Ph.D. degree in computer science from UCLA in 2008. He is currently a member of technical staff in Bell Labs, Alcatel-Lucent. His research interests include distributed systems, mobile wireless networking systems, and performance modeling/evaluation.

Marios Lestas received the B.A and M.Eng degrees in Electrical and Information Engineering from the University of Cambridge U.K and the Ph.D degree in Electrical Engineering from the University of Southern California in 1999, 2000 and 2005 respectively. From 2007 until 2009 he was a visiting lecturer at the Department of Computer Science of the University of Cyprus. He is currently a special scientist and a postgraduate researcher at the Cyprus University of Technology. He is also a member of the executive board of Transim Transportation Research Ltd. He has worked for a number of projects funded by the European Commission and the Cyprus Research Promotion Foundation. His research interests include application of non-linear control theory and optimization methods in Computer Networks.

Thomas D.C. Little is a professor in the Department of Electrical and Computer Engineering at Boston University. He is Associate Chair for Graduate Studies for the department and is director of the Multimedia Communications Lab where he is involved in the development of enabling technologies and applications for networked and distributed systems. Recent efforts include research in video sensor networks and streaming in wireless settings, ubiquitous optical networking with visible light, vehicle-to-vehicle/infrastructure (V2X) communications, and the application of wireless sensors in health monitoring. Dr. Little received the BS degree in biomedical engineering from Rensselaer Polytechnic Institute in 1983, and the MS degree in electrical engineering and PhD degree in computer engineering from Syracuse University in 1989 and 1991. He is a Senior member of the IEEE, a member of the IEEE Computer and Communications Societies and a member of the Association for Computing Machinery. He serves on the editorial board of the Journal of Multimedia Tools and Applications, and on various program committees.

J. Antonio Garcia-Macias holds a Ph.D. degree in Computer Science from the Institut National Polytechnique de Grenoble (INPG), France. He is currently a researcher at CICESE's Computer Science Department, working in the fields of ubiquitous computing and next generation communication protocols and networks. He has published numerous works in subjects related to wireless ad-hoc networks, novel human-computer interfaces for context-aware environments, reprogramming and data dissemination in wireless sensor networks, and ambient-assisted living applications. He is also the founder of a startup company in the field of wireless sensor and actuator networks.

Aldo Mendez obtained his BS in engineering from the Universidad Veracruzana (1995), MSc from CENIDET (1997) and his PhD from the CICESE (2003) all them in Mexico. He has been member of the scientific staff of Electronics and Telecommunications department at UAT since 2004. His current research interests include MAC and scheduling modeling for mobile communications.

Yiannos Mylonas received his B.Sc in Computer Engineering from Oregon State University in 1998. In 2001, he received his M.Sc in Computer Science from University of Cyprus. He is currently pursuing his PhD degree at University of Cyprus under the supervision of Prof. Andreas Pitsillides. From 1998 until 1999 he worked for Intel Corporation as a product support engineer. Since 2001, he is working as a Special Teaching Staff at the department of Computer Science at the University of Cyprus. His research interests include Intelligent Transportation Systems (ITS), and Vehicular Ad Hoc Networks.

Andreas Pitsillides received the B.Sc. (Hns) degree from University of Manchester Institute of Science and Technology and PhD from Swinburne University of Technology, Melbourne, Australia, in 1980 and 1993 respectively. He is a Professor, Department of Computer Science, University of Cyprus, and heads the Networks Research Laboratory (NetRL). Andreas is also a Founding member and Chairman & Scientific Director, of the Cyprus Academic and Research Network (CYNET) since its establishment in 2000. Prior to that he has worked in industry for six years (Siemens 1980-1983, Asea-Brown Boveri, 1983-1986), and from 1987 till 1994 had been with the Swinburne University of Technology (Lecturer, Senior Lecturer 1990-1994, and Foundation Associate Director of the Swinburne Laboratory for Telecommunications Research, 1992-1994). In 1992, he spent a six month period as an academic visitor at the Telstra (Australia). Andreas's research interests include fixed and wireless Networks (ad-hock and sensor networks, TCP/IP, WLANs, UMTS, 3rd Generation mobile networks and beyond), flow and congestion control, resource allocation and radio resource management, and Internet technologies and their application in Mobile e-Services, e.g. in Tele-Healthcare. He has a particular interest in adapting tools from various fields of applied mathematics such as non-linear control theory, computational intelligence, complex systems and nature inspired techniques, to solve problems in computer networks. Andreas has published over 200 research papers and book chapters, he is the co-editor with Petros Ioannou of the book on Modelling and Control of Complex Systems (CRC Press, ISBN: 978-0-8493-7985-0, 2007,), presented invited lectures at major research organisations, has given short courses at international conferences and short courses to industry. Andreas work has been funded by the European Commission IST program, the Cyprus National Research Promotion Foundation (RPF), the Cambridge Microsoft Research Labs, the University of Cyprus, the Swinburne University of Technology, and the Australian Government research grants board, with total funding exceeding 10 million Euro (over 4 million as PI or Co-PI). Examples of recent projects are: GINSENG, C-CAST, MIND2C, EM-VANETS, M-POWER, C-MOBILE, MOTIVE, B-BONE, E-NEXT, SEACORN, VIDEO, ADAVIDEO, HEALTHSERVICE24, LINKCARE, GEANT, DITIS. Andreas serves/served on the executive committees of major conferences, as e.g. INFOCOM, WiOpt, ISYC, MCCS, and ICT. He is a member of the IEEE (M'89, SM'2005), of the International Federation of Automatic Control (IFAC) Technical Committee TC 1.5 on Networked Systems and TC 7.3 on Transportation Systems, and of the International Federation of Information

Processing (IFIP) working group WG 6.3: Performance of Communications Systems. Andreas is also a member of the Editorial Board of Computer Networks (COMNET) Journal.

Akbar Ghaffarpour Rahbar received his B.Sc. and M.Sc. degrees in computer hardware and computer architecture both from Iran University of Science and Technology, Tehran, Iran in 1992 and 1995, respectively. He joined the Department of Electrical Engineering, Sahand University of Technology, Tabriz, Iran in 1995. He received his Ph.D. degree in computer science from University of Ottawa, Canada in 2006. He is currently an assistant professor at Department of Electrical Engineering, Sahand University of Technology. His main research interests are: scheduling in computer networks; VANET; optical networks; network modeling, analysis, and performance evaluation.

G. Raghavendra Rao is currently working as the Principal, NIE Institute of Technology, Mysore India. He received his Masters in Engineering from Indian Institute of Science Bangalore in the year 1987 and his Ph.D. from University of Mysore in the year 1999. He has published several papers in International Conferences and Journals. His current research interest includes Genetic Algorithms, Wireless Networks, Cryptography and Network Security. He is a member of IEEE, ACM and ISTE.

Victor Rangel received the B.Eng (Hons) degree in Computer Engineering in the Engineering Faculty from the National Autonomous University of Mexico (UNAM) in 1996, the M.Sc in Telematics at from the University of Sheffield,U.K. in 1998, and the Ph.D. in performance analysis and traffic scheduling in cable networks in 2002, from the University of Sheffield. Since 2002, he has been with the School of Engineering, UNAM, where he is currently a Research-Professor in telecommunications networks. His research focuses on fixed, mesh and mobile broadband wireless access networks, QoS over IP, traffic shaping and scheduling.

Danda B. Rawat received the Bachelor's Degree in Computer Engineering in 2002 from the Department of Electronics and Computer Engineering, Pulchowk Campus, Institute of Engineering, Tribhuvan University, Nepal. After graduation because of his high academic performance he was appointed as an instructor (assistant lecturer) at the same department and worked as an instructor till June 2006. He also worked as a Network Engineer at Center for Information Technology, Institute of Engineering, from June 2003 to July 2004. He received the Master's Degree in Information and Communication Engineering with First class first with distinction from the same university in the year 2005. He also worked as an ICT (Information and Communication Technology) Officer for Government of Nepal from January 2004 to December 2006. He is currently working toward the PhD degree at the Department of Electrical and Computer Engineering, Old Dominion University, Norfolk, VA, USA. His research interests are in the areas of wireless communications, wireless cellular/ad-hoc networks, and vehicular communications. He is the recipient of Outstanding PhD Researcher of the Year Award 2009 given by the Department of Electrical and Computer Engineering, Old Dominion University, Norfolk, VA, USA.

Taka Sakurai received the B.Sc. degree in applied mathematics and B.E. degree in electrical engineering from the University of Adelaide in 1988 and 1989, respectively, and the Ph.D. degree in electrical engineering from the University of Melbourne in 2003. From 1991 to 1997, he was a Research Engineer at Telstra Research Laboratories. Subsequently, he held research and development roles at NEC and Lucent Technologies. From 2003 to 2005, he was with the Department of Electrical and Electronic

Engineering, University of Melbourne. Currently, he is with the Chief Technology Office of Telstra Corporation, and an Honorary Fellow of the University of Melbourne. His research interests are in the areas of performance analysis of next-generation wireless networks, design of MAC protocols for wireless LANS and sensor networks, and computational probability.

Jose Santa received the M.S. degree in Computer Science Engineering in 2004 and the M.S. degree in Advanced Information and Telematic Technologies in 2008, both from the University of Murcia (UMU), Spain, and the PhD in Computer Science, from the same university, in 2009. Since 2004 he is a researcher with Department of Information and Communication Engineering, at UMU. During the last three years, he has combined his research with teaching tasks in the area of Electronic Technology.

Raúl Aquino Santos graduated from the University of Colima with a BE in Electrical Engineering, received his MS degree in Telecommunications from the Centre for Scientific Research and Higher Education in Ensenada, Mexico in 1990. He holds a PhD from the Department of Electrical and Electronic Engineering of the University of Sheffield, England. Since 2005, he has been with the College of Telematics, at the University of Colima, where he is currently a Research-Professor in telecommunications networks. His current research interests include wireless and sensor networks.

Weihua Sun received his B.E., M.E., and D.E. degrees in information and computer science from Osaka University in 2003, 2005 and 2008, respectively. He is working on development of protocols and applications on MANETs and VANETs.

Manabu Tsukada is a Ph.D student at MINES ParisTech and works as researcher at INRIA. He has studied in Jun Murai laboratory in Keio University from September 2002 to May 2007. He got BS (2005) and MS (2007) from Keio University. His research interests are mobility support for next generation Internet (IPv6) and communications for intelligent vehicles.

Hai L. Vu (S'97*M'98-SM'06) received the B.Sc./M.Sc. and Ph.D. degrees in electrical engineering from the Technical University of Budapest, Budapest, Hungary, in 1994 and 1999, respectively. From 1994 to 2000, he was a Research Engineer with Siemens AG, Hungary. During this period, his focus was on performance measurements, Internet quality of service, and IP over ATM. During 2000-2005, he was with the Department of Electrical and Electronic Engineering, University of Melbourne, Melbourne, Australia. In 2005, he joined Swinburne University of Technology and is with the Centre for Advanced Internet Architectures (CAIA). He is currently an Associate Professor at the Faculty of Information and Communication Technologies (FICT), Swinburne University of Technology, Hawthorn, Victoria, Australia. Dr Vu has authored or coauthored over 90 scientific journals and conference papers. His research interests are in data network modeling, performance evaluation of wireless and optical networks, network security and telecommunication networks design.

Andreas Xeros received his B.Sc degree from the Computer Engineering and Informatics department of the University of Patras in 2002. Upon completion of his undergraduate studies he earned a fellowship from the University of Southern California to continue his studies there. In 2004 he received his Master's Degree in Computer Science with specialization in Multimedia and Creative Technologies from U.S.C. He is now in the fourth year of the PhD program of the University of Cyprus. His research interests include Information Dissemination in Vehicular Ad Hoc Networks (VANETs), Vehicular Traffic modeling and Graph Theory. His work focuses on the application of graph theoretic algorithms to improve information dissemination speed in VANETs and increase information delivery probability. He also studies the applicability of Information Hovering in VANETs.

Hirozumi Yamaguchi received his BE, ME and Ph.D. degrees in Engineering from Osaka University, Japan. He is currently an Associate Professor at Osaka University. His current research interests include design and implementation of distributed systems and communication protocols, especially protocols and services on mobile ad hoc networks and application layer multicast. Also, he is working on some issues of wireless network simulations. He is a member of IEEE.

Gongjun Yan received a B.S. in Mechanic Engineering from the Sichuan Institute of Technology in China in 1999 and began his M.S. in Computer Science at the University of Electronics Science and Technology of China in 2001. In 2005, Gongjun began work on his Ph.D. at Old Dominion University in Computer Science. He has been working on the issues surrounding Vehicular Ad-Hoc Networks and Wireless Communication. He has published about 30 papers and book chapters, entitled with 3 patents, acted as conference chairs/co-chairs for 6 conferences and reviewed about 50 papers and manuscripts. Recently Gongjun received the Best Student Paper Award at the 9th IEEE Conference on Service Operations, Logistics and Informatics (SOLI) held in Chicago in July, 2009. He also received a travel grant from U.S National Research Foundation for the sixth IEEE International Conference on Mobile Ad-hoc and Sensor Systems (IEEE MASS 2009).

Index